Globalization and Its Socio-Economic Consequences, Volume I

Tomas Kliestik / Elvira Nica (eds.)

Globalization and Its Socio-Economic Consequences, Volume I

23rd International Scientific Conference Proceedings

PETER LANG

Berlin - Bruxelles - Chennai - Lausanne - New York - Oxford

Library of Congress Cataloging-in-Publication
A CIP catalog record for this book has been applied for at the Library of Congress.
Library of Congress Control Number: 2025930537

Bibliographic information published by the Deutsche Nationalbibliothek
The Deutsche Nationalbibliothek lists this publication in the Deutsche Nationalbibliografie; detailed bibliographic data is available on the Internet at http://dnb.d-nb.de.

ISBN 978-3-631-92465-5 (Print)
E-ISBN 978-3-631-92474-7 (E-PDF)
E-ISBN 978-3-631-92475-4 (E-PUB)
DOI.10.3726/b22205

Published by Peter Lang GmbH, Berlin, Germany

info@peterlang.com - www.peterlang.com

This publication has been peer reviewed.

Contents

Cristina Alpopi[1,*] Armenia Androniceanu[1], Elvira Nica[1], and Mihaela Melenciuc[1]

Digital Services in Central and Eastern European Capitals: A Citizen's Perspective Analysis

Abstract:
Research background: The advances in digital technology have facilitated the development of smart cities. The research context reflects the complexity and diversity of contemporary urban issues and attempts to find innovative solutions in order to address these challenges.
Purpose of the article: This study aims to evaluate and compare the level of development of digital services in eleven Central and East European capitals, according to their citizens' perceptions.
Methods: The method used for the evaluation was the Minimax Technique, which allowed us to develop a detailed analysis of the quality of the existing digital services from each city. Based on the data about the digitalization of public services and social life, a city rank was determined to illustrate both the digital level of the infrastructure and public services from the perspective of a smart city.
Findings & Value added: The results revealed significant differences between the cities in terms of citizens' perception of digital services. Vilnius has obtained the highest evaluation city rank. This study is an important step in evaluating smart cities from Eastern Europe and provides useful information both for city managers and politicians. The obtained research results can be useful for the managers of the analyzed European capitals to make the necessary changes in city strategies for improving citizens' perceptions and transforming them into modern and efficient smart cities.

Keywords: *smart city, urban digitalisation, urban mobility, digital transformation*

JEL Classification: *O18; O33*

* Corresponding author: cristina.alpopi@ase.ro
1 Bucharest University of Economic Studies, Faculty of Administration and Public Management, Bucharest, Romania

1 Introduction

Smart cities are a field of urban research and development that has caught the attention of the contemporary world in an unprecedented manner. On the background of the 21st century's technological and social rapid changes, the cities have become epicentres of innovation and adaptation to the new challenges of the modern society. In an increasingly urbanized world, the smart city concept has evolved beyond being just a trendy term and has become an imperative necessity for the sustainable development of the urban communities.

Organizational, technological and social changes in modern cities are motivated by their aspiration to contribute to solving the climate crisis. Therefore, smart cities aim at harmonizing the social, cultural and environmental aspects in a global approach that combines participatory governance with an efficient management of the natural resources. The goal is to meet the needs of the institutions, communities and citizens (Săvulescu & Antonovici, 2014).

In order to understand the "smart city" concept, a term that has become more and more popular in the scientific literature and the international policies during these last decades, it is important to acknowledge that cities are considered to be key elements for the future of mankind. They play a crucial role in all social and economic aspects worldwide, having a recognized impact on the environment (Albino et al., 2015).

Urban planning based on the "smart city" concept will overcome urban challenges, such as crowded transport, electricity network with high carbon emissions, infrastructure maintenance and repair, as well as urban security and policy (Al Sharif & Pokharel, 2022). In the European Union there are multiple regulations and initiatives aimed at developing and promoting smart and sustainable cities. These are meant to support the urban transformation in a more efficient, more sustainable direction, more oriented towards the needs of the citizens. Below are a few of the main European regulations and initiatives concerning smart cities (European Commission, 2023):

1 **Urban Agenda for the EU** – This initiative promotes the cooperation between cities and Member States of the EU in approaching major urban challenges.
2 **EU Funding for Smart Cities** – The Horizon 2020 Programme and, more recently, The Horizon Europe Programme have provided funding for research and development projects in the smart city field. These programmes support the innovation and the adoption of smart technologies within cities.
3 **Directives on Energy Efficiency** – Directive 2012/27/UE and Directive 2018/844/UE lay down requirements for improving the energy efficiency in buildings and urban transport.

4 **GDPR (General Data Protection Regulation)** –Smart cities collect a significant amount of data to improve services and the urban infrastructure and the GDPR guarantees the protection of the citizens' personal data.
5 **"Smart and Sustainable Cities" Initiative (Covenant of Mayors for Climate and Energy)** – This is a collaboration agreement between the local and regional authorities to fight against climate change and to promote renewable energy.
6 **Digital Europe Programme** – This programme aims at promoting digitalisation in Europe and supporting the development of digital technologies, including those related to smart cities.

In this context, there are documents assumed by the Member States of the European Union (EU) concerning smart cities that may vary according to the country and the national or regional strategies. Nevertheless, there are certain types of joint initiatives and documents which are assumed or developed by many Member States in the smart city development context. Here are a few of these (European Commission, 2023):

1 *National Strategies for Smart Cities*
2 *Sustainable Urban Plans or Agendas*
3 *Agreements with the Local Authorities*
4 *Research and Development Initiatives*
5 *Local Legislation and Urban Regulations*
6 *Public-Private Partnerships*
7 *Funding Programmes* This scientific study focuses on exploring and analyzing the smart city phenomenon, placing under a magnifying glass the various aspects that define it and their impact on urban life. Smart cities are characterized by an extensive use of advanced technologies in order to improve the efficiency, the quality of life and the sustainability in our crowded cities. They integrate elements such as information and communication technologies, data management, renewable energy, smart mobility, participatory governance and many more to create a safer, healthier and more connected urban environment.

1.1 The Stage of Knowledge in the Field

The smart city concept is an innovative approach of the urban development, using technology to improve the quality of life for the citizens and to increase the efficiency of the public services. The technological infrastructure, the energy efficiency, the urban mobility, the participation of the citizens in taking decisions and the security of the data are a few of the key aspects taken into consideration by smart cities. However, it is important to bear in mind the need to ensure a sustainable development and that the welfare and safety of the inhabitants must be at the heart of all efforts (Ionica, 2023).

A smart city is that environment where, by using digital and communication technologies for the benefit of its inhabitants and their businesses, the traditional networks and services become more efficient (Israilidis et al., 2021).

According to Androniceanu and Georgescu (2023), the "Digital First" principle represents the orientation that some public administrations in the member states of the European Union have to plan their policies and strategies. The coherent approach at the national level regarding the reuse of public data can contribute to improving the quality of services provided to citizens and private companies by the public administration. By leveraging existing data, the administration can support decision-making in key sectors of the public sector with increased efficiency. At the same time, administrations produce the data and infrastructure needed to facilitate the re-use of this data by public and private sector organizations, thus helping to boost economic competitiveness.

Lytras and Visvizi (2018) believe that the future of the cities is a "smart" one, as there are various commercial partnerships and research organizations worldwide seeking to contribute to the creation of applications for smart cities.

Accordingly, smart cities are characterized by a variety of elements and features and different authors and experts have highlighted these aspects in different ways. In the following, there several key elements presented, characterizing smart cities from the point of view of different authors:

- **Use of Advanced Technology:** Smart cities are based on state-of-the-art technology, such as the Internet of Things (IoT), sensors, data management systems and artificial intelligence (IA), to collect, monitor and analyze information throughout the city (Giffinger et al., 2007);
- **Extended Connectivity:** Smart cities are characterized by an extended and efficient communication infrastructure, enabling connectivity and easy access to services for all the inhabitants and economic operators (Hollands, 2008);
- **Sustainability and Energy Efficiency:** Smart cities place a special emphasis on reducing resource consumption, efficient energy management and environmental protection. They aim at being sustainable and reducing the carbon footprint (Caragliu et al., 2011);
- **Smart Mobility:** Smart cities develop intelligent transport systems, that encompass an efficient public transport, a sustainable mobility (bicycles,

electric vehicles), as well as solutions to reduce congestions and improve the mobility (Giffinger et al., 2007);

- **Participatory Governance:** Smart cities actively involve the citizens and the communities in the decisional process and encourage the participation of the public in the development of the city (Nam & Pardo, 2011);
- **Quality of Life:** Smart cities strive to improve the quality of life for their inhabitants by providing better public services, including education, health-care, culture and recreation (Allam & Newman, 2018);
- **Innovation and Creative Economy:** These cities promote innovation and economic development by supporting creative and technological business ecosystems, as well as by creating collaborative working spaces (Caragliu et al., 2011);
- **Resilience and Safety:** Smart cities are prepared to cope with natural threats or social challenges by developing crisis management plans and early warning systems (Hollands, 2008);
- **Cultural and Social Diversity:** These cities value the cultural diversity and promote the social inclusion of all groups of inhabitants. They encourage the exchange of cultures and experiences (Caragliu et al., 2011);
- **Administrative Efficiency:** Smart cities use technology to improve the efficiency and transparence of the public administration, reducing the bureaucracy and unnecessary spending (Nam & Pardo, 2011).

These elements are only a few of the main characteristics attributed to smart cities by various authors and experts. It is important to understand that the smart city concept is dynamic and adapts to local needs and conditions and that the characteristics can vary from one city to another, according to their objectives and priorities.

Tsun Lai and Cole (2023) assess that "smart city" is a basic characteristic of the modern urban development. In the literature there are multiple smart city indices presented, by means of which their performances are successfully compared. It is important to identify those indices that enable different comparisons between the cities. The authors, in the "Measuring progress of smart cities: Indexing the smart city indices" paper, propose a method for evaluating the accuracy and quality of the existing smart city indices according to five criteria – Credibility, Reliability, Methodology, Versatility and Precision.

Digital Cities Index (DCI) 2022, developed by Economist Impact, provides a way to evaluate the digitalisation degree in 30 cities around the world. By analysing the key pillars of the digital connectivity, services, culture and sustainability, this index reflects the efforts and progresses of the cities in adopting smart technologies and sustainable practices.

Smart cities have appeared as an important concept in urban development, intended to improve the quality of life for the citizens by implementing smart technologies, supporting urban innovation, increasing the economic productivity and approaching common problems such as urbanization, climate crisis and the shortage of raw materials. Smart city technologies have appeared in various fields, creating implications and bringing benefits for the housing sector, energy, economy, medical care, infrastructure, environment, government etc. (Alshamaila et al., 2023).

In the context of these evaluations and definitions of the smart cities, it is obvious that the "smart city" concept continues to have a significant impact on the modern urban development. The development and implementation of smart technologies in the cities is an ongoing process, with significant benefits for the citizens and the society as a whole.

1.2 Key Dimensions of the Smart Cities

Starting from the idea mentioned above, different authors define in different manners the dimensions incorporated by a smart city, each characteristic with the corresponding type and number of factors. The smart city key dimensions are essential tools for evaluating, planning and developing cities in a more efficient and sustainable manner, and also more oriented towards the needs of the citizens. These dimensions offer a structure and framework to approach the smart urban development and to measure the progress in this respect.

Accordingly, Camboim et al. (2019) have identified four key dimensions of the smart cities: city governance, configuration of the urban environment, technical and economical dynamics and socio-institutional structure. Giffinger et al. (2007) have identified six key characteristics of the smart city: smart economy (competitiveness), smart environment (natural resources), smart governance (participation), smart life (quality of life), smart mobility (transport and ICT) and smart people (social and human capital). Sharifi (2019) has conceived a model in which he classified the indicators of a smart city by seven representative themes: economy, governance, people, mobility, environment, life and data. Bosh et al. (2017) suggested five other key dimensions, which define the framework of a smart city: people, prosperity, planet, governance and propagation. Zhu et al. (2019) have identified eight directions for the development of the smart city in China: smart community, smart governance, smart logistics, smart transport, smart medicine, smart energy, smart materials and smart constructions. Sen et al. (2018) proposed a smart city framework that contains six urban fields: economy, education, mobility, life and environment and security. Lim and Maglio (2018) conceived 12 characteristics of the smart cities encompassing smart devices, smart energy, smart environment, smart transport, smart houses, smart buildings, smart logistics, smart health, smart agriculture, smart security, smart hospitality and smart education.

Basically, smart cities use technology to bring significant improvements in each of these fields, making them more efficient, more accessible and more convenient for the inhabitants. By integrating the technology in these aspects of the urban life, more connected and more intelligent cities are created, which respond better to the needs and requirements of the modern society.

2 Methods

The general objective pursued in this paper is to evaluate and compare the development level of the technological services in 11 East European capitals, including Bucharest, from the perspective of the citizens' perception (120 from each city) regarding the technological pillar which describes the existing services in each city, with the purpose of achieving a ranking of these that would show the position each one has in their endeavour to become a smart city. The technological pillar is evaluated through 5 fields (see Appendix 1), respectively: health and safety, mobility, recreational activities, work and school and governance, and the data employed were drawn from the 2023 IMD Smart City Index Report, for each city.

Each field has a number of services carried out in each city for the benefit of the citizens, with the purpose of ensuring the advance towards a smart city. Accordingly, the health and safety field encompasses services such as: online reporting of the city's maintenance problems, applications or sites allowing the citizens to quickly transmit unwanted situations so that these cand be solved, access to various city services through Wi-Fi, surveillance cameras giving the citizens a feeling of safety, websites or applications that allow citizens to obtain information on the efficient monitoring of the air pollution, online appointment of the medical check-ups which improves the access and reduces reduce queue times etc.

The mobility field refer to services such as: car-sharing applications to reduce traffic congestion, applications ensuring the directioning to available parking spaces to reduce travel times, bicycle rental to reduce traffic congestion, online appointment and ticket sale for an easier use of the public transport, offering information related to traffic congestion in the city by means of mobile phones etc.

In support of the recreation activities, online ticket sale services are provided for shows and museums, making the participation in these events much easier.

As regards "work and school," the online applications facilitate employment opportunities and simplify the business opening process. Also, the high speed Internet facilitates the connectivity needs and the educational institutions offer the possibility of acquiring good IT knowledges.

In terms of governance, the public access to the city's finances in the online environment reduces the corruption, the online processing of the identification documents reduces waiting times, the existence of online platforms where citizens can express their ideas improve their life and the possibility to vote online improves the voting participation rate.

Starting from the assumption that the implementation of smart technologies in smart cities has a significant impact on the quality of life for the inhabitants and on the efficiency of the urban functioning, the hypothesis of the study is that the cities adopting these smart technologies will have significant improvements regarding health and safety, mobility, recreational activities, jobs and education, as well as the quality of the local governance.

In order to reach the general objective of the study, the following steps have been taken:

1 Literature review: A detailed analysis of the literature was made to identify the existing studies and theories regarding smart cities and the impact of the smart technologies on the urban development, as well as the characteristics of the smart cities.
2 Data Collection: Relevant statistical data from the 2023 IMD Smart City Index Report were collected for the 11 East European capitals, Bucharest included, regarding the technological pillar.
3 Data Analysis and Methodology: The collected data were analyzed by means of the "Minimax Technique," to identify the minimum and maximum value of the criteria relevant to the technological pillar.
4 Result Interpretation: The results were interpreted in the context of the existing theories and of the general objective pursued, as well of the initial hypothesis.
5 Formulation of the study's conclusions.

In this manner, the Minimax Technique was employed as an evaluation and classification tool to reach the general objective of the study, giving a clear perspective on the citizens' perception regarding the technological pillar from each smart city and highlighting the relative position of these in relation to others. This enabled the achieving of a ranking illustrating the position of each city in their endeavour to become smart cities. In this context, the Minimax Technique was the right choice, involving steps such as identifying the evaluation criteria, data scaling, assigning criteria weights, calculating total scores and city ranking.

3 Results and Discussions

We will further present the analysis of the research results, highlighting the findings obtained by applying the Minimax Technique in evaluating and ranking the 11 East European capitals, Bucharest included. This analysis will provide a detailed perspective on the position of each city as regards the citizens' perception on the technological pillar of the city, as well as a comparison of these results between the cities.

3.1 Analysis of the Research Results

As we can notice, the table data from the Appendix 1 do not have a measuring unit, since the services presented in our analysis are diverse and cover a wide range of aspects related to the technological pillar of the smart cities. This diversity in criteria and indicators may complicate the direct comparison of the cities' performances, as the natural differences between services and values could distort the results and could offer an incorrect picture of the situation.

To approach this issue and to smooth the data, we used the Minimax normalisation technique. Normalisation is an important step in data analysis when working with criteria which vary significantly in amplitude and measuring units. This technique allows us to bring all data at the same scale, so that we can accurately compare the performance of the cities within our analysis.

By applying the Minimax Technique, we have succeeded in transposing all data in an interval ranging between 0 and 1 (see Appendix 2), where 0 means the worst possible performance and 1 is the best possible performance, intermediate values being calculated by means of the relation (1):

$$U_{(x)} = \frac{U - \min U}{\max U - \min U} \tag{1}$$

where :

$U_{(x)}$ ranges between 0 and 1;
U original value that must be normalised;
min U minimum value;
max U maximum value.

This normalisation process enabled a relative comparison of the cities based on the perception of the citizens regarding the technological pillar, without being influenced by the initial absolute values of the criteria.

Analyzing Appendix 2, we can notice that for each criterion associated to the 5 services in each city, we have individual utility values and, in the end, we calculate the total utility for each city. This approach allows us to dissect and evaluate in a detailed manner the contribution of each criterion to the general perception of the citizens regarding the technological pillar of their city.

By individual breakdown and evaluation of the criteria, we can identify the strengths and weaknesses of each city in terms of technological services. This offers us a more detailed picture of the manner in which the citizens perceive the quality and efficiency of these services, according to their various aspects.

The total utility, which is the sum of the individual utilities of each criterion, offers us a global measure of the citizens' general perception on the technological pillar of the city. This is an important indicator that allows us to compare cities with each other as regards their performance in the technology field and to identify the cities that stand out through high- quality technological services, as well as those that might need significant improvement in this area.

In terms of health and safety, Vilnius ranks first in this field, with a total utility of 5.04, outlining a high level of positive perception of the technological services related to health and safety. Bucharest is on the 8th place with 2,17, which also indicates a relatively positive perception of these services and distinguishes itself particularly in criteria such as online reporting of the maintenance problems and access to online medical services. Ljubljana, Budapest and Zagreb are among the cities ranking lower in this field.

The mobility field is led by Warsaw, with a total utility of 4,37, while Bucharest is on the 9th place with a total utility of 1.87, followed by Tallinn (1,86) and subsequently by Zagreb (0,2). This field analyses the aspects connected to traffic management, access to public transport and facilitation in crossing the city. Vilnius, situated on the 2nd place, and Budapest, on the 3rd, also stand out for good performances in this area.

For the recreational activity field, the utility values are relatively low for all the cities, with Bucharest situated on the 8th place. This field is focused on facilitating the citizens' participation in cultural and recreational events and Tallinn city holds the maximum value (1) in this respect, while Riga has the minimum value (0).

In terms of work and school, Vilnius is situated on the first place again, with a value of 3,48 and Bucharest has a total utility of 0.98, ranking last. This field analyses the access to employment, education and professional development opportunities.

In the governance field, we can notice that Tallin city is once again on the first place with a value of 3,24, while Bucharest is on the 10th place, with a total utility of 0.30. This field examines the aspects related to the transparence of the governance and civic engagement.

In the total of all fields, Bucharest holds the 10th place in the general ranking, with a total utility of 5.43. Warsaw ranks first, with a total utility of 15.14.

3.2 Conclusion

Considering the results obtained, we believe that the general objective of the study was reached. The analysis based on the Minimax technique allowed the evaluation and comparison of the performances of the various East European capitals in terms of aspects connected to smart cities.

The study provided a detailed picture of the citizens' perception regarding the technological services from their cities and outlined the significant differences between these cities. This enabled the identification of the strengths and of the areas that require improvements in each analyzed capital.

In the work and education field, a significant difference is noticed between the evaluated cities. Vilnius holds the top position with an impressive evaluation of 3,48, which suggests that the citizens of Vilnius perceive a favourable environment for the access to employment, education and professional development opportunities. This probably indicates the presence of efficient technological services and well-developed educational policies in Vilnius.

In contrast, Bucharest is at the opposite end of the ranking, with a total evaluation of only 0,98. This suggests that, in the perception of the citizens from Bucharest, the access to employment and education opportunities might be considered suboptimal or requiring significant improvement. This might can be a signal for the local authorities and governing bodies to conduct a more careful analysis of the existing technological services and educational policies, in order to make adjustments and improvements that would better support the needs of the inhabitants.

The general ranking of the smart cities, based on the total evaluation of all the analyzed fields reveals an interesting perspective on the position of Bucharest compared to other East European capitals. With a total utility of 5,43, Bucharest holds the 10th position in the general ranking.

On the other hand, Warsaw is at the top of this ranking, with an impressive total evaluation of 15,14. This suggests that in the citizens' perception and in terms of technological services related to various aspects of the urban life, Warsaw distinguishes itself as the undoubted leader of the region. This top position might be the result of an efficient smart city development policy and of significant investments in technology and digital infrastructure.

While Bucharest is at the bottom of this ranking, this does not have to be a disappointing evaluation. Instead, it can be seen as an opportunity to identify the areas that require significant improvements and to develop strategies and projects for increasing the quality of life for the citizens by means of technology and of the smart city concept.

The general ranking reflects the ongoing importance of developing smart cities in the East European region and the competition to become leaders in this field. It is crucial that cities continue to invest in innovation and technology in order to improve public services, support the economic growth and meet the changing needs of the citizens.

In summary, this study is an important step in evaluating smart cities from the Eastern Europe and offers a solid basis for taking decisions and for the strategic development of these cities. Taking into account that smart cities continue to be an important trend in urban development, this type of research remains essential to support the progress and innovation in our urban communities.

Acknowledgment

The paper has been prepared under the research project with the title: Digitization, digital transformation, and artificial intelligence in public administration, 2023, financed by the Bucharest University of Economic Studies and is part of the research strategy of the International Centre for Public Management.

References

Al Sharif, R., & Pokharel, S. (2022). Smart City dimensions and associated risks: Review of literature. *Sustainable Cities and Society, 77*, Article 103542.

Albino, V., Berardi, U., & Dangelico, R. A. (2015). Smart Cities: Definitions, dimensions, performance, and initiatives. *Journal of Urban Technology, 22*(1), 3–21.

Allam, Z., & Newman, P. (2018). Redefining the smart city: Culture, metabolism and governance. *Smart Cities, 1*(1), 4–25.

Alshamaila, Y., Papagiannidis, S., Alsawalqah, H., & Aljarah, I. (2023). Effective use of smart cities in crisis cases: A systematic review of the literature. *International Journal of Disaster Risk Reduction, 85*, Article 103521.

Androniceanu, A., & Georgescu, I. (2023). Public Administration Digitalization and Government effectiveness in EU countries. *Central European Public Administration Review, 21*(1), 7–30.

Bosh, P., Jongeneel, S., Rovers, V., Neumann, H.-M., Airaksinen, M., & Huovila, A. (2017). CITYkeys indicators for smart city projects and smart cities. https://www.researchgate.net/publication/326266723_CITYkeys_indicators_for_smart_city_projects_and_smart_cities?channel=doi&linkId=5b434e4f0f7e9bb59b187e77&showFulltext=true

Camboim, G. F., Zawislak, P. A., & Amarante Pufal, N. (2019). Driving elements to make cities smarter: Evidences from European projects. *Technological Forecasting and Social Change, 142,* Article 154–167.

Caragliu, A., Del Bo, C., & Nijkamp, P. (2011). Smart cities in Europe. *Journal of Urban Technology, 18*(2), 65–82.

Economist Impact. (2022). Digital Cities Index 2022 Executive Summary. https://impact.economist.com/projects/digital-cities/2022-executive-summary/.

European Commission. (2023). Official website of European Commission. https://commission.europa.eu/

Giffinger, R., Fertner, C., Kramar, H., Kalasek, R., Milanović, N., & Meijers, E. (2007). Smart cities – Ranking of European medium-sized cities. http://www.smart- cities.eu/download/smart_cities_final_report.pdf

Hollands, R. G. (2008). Will the real smart city please stand up? City: Analysis of urban trend, culture, theory. *Policy, Action, 12*(3), 303–320.

IMD World Competitiveness Center. (2023). IMD Smart City Index Report 2023, p. 36. https://imd.cld.bz/IMD-Smart-City-Index-Report-20231/36/

Ionica, A. (2023). Orasele inteligente: Unde tehnologia intalneste viata urbana. https://smartcityblog.ro/orasele-inteligente-unde-tehnologia-intalneste-viata-urbana/

Israilidis, J., Odusanya, K., & Mazhar, M. U. (2021). Exploring knowledge management perspectives in smart city research: A review and future research agenda. *International Journal of Information Management, 56*, Article 101989.

Lim, C., & Maglio, P. (2018). Data-Driven understanding of smart service systems through text mining. *Service Science, 10*(2), 154–180.

Lytras, M. D., & Visvizi, A. (2018). Who uses smart city services and what to make of it: Toward interdisciplinary smart cities research. *Sustainability, 10*(6), Article 1998.

Nam, T., & Pardo, T. A. (2011). Conceptualizing smart city with dimensions of technology, people, and institutions. *Proceedings of the 12th annual international digital government research conference: Digital government innovation in challenging times* (pp. 282–291).

Săvulescu, C., & Antonovici, C. G. (2014). Orasul inteligent–ecosistem de inovare si adaptare. *Smart Cities International Conference (SCIC) Proceedings*, Vol. 2 (pp. 11–21).

Sen, R., Eggers, D. W., & Kelkar, M. (2018). Building the smart city, Deloitte center for Government Insights. https://www2.deloitte.com/content/dam/Deloitte/us/Documents/public-sector/us-fed- building-the-smart-city.pdf

Sharifi, A. (2019). A critical review of selected smart city assessment tools and indicator sets. *Journal of Cleaner Production*, *233*, 1269–1283.

Tsun Lai, C. M., & Cole, A. (2023). Measuring progress of smart cities: Indexing the smart city indices. *Urban Governance*, *3*(1), 45–57.

Zhu, S., Li, D., & Feng, H. (2019). Is smart city resilient? Evidence from China. *Sustainable Cities and Society*, *50*, Article 101636.

Appendix 1 – Values corresponding to the 5 fields of the technological pillar, regarding the existing services in the cities

	Bucharest	Budapest	Bratislava	Warsaw	Prague	Sofia	Vilnius	Riga	Tallinn	Zagreb	Ljubljana
1. Health and safety											
1. the online reporting of a city's maintenance problems offers quick solutions	46,3	36,0	48,3	51,3	52,6	46,8	53,5	47,2	54,3	34,0	47,1
2. an application or a site allows the citizens to quickly eliminate unwanted aspects	52,4	55,5	51,5	62,2	64,1	51,9	73,9	53,1	55,9	47,9	46,9
3. free public Wi-Fi has improved the access to the city's services	48,6	53,3	55,0	62,6	56,4	54,9	64,0	55,3	62,5	56,8	59,8
4. surveillance cameras made the citizens feel safer	47,2	53,8	52,9	55,2	62,7	49,7	59,2	55,6	64,0	43,1	40,3
5. a website or an application allows the citizens to get information on efficient air pollution monitoring	52,6	43,3	36,8	64,4	46,1	55,7	56,5	40,8	38,5	45,1	52,7
6. the online appointments for the medical check-ups have improved access and have reduced waiting times	58,6	47,0	60,8	66,4	63,5	58,4	60,2	63,1	69,7	48,1	49,6
2. Mobility											
1. car-sharing applications have reduced traffic congestion	35,9	36,2	34,6	49,1	35,0	38,8	37,4	35,6	34,5	28,5	37,5

(continued on next page)

Appendix 1 Continued

	Bucharest	Budapest	Bratislava	Warsaw	Prague	Sofia	Vilnius	Riga	Tallinn	Zagreb	Ljubljana
2. the applications directing people towards available parking spaces have reduced travel time	40,4	45,6	36,4	50,7	47,1	47,5	47,9	38,9	36,8	29,7	45,5
3. bicycle renting has reduced traffic congestion	41,9	48,6	49,4	59,6	42,3	41,9	42,9	42,5	37,6	28,3	65,8
4. online appointment and ticket sale led to an easier use of the public transport	54,4	72,7	66,7	71,8	72,2	55,9	75,8	64,2	76,8	54,4	67,4
5. information on traffic congestion in the city are provided by means of the mobile phones	46,7	57,1	36,7	50,1	44,6	53,3	55,4	49,4	25,9	32,4	44,5
3. Recreational activities											
1. the online purchasing of tickets to shows and museums has simplified the participation in these events	75,1	80,3	78,5	78,7	80,2	74,7	81,2	73,9	84,4	77,2	75,8
4. Work and school											
1. online access to employment opportunities has simplified this activity	63,0	73,2	69,8	78,7	74,2	70,4	76,1	72,5	79,7	66,5	67,6
2. the IT abilities are properly learnt in schools	41,4	51,1	50,0	58,7	53,3	51,2	67,2	42,5	59,7	58,1	49,6

3. online services provided by the city made the business opening process easier	38,8	50,7	38,1	63,7	49,0	50,5	56,2	47,5	58,3	47,4	50,8
4. high-speed internet and its reliability meet the connectivity needs	77,6	67,8	69,8	71,3	69,2	71,7	78,2	70,8	73,3	60,3	70,2
5. Governance											
1. online public access to city's finances has reduced corruption	23,0	30,6	30,2	45,2	35,4	28,4	35,3	25,3	37,6	26,1	29,8
2. online voting has improved the voting participation rate	32,0	51,0	40,5	57,6	46,7	36,2	43,8	36,4	73,2	36,5	36,3
3. online platforms where citizens can express their ideas have improved city life	37,9	45,2	41,6	63,7	52,1	43,0	46,8	37,5	52,3	35,8	43,0
4. online identification document processing has reduced waiting times	52,7	65,7	54,5	67,3	63,6	57,3	66,5	45,3	76,7	55,8	47,5

Appendix 2 – The normalised value table for the 5 fields of the technological pillar, as regards the existing services from the cities

	Bucharest	**Budapest**	**Bratislava**	**Warsaw**	**Prague**	**Sofia**	**Vilnius**	**Riga**	**Tallinn**	**Zagreb**	**Ljubljana**
1. Health and safety											
1. the online reporting of a city's maintenance problems offers quick solutions	0,60	0,09	0,70	0,85	0,90	0,63	0,96	0,65	1	0	0,64
2. an application or a site allows the citizens to quickly eliminate unwanted aspects	0,20	0,31	0,17	0,56	0,63	0,18	1	0,22	0,33	0,03	0
3. free public Wi-Fi has improved the access to the city's services	0	0,30	0,41	0,90	0,50	0,40	1	0,43	0,90	0,53	0,72
4. surveillance cameras made the citizens feel safer	0,29	0,56	0,53	0,62	0,94	0,39	0,79	0,64	1	0,11	0
5. a website or an application allows the citizens to get information on efficient air pollution monitoring	0,57	0,23	0	1	0,33	0,68	0,71	0,14	0,06	0,30	0,57
6. the online appointments for the medical check-ups have improved access and have reduced waiting times	0,51	0	0,60	0,85	0,72	0,50	0,58	0,70	1	0,04	0,11
Total health and safety	**2,17**	**1,49**	**2,41**	**4,78**	**4,02**	**2,78**	**5,04**	**2,76**	**4,29**	**1,01**	**2,04**
2. Mobility											
1. car-sharing applications have reduced traffic congestion	0,35	0,37	0,29	1	0,31	0,5	0,43	0,34	0,29	0	0,43

2. the applications directing people towards available parking spaces have reduced travel time	0,50	0,75	0,31	1	0,82	0,84	0,86	0,43	0,33	0	0,75
3. bicycle renting has reduced traffic congestion	0,36	0,54	0,56	0,83	0,37	0,36	0,38	0,37	0,24	0	1
4. online appointment and ticket sale led to an easier use of the public transport	0	0,81	0,54	0,77	0,79	0,06	0,95	0,43	1	0	0,58
5. information on traffic congestion in the city are provided by means of the mobile phones	0,66	1	0,34	0,77	0,59	0,87	0,94	0,75	0	0,20	0,59
Total mobility	**1,87**	**3,47**	**2,04**	**4,37**	**2,88**	**2,63**	**3,56**	**2,32**	**1,86**	**0,20**	**3,35**
3. Recreational activities											
1. the online purchasing of tickets to performances and museums has simplified the participation in these events	0,11	0,60	0,43	0,45	0,60	0,07	0,10	0	1	0,31	0,18
Total recreational activities	**0,11**	**0,60**	**0,43**	**0,45**	**0,60**	**0,07**	**0,10**	**0**	**1**	**0,31**	**0,18**
4. Work and school											
1. online access to employment opportunities has simplified this activity	0	0,61	0,40	0,94	0,67	0,44	0,78	0,56	1	0,20	0,27
2. the IT abilities are properly learnt in schools	0	0,38	0,33	0,67	0,46	0,37	1	0,04	0,70	0,64	0,31
3. online services provided by the city made the business opening process easier	0,02	0,49	0	1	0,42	0,48	0,70	0,36	0,78	0,36	0,49

(continued on next page)

Appendix 2 Continued

	Bucharest	Budapest	Bratislava	Warsaw	Prague	Sofia	Vilnius	Riga	Tallinn	Zagreb	Ljubljana
4. high-speed internet and its reliability meet the connectivity needs	0,96	0,41	0,53	0,61	0,49	0,63	1	0,58	0,72	0	0,55
Total work and school	**0,98**	**1,89**	**1,26**	**3,22**	**2,04**	**1,92**	**3,48**	**1,54**	**3,2**	**1,2**	**1,62**
5. Governance											
1. online public access to city's finances has reduced corruption	0	0,34	0,32	1	0,55	0,24	0,55	0,10	0,65	0,13	0,30
2. online voting has improved the voting participation rate	0	0,46	0,20	0,62	0,35	0,10	0,28	0,10	1	0,10	0,10
3. online platforms where citizens can express their ideas have improved city life	0,07	0,33	0,20	1	0,58	0,25	0,39	0,06	0,59	0	0,25
4. online identification document processing has reduced waiting times	0,23	0,64	0,29	0,70	0,58	0,38	0,67	0	1	0,33	0,07
Total governance	**0,30**	**1,77**	**1,01**	**2,32**	**2,06**	**0,97**	**1,89**	**0,26**	**3,24**	**0,56**	**0,72**
TOTAL	**5,43**	**9,22**	**7,12**	**15,14**	**11,57**	**8,37**	**14,07**	**6,88**	**13,59**	**3,28**	**7,91**
Ranking position	**10**	**5**	**8**	**1**	**4**	**6**	**2**	**9**	**3**	**11**	**7**

Cristina Alpopi[1,*], Elvira Nica[1], Cristina Manole[1], and Anamaria Mişa[1]

Digital Maturity of Cities. A Comparative Study

Abstract:
Research background: Urban digitalization is vital for addressing the complex challenges faced by rapidly growing urban populations. Many researchers believe that smart cities offer solutions to resource management, environmental sustainability, economic growth, and overall quality of life.
Purpose of the article: The digital development gaps of cities and the complexity of the "smart city" concept are becoming fundamental topics in the states' agenda. In this sense, it is necessary to identify those successful urban concentrations so as to constitute models to inspire the communities left behind from this point of view.
Methods: This article used the method of comparative analysis of data from the Digital City Index to determine the digital maturity stage of cities
Findings & Value added: Our research reveals interesting insights regarding the four criteria analyzed: connectivity, services, culture and sustainability. At the same time, it brings new insights by highlighting specific correlations between the digital transformation and variables such as the development stage of the cities or the continent of which they are a part. The study has its limits in that it uses data that can be correlated. However, it is not sufficient to establish causality. As the concept of "smart city" is a particularly complex one, of course that our research can advance with an analysis of factors that were not taken into account in the DCI report. Our study can be useful to the public management in Romania so that they can make effective decisions in accelerating the digital transformation in the cities of our country.

Keywords: *digitalisation, smart cities, DCI, urban digitalisation, technology*

JEL Classification: *H83; O31; O38*

* Corresponding author: cristina.alpopi@ase.ro
1 Bucharest University of Economic Studies, Faculty of Administration and Public Management, Bucharest, Romania

1 Introduction

1.1 Urban Digitalisation

The international pressure on the security, competitiveness and sustainability of cities is becoming a constant in our lives. Of course, in the last two decades, a global priority has been to integrate the smart city model into the agenda of as many states as possible. (Albino et al., 2015). Smart cities are currently at the heart of the European Commission's (EC) strategic vision for a modern, competitive and climate-neutral economy (European Commission, 2022). Moreover, the European Commission (2022) launched a new digital strategy that establishes a new vision that addresses the opportunities for digital transformation of a post-pandemic scenario and supports the achievement of the strategic priorities of the European Union until 2030. The European Union's digital strategy is shaped around the so-called "European Digital Decade" concept, which reiterates the crucial importance of the digital transformation process. If the first narratives in this field was referring to the efficiency of public management and the adequate use of resources, nowadays, the central goal of smart city policies became the formation of sustainable, climate-neutral cities. (Biesaga et al., 2023) The digital strategy of the European Union will seek to implement a sustainable vision, created around the individual "for the digital society throughout the digital decade" so that citizens and companies are determined to perform (European Commission, 2022).

We are all citizens of a digital world, a world that confronts us with new possibilities, new rights, new duties (Isin & Ruppert, 2020). Digital citizens use ICT technologies to relate, communicate, access information and socialize in economic and political activities (Ciancarini et al., 2023). Thus, we can say that technology has acquired a fundamental role in the lives of people and the entire community, the digital transformation of cities continuing to bring countless advantages to both citizens and public institutions and stakeholders. The current agenda of smart cities involves the adoption of socio-technical innovation with the promise of merging information and communication technologies (ICT) in the desire to increase the economic and sustainable performance of cities. Researchers believe that this digital transformation will also bring with it a better quality of life for residents (Karvonen et al., 2020).

The management of relationships involving the state, regions, local authorities, and the communication between public administration entities and citizens now relies more and more on these technological advances. Effective governance is built upon principles of government openness, transparency, accountability, and active community involvement in shaping and implementing policies. Digital technologies ensure that these processes are accessible and user-friendly (Androniceanu et al., 2022) The development of cities (their growth and concentration) has led to increasing pressure to identify solutions amid a global effort to sustainably meet people's demands. In this context, pressures are described as, in particular, environmental, economic and social (United Nations Human Settlements Programme, 2009). For most cities in the European Union, the solution to these challenges is the smart city. Urban digitization refers to the adoption of cutting-edge ICT solutions (mostly data-driven) to inform and integrate problem-solving into urban processes (Millard et al., 2014). Therefore, the digital transformation of cities, namely urban digitization, is understood as a continuous process, with a flexible evolution, which will be shaped according to various factors such as: technological innovations, economic development, crisis situations, strategic priorities.

Digitization will lead to the transformation to new forms of organization and social mechanisms, to new types and institutional models, generating regenerative effects on the whole society, contributing to the increase of the quality of life of all citizens. The conclusions of a group of researchers (Evans et al., 2019) emphasize the fact that the digital transformation of cities is not an issue related only to the technological agenda, but a complex socio-technical process that involves fundamental social, political and cultural. Thus, the great challenge is "to identify and shape the relationships between technological innovation and the society of smart cities by conveying collective interests and serving as a guardian of the public good" (Karvonen et al, 2019). Once the utility and benefits of urban digitization are established, it can be stated that the digital transformation of Romanian cities is more than a wish. However, according to the "Digital Economy and Society Index" (DESI), recorded after 2020, Romania ranks last among the 27 member states of the European Union (EU). This situation makes the phenomenon of urban digitization in Romania an interesting issue for researchers to analyze in order to outline the scientific contexts and, of course, to identify and propose specific solutions for the progress of our country. The present study carries out an analysis of the digital transformation situation of the states in the world in accordance with the "Digital Cities Index" (DCI). This comparative analysis will help us in establishing those models to follow on different issues analyzed by DCI. Our benchmarking research brings relevant insights into evaluating the digital performance of cities. This helps identify best practices and strategies that can be adopted from leading cities to drive local digital transformation in our country.

1.2 Literature Review

In different countries of the world, the development stages and development paths of ICT vary a lot, hence the significant differences of an economic and social nature between different states. For example, the fourth industrial revolution related to ICT is taking place globally, in France (Nouvelle France Industrielle), in Germany (Industrie 4.0), in Sweden (Produktion 2030), Austria (Produktion der Zukunft), Italy (Fabbrica Intelligente) and so on It is obvious that most EU member states are moving towards a digital economy, but it is a reality, at the same time, that there is a significant development gap in terms of its social benefits (Gao et al., 2022). Reis and Melão (2023) emphasize that digitalization is generally associated with the transformation of traditional processes into digital processes or that digitalization is a process of transforming analog data into digital data sets, which leads to the creation of value and the improvement of customer experience Digital development has become a driving force in economic development (Peng et al, 2023) allowing smart cities to do more with fewer resources(Maiurova et al., 2022).

Jiang et al. (2023) show that urban digital transformation can promote resource sustainability through technological innovation, structural transformation and reallocation of capital and that the implementation of urban digital transformation in resource-poor eastern cities and cities with unreasonable industrial structures has a more favorable effect on the sustainability of resources. Urban digital transformation facilitates urban economic and social activities, infrastructure and urban governance through elements of data and digital technologies, improving the efficiency of urban management and living standards. The progress of digital technologies promises "smarter" cities, thus more sustainable, more democratic and more accessible. Van Holstein et al. (2021) suggested that smart city development redistributes and consolidates rather than equalizes, providing unequal access to opportunities to practice urban citizenship. The authors draw attention to the unequal racial and gender results of digital inequality, because technologies can replicate and amplify oppressive and discriminatory structures. The same paper analyzes the unequal effects of the digitization of urban services, with a specific focus on people with intellectual disabilities, as a highly marginalized group of people who face a distinct set of barriers when accessing and using digitization services (Van Holstein, 2021).

In many countries, significant funding is provided for the construction of resilient, safe, sustainable and equitable transport infrastructures, with an obvious need for initiatives to digitize and inventory road assets, especially through the adoption of innovative technologies such as remote sensing, the Internet of Things and artificial intelligence, for asset management. The digitization and management of road assets are generally driven by transport planning and maintenance objectives, such as improving road safety, reducing congestion and increasing transport efficiency (Li et al., 2023). Traffic control infrastructures (ITC), elements such as traffic signs and signals, pavement markings, etc., play an important role in managing traffic flows and improving road safety. They provide information about the current state of the roads, restrictions and prohibitions, warnings and other useful information for traffic participants. Digitized and timely updated ITCs can benefit transportation management and lay a solid foundation for promoting the implementation of connected and autonomous vehicles, as well as the establishment of intelligent transportation systems (Li et al., 2023).

It is essential to assess the possibilities and obstacles regarding the different optimization scenarios for old buildings. Denmark is a leader in digitizing building data and making it accessible to the public, either through demolition and the construction of new ones, or through renovation (Andersen et al., 2021). The construction sector is a significant contributor to global environmental impacts such as global warming due to greenhouse gas emissions. Indeed, the construction sector was responsible for almost 40 % of all energy- related CO2 emissions in 2018. In addition, construction and demolition waste is responsible for 34 % of urban waste produced by OECD countries. In reality, like urbanization, the demand for new buildings will continue to grow. In 2018, 55 % of the world's population lived in urban areas, which is expected to increase to approximately 68 % by 2050. Urbanization creates a demand for more housing, resulting in increased levels of demolition and new construction (Andersen et al., 2021).

A Danish case study shows that the environmental impact of renovating an old building can be reduced to 40 % of the environmental impact associated with the construction of a new building of similar size. In addition, an analysis of sixteen buildings by engineering company Rambøll showed an advantage in choosing to renovate rather than demolish and replace in terms of CO2 emissions and costs in all sixteen cases. To provide accurate information about the potential for renovation, as opposed to demolition and reconstruction, assessments of improvement options are needed in the early planning stages. A potential way to optimally choose options is to use automation and building information modeling, so digitizing and using data to create information about materials and buildings (Andersen et al., 2021). Dumitrescu (2022) appreciates that, taken together, the general mayor's office of the city of Bucharest and the sectoral mayor's offices of the capital carried out the most smart city projects, according to the report Scanning Smart Cities in Romania for 2022. Broken down by general mayor's office, Cluj-Napoca is the city with the most numerous smart city projects (63), followed by Iasi (56) and Bucharest (54).

2 Methods

In order to analyze the situation of cities all over the world regarding the transition to the desired "smart city," we used the Digital Cities Index ranking. Developed by Economist Impact and supported by NEC, this is a ranking system that assesses the level of digitization and technological progress in different cities around the world. It provides insight into how well cities are using digital technologies and data-driven solutions to improve urban life, governance and economic development. The specific criteria and methodology for calculating the Digital Cities Index may vary depending on the organization or research institution conducting the assessment.

To carry out this data comparison study, we used the latest DCI ranking – "Making digital work for cities: A global benchmark of urban technology." Following its analysis, we have selected those states and cities that can be considered models of best practices in certain fundamental components of digital transformation. Thus, we presented their situation and provided some examples of successfully completed processes.

In order to identify best practices of certain cities in the world, we used comparative analysis. Comparative scientific research methodology involves the systematic comparison of different variables, cases or groups to identify patterns, relationships and differences between them. This type of research aims to explore how and why certain variables behave differently or similarly, under different conditions (Ragin, 1987). Benchmarking a Digital City Index (DCI) involves assessing and comparing the digital maturity or readiness of different cities or regions. As the first stage of the comparative analysis, we identified the data of the most recent DCI ranking published during the past year. Afterwards, we collected the data for each city or region that we thought that it was relevant to present. According to the DCI, this data can include information on broadband access, digital literacy rates, availability of digital government services, technology startups and more. Due to the diversity and complexity of the data, we further divided the analysis into four segments according to the four fundamental indicators that the studied index takes into account when analyzing a city's digital performance: connectivity, services, culture and sustainability. Each of these pillars has various sub-branches and characteristics that we have summarized in Table 1. In order for our analysis to be relevant, we have highlighted which are those urban areas that have become centers of excellence according to the criteria presented in this table. The ranking is made following an objective process of quantitative and qualitative analyses, but without neglecting the citizens' perception. The results take into account the survey carried out on a sample of 3000 inhabitants living in the cities evaluated in DCI. Among the quantitative metrics we mention, for example, the speed of the Internet, and among the qualitative ones we mention the plans regarding technology such as smart city strategies.

This analysis can be valuable for various purposes such as investment decisions, urban planning and policy development. For our country, the purpose of such a study is to analyze the current state of affairs in Romania, in this context of digital transformation and, of course, to offer decision-makers, businesses and the public a reference point for understanding the level of digitization and technological readiness of cities, which can be useful for investment strategy, policy planning and measuring competitiveness and general quality of life in different urban areas. In recent years, significant shifts have taken place in the realm of public administration in Romania. These changes reflect a clear commitment from both central and local authorities to expedite the process of digital transformation. This involves the adoption of electronic identity solutions, the promotion of interoperable digital systems, the utilization of artificial intelligence applications, the establishment and operationalization of a government cloud, and various other initiatives(Androniceanu, 2023) Of course, the process of urban digital transformation is a particularly complex one, and the states have not yet discovered an ideal "recipe" in this direction, but the analysis below gives us a good overview that can be used as a starting point for creating a more integrated strategy.

3 Results and Discussions

The Digital Cities Index 2022 shows that, in the last decade, cities around the world have built digital infrastructure and integrated digital technologies into urban services, and to make cities safer and cleaner, smarter and more inclusive, they have integrated a series of of tools: artificial intelligence, the Internet of Things, cloud computing and 5G connectivity. Despite this integration of capabilities, the digital transformation of cities is seen as a long-term, complex process, for which challenges and pitfalls are expected, including social reaction and opposition. The Digital Cities Index (DCI) 2022 presents a ranking of 30 cities in the world based on 4 thematic pillars: connectivity, services, culture and sustainability.

Table 1. General framework of the Digital Cities Index.

Digital Cities Index			
1. Connectivity ▼	**2. Services** ▼	**3. Culture** ▼	**4. Sustenability** ▼
• Digital Infrastructure • Quality • Accesibility	• E-government services for residents and the business environment • Digital finance • Transportation • Health • Education • Retail and hospitality	• Digital inclusion • Government support • Innovative ecosystem • Public attitude and involvement	• Effective management of resources • Reduction of emissions • Pollution • Circular economy

Source: Author's analysis based on Digital Cities Index, 2022.

In what follows, we will analyze the situation in different states/cities among those included in the DCI, including Romania/Bucharest from the point of view of digital transformation.

3.1 Connectivity

In many DCI cities, connectivity levels are too low to enable comprehensive digital transformation.

In the top 10 most connected cities in DCI 2022, Denmark ranks 1st in the population's use of digital technology for the interface with public services. Copenhagen is among the world leaders in the use of digital technology for traffic control and pollution reduction, the use of GPS in public transport and the use of sensors in the waste system. Copenhagen is followed by Singapore, Zurich, Beijing, Sydney, Amsterdam, Hong Kong, New York, Washington and Seoul.

From the point of view of the digital quality of life, the USA ranks first, and Israel occupies the leading position in Asia. Among African countries, South Africa records the highest digital quality of life, and in Oceania, New Zealand surpassed Australia in various digital domains in 2022 .

In DCI 2022, Romania is not in the top 10 countries in the world, but the Digital Quality of Life Index 2022 places it in 34th place in the world in relation to general digital well- being. Among the pillars of the urban digitization indices, Romania's weakest point is for e-government (58th place worldwide), and the best score is recorded in terms of internet quality (13th place globally) and is 41 % better than the global average. Internet accessibility services place Romania in 18th place, and e-security and electronic infrastructure in 20th and 53rd places, respectively. As for the speed of the mobile Internet, it has improved in Romania, reaching to be surpassed by Bulgaria, but the fixed Internet in broadband it is superior to the mobile one in the global ranking.

From the point of view of mobile data accessibility, the first 5 cities with the lowest average costs for 1 GB of mobile data as a percentage of personal income are: Paris, Rome, Sydney, Copenhagen and Singapore, and the 5 cities with the highest costs mediums are: Manilla, Buenos Aires, Seoul, Auckland and Dubai (The Economist Group, 2022).

In Eastern Europe, Moldova is the cheapest ($0.26), followed by Poland ($0.41), Romania ($0.45) and Montenegro ($0.60). Greece is the most expensive in the region, where 1GB of mobile data costs $5.3 on average. In Romania, the average cost for 1 GB of mobile data is more than 12 times lower than in the USA in 2022 (Fodor, 2022).

In Western Europe, the cheapest mobile data is in France, Italy and San Marino, located below 0.25 USD, and the UK has an average cost of 0.79 USD, being the 7th cheapest in Europe by West and on the 59th cheapest place in the world (Fodor, 2022).

Asian countries make up a third of the top 20 cheapest countries for mobile data, with India ($0.17) and Nepal ($0.27) rounding out the top ten. Japan at $3.85 is above the global average of $3.12, while South Korea is the most expensive in the region ($12.55) (Fodor, 2022).

5G technology is the engine for the urban digital transformation, allowing activities that were not possible before. As 5G spreads, they will be able to offer basic advantages for urban services such as: interventions in emergency situations and public safety, education, e- commerce, industrial production, transport with autonomous and remotely controlled vehicles, optimization of supply chains by reacting in real time, etc. (The Economist Group, 2022). Regarding the 5G technology adopted in Europe, it can be stated that Finland is on the 1st place and Germany on the 8th place. The countries of South-Eastern Europe are at the bottom of the ranking, for example Cyprus 28, Albania 34, Bosnia and Herzegovina 36. In general, the richer a country is, the easier the conditions for introducing 5G are met. (The Economist Group, 2022).

3.2 Services

Municipal services have an impact on businesses and citizens' lives, and their efficiency can be increased through digital technology. The key indicators of this DCI pillar are: e- government portals for citizens and the business environment, digital technologies for biometric identification at airports and integrated applications in public transport, digital platforms for health and education, etc.

Singapore is the world leader in e-government, followed by São Paulo, where programs are implemented that allow access to public services from home. New Delhi ranks 3rd in e- governance services for residents and businesses, and in Seoul citizens are provided with services through which they can consult virtually with municipal officials.

Among the top cities that provide mobile applications allowing travel planning, issuing tickets, access to various attractions, digital tourist subscriptions, cities such as: Bangkok, Berlin, Copenhagen, Dubai, Paris, Seoul and Zurich can be listed.

Other types of services consist of the presence and adoption of telehealth and telemedicine, the issuance of electronic health records, access to programs for the prevention of diabetes, where New York ranks first.

In the field of digital financing, out of the first 10 places, 5 are occupied by Asian cities such as: Beijing, Seoul and Hong Kong. China and India are two world leaders in digital financing. Among the countries of the world that have adopted the mobile payment method in the highest percentage (as a percentage of the number of smartphone users) are: China, India, USA, Japan, Italy, UK, Russia, France and Germany. Five Asian cities are among the top 10 in the field of digital financing: Beijing, Seoul, Hong Kong, New Delhi and Singapore (The Economist Group, 2022). In the countries of South-Eastern Europe, the level of digital financial inclusion has increased in recent years, but it is on average lower than in the OECD countries.

3.3 Culture

The population of developing countries has higher digital skills than that of developed countries. Thus, the first 7 cities in the ranking of those that use digital platforms to the greatest extent are: New Delhi, Dubai, Jakarta, Beijing, Mexico City, Manila and Bangkok. The biggest involvement of citizens on e-government platforms is the inhabitants of cities in developing countries in Asia.

European and US cities lead the rankings in terms of openness to artificial intelligence used in traffic optimization, energy use, design and planning of urban services, etc. Artificial intelligence in public services is mostly used in 6 cities in Europe and the USA, such as: Dallas, New York, Washington, London, Berlin and Frankfurt. On the 7th and 8th places are the Asian cities Singapore and Seoul.

Western cities offer the strongest freedoms and guarantees in using the Internet, and Asia and the Middle East sustenabilitateare in last place. Regarding the average score of the indicator that illustrates the freedom of the Internet, the ranking is as follows: Europe (78.3), USA (78.0), Oceania (75.0), Latin America (65.0), Asia (51, 4) and the Middle East (27.0).

3.4 Sustainability

European cities invest significantly in air pollution control and monitoring, intelligent lighting, intelligent utility management, improving energy and resource efficiency, waste management. Technology can also help prevent natural disasters. Certain cities are using social media to track the progress of floods and earthquakes while micro sensors detect urban heat nuclei. These represent areas where temperatures are higher due to the fact that we very often encounter materials that capture heat (glass/concrete).Digital technologies such as artificial intelligence and Internet of Things can help improve energy and resource efficiency internationally – we are now talking about water, street lighting or efficient waste collection. Ten cities from DCI obtained maximum scores at the level of the use of digital technologies, for the management of smart utilities, and Barcelona is in first place. Amsterdam, Copenhagen, Frankfurt and Madrid scored well for intelligent traffic management. Amsterdam has invested substantially in traffic management for adaptive control of traffic lighting, analysis of traffic trends to improve situational assessment and reduce the number of accidents. In this regard, at the opposite end are cities of developing countries in Asia, such as: Manila, New Delhi, Tokyo, Bangkok, Seoul and Jakarta. The sharing economy is a solution where goods and resources can be used by more individuals or groups and helps with sustainability goals such as reducing waste. An example would be car sharing platforms to reduce traffic and pollution..Some cities have explicit plans, policies or frameworks for supports the collaborative economy: Amsterdam, Beijing, Copenhagen, Kuala Lumpur, Seoul, Sydney and Toronto. However, most of the the analyzed cities (23) have no plan in this direction.

3.5 Analysis

In the past decade, an increasing number of cities have aimed to harness the potential of cutting-edge technologies like AI, the Internet of Things (IoT), and cloud computing. These advancements have been greatly accelerated by the arrival of 5G connectivity. The COVID- 19 pandemic has prompted many cities to enhance their digital infrastructure in ways that might become permanent. Alongside the improved quality and affordability of digital technologies, cities now possess a wealth of experience to guide them in making informed decisions.

Experts observe that the concept of smart cities has evolved significantly. Initially characterized by top-down technocratic approaches and a fascination with impressive technology without a clear understanding of the problems it should address or its unintended consequences, there's now a shift toward a new era. In this new era, urban technology decisions are made through dialogue with urban constituents, including citizens and businesses. One solution is identifying the problem to be solved and then selecting the appropriate technology to address it, rather than starting with a predetermined technology and searching for a problem to apply it to. Hunter urges cities to focus on the specific challenges faced by their communities and to carefully assess how available technologies can be applied, to avoid falling into the trap of investing in flashy but ultimately unhelpful solutions.

The utility of the Digital Cities Index lies in its ability to provide a comprehensive assessment of a city's digital ecosystem and its impact on various aspects of urban life and development. In the analysis above, we took the data provided by DCI and presented the situation regarding the 4 pillars that DCI considers: connectivity, culture, services and sustainability. As we presented above, in all 4 chapters, there are states that can serve as models of good practice for our country so that we can make progress on digital transformation. Unfortunately, although in Romania there is an institution with specific responsibilities, the DSI ranking does not recognize performance in this direction. This situation is confirmed by the fact that the report taxes our country, in particular, in the e- government chapter (The Economist Group, 2022). As I presented above, Romania does not have a convincing performance except at the point of connectivity, the performance of the Internet being already a well-known information and an aspect appreciated at the international level. However, if we refer to the rest of the chapters, we are far from the performance of the Danish state regarding the use of digital technologies or the functions provided by Singapore in terms of e-government.

The DCI ranking serves as a valuable tool for stakeholders, including governments, businesses, researchers and the public, to understand, assess and improve the digital readiness and competitiveness of cities and regions. However, the presented hierarchy has its limits due to the fact that it is constructed by an organization that may have a subjective approach depending on its priorities and biases. Also, we cannot fail to note the fact that urban digitization is a particularly complex process that involves numerous fields that were not taken into account in the construction of the index. DCI may not cover all aspects of a city's digitization efforts. For example, they may not capture the quality of digital education, citizen engagement or specific cultural and creative digital initiatives. However, the above analysis is representative of the digital transformation process of cities / states but the results should be taken carefully without limiting the process to this ranking.

3.6 Conclusions and Limits

Over time, there have been various attempts to outline patterns, methodologies or support tools to succeed in accelerating the digital transformation process

(Csukas et al., 2020). The developments made by different stakeholders or social actors had their specific limitations. Thus, analyzes coordinated by private providers are too narrow in scope and are reduced to urban aspects related to their products and services (Robinson, 2015). Furthermore, the approaches proposed by the management of certain public administrations or academic staff are too specific to a certain type of city (Millard et al., 2014) while the approaches wider ones are too generic. However, "digitalization in cities presents the potential for highly inclusive, evidence-based urban planning decision-making, responding to the increasing pressures cities face" (Csukas et al., 2020). As experimental learning and testing (Cook et al., 2019) are fundamental in the process of urban digitization, it is necessary to persist in the process of analyzing and researching the phenomenon. The article proposed by us is based on DCI rankings, internationally recognized hierarchies for their complexity. Sure they can suggest correlations between digitization and various outcomes, but they may fail to establish causation. Certainly there are other factors, other than digitization, factors that can influence the performance of a city and were not analyzed by the DCI. At the same time, there is no standard definition of what constitutes a "digital city." Different components of the process can be measured differently, making it difficult to create a universally accepted reference standard. Last but not least, the level of digitization and technology adoption can vary significantly between regions and cultures. DCI may not always take these variations into account adequately. Although our research is a dashboard of the state of global digitization, we can explore this idea of regional diversity in our next studies to be able to narrow the analysis on possible directions that our country could take in the future.

Acknowledgment

The paper has been prepared under the research project with the title: Digitization, digital transformation, and artificial intelligence in public administration, 2023, financed by the Bucharest University of Economic Studies and is part of the research strategy of the International Centre for Public Management.

References

Albino, V., Berardi, U., & Dangelico, R. M. (2015). Smart cities: Definitions, dimensions, performance, and initiatives. *Journal of Urban Technology, 22*(1), 3–21.

Andersen, R., Jensen, L. B., & Ryberg, M. (2021). Using digitized public accessible building data to assess the renovation potential of existing building stock in a sustainable urban perspective. *Sustainable Cities and Society, 75*, Article 103303.

Androniceanu, A. (2023). The new trends of digital transformation and artificial intelligence in public administration. *Administratie si Management Public, 40*, 147–155.

Androniceanu, A., Georgescu, I., & Sabie, O.-M. (2022). The impact of digitalization on public administration, economic development, and well-being in the EU countries. *Central European Public Administration Review, 20*(2), 9–31.

Biesaga, M., Domaradzka, A., Roszczyńska-Kurasińska, M., Talaga, S., & Nowak, A. (2023). The effect of the pandemic on European narratives on smart cities and surveillance. *Urban Studies, 60*(10),1894–1914.

Ciancarini, P., Giancarlo, R., & Grimaudo, G. (2023). *Digital transformation in the public administrations: A guided tour for computer scientists*. https://arxiv.org/abs/2305.05551.

Cook, M., Horne, R., Potter, S, & Valdez, A. M. (2019). Exploring the epistemic politics of urban niche experiments. In Jensen, Jens Stissing; Cashmore, Matthew; & Späth, Philippeds. *The politics of urban sustainability transitions: Knowledge, power and governance* (pp. 125–147). Routledge,

Csukás, M. S., Bukovszki, V., & Reith, A. (2020). Challenges and solutions for organizational design in urban digitalization. *European Journal of Sustainable Development, 9*(2), 615–629.

Dumitrescu, R. (2022, 15th July). *Bucharest tops ranking of smart city projects, report shows*. https://www.romania-insider.com/bucharest-tops-ranking-smart-city-projects- report.

European Commission. (2021). Digital Economy and Society Index (DESI) 2021. https://digital-strategy.ec.europa.eu/en/library/digital-economy-and-society-index-desi-2021

European Commission. (2022). Digital Economy and Society Index (DESI) 2022. https://digital-strategy.ec.europa.eu/en/library/digital-economy-and-society-index-desi-2022.

European Parliament, Directorate-General for Internal Policies of the Union, Millard, J., Thaarup, R., & Pederson, J. (2014). Mapping smart cities in the EU, *Publications Office*. https://data.europa.eu/doi/10.2861/3408.

Evans, J., Karvonen, A., Luque, A., Martin, C., McCormick, K., Raven, R., & Palgan, Y. V. (2019). Smart and sustainable cities? Pipedreams, practicalities and possibilities. *Local Environment, 24*(7), 557–564.

Fodor, S. (2022). Ranking: Price of 1GB of mobile data in RO, 12 times cheaper than in the US. https://www.romania-insider.com/price-one-gigabyte-mobile-data-ro-jul-2022.

Gao, D., Li, G., & Yu, J. (2022). Does digitization improve green total factor energy efficiency? Evidence from Chinese 213 cities. *Energy, 247*, Article 123395.

Isin E., & Ruppert, E. (2020). *Being digital citizens* (2nd ed.). Rowman & Littlefield Publishers.

Jiang, Z., Zhang, X., Zhao, Y., Li, C., & Wang, Z. (2023). The impact of urban digital transformation on resource sustainability: Evidence from a quasi-natural experiment in China. *Resources Policy*, *85,* Article 103784.

Karvonen, A., Matthew, C., & Håvard, H. (2020). Urban planning and the Smart City: Projects, practices and politics. *Urban Planning, 5*(1), 65–68.

Maiurova, A., Kurniawan, T. A., Kustikova, M., Bykovskaia, E., Othman, M. H. D., Singh, D., & Goh, H. H. (2022), Promoting digital transformation in waste collection service and waste recycling in Moscow (Russia): Applying a circular economy paradigm to mitigate climate change impacts on the environment. *Journal of Cleaner Production*, *354*, Article 131604.

Li, M., Li, X., Wu, D., Zou, L., & Huang, X. (2023). Digitizing and inventorying traffic control infrastructures: A review of practices. *Transportation Research Interdisciplinary Perspectives, 21*, Article 100879.

Peng, H., Zhang, Y., & Liu, J. (2023). The energy rebound effect of digital development: Evidence from 285 cities in China. Energy, 270, 126837. https://doi.org/10.1016/j.energy.2023.126837

Ragin, C. (1987). *The comparative method: Moving beyond qualitative and quantitative strategies*. University of California Press.

Reis, J., & Melão, N. (2023). Digital transformation: A meta-review and guidelines for future research. *Heliyon*, *9*(1), Article e12834.

Robinson, R. (2015). 6 inconvenient truths about Smart Cities. *The Urban Technologist*. http://theurbantechnologist.com/2015/02/15/6-inconvenient-truths-about-smart-cities.

The Economist Group. (2022). *Digital City Index*. https://impact.economist.com/projects/digital-cities/#:~:text=The%20Digital%20Cities%20Index%20%28DCI%29%202022%2C%20developed%20by,digitisation%20in%20a%20selection%20of%2030%20global%20cities.

United Nations Human Settlements Programme. (2009). *Planning Sustainable Cities: Global Report on Human Settlements 2009*. https://unhabitat.org/planning-sustainable- cities-global-report-on-human-settlements-2009.

Van Holstein, E., Wiesel, I., Bigby, Ch., & Gleeson, B. (2021). People with intellectual disability and the digitalization of services. *Geoforum, 119*, 133–142.

Tomas Barcak[1,*], and Zdenek Franek[1]

Use of Unified Modelling Language and Enterprise Resource Planning System to Improve the Quality of Management and Production in a Manufacturing Company

Abstract:
Research background: The issue of optimization and control of production quality in manufacturing companies is closely related to the theory of enterprise resource planning (ERP) information systems. The graphical modelling tool UML (Unified Modelling Language) is used to model the processes in manufacturing companies and the properties of information systems. Another starting point is advanced statistical datamining methods, which use data sources from the ERP and which are then used in the modelling of product quality optimisation.
Purpose of the article: The aim of this paper is to present the results of research in the area of improving the quality and efficiency of production using data from ERP and modelling business processes using UML. The data repository of an enterprise information system is used as the source of the investigated and processed data, which is used for statistical analysis and subsequent modelling of production optimization a manufacturing company.
Methods: Data are processed using statistical methods and business processes are then modelled using the knowledge of operators and technical staff. The graphical modelling language UML was used to advantage in the modelling process.
Findings & Value added: The results of the research and modelling of production processes have a direct impact on resource planning in the enterprise information system (ERP) and production quality improvement. Modeling using the UML tool in conjunction with statistical methods and data from the ERP system is an original approach that provides the management of manufacturing enterprises with a useful tool for optimizing production management.

Keywords: *Modelling, UML, ERP system, business processes, production quality*

JEL Classification: *H8; C61; C63*

* Corresponding author: barcak@opf.slu.cz; franek@opf.slu.cz

1 Silesian University in Opava, School of Business Administration in Karvina, Department of Informatics and Mathematics, Univerzitní náměstí 1934/3,733 40 Karviná, Czech Republic

1 Introduction

Every organization – a company, a manufacturing enterprise or a government institution, produces a large amount of data through its information system, usually as a result of economic, logistic, operational or production processes. According to Karimi et al. (2007), based on empirical data, it has been found that the extent of ERP system implementation affects the results of business processes. This paper focuses on quality optimization in manufacturing companies. During the production process, a large amount of data is generated and stored in the databases of the enterprise information system – ERP system (Hoeven, 2009). Data from the entire production process is stored, i.e., from the inputs (material purchase), through the production process to the evaluation of the product quality and its sale to customers.

In the process of production planning, it is a necessary condition to maintain the required quality of production and to respect all limiting conditions of the production process (capacity, technological, etc.) (Švec et al., 2016). In today's industrial enterprises, more and more emphasis is being placed on the quality of products at each stage of production. With the increasing modernization of business and the development of automation technology, many plants are switching to automated management (David et al., 2019).

This paper deals with the streamlining of production processes to achieve the best possible product quality. For this purpose, data from ERP system is used and imported for statistical evaluation and feedback to the production process. The UML modelling language (ISO/IEC 19505–1, 2012) is used to describe the process. Among the UML diagrams, the following are used: a USE CASE diagram showing the roles of managers in modelling production quality improvement, a class diagram modelling data storage and relationships between objects, and an activity diagram modelling the quality improvement process algorithm using statistical methods. Advanced software is used for statistical analyses, including state-of-the-art statistical methods, including data mining methods. Comprehensive ERP systems must correspond to the adopted business (business) strategy and be in line with the chosen production management concept (Weske, 2007; Pecoraro & Luzi, 2022). It is important that all necessary data is concentrated in the ERP system and the method of data storage in the centralized database of the ERP system is convenient for performing various analyses. The aim of this paper is to show how this data can be used with the involvement of the company's employees to optimize the production process with an impact on product quality.

2 Methods

2.1 ERP Systems

The abbreviation ERP is based on the English name Enterprise Resource Planning. However, this name must not confuse us. It is related to the history of ERP system development, which will be mentioned below. Today, ERP can be briefly defined as an integrated software system that supports the planning and management of all major processes in an enterprise (Balić et al., 2022). An important feature of an ERP system is the use of standardized approaches to these processes. Standardized approaches emerge as generalizations of known and best practices in a large number of organizations (Zafar et al., 2019). An ERP system typically contains the following subsystems: Purchasing, Manufacturing, Sales, Finance, Human Resources (HR and Payroll). These subsystems represent the core of an ERP system, usually also related to the definition of an ERP system in a narrower sense.

Other modules such as Customer Relationship Management (CRM), Service, Management Information Systems of different levels, E-commerce, Supplier Relationship Management (SCM) and others are connected to this core. Thus, ERP systems are systems that integrate the core business subsystems into a single entity (core ERP). The downstream modules extend the core ERP into ERP in a broader sense. In this way, an ERP system in the broader sense can be considered as the entire information system of an enterprise. A summary of the functions of an ERP system is given in Figure 1.

The core is followed by other modules, namely supplier relationship management on the input side and customer relationship management, which includes e-commerce on the output side. The core and additional functions are followed by support for management functions, in particular the Decision Support System (DSS), Executive Information System (EIS), data warehouse, general Business Intelligence modules and others. The definition of an ERP system in a broader and narrower sense makes it clear that it is a large system both in terms of software modules and technical and communication support (hardware, network management, system software) (Slaninová & Vymětal, 2023).

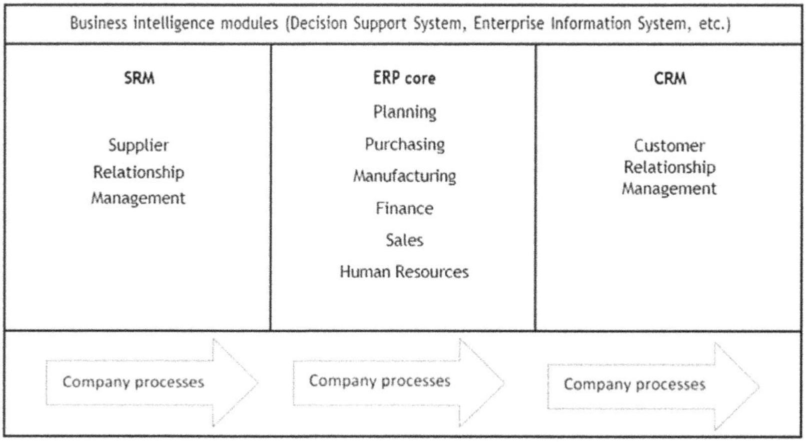

Figure 1. ERP system overview.
Source: Slaninová & Vymětal (2023)

The above figure shows that the ERP system covers a substantial part of the company's processes. (Slaninová & Vymětal, 2023).

The production quality data is contained in the production subsystem. It is essential that the ERP data can be exported for data processing by statistical methods or statistical software. The ideal situation is when a matrix with both data having an impact on production quality (the so-called independent variables) and data with quality assessment (the so-called dependent variables) is exported. A possible procedure for exporting data from an ERP system is shown in Figure 2.

The data from the ERP system on the quality of the product with the parameters under which it was created must be subjected to further analysis. All employees involved in the production must be involved in this process. These are in particular the company management, technical control staff, researchers, etc. It depends on the capabilities of the ERP system whether it has sufficient support for such analysis. For the analyses it is necessary to use other software, in particular statistical software, process modelling software and sometimes it is necessary to develop a custom extension to evaluate the quality of production. The next part of the article shows how to proceed and what resources can be used.

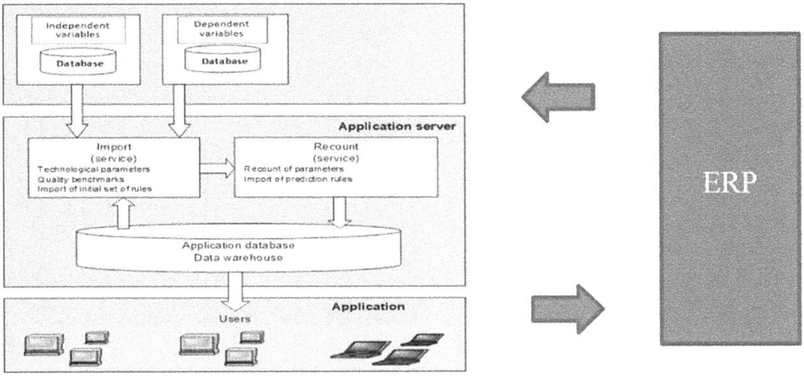

Figure 2. Export of data from ERP system for statistical analysis and production quality improvement.

Source: own

2.2 Statistical Methods and Data Mining for Production Quality Improvement

Overview of statistical methods for the evaluation of casting parameters and slab quality:

- Descriptive statistics of measured variables,
- frequency histograms,
- data filtering and cleaning,
- correlation analysis,
- regression analysis,
- hypothesis testing,
- classification tables
- factor analysis
- clustering methods, segmentation and typology generation
- multidimensional scales (perceptual maps and relationship mapping).

Knowledge mining from databases is the process of non-trivial extraction of implicit, previously unknown and potentially useful information from data. This process consists of a series of steps in which the data is sequentially prepared for analysis, analyzed, and the extracted knowledge is evaluated and used to solve a given problem. In contrast to the use of statistical methods, the knowledge mining process also emphasizes the preparation of data for analysis and the interpretation of the knowledge obtained. A comprehensive methodology is described in the literature (Aalst 2011), which is schematically illustrated in Figure 3.

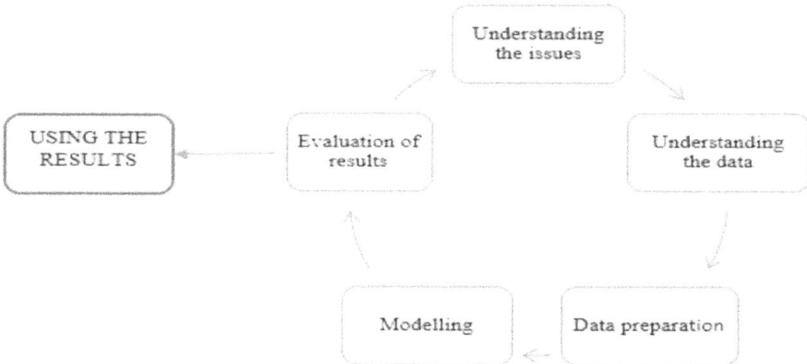

Figure 3. Methodology datamining.
Source: own

The computational core of the whole process of knowledge extraction from databases is the use of analytical methods. This step is called data mining, modelling or analysis in English literature (O'Reilly et al., 2022).

Overview of data mining methods:

Neural networks, cluster analysis, decision trees, association rules, logistic regression.

Data mining methods are incorporated into statistical software "packages" such as IBM SPSS Statistics©, STATISTICA©, MATLAB© and others.

2.3 Process Modelling and Unified Modelling Language

The UML modelling language is a set of graphical notations for expressing analytical and design models (Page-Jones, 1999). UML is a language that provides the assumptions and capabilities for modelling simple and complex applications using the same formal syntax. UML serves well in creating both simple and complex applications while using the same formal syntax.

An overview of UML diagrams (Franěk, 2018) is presented in Figure 4.

STATIC STRUCTURE	DYNAMICAL BEHAVIOUR	MODULE MANAGEMENT
Class Diagram	Use CASE diagram	Packages
Object Diagram	Sequence Diagram	Subsystems
Component Diagram	Activity Diagram	Models
Deployment Diagram	Collaboration Diagram	
	State Chart Diagram	

Figure 4. Overview of UML diagrams by type of destination
Source: own

The UML modeling graphical language is an ideal means of sharing workflows for developers, testers, as well as system specifiers and users. It is also used to clarify user requirements for the system being developed. UML diagrams always focus on just one view of the problem at hand. The proposed system captures the whole by a complex of individual UML diagrams (Arlow & Neustadt, 2005).

The modeling techniques using UML support the most well-known UP (Unified Process) and RUP (Rational Unified Process) methodologies.

Although the modelling language is mainly intended for the development of information systems software, it can serve equally well in modelling production quality improvement processes (Penker & Eriksson, 1999, OMG BPMN, 2014). These issues are closely related in that it is necessary to export the data from the ERP system, prepare the data for processing by standard statistical software, and reverse engineer the findings into the ERP system. The practical part of the paper demonstrates how UML can be used.

Class Diagram, Use CASE diagram and Activity diagram (Fowler, 2003) were used for the practical part of the article.

3 Results

3.1 Definition of the Problem

Evaluation of the quality of slabs at the continuous casting plant is part of the information system of the steel plant. The continuous casting plant (CCP) is part of metallurgical production. In order to improve quality, it is necessary to develop a comprehensive system for long-term monitoring of casting parameters and their influence on the quality of the pre- cast. The proposed procedure and process work with all data available from the CCP process. It is based on the ERP system data and from there the data is exported and paired with other measured data directly from the CCP casting machine and the casting temperature model. The system includes data uploading and filtering, data sorting, storage in a relational database system, data aggregation and graphical interpretation.

Data selection functions are available for the analysis methods. The user can transform the data into a matrix of causes – measured variables and consequences – qualitative indicators. Over such narrowed data, the steelworks employees perform statistical analyses of the casting process (Pyszko et al., 2018). The system allows the selected data to be exported to other statistical programs for more detailed analyses. After the statistical analyses are evaluated by the head of the CCP, operation, researchers and the staff of the Department of Management Technology and Quality Control, adjustments and changes are proposed for planning further production. These changes, after approval by the company management are implemented back into the ERP system.

3.2 Data Hierarchy

Data storage is performed according to the hierarchy of defect occurrence: data to the sequence, melt, slab, measured quantities (called channels) from the casting machine, data on the quality of slabs and the products rolled from them (Franěk et al., 2015), see Figure 5.

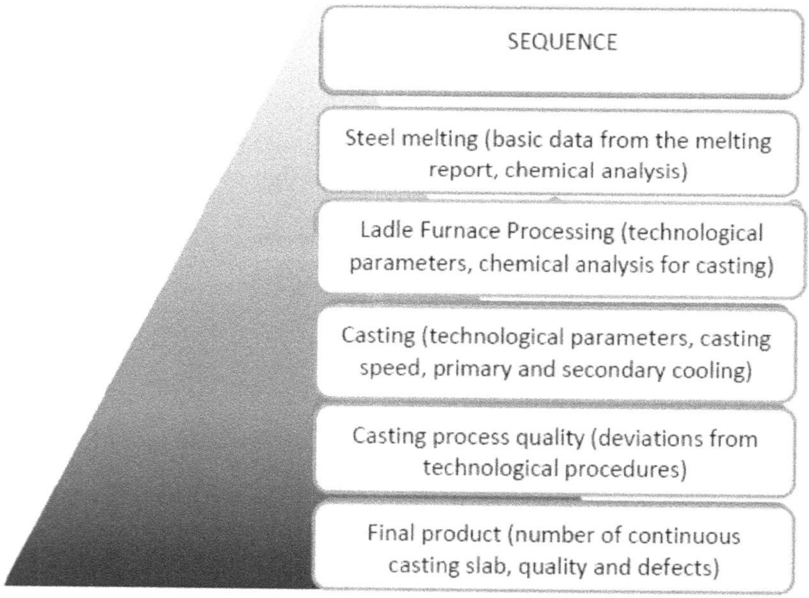

Figure 5. Data storage hierarchy.
Source: own

Files are divided into items with their attributes. There are about 400 items in the whole system, and if we add to this that the technological parameters, the so-called channels, are measured every 10 seconds, a considerable amount of data is generated.

3.3 Data Storage Structure – Class Diagram

The data structure and the relationships between objects are best captured in the UML class diagram, see Figure 6. This is then detailed into a final class diagram with items (attributes) and operations (algorithms).

By combining the files on casting parameters and precast quality, it is possible to create a basic and important activity for determining the quality level of the precast and, more importantly, for establishing plausible limits for the individual parameters beyond which a defect occurs. This activity mainly involves statistical investigations of large files.

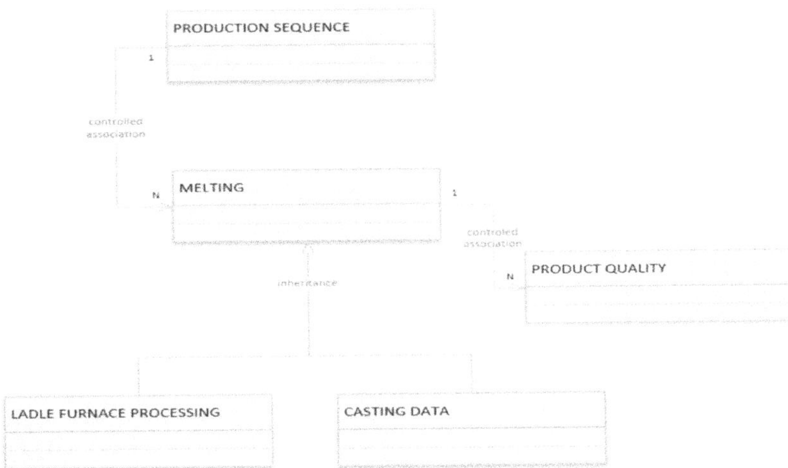

Figure 6. Class diagram.

Source: own

3.4 Use Case Diagram for Quality Optimization

Use cases accurately capture the functionality covered by the system and thus clearly define the scope of work. Each use case describes one of the behaviors of the system, thus describing one of its desired functionalities. The USE CASE also identifies the users of the system, called actors, and defines their individual roles. Each actor performs certain activities in the optimization system, which are described in the scenarios. An example of the USE CASE diagram for our example of quality optimization at the ZPO is shown in Figure 7.

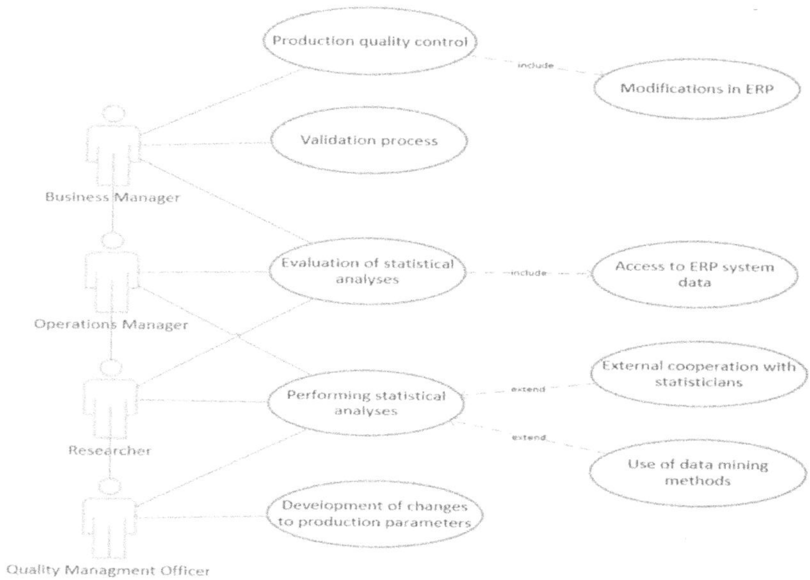

Figure 7. Use case quality optimization.
Source: own

For each individual case (in the ellipse), a scenario is developed describing in more detail the activities required to fulfil the purpose of the process. For example, statistical analyses may be described in detail and may not be performed by a single worker, but by a whole team of workers. The description of individual use case scenarios is beyond the scope of this paper.

3.5 Activity Diagram

An Activity Diagram is a type of interaction diagram that is used to describe workflows. It also allows you to graphically model individual use cases as a sequence of actions. The Activity Diagram in Figure 8 describes the process of optimizing the quality of production at a ZPO using statistical methods. It is a basic simple diagram demonstrating their meaning. In real operations, activity diagrams are more complex and show a sequence of activities that support both sequential and parallel behavior. Activity diagrams are probably the most difficult part of the UML.

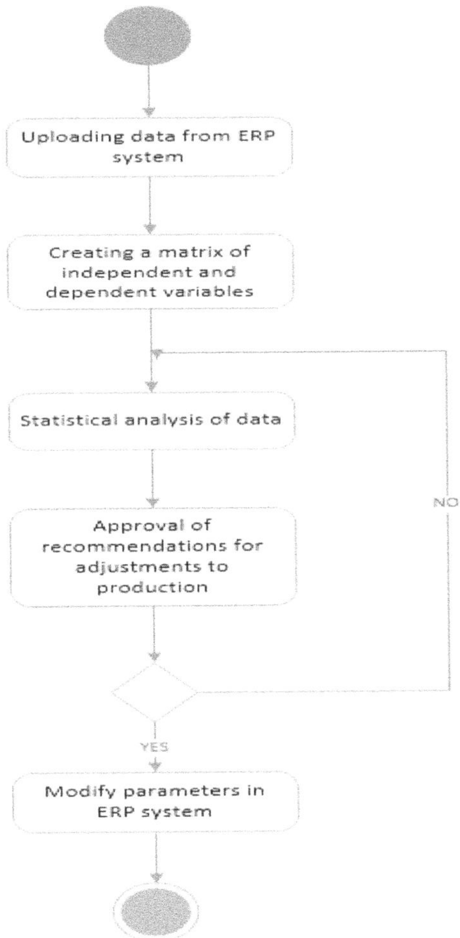

Figure 8. Activity diagram.

Source: own

4 Discussion

The procedure was verified in the conditions of a metallurgical enterprise, specifically for a continuous steel casting plant. It was practically verified that the procedure is feasible and is particularly suitable for enterprises with measurable production parameters and with measurable product quality parameters. In writing this article, the authors of the article have based their own knowledge and experience in the problems of production in metallurgical enterprises. In doing so, advanced statistical methods of datamining were used (Franěk et al., 2020).

The obtained findings and methodology can be generalized for medium and large enterprises that use an ERP system and their production leads to a final product that can be evaluated by ordinal variables.

5 Conclusion

The article gives an overview of a possible procedure for optimizing production quality. As the first starting point for a solution, the ERP system, which every manufacturing company is already equipped with, was described. The second basis of the solution is the use of statistical methods, including data mining methods, and finally, the third element is modelling with the UML graphical language. These three theoretical bases have been combined into a methodology for how to optimize production processes and continuously improve production quality in a manufacturing company.

The main contribution of this approach is the analysis and proposal to create a software module that is interfaced with the ERP system, as illustrated in Figure 2. According to the requirement of the company management, this software module can be integrated directly into the ERP system. In the analysis of the creation of the module described above, the graphical modelling language UML was used to great advantage. This tool helps workers of various professions to understand the problem being solved.

Acknowledgments

"This paper was supported by the Ministry of Education, Youth and Sports Czech Republic within the Institutional Support for Long-term Development of a Research Organization in 2023."

References

Aalst, W. (2011). *Process mining: Discovery, conformance and enhancement of business processes*. Springer-Verlag.

Arlow, J., & Neustadt, I. (2005). *UML 2 and the unified process: Practical object-oriented analysis and design*. Addison-Wesley.

Balić A., Turulja, L., Kuloglija, E., & Pejic-Bach, M. (Pejic-Bach, Mirjana). (2022). ERP quality and the organizational performance: Technical characteristics vs. information and service. *Information*, *13*(10), Article 474.

David, J., Garzinová, R., Barčák, T., Sláčala, J., & Shmeleva, N. (2019). Digitization of embossed numbers on continuous steel casting billets. *METAL 2019, Ostrava: Tanger, 2019. 28th International Conference on Metallurgy and Materials* (pp. 1892–1897).

Fowler, M. (2003). *UML distilled: A brief guide to the standard object modeling language*. Addison Wesley.

Franěk, Z., & Pyszko, R. (2020). *Logit Model and Prediction Quality of Continuously Cast Slabs. METAL 2020, Ostrava: Tanger, 2020. 29th International Conference on Metallurgy and Materials* (pp.1232–1237).

Franěk, Z. (2018). *Objektové metody modelování, učební text*. Karviná: Slezská univerzita.

Franěk, Z., Masarík, M., & Šmid, J. (2015). Determination of the cause of the formation of transverse internal cracks on a continuously cast slab. *Materiali in Tehnologie*, *49*(2), 285–290.

ISO/IEC 19505-1. (2012). *Information technology – Object Management Group Unified Modeling Language (OMG UML) – Part 1: Infrastructure*. https://www.iso.org/standard/32624.html.s

Karimi, J., Somers, T. M., & Bhattacherjee, A. (2007). The impact of ERP implementation on business process outcomes: A factor-based study. *Journal of Management Information Systems*, *24*(1), 101–134.

O´Reilly, J. A., Wehrman, J., & Sowman P. F. (2022). A guided tutorial on modelling human event-related potentials with recurrent neural networks. *Sensors*, *22*(23), Article 9243.

OMG BPMN. (2014). *Business process model and notation*. https://www.omg.org/spec/BPMN

Page-Jones, M. (1999). *Fundamentals of Object-Oriented Design in UML*. Pearson India.

Pecoraro, F., & Luzi, D. (2022*)*. Using unified modeling language to analyze business processes in the delivery of child health services. *International Journal of Environmental Research and Public Health*, *19*(20), Article 13456.

Penker, M., & Eriksson, H. E. (1999). *Business modeling with UML: Business patterns at work*. Wiley.

Pyszko, R., Franek, Z., Príhoda, M., Velicka, M., & Sikora, K. (2018). Monitoring and simulation of the unsteady states in continuous casting. *Materiali in Tehnologie*, *52*(2), 111–117.

Slaninová, K., & Vymětal, S. (2023). *Podnikové informační systémy - ERP*. Distanční studijní text. Karviná: Slezská univerzita.

Švec, P., Frischerová, L., Barčák, T., & David, J. (2016). Usage of analytical diagnostic for operational control support on steelworks. *METAL 2016, Ostrava: Tanger, 2016. 25th Anniversary International Conference on Metallurgy and Materials* (pp. 2049–2054).

Van der Hoeven, H. (2009). Erp and Business Processes. Aeon Publishing Inc.

Weske, M. (2007). *Business process management - Concepts, languages, architectures*. Springer-Verlag.

Zafar I., Azam, F., Anwar, M. W., Maqbool, B., Butt, W. H., & Nazir, A. (2019). A novel framework to automatically generate executable web services from BPMN models. *IEEE Access*, *7*, 93653–93677.

Radka Bauerova,[1,*], and Lucie Vavruskova[1]

Exploring the Metaverse Gold Rush: Understanding Consumer Behaviour and Usage Implications within a Globalized Virtual Realm

Abstract:
Research background: In the rapidly evolving environment of virtual reality and digital connectivity, the concept of the metaverse has emerged as a dynamic domain with profound implications for consumer behaviour and globalized interactions. As the influence of the metaverse expands across borders, its potential use is becoming a key issue. In this paper, the focus is on this dynamic environment to explore the interplay between consumer behaviour and the global implications of the metaverse.
Purpose of the article: The central purpose of this article is to unravel the intricate dimensions of customer behaviour and usage patterns in the metaverse, investigating their impact on globalized interactions. By analysing willingness to test new products for monetary rewards, apprehensions regarding user behaviour data collection, content creation abilities, proclivity to invest in metaverse technologies, and purchasing behaviour within the metaverse, this study sheds light on the complex dynamics that define this virtual frontier.
Methods: This study focused on the dynamics of the metaverse and its implications in a globalized context through the method of questioning through a structured questionnaire. The data collection was carried out through an online panel of the research agency Ipsos. The study involves a diverse sample to ensure representation across geographical, demographic, and socio-economic strata.
Findings & Value added: This study reveals the spectrum of attitudes within the use of the metaverse and the associated global implications. The unique dynamics of metaverse consumption challenge traditional models and require adaptive business strategies.

Keywords: *consumer behavior, digital environment, globalized interactions, metaverse, virtual reality*

JEL Classification: *M20; M39; O33*

* Corresponding author: bauerova@opf.slu.cz
1 Silesian University in Opava, School of Business Administration in Karvina, Univerzitní náměstí 1934/3, 733 40 Karviná, Czechia

1 Introduction

The advent of the metaverse, an expansive and immersive digital realm, has ushered humanity into a new era of virtual interconnectedness. This evolving frontier has captivated the collective imagination and garnered remarkable attention from technologists, businesses, and scholars alike. Within this burgeoning metaverse ecosystem, users engage in multifaceted activities, from social interactions to commerce, entertainment, and content creation, all within a hyper-realistic digital domain. As the metaverse continues to expand its influence, it presents a compelling intersection between technology, consumer behaviour, and globalization. This paper embarks on a comprehensive exploration of the metaverse's implications in the context of globalization. The metaverse, often described as a digital mirror of the physical world, has not only transformed the way we interact with digital technology but also revolutionized the avenues for consumption, socialization, and personal expression. This paper delves into the multifaceted dimensions of the metaverse, dissecting the intricate dynamics that govern consumer behaviour and usage patterns within this virtual expanse.

As the metaverse takes center stage in the global digital landscape, its potential for both innovation and exploitation becomes increasingly pertinent. This paper seeks to provide valuable insights for stakeholders, including businesses, policymakers, and researchers, to navigate this transformative terrain ethically and effectively. By shedding light on the metaverse gold rush and its far-reaching implications, this study aims to contribute to the evolving discourse surrounding virtual reality, consumer behaviour, and globalization in the digital age. Consumer behaviour has recently been influenced by, among other things, the FoMO (Fear of Missing Out) phenomenon, so one of the assumptions of this study is that people who are most susceptible to this phenomenon (those with higher FoMO scores) will have a more positive attitude towards buying a product in the metaverse because they will not want to feel that they have missed out.

1.1 Metaverse

In recent years, the burgeoning field of virtual environments has garnered substantial scholarly and public attention. Notably, the metaverse has emerged as a phenomenon with distinctive attributes, marking a departure from conventional global cultural influences. Its impact and reach are characterized by distinctive features that set it apart from prior cultural phenomena. The metaverse market is forecasted to reach $280 billion by 2025, with the VR sector within the metaverse estimated to surge from $33 billion in 2020 to $338.1 billion in 2025 and a staggering $1.92.4 trillion by 2030. (Jeon, 2021). While no existing metaverse perfectly aligns with the ideal metaverse criteria, several notable platforms, including Second Life, Roblox, Decentraland, and Fortnite, exhibit key features like proprietary ecosystems (user-generated content, economies, currencies, artificial intelligence), interactive elements (creators, VR/AR), and integration with blockchain technology.

Scholars have extensively referred to the metaverse as a virtual world platform, notable for its striking resemblance to the physical world and its dense interconnectedness with it (Seo et al., 2023). This digital expanse is increasingly recognized for its capacity to provide immersive experiences while fostering the creation of robust social connections among users (Buhalis et al., 2023). Its ubiquitous presence is observed across both industrial and academic domains on a global scale, underscoring its significance (Zhang et al., 2022).

The overarching aim of the metaverse is to establish an immersive virtual realm wherein users engage with the digital environment alongside real-world counterparts (Chen, 2022). In this intricate digital realm, a distinct tension arises between the digital and physical realities, manifesting in the form of a 3D object-based world, which facilitates the construction of a comprehensive 3D network within a virtual space. Users navigate a diverse array of activities within this network, fostering extensive social interactions and networking (Al-Ghaili et al., 2022).

1.1.1 Perception of the Metaverse

The metaverse holds substantial promise for organizations in terms of innovative business models and enhanced operational capabilities, thereby attracting scholarly attention (Dwivedi et al., 2022). Simultaneously, individuals who opt to engage in this digital domain can significantly enrich their experiences while forging novel interactions with the virtual environment. As exemplified by Facebook, noteworthy strategic developments have been undertaken, focusing on novel customer channels for direct marketing and sales. These endeavors are characterized by the integration of digital offers and emerging technologies. Capitalizing on well-established user interactions, Meta Platforms, the parent entity of the Facebook social platform, can extend its strategic initiatives by introducing new hardware solutions tailored to the existing customer base. Consequently, this strategic evolution culminates in a continuity of customer channels throughout the final operational phase (Kraus et al., 2022).

However, the adoption of virtual environments may not be devoid of concerns. Privacy apprehensions in such spaces can potentially engender discomfort among users, consequently influencing their perception of this immersive world (Stephan & Stephan, 2017). Conversely, certain users immersed in virtual environments may develop a profound attachment to this digital realm, surpassing their connection to physical places in the tangible world. This phenomenon can contribute to the emergence of viral destinations and engender a profound sense of attachment within the metaverse community (Oleksy et al., 2023).

1.1.2 Content Creation and Problems in Metaverse

Among one of the most important factors that can influence the emergence of content into the metaverse is the monetary factor that can help the economic system (Weinberger, 2022). Thus, monetary factors, such as financial investments and revenue generation, are critical drivers in shaping the metaverse's economic ecosystem. Essentially, it suggests that content creators, businesses, and individuals are incentivized to participate in the metaverse primarily due to the potential for financial gains. This could include creating and selling virtual products, services, or experiences, which contribute to the overall economic structure of the metaverse. This highlights how financial incentives are a powerful force shaping the evolution and growth of the metaverse.

In recent years, as highlighted by Hwang (2023), the metaverse has evolved into a creative domain that accommodates users' problem-solving and curiosity-driven activities. However, it is noteworthy that users may encounter adverse experiences primarily stemming from technical challenges. Wang et al. (2023) contribute to this discourse by discussing the enhancement of metaverse content, categorizing it into four distinct segments: viral 3D reconstruction, data-driven generation, and the progressive refinement of antiquated content. Beyond its creative and recreational potential, the metaverse has also found relevance in religious contexts. Yamac (2023) raises pertinent concerns regarding the potential for religious authority misuse within this virtual sphere.

The metaverse presents a multifaceted landscape with associated security implications, including data breaches, theft, injection attacks, and authentication vulnerabilities. Notably, it introduces novel challenges, exemplified by the potential intrusion into an individual's physical body via brain-computer interfaces connected to the metaverse (Huang et al., 2023). These emergent issues, while paramount, are not exhaustive; additional concerns encompass mental and physical health (Leenes, 2009). This suggests that the metaverse, while offering numerous advantages, introduces security challenges that are not encountered in conventional digital spaces. These concerns are significant and should not be ignored. Therefore, the need for comprehensive investigation and management of safety and well- being issues within the metaverse ecosystem can be seen here.

2 Methodology

A quantitative research approach was employed to investigate the attitudes and behaviors of participants within the metaverse. The primary data collection instrument was a structured survey questionnaire. Given the nascent nature of the metaverse concept, a brief yet informative explanation was provided within the questionnaire to ensure clarity for respondents less familiar with the term. The questionnaire provided an explanation of the metaverse concept as follows: "The metaverse can be imagined as a virtual environment that can be entered instead of just viewing a flat screen. It is a world of unlimited possibilities, interconnected communities, of places for virtual meetings, work, and for play. Special virtual and augmented reality headsets such as glasses, smartphones, and other devices that work with these technologies play a major role in the metaverse."

The questionnaire encompassed various dimensions related to metaverse engagement, including willingness to test new products, privacy concerns, content creation, technology investment, and purchasing behaviors. A 7-point Likert scale was employed to gauge participants' responses to various survey items. The Likert scale ranged from 1 (Strongly Disagree) to 7 (Strongly Agree), allowing participants to express their level of agreement or disagreement with the statements presented in the questionnaire. This scale offered a quantifiable framework for capturing the nuances of participant sentiments and perceptions regarding metaverse-related phenomena.

2.1 Sample Characteristics

The participants were sourced from the Ipsos respondent panel, which includes individuals from diverse demographic and geographic backgrounds across the Czech Republic. The sample was selected through a random sampling method, ensuring a representative cross- section of the population.

Table 1. Characteristics of the respondent sample.

Segmentation variable	Segments	Sample (N=525)	Sample %
Gender	Male	271	51.6
	Female	254	48.4
Generation	Generation Z	74	14.2
	Generation Y	135	25.7
	Generation X	261	49.7
	Baby Boomers	55	10.5
Education	Primary school	59	11.2
	Secondary school with apprenticeship	203	38.7
	Secondary school	179	34.1
	College	84	16.0

Source: own research

This research adhered to ethical guidelines and principles in data collection and analysis. Respondents were informed about the voluntary nature of participation and the confidential handling of their responses. The survey methodology, incorporating the 7-point Likert scale, facilitated a comprehensive exploration of participant attitudes and behaviors within the metaverse, providing valuable insights into the evolving landscape of virtual engagement.

2.2 Measures

In this study, *Fear of Missing Out* was measured using the 10-item fear of missing out scale according to Przybylski et al. (2013). The scale demonstrated optimal internal consistency (α = .861) and individual scores were calculated for each participant by taking the average across all ten items (M = 3.587, SD = 1.108).

Attitude toward the buy product in the metaverse was measured using 6-item asked participant to assess this activity from the point of view of saving time, saving physical effort, effectiveness, simplicity, usefulness and convenience. These six items were summed to create one attitude score for each participant (α = .938, M= 4.388, SD = 1.381).

Willingness to test products in the metaverse was assessed using a single-item question that asked participant to rate how much they agreed with the statement that they would be willing to test new products for money in the metaverse (M = 4.50, SD = 1.761). Attitudes towards content creation in the metaverse were assessed using a single-item question in which participants were asked to rate how much they agreed with the statement that all metaverse users should be able to create content in the metaverse, not just professional designers (M = 4.37, SD = 1.601). Privacy concerns were assessed using a single-item question in which respondents commented on how much they agreed with the statement that they feared their privacy would be compromised if behavioral data was collected about them in the metaverse, i.e., information about their habits, activities and decisions (M = 4.78, SD = 1.820). Willingness to purchase new technologies to enter the metaverse was assessed using a one-item question asking respondents to indicate the extent to which they agreed with the statement that they would be willing to purchase new technologies for spending time in the metaverse, such as augmented, mixed and virtual reality technologies (virtual and augmented reality glasses were given as an example) (M= 3.67, SD = 1.715).

3 Results

This section presents the study's findings. Initially, it delves into variables that exhibited discrepant results among distinct respondent segments. Notably, interaction effects between Fear of Missing Out (FoMO), generational cohorts, and educational attainment were detected for specific variables. Gender, however, did not reveal any discernible interaction effects. Subsequently, a comprehensive overview of the results derived from the frequency analysis is presented.

3.1 FoMO and Attitude to Buy Products in the Metaverse

To test the hypothesis that FoMO would be positively related to attitude to buy products in the metaverse, the regression analysis was perform. Indeed, Fear of Missing Out has been found to be related to the attitude to buy product in the metaverse. That is, respondents have a more positive attitude towards buying a product in the metaverse the higher their FoMO score ($\beta = 0.545$, $p < 001$). This confirms the assumption that people who are most susceptible to this phenomenon (with higher FoMO scores) will have a more positive attitude towards buying a product in the metaverse because they won't want to feel like they missed out.

3.2 Generational Differences

When the results were looked at by generation using the Kruskal Wallis Test (Table 2), it was found that with the exception of two statements, there were no differences in the responses. Only the statement that they would be willing to purchase new technology to spend time in the metaverse and that they find shopping for products using the metaverse useful differed between generations.

Table 2. Significant results of the effect of generation on the variables.

Dependent variable	Results of Kruskal-Wallis H Test	Generation
Willingness to buy new technology to spend time in the metaverse	Chi-Square	14.666
	Df	3
	Sig.	0.002
The usefulness of shopping for products through the metaverse	Chi-Square	10.349
	Df	3
	Sig.	0.016

Source: own research

The results show that older generations of consumers (Generation X and Baby Boomers) are less willing to purchase new technologies for spending time in the metaverse. For Baby Boomers, this reluctance is strongest, with more than half of participants from this generation not purchasing new technology for this purpose and only 18 % of participants from this generation responding that they would be willing to take this step. Generation X is slightly more supportive in this regard, with up to 31 % of participants from this generation willing to purchase new technology for this purpose. Generation Y consumers were the most willing in this area, with up to 47 % of them willing to purchase new technologies for spending time in the metaverse, followed by Generation Z, where up to 45 % said the same.

In the case of buying products through the metaverse, perceived usefulness decreases with each previous generation of consumers. Generation Z perceives shopping for products in the metaverse as the most useful, with up to 68 % of consumers saying so. Up to 60 % of Gen Y consumers think shopping for products in the metaverse is useful. Even more, half of Generation X users rated shopping for products in the metaverse as useful. Baby Boomers, however, are slightly more negative in their assessment, with only 40 % of consumers in this group rating metaverse shopping as such.

3.3 Educational Differences

Looking at the responses by educational attainment, using the Kruskal Wallis Test (Table 3), it was found that there were no differences in responses except for three statements. In this case, only the statements related to privacy concerns, ability to create content and illustrating how to create content in the metaverse were answered differently by the respondents.

The results show that the more educated consumers are, the more concerned they are about privacy risks when behavioral data is collected about them in the metaverse. While only 40 % of consumers with a primary education share this concern, up to 70 % of consumers with a college degree do. When it comes to the ability to create content in the metaverse, consumers with a college degree are the most likely (61 %) to think that all metaverse users should be able to do so. Consumers with a secondary school education follow closely behind (56 %). Also, illustrating how to create content in the metaverse would be most welcomed by consumers with a college degree, as many as 75 % of them. Consumers with a secondary education are again close behind (73 %).

Table 3. Significant results of the effect of education on the variables.

Dependent variable	Results of Kruskal-Wallis H Test	Education
Privacy concerns if data on user behavior in the metaverse is collected	Chi-Square	17.358
	Df	3
	Sig.	0.001
Ability to create content in the metaverse by all users	Chi-Square	8.521
	Df	3
	Sig.	0.036
Illustrating how content can be created in the metaverse	Chi-Square	8.018
	Df	3
	Sig.	0.046

Source: own research

3.4 Frequency Analysis Results

In the last section, the authors examined the data using frequency analysis to extract information from questions where no differences in responses were found by the consumer segments studied. The first figure shows the results in terms of attitudes towards buying products in the metaverse.

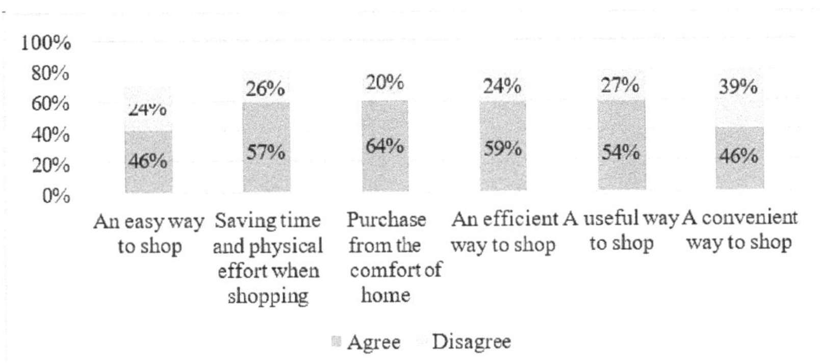

Figure 1. Attitude to buy products in the metaverse.
Source: own research

From a global standpoint, more than half of consumers view the act of buying products within the metaverse as an opportunity to conduct transactions in the convenience of their homes, thereby yielding time and physical effort savings in the shopping process. This mode of shopping is widely regarded as an efficacious and utilitarian approach (useful way to shop). A still large percentage of consumers (46 %) agree that shopping in the metaverse is an easy and convenient way to shop. An almost balanced ratio in consumer attitudes (agree/disagree) can be seen in the statement that shopping for products in the metaverse is a convenient way to shop.

The second figure shows the results of exploring views on metaverse adoption. These are statements that are linked to the issue of the use of the metaverse environment itself and that may have an impact on the globalisation potential.

An interesting finding is that up to 66 % of consumers are interested in a demonstration of how to create content in the metaverse. This indicates a strong willingness to engage metaverse users in creating content. In addition, more than half of consumers think that everyone should be able to create content in the metaverse. The metaverse environment also represents an interesting potential for product testing on a global scale, as up to 56 % of consumers are willing to test new products for money in the metaverse. Unfortunately, up to 60 % of consumers are concerned about privacy when using Metaverse. Another negative finding is that only 36 % of consumers are willing to purchase new technologies to enter the metaverse.

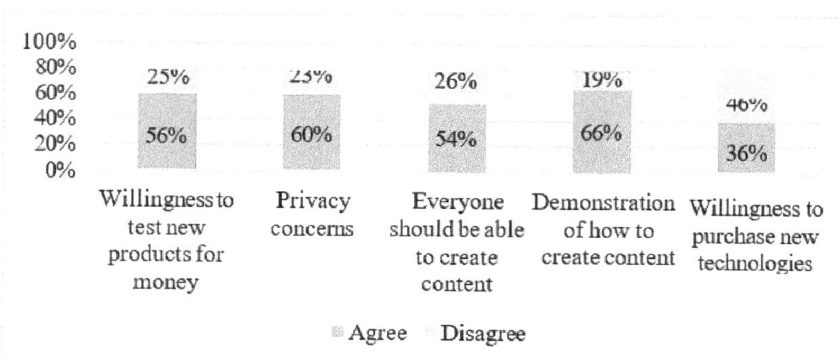

Figure 2. Exploring Perspectives on Metaverse Adoption.
Source: own research

4 Discussion

The findings of this study illuminate intricate dynamics within the metaverse landscape, particularly in relation to Fear of Missing Out (FoMO), generational cohorts, educational attainment, and consumer attitudes and behaviors. The analysis reveals a positive relationship between FoMO and the attitude towards purchasing products in the metaverse. Respondents who exhibited higher FoMO scores were more inclined to have a positive attitude towards metaverse shopping. This correlation substantiates the hypothesis that individuals most susceptible to FoMO tend to view metaverse shopping favorably, driven by the desire to avoid missing out on experiences.

Generational disparities were evident in certain aspects of metaverse engagement. While the majority of responses exhibited uniformity across generations, differences emerged concerning the willingness to purchase new technology for metaverse immersion and perceptions of metaverse shopping usefulness. Older generations, such as Generation X and Baby Boomers, displayed a decreased inclination to invest in new technologies for metaverse participation, with Baby Boomers exhibiting the highest reluctance. Conversely, Generation Y and Generation Z participants exhibited greater readiness to embrace metaverse technology. In terms of metaverse shopping usefulness, a notable decline was observed across previous generations, with Generation Z perceiving it as the most useful, followed by Generation Y and Generation X. Baby Boomers, however, held a more skeptical view.

The study found distinctions in responses related to privacy concerns, content creation ability, and the desire for guidance in content creation based on respondents' educational attainment. Higher-educated individuals expressed increased apprehension regarding privacy risks in metaverse data collection. Additionally, those with higher education were more likely to support universal content creation abilities in the metaverse and exhibited a greater desire for instructional guidance in this regard. These findings underscore the nuanced influence of educational background on metaverse-related perceptions.

At a global level, consumers perceive metaverse shopping as a convenient and efficacious way to conduct transactions, emphasizing its utility and time-saving potential. A substantial proportion of respondents expressed interest in demonstrations of content creation in the metaverse, highlighting a strong inclination towards involving users in content generation. Furthermore, a notable percentage of consumers believe that everyone should have the capability to create content in the metaverse. However, concerns about privacy in the metaverse and reluctance to invest in new technologies for metaverse entry pose challenges to its broader adoption.

Acknowledgments

Publication of this paper was supported by the Student Grant Competition Project: "Specifics and use of virtual reality in companies in selected work activities and internal team communication." The support is gratefully acknowledged.

References

Al-Ghaili, A. M., et al. (2022). A review of metaverse's definitions, architecture, applications, challenges, issues, solutions, and future trends. *IEEE Access, 10*, 125835–125866.

Buhalis, D., Lin, M. S., & Leung, D. (2023). Metaverse as a driver for customer experience and value co-creation: Implications for hospitality and tourism management and marketing. *International Journal of Contemporary Hospitality Management, 35*(2), 701–716.

Chen, S. C. (2022). Multimedia research toward the metaverse. *IEEE MULTIMEDIA, 29*(1), 125–127.

Dwivedi, Y. K., et al. (2022). Metaverse beyond the hype: Multidisciplinary perspectives on emerging challenges, opportunities, and agenda for research, practice and policy. *International Journal of Information Management, 66*.

Huang, Y., Li, Y., & Cai, Z. (2023). Security and privacy in metaverse: A comprehensive survey. *Big Data Mining and Analytics, 6*(2), 234–247.

Hwang, Y. (2023). When makers meet the metaverse: Effects of creating NFT metaverse exhibition in maker education. *Computers & Education, 194*.

Jeon, J. E. (2021). The effects of user experience-based design innovativeness on user-metaverse platform channel relationships in South Korea. *Journal of Distribution Science, 19*(11), 81–90.

Kraus, S., Kanbach, D. K., Krysta, P. M., Steinhoff, M. M., & Tomini, N. (2022). Facebook and the creation of the metaverse: Radical business model innovation or incremental transformation? *International Journal of Entrepreneurial Behavior & Research, 28*(9), 52–77.

Leenes, R. (2009). Privacy regulation in the metaverse. In *Handbook of research on socio-technical design and social networking systems*. New York, NY, USA: Information Science Reference, 123–136.

Oleksy, T., Wnuk, A., & Piskorska, M. (2023). Migration to the metaverse and its predictors: Attachment to virtual places and metaverse-related threat. *Computers in Human Behavior, 141*.

Przybylski, A. K., Murayama, K., DeHaan, C. R., & Gladwell, V. (2013). Motivational, emotional, and behavioral correlates of fear of missing out. *Computers in Human Behavior, 29*(4), 1841–1848.

Seo, S., Seok, B., & Lee, Ch. (2023). Digital forensic investigation framework for the metaverse. *The Journal of Supercomputing, 79*, 9467–9485.

Stephan, W. G., & Stephan, W. C. (2017). Intergroup threats. In C. G. Sibley & F. K. Barlow (Eds.), *The Cambridge handbook of the psychology of prejudice* (pp. 131–148). Cambridge University Press.

Wang, J., Chen, S., Liu, Y., & Lau, R. (2023). Intelligent Metaverse Scene Content Construction. *IEEE Access, 11*, 76222–76241.

Weinberger, M. (2022). What is metaverse? A definition based on qualitative meta- synthesis. *Future Internet, 14*(11), 1–16.

Yamac, M. (2023). Religious and social manifestations in the metaverse. *Dinbilimleri Akademik Arastirma Dergisi – Journal of Academi Research in Religious Sciences, 23*(1), 31–64.

Zhang, X., Yang, D., Yow, C. H., Huang, L., Wu, X., Huang, X., Guo, J., Zhou, S., & Cai, Y. (2022). Metaverse for cultural heritages. *Electronics, 11*(22), 3730.

Nikola Biskupi[1,*], Kresimir Buntak[1], Ivan Cvitkovic[1], and Matija Kovacic[1]

Digital Twin Technology in the Function of Risk Management of Logistics Processes

Abstract:
Research background: Logistics processes bring numerous risks in their management. Risks should be minimized to make them easier to manage. The technological solution of a Digital Twin (DT) can significantly help in this. This article aims to explore possible solutions and methods related to the implementation of DT in logistics.
Purpose of the article: The purpose of the article is to show the different applications and methods of implementing DT within logistics processes. The authors mentioned in the article in their literature cite various examples of application and methods of this technology.
Methods: One research method was used in the paper, which was based on the study of other authors and their literature. In addition to Web of Science and Scopus, other research platforms were also used. In order for the research process itself to be of higher quality, it was guided by given keywords.
Findings & Value added: For the implementation of this technology, a good technological background must be provided. After that, it starts creating the architecture that represents the basis for implementation, and consists of physical entities, its virtual representation, bi-direct information and a database. LAMBDA is an architectural principle suitable for a digital twin. In practice, there are also some good examples of the application of the mentioned technologies (FlexSim packaging, shipments, etc.).This technology enables the minimization of logistical risks due to better quality control. But the research shows that there is a weak direct connection between the digital twin and risk management by other authors.

Keywords: *Digital Twin in logistics, digital risk management, Digital Twin architecture, LAMBDA architecture, logistics risk platforms*

JEL Classification: *C88; C89; L52; M15*

* Corresponding author: nibiskup@unin.hr
1 University North, Department for Logistics and Sustainable Mobility, Trg dr. Žarka Dolinara 1, 48000 Koprivnica, Croatia

1 Introduction

Each component in the logistics process must be well managed and connected to other components in order for such a chain to be functional. A quality ability to manage logistics processes brings considerable benefits for the stated purpose. The use of technology in logistics management is not new, but the technology that will be covered in this chapter is still in its infancy. It is digital twin technology. The first appearance of the concept could be linked to the application of the virtual Apollo 13 in 1970 by NASA (Csaba, 2021). In order to implement the digital twin system in any segment of logistics management, its requirements must be met, and these are the elements of the foundation for the introduction of such a system. Under the elements of the foundation, five technological trends are understood: the Internet of Things (IoT), Cloud technology, API and open standards, Artificial Intelligence (AI) and digital reality technologies (Dohrmann et al., 2019.). After all the prerequisites have been met, i.e., the foundation elements for the digital twin have been laid, it is necessary to build a good foundation. Foundations are defined by architecture consisting of several elements. These include: physical entity, its virtual representation, bi- direct information and database (National Institutes of Health, 2021.). The elements of digital twin technology have clear technological definitions and therefore can guide implementations of different digital twins (Jeong et al., 2022) Challenges that affect logistics processes, i.e., supply chains, can be demand for individualized products, shortening of product life and thus innovation cycles, larger supply chains and shorter batch sizes, etc. (Malagón-Suárez & Orjuela-Castro, 2022.). It is important to recognize all the mentioned challenges and ultimately reduce them to a minimum. Likewise, by properly managing the challenges, it is necessary to eliminate them as soon as possible. All that is needed at that point is to use all existing management tools and skills. Digital twin refers to the state of mutual symbiosis between digital entities and physical entities. Digital twin technology is a technology that integrates data, models and physical entities. Digital twins refer to the mapping of collections of entities in the digital world. (Buntak et al., 2021.) Such technology requires constant improvements. What the authors state that technologies and tools for dat processing and analysis will be the main drivers of further improvements in Digital Twins (Botin-Sanabria et al., 2022). Risks in logistics management are inevitable. The larger the supply chain and its network, the greater the chances of a certain risk occurring. Some authors define risk as the possibility of loss or an unfavorable outcome associated with an action (Crane et al., 2013.). Risk management consists of several steps: (1) Risk identification, (2) Risk measurement, (3) Assessments of risk tolerance, (4) Assessments of risk tolerance and preferences, (5) Setting goals in risk management, (6) Identification of effective risk management tools, (7) Chooses professional help, (8) Making decisions and implementing the plan and (9) Evaluation of results. All of the this can achieve risk reduction in logistics can be facilitated through the digitization of risk management, i.e., the digital twin of logistics management. Risks cannot be exploited, but they can be mitigated by actions to reduce risk, which is done through risk management strategies (Botha & Badenhorst-Weiss, 2019.). These steps are important for risk management within any organization, process, activity, etc., including within logistics processes. It is assumed that in the literature of other authors there are still not enough examples of the implementation of digital twin technology within logistics processes in the function of management, i.e., minimizing potential risks. The above is put forward as a hypothesis of this article.

2 Methods

When researching this paper, the Web of Science (WoS) and Scopus databases, as well as other relevant databases, were taken into account. During the research, the goal was to take into account only those articles whose authors connect the three parts, namely digital twin, risks and logistics processes. Articles that connect not only three parts, but also those that connect only two parts (e.g., digital twin and logistics processes) were taken into account. Each of the articles offered has been studied in detail in order to discover the possible link that is sought in this research. Articles no older than five years were considered. After a detailed research of the articles, data was obtained that give us relevant and true information according to which we can present the results.

3 Results

By analyzing the research, we divided the results into two groups. The first group are results that do not have direct links to risk management within logistics processes and digital twin technology, but they can still indirectly help with logistics risk management. Another group of results can help with risk management and they have a direct link between risk management and digital twin technology.

3.1 Indirect Results

The application of digital twin technology can be found in different segments of the supply chain. Accordingly, applications in some of these segments presented by a team of experts from DHL will be presented below.

One of the examples of application is in the packaging of goods and containerization. The application in this case was necessary because the tracking and management of packaging turned out to be a big challenge in logistics management. For example, when it comes to e- commerce, it encourages increased demand, seasonal volatility and variety of product packaging, which significantly affects the production of a larger amount of waste and reduces operational efficiency due to poor volume utilization. In this case, digital twin technology could help in the development of stronger, lighter and environmentally friendly packaging materials. Likewise, digital twins could in this case help companies to understand and predict the future performance of new packaging materials by modeling the behavior of materials under temperature, vibration and other loads during transport. In addition to packaging, this technology can be of great help in the management of container fleets, because the challenge here is tracking containers from point A to point B. In addition, there is also the possibility of monitoring or checking damage that can endanger the condition of the product, and thus represent danger to personnel and the environment. An example of the use of digital twin technology in this case was developed by the German startup Metrilus in such a way that they developed a detailed representation of the container in digital form and thus enabled the automated identification of potential problems related to damage of the container. For example, this information could in the future be combined with historical container movement data to create a digital twin that will be able to make decisions about whether the damage can be repaired or whether the container must still be decommissioned. Likewise, collecting data for container fleets could help logistics companies make optimal decisions about fleet size and distribution, and could reveal underlying problems such as container design errors or mishandling. (Dohrmann et al., 2019.)

The next use of this technology is in shipping. If production and packaging data were combined, it could help companies improve their efficiency through automatic packaging selection and packaging strategy. For example, products that are of high or sensitive value, they already have a practice of having sensors on them and thus are sent as a shipment. It enables monitoring of temperature, package orientation, impact or vibration. There are sensor variants like Roambee, Blulog, Kizy and others that offer a growing array of data points that allow for continuous data transmission as the shipment progresses. Technology in this case would be the database that was collected through the aforementioned sensors. (Dohrmann et al., 2019.)

Digital twins can be used in warehouse management. For example, digital twins in this case could combine a 3D model of a warehouse facility with IoT data collected from warehouse platforms. Digital twins used in warehouse facilities and systems can assist in the design and layout of new facilities. This enables companies to optimize the use of their warehouse spaces and simulate the movement of products, workers and material handling equipment within facilities. It is important that the digital twin is constantly updated during warehouse operations with data collected from various automation technologies within the warehouse. These include inventory counting systems, automated guided vehicles, order picking systems and automated storage and retrieval equipment. Likewise, facility data can be used to increase warehouse staff productivity. This can be achieved by virtual training of employees using VR glasses (eg Google Glass Enterprise Edition or Microsoft HoloLens). (Dohrmann et al., 2019.) There is also a FlexSim platform for warehouse management (Huihui et al., 2016). FlexSim is a 3D simulation software that models, simulates, predicts and visualizes systems such as scalding systems and others (Medan & Ravainagy, 2022). With the mentioned software, it is possible to monitor problems and find alternative solutions in a relatively short time (Luscinski & Ivanov, 2020). An example of a 3D model of the logistics distribution center infrastructure is shown in Figure 1. The model was created at the University North.

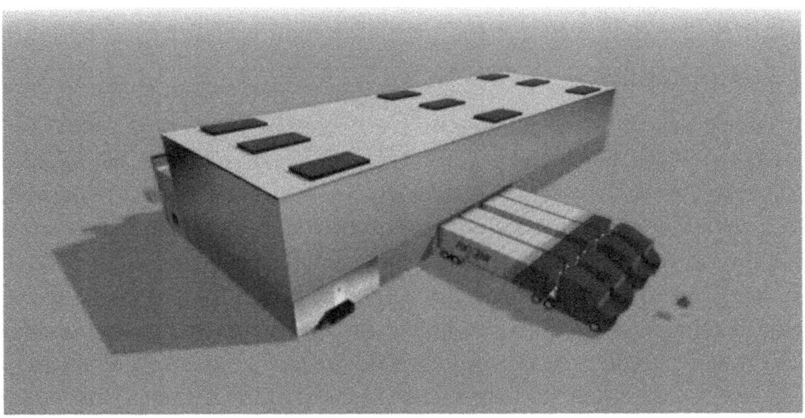

Figure 1. FlexSim digital twin of warehouse infrastrukture created by University North, Croatia.

Source: authors

Logistics, in addition to the logistics infrastructure, also consists of the suprastructure, information systems and people who manage within the entire system. This example can easily be seen in large logistics centers such as airports or seaports. Today, such centers have systems for exchanging information with certain shortcomings, which creates a great challenge to their efficiency. The participants of the aforementioned system rely on offline processes that are most often subject to errors and delays. To solve these problems, a project using digital twin technology is being developed in Singapore. The project is led by the Port Authority of Singapore, which is working with other partners, such as the National University of Singapore, to develop a digital twin of the country's megahub for container traffic. This project has already proven effective at an early stage as the partners used their digital models to accelerate the generation of potential layouts and used simulation systems to evaluate different operational scenarios. The project holder hopes that the digital twin will optimize the management of the new facility, for example, with the help of simulation it will be possible to choose the optimal location for the berth of vessels of any size, taking into account certain components such as assets, space, personnel required for loading and unloading operations, as well as the need to share these resources between multiple vessels at any given time. What will be required of all stakeholders who will use the port facility is to manage and maintain a digital twin of their assets and personnel and to share their data with other stakeholders. (Dohrmann et al., 2019.)

3.2 Direct Results

With this group of literature, we got several authors. (Greis et al., 2021) mentions a digital twin-based architecture that enables manufacturers to proactively manage supply chain risk in an increasingly complex and dynamic environment. This is an integrated framework that has "sense and respond" capabilities, i.e., the ability to sense potential supplier and manufacturing risks that affect the customer's final delivery, update expected delivery dates for customers, and recommend mitigation steps that minimize any anticipated disruptions. Its function is to sense disruptions in a supplier's facility further upstream in the supply chain and use the predictive capabilities of its machine learning-based engine to initiate and support adaptive changes in the manufacturer's MES system. An architecture suitable for a digital twin is called LAMBDA. Its goal, as stated by (Suthakar et al., 2021), is to meet the requirements for any infrastructure that is fault-tolerant, robust, or prone to human as well as hardware errors. The reason is its ability to function in different ways, in situations where it is crucial to ensure that the system has low latency while providing regular updates to users. Such a system according to LAMBDA is linearly mounted and scales outwards. The Lambda implementation is realized with a modified SMACK (Spark, Mesos,

Akka, Cassandra and Kafka) stack in Figure 2 (Haße et al., 2019.). This stack is a distributed big data for streaming data processing.

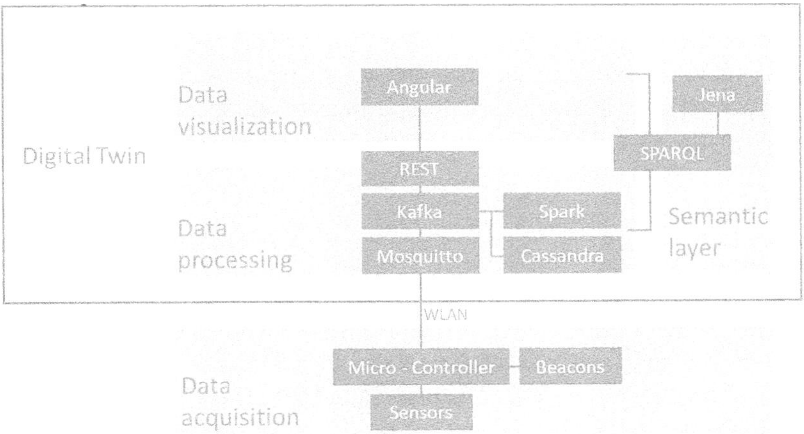

Figure 2. Lambda architecture for real-time IoT analytics in logistics.
Source: authors according to (Haße et al., 2019).

Authors like (Lee & Lee, 2021) talk about the risks of deviations from the schedule in the logistics process of modular construction, which can nullify their advantages and thus hinder their wide application. We already know that a digital twin is a virtual replica of a physical module that updates its virtual assets e.g., based on Building Information Modeling (BIM) in near real time using Internet of Things (IoT) sensors. Virtual assets are transferred and exploited for logistics simulation in a geographic information system (GIS)-based routing application. This model was tested in the case of a project where the modules are manufactured in a factory, delivered to the construction site by truck and assembled on site. The results of these authors showed that potential logistical risks and the exact arrival time of modules can be detected based on this technology. Reliable risk prediction as in this case enabled efficient supply chain coordination, which can improve project performance and widespread adoption of modular construction.

The following authors link the digital twin to logistics processes for Covid-19 vaccines. This topic appeared after the outbreak of the pandemic and the discovery of the start of vaccine production. The distribution of vaccines brings a large number of risks, which gave rise to the idea of connecting a digital twin with risk management. The study presented by (Lam et al., 2023) presents a risk analysis model based on cold chain digital twins that is designed to manage and monitor the vaccine delivery process with a high level of reliability and traceability. The model enables the integration of the Internet of Things (IoT) and digital twins to collect data on environmental conditions and shipment movements, and to connect physical cold chain logistics with the digital world. Thus, by simulating cold chain logistics in a virtual environment, risks can be predicted in advance to prevent any disruption within the vaccine cold chain.

4 Discussion

Through this research, we discovered that there are two groups of literature by authors. The first group indirectly links digital twin technology with risk management within logistics processes. The authors mention different ways and methods of applying such technology within logistics processes. The most specific use is mentioned by a team of experts from DHL. These are applied technologies in the packaging of goods and containerization. The model offered in this case enables the prediction of the future state of the performance of new packaging materials by modeling the behavior of the material under temperature, vibration and other loads during transport. The authors also mention the great help of this technology in the management of container fleets, because here the challenge is to track containers from point A to point B. In addition, there is also the possibility of monitoring or checking damage that can threaten the condition of the product, time and pose a danger to personnel and the environment. Also mentioned is the German startup Metrilus, which developed a detailed representation of the tank in digital form, and thus enabled the automated identification of potential problems associated with damage to the tank. Collecting data for container fleets could help logistics companies make optimal decisions about fleet size and distribution, and could reveal underlying problems such as container design errors or mishandling. The authors also mention the use of DT technology in shipping in such a way that delivery conditions are monitored via sensors. It is also important to mention the use of DT technology in warehouse management in such a way as to enable the display of warehouses and warehouse processes in 3D form through warehouse platforms. This method enables the simulation of movement of products, workers and material handling equipment within facilities. These results give us insight into solving challenges within certain elements of logistics processes. Likewise, they can influence risk reduction within logistics processes, although this group of authors does not mention risk management in this context or directly link it to digital twin technology. On the other hand, the next group of authors directly linked digital twin technology with risk management within logistics processes. Certain authors offer an integrated framework that has "sense and respond" capabilities, i.e., the ability to sense potential supplier and manufacturing risks affecting the customer's final delivery, update expected delivery dates for customers, and recommend mitigation steps that minimize any anticipated disruptions. Other authors mention risks in terms of deviations from the schedule in the logistical process of modular construction. Their results showed that potential logistics risks and exact module arrival times can be detected based on this technology. This kind of risk prediction enables effective supply chain coordination, which can improve project performance and the widespread use of modular construction. In this group of literature, the authors have also included digital twin technology with vaccine distribution, and such a model enables the integration of the Internet of Things (IoT) and digital twins to collect data on environmental conditions and the movement of shipments, and to connect the physical logistics of the cold chain with the digital world in order to minimize of all possible risks. According to these results, we see that the authors weakly and to a lesser extent connect digital twin technology with risk management. We can conclude that, to a greater extent, this technology can be indirectly associated with risks. Therefore, the hypothesis of this research is confirmed that there is a weak connection between digital twin technology and risk management within logistics processes due to the scarcity of the results of this research. In the future, researches should be done to show whether improvements have been detected or whether the situation remains unchanged in the use of digital twin technology in risk management within logistics processes.

References

Botha, A., & Bdenhorst-Weiss, J. A. (2019). Risk management in a bulk coal export logistic chain: A stakeholder perspective. *Journal of Transport and Supply Chain Management*, *13*, Article a424.

Botin-Sanabria, D. M., Mihaita, A. S., Peimpert-Garcia, R. E., Ramirez-Moreno, M. A., Ramirez-Mendoza, R. A., & Lozoya-Santos, J. J. (2022). Digital twin technology challenges and applications: A comprehensive review. *Remote Sensing*, *14*(6), Article 1335.

Buntak, K., Biskup, N., Cesarec, B., & Brlek, P. (2021). Digital twin cities. In O. Filiposki, D. Metodijeski, & D. Zlatovic (Eds.), *Proceedings of the 5th International Scientific and Professional Conference "The Challenges of Today"* (pp. 453–462). Polytechnic of Sibenik.

Crane, L., Gantz, G., Isaacs, S., Jose, D., & Sharp, R. (2013). *Introduction to risk management* (2nd ed.). Extension Risk Management Education and Risk Management Agency. https://extensionrme.org/Pubs/Introduction-to-Risk-Management- ENGLISH.pdf

Csaba, R. (2021). Digital twin technology – External data resources in creating the model and classification of different digital twin types in manufacturing. In J. Vancza, & P. Maropoulos (Eds.), *10th CIRP sponsored conference on digital enterprise technolgies (DET 2020) – Digital technologies as enablers of industrial competitiveness and sustainability*, *54*, 209–215.

Jeong, D. Y., Baek, M. S., Lim, T. B., Kim, Y. W., Kim, S. H., Lee, Y. T., Jung, W. S., & Lee, I. B. (2022). Digital twin: Technology evolution stages and implementation layers with technology elements. *IEEE Access*, *10*, 52609–52620.

Dohrmann, K., Gesing, B., & Ward, J. (2019). Digital twins in logistics. *DHL Customer Solutions & Innovation.*

Greis, N. P., Nogueira, M. L., & Rohde, W. (2021). Digital twin framework for machine learning-enabled integrated production and logistics processes. In A. Dolgui, A. Bernard, D. Lemoine, G. VonCieminski, & D. Romero (Eds.), *Advances in production management systems: Artificial intelligence for sustainable and resilient production systems*, *630*, 218–227

Haße, H., Li, B., Weißenberg, N., Cirullies, J., & Otto, B. (2019). Digital twin for real- time data processing in logistics. In Kersten, W. Blecker, T. Ringle, M. Christian (Eds.), *Artificial intelligence and digital transformation in supply chain management: Innovative approaches for supply chains. Proceedings of the Hamburg International Conference of Logistics* (pp. 4–28).

Huihui, S., Xiaoxia, M., & Xiangguo, M. (2016). Simulation and optimization of warehouse operation based on Flexsim. *Journal of Applied Science and Engineering Innovation*, 125–128.

Lam, H. Y., Tang, V., & Ho, G. (2023). A digital twins model for analyzing and simulating cold chain risks. *2023 International conference on artificial intelligence in information and communication* (pp. 259–263).

Lee, D., & Lee, S. (2021). Digital twin for supply chain coordination in modular construction. *Applied Sciences-Basel*, *11*(13), Article 5909.

Luscinski, S., & Ivanov, V. (2020). A simulation study of industry 4.0 factor on the ontology on flexibility with using flexsim® software. *Management and Production Engineering Review*, *11*(3), 74–83.

Malagón-Suárez, C. P., & Orjuela-Castro, J. A. (2022). Challenges and trends in logistics 4.0. *Ingeniería*, 1–28.

Medan, N., & Ravai-nagy, S. (2022). Modelling, simulating and analysing a process flow for a machining part using flexsim software. *Acta Technical*

Napocensis Series – Applied Mathematics Mechanics and Engineering, *65*(4), 1229–1234.

National Institutes of Health. (2021). Digital Twins Part 1: Introduction. *Technical Bulletin.*

Suthakar, U., Magnoni, L., Smith, D. R., & Khan, A. (2021). Optimised Lambda architecture for monitoring scientific infrastructure. *IEEE Transaction on Parallel and Distributed Systems*, *32*(6), 1395–1408.

Dumitru Alexandru Bodislav[1,*], Florina Bran[1], Ioan I. Gâf-Deac[2], Otilia Ganea[3], and Maria Loredana Popescu[1]

Globalization Based on Transformation and Digitalisation

Abstract:
Research background: This comprehensive study engages with a broad spectrum of literature from various disciplines to uncover the mechanisms through which digitalization has accelerated and transformed globalization. It focuses on the profound impact of digital innovations on societal and structural dynamics, thereby shedding light on the accelerated pace of global change in the digital era.
Purpose of the article: The article aims to explore the transformative processes instigated by digital advancements, dissecting their effects on economic structures, labor markets, and cultural expressions. It seeks to understand how these digital innovations are reshaping the global landscape, underscoring their significance in the context of an interconnected world.
Methods: Utilizing a critical analysis methodology, the study meticulously examines specific case studies that illustrate the complex relationship between globalization, digitalization, and transformation. This approach allows for a detailed exploration of the nuanced interactions and consequences of these phenomena.
Findings & Value added: The study reveals the dual role of digitalization in the context of globalization, acting both as a catalyst and a driver of change. It identifies the challenges and potential benefits arising from this convergence, stressing the importance of adaptive policymaking and governance in leveraging these changes for societal benefit. The paper significantly contributes to a nuanced understanding of the interplay between globalization, digitalization, and transformation, offering insights into managing these forces for a more equitable and sustainable future.

Keywords: *globalization, digitalization, well-being, transformation*

JEL Classification: *F60; F63*

* Corresponding author: carmen-valentina.radulescu@eam.ase.ro
1 Bucharest University of Economic Studies, Romana Square, no. 1, district 1, Bucharest, Romania
2 Ec./Technical Science, Sci. Research., INCE C. Kiritescu / Romanian Academy, Romania
3 Romanian Academy, Research Institute for Quality of Life – ICCV

1 Introduction

The development of digitization has had a huge impact on the quick speed of globalization in the 21st century. The convergence of these two formidable forces has engendered a new terrain that impacts all facets of society, including economics and labour markets, as well as culture and government (Burlacu et al., 2022).

The primary objective of this research study is to provide a comprehensive understanding of the processes by which globalization has been expedited and altered because of digitalization. Additionally, it aims to analyze the interdependent nature of these two phenomena. Furthermore, this study examines the consequences of this interaction on policy formulation, governance practices, and the implementation of inclusive development methods.

This study embarks on a comprehensive exploration of how digitalization has catalysed and reshaped the process of globalization in the 21st century, focusing on the symbiotic relationship between these two phenomena and their impact across various societal facets. Drawing insights from a diverse array of scholarly works, the study presents an interwoven narrative. Beginning with Burlacu et al. (2021), who underscore the profound influence of digitalization on globalization's pace, the study then integrates perspectives from Gereffi et al. (2005), who delve into the governance of global value chains. This is juxtaposed with insights from Georgescu (2023), discussing modern leadership in business organizations amid economic disruptions.

Further enriching the discourse, Rădulescu et al. (2020) offer perspectives on entrepreneurial education within the context of sustainable business development, while Shapiro and Varian (1999) present a strategic guide to navigating the network economy. This eclectic mix of viewpoints is further enhanced by Castells' (1996) seminal work on the rise of the network society and Chesbrough's (2003) exploration of open innovation as a new imperative in technology.

The study also weaves in Levitt's (1983) foundational work on market globalization and Graham's (2010) research on neogeography and virtual Earth. This is complemented by Goldin and Reinert's (2006) discussion on globalization for development and Dutton and Blank's (2011) cultural analysis of the Internet in Britain.

Mowery and Rosenberg's (1993) insights on the U.S. National Innovation System and Ohmae's (1990) perspective on the interlinked economy offer additional depth. Finally, Chua's (2018) exploration of the rise of Digital China offers a contemporary viewpoint, situating the study within a broader, global context.

Continuing with the interdisciplinary approach, this study further incorporates the insights of Benkler, Bessen and Hunt, and Bodislav, each contributing unique perspectives on the intersection of digitalization and globalization.

Yochai Benkler's seminal work, "The Wealth of Networks" (2006), delves into how social production transforms markets and freedom, offering a critical analysis of how network- based production models are reshaping economic and social systems. Benkler's thesis is integral to understanding the evolving nature of digital economies in the context of global interconnectedness.

The study also examines the work of Bessen and Hunt (2007), who provide an empirical perspective on software patents through their article in the Journal of Economics & Management Strategy. Their analysis of the impact of intellectual property rights on innovation in the software industry offers valuable insights into the complex relationship between legal frameworks, technological innovation, and global market dynamics.

Bodislav et al. (2016) focuses on the application of business intelligence in economic decision-making. This work highlights the increasing relevance of artificial intelligence and data analytics in financial markets, underscoring the role of digital technologies in shaping modern economic strategies and investment practices.

Through the integration of these diverse perspectives, the study paints a comprehensive picture of the multifaceted impacts of digitalization on global economic structures, market dynamics, and the shifting paradigms of production and innovation. This amalgamation of viewpoints underscores the complexity of the digital-global interface and its far-reaching implications for markets, governance, and societal freedoms.

2 Methodology

In our research, we adopted a critical analysis methodology, centered on the meticulous examination of specific case studies. These studies have been selected to illustrate the complex relationship between globalization, digitalization, and transformation. We chose cases that reflected both the positive and negative impacts of digitization in the context of globalization, thus providing a balanced perspective.

We used a critical analytical approach to dissect each case study, evaluating the data sources, context, methodology applied, and conclusions drawn in the original studies. The importance of integrating theories from existing literature has not been neglected; theories from economics, sociology, and political science were used to contextualize and interpret the results of each case study.

A crucial aspect of the research was examining the long-term impact of digitization within globalization. This included close attention to the resulting socio-economic and cultural changes. The study benefited from an interdisciplinary approach, integrating various perspectives and analytical frameworks to provide a comprehensive view of the subject of study.

Discussions and implications of each case study follow, allowing us to interpret the results and explore their implications for the broader understanding of the interplay between globalization, digitalization and transformation. Finally, we synthesized findings from different case studies to formulate conclusions that reflected the complexity and multidimensionality of the relationship between globalization and digitization.

3 Research

3.1 Globalization in the Digital Age

The concept of globalization, which has historically been characterized by the growing interdependence between nations and individuals, has seen a significant shift in the era of digitalization (Burlacu et al., 2023). The rapid advancement of digital technology has greatly improved the efficient and swift movement of information, money, and products across international boundaries (Calin et al., 2022). This section examines the impact of digitalization on globalization processes, with a specific emphasis on its role in accelerating and reshaping economic transitions and labour markets (Profiroiu et al., 2020).

The phenomenon of globalization, characterized by heightened levels of interconnection and interdependence between countries and individuals, has seen a significant shift in the era of digitalization. The emergence of digital technology has initiated a profound transformation that is reconfiguring the global terrain in new ways (Mogos et al., 2021). This part delves into the fundamental aspects of globalization in the digital era, including the increased speed of information dissemination, the transformation of corporate practices, and the significant ramifications for society.

The digital era is distinguished by the expeditious dissemination of information and ideas on a global scale. The advent of digital technology, such as the internet and social media platforms, has significantly disrupted traditional geographical limitations, facilitating the rapid dissemination of news, views, and cultural manifestations. The dissemination of information is no longer limited by geographical boundaries, as people now can establish global connections with a simple click. The rapid transmission of information has not only facilitated the equal access to knowledge but also magnified the impact of a worldwide public forum.

The advent of digitalization has brought about significant transformations in the way organizations function and engage with one another on a worldwide level. The advent of e-commerce, digital platforms, and the sharing economy has caused significant disruptions in conventional businesses, hence giving rise to new economic paradigms. In the contemporary business landscape, companies have gained the ability to effortlessly engage with customers on a global scale, therefore augmenting their market reach and fundamentally altering the dynamics of competition (Radulescu et al., 2020). Furthermore, the advent of digitization has resulted in the emergence of remote work and the gig economy, hence causing a convergence of conventional employment boundaries and a fundamental alteration of labour markets.

The process of digitization facilitates the proliferation of cultural variety by enabling the worldwide dissemination of ideas and expressions. However, it also gives rise to apprehensions over the potential for cultural uniformity. The ubiquity of Western digital platforms and information has created discourse about the hegemony of certain cultural narratives. Concurrently, the process of digitization has provided disadvantaged groups with the means to disseminate their narratives and safeguard their cultural legacy on an international platform, therefore questioning the concept of a one, prevailing culture.

The advent of the digital era has provided individuals with a platform for the construction and manifestation of their identities. Individuals can construct and manage virtual identities on the internet, therefore establishing connections with individuals and groups that have similar interests, regardless of geographical boundaries. Social media platforms have emerged as crucial instruments for the construction and influence of individual and communal identities. Nonetheless, the digital domain also presents concerns over the genuineness of information and the convergence of one's online and offline identities.

The increasing digitization of globalization has led to a heightened emphasis on the management of data and the protection of privacy, emerging as a significant area of concern. The proliferation of data collected and disseminated on a worldwide scale gives rise to inquiries about monitoring, security, and the ethical use of information. Achieving a harmonious equilibrium between the advantages offered by data-driven technology and the safeguarding of personal privacy is a persistent and complex endeavour.

Governments are confronted with the intricate challenge of effectively regulating the digital realm while concurrently fostering innovation and facilitating economic progress. Achieving a harmonious equilibrium between cybersecurity, data protection, and the unrestricted availability of information necessitates the implementation of flexible and adaptable legislative frameworks. The need of international collaboration is essential in tackling worldwide issues, including but not limited to cyber threats and the movement of data over national borders.

Although digitization presents significant potential, it also amplifies existing imbalances. The digital divide, which refers to the disparity between those who have access to digital technology and those who do not, continues to be a significant concern. It is essential to establish a connection between different groups to guarantee universal access to the advantages of globalization in the era of digitalization, irrespective of geographical location or socioeconomic standing.

In summary, the advent of globalization in the digital era has resulted in a complex and diverse phenomenon that has fundamentally altered our modes of interaction, commercial practices, and self-conceptions. The advent of technology has expedited the dissemination of information, changed the landscape of commercial activities, and created novel platforms for artistic manifestations. Nonetheless, it also poses some issues pertaining to data, privacy, and diversity. Effectively traversing this emerging domain necessitates the implementation of flexible policies, fostering international collaboration, and acquiring a profound comprehension of the ever-changing interplay between globalization and digitalization. As society navigates the ongoing challenges posed by these transformations, it becomes imperative to effectively use the opportunities presented by the digital era to promote the common welfare of global communities.

3.2 Digitalization and Economic Transformation

The process of digitalization has emerged as a significant catalyst for economic transformations on a global scale. The advent of e-commerce, the emergence of the sharing economy, and the proliferation of digital platforms have significantly impacted conventional businesses while also generating novel economic prospects. This section examines the effects of digitalization on worldwide economic frameworks, specifically addressing the redistribution of wealth and the difficulties presented by digital monopolies.

The realm of economics is now experiencing a significant shift due to the continuous progression of digitization in the modern era. This section examines the impact of digitalization on economic structures, the redistribution of wealth, and the disruption of old business models.

The exponential expansion of e-commerce stands out as a prominent manifestation of economic revolution facilitated by digitization. The advent of online retail platforms has significantly impacted the conventional brick-and-mortar businesses, hence providing customers convenient access to an extensive range of items and services via a simplified digital interface. Companies can access international markets, therefore increasing their pool of customers and possible sales. The transition has resulted in a modification in consumer behavior, as individuals are more inclined towards the ease and many options provided by electronic commerce.

The advent of digitalization has also facilitated the emergence of the sharing economy, which is distinguished by the presence of platforms such as Uber, Airbnb, and TaskRabbit. These platforms enable peer-to-peer transactions, providing people with the opportunity to generate income from assets that are not fully used, such as automobiles and spare rooms. The sharing economy poses a significant threat to conventional business models by eroding the distinction between customers and service providers. The advent of this phenomenon presents new avenues for people to generate money, whilst causing significant disruptions within well-established sectors.

The notion of "creative destruction" as proposed by Joseph Schumpeter has heightened significance within the context of the contemporary digital era. Start-ups and technology start-ups consistently provide revolutionary digital solutions that challenge existing sectors. The phenomenon of creative destruction has the potential to foster economic expansion and enhance efficiency, although it may also result in job displacement and market instability. In light of the rapid evolution of industries, the capacity to adapt has emerged as a critical factor for both firms and people.

The process of digitization has been essential in promoting innovation; nevertheless, it has also given rise to apprehensions over the potential for monopolistic behaviors. The market dominance attained by technology giants such as Google, Amazon, Facebook, and Apple (together referred to as GAFA) presents significant obstacles to ensuring fair competition. The consolidation of power within a small number of corporations has the potential to impede the progress of innovation and restrict the range of options available to consumers. The inclusion of antitrust legislation and discussions around the fragmentation of digital monopolies have been more prominent among legislators.

The process of digitalization is facilitating the use of automation throughout several industries, ranging from production to customer service. Although automation has the potential to enhance efficiency and save expenses, it also gives rise to apprehensions over the displacement of jobs. The nature of labour is undergoing a transformation, characterized by an increasing focus on skills that are pertinent to a digital economy. Governments and companies are confronted with the imperative of enhancing the skill sets of the workforce to effectively respond to these transformations and mitigate possible disparities within the labour market.

The process of digitalization has been crucial in generating novel economic prospects within several areas, including artificial intelligence, data analytics, and cybersecurity. The burgeoning sectors has the capacity to provide employment opportunities with lucrative remuneration and stimulate economic expansion. It is essential to allocate resources towards education and training initiatives to adequately equip the workforce for the jobs, hence maximizing the potential benefits that these possibilities provide.

The gig economy, which is distinguished by the prevalence of temporary contracts and independent labour arrangements, has seen significant growth in the era of digitalization. Although it provides employees with flexibility, the gig economy is characterized by a lack of job security, benefits, and safeguards often associated with regular employment. The task of reconciling the advantages and difficulties associated with the gig economy continues to provide a multifaceted dilemma for policymakers.

The process of digitalization has had a profound impact on the realm of international commerce. The use of e-commerce and digital platforms facilitates the participation of firms, regardless of their scale, in cross-border commercial activities. Nevertheless, it is essential to confront the regulatory and fiscal obstacles associated with digital commerce to provide equitable conditions for enterprises and facilitate equitable revenue generation for governments.

In summary, digitization is a formidable catalyst that is fundamentally transforming the global economy. The advent of e-commerce, the sharing economy, and digital platforms has resulted in the emergence of alternative business models that provide a threat to conventional practices. While promoting innovation and facilitating economic progress, this phenomenon also gives rise to apprehensions over competitiveness, displacement of jobs, and disparities in economic distribution. Effectively navigating the intricate terrain of digital economic change requires the implementation of proactive policies, substantial investment in workforce development, and a steadfast dedication to confronting the obstacles and capitalizing on the possibilities afforded by this ongoing digital revolution. In light of the ongoing progression of the digital era, it is imperative for companies, employees, and politicians to effectively adjust and respond to its economic ramifications.

3.3 Cultural Transformation in the Digital Age

In addition to its impact in the field of economics, digitization has also been instrumental in driving cultural shift. The advent of social media, online communities, and digital content production has facilitated the emergence of new cultural manifestations and identities. This section delves into the effects of digitalization on culture, including topics such as cultural homogeneity, the construction of identity, and the preservation of cultural heritage.

The advent of the digital age has initiated a paradigm shift in cultural dynamics, fundamentally altering the way cultures engage in the production, dissemination, and engagement with cultural artifacts. This section examines the significant influence of digitalization on culture, examining both the potential for increased variety and the obstacles posed by cultural uniformity.

The advent of digitalization has significantly expanded the accessibility and inclusivity of artistic expression in unprecedented ways. The emergence of social media, online communities, and digital content platforms has provided people and organizations with platforms to engage in the creation, curation, and dissemination of cultural material. The proliferation of material provided by users has resulted in the emergence of a wide range of culturally varied and ever-evolving expressions.

The advent of the digital age has effectively eliminated geographical barriers, facilitating extensive cultural interactions on a worldwide level. Individuals can establish connections with individuals residing in other regions throughout the globe, so facilitating the sharing of cultural knowledge and promoting the development of cross-cultural comprehension. Online communities that revolve on common interests or identities have the ability to surpass conventional cultural limitations.

The use of digital technology has played a significant role in the conservation and revitalization of cultures that are at risk of extinction or neglected (Burlacu et al., 2019). The use of online archives, digital libraries, and collaborative endeavours facilitates the process of documenting and disseminating cultural material. Digital resources may be used by Indigenous groups as a means to transmit cultural practices and languages to subsequent generations.

The process of digitization has been shown to have a dual effect on cultural dynamics, as it simultaneously fosters the proliferation of cultural variety while also giving rise to apprehensions over cultural uniformity. The prevalence of Western digital platforms and material has the potential to overwhelm local cultures and narratives in some instances. The subject of the potential emergence of a global monoculture is a matter of ongoing discourse, as many cultures undergo adaptations in response to digital trends and the proliferation of popular material.

The advent of the digital era has transformed into a realm whereby individuals engage in the process of constructing and navigating their identities. Individuals could construct virtual identities, delve into various aspects of their personality, and establish connections with groups that share similar interests in the online realm. Nevertheless, the emergence of this digital domain also gives rise to inquiries over the genuineness of online personas and the possibility of adopting performative identities.

The advent of digitalization has led to the emergence of several online communities and subcultures, each characterized by its own set of values, rules, and cultural manifestations. Digital places, such as gaming communities and fandoms, provide people with a feeling of belonging and a shared sense of identity.

The advent of the digital era has also presented a series of issues pertaining to the dissemination of disinformation and the exacerbation of cultural divide. The accessibility and efficiency of internet platforms facilitate the fast propagation of inaccurate or deceptive narratives. Digital echo chambers have the potential to strengthen pre-existing opinions, hence exacerbating society divisions.

The advent of digital tools and platforms has facilitated the democratization of creative expression, hence fostering cross-border cooperation. The ability for musicians, artists, and producers to engage in worldwide collaborations enables them to surpass conventional limitations and generate unique works that are culturally diverse.

The advent of digitalization has expanded the boundaries of creative expression. The use of virtual reality (VR) and augmented reality (AR) technology enables artists to create immersive and interactive experiences that question conventional understandings of art and culture.

Governments and cultural organizations are now facing the challenges posed by the digital revolution of culture. In the digital realm, individuals are faced with the task of effectively addressing several challenges pertaining to copyright, cultural preservation, and cultural representation. The task of establishing digital governance structures that both safeguard cultural heritage and foster innovation is a multifaceted undertaking.

In summary, cultural revolution in the era of digital technology is a complex and multidimensional phenomenon. The phenomenon provides avenues for the promotion of cultural variety, the safeguarding of cultural heritage, and the facilitation of global interaction. However, it also poses issues pertaining to the erosion of cultural distinctiveness, the dissemination of inaccurate information, and the exacerbation of societal divisions. In the context of contemporary societies' engagement with the digital realm, it becomes imperative to effectively manage the tension between promoting cultural innovation and safeguarding cultural legacy. The advent of the digital era presents an unparalleled prospect for cultural enrichment and intercultural interaction, with the decisions taken in the present having a lasting impact on the cultural milieu for future generations.

4 Discussion

The interaction between digitization and change is intricate and diverse. Digital breakthroughs have the capacity to function as both catalysts and disruptors of transformative processes. This section examines case studies that demonstrate the mutually reinforcing relationship between digitization and transformation, providing insight into the underlying dynamics.

The current situation involves a dynamic interaction between digitization and change, which has had a profound impact on all aspects of human existence. This section examines the interconnectedness between digitization and transformation, investigating how these two phenomena mutually reinforce and redefine one another, eventually impacting our society, economy, and personal encounters.

Digitalization acts as a catalyst for change across several domains. It facilitates the acceleration of change by the provision of tools and technology that allow innovative approaches to cognition, labour, and lifestyle. The integration of digital technology across diverse industries, such as healthcare and education, has resulted in significant transformations in operational methods, frequently requiring the establishment of novel standards and approaches.

Data, a term sometimes likened to the "new oil" within the context of the digital era, serves as a catalyst for driving transformative processes. The act of gathering, examining, and using large quantities of data enables firms to make well-informed choices, enhance operational efficiency, and provide tailored experiences. The transformative influence of data extends to other domains, including healthcare, where the use of predictive analytics enhances the quality of patient care, and marketing, where data-driven insights contribute to the refinement of client interaction strategies.

Certain industries are especially well-suited for change in the digital age. The financial sector has seen substantial upheaval due to the emergence of financial technology (fintech), which has facilitated the implementation of efficient digital payment systems, peer-to-peer lending platforms, and the widespread use of cryptocurrencies. The energy industry is now experiencing a shift towards sustainability, characterized by the integration of digital technologies that boost the production and use of renewable energy sources (Angheluta et al., 2019).

The advent of digitalization has brought about a paradigm shift in the manner in which cultural material is both consumed and produced. The democratization of cultural expression has been facilitated by the advent of streaming platforms, social media, and user-generated material. The advent of digital technologies has brought about a significant cultural revolution, leading to the reconfiguration of several domains such as entertainment, media, and activism. Notably, the emergence of online movements has enabled the rapid mobilization of worldwide support (Rădulescu et al., 2023).

Organizations across all sectors are undertaking digital transformation initiatives to sustain competitiveness. The incorporation of digital technologies, including artificial intelligence, the Internet of Things (IoT), and cloud computing, facilitates the optimization of operations, improves consumer experiences, and enables the exploration of novel avenues for generating money.

The dynamic relationship between digitization and transformation is marked by mutual reinforcement. The process of digitalization speeds up transformation by offering the necessary tools and resources to foster rapid innovation and adaptability. Concurrently, transformational processes serve to inspire more digitalization efforts as firms strive to harness technology for the sake of expansion and enhanced operational effectiveness.

The interaction between digitization and transformation offers significant potential, but it also presents several obstacles. The accelerated rate of change has the potential to give rise to several challenges, including opposition, disparities in skills, and ethical quandaries. The goal of ensuring that digital transformation is in line with social values and inclusion is a multifaceted endeavour.

The interaction is characterized by the essential presence of ethical components. The process of digitalization gives rise to ethical concerns pertaining to the domains of privacy, data security, and algorithmic prejudice. The achievement of ethical digital transformation necessitates the proactive resolution of these challenges, while simultaneously optimizing the advantages derived from innovation.

The ongoing processes of digitization and transformation give rise to a multitude of potential outcomes for the future. Artificial intelligence, quantum computing, and augmented reality have the potential to initiate significant shifts in several sectors, challenging established paradigms and facilitating transformative changes.

Within the context of this dynamic, it is the people who possess the authority to effectively adjust and use the inherent capabilities of digital transformation.

The acquisition of knowledge and skills throughout one's lifetime, proficiency in digital technologies, and the capacity to adjust and respond effectively to evolving circumstances are essential for successfully navigating the dynamic and ever-changing environment.

In summary, the dynamic relationship between digitization and change is a defining factor in our modern society. Digitalization has a pivotal role in driving the process of transformation, while the process of transformation, in turn, fosters more digitalization. The tandem in question has a significant impact on several aspects of human activity, including work processes, communication patterns, creative endeavours, and overall lifestyle. To fully engage with this dynamic interaction, it is necessary to adopt a proactive approach, demonstrate ethical consciousness, and dedicate oneself to using its capacity for the collective benefit of people, communities, and global economies. In the current era of digital advancements, it is crucial to comprehend and influence the dynamic relationship between these influential factors, as it will play a crucial role in determining our shared destiny.

References

Angheluta, S. P., Burlacu, S., Diaconu, A., & Curea, C. S. (2019). The energy from renewable sources in the European Union: Achieving the goals. *European Journal of Sustainable Development, 8*(5), 57.

Benkler, Y. (2006). *The wealth of networks: How social production transforms markets and freedom*. Yale University Press.

Bessen, J. E., & Hunt, R. M. (2007). An empirical look at software patents. *Journal of Economics & Management Strategy, 16*(1), 157–189.

Bodislav, D. A. (2016). Business intelligence for decision making in economics. In C. Dunis, P. Middleton, A. Karathanasopolous, & D. A. Bodislav (Eds.), *Artificial intelligence in financial markets. New development is quantitative trading and investment* (pp. 125–158). Palgrave Macmillan.

Burlacu, S., Alpopi, C., Mitrită, M., & Popescu, M. L. (2019). Sustainable e-Governance and human resource development. *European Journal of Sustainable Development, 8*(5), 16–20.

Burlacu, S., Pargaru, I., Iacob, O. C., & Gombos, S. P. (2022). Digital Public Administration and the perspectives of Sustainable Development in Romania. *European Journal of Sustainable Development, 11*(4), 230–236.

Burlacu, S., Popescu, M. L., Diaconu, A., & Sârbu, A. (2021). Digital Public Administration for Sustainable Development. *European Journal of Sustainable Development, 10*(4), 33–40.

Burlacu, S., Rădulescu, C. V., Bălu, E. P., & Dobre, F. (2023). Socio-cultural sustainability for resilience in public services: Strategies for achieving inclusive and equitable service delivery. *European Journal of Sustainable Development, 12*(3), 29–29.

Calin, A. M., Burlacu, S., Mocanu, V., & Popescu, M. L. (2022). Digital Public Management Governance. *8th BASIQ International Conference on New Trends in Sustainable Business and Consumption* (pp. 101–108).

Castells, M. (1996). *The rise of the network society. The information age: Economy, society, and culture.* Wiley-Blackwell.

Chesbrough, H. W. (2003). *Open innovation: The new imperative for creating and profiting from technology.* Harvard Business Press.

Chua, R. Y. J. (2018). *The rise of Digital China: Encounters between state, market, and society.* Oxford University Press.

Dutton, W. H., & Blank, G. (2011). *Cultures of the Internet: The Internet in Britain.* Oxford University Press.

Georgescu, R. I. (2023). Modern leadership in business organisations during economic disruption. *Theoretical and Applied Economics, 30*(2), 73–82.

Gereffi, G., Humphrey, J., & Sturgeon, T. (2005). The governance of global value chains. *Review of International Political Economy, 12*(1), 78–104.

Goldin, I., & Reinert, K. (2006). *Globalization for development: Trade, finance, aid, migration, and policy.* World Bank Publications.

Graham, M. (2010). Neogeography and the Palimpsests of place: Web 2.0 and the construction of a virtual Earth. *Tijdschrift voor Economische en Sociale Geografie, 101*(4), 422–436.

Levitt, T. (1983). The globalization of markets. *Harvard Business Review, 61*(3), 92–102.

Mogos, R. I., Negescu-Oancea, M. D., Burlacu, S., & Troaca, V. A. (2021). Climate change and health protection in European Union. *European Journal of Sustainable Development, 10*(3), 97–108.

Mowery, D. C., & Rosenberg, N. (1993). *The U.S. National Innovation System.* Oxford University Press.

Ohmae, K. (1990). *The borderless world: Power and strategy in the interlinked economy.* Harper Business.

Rădulescu, C. V., Burlacu, S., Bodislav, D. A., & Bran, F. (2020). Entrepreneurial education in the context of the imperative development of Sustainable business. *European Journal of Sustainable Development,* 9(4), 93–93.

Rădulescu, C. V., Mănescu, C. O., Popescu, M. L., & Burlacu, S. (2023). Sustainable development in Public Administration: Research, practice, and education. *European Journal of Sustainable Development*, *12*(4), 27–27.

Shapiro, C., & Varian, H. R. (1999). *Information rules: A strategic guide to the network economy*. Harvard Business School Press.

Josef Botlik[1,*], Milena Botlikova[2], Zaneta Rylkova[1], Lucie Waleczek Zotykova[1], and Tereza Ikasova[1]

Mapping the Potential of 3D Printing in the Corporate Environment

Abstract:
Research background: 3D printing technologies have a significant potential to influence Industry 4.0 and the global economy. A significant increase in the adoption of 3D printing technologies has been observed in various areas of human work and corporate processes. The breadth of application gives companies independence in the global market and opens up new possibilities in supplier-customer relationships, inventory management, and logistics processes.
Purpose of the article: Companies are increasingly utilizing products from so-called additive manufacturing and looking for ways to increase manufacturing variability, which brings new technical challenges and requirements for key knowledge of their own manufacturing processes, the field of 3D printing technologies, material assortments, as well as the need to change perspectives on the product lifecycle, distribution chains, and business models.
Methods: The survey was primarily conducted on a theoretical level on the basis of published statistical data of the CZSO and EUROSTAT, discussions on social networks, and AI, followed by a comparison of development dynamics.
Findings & Value added: On the basis of the research, the fact was identified that a significant, yet underestimated, factor is the low or non- existent awareness of companies and the private sector about these technologies, the complexity of these processes, and the actual real possibilities

Keywords: *3d printing, companies, processes, globalization, problems*

JEL Classification: *D29; E23; F63*

* Corresponding author: botlik@opf.slu.cz

1 University Silesian University in Opava, School of Business Administration in Karvina, Univerzitní náměstí 1934/3, 733 40 Karviná, Czechia

2 University Silesian University in Opava, Faculty of Philosophy and Science in Opava, Masarykova třída 343/37, 746 01 Opava, Czechia

1 Introduction

The importance of 3D printing is indisputable, especially in a globalized world, it plays a significant role in the innovation potential of companies and in the restructuring of supplier- customer relationships. "3D printing is poised to change the world as we know it. Consumer goods will be personalized and produced on demand, while manufacturers will be able to use 3D printing to come up with radically new designs for everyday objects" (Deighton, 2014). A characteristic and essential feature of 3D printing is the fact that it is rapidly evolving, thus creating a lot of uncertainty in the manufacturing process. 3D printing has not yet reached its full potential, but it has already changed the way things are done in product design, prototyping, personalized products, and in some cases, mass production. Huge economic potential for companies is represented by technology, a technological form of the production process in which products are created by various forms of gradual, controlled addition of materials (as opposed to machining materials), where an object is created by laying continuous layers of material until the project or product is completely completed. This is referred to as additive technology. This technology also includes the area of 3D printing, which is used to create three-dimensional solid objects from digital files (especially in industry and healthcare). Despite the fact that these are progressive technologies, here too, we will encounter a number of problems, starting with technological problems and ending with ignorance of technology or uninformed company management. Various problems then lead to economic losses, bad results, or even (in the worst case) fires or destruction of technological components, which can lead to a reluctance to use these technologies. An increase in new legal issues, copyright of printed works, protection of digital 3D models, or product liability can also be significant. In particular, uninformed management of companies, exaggerated expectations, and biased material or personnel security are negative factors that prevent (due to ignorance of company needs and material-technical problems) the productive use of additive technologies, especially in the segment of small and medium-sized companies. The field of 3D printing, even though this technology is experiencing a boom, brings pitfalls and problems that companies and individuals do not know in advance and are unable to react to them realistically on their own. Therefore, it is necessary to prepare companies and individuals for 3D printing technologies (3DPT), not only for issues related to calibration, installation, selection of suitable types of printing technologies and materials, 3D modelling, the printing process, and subsequent activities, but also the usability of products, suitability use, or the pitfalls of implementing this technology in a corporate environment.

1.1 Current State of Knowledge

The current state of knowledge is presented at the level of 3DPT knowledge, its usability in general, in the corporate environment and in the educational process, possibly in relation to forms of evaluation of usability and benefits. The necessity and expediency of research directed in this way is evidenced by the fact that there is only one comprehensive research available in the environment directed at Czech companies when the company 3Dwiser already conducted a unique survey among companies from the Czech Republic, Slovakia, Hungary, and Romania focused on 3DPT in Central Europe (Wade et al., 2017), the research mainly concerned the following areas: the additive manufacturing market and its expected development, the use of 3DPT in companies, internal versus external use of 3DPT, types of 3D printers and technologies used, how companies perceive 3DPT technology, benefits of 3DPT according to business customers, and satisfaction with 3DPT. Although 3DPT is a set of digital manufacturing technologies, its adoption rate is not yet what the market expected. Therefore, from the point of view of corporate use, some research focuses on researching the organizational perspective and the factors that influence the adoption of 3DPT. For example, a study (Jo & Chen, 2018). represents research to develop a proper evaluation model that can prioritize the impact of these factors. Creating a similar evaluation model is also one of the goals of this project. One of the reasons for the low rate of transformation into the 3D industry is the generally low knowledge of companies in terms of related processes. Although companies perceive 3DPT as a revolutionary technology, they are not willing to change their decisions, for example, about corporate resources or supply networks and processes; these facts were published e.g., in (Davis et al., 2019). Especially for the SME segment, one of the effects of 3DPT is the ability to reverse the trend of global specialization of production systems and enable geographic dispersion closer to end users (Laplume et al., 2016) thereby increasing competitiveness. It can also be stated that it is currently not possible to separate the production of 3D printing equipment and 3D printing products, it is rather necessary to talk about the general corporate environment and the 3D industry, in this sense, there are studies conducted among SME companies (Wozniak et al., 2021) that demonstrate the willingness of companies to develop their activities and improve their position on the market by using 3DPT. Especially in the context of the limited possibilities of SME companies, there are also studies identifying the role of online markets for 3DPT platforms (Walsh et al., 2017). Already in the past, it was possible to find analyses from the field of product development and rapid prototyping in the product life cycle, which proves that 3DPT copies the knowledge of standard technological processes (Chuchro et al., 2008). In the literature, we will encounter not only the possibilities of 3D printing, but currently there is also research presenting business models (e.g., simulation of the business model of a company using 3DPT (Jin et al., 2021)), or studies devoted to the impact of 3DPT on new business models (Montes, 2016). There are also studies investigating the possibilities of further incorporating 3D printing into the manufacturing industry (Mavri & Mennis, 2022). Another area of corporate use consists of the implementation of non-standard components and tools where it is necessary to modify existing technologies (Schneider & Gärtner, 2022), through replications and reconstructions (including cultural heritage) (De la Torre-Cantero et al., 2015), to 3D printing production of purpose-built modular robotic tools (Mitsuhashi et al., 2015). Concepts are moving into previously unconsidered trends (Ice printing, Green printing), as mentioned by e.g., Garg et al. (2022) or Scaffaro et al., (2023). Innovative approaches can be traced in (Delmotte et al., 2020) when 3DPTs secured the identification watermarks of 3D objects. A wide spectrum of use is also indicated by Spahiu et al., (2020), when the use outside the standard (usually medical and technical) fields, but also in the textile industry, design, etc. (Wade et al., 2017). The importance of the 3DPT segment in the corporate environment is evidenced by the fact that, according to the CZSO (CZSO, 2023a), the use of printing (2019 data) is almost evenly distributed between companies with up to 250 employees and over 250 employees (the percentage of companies using 3D printing is 36.2 % / 40.3 %; average 12.9 %), most companies use their own or rented printers (21.8 % / 36.8 %; 10.9 %), 23.2 %/35 used prints to produce prototypes or models .9 %; 11.3 % of companies, which means that almost a third of companies with up to 250 employees use 3D printing for purposes other than the production of prototypes and models. This fact shows the necessity of research into the areas of 3DPT use in the corporate environment, the importance of 3DPT has reached such parameters that there is talk of a new industry, at MSV in Brno 2022, for example, the Forum of Additive Manufacturing 2022 was an associated event (Kuruc, 2022). The relevance of the topic can be further demonstrated by the increase in research outputs in this segment, in the ProQuest database 44697 results were found for the query "3D printing," the vast majority during the last 5 years (35717), 3295 occurrences in the last 12 months. For the combination "3d print enterprises," the number of results decreased to 2516/1374/139 results, for the combination "3d print business," the frequencies were: 5508/3147/302/208. Google returned 409,000 results for the query "3D courses" (March, 2023).

2 Methods

2.1 Methods and Data

The presented part of the research is primarily based on CZSO data, which is further refined on the basis of the company environment and Eurostat statistics. The default mathematical statistical method is comparison and regression analysis. As part of the comparison, the importance of companies is compared on the development of the number of companies of the relevant size in the Czech Republic and the degree of deployment of 3DPT in the Czech Republic. The methodology is based on the fact that information about 3D printing belongs to the data processed by the Czech Statistical Office (CZSO, n.d.). The second important factor is the fact that the Document of the National RIS3 strategy for the period 2021–2027, which was approved by the government of the Czech Republic on 25/01/2021, contains the indicator D06b "Companies in the Czech Republic using 3D printing" as part of contextual indicators D (DATASET 3.1 a) (MIT, n.d.). Based on these factors, the following analyses were performed: comparison of the development of 3D printers used in the corporate sector according to the CZSO classification (10–50 employees, 50–500 employees, more than 500 employees). The priority 4 areas of deployment were compared. The use of own 3D printing was evaluated compared to outsourced 3D printing. Furthermore, the use for the production or pre-production phase was compared. The evaluation was also carried out according to the partial classification of economic activities according to the CZ-NACE. Not all economic activities could be identified and assigned values, because their classification differs in 2019 and in 2021, for example, "Trade and repair of motor vehicles" in 2021 cannot be matched with "Wholesale and retail trade; repair and maintenance of motor vehicles." Some activities, such as "Activities of travel agencies and offices" are not reported data, however, it cannot be distinguished whether it is missing data or whether the industry does not use 3D printing technology. The slope method (1) was used as part of the regression analysis, the dynamics of the use of 3DPT was identified using the regression line, and the changes in dynamics were evaluated.

$$b = \frac{\Sigma(x-\bar{x})\cdot(y-\bar{y})}{\Sigma(x\cdot\bar{x})^2} \quad (1)$$

where y are the dependent values (numbers of enterprises), x is the independent variable, (years), $\bar{x}$ and $\bar{y}$ are the mean values of the sample. The CZSO data “Economic entities by number of employees, Entities with identified activity” were used for the calculation. These data are classified into the groups “not specified,” “without employees,” “1 – 5 employees,” “6 – 9,” “10 – 19,” “20 – 24,” “25 – 49,” “50 – 99,” “100 – 199,” “200 – 249,” “250 – 499,” “500 – 999,” “1000 – 1499,” “1500 – 1999,” “2000 – 2499,” “2500 – 2999,” “3000 – 3999,” “4000 – 4999,” “5000 – 9999,” “10000 and more” (scale 2). On the basis of data from 2008 to 2022, estimates were calculated for the groups of enterprises 10–49, 50–250, and 250+ (scale 1) according to the average size of the enterprise, based on the average number of enterprises in scale 2 and the average number of employees. Subsequently, the data were normalized to the interval <0, 1>, based on the normalized data, the slope of the guideline was calculated using the Slope (1) function, and the growth dynamics of the number of enterprises in the selected group was determined according to scale 2.

2.2 Research Background, Research Question, Hypotheses

Methods and data are based on research “3D printing technology as a tool for the competitiveness of companies – research on the conditions for the use of 3D printing in a corporate environment with an output aimed at the level of education,” which aims to map the needs, requirements and possibilities of using 3D printing, especially in the corporate sphere, the identification and concretization of problematic areas and the proposal of recommendations related to 3D printing technologies in order to create the prerequisites for the implementation of the knowledge needed in this sector into the learning process based on the needs of the corporate and private sectors. The field of research is directed to the identification of needs and critical points related to the implementation of 3D printing technologies in the corporate environment, which would allow businesses and individuals to effectively use this technology, at the same time, a set of recommended educational activities would be created (de la Torre-Cantero et al. 2015). The presented part of the research is devoted to the creation of weights and criteria for the identification of business segments that use, or have the potential to use, additive technologies.

Within the presented research (not this contribution), the following research questions were formulated:

> Q1: How challenging is the process of implementing 3DPT into company processes?
> Q2: Are companies currently willing to implement 3DPT into processes?

In connection with these questions, the investigated areas were specified in the hypotheses. H1: Firms consider 3DPT as standard production tools.

H2: Companies assume that they can manage the implementation of 3DPT by themselves. H3: Companies are aware of the complexity of the 3DPT implementation process and are willing to accept external cooperation in this sense (training, service, consulting, etc.).

H4: Firms are able to specify requirements for 3DPT implementation.

H5: Firms expect that 3DPT will significantly change their supply-customer chains. H6: Firms assume that 3DPT will significantly change their business models.

H7: Companies assume the applicability of 3D printing in managerial processes.

3 Results and Discussion

The presented part of the research maps the corporate segment using 3D printing technology and key areas that may be significant for identifying the analyzed factors. The table in Figure 1 (to preserve the graphical visualization of the data, the table created in MS Excel is inserted as an image) shows the percentage of companies using 3D printing in a given segment and industry. The Slope column contains the rates of change of the regression line (1), interlaced with the values of 2019 and 2021, it is graphically highlighted for better visualization. As already mentioned, some statistical values show a certain degree of implausibility, so it is not provable whether the values marked in red in the Slope column are due to the decline of 3D printing in these sectors, or whether it is a statistical error caused by a different interpretation of the input data. The division of companies into 3 groups according to the number of employees is given by the statistical data of the CZSO.

3.1 Analysis of the Corporate Environment

Two important conclusions can be seen from the Figure 1. There is an increase in the use of 3D printing technologies in company processes, with the highest share reported by companies with more than 250 employees, these companies also show the highest dynamics. In the given breakdown by economic activities, the highest dynamics are shown in the sectors "Professional, scientific, and technical activities" and "Telecommunication activities," while the highest share of the use of 3D printing is in "IT activities," "Manufacturing industry," and "Telecommunication activities." The "Professional, scientific, and technical activities" segment also shows a significant share. Based on CZSO (2023b) where it is stated that "*In 2021, 52 % of large industrial enterprises printed three-dimensional objects. 49 % of enterprises from the electronic industry and 35 % of the companies from the automotive industry used 3D technology. Outside of the industry, 3D printing is most often used by entities from the Research and Development sector (CZ-NACE 72), where 43 % of enterprises were concerned,*" the data of the CZSO were further mined for the identification of the sector (data from 2019, table data for 2021 were not yet available).

Total businesses (10+)	6,25	7,20	0,48
1 10–49 employees	4,32	4,90	0,29
2 50–249 employees	10,35	12,40	1,02
3 250 + employees	25,79	32,60	3,41
1 Manufacturing industry	12,9	15	1,053
2 Production and distribution of energy, gas, heat	---	5,2	--
3 Construction industry	2,2	1,2	-0,488
4 Trade and repair of motor vehicles	4,2	2,7	-0,753
5 Wholesale	5,1	3,9	-0,588
6 Retail	3,2	2,8	-0,182
7 Transport and storage	0,5	0,8	0,134
8 Accommodations	0,1	1,7	0,800
9 Catering and Hospitality	0,4	0,6	0,100
10 Audiovisual activities; publishing	7,2	7,5	0,137
11 Telecommunication activities	10,0	14,7	2,375
12 IT activities	15,5	16,5	0,483
13 Real estate activities	1,4	2,3	0,440
14 Professional, scientific and technical activities	5,8	10,4	2,291
15 Other administrative and support activities	2,9	5,1	1,104

Figure 1. Businesses using 3D print.
Source: Own research, data from the CZSO (2023)

Sectors with a share higher than 40 % are listed in the table in Figure 2, the table is again converted into a picture for the sake of graphic visualization. Values are highlighted in color from lightest to darkest (from lowest to highest). In the graph column, there is a share according to the size of the company. A value of more than 75 % was identified in the 250+ segment. The figure shows that in all these sectors the largest percentage share is companies 250+, on the other hand, companies 10–49 have a no smaller share.

CZ NACE	employees			graph
	10–49	50–249	250 +	
Manufacture of computers, electronic and optical instruments and equipment (26)	26,2	38,1	75,6	
Manufacture of electrical equipment, manufacture of machinery and equipment n.e.c. (27–28)	14,8	25,5	52,0	
Automotive industry and production of other means of transport (29–30)	10,4	28,5	49,2	
Furniture production; Other manufacturing industry; Repairs and installations of machinery and equipment (31–33)	11,0	14,1	42,6	
Chemical, pharmaceutical, rubber and plastic industry; Glass and building materials industry (19–23)	7,8	25,8	40,3	
Manufacturing - C (10-33)	8,0	18,2	40,3	

Figure 2. Top economic activity with 3d printing.
Source: Own research, data from the CZSO (2023)

Subsequently, the printing methods and processes in which 3D printing is applied in individual industries and segments were compared. It was investigated whether companies use their own 3D printing or outsource services. Furthermore, it was determined whether companies use 3D printing for the creation of prototypes or for their own production processes. Figure 3 shows that all segments of companies use more 3D printing technology on average to create models and prototypes, the largest share, almost 60 %, is held by companies 50–249. For all segments, this share is greater than 50 %. If we compare the share of outsourcing and in-house 3D printing, companies 250+ use outsourcing the least, and companies 10–49 the most.

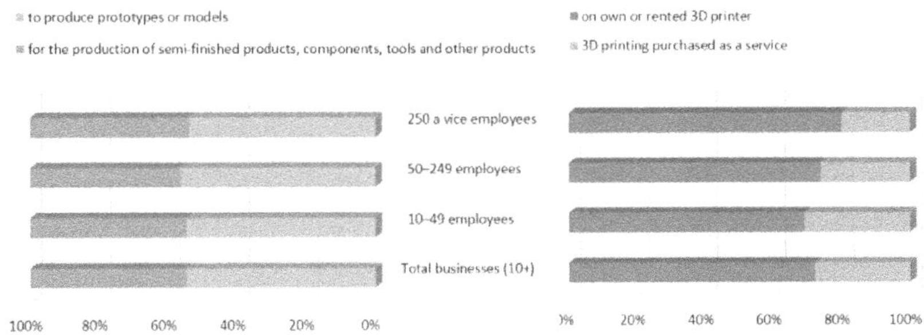

Figure 3. Outsourcing and prototyping – enterprise segment.
Source: Own research, data from the CZSO (2023)

However, these individual average values in the use of 3D printing vary significantly across industries. It can be seen in Figure 4 that "Trade and repair of motor vehicles" makes significant use of outsourcing, and "Real estate activities" have a higher proportion of outsourcing. If we evaluate the rate of manufactured prototypes and models, they are least used in "Retail," where their share is around 40 %. The graph also shows that "Activities of travel agencies and offices" either do not use 3D printing, or the required data for the given sector does not exist.

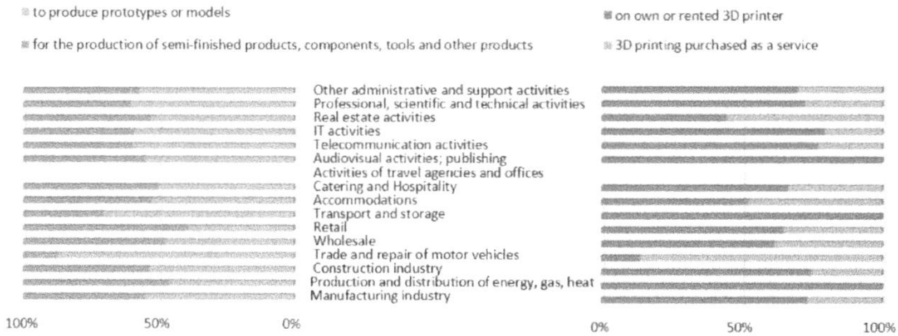

Figure 4. Outsourcing and prototyping – industry, CZ NACE.
Source: Own research, data from the CZSO (2023)

For further classification, companies were divided into 4 quadrants according to the use of their own/rented 3D printers and according to the use of the product. The share of one component to the total amount, expressed as a percentage, was used for the classification, the more the sector is to the left of the graph, the greater the proportion of prototypes than products, the lower the sector is, the greater the proportion of outsourcing than own 3D printing (2).

$$f(x,y) = \begin{cases} \left(\frac{service*100}{service+own}\right), & x = 0 \div 100\% \\ \left(\frac{product*100}{prototypes+product}\right), & y = 0 \div 100\% \end{cases} \qquad (2)$$

The figure shows a cluster of sectors 1, 3, 11, 12, 14, and 15, with a slightly predominant share of prototyping and approximately one-third share of in-house printing. Furthermore, groups 2, 7, and 10 can be seen, where the share of outsourcing is zero (or it may be a statistical error when data on outsourcing are missing). Of all sectors, activity 4 shows a significant deviation, where there is a high proportion of outsourcing and prototyping. Figure 5 also shows values that indicate the percentage of companies that use 3D printing according to individual forms of use in sectors.

no	own	service	prototypes	production
1	12.8	4.6	13.7	11.4
2	4.6		3.5	4.1
3	1.2	0.4	0.9	0.8
4	0.4	2.5	2.7	0.4
5	3.4	2.1	3.1	3.5
6	2.6	1.4	1.4	2.2
7	0.8	0	0.7	0.3
8	1.2	1.1	1.2	1.1
9	0.6	0.3	0.3	0.3
10	7.1	0	6.6	5.4
11	14.7	4.3	14.1	9.7
12	14.8	3.8	14.6	10.2
13	1.3	1.6	1	0.9
14	8.5	3.2	9.2	6.1
15	4.7	2	4.5	3.4

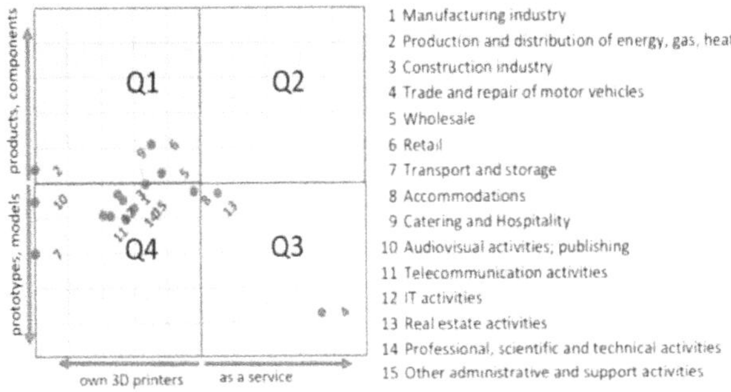

Figure 5. Outsourcing and prototyping – classification to quadrants.
Source: Own research, data from the CZSO (2023)

The graph in Figure 6 on the right shows the guideline for the 15-year interval 2008–2022, and further in the years 2021–2022, 2020–2022, 2019–2022, and 2018–2022. This determines the dynamics of the development of enterprises of the appropriate size. Although it is evident that the 250+ segment shows the greatest dynamics in the entire 15-year interval, in recent years, the 50–249 companies have shown the greatest dynamics in the monitored segments. For comparison, the dynamics of enterprises without employees and up to 9 employees is also shown; segments 1–9 show the highest dynamics in the last 2 years. The left part of the graph shows the normalized values of the development of the number of enterprises in a fifteen-year interval and the direction of the trend. Graphs are processed in MS Excel.

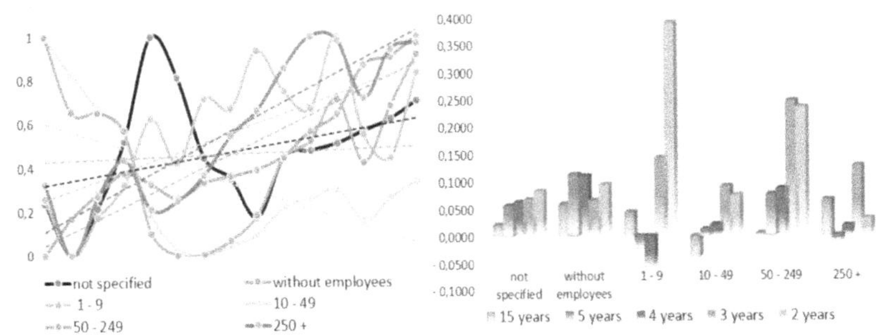

Figure 6. Function Slope on different intervals.
Source: Own research, data from the CZSO (2023)

Furthermore, 4 evaluation weights (sc1 – sc4, Figure 7) were calculated for subsegments of enterprises (according to scale 2). The weight sc1 expresses the number of enterprises in the given segment relative to the average number of employees in the given segment. The resulting values were normalized to the interval <0.1> (3).

$$ i=1; \quad \underset{k}{avg}\ Enn * \frac{\sum_{i=2}^{20} (avg_k En_i) * \frac{l_i + j_i}{2}}{\sum_{i=2}^{20} avg_k En_i}; \quad k=2008 \div 2022 \qquad - min_i \tag{3} $$

Where i is the segment according to scale 2 (1 – 20), Enik is the number of companies in the given segment i in year k (k=2008 – 2022), Enw is the number of companies without employees (i=2) and Enn is the number of companies not specifying the number of employees (i=1), avg is the average, l, j are the upper and lower limits of the given segment interval (for segment 10000+, l=j=10000). The values sc2, sc3 and sc4 are similarly ((value-min)/(max-min)) normalized values of the function Scope (1) calculated for 15-year, three-year, and two- year intervals. The resulting weight for further comparisons was calculated as a simple sum of partial weights, which was again normalized to the <0.1> interval. The partial weight coefficients take into account the size of the company, including the ratio to the number of employees, and the dynamics during the monitored period, and favor companies with dynamics over the last period. The mentioned procedure contains an element of uncertainty, when the estimate of the number of employed persons for the "not specified" segment is estimated as the average of the other segments, since it is statistically assumed that the population sample is evenly represented.

10000 +	5000 - 9999	4000 - 4999	3000 - 3999	2500 - 2999	2000 - 2499	1500 - 1999	1000 - 1499	500 - 999	250 - 499	200 - 249	100 - 199	50 - 99	25 - 49	20 - 24	10 - 19	6 - 9	1 - 5	without employees	not specified	sum	ent
0,05	0,09	0,01	0,02	0,00	0,02	0,04	0,10	0,26	0,28	0,05	0,30	0,33	0,26	0,04	0,22	0,10	0,35	0,55	,00		sc 1
0,65	0,91	0,70	,21	0,63	0,5[illegible]	0,97	0,90	0,78	1,00	,21	0,42	0,48	0,40	0,04	0,00	0,05	0,81	0,93	0,60		sc 2
0,20	0,15	0,21	0,59	0,00	0,54	0,54	0,27	0,55	0,56	0,77	1,00	0,57	0,72	,52	0,38	0,46	0,53	0,43	0,43		sc 3
0,36	0,33	0,49	0,68	0,00	0,82	0,75	,47	0,76	0,60	1,00	1,00	0,73	0,83	,69	0,63	0,77	0,97	0,70	0,69		sc 4
1,27	1,48	1,41	1,50	0,63	1,89	2,31	1,74	2,35	2,44	2,03	2,72	2,11	2,21	1,31	1,23	1,38	2,67	2,60	2,72		sum
0,30	0,40	0,37	0,41	0,0[illegible]	0,60	0,80	0,53	,82	0,8[illegible]	0,6[illegible]	1,00	,71	,75	,32	0,28	0,36	0,97	,94	1,00		weight

Figure 7. Calculated weights according to scale 2.
Source: Own research, data from the CZSO (2023)

On the basis of the established weights, the segments dominant in the use of 3D printing can be corrected. It is obvious that companies without employees, or small companies with up to five employees, will also play an important role. Similar potential can be expected in the 50–249 segment. Even if, from the perspective of long-term development, larger companies show dynamic potential, when taking current developments into account, the dominance of companies in the 100–199 segment is evident. If in this comparison we break down the values of the use of 3D printing into individual segments, as shown in Figure 3, we get the theoretical share of the use of 3D printing in the segment according to scale 2. It is obvious from Figure 8 that there has been a breakdown of the potential segment of the use of additive technology.

The picture does not take into account the possible development in the segment of small companies and companies without employees, because it was not possible to spread the spectrum of the use of 3D printing to these segments, due to the lack of statistical data. In the right part of the figure, the share of the respective form used by 3DPT is compared to the total number of companies.

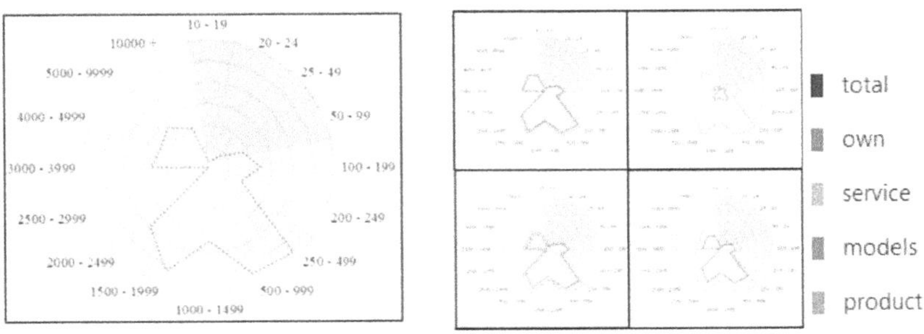

Figure 8. Using 3D prints according to scale 1and scale 2 – compare.
Source: Own research, data from the CZSO (2023)

3.2 Summary and Discussion

The presented part of the research maps the company environment and the current state of implementation and use of additive technologies, respectively. 3D printing technology in the Czech Republic. At this stage, the standard questionnaire survey, which can be considered obsolete today, was abandoned, and the potential of social networks and AI in combination with official statistics was used for further research. Based on analyses of primary statistical data available on official statistical portals (Eurostat, Czech Statistical Office), awareness of

3D printing in the corporate and private sector was mapped, then priority areas of problems and related terms were indicated, which were further compared and specified using reconnaissance of available (especially internet) sources, this knowledge was further expanded using information from professional forums (Conference Technological trends in 3D printing, Workshops of the National Center for Industry 4.0, Seminars Technological trends in the use of 3D printing in industry, Forum additive manufacturing, etc.) and through artificial intelligence analyzes (ChatGPT and Bing). At the same time, the obtained information was cross- compared and refined using social networks, especially through available Facebook groups (3d Printing for Beginners and Pros, 47.3 thousand members; 3D Printing World, 24.5 thousand members; 3D printing, 24.3 thousand members; 3D Printing/ 3 groups with the same name/ 19.8/ 9.8/ 8.2/ thousand members; 3D printing for beginners and advanced. Advice, tips and recommendations, 11.9 thousand members; Free 3d model stl 3d printing, 11.1 thousand members; 3D PRINT USEFUL / 3D PRINT USEFUL, 10.9 thousand members; 3D PRINTING COMMUNITY, 7.4 thousand members). The groups were chosen based on the selection of TOP 10 groups according to the number of members, the groups were selected with regard to the regional limitations of Facebook, and the original (in some cases Czech) names of the groups are given. In total, the discussions of groups numbering more than 150 thousand people were monitored in this way, this phase of the preliminary research took place from March to August 2023. Based on these discussions, two distinct sets of problems were identified. The first file mainly concerns individual printing, so it is also related to the company segment "without employees," or "1–9" employees. At this level, one can start especially from the environment of social networks, where (in the previously mentioned groups) the following are priority topics: used materials and temperatures, collapse and deformation of the printed model, problems with calibration, time and quality of printing, problems related to a stable environment for prints and problems related to printer hardware (nozzles, firmware, etc.). To a lesser extent, the issue of copyright, performance, service, etc. is addressed here. The cost of printing is only marginally mentioned. In contrast, AI-based discussion (especially Bing) present corporate issues, including information on fairs, workshops, and marketing. Initial and operational costs, the demand for expertise, quality, and reliability of the printing in the company process, and the limited print size are listed as priority areas. In the segment of "routine" operation, there are priority issues related to IT infrastructure, design and modelling capabilities, security and protection of intellectual property, and legal and regulatory issues. The segment of large companies hardly addresses the quality and reliability of printing, as it considers it a standard technological parameter. Generally, from a scan of the available documents, AI identifies as a substantial, general set of key issues in the corporate environment: Equipment costs, Materials costs, Employee training, Expertise, Print speed, Print quality, Material limitations,

Equipment maintenance, 3D modelling software, Compatibility with existing systems, Intellectual property, Regulation and certification, Safety and health at work, Recycling of materials, Supply chains, Scalability of production, Space requirements, Energy consumption, Life of products, and Postprocessing (finishing work).

4 Conclusion

The conclusions of the presented part of the research can be summarized in concrete findings. In the future, the perspective company segment will be two company segments. The first will be companies with up to 10 employees, which will use 3DPT as a small-series or additional technology. The second group consists of companies on the border between the segment of medium and large companies, with an approximate size of 200–500 employees. According to economic activities, the sectors "Professional, scientific and technical activities" and "Telecommunication activities" show the highest dynamics, while the highest share of the use of 3D printing is in "IT activities," "Manufacturing industry" and "Telecommunication activities." The "Professional, scientific and technical activities" segment also shows a significant share. It is therefore evident that the research must continue to be directed to the identified company segments that already use 3DPT and to try to transfer the experience gained, which of course may interfere with the company's know-how. Other conclusions can be summarized in general findings. Additive technologies have become an integral part of production. It can be stated that the "start-up" period has ended, it can be stated that 3D printing has transformed into a standard production technology. As a technology, it requires the relevant specific working environment (temperatures, materials, times, etc.), technological standards, procedures, processes, and legal and personnel security. Research has shown that 3D printing technology has a similar behavior in the corporate environment as other manufacturing technologies. It is necessary to distinguish small-scale production and prototyping from high-end production of specialized products. As was shown in discussions on social networks, there is a relatively large community dedicated to "cheap" 3D printing and model development, using hardware in price ranges up to 1000 Euros, on the other hand, large companies and specialized workplaces use technologies priced at hundreds of thousands of Euros.

Motivation for further research can be sought at the level of identification of weak and strong points related to the implementation of 3DPT in a company environment.

Acknowledgments

The contribution was processed within Institutional Support Project IP/08/2023 of the University of Silesia in Opava, School of Business Administration in Karvina "3D printing technology as a tool for companies' competitiveness – research into the conditions of usability of 3D printing in a corporate environment with an output targeted at the level of education."

References

Chuchro M., Czekaj J., & Ruszaj A. (2008). Seminarium: Techniki szybkiego prototypowania w cyklu życia produktu. *Mechanik, 12*, 1063–1070.

CZSO. (n.d.). *Podniky a ICT zdroje dat metodika setreni*. https://csu.gov.cz/podniky-a-ict-zdroje-dat-metodika-setreni

CZSO. (2023a). *Využívání informačních a komunikačních technologií v podnikatelském sektoru – 2023*. https://csu.gov.cz/produkty/vyuzivani-informacnich-a-komunikacnich-technologii-v-podnikatelskem-sektoru-2023

CZSO. (2023b). 3D tisk proniká do průmyslu i do dalších oborů. CZSO. https://csu.gov.cz/produkty/3d-tisk-pronika-do-prumyslu-i-do-dalsich-oboru

Davis, E. R., et. al. (2019). An analytics framework for structuring 3D printing deployment decisions. *Annual Reliability and Maintainability Symposium (RAMS) – R and M in the Second Machine Age – The Challenge of Cyber Physical Systems* (pp. 1–6).

de la Torre-Cantero, J., Saorín, J. L., Meier, C., Melián-Díaz, D., & Aemán, M. D. D. (2015). Creating replicas of scultural heritage through 3D reconstruction and low cost 3D printer in Education. *Arte individuo y sociedad, 27*(3), 427–444.

Delmotte, A., Tanaka, K., Kubo, H., Funatomi, T., & Mukaigawa, Y. (2020). Blind watermarking for 3-D printed objects by localifying layer thickness. *IEEE Transactions on Multimedia, 22*(11), 2780–2791.

Deighton, B. (2014, April, 25). *What does the future hold for 3D printing?* Horizon. https://ec.europa.eu/research-and-innovation/en/horizon-magazine/what-does-future- hold-3d-printing

Garg, A., Yerneni, S. S., Campbell, P., LeDuc, P. R., & Ozdoganlar, O. B. (2022). Freeform 3D ice printing (3D-ICE) at the micro scale. *Advanced Science, 9*(27), Article 2201566.

Jin, Y. R., Campbell, R., Tang, J. N., Ji, H. S., Song, D. R., & Liu, X. Q. (2021). Designing and simulating a "mass selective customization-centralized manufacturing" business model for clothing enterprises using 3D printing. *Rapid Prototyping Journal, 27*(9), 1664–1680.

Kuruc, J. (2022). *Nové průmyslové odvětví. Přednosti a strasti profesionálního 3D tisku*, Živě.cz. https://www.zive.cz/clanky/nove-prumyslove-odvetvi-predno sti-astrasti- profesionalniho-3D-tisku/sc-3-a-219411/default.aspx

Laplume, A., Petersen, B., & Pearce, J. (2016). Global value chains from a 3D printing perspective. *Journal of International Business Studies, 47*(5), 595–609.

Mavri, M., & Mennis, V. (2022). Is COVID-19 the "Catalyst" to Incorporate 3D Printing Technology into the Manufacturing Industry? *3D Printing and Additive Manufacturing, 9*(5), 450–459.

Ministry of Industry and Trade [MIT]. (2023). *Národní výzkumná a inovační strategie pro inteligentní specializaci České republiky*. MIT. https://www.agent ura-api.org/wp-content/uploads/2023/04/priloha-9-narodni-ris3-strate-giepriloha-3.pdf

Mitsuhashi, K., Ohyama, Y., Hashimito, H., & Ishijma, S. (2015). Production and education of the modular robot made by 3D printer. *10th Asian Control Conference (Ascc)* (pp. 1–5).

Montes, J. O. (2016). Impacts of 3D printing on the development of new business models technology and service complementarity in Industry 4.0. *2016 IEEE European Technology and Engineering Management Summit (E-Tems).*

Scaffaro, R., Citarrella, M. C., & Morreale, M. (2023). Green composites based on Mater-Bi® and *Solanum lycopersicum* plant waste for 3D printing applications. *Polymers, 15*(2), Article 325.

Schneider, L., & Gärtner, H. (2022). Additive manufacturing for lab applications in environmental sciences: Pushing the boundaries of rapid prototyping. *Dendrochronologia, 76*, Article 126015.

Spahiu, T., Canaj, E., & Shehi, E. (2020). 3D printing for clothing production. *Journal of Engineered Fibers and Fabrics, 15*, Article 1558925020948216.

Wade, R; Girlanda, N., & Podrost, G. (2017). Challenges of 3D printing for home users. In A. Berg, E. Bohemia, L. Buck, T. Gulden, A. Kovacevic, & N. Pavel (Eds.), *19th International Conference on Engineering and Product Design Education (E&PDE), Building Community: Design Education for a Sustainable Future* (pp.478–482).

Walsh, G. S., Przychodzen, J., & Przychodzen, W. (2017). Supporting the SME commercialization process: The case of 3D printing platforms. *Small Enterprise Research*, *24*(3), 257–273.

Wozniak, J., Budzik, G., Przeslowski, L., & Chudy-Laskowska, K. (2021). Directions of the development of the 3D Printing Industry as exemplified by the Polish Market. *Management and Production Engineering Review*, *12*(2), 98–106.

Yeh, C. C., & Chen, Y. F. (2018). Critical success factors for adoption of 3D printing. *Technological Forecasting and Social Change*, *132*, 209–216.

3DWiser. (n.d.a). 3D tisk ve střední Evropě. 3DWiser. https://3Dwiser.com/3D-tisk-ve- stredni-evrope-unikatni-pruzkum-2021/

Florina Bran[1,*], Dumitru Alexandru Bodislav[1], Raluca Florentina Crețu[1], Victor Adrian Troacă[1], and Carol Cristina Gombos[1]

Globalization as a Tool for Sustainable Development

Abstract:

Research background: This paper provides a critical analysis of the complex interplay between globalization, sustainability, and development, investigating the diverse factors that influence the current global environment. The ongoing process of globalization is reshaping economic, social, and environmental frameworks, thereby emphasizing the crucial importance of sustainable development.

Purpose of the article: The aim of this research is to provide a comprehensive understanding of the synergistic effects, conflicting dynamics, and possible compromises inherent in the trilateral interaction of globalization, sustainability, and development. The paper seeks to offer a comprehensive analysis of interdisciplinary scholarship to illuminate the dual impact of globalization on sustainable development goals, encompassing both its facilitative and obstructive aspects.

Methods: This study examines the potential of globalization's economic interconnections to enhance development prospects, while also considering the simultaneous ecological pressures and socio-economic disparities that may be exacerbated as a result. The research employs a range of case studies to elucidate the intricate nature of converting globalized systems into sustainable results at the local level.

Findings & Value added: This paper underlines the importance of technology, innovation, and inclusive governance in harnessing globalization for sustainable development. It stresses tailoring strategies to cultural and regional specifics for global sustainability, combining empirical data and theory to explore the interplay between globalization, sustainability, and development. The study advocates for comprehensive strategies leveraging globalization's transformative power for equitable development and addressing global issues, guiding towards a sustainable, inclusive future.

Keywords: *globalization, sustainability, development, evolution*

JEL Classification: *F60; F63*

* Corresponding author: carmen-valentina.radulescu@eam.ase.ro

1 Bucharest University of Economic Studies, Romana Square, no. 1, district 1, Bucharest, Romania

1 Introduction

Globalization, a multifaceted phenomenon, has significantly impacted the world in the past few decades (Burlacu et al., 2018). While it is often associated with economic integration, it extends far beyond trade and commerce (Burlacu et al., 2023). Globalization has transformed societies, cultures, and environments, and its influence on sustainable development is a topic of intense debate (Popescu et al., 2021). This essay explores the relationship between globalization and sustainable development, highlighting both its positive and negative aspects.

Before delving into the relationship between globalization and sustainable development, it is essential to define these concepts:

- Globalization: Globalization refers to the increasing interconnectedness and interdependence of countries through the exchange of goods, services, information, and ideas across national borders. It encompasses economic, political, social, and cultural aspects (Rădulescu et al., 2020a).
- Sustainable Development: Sustainable development is a holistic concept that aims to meet the needs of the present without compromising the ability of future generations to meet their own needs. It involves economic growth, social inclusion, and environmental protection (Bodislav, 2013).

Positive aspects of globalization for sustainable development:

- Economic Growth: Globalization has facilitated economic growth in many parts of the world. The flow of investments, technology, and expertise across borders has led to the expansion of industries and the creation of jobs, ultimately improving the standard of living for many (Stiglitz, 2002).
- Reducing Poverty: The integration of developing countries into the global economy has lifted millions out of poverty. Access to global markets provides opportunities for income generation and poverty reduction (Levitt, 1983).
- Technological Advancements: Globalization accelerates the dissemination of technology and knowledge. Innovations in healthcare, agriculture, and communication have improved living conditions and access to education.
- Cultural Exchange: Increased cultural exchange is a positive aspect of globalization. It fosters understanding, tolerance, and the appreciation of diverse cultures, contributing to social cohesion (Tomlinson, 1999).
- Global Collaboration: Globalization has necessitated international cooperation on issues like climate change, public health, and security. These collaborative efforts are essential for addressing global challenges (Thomas & Greenberg, 1988).

Negative aspects of globalization for sustainable development:

- Income Inequality: While globalization can reduce poverty, it often exacerbates income inequality within and between countries. The benefits of globalization are not evenly distributed, and marginalized populations may be left behind.
- Environmental Degradation: Rapid industrialization and global trade have put immense pressure on natural resources and ecosystems. Unsustainable consumption and production patterns contribute to environmental degradation.
- Cultural Homogenization: Globalization can lead to cultural homogenization, as dominant Western cultures and values are spread worldwide, potentially eroding local traditions and identities.
- Labour Exploitation: In pursuit of cost savings, some multinational corporations engage in exploitative labour practices in developing countries, undermining social and labour rights.
- Dependency: Developing countries may become overly dependent on a few key industries or foreign aid, making them vulnerable to global economic fluctuations and geopolitical pressures.

Achieving a balance between globalization and sustainable development requires a comprehensive approach that maximizes the benefits of globalization while minimizing its negative impacts (Radulescu et al., 2020b). Here are some strategies:

- *Inclusive Economic Policies:* Governments and international organizations should implement policies that ensure the benefits of globalization are distributed equitably. This includes progressive taxation, social safety nets, and measures to support marginalized communities (Belostecinic et al., 2022).
- *Environmental Regulations:* To combat environmental degradation, strict regulations and international agreements on issues like carbon emissions and biodiversity protection are essential. Encouraging sustainable practices in industries is crucial (Mogos et al., 2021).
- *Cultural Preservation:* Efforts should be made to preserve and celebrate local cultures and traditions. Promoting cultural exchange without erasing indigenous identities is vital (Diaconu et al., 2019).
- *Fair Trade Practices:* Encouraging fair trade practices ensures that workers are treated ethically and paid fair wages in global supply chains (Radulescu et al., 2020a).

- *Investing in Education:* Education is key to harnessing the benefits of globalization. Access to quality education equips individuals with the skills needed to participate in the global economy.
- *Global Governance:* Strengthening international organizations and mechanisms for global governance is necessary to address transnational challenges effectively (Calin et al., 2022).

Globalization is a powerful force that has the potential to both advance and hinder sustainable development (Burlacu et al., 2021). Its impact is complex, with both positive and negative consequences. To harness globalization as a tool for sustainable development, it is crucial to adopt a balanced approach that prioritizes economic growth, social equity, and environmental stewardship (Rich, 2002). By addressing the challenges posed by globalization and leveraging its opportunities, we can work towards a more equitable and sustainable world for current and future generations (Radulescu et al., 2020a). The development of digitization has had a huge impact on the quick speed of globalization in the 21st century (Nye, 2000). The convergence of these two formidable forces has engendered a new terrain that impacts all facets of society, including economics and labor markets, as well as culture and government (Newell & Wheeler, 2006). The primary objective of this research study is to provide a comprehensive understanding of the processes by which globalization has been expedited and altered because of digitalization. Additionally, it aims to analyze the interdependent nature of these two phenomena. Furthermore, this study examines the consequences of this interaction on policy formulation, governance practices, and the implementation of inclusive development methods. This study seeks to provide a complete knowledge of the intricate interplay of globalization, change, and digitalization by means of a critical analysis and evaluation of individual case studies.

1.1 Labor Markets in the Digital Era

The advent of digitalization in labor markets has resulted in substantial transformations in the characteristics of employment. The prevalence of automation, remote labor, and gig employment has led to a significant transformation of conventional employment structures. This section provides an analysis of the impact of digitalization on the global labor market, highlighting the many possibilities and problems it has presented. Additionally, it explores the consequences of digitalization on income inequality and job security (Popescu et al., 2021).

The advent of the digital age has brought about significant changes in labor markets, resulting in a fundamental restructuring of work dynamics, employment associations, and the requisite skill sets for the workforce (Henriques & Richardson, 2004). This section examines the fundamental dynamics of labour markets in the era of digitalization.

The advent of digitalization has resulted in the emergence of novel work modalities that surpass conventional office environments and standard working schedules. The prevalence of remote work has been on the rise, driven by the widespread use of digital technology and communication platforms. The flexibility confers advantages to both businesses and people, facilitating the use of a diverse talent pool on a worldwide scale and enhancing the equilibrium between work and personal life.

The gig economy is a prominent feature of the contemporary digital landscape, distinguished by its reliance on temporary agreements and independent employment. Digital platforms such as Uber, Upwork, and Fiverr facilitate the connection between employees and various jobs and projects, giving them the autonomy to choose their own work schedule and methods. Although the gig economy provides individuals with a certain degree of flexibility, it often fails to give the stability and employment advantages typically associated with traditional forms of work.

The use of artificial intelligence and robotics in automation has the capacity to bring about substantial transformations in labor markets. The automation of routine and repetitive work is progressively becoming more prevalent, potentially resulting in employment displacement within certain sectors. Nevertheless, the use of automation may also give rise to novel positions and prospects, especially within technology-centric domains.

As the labor markets undergo changes, there is a corresponding need for the workers to acquire new skills. There is now a significant need for skills such as digital literacy, data analysis, coding, and problem-solving. The acquisition of knowledge and the capacity to adapt are crucial to remain relevant within a swiftly evolving employment environment. Governments and educational institutions are collaborating to implement training and upskilling initiatives aimed at equipping employees with the most sought-after skills.

The process of digitalization has the potential to amplify existing imbalances within the labor market. Individuals who possess digital abilities may have enhanced employment chances and increased earning capacity, whilst those who lack proficiency in this domain may encounter restricted career options. Addressing the issue of bridging the digital gap is of utmost importance due to its potential to exacerbate disparities in economic and social equity.

The advent of digital platforms and online markets has facilitated the empowerment of people, enabling them to assume the roles of entrepreneurs and freelancers. The pursuit of self-employment provides individuals with a sense of independence and adaptability, although it also entails the responsibility of managing benefits and preparing for retirement solely on the part of the person. Policymakers are now faced with the challenge of devising strategies to expand conventional employment safeguards to accommodate the expanding sector of the workforce.

In the contemporary digital age, labor markets often need a delicate balance between the desirable attributes of flexibility and job security. Although gig labor and remote work provide employees the advantage of autonomy, it is important to note that these workers often face challenges related to limited access to healthcare, retirement benefits, and employment security. Policymakers are now engaged in the examination of strategies to achieve a harmonious equilibrium between these conflicting objectives.

The process of digitalization has significantly contributed to the facilitation of talent mobility on a worldwide scale. Organizations could access a heterogeneous labor force originating from many geographical locations, hence promoting the generation of novel ideas and facilitating intercultural cooperation. Nevertheless, these circumstances also give rise to inquiries over immigration rules, work permits, and the ramifications on domestic labor markets.

The role of governments in influencing labor markets in the digital age is of utmost importance. In the context of the gig economy, it is essential to consider and tackle pertinent concerns pertaining to labor rights, worker categorization, and taxes. Furthermore, it is possible to provide incentives for firms to allocate resources towards workforce development initiatives, while also establishing safety nets to support employees amidst the dynamic and evolving nature of the labor market (Sen, 1999).

The prospects of labor in the digital age provide a combination of exhilarating opportunities and formidable obstacles. Although digitization has several prospects for enhancing efficiency and fostering innovation, it also introduces concerns over job security and the equitable distribution of economic benefits. The successful transition to the evolving work landscape requires a collective endeavor including governmental bodies, enterprises, and employees, aimed at ensuring equitable distribution of the advantages stemming from digitization.

In summary, the labor markets in the digital age exhibit dynamic transformations and a notable transition towards adaptability and proficiency in digital competencies. The ongoing transformation of the labor landscape due to technological advancements necessitates the adoption of a lifelong learning mindset by people, with the implementation of laws by governments and corporations that safeguard workers' rights and foster an inclusive environment for economic development. The dynamic characteristics of labor markets provide many problems and prospects, necessitating societal adjustments to guarantee inclusivity in the contemporary work environment.

1.2 Policy, Governance, and Inclusive Development

The ramifications of the interplay between digitization and globalization have far-reaching effects on the domains of policy and governance. Policymakers are confronted with the task of formulating adaptable frameworks that effectively use the advantages of digitalization while also addressing and minimizing its associated hazards (Fukuyama, 1989). This section examines the influence exerted by governments and international organizations on the trajectory of globalization in the era of digitalization.

In the intricate and swiftly changing environment of the 21st century, policy and governance assume a crucial role in determining the course of countries and regions. This section delves into the complex interplay between policy, governance, and inclusive development, highlighting the significance of these elements in attaining societies that are both fair and enduring.

Policy functions as the foundational framework for the development of a country. Government choices span a broad spectrum, including many aspects such as economic laws, social programs, environmental safeguards, and healthcare standards. Well-crafted policies serve as the fundamental basis for fostering inclusive growth.

Governance refers to the procedural framework through which policies are executed and institutions are administered. Efficient, transparent, and accountable policy execution is a hallmark of effective government. Additionally, it assumes a crucial function in facilitating citizen participation, advocating for the principles of justice, and safeguarding fundamental human rights (Meadows et al., 1972).

Inclusive development is a fundamental idea that prioritizes the provision of equal opportunities, fair distribution of resources, and the enhancement of social well-being (Georgescu, 2023). The primary objective is to promote equitable distribution of the advantages derived from economic growth and development, with the goal of inclusivity and leaving no individual or group marginalized. Inclusive development strategies provide a primary focus on vulnerable populations, with the aim of diminishing inequities and promoting social cohesion.

Inclusive development approaches directly address the issue of inequality. Redistributive policies include several strategies, including progressive taxation, the establishment of social safety nets, and the provision of accessible and high-quality education and healthcare services (Rădulescu et al., 2020b). The primary objective of these programs is to alleviate poverty among the most marginalized individuals, while concurrently fostering a more equitable allocation of economic resources.

The need of achieving inclusive growth necessitates the simultaneous pursuit of environmental sustainability. The implementation of policies and governance systems that place sustainability as a top priority is vital in safeguarding the earth for future generations. This encompasses strategies aimed at mitigating climate change, preserving finite resources, and fostering the use of environmentally sustainable technology.

The implementation of policy is contingent upon the presence of effective governance. To guarantee the effective implementation of policies and prevent corruption, it is essential to establish institutions that prioritize transparency and accountability. The establishment and implementation of robust regulatory frameworks and effective supervision mechanisms play a crucial role in the attainment of policy goals.

Citizen participation is a crucial factor in the success of inclusive development. It is important for governments to provide avenues for public engagement in decision-making procedures, enabling them to express their concerns and ensure institutional transparency and responsibility. The inclusion of information accessibility, freedom of speech, and open conversation are fundamental elements within the framework of participatory government.

In the contemporary global landscape, the significance of international collaboration cannot be overstated in fostering equitable growth. The resolution of global concerns, such as climate change, pandemics, and migration, necessitates the implementation of collective action and policy coordination across states. Multilateral organizations and agreements serve as effective mechanisms for tackling these complex problems (Mogos et al., 2021).

In an epoch characterized by expeditious technical progress and unanticipated catastrophes, it is essential for policy to demonstrate adaptability. It is essential for governments to possess the capability to promptly adapt policies considering developing difficulties, including domains such as technology, public health, and the economy.

The objective of inclusive development strategies is to construct resilient societies capable of withstanding shocks and crises, all the while prioritizing fairness and social well- being. This entails allocating resources towards the development of healthcare facilities, the establishment of robust social safety nets, and the enhancement of education systems to adequately equip individuals for forthcoming difficulties.

In summary, the interaction of policy, governance, and inclusive development plays a pivotal role in the advancement and welfare of societies. The establishment of well-crafted policies, transparent governance institutions, and a steadfast dedication to inclusive development ideals serve as the fundamental pillars for fostering a just and enduring future. In the context of the contemporary period, it is imperative for governments and policymakers to maintain a steadfast commitment towards promoting comprehensive development that ensures the inclusion of all individuals, empowers marginalized populations, and preserves the environment for the benefit of future generations.

2 Methods

Our research focuses on examining the impact of digitization on labor markets in the context of globalization. The main aim is to analyze how digitization has reshaped the structure of the labor market, while influencing sustainable development and globalization.

We adopted a qualitative, case-based approach to explore the impact of digitization on labor markets. Data was collected from a variety of sources, including academic articles, government reports, specialist publications and interviews with experts in the field of labor market, digitization, and globalization. We used academic databases and digital archives to ensure the validity and relevance of the information. The collected data were subjected to a thematic analysis to identify emerging trends and patterns. We used qualitative analysis software to facilitate data organization and interpretation. Through this analysis, we have explored the impact of digitization on forms of employment, changes in skill requirements, labor market inequalities and how these elements interact with the globalization process.

To provide a deep understanding, we have selected specific case studies that illustrate different aspects of the impact of digitization on labor markets in the context of globalization. These case studies included examples from companies adopting remote working, the gig industry (collaborative economy), and the impact of automation in various sectors.

2.1 Adaptive Strategies for Societal Well-being

Expanding on the analysis of policy and governance, this part underscores the significance of adaptive methods that foster societal well-being within the process of digitalization- induced globalization. The integration of inclusive development, digital literacy, and ethical issues is crucial within these tactics.

In a dynamic global landscape characterized by rapid technological progress, environmental complexities, and demographic fluctuations, the implementation of adaptive methods becomes imperative to safeguard the overall welfare of society. This section examines the importance of adaptive methods, their function in tackling intricate problems, and their capacity to promote resilience and prosperity.

Adaptive methods emerge because of the ever-changing and uncertain characteristics of modern society. The recognition of the perpetual nature of change and the need of proactive adaptation are acknowledged as essential factors for achieving success during ever-evolving obstacles.

Numerous contemporary socioeconomic challenges exhibit a complex and interdependent nature. Adaptive techniques provide a comprehensive approach to tackling these intricacies, acknowledging the need for flexibility, context sensitivity, and inclusivity in devising solutions.

Environmental sustainability is widely recognized as a prominent problem in contemporary society. In this context, adaptive strategies include a range of policies and practices aimed at mitigating the environmental effects of human activity, as well as equipping communities to cope with the repercussions of climate change.

The significance of adaptive strategies in the field of public health has been highlighted by the COVID-19 pandemic. The implementation of adaptive measures, including as the expedited development of vaccines and the establishment of flexible healthcare systems, played a crucial role in minimizing the repercussions of the disaster.

In the context of a worldwide economy, the implementation of adaptive techniques becomes imperative to ensure economic resilience. To effectively respond to economic shocks, market upheavals, and technological breakthroughs, it is essential for governments and enterprises to possess the ability to adapt and innovate.

The prioritization of fair policies and practices is a key aspect of adaptive solutions within the domain of social inclusion. The objective is to mitigate inequalities in educational, healthcare, and economic access, hence fostering inclusive prosperity for all individuals within the community.

The establishment of robust governance mechanisms is crucial for the successful implementation of adaptive tactics. It is important for governments to exhibit responsiveness to dynamic conditions, maintain transparency in the process of decision-making, and demonstrate a willingness to engage in collaborative efforts with a wide range of stakeholders.

In the era of digitalization, there is a pressing need for the development of flexible approaches that effectively use the capabilities of technology while concurrently addressing and minimizing its associated hazards. To ensure the protection of privacy and security in an ever more interconnected global landscape, policymakers must undertake the necessary adjustments to rules and cybersecurity protocols.

The use of adaptive techniques in the field of education acknowledges the notion that the process of acquiring knowledge and skills extends over an individual's whole lifespan. The organization fosters a culture that prioritizes ongoing skill enhancement and embraces progressive methodologies in the realm of education and training.

Numerous global concerns, such as pandemics and climate change, need the imperative of international collaboration. Adaptive tactics include diplomatic endeavors aimed at establishing collaborative relationships and agreements that successfully tackle common difficulties (Hardin, 1968).

The formulation of adaptive strategies necessitates the achievement of equilibrium between immediate need and future objectives. While it is crucial to prioritize the resolution of urgent problems, it is as essential to engage in future-oriented planning and allocate resources towards the development of sustainable solutions.

Adaptive solutions are grounded in ethical concepts, which serve to uphold human rights, inclusiveness, and ethical standards in addressing social difficulties. These factors play a crucial role in shaping decision-making processes under intricate and dynamic circumstances.

To effectively implement adaptive methods, it is essential to establish procedures that facilitate the measurement of success and ensure accountability. The implementation of robust monitoring and evaluation mechanisms is crucial in ensuring the efficacy and adaptability of policies and initiatives considering changing conditions.

The basic objective of adaptive methods is on the aspiration to construct societies that possess resilience. These communities possess superior capabilities to endure disturbances and adjust to evolving circumstances, consequently augmenting the welfare of their constituents.

In summary, the implementation of adaptive solutions is crucial in effectively navigating an unpredictable future and safeguarding the overall welfare of society. The organization provides a flexible and adaptable strategy for tackling intricate and interrelated issues, ranging from the preservation of the environment to the promotion of public health and the enhancement of economic resilience. As societies undergo ongoing transformations, the capacity to adjust and generate novel ideas will serve as a fundamental element for achieving prosperity and resilience, therefore ensuring the welfare of present and forthcoming cohorts.

3 Results

The study revealed that digitization has significantly transformed traditional employment structures. The emergence of remote work and employment in the gig (collaborative) economy has become increasingly prevalent, characterized by flexibility and autonomy.

These new forms of employment offer opportunities for work-life balance, but also raise concerns about job security and the lack of traditional employment benefits.

Our analysis identified a shift in skills requirements due to digitization. There is an increased demand for digital literacy, technical skills, and adaptability in the labor market. Workers with advanced digital skills find more opportunities, while those without such skills face possible marginalization. This change requires a reassessment of education and training programs to align with the evolving demands of the labor market.

Digitization has contributed to widening inequalities in the labor market (Dollar & Kraay, 2002). While it has created new opportunities for some, it has also exacerbated existing disparities, particularly affecting low-skilled workers and those in sectors less adaptable to digital transformation. The study highlighted the need for policy interventions to address these growing inequalities.

The research found a complex interplay between digitization and globalization in labor markets. Digitization has facilitated the process of globalization, enabling cross-border interactions and remote work opportunities. However, it has also led to challenges such as the outsourcing of jobs and increased competition in the global labor market.

A significant result of the study is the impact of automation on employment. Automation has led to the disappearance of jobs in certain sectors, especially those involving repetitive tasks. However, it has also created new job opportunities in fields that require advanced technical skills. This dual effect of automation underscores the importance of reskilling and upskilling the workforce.

The study highlights several policy implications, including the need for governance structures that can quickly adapt to the changes brought about by digitization. Policies are needed to support transitioning workers, promote fair labor practices, and ensure equitable access to digital tools and training.

From an economic point of view, digitization has led to an increase in productivity and efficiency in some sectors. Socially, however, the results point to potential risks, including social isolation due to remote work and challenges in maintaining work-life balance. The study calls for a holistic approach to leverage the benefits of digitization while minimizing the adverse social impact.

4 Discussion

In summary, the intricate and evolving connection between globalization and sustainable development within the framework of an effective labor market is a subject of academic inquiry. This study has examined the impact of globalization on labor markets, social welfare, and the overarching objectives of sustainability.

Globalization, characterized by its capacity to foster heightened economic expansion, technical progress, and international collaboration, presents prospects for enhancing labor market efficacy and overall welfare. The phenomenon under consideration has the potential to provide employment opportunities, facilitate the dissemination of important expertise and information, and contribute to the alleviation of poverty in many geographical areas. Furthermore, globalization has the potential to facilitate the effective distribution of resources and workforce, hence augmenting productivity, and competitiveness.

Nevertheless, it is essential to acknowledge that globalization has the potential to aggravate economic inequality, erode worker rights, and contribute to environmental damage. The equitable distribution of advantages derived from globalization is not uniform, hence presenting problems for excluded communities in their pursuit of accessing these possibilities. Furthermore, the prioritization of immediate economic benefits within the context of globalization may sometimes result in the detriment of long-term sustainability and the overall welfare of society.

To achieve a harmonious equilibrium between globalization, labor market efficiency, and social well-being, it is imperative to develop policies and methods that effectively tackle these complex difficulties. To effectively manage the consequences of globalization and optimize its advantages, it is crucial to implement inclusive economic policies, environmental legislation, equitable labor practices, and educational initiatives.

The achievement of sustainable development in efficient labor markets via globalization is contingent upon the collaborative efforts and adaptability of governments, international organizations, and stakeholders in response to the evolving global environment. By placing equal importance on economic development, social equality, and environmental stewardship, it is possible to construct a global society that is more resilient and fairer, ultimately promoting the welfare of all individuals. Attaining this equilibrium is a multifaceted and continuous endeavor, however it is necessary for a thriving and enduring future.

References

Belostecinic, G., Mogoş, R. I., Popescu, M. L., Burlacu, S., Rădulescu, C. V., Bodislav, D. A., & Oancea-Negescu, M. D. (2022). Teleworking – An economic and social impact during COVID-19 pandemic: A data mining analysis. *International Journal of Environmental Research and Public Health, 19*(1), Article 298.

Bodislav, D. A. (2013). *The optimal corporative model for sustainable economic growth for an emergent country*, ASE Publishing.

Burlacu, S., Gutu, C., & Matei, F. O. (2018). Globalization-Pros and Cons. *Quality- Access to Success, 19*, 122–125.

Burlacu, S., Popescu, M. L., Diaconu, A., & Sârbu, A. (2021). Digital Public Administration for sustainable development. *European Journal of Sustainable Development, 10*(4), 33–40.

Calin, A. M., Burlacu, S., Mocanu, V., & Popescu, M. L. (2022). Digital Public Management governance. *8th BASIQ International Conference on New Trends in Sustainable Business and Consumption* (pp.101–108).

Diaconu, A., Popescu, M.-L., Burlacu, S., Buzoianu, O., & Cristian, A. (2019). Strategic options for the development of renewable energy in the context of globalization. In I. Popa, C. Dobrin, & C. N. Ciocoiu (Eds.), *Proceedings of the 13th International Management Conference: Management Strategies for High Performance* (pp. 1022–1029).

Dollar, D., & Kraay, A. (2002). Inequality, globalization, and world politics. *World Bank Research Observer, 17*(2), 159–190.

Fukuyama, F. (1989). The end of history? *The National Interest, 16*, 3–18.

Georgescu, R. I. (2023). Modern leadership in business organizations during economic disruption. *Theoretical and Applied Economics, 30*(2), 73–82.

Hardin, G. (1968). The tragedy of the commons. *Science, 162*(3859), 1243–1248.

Henriques, A., & Richardson, J. (2004). The triple bottom line: What is it and how does it work? *Indiana Business Review, 79*(1), 4–8.

Levitt, T. (1983). The globalization of markets. *Harvard Business Review, 61*(3), 92–102.

Meadows, D. H., Meadows, D. L., Randers, J., & Behrens III, W. W. (1972). *The limits to growth.* Universe Books.

Mogos, R. I., Negescu-Oancea, M. D., Burlacu, S., & Troacă, V. A. (2021). Climate change and health protection in European Union. *European Journal of Sustainable Development, 10*(3), 97–108.

Newell, P., & Wheeler, J. (2006). Globalization and Sustainable Development: False twins? *Global Environmental Politics, 6*(3), 70–94.

Nye, J. S. (2000). Globalization and its challenge to State Sovereignty. In R. Schneider, & J. D. Schneider (Eds.), *Globalization and the challenge to State Sovereignty* (pp. 9–23). Lexington Books.

Popescu, M. L., Gombos, S. P., Burlacu, S., & Mair, A. (2021). The impact of the COVID-19 pandemic on digital globalization. *SHS Web of Conferences*, 129, Article 06008.

Radulescu, C. V., Bran, F., Burlacu, S., Dobrea, C. R., & Diaconu, S. (2020a). Challenges Regarding food resources in the context of globalization and population growth. *Proceedings of the International Conference on Economics and Social Sciences* (pp. 1041–1052). Sciendo.

Radulescu, C. V., Burlacu, S., Bodislav, D. A., & Bran, F. (2020b). Entrepreneurial education in the context of the imperative development of sustainable business. *European Journal of Sustainable Development, 9*(4), 93–93.

Rich, B. (2002). Globalization and the environment: Greed, corruption, and the coming collapse of the ecosystem. *North Carolina Journal of International Law and Commercial Regulation, 27*(2), 431–480.

Sen, A. (1999). Development as freedom. Alfred A Knopf Inc.

Stiglitz, J. (2002). *Globalization and its discontents.* W. W. Norton & Company.

Thomas, D. S. G., & Greenberg, J. B. (1988). The globalization of environmental crisis. *Geographical Journal, 154*(2), 125–137.

Tomlinson, J. (1999). *Globalization and culture.* Chicago University Press.

World Commission on Environment and Development. (1987). *Our common future.* Oxford University Press.

Veronika Bumberová[1,*], and Lucie Kaňovská[1]

Product-related Services Provided by Electrical Engineering Manufacturers in the Visegrad 4 Countries

Abstract:
Research background: Many of engineering manufacturers provide service offer based on technologies in the context of Industry 4.0 as digitized or remote (so- called smart services). However, there is limited empirical evidence to examine which after-sales product services are in practice adopted and supported by technologies by manufacturers in the V4 countries.
Purpose of the article: This article presents empirical evidence on the after-sales product services offered, such as monitoring, diagnostics, repair and maintenance, offered by small to large manufacturers in V4 countries. The current study seeks to map the occurrence of after-sales product services provided by manufacturers from the electrical industry with the potential of digitization and remote support.
Methods: Through secondary research of data obtained from the ORBIS EUROPE global database, this study applies archival research and content analysis of data from approximately 2,000 electrical engineering manufacturers from NACE Rev 2. 26 and 27, which are analyzed in more detail as those sectors, that have the largest share of product support and maintenance service offerings.
Findings & Value added: Of the total number of producers from the electrotechnical sector of the V4 countries, 20.62 % are oriented towards the provision of product after-sales services with the potential of digitization or remote support. Hungary and the Czech Republic have the relatively highest share of the offer of support services for products with regard to the number of producers in the country. The potential of services in the context of Industry 4.0 is presented at the end of this study.

Keywords: *electrical engineering companies, smart services, Industry 4.0, product-related services, Visegrad 4 countries*

JEL Classification: *O14; D22; L63*

---

* Corresponding author: Veronika.Bumberova@vut.cz
1 Brno University of Technology, Faculty of Business and Management, Czech Republic

1 Introduction

To survive in developing economies in Europe, manufacturing firms need to move up the value chain, innovate and create even more sophisticated products and related services, so they do not have to compete on the basis of cost. Many of these services are supported by technologies in the context of Industry 4.0 as remote and digitized. The study deals only with industrial services that does not create a new finished product defined in PRODCOM. These are only services aimed at completing the product and ensuring its useful function such as repairs and maintenance, installation and assembly, modifications, etc. (CSO, 2023).

The field of machine and equipment maintenance offers wide application possibilities in the field of data analytics, which as a result enables more efficient use of resources. Although some companies in the environment are starting to deal with the area of maintenance based on data analytics and are recording the first positive experiences, especially in the cost area, awareness of these trends is very low (Industry 4.0 Initiative, 2017).

In our contribution, we therefore focused on research in the field of after-sales customer care, where we found out how much these services (repairs, maintenance, monitoring and diagnostic services) are provided to SMEs in 4 countries, specifically in the Czech Republic, the Slovak Republic, Poland and Hungary, which are countries referred to as countries of the Visegrad Treaty, V4. This area of research has limited empirical evidence, especially regarding the supply of these services, on how producers in the Visegrad Four countries are received in practice.

Although the number of studies dealing with the issue of servitization of manufacturers is increasing, even at the global level (e.g., Neely et al., 2008, Mastrogiacomo et al., 2019), studies focusing on the area of services that are supported by technology and digitized (so-called "smart" or remote) are lacking. Manufacturers are able to generate additional revenues (Rachinger et al., 2019) and do it so more stably because long-term contracts replace sales (Rymaszewska et al., 2017) with using smart services.

1.1 Product-related Services Offered by Manufacturing Firms

Most manufacturers today offer services alongside their products, so called "accompanying services," from the basic to the advanced. Basic services care about product functionality, such as pre- and post-sale services. Advanced services try to avert product breakdowns by using e.g., preventive maintenance processes, training, and maintenance contracts. Moreover, advanced services help to create value with customers up to a service business model (Kindström, 2010). Based on Fischer et al. (2012), the expansion of accompanying service offerings includes three service categories as *(1) customer services, (2) product-related services and (3) services supporting business needs.*

Basic and advanced services can be included in the second category as product-related services. Also, a complex solution is a possibility of service offering, where end-users are not required to deal with technical issues related to the product, because everything is organized by the supplier, e.g., regular inspections, repairs, and ensured for the general trouble-free operation of the product. According to Mastrogiacomo et al. (2019), product support and maintenance services solve potential operational problems during the life cycle of the product, offering spare parts and skilled labour capable of repairing or updating the product features. Possible support services are also those that allow the regular functioning of the product. Then these services based on technologies with HW/SW support are called "smart services" (Grubic & Peppard, 2016; Suppatvech et al., 2019; Blichfeldt & Faullant, 2021). Smart services can be one of the enablers of servitization (e.g., Grubic & Peppard, 2016; Neu & Brown, 2008). They are the application of specialized competences, through deeds, processes, and performances that are enabled by smart products (Beverungen et al., 2017).

A worldwide focused study by Mastrogiacomo et al. (2019) claim that NACE categories 26 and 27 are those companies that have the largest share of product support and maintenance service offerings (between 31–33 %). A higher share is only recorded by productions from the NACE category 28 – 30. In general, the companies producing computer, electronic and optical products (NACE 26) and machinery of equipment (NACE 28) have a higher propensity to servitization: nearly half of the companies (49 %) are servitised, and the proportion of companies offering more than one service is close to 30 % (Mastrogiacomo et al., 2019).

The area of machinery and equipment maintenance includes many opportunities to use data analytics, which helps to make the resources used more efficient. However, the awareness of these trends among enterprises is very low. However, the situation is starting to change and some enterprises are seeing the first positive experiences in the maintenance area, especially in the cost area. This involves the analysis of data from production systems and sensors, whereby, by modelling the dependencies of individual parameters, fault conditions leading to a reduction in performance or failure of the technology can be identified before they occur. The outputs of these analyses should then feed into preventive and predictive maintenance plans linked to the above mentioned maintenance strategy. In addition, maintenance plans are based on the need to maintain more or less all assets in a state of 100 % uptime, which results in particularly inefficient use of resources (finance, personnel, spare parts) within the maintenance budget. Most manufacturers use IoT technologies for provision basic product-related services, such as time and material repairs and required warranty services (Paiola & Gebauer, 2020).

1.2 Brief Overview of the Visegrad V4 Countries

This chapter briefly describes the importance of the electrical engineering industry (NACE 26 and NACE 17) in the Visegrad countries where the research was carried out.

1.2.1 Czech Republic

Manufacturing has historically been strong in the Czech Republic both in gross value added and employment. It is expected that service will contribute a larger share of GVA in the future, as in other EU countries. After the automotive industry, the electrical industry is one of the key sectors of the Czech economy and is one of the most important and decisive sectors within the manufacturing industry (BusinessInfo, 2023). The share of the NACE 26 sector in the Czech Republic compared to the NACE 27 sector in terms of the number of economic entities is 1/3 (Czech Statistical Office, 2023). The Electronic Component Manufacturing in Czechia industry is valued at €615.6m and is ranked 11th in Europe in 2023 (of 22 total EU countries). The industry's rank (11th) has remained the same since 2018. The Electronic Component Manufacturing in Czechia industry is the 122nd largest industry in Czechia in 2023 (of 218 total industries that IBISWorld tracks). The industry's rank (122nd) has remained the same since 2018. The market size of the Electronic Component Manufacturing in Czechia industry has grown 2.6 % per year on average between 2018 and 2023 (IBISWorld, 2022c).

The document "Industry 4.0 Initiative" from the Czech Ministry of Industry and Trade states that the approach in the area of maintenance of machinery and equipment is at different levels in the conditions of Czech manufacturing companies, but it mainly depends on the type of technology used (Ministry of Industry and Trade, 2017). Over 50 % of Czech companies do not have a maintenance management strategy Ministry of Industry and Trade (2020).

1.2.2 Hungary

The electronics industry is one of Hungary's main industries and accounts for approximately 22 % of manufacturing production. Hungary is the largest producer of electronics in Central Europe and is responsible for approximately 26 % of all electronics produced in the region. The industry directly employs approximately 115,000 people. Germany is the main trading partner and most of its exports go to other European countries.

Hungary is the largest electronics producer by size among the new EU members, followed by the Czech Republic and Poland. While the Czech Republic is more specialised in the production of personal computers, Hungary has managed to enable the rapid growth of the electronics industry, which is more dedicated to mobile phones. Moreover, Hungary has a significant share of European PC production and the country is well positioned in Central and Eastern Europe in the production of consumer goods (TVs and VCRs) (Portal, 2022).

The most profitable category in the Hungarian consumer electronics market in 2020 was computing, which accounted for the majority of sales; a total of US$719 million. The turnover of the computer, electronics and optical equipment industry shrank to €14.3 billion. This means a loss of 414.5 million euros in 2020. This decline was preceded by an increase in industry turnover. Despite a slower than expected digital transformation (including a hesitation to adopt the cloud), the Hungarian ICT sector is extremely important (Statista, 2023).

The Electronic Component Manufacturing in Hungary industry is valued at €1.4bn and is ranked 6th in Europe in 2023 (of 22 total EU countries). The industry's rank has fallen from 2018 when it was ranked 7th. The Electronic Component Manufacturing in Hungary industry is the 62nd largest industry in Hungary in 2023 (of 297 total industries that IBISWorld tracks). The industry's rank (62nd) has remained the same since 2018. The market size of the Electronic Component Manufacturing in Hungary industry has grown 5.4 % per year on average between 2018 and 2023 (IBISWorld, 2022b).

1.2.3 Slovak Republic

The Slovak economy is strongly focused on industry, which employs almost 700,000 people. people. The economy is vitally dependent on the automotive industry. It creates 13.9 % of GDP and makes up almost half of exports and industrial production. There are four car manufacturers in Slovakia and more than 350 suppliers for these car manufacturers. Slovakia is the world's largest producer of passenger cars per 1,000 inhabitants. Other important industrial sectors include electrotechnical and chemical industries and metallurgy (BusinessInfo, 2023). The electrotechnical industry is represented by several international companies. 3. the most significant influence on industrial production in June 2023 was the production of electrical equipment (13.9 %) (Slovak statistics and demography, 2023).

The Electronic Component Manufacturing in Slovakia industry is valued at €535.1m and is ranked 12th in Europe in 2023 (of 22 total EU countries). The industry's rank (12th) has remained the same since 2018. The Electronic Component Manufacturing in Slovakia industry is the 88th largest industry in Slovakia in 2023 (of 286 total industries that IBISWorld tracks). The industry's rank (88th) has remained the same since 2018. The market size of the Electronic Component Manufacturing in Slovakia industry has grown 2.3 % per year on average between 2018 and 2023 (IBISWorld, 2023d).

1.2.4 Poland

Services are the dominant sector of the Polish economy, accounting for 58 % of GDP. Industry, agriculture and mineral extraction are also very strong. Poland has the third largest agricultural area in the EU and since 2004 Polish farmers have been net beneficiaries of EU Common Agricultural Policy funds (mainly direct payments). The main industries are engineering, metallurgy, automotive, chemical, electrical, textile and food processing. Mining and mineral processing play an important role. The vast majority of Poland's international trade is with EU countries. Poland's main trading partner is Germany. Both in terms of imports and exports. The basis of Polish exports is the engineering industry, which accounts for 37 % of Polish exports (BusinessInfo, 2023).

The Electronic Component Manufacturing in Poland industry is valued at €2.7bn and is ranked 5th in Europe in 2023 (of 22 total EU countries). The industry's rank (5th) has remained the same since 2018. The Electronic Component Manufacturing in Poland industry is the 114th largest industry in Poland in 2023 (of 300 total industries that IBISWorld tracks). The industry's rank (114th) has remained the same since 2018. The market size of the Electronic Component Manufacturing in Poland industry has grown 2.7 % per year on average between 2018 and 2023 (IBISWorld, 2022a).

2 Research Methodology and Sampling

The research was carried out using archival and content analysis of secondary data obtained from global database. The goal is to map servitization of electrical engineering manufacturers in current situation in V4 and determine the potential of the offer in the form of digitization or remote provision (smart services) of the after-sales product service. The data used in the study is drawn from the ORBIS EUROPE database contains information on more than 110 million companies from Europe. Data were downloaded in the first week of June 2023. There was a three-phase process of finding and editing the data and sample for subsequent analysis.

In the first part, we excluded companies with no recent financial data and public authorities, states, government. We involved all companies within Czech Republic, Hungary, Poland and Slovakia covering 6,297,561 companies. Further, we involved all companies with primary NACE Rev 2 codes in the range 26 and 27 inclusive. This search resulted in the identification of 24,586 companies. The third search involved adding a control from company size. Only companies with over 10 employees were included in the sample. This resulted in the sample being reduced to approximately 2,000 companies.

The second part consisting content analyze via text coding. The database contains a field of "full overview" for each firm. This field includes primary and secondary activity of the firm (Nace Rev 2), US SIC and NAICS 2022 codes (derived from NACE Rev. 2 codes), a text-based description of history, trade description, and product and service offer. Within the analysis of economic activities, it is possible to easily search for repair and maintenance services, which are registered as specialized maintenance, repair and installation of machinery and equipment generally belong to section 33. Unfortunately, remote or smart services such as monitoring, diagnostic, maintenance and repair based on technology are not anchored in primary/secondary or "ancillary" economic activities (except Nace 80.20) A certain signal may evoke the presence of an activity under section 62.0, however it is not authoritative.

So, the third step, was selected companies via Boolean operators through activity text search tool of database, which must contain: (1) mainten* or (2) monitor* or (3) diagnos* or (4) repair*. The ordered database provided a sample size of 467 firms. After manual control, we excluded 32 companies in data set due to the absence of focus on manufacturing. The overall sample cover 412 manufacturers from electrical engineering sector. The final step was carried out manually by a single coder. The coder reviewed the descriptions of each of the firms in terms of trade description, product and service offer in dataset and analyzed website information of each company, seeking to identify areas (words or phrases) covering digitation, remote, online ("open") services, life-cycle services of providing after-sale service offer to customers (as you can see on Table 1).

Table 1. Example of data structure within content analysis.

The name of the company	**CATTRON S.R.O.**
Country ISO code	**CZ**
NACE Rev 2 main sector	**Manufacturing (C)**
Primary code	**26.30 – Manufacture of communication equipment**
Trade description, products & services: [Source: Bureau van Dijk 2023 and companies websites]	Engaged in the production and manufacture of a wide range of products such as radio remote control systems, etc. It also offers services such as **troubleshooting, installation and testing, equipment repair and maintenance** with customizable and tailored service agreements. **Cloud-Based (Smart) Remote Monitoring** – RemoteIQ. Repair & maintenance – depot service such as troubleshooting, repair and maintenance of equipment. Installation & testing, 24/7 technical support **FAULT DIAGNOSTICS, QR-ASSIST™** – Software-based, diagnostic QR code management tool.

Source: Authors (2023)

3 Results and Discussion

From the total manufacturing companies from electrical engineering sector in V4, 20.62 % are oriented towards providing after-sale or product supporting services with potential of digitization or remote (technology) support. The Hungary and Czech Republic have the relative the highest share of product supporting services as you can see on Table 2. Although Poland represents the largest market in terms of the number of manufacturers, however their offer does not include such a share of supporting product related services.

Given that the size of the countries varies, the following Figure 1 visually shows the relative calculation of the number of servitized producers with regard to the size of the market, i.e., the total number of electrical engineering manufacturers (up to 10 employees) in a given country. Slovakia and Poland rank among the countries with the lowest share of product-related services.

Table 2. The general share of manufacturers in V4 as total sample.

Countries of V4	**Total No. of manufacturers (up to 10 employees)**	**Relative frequencies (V4)**	**Total no. of manufacturers with product-related servic es (at least one service offer)**	**Relative frequencies (V4)**
Hungary	491	24.6 %	198	48.1 %
Czech Rep.	447	22.4 %	147	35.7 %
Poland	882	44.1 %	51	12.4 %
Slovakia	178	8.9 %	16	3.9 %
Total (V4)	*1998*	*100.0 %*	*412 (20.62 %)*	*100.0 %*

Source: Authors (2023)

According to NACE Rev 2 classification of primary and secondary economic activity and trade overview of each firm, there is a dominance of repair and maintenance service offerings of manufacturers in the countries of V4. However, a small number of manufacturers present themselves with after-sale product services such as monitoring and diagnostic.

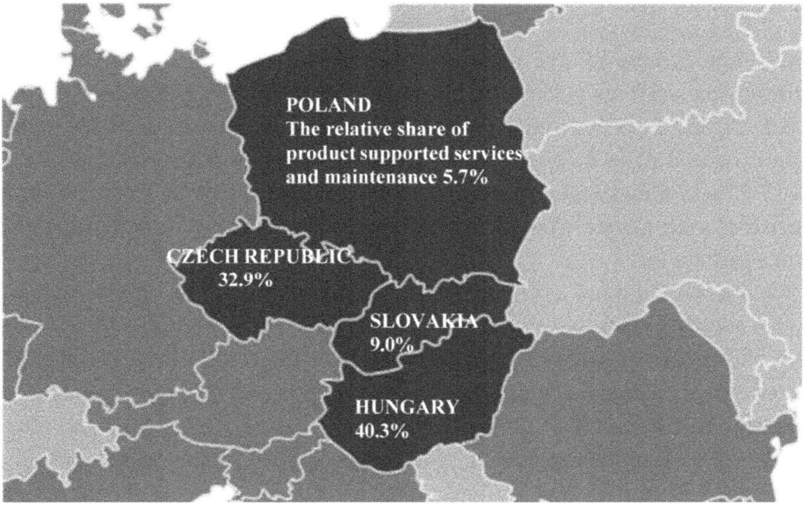

Figure 1. Relative share of services offer by manufacturers according to individual markets

Source: Authors (2023)

Here, it is necessary to emphasize the differences in the digitization of services for products whose services are a necessary part of the product for functioning and products where the given services appear as an add-on and thus create customer support during the life cycle as an advantage. In the case of monitoring services, diagnostics, which are an integral part of the product, this is primarily a category of manufacturers focusing on the production of measuring, precision instruments, protective automation etc. Often these manufacturers consider these advanced, remote services as the basis and necessity for providing their products. Therefore, we did not consider the main economic activity from the point of view of firm engaged in manufacture of monitoring and diagnostic equipment for clients, as a supporting/additional service for the client within the after-sales life cycle. A typical representative of this category is Nace Rev 2 26.51 – Manufacture of instruments and appliances for measuring, testing and navigation.

3.1 Service Offer According to Selected Characteristics

Within the sample of 412 manufacturers providing product supported and maintenance services within the V4 countries, 49.5 % of producers are from NACE 26 and 50.5 % from NACE 27. The size representation of the sample within the countries follows general trend, except Czech Republic, where the NACE 27 sector dominates in the area of service supply (60 %). These results are consistent with general statistical information providing state statistical office from country.

The following Figure 2 already shows the differences in the representation of service supply within these two NACE sectors. As can be seen, NACE 26 dominates within monitoring and diagnostic services. The result can be connect with the previous conclusions, where category Nace 26 is able to acquire, analyze and generate data for warnings, preventive maintenance etc. based on product functionality (e.g., monitoring, testing, diagnostic devices for the client). NACE 27 dominates within maintenance and repair services, however there are no such differences between sectors.

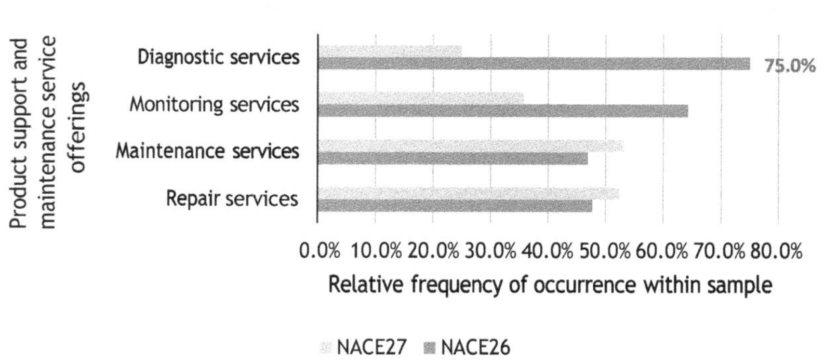

Figure 2. Relative share of NACE codes according to supported services and maintenance

Source: Authors (2023)

The previous study by Mastrogiacomo et al. (2019) claim, that as the size of the company increases, there is a proportional increase in the level of servitization, similar considerations hold for service variety i.e., larger manufacturing companies tend to offer a wider range of services. The reasons are often connected to the greater availability of financial and human resources, which allows and enhances the diversification of each company's offering while reducing the reluctance to face and overcome servitization barriers.

Overall, 51,5 % of small manufacturers, 32,3 % of medium-sized companies and 16,3 % of large producers are represented in the sample of V4 landscape producers. Again, the size representation of the sample within the countries follows general trends, however, in Poland there are more medium-sized (40.0 %) and large manufacturers (35.1 %) than small (20.3 %). As can be seen on Figure 3, it could be inferred, that large and medium-sized enterprises offer services to greater extent in the after-sale product life cycle. A small companies focus mainly on repair and maintenance services (99–100 %), monitoring and diagnostics make up only 0.9 %.

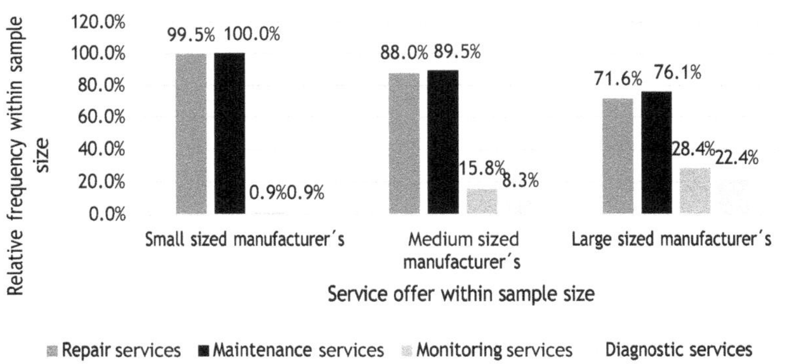

Figure 3. The range of product-services offered according to size of manufacturers.
Source: Authors (2023)

3.2 Potential of Services as Remote and Digitized in V4 Landscape

From the content analysis of the database and web presentations of the companies, it emerged that 60 % of the companies in the sample offer after-sales product services with the support of technology (remote, digitized). This represents 12.5 % of all manufacturers within the V4. Further, from the finding emerges that services related to the product life cycle supported by technology are mainly monitoring and diagnostics services (see Figure 4). Remote maintenance or repairs occur to a much lesser extent. It can be said, that maintenance and repairs are considered still as a basic service linked to the physical presence of the highly qualified employees at the client's place of work or the manufacturer's (or business partners) specialized premises.

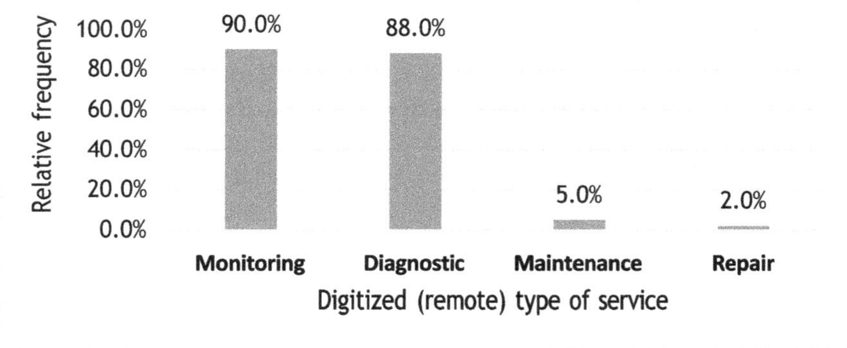

Figure 4. Digitized (remote) service offer of manufacturers in V4 sample.
Source: Authors (2023)

4 Conclusion

Current study seeks to explore empirically the phenomenon of servitization within product related after-sale services that provide manufacturers from electrical industry. The aim was to map product-related services of electrical engineering manufacturers in current situation in V4 and determine the potential of the offer in the form of digitization or remote provision (smart services) of the after-sales product service. The results show, that of the total number of producers within the territory of V4, 20.62 % are oriented towards providing product after-sale additional services with potential of digitization or remote (technology) support. However, within this sample of 412 manufacturers, 60 % of the manufacturers offer after-sales product services with the support of technology (remote, digitized). This represents 12.5 % of all manufacturers within the V4. Further, from the finding emerges that services related to the product life cycle supported by technology are mainly monitoring and diagnostics services and much less remote maintenance or repair.

In addition, it can be said, that in many cases, the service offering is outsourced or left to the customer's investment to create their own team. Everything is based on customer tailored services (requirements) and mutual agreement. It was also found, that many companies offer these services within a corporate group of collaborating companies or as part of the offering of the parent company that controls.

4.1 Limitation and Further Development of the Research

Research in this area must be supplemented by primary data collection from the manufacturers themselves. The mere use of secondary sources of databases and economic activities (primary/secondary), including company websites, is not sufficient to clarify the issue. We have to consider two essential factors:

1 Additional, support services are not traceable within the secondary economic activity (code) within the entity's added value. Possible reasons could be outsourcing, feedback and notification from the customer rather than from the manufacturer, the customer creates its own support team.
2 Low level of presentation of supporting and additional product services on company websites, including in the context of strategic cooperation within a corporate or collaborating network.

A small number of producers (especially small ones) present themselves with an offer of supporting/additional activities in the field of monitoring and diagnostic services (public data, websites). It is possible that there is customer feedback and notification for their products, rather than ongoing (regular) physical inspection by manufacturers or remote service personnel. The question may also be related to the internal characteristics of the products offered by different commodity sectors, the ICT/IS system, but also to the specificity of the market segment. This is a collection of factors for which no conclusions can be drawn without further verification.

References

Beverungen, D., Matzner, M., & Janiesch, C. (2017). Information systems for smart services. *Information Systems and e-Business Management*, *15*(4), 781–787.

Blichfeldt, H., & Faullant, R. (2021). Performance effects of digital technology adoption and product & service innovation–A process-industry perspective. *Technovation*, *105*, Article 102275.

Businessinfo.cz (2023) Slovensko. https://www.businessinfo.cz/navody/polsko-souhrnna- teritorialni-informace/2#1-zakladni-informace-o-teritoriu

Czech statistical office. (2023). https://www.czso.cz/csu/czso/katalog-produktu (2023).

Fischer, T., Gebauer, H., & Fleisch, E. (2012). Service business development: strategies for value creation in manufacturing firms. Cambridge: Cambridge University Press.

Grubic, T., & Peppard, J. (2016). Servitized manufacturing firms competing through remote monitoring technology: An exploratory study. *Journal of Manufacturing Technology Management*, *27*(2), 154–184.

Ibisworld. (2023a). *Electronic Component Manufacturing in Poland – Industry Statistics 2008–2026*. Ibisworld. https://www.ibisworld.com/poland/industry-statistics/electronic- component-manufacturing/1635/

Ibisworld. (2023b). H*ungary Industry Statistics*. Ibisworld. https://www.ibisworld.com/slovakia/industry-statistics/electronic-component-manufacturing/1635/ (2023)

Ibisworld. (2023c). *Industry Statistics – Czechia*. Ibisworld. https://www.ibisworld.com/czechia/industry-statistics/

Ibisworld. (2023d). *IndustryStatistics–Slovakia*. Ibisworld. https://www.ibisworld.com/slovakia/industry-statistics/electronic-component- manufacturing/1635/ (2023)

Kindström, D. (2010). Towards a service-based business model–Key aspects for future competitive advantage. *European Management Journal*, *28*(6), 479–490.

Mastrogiacomo, L., Barravecchia, F., & Franceschini, F. (2019). A worldwide survey on manufacturing servitization. *The International Journal of Advanced Manufacturing Technology*, *103*(9–12), 3927–3942.

Neely, A. (2008). Exploring the financial consequences of the servitization of manufacturing. *Operations management research*, *1*, 103–118.

Neu, W. A., & Brown, S. W. (2008). Manufacturers forming successful complex business services: Designing an organization to fit the market. *International Journal of Service Industry Management*, *19*(2), 232–251.

Ministry of Industry and Trade. (2020). Národní RIS3 strategie. https://www.mpo.cz/assets/cz/podnikani/ris3-strategie/dokumenty/2022/1/RIS3-Strategie_A_RIS3-Strategie_.pdf (2020)

Ministry of Industry and Trade. (2017). Industry 4.0 Initiative. https://www.mpo.cz/cz/rozcestnik/ministerstvo/aplikace-zakona-c-106-1999-sb/informace-zverejnovane-podle-paragrafu-5-odstavec-3-zakona/-iniciativa-prumysl-4-0-230485/ (2017)

Paiola, M., & Gebauer, H. (2020). Internet of things technologies, digital servitization and business model innovation in BtoB manufacturing firms. *Industrial Marketing Management*, *89*, 245–264.

Portal, L. (2022). Rozvoj elektronického průmyslu: příležitost, kterou Maďarsko nesmí promarnit. Blue Europe. https://www.blue-europe.eu/cs/analyza-a-vyzkum/rozvoj- elektronickeho-prumyslu-prilezitost-kterou-madarsko-nesmi-promarnit/

Rachinger, M., Rauter, R., Müller, C., Vorraber, W., & Schirgi, E. (2019). Digitalization and its influence on business model innovation. *Journal of Manufacturing Technology Management*, *30*(8), 1143–1160.

Rymaszewska, A., Helo, P., & Gunasekaran, A. (2017). IoT powered servitization of manufacturing–an exploratory case study. *International Journal of Production Economics*, *192*, 92–105.

Slovak statistics and demography (2023). Priemyselná produkcia v marci 2023. Avaiable at: https://www.susr.sk/wps/portal/ext/products/informationmessages/inf_sprava_detail/!ut/p/z1/pVRNV6MwFP0tLlimeZBAwuzQ0bZO-1dPptLVsPAFCi3wEIaVTf_2kVefozNjqGRZJgHtf3n1fOMS3OKxEly2FzlQlC-vO-CL27MRvy01M7ADgdERhefptcD84unP7UxfM94KwfDCgbAfBR34VhM-Jh-98eEQEBw-Jp_c-afG_7ACyg7t29m9jMf3nkCOMaf4RCHcaVrvcILFbVihdocZVWKRK4tMAfVlEZNV0nU1o3othaIJl5lnQU-pxEkPELci31EozRBEXNs5HBIfIiZ7SZ8Z76OswQvPoSeH4tXeFjtpM3xJQ6zqOxt4rIHPZtRZnOfEs92GPX-ILiPZ_cNDGBjZqtLyp8a3L7otaLXRGqP9n8roL6UW60TcSwvyQrRZmuUizo-QBpGppQZPJVlaZREqLR5WjunmOkonWo2hEsv_ZbRPR5apDtUoKgV4Zkk-G3rrsEU45uGCDQ32AQy7L6m-XtSxNjkqRN0rmqlJlFucC7VGtNrdaEMtqa9xUupGRBevcuN4JLQv5R-gczjzq2JT7DjHng36gem1smaV4EvZSJb-_ZBa4DnE9CRLZ4EaIxi4gX0YEpdRJzS0JTSF96wJ3fd9k0OUUHNsm_JPZOx6KSjQqMclax3p7IBSMMyCMcWoy4rnkcBUd6Z6ulTo3O_jEjVxCk-alND9HELML3fURsGseESZel-3uc5ursamm6SOjVzrTCtx-lBlVEuKE2Mp-WNbHrrxkykldZ1-8UCCzabTW-p1LKQvViVFvyLslKtkfYWabo03DdiMB6P-J6PZDPoz5wKGxO7D9XRqutY7AvjxAjg0-I71-sLMCvburLAZnneZ3OBptctBgSefHEUD2NXA4Wn0H2XwqSFal9NpyckW9ecojNyiK3f7lhTdKJ0M791lefd1FJyc_AIG-sao/dz/d5/L2dBISEvZ0FBIS9nQSEh/

Statista.(2023).Consumer electronics in Hungary – Statistics & facts. https://www.statista.com/topics/8250/consumer-electronics-in-hungary/#topicOverview (2023)

Suppatvech, C., Godsell, J., & Day, S. (2019). The roles of internet of things technology in enabling servitized business models: A systematic literature review. *Industrial Marketing Management*, *82*, 70–86.

Sorin Burlacu[1,*], Carmen-Valentina Rădulescu[2,*], Cristina Dima[3], and Cătălin Răzvan Dobrea[3]

The Digital Transformation of Public Administration: An Analysis of the Impact of Globalization on Sustainable Development Strategy

Abstract:
Research background: This study explores the digital transformation of public administration, focusing on the impact of globalization on sustainable development strategies. By examining the integration of digital technologies within governmental processes, the research aims to understand how the interconnectedness of global economies and cultures influences administrative policies towards long-term sustainability. The analysis seeks to reveal insights into how modern public administrations can leverage digital advancements to navigate the challenges and opportunities of globalization, all while aligning with broader social, environmental, and economic goals.
Purpose of the article: The purpose of this article is to analyze the role of digital transformation in public administration and investigate how globalization affects strategies for sustainable development. The research aims to uncover insights that could inform policymaking, administrative practices, and technological adoption, contributing to more effective governance that aligns with global sustainability goals.
Methods: A qualitative approach was used in the research. The main research tool was the case study, where examples of administrative transformations from various countries

* Corresponding author: carmen-valentina.radulescu@eam.ase.ro
1 Bucharest University of Economic Studies, The Faculty of Administration and Public Management, 6 Piata Romana, 1st district, Bucharest, 010374 Romania
2 Bucharest University of Economic Studies, The Faculty of Agrifood and Environmental Economics, 5–7 Mihail Moxa Street, District 1, 010961, Bucharest, Romania
3 Bucharest University of Economic Studies, The Faculty of Management, 2–10 Caderea Bastiliei Street, District 1, 010615, Bucharest, Romania

were analyzed. In addition to these methods, a literature review was conducted to outline a theoretical framework and better understand existing discussions in the field.
Findings & Value added: The findings are expected to reveal a multidimensional relationship between digital transformation, globalization, and sustainable development. The value added by this research could include a new conceptual framework for understanding the intersection of these domains, practical guidelines for administrators, and policy recommendations that reflect the complexities of modern governance.

Keywords: *digital transformation, public administration, globalization, sustainable development, governance*

JEL Classification: *H11*; *O33*; *O38*; *F63*; *Q01*

1 Introduction

In the vast tapestry of our interconnected world, the digital realm has emerged as the predominant platform upon which societies, economies, and politics interweave. The arena of public administration, which once operated within the tangible confines of bureaucratic walls, is now being swiftly redrawn by digital lines, creating a canvas that is both expansive and intricate (Negescu et al., 2021). Yet, as with any profound transformation, the digital metamorphosis of public administration is not merely an outcome of technological advancement in isolation. It is also deeply influenced by the omnipresent currents of globalization (Ridei et al., 2022).

Globalization, often visualized as the intricate web of economic, cultural, and political connections spanning across continents, has in recent decades become an inexorable force shaping national agendas and strategies (Shtets et al, 2020; Salih, 2020). One of its most poignant implications is its impact on sustainable development, a concept that has evolved from being an environmental catchphrase to an integral component of strategic planning across nations. Given this backdrop, the intersection of digital transformation in public administration with the overarching strategies of sustainable development under the influence of globalization offers a research mosaic that is rich, timely, and critically relevant.

This article seeks to voyage into this intersection, unraveling the layers through which globalization catalyzes, challenges, and reshapes the digital journey of public administration. More so, it aims to understand how this interplay, in turn, reflects upon and redirects sustainable development strategies. By diving into this exploration, we hope to paint a comprehensive picture of our present, to better forecast and sculpt our shared digital and sustainable future in an era of relentless global interconnectivity.

1.1 Literature Review

The digital transformation of public administration is not a siloed phenomenon, but a significant aspect of an increasingly interconnected global narrative. The 21st century has borne witness to a series of revolutions, not least of which is the digital one, set against the backdrop of relentless globalization and pressing demands for sustainable development.

Diving into the specifics, Androniceanu et al. (2017) brought forth insights on the new digital trends within business realms in Romania, pointing out the shifting behaviors of young consumers in a digitalized environment. Such findings on the nexus of technology and its societal influence are further elaborated upon by Burlacu et al. (2022), who detail the ramifications of digital globalization on both the economic and societal tapestry. Their in- depth examination, readily accessible through an online conference paper, is a testament to how digital reach has permeated academic exchanges.

The significance of adaptive digital content in education is emphasized by Burlacu et al. (2021), which aligns with the broader narrative on the digital transformation of various sectors. This perspective complements their other research on the fundamentals of designing digital content for e-learning, signifying the breadth of digital integration across diverse platforms (Burlacu et al., 2013).

Delving deeper into the nexus of globalization and digital transformation, the works of Burlacu et al. (2021) and Rădulescu et al. (2023) are pivotal. They explore the terrain of digital globalization, its multifaceted impacts on economic and social spheres, and specifically its implications during unprecedented challenges like the COVID-19 pandemic.

Moreover, with sustainable development being a cornerstone of this discussion, the research by Rădulescu et al. (2018) and Burlacu et al. (2023) specifically targeting digital public administration as a driver for sustainable progress is pivotal. This intersection of digitalization, public administration, and sustainable growth is also enriched by Calin et al. (2022), which provides a robust framework on digital public management governance.

The challenges and opportunities presented by such transformative waves have not gone unnoticed in the broader academic community. Noteworthy contributions by Armenia et al. (2021), Viana (2021), and Burlacu et al., (2022) provide comprehensive overviews, from measuring outcomes of digital transitions to system approaches, and the evolution from e- Government paradigms to full-fledged digital governance.

To understand this transformation's broader milieu, the works of Farazmand & Pinkowski (2006), McGrew & Held (2002), and Farazmand (2012) delve into globalization's dynamics, governance structures, and the futuristic challenges and opportunities for public administration. These comprehensive texts offer an enriched understanding of the global framework within which digital transitions occur.

Recent studies such as Belyakova (2022), Kysh (2022), and Göksan (2023) further reiterate the vital role of institutional support, the achievements, and the challenges in the digital overhaul of public administration. Notably, Datta (2022) integrates the discourse on digital transformation within the broader context of a globalized world, enriching our understanding of technology's role in shaping global narratives.

In summation, the literature underscores a multifaceted exploration of the digital transformation of public administration, pivoting on the axes of globalization and sustainable development. The references cited herein present a kaleidoscope of perspectives, painting a holistic picture of a world in flux, teetering on the cusp of digital promise and challenges.

2 Methodology

To delve into the nuances of how globalization trends influence sustainable development strategies in the context of the digitalization of public administration, a qualitative approach was used from several perspectives:

1. *Analysis of the case study:* A selection of countries, which varied both geographically and economically, served as reference points. This allowed a comparative view of digitization experiences and sustainable development approaches. For each nation, specific digitization initiatives and projects were identified, focusing on their impact on sustainable development policies.
2. *Semi-structured interviews:* Interviews were conducted with decision-makers and administrators from the public administration sectors, as well as with citizens. Designed to gather insights into perceptions of digitalization, challenges faced, and opportunities recognized, semi-structured interviews were conducted.
3. *Document analysis:* A systematic collection of relevant documents was carried out. This included government reports, official documents, case studies and material published by international organizations. Such documents provided insights into the legislative and institutional context of digitization, together with sustainable development strategies adopted at the national level.
4. *Literature review:* To establish a robust theoretical framework and discern current discourses in the field, a systematic literature review was undertaken.

The sources chosen incorporated specialist articles, studies and reports published in the previous decade. This analysis facilitated the identification of trends, dominant views, and areas requiring further investigation.

3 Findings

A thorough examination of the data illuminated insightful correlations between the digital transformation in public administration and the overarching influence of globalization on sustainable development strategies.

A. Comparative Analysis of Digital Transformation Initiatives Across Countries

To understand the intricacies of digital transformation across various geographies, Table 1 provides a comprehensive overview of the digital initiatives undertaken by select nations, offering a comparative understanding of their benefits and challenges.

Table 1. Comparative analysis of digital initiatives.

Country	Initiative Overview	Key Benefits	Challenges
Romania	E-governance & Open Data Portals	Increased Transparency & Efficiency	Cybersecurity Concerns
Estonia	e-Residency & Digital Identity	Global Citizen Integration	Data Privacy Concerns
Finland	Virtual City Platforms & E- services	Improved Urban Sustainability	Integration with Legacy Systems
Bulgaria	E-taxation Platforms	Efficient Tax Management	Skill Development Needs
Singapore	Smart Nation & Digital Government Initiatives	Enhanced Public Services Accessibility	Data Management & Security
South Korea	Digital New Deal & e- Government Services	Economic Revitalization & Efficiency	Infrastructure Maintenance

Source: Author's contribution

The Table 1 highlights the customized strategies that countries have adopted, pivoted on their unique administrative needs and socio-economic conditions. While Estonia has championed the cause of e-Residency to involve global citizens, Romania's focus on e- governance is more aligned towards enhancing national transparency.

B. Thematic Evolution in the Digital Transformation Journey

An in-depth document analysis shed light on the central themes prevalent in the digital transformation discourse.

Table 2. Core themes from document analysis and their manifestations.

Theme	Romania	Estonia	Finland	Bulgaria	Singapore
Integration	E-services linkage	Single e-identity	Cross-sectoral platforms	Unified tax systems	Holistic Smart Nation plan
Capacity Building	Digital academies	e-Skill initiatives	National digital training	Digital literacy programs	Tech skill incubation
Security & Ethics	GDPR compliance	Digital oaths	Data transparency laws	Cybersecurity initiatives	Ethical AI guidelines
Public Participation	Open data portals	Citizen feedback platforms	Co-design of e-services	Public digital consultations	Citizen innovation labs
Infrastructure & Tech	Cloud adoption	5G rollout	Digital twin cities	Broadband expansion	Smart urban solutions

Source: Author's contribution

Table 2 underscores that while the overarching themes of digital transformation are consistent, their manifestations vary. For instance, while Finland leans into the creation of digital twin cities under its infrastructure theme, Estonia prioritizes the rapid deployment of 5G technology.

C. Overview of Country-specific Initiatives

As public administrations worldwide embark on their respective journeys of digital transformation, the initiatives they undertake reflect not only an effort to streamline governance but also a stride towards global sustainable development goals (SDGs). Drawing from a selection of countries that represent various stages of digitalization and diverse geographical contexts, Table 3 elucidates specific digital initiatives and their consequential impact on the United Nations' SDGs. This comparison underscores the multifaceted benefits of digital interventions in public sectors, emphasizing their broader implications for achieving sustainable development.

Table 3. Overview of country-specific initiatives

Country	Initiative Name	Brief Description	Impact on Sustainable Development
Romania	"Digital Romania"	Streamlining online public services and enhancing internet accessibility in rural areas	Positive influence on SDG 9 (Infrastructure, Industrialization, and Innovation) and SDG 10 (Reduced Inequality)
Estonia	"Digital Nomad Visa"	Encouraging global professionals to work remotely, capitalizing on Estonia'sdigital-first environment	Contributes to SDG 8 (Decent Work and Economic Growth) and SDG 10 (Reduced Inequality)
Finland	"KIRA-digi"	Digitalization of the built environment and real estate, integrating with e-services	Enhances SDG 11 (Sustainable Cities and Communities)
Bulgaria	"Vivacom Art Hall"	Digital space merging modern art and technology, promoting both culture and innovation	Influences SDG 4 (Quality Education) and SDG 11 (Sustainable Cities and Communities)
Singapore	"Smart Nation	Deployment of sensors and IoT devices for data	Directly targets SDG 9 (Infrastructure, Industrialization, and
	Sensor Platform"	centralization and urban planning	Innovation) and SDG 11 (Sustainable Cities and Communities)

Source: Author's contribution

This table provides a detailed linkage between digital transformation initiatives in selected countries and their aligned Sustainable Development Goals (SDGs). It is evident that while digitalization serves an intrinsic value in modernizing public administration, its extrinsic value significantly influences the broader sustainable development narrative.

D. Key Themes from Literature Review on Digital Transformation in Public Administration

The digital transformation of public administration is a multifaceted topic, with myriad influences and implications. To navigate the wealth of insights and conclusions derived from the extensive literature review, a conceptual diagram has been devised. This diagram seeks to distill the essence of our literary exploration, encapsulating the central ideas, their sub- themes, and the intricate web of interrelationships that bind them. By presenting the information in this structured visual manner, we aim to provide a holistic overview of the digital transformation discourse, aiding in the comprehension and assimilation of its vast and varied components.

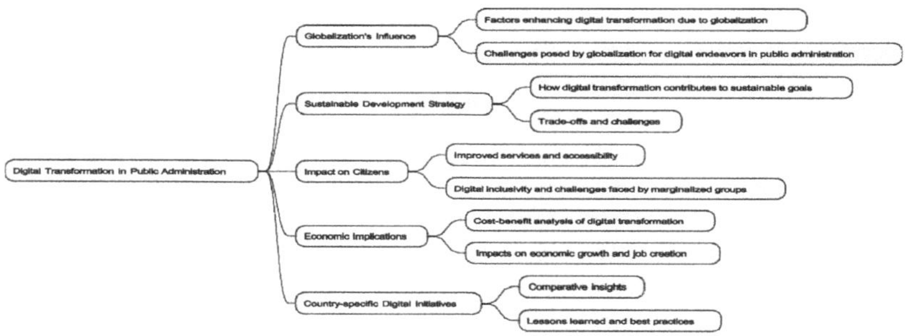

Figure 1. Key Themes from Literature Review on Digital Transformation in Public Administration.

Source: Author's contribution

At the heart of the diagram lies the pulsating essence of our exploration: the digital transformation in public administration. This central theme resonates with global significance, as administrations worldwide grapple with the challenges and opportunities presented by rapid technological advancements. Branching out from this nucleus are sub- themes that capture the diversity of factors influencing, and influenced by, digital transformation. For instance, the influence of globalization is evident, as it has both propelled and complicated the journey of digital transformation in public sectors. Its two-way arrows to economic implications suggest the reciprocity of these themes; globalization shapes economic outcomes of digital transformation and vice-versa.

Sustainable development, another pivotal theme, paints a picture of a future where digital initiatives harmoniously coexist with our environmental and societal goals (Rădulescu et al. 2022). The interconnectedness between digital transformation's impact on citizens and country-specific digital initiatives sheds light on the tangible manifestations of these changes in everyday life and governmental strategies.

In sum, the diagram is a testament to the complexity and richness of the topic at hand. It offers a bird's-eye view of the landscape of digital transformation in public administration, highlighting its multifarious dimensions and their intricate interplay.

4 Results and Discussion

Based on the methods applied in this study, we obtained the following significant results:

A. *Technology development in public administration:* Case studies from various countries have highlighted that digitization has become a central element in administrative reform. For example, in Romania, the introduction of e-government portals has improved transparency and efficiency, while in Norway, e-health has become a vital tool for public health management.
B. *Interconnection in the global context:* Highlighted through the documentary analyses, digital technologies were observed to facilitate increased global connectivity. This allowed public administrations to quickly learn from other nations and adopt best practices.
C. *Technology and Sustainability:* Interviews with decision makers highlighted that digitization not only facilitates daily operations but is also crucial for monitoring and implementing sustainable development goals.

Analyzing the results, we can formulate some essential discussions:

A. *Digitization as a catalyst for efficiency:* While many countries have begun the digital transition to streamline administrative operations, the impact is much deeper. Digital transformation is not just about automation or efficiency; it is about reinventing the way public administration perceives and interacts with its citizens.
B. *Globalization and adaptability:* In a constantly evolving global context, adaptability becomes a vital feature for public administrations. The ability to learn and adapt to rapid change is essential not only to keep up, but also to proactively anticipate and navigate future challenges.
C. *Digitization and Sustainability – Two sides of the same coin?:* Findings suggest that technology and sustainable development are not just allies, but intrinsically linked. Technology can provide the tools needed to measure, track and achieve sustainable development goals.
D. *Cultural sensitivity in digital transformation:* Discussions with decision makers also highlighted the importance of maintaining cultural sensitivity when implementing digital initiatives. Each country, region or locality has its own cultural context, and digital solutions must take this into account to be truly effective and inclusive.

5 Conclusion

The digital transformation of public administrations in the era of technological acceleration, in the context of ubiquitous globalization and directed towards the strategic goals of sustainable development, was the focus of this study. The findings offer us a panorama in which administrative dynamics are increasingly influenced by digital strategies, largely shaped by global currents, but always firmly oriented towards sustainable development.

Digital Transformation as Pivot: At the heart of administrative evolution is digital transformation. It is no longer a luxury, but a necessity. As the case studies highlighted, digital mechanisms are not just simple tools; they have become central to the way public administrations operate, interact and deliver services. From real-time data analytics that guide decisions to e-government platforms that ensure inclusion, the digital side of public administration is demonstrably more transparent, efficient and responsive.

Dual Role of Globalization: Globalization, with its vast influence, has introduced both challenges and opportunities. From an administrative perspective, globalization requires agility; the ability to quickly adapt to emerging trends internationally. However, globalization also introduces international best practices, cross-border collaborations and shared visions of a sustainable future. The permeation of global culture and economics in administrative strategies has led to a more harmonized vision of sustainability.

Sustainable Development – Guiding Lighthouse: Amid technological and global waves, sustainable development remains the strategic compass. The interviews indicated a deep understanding among decision makers that digital transformation, while essential, must be navigated in a way that aligns with long-term sustainability. The challenges of globalization, from economic disparities to cultural differences, can be mediated when the administrative lens is focused on global sustainability goals.

Interconnected Trajectories: A significant achievement of this research is that the trajectories of digital transformation, globalization and sustainable development are not parallel; they are deeply interconnected. Digital tools are not only influenced by global trends, but are essential tools in updating sustainable practices. Similarly, the challenges and opportunities presented by globalization can be mediated and maximized through digital strategies, with sustainability as a fundamental principle.

Recommendations and ways forward: The study suggests that modern public administrations adopt an integrated approach. Embracing digital advancements is just the beginning; it is equally essential to continuously update these tools in line with global best practices and within the framework of sustainable development. Decision makers are encouraged to adopt a globally conscious perspective, informed by international trends but localized to meet specific administrative needs. The focus on training and upskilling administrative staff in digital tools, global trends and sustainability measures is more crucial than ever.

Essentially, this study emphasizes the importance of an integrated perspective in public administration, where the digital, global and sustainable dimensions are not individual domains, but a cohesive and interconnected triad. The administrative blueprint of the 21st century, as revealed, is one of digital agility, global sensitivity and unwavering commitment to sustainable development.

References

Androniceanu, A., Burlacu, S., Drăgulănescu, I. V., & Nicolae, E. E. (2017). New trends of businesses digitalization in Romania and the behaviour young consumers. In V. Dinu (Eds.), *BASIQ International Conference: New Trends in Sustainable Business and Consumption* (pp. 27–35).

Armenia, S., Casalino, N., Gnan, L., & Flamini, G. (2021). A systems approach to the digital transformation of public administration. *Prospettive in organizzazione*, 14.

Belyakova, O. V. (2022). Digital transformation of public administration: Achievements and problems. In S. I. Ashmarina, V. V. Mantulenko, M. I. Inozemtsev, & E. L. Sidorenko (Eds.), *Global Challenges and Prospects of The Modern Economic Development. European Proceedings of Social and Behavioural Sciences* (pp. 174–180).

Burlacu, S., Ciobanu, G., Troaca, V., & Gombos, C. (2021). The Digital Finance – Opportunity of development in the new economy. *Proceedings of the International Conference on Business Excellence, 15*(1), 392–405.

Burlacu, S., Diaconu, A., Mocanu, V., & Gombos, S. P. (2022). The effects of digital globalization on economics and society. *8th BASIQ International Conference on New Trends in Sustainable Business and Consumption* (pp. 95–100).

Burlacu, S., Enache, A. C., & Stefan, C. (2013). INcreator-innovative software tool for creation of adaptive education digital content. In *The International Scientific Conference eLearning and Software for Education* (Vol. 2, p. 238). "Carol I" National Defence University.

Burlacu, S., Grigorescu, S. D., Stefan, C., & Popescu, C. (2013). Basics of design and testing of a digital content generator tool for e-learning. *2013 8th International Symposium on Advanced Topics in Electrical Engineering (ATEE)* (pp. 1–4). IEEE.

Burlacu, S., Rădulescu, C. V., Bălu, E. P., & Dobre, F. (2023). Socio-cultural sustainability for resilience in public services: Strategies for achieving inclusive and equitable service delivery. *European Journal of Sustainable Development, 12*(3), 29–29.

Burlacu, S., Pargaru, I., Iacob, O. C., & Gombos, S. P. (2022). Digital Public Administration and the perspectives of Sustainable Development in Romania. *European Journal of Sustainable Development, 11*(4), 230–236.

Burlacu, S., Popescu, M. L., Diaconu, A., & Sârbu, A. (2021). Digital Public Administration for Sustainable Development. *European Journal of Sustainable Development, 10*(4), 33–40.

Calin, A. M., Burlacu, S., Mocanu, V., & Popescu, M. L. (2022). Digital Public Management Governance. *8th BASIQ International Conference on New Trends in Sustainable Business and Consumption* (pp.101–108).

Datta, P. M. (2022). Digital transformation in a globalized world. *Global technology management 4.0: Concepts and cases for managing in the 4th industrial revolution* (pp. 227–260). Cham: Springer International Publishing.

Farazmand, A. (2012). The future of public administration: Challenges and opportunities – A critical perspective. *Administration & Society, 44*(4), 487–517.

Farazmand, A., & Pinkowski, J. (Eds.). (2006). *Handbook of globalization, governance, and public administration*. CRC Press.

Göksan, G. (2023). Digitalization in Public Administration. *Two faces of digital transformation* (pp. 47–57). Emerald Publishing Limited.

Kysh, L. (2022). Institutional support for the digital transformation of public administration. *Knowledge, Education, Law, Management, 3*(47), 125–130.

McGrew, A., & Held, D. (2002). *Governing globalization: Power, authority and global governance*. Polity Press.

Negescu, M. D. O., Burlacu, S., Biner, M., Gombos, S. P., Kant, A., & Troacă, A. V. (2021). Paradigms of Public Administration Digitalization in the context of the Covid-19 pandemic. *Proceedings of Administration and Public Management International Conference, 17*(1), 109–115.

Rădulescu, C. V., Mănescu, C. O., Popescu, M. L., & Burlacu, S. (2023). Sustainable Development in Public Administration: Research, Practice, and Education. European Journal of Sustainable Development, 12(4), 27–27.

Rădulescu, C. V., Angheluță, P. S., Burlacu, S., & Kant, A. (2022). Aspects regarding renewable sources in the European Union. *European Journal of Sustainable Development, 11*(3), 93–93.

Rădulescu, C. V., Dobrea, R. C., & Burlacu, S. (2018). The business management of distress situations. In I. Popa, C. Dobrin, & CN. Ciocoiu (Eds.), *The*

12th International Management Conference "Management Perspectives in the Digital Era" (pp. 741–747).

Ridei, N., Wojciech, W., Tytova, N., Stepanenko, L., & Armen, A. (2022). Digital transformation of public administration: Sociocultural forms of organization in education, science and innovation. *Cuestiones Políticas*, *40*(73), 868–882.

Salih, A. (2020). *Cross-cultural leadership: Being effective in an era of globalization, digital transformation and disruptive innovation*. Routledge.

Shtets, T., Lupak, R., & Vasyltsiv, T. (2020). General aspects of state policy for the digital transformation of the national economy. *International Independent Scientific Journal*, (20–2), 14–19.

Viana, A. C. A. (2021). Digital transformation in public administration: From e- Government to digital government. *International Journal of Digital Law*, (1), 29–44.

Marie Cerna[1,*], Jana Sturcova[1], and Adela Berankova[1]

Digitalization in the Area of Taxes and Accounting

Abstract:
Research background: Legislation, especially legislation in the area of taxes and accounting, is associated with frequent changes caused by many factors to which, among the others, belong the necessity to include to this norms current changes in standard human activities, business operations or economic transactions that are enabled by technical development and ensured by the possibility to use new tools for data processing. That is the reason for discussing positive, and also negative, impact of new technologies on economic subjects.
Purpose of the article: Purpose of this contribution can be described as identification and assessment of suitable possibilities for digital transformation of selected processes in the area of taxes and accounting in conditions of selected economic subjects operating in the Czech Republic.
Methods: During the research were used these methods: literary research of the current state in analyzed area, comparison of author's findings and approaches proposed by the authors of articles and other sources focused on this issue and model case of digitalization possibilities in selected accounting unit.
Findings & Value added: Authors formulated, based on conducted research, positive and also negative impacts of digital transformation in tax administration and accounting management. They also compiled list of recommendations supporting digital transformation of the selected accounting unit. As written at the beginning, legislation in the rea of taxes and accounting changes quite often, therefore it can be expected that these two areas will remain suitable environment for further research.

Keywords: *accounting, taxes, digitalization*

JEL Classification: *M41; M48; K34*

* Corresponding author: macerna@fek.zcu.cz
1 University of West Bohemia, Faculty of Economics, Univerzitní 8, Pilsen, Czech Republic

1 Introduction

Digitalization can be taken as still interesting and current issue influencing so significantly many areas of people's daily lives: sector of public services represented by education or health care, or individual sectors of industry like transportation, entertainment, etc.

Even if the sense of the word digitalization is still being refined, it is possible to find definitions of this word in scientific literary sources. In sources written in English, reader often finds two words, digitalization and digitization. The problem in terminology may arise when trying to translate these words to other languages, because languages like for example Czech use these words often as the synonyms. This usually doesn't matter in common speech, but when trying to go deeper into this problem, ambiguities may arise. When strictly dividing the terms digitalization and digitization, their meaning can be understood as it is done by Samoilenko (2022).

To be able to understand the word digitalization, it is essential to clarify the term digitization first. Samoilenko (2022) defines digitization as 'the process of using digital information technologies to convert analog data into its digital counterpart.' In this point of view, digitization represents kind of tool enabling its user to reach the goal of digitalization, which is often represented by the effort to improve existing way of ensuring standard processes, their changes or creation of completely new version of these processes.

Digitalization is by Schallmo and Williams (2018) and i-SCOOP (2016) defined as: 'Digitalization means the use of digital technologies and of data (digitized and natively digital) in order to create revenue, improve business, replace/transform business processes (not simply digitizing them) and create an environment for digital business, whereby digital information is at the core.' It is seen similarly by Polanco (2023) who analyses this area focusing on example of investments in digital assets or by Adomako and Nguyen (2023) defining the goals of digitalization as 'increase efficiency, reduce costs, and enhance the ability of organizations to deliver products and services to customer in a fast and agile manner'. To do so, digitalization as the process uses a lot of information, communication technologies and other tools or services like for example 'Government as a Platform' (GaaP) (Zaramenskikh and Fedorova, 2020) with the intention to support many human activities and also what Khrypko et al. (2023) describe as 'advancing sustainable development'.

Tendencies leading to support of digitalization are visible in many areas. Purpose of this contribution was described as identification and assessment of suitable possibilities for digital transformation of selected processes in the area of taxes and accounting in conditions of selected economic subjects operating in the Czech Republic. Therefore, literary research and analysis mentioned in the following part of this contribution will focus specifically on these areas.

2 Methods

To be able to compile this contribution, its authors had to use these methods:

- Literary research of the current state in analyzed area.
- Comparison of author's findings and approaches proposed by the authors of articles and other sources focused on this issue.
- Analysis of the current requirements set for digitalization of taxes and accounting by the Czech legislative (Act no. 12/2020 Coll., on the Right to Digital Services and to amend certain Acts and other relevant acts).
- Model case of digitalization possibilities in selected accounting unit.

3 Results

3.1 Results of the Conducted Literary Research

With respect to the fact that digitalization is often solved issue, it was necessary to conduct thematic literary research to be able to identify how (from which point of view) is this problem solved by other authors from the Czech Republic and also from other countries.

It was necessary to find out if, how and how often is the issue of digitalization solved in connection with accounting and taxes, and what are the results of identified researches.

Use of this type of literary research (not focused on just one individual database) was suitable for obtaining general overview of this issue and for better understanding to this issue and its current tendencies. It was then also possible to estimate further development of this area. Selected literary sources with the added value for the authors' own research are visible in the following table (Table 1). To compare approaches to the issue, current sources (publication years 2022 and 2023) were used most often.

Table 1. Selected literary sources – part of output of conducted thematic literary research.

Name of the author	Title of the source	Key issues	Publication date	Source	Publisher
Samoilenko, S.V.	Digitalization. Contexts, Roles, and Outcomes.	digitalization, tax, accounting,	2022	book	CRC Press
Evans, Ch., Kim, Ch.J., Taghizadeh-Hesary, F., & Hendriyetti, N.	Taxation in the Digital Economy	accounting, dig. economy, audit	2022	book	Taylor & Francis
Özen, E., Boz, H., & Grima, S.	The New Digital Era	accounting, dig. economy, assets	2022	book	Emerald Publishing Limited
Alareeni, B.A.M., & Elgedawy, I.	Artificial Intelligence (AI) and Finance	AI, accounting, dig. transformation	2023	book	Springer
Segura, E.A.	Holistic Approach to New Technologies for Secure Accounting Management	accounting, technologies, automating	2023	book	Editorial Dykinson, S.L.
Lowe, A., Svanberg, J., Öhman, P., & Rana, T.	Handbook of Big Data and Analytics in Accounting and Auditing	accounting, auditing, AI, data analytics	2023	book	Springer Nature Singapore
Rumyantseva, A., Sintsova, E., Anyigba, H., & Vasilenko, N.	Finance, Economics, and Industry for Sustainable Development	age tech, costs,	2022	conf. proceed.	Springer

Source: authors (2023)

Bibliometric analysis (BA) was done just for the authors' use to let them see, how many sources focusing on this issue are available in the Web of Science database (WoS) and what are the key words represented in these sources. Authors were particularly looking for articles focused on the interconnection of tax, accounting and digitalization issue. Part of this research output showing 32 sources found by WoS is represented by Figures 1 and 2 processed with the R software.

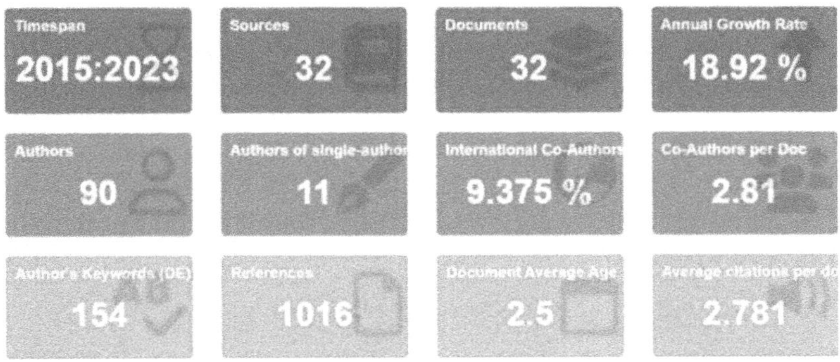

Figure 1. BA – WoS sources by relevance for authors purposes – main data.
Source: authors (2023)

Figure 2. BA – WoS sources by relevance for authors purposes – key words.
Source: authors (2023)

Bibliometric analysis was done with the intention to find out if there are similar contributions focused on the solved issue which are furthermore compiled using the standard currently used research paper structure defined as IMRaD. Simultaneously was conducted the standard thematic literary research including also different sources than those from the Web of Science database, because synthesis of the existing literature focused on a research topic was definitely what the authors needed to be able to form their own opinion and process their own outputs.

3.2 Current State of Taxes and Accounting Digitalization in the Czech Republic

3.2.1 Digitalization in the Czech Republic Generally

In the Czech Republic exists the program called 'Digital Czech Republic' that by the Ministry of the Interior of the Czech Republic (2023) represents 'a set of concepts ensuring the long- term prosperity of the Czech Republic in the environment of the ongoing digital revolution.' 'Digital Czech Republic' represents one logical complex with a large number of internal links. The focus on different beneficiaries and differences caused by variable legislative setting can be identified in this strategy. This program is built on three main pillars:

- Digital public administration.
- Interaction of the Czech Republic in the European Union (EU) in the digital agenda.
- Preparation and interaction of society and economy of the Czech Republic for consumption of digitalization.

Progress of the EU countries in the area of digitalization is evaluated using the digital economy and society index (DESI). Based on the European Commission data, it is possible to assume that the establishment of the "Digital Czech Republic" program in 2018 led to a shift in the Czech Republic in the area of digitalization (integration of digital technology) on an international scale (Figure 3). In the year 2022 was the Czech Republic on the 19th place among other EU countries.

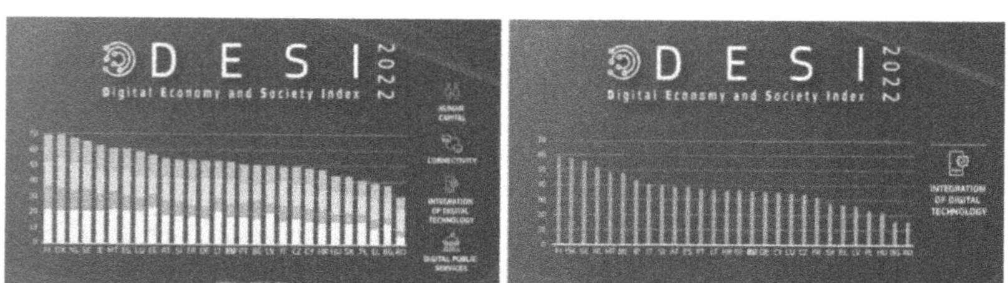

Figure 3. DESI – position of the Czech Republic.

Source: European Commission (2023)

Digitalization is influenced by various factors to which belongs also legislative framework existing in individual countries to improve the process of digitalization. This contribution focus on the area of taxes and accounting, therefore it is necessary to mention existing legislative framework supporting process of public administration digitalization and access of citizens to digital public services. Problems related with this issue are solved by the Act no. 12/2020 Coll., on the Right to Digital Services and to amend certain Acts which has experienced changes in the past two years. A qualitative shift and other economic benefits are expected from the introduction of digitalization. Expected positive effects were described based on the authors experience mostly as reduction of the administrative burden for tax authorities and taxpayers, easier and faster data and information sharing and processing, decrease of possible fraud occurrence, increase of data quality or time and cost savings. There exist also described negative effects of digitalization like safety of data insufficiency, loss of hardware or software failures or human factor failure. These negative effects are not mentioned in related literary sources (Cardinali et al., 2022; Ruiz, 2022; Trachova et al., 2021; Vishnevsky, 2022) as often as those positive ones.

3.2.2 Digitalization in Taxes

Digitalization has many impacts on taxation. It affects tax policy and tax administration and offers new tools. The tax administration can thus work with the advantages associated with developments in artificial intelligence, robotics and technological advances that serve to secure the tax system. In the Czech Republic, the digitalization of tax administration is handled by the Digital Information Agency, whose task is setting new standards, introduction of a comprehensive methodology and supervision of the digitalization process. It will be possible to ensure the governance of public affairs, for example, by using these tools:

- eGovernment.
- Czech POINT.
- Data box.
- 'My Taxes'.
- Electronic submission of tax returns – Electronic submissions for financial administration (EPO).
- Electronic submission of tax returns – Tax information box PLUS (DIS+).

3.2.3 Digitalization in Accounting

Economic entities that have an obligation to keep accounts or entities that choose to keep accounts on a voluntary basis have a choice of several options they can use for keeping accounting:

- Internal accounting (accounting by own employees – own software).
- Outsourcing (process by which an organization transfers the management of its accounting to an external firm or experts who specialize in providing accounting services).
- Cloud (software on which the accounting is operated performs its function instead of company computers on remote servers).

As part of the digitalization of accounting, it is necessary to work with digital technologies. These technologies must be ensured in order to make a smooth transition to fully digitalized accounting. Among the digital services used in accounting belong:

- Data mining.
- Electronic signature.
- Time stamp.

Extracting data from documents is one of the essential steps of digitalization. It is the process during which data is extracted from a document and its subsequent transformation into usable information is performed (digitization).

According to Act No. 227/2000 Coll., Electronic Signature Act and Amendment of Certain Other Acts (Electronic Signature Act) an electronic signature means 'data in electronic form that is attached to or logically connected to a data message, and which serves as a method to unambiguously verify the identity of the signed person in relation to the data message'. A time stamp is a kind of service making possible to clearly demonstrate time of document creation (electronic documents with legal consequences). This service is necessary if an accounting unit intends to keep its accounting in a fully digitized form.

In part 3.2 were introduced tools and methods used in the Czech Republic when digitalizing tax and accounting processes. Next part focuses on use of methods for tax and accounting digitalization in the conditions of real accounting unit.

3.3 Digitalization Possibilities in Selected Accounting Unit

In this part of the contribution, the authors try to describe the process of digital transformation of accounting management and tax administration in the selected accounting unit. These are the digital transformation solutions that are currently available and that the accounting unit can use, even if they have set the financial and time limits.

Analyzed accounting unit focuses on activities like property and real estate management, construction modifications and reconstructions, maintenance of the grounds (lands), accounting and tax consulting, assembling computers, smart home and IT consultancy. This company belongs to small accounting units as they are defined by the Act no. 563/1991 coll., Accounting act.

3.3.1 Digitalization in Taxes

The company (limited liability company) is subject to corporate income tax and value added tax (VAT). In connection with VAT, the company also has the obligation to submit a monthly VAT control report to the tax administrator. Company uses tax information box PLUS, but mostly for the communication with state authorities. It is also used for electronic submission of tax returns. Company enters this box by portal 'My Taxes'.

The company uses this method for submitting tax returns to the corporate income tax, VAT control reports and VAT returns. Full digitalization is used in the processing of VAT control reports and VAT returns. Tax returns to the corporate income tax is still processed manually by filling the information into the relevant fields in the tax forms.

The possibilities of the company in the digital transformation of tax administration can be considered limited. There are programs providing services more or less identical to those available on the Financial Administration portal. On the basis of a personal consultation with the responsible employees of the company, it is possible to state that the most advantageous option for an economic entity within the tax forms filling framework appears to be use of services of additional programs (electronic submissions manager) from the company, which also provides the company with accounting software.

To summarize, it is possible to state that digitalization is, in the case of analyzed company, possible in the field of submitting VAT control reports and VAT returns. Digitalization in the area of submitting corporate income tax returns would mean switching to another accounting software, which is currently not feasible.

3.3.1 Digitalization in Accounting

Analyzed company uses the most common method of keeping accounting records, using accounting software that can only be accessed from specific user devices. Company uses the MRP accounting software for accounting which is then used as the data base for tax reports compilation.

Currently, the company enters all data from invoices and other accounting documents manually. Partial automation can only be found in the established suppliers' agenda. The fundamental problem can be seen in the fact that documents in paper form are not organized in a single location. The digital transformation process could therefore bring significant benefits.

Based on personal interview with employees of the company were identified their needs and finally was found the suitable tool which will help to simplify the accounting processes, services provided by Wflow.com. Wflow.com provides the possibility to link the offered services with the MRP accounting software used by analyzed accounting unit.

The result of digitalization of these processes can be considered as time savings, increased efficiency consisting in the decrease of routine tasks, easily searchable and available data accessible from anywhere, decrease of unwanted errors and data security itself.

Recommendations for digitalization reachable by the analyzed accounting unit are summarized in Table 2.

Table 2. Recommendations to digital transformation for analyzed accounting unit.

Solved area	Further specification	Current state of processing	Digitalization - possible	Recommended tool
Taxes	Corporate income tax	manually	no	-
Taxes	VAT returns	automatically	yes	electronic submissions manager
Taxes	VAT control returns	automatically	yes	electronic submissions manager
Accounting	all accounting processes	manually	yes	services by Wflow.com (data mining)

Source: authors (2023)

4 Discussion

Authors formulated, based on conducted research, positive and also negative impacts of digital transformation in tax administration and accounting management. Their approach is very similar to approaches presented by other authors focusing on this area.

They agree with the statement by Loginova (2022) concerning the role of the state in this area presenting thought that 'the effective application of tax policy instruments can contribute to success of the jurisdiction in winning in global tax competition game. This is particularly important in context of digitalization and for attracting investments and parts of activities of multinational enterprises to the territory of the state.' Zaramenskikh and Fedorova (2020) further deal in their contribution with the idea to create digital platform (within the GaaP model) that will be used to enable digitalize provision of services provided by government authorities. State will accept the role of 'moderator of digital ecosystem' enabling to combine effectively policies and institutions which should lead to development of interested parties, citizens, business and non-profit organizations. Ponomareva (2022) view supports the idea of changes necessary in the area of taxation, because she writes that 'problem with taxation of the digital economy is highlighted: tax systems laid down in the 1920s traditionally take into account the principles of the source of income and residency. In the new world of globalization and the digital economy, these principles have become significant obstacles to international trade'.

To sum up taxes and accounting are areas associated with frequent changes leading to 'updates' created in a form of amendments and additions to the legislation or to 'upgrades' in a form of new act creation. Therefore, it can be expected that taxes and accounting will remain the suitable environment for further scientific researches. Even if there exists the tendency to bring these areas together in individual EU countries, there still exist many specific issues solved by each national country individually. From the point of view of economic entity (accounting unit) implementing the subject of its activity in a given country, it is always absolutely necessary to consider all the relevant risks (Vladimirovna et al., 2023) and potential threats associated with it during its digital transformation, and then take measures to reduce (minimize) these risks.

Acknowledgments

This paper was created within the project SGS-2023-007 'Current Challenges and Problems of Modern Society from the Perspective of Finances and Accounting' at the University of West Bohemia, Faculty of Economics.

References

Act no. 12/2020 Coll., on the Right to Digital Services (CZ).

Act No. 227/2000 Coll., Electronic Signature Act and Amendment of Certain Other Acts (Electronic Signature Act) (CZ).

Act No. 563/1991 Coll., Accounting act (CZ).

Adomako, S., & Nguyen, N. P. (2023). Digitalization, inter-organizational collaboration, and technology transfer. *The Journal of Technology Transfer*.

Cardinali, S., Pagano, S., Carloni, E., Giovannetti, M., & Governatori, L. (2022). Digitalization processes in small professional service firms: Drivers, barriers and emerging organisational tensions. *Journal of Service Theory and Practice*, *33*(2), 237–256.

European Commission (EC). (2023, September 20). *Integration of Digital Technology by Enterprises in the Digital Economy and Society Index*. EC. https://digital-strategy.ec.europa.eu/en/policies/desi-integration-technology-enterprises

I-SCOOP. (2016). *Digitization, digitalization and digital transformation: The differences*. https://www.i-scoop.eu/digitization-digitalization-digital-transfo rmation- disruption/

Khrypko, S., Yang, Q., Ishchuk, A., Zabolotnyuk, V., Zabolotniuk, I., & Salo, H. (2023). The role of the virtual economy in advancing Sustainable Development: Exploring network semantics, cyber risks, and digitalization. *European Journal of Sustainable Development*, *12*(2), 107–118.

Loginova, T. A. (2022). Tax regulation of enterprise R&D expenditures: Special aspects and problems of regulation. *Pravopriemenenie-law Enforcement Review*, 6(1), 111–123.

Ministry of the Interior of the Czech Republic (MVCR). (2023, September 20). *Government Council for Information Society*. MVCR. https://www.mvcr.cz/webpm/clanek/rada-vlady-pro-informacni-spolecnost.aspx?q=Y2hudW09Ng%3D%3D

Polanco, R. (2023). The impact of Digitalization on International Investment law: Are investment treaties analogue or digital? *German Law Journal*, *24*(3), 574–588.

Ponomareva, K. (2022). Tax challenges arising from the digitalisation of the economy: The development of the OECD Project and possible implementation. *Bricks Law Journal*, *9*(4), 41–63.

Ruiz, M. A. G. (2022). The alignment of taxation and sustainability: Might the digital controls of non-financial information become a universal Panacea? *Review of European and Comparative Law*, 50(3), 61–83.

Samoilenko, S. V. (2022). *Digitalization. Contexts, roles, and outcomes*. CRC Press.

Schallmo, D. R. A., & Williams, Ch. A. (2018). *Digital transformation now! Guiding the successful digitalization of your business model*. Springer.

Trachova, D., Diachek, S., Vyhovska, N., Havryliuk, O., Chaban, Ch., & Kadatska, T. (2021). Conceptual framework for digitalization of depreciation policy. *Independent Journal of Management & Production, 12*(3), S41–S53.

Vishnevsky, V. P., Goncharenko, L. I., Dementiev, V. V., & Gurnak, A. V. (2022). The principles of taxation for digital economy. *Terra Economicus, 20*(2), 59–71.

Vladimirovna, M. E., Vladimirovna, P. S., Nikolaevna, B. A., & YuliaSergeevna, S. (2023). Manageability and tax risks in the digital economy. *Pacific Business Review International, 15*(8), 65–71.

Zaramenskikh, E., & Fedorova, A. (Eds.). (2020). *Digital transformation and new challenges. digitalization of society, economics, management and education*. Springer.

Radim Dolak[1,*], and Michal Halaska[1]

Process Mining and Global Business Services

Abstract:
Research background: Global Business Services (GBS) is a business approach that aims to consolidate and streamline the delivery of shared services across different functions and geographies within a company. This approach is designed to centralize and optimize business processes, such as finance and accounting, human resources, information technology, procurement, or customer service. The main benefits should be improving operational efficiency, reducing costs, enhancing service quality, and improving the overall business performance.
Purpose of the article: The aim of the paper is to present the results of the current state of Global Business Services in connection with Enterprise Resource Planning systems and Process Mining software tools.
Methods: Garner analysis, statistical data provided by https://www.statista.com/, and analysis of integration of global enterprise resource planning systems with Process Mining software tools were used.
Findings & Value added: The results of the paper illustrate the importance of Global Business Services in connection with Enterprise Resource Planning systems and Process Mining software tools.

Keywords: *Global Business services, Process Mining, Enterprise Resource Planning systems*

JEL Classification: *C61; C63; C88; L86*

1 Introduction

We are living in a global digital society that is based on the widespread interconnection of people, organizations, services, and devices around the world through digital technologies. Global Business Services (GBS) is the evolution of Shared Services and Business Process Outsourcing (BPO), both focused on process efficiency improvement and cost reduction. GBS is a strategic approach

* Corresponding author: dolak@opf.slu.cz
[1] Silesian University in Opava, School of Business Administration in Karvina, Univerzitní náměstí 1934/3, 733 40 Karviná, Czechia

that has gained popularity among large, multinational corporations looking to enhance their operational agility and competitiveness in the global marketplace. This approach is designed to centralize and optimize business processes, such as finance and accounting, human resources, information technology, procurement, or customer service. The main benefits should be improving operational efficiency, reducing costs, enhancing service quality, and improving the overall business performance. It is a key pillar of a digital strategy that helps companies navigate the Transformative Age. (EY, n.d.) We can find European cases in the edited book called "Outsourcing in European Emerging Economies: Territorial Embeddedness and Global Business Services" (Mamica, 2020). This book presents a variety of international studies exploring the cities of the experiences of the service hubs of Brno, Bratislava, Budapest, Krakow, and Prague.

There are some novel approaches that help in the effectiveness and evolution of Global Business Services such as Process Mining (PM) or Robotic Process Automation (RPA).

Process Mining is a field of data science that involves the analysis of event data recorded by an organization's information systems to discover, monitor, and improve real processes. Böhm et al. (2022) deal with Process mining at Lufthansa CityLine, Guzzo et al. (2022) deal with Process mining applications in the healthcare domain, Erdogan and Tarhan (2022) deal with Multi-perspective process mining for emergency process and Corallo et al. (2020) deal with Process mining and industrial applications. There is also paper called "From event logs to goals: a systematic literature review of goal-oriented process mining" written by Ghasemi and Amyot (2020) or paper "How is process mining technology used by organizations? A systematic literature review of empirical studies" written by Thiede et al. (2018) that is a review of empirical studies on process mining in order to understand its use by organizations. "Process mining can help Global Business Services (GBS) organizations overcome key process visibility and transparency challenges by providing fact-based views on business processes and providing valuable data-based insights" (Celonis, 2022).

How does process mining benefit GBS organizations in enabling intelligent and efficient processes? There are the following main benefits according to Celonis (2022):

- Process discovery.
- Process standardization.
- Process conformance.

- Process monitoring.
- Process simulation.
- Process improvement.
- Action triggers.

Robotic Process Automation is a technology that uses software robots or “bots” to automate repetitive and rule-based tasks within business processes. The study provided by Fernandez and Aman (2021) is conducted using an in-depth case study approach and interviews at one of the world’s largest oil and gas organizations in the GBS industry. The result of the study showed that the organization is facing various challenges and issues during and after implementing the RPA technology in its organization. Willcocks et al. (2017) deal with a case study that presents a series of dilemmas facing senior executives thinking through the potential application of robotic process automation (RPA) into human resource (HR) functions and global business service (GBS) operations.

2 Methods

The main method used in this paper is the analysis of secondary sources. Garner analysis or reports were used, as well as statistical data provided by this website https://www.statista.com/

There is also a web search focusing on the availability of software solutions in the global market in the field of ERP and Process mining tools collaboration or integration.

Gartner states that Process mining tools must include the following features: Process models and analysis, Journey models and analysis, Comparative process mining, Process model enhancement, Data access and preparation, Business activity monitoring and management, and advanced process analysis. (Apromore, 2023)

3 Results and Discussion

The introduction will define basic terms such as Global Business Services, Global ERP systems, and Process mining software tools. There will also be carried out research on currently available software tools in the field of ERP and Process mining tools collaboration or integration. This research will be processed based on searches for available software solutions in the global market.

3.1 Global Business Services

We can see quarterly worldwide Global Business Service (GBS) setups and expansions by type 2018–2022 in the following Figure 1 provided by Statista Research Department (2023).

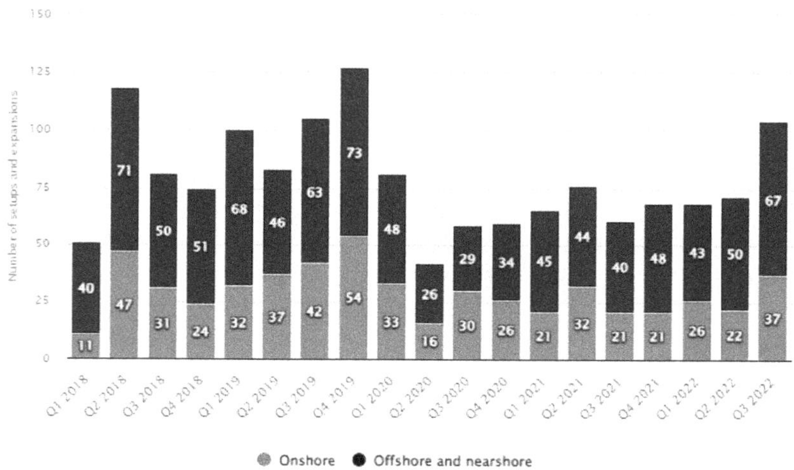

Figure 1. Global Business Service.
Source: Statista (2023)

Global Business Services (GBS) is one of the most popular areas of corporate development in driving optimized performance across business support services. Today, GBS is often the delivery engine for digital transformation, an industry that is projected to grow dramatically from USD 1.8 trillion in 2022 to 2.5 trillion in 2025, besides being the #1 priority for most boards and CEOs. (SSON, n.d.) What is the State of Global Business Services in 2023 and Beyond? "GBS is in growth mode and promises wins in key strategic areas" (Hodge, 2023).

3.2 Global ERP Systems

Enterprise Resource Planning (ERP) systems also play an important role. What is the difference between a global ERP system and a standard ERP system? "Global ERP systems contain the same features and benefits that you would find with a more traditional ERP system, as well as other features that are essential for companies operating in multiple countries. These additional features address the scenario, such as" (Microsoft, n.d.):

- Multiple currencies.
- Multiple languages.
- Tax rules in different geographic areas.

Popular global ERP vendors include for example SAP S/4HANA, Microsoft Dynamics 365, NetSuite ERP, Oracle Cloud ERP, Odoo, etc. We can see the global overview of ERP/CRM systems leader by Gartner. in the following Figure 2.

Figure 2. Global overview of the leader of ERP/CRM systems by Gartner.
Source: Gartner (2023)

"SAP S/4HANA Cloud is ERP for every business need – from mission-critical operations to business model innovation" (SAP, n.d.).

Microsoft Dynamics 365 is a cloud-based and on-premises suite of business applications with an enterprise information system designed for the management of companies of all sizes. It helps increase productivity and competitiveness by consolidating and standardizing all processes, providing an overview of what is happening in the organization across all agendas. It allows you to work efficiently, respond to new trends and facilitate compliance with statutes and regulations. The individual interconnectable modules of this enterprise systems platform include an advanced solution for financial management, controlling, sales, purchasing, logistics, production and services. "Dynamics NAV is an enterprise resource planning (ERP) application that helps with finance, manufacturing, customer relationship management (CRM), supply chains, analytics and e-commerce for small and medium-sized companies and local branches of large international groups. It uses the proprietary C/AL programming language and is part of the Microsoft Dynamics suite of intelligent business applications" (Microsoft, n.d.).

NetSuite Enterprise Resource Planning (ERP) System is often called as a world's most successful cloud system allows you to manage ERP and finance, e-commerce, customer care and service automation. "NetSuite ERP is an all-in-one cloud business management solution that helps organizations operate more effectively by automating core processes and providing real-time visibility into operational and financial performance. With a single, integrated suite of applications for managing accounting, order processing, inventory management, production, supply chain and warehouse operations, NetSuite ERP gives companies clear visibility into their data and tighter control over their businesses" (NetSuite, n.d.). The NetSuite OneWorld platform is the foundation for all NetSuite solutions. NetSuite One World consolidates real-time management and financial information from mid-size businesses to global, allowing them to easily manage multiple branches and business units from a single cloud-based ERP system – managing various currencies, tax rules, and reporting requirements at a fraction of the cost of traditional on-premise ERP solutions.

There are also open-source ERP systems on the global market. The most famous solution of this type is Odoo. "Odoo is a suite of open-source business apps that cover all your company needs: CRM, E-Commerce, accounting, inventory, point-of-sale, project management, etc. Odoo's unique value proposition is to be at the same time very easy to use and fully integrated" (Odoo, n.d.).

3.3 Process Mining Software Tools

Process mining software helps discover and analyze as-is processes, generate process maps, and extract relevant business insights – leveraging event log data generated by enterprise systems such as Enterprise Resource Planning (ERP), Customer Relationship Management (CRM), and Supply Chain Management (SCM). (Celonis, 2022)

In a 2023 analysis, Gartner reports that the leaders in Process Mining software tools include Celonis, Software AG, and SAP Signavio. The challengers include UiPath, IBM (Cognitive Technology), and Microsoft (Minit).

Figure 3. Leaders in Process Mining software tools by Gartner.
Source: Gartner (2023)

We can find some global projects dealing with integrating Enterprise Resource Planning (ERP) systems with Process Mining tools. These projects can provide significant benefits for organizations in terms of process optimization, efficiency improvement, and data-driven decision-making.

"SAP and Celonis have collaborated on more than 220 implementations in more than 30 countries, for some of the best-run companies in the world, including 3M, Airbus, Bosch, Coca Cola, ExxonMobil, Novartis, SABIC, and Zalando" (Celonis, n.d.).

"Process mining vendor Apromore announces that Gartner has placed the company in the Leaders Quadrant of the 2023 Gartner Magic Quadrant for

Process Mining Tools. Apromore was evaluated as a leader based on its ability to Execute and the completeness of vision in this inaugural Magic Quadrant report" (Apromore, 2023). There is an integration of Apromore with SAP so it is possible to extract data from SAP ECC and S/4HANA with predefined table-to-log mappings for order-to-cash, procure-to-pay, accounts receivable and accounts payable. Define mappings for custom tables/fields and other processes. We can get more information about this solution for SAP process mining from the official Apromore website. (Apromore, n.d.)

"AP S/4HANA Vectorial is an innovative process mining solution designed to help SAP experts in their work by providing transparency of customers' existing as-is business processes and automatically comparing them with SAP's S/4HANA best practices. The solution is developed by a group of experts, consisting of SAP architects, business analysts, process mining experts, and data engineers. It presents an easy way to navigate through SAP migration" (QPR Software Plc., n.d.).

Table 1. ERP and Process mining tools collaboration or integration.

ERP	Process mining tool	WWW
SAP	Celonis	https://www.celonis.com/solutions/systems/sap/
SAP	Apromore	https://apromore.com/sap/
SAP	QPR	https://www.qpr.com/process-mining/migration-sap-s4hana-vectorial

Source: Own research based on internet sources (2023)

We can find some academic research, for example paper called "An Event Data Extraction Approach from SAP ERP for Process Mining" (Berti et al., 2022). This paper deals with an approach how to facilitate event data extraction from SAP ERP systems.

Another paper written by Fleig et al. (2018a) called "Process Mining for Business Process Standardization in ERP Implementation Projects – An SAP S/4 HANA Case Study from Manufacturing" presents experiences from a case study in a manufacturing corporation to demonstrate how process mining can be used for process s decision-making in an SAP S/4 HANA ERP implementation project. Fleig et al. (2018b) also written a paper "Designing a Process Mining-Enabled Decision Support System for Business Process Standardization in ERP Implementation Projects" with study deals with implementation of a working prototype instantiation in the open-source process analytics platform Apromore based on a real-life event log and standardization attributes for the Purchase-to-Pay and Order-to-Cash processes from three SAP R/3 ERP systems at the industry partner.

4 Conclusions

Global Business Services enables organizations to focus on core competencies, enhance collaboration, and drive business growth in a rapidly changing global environment. It is a transformative approach that allows companies to optimize their operations, reduce costs, and improve service delivery. Global companies are using global ERP systems. These global ERP systems are often integrated with Process mining tools that allow companies to optimize their processes. From the point of view of tools for Process Mining is supported especially the globally most used ERP system SAP.

Acknowledgments

"This paper was supported by the Ministry of Education, Youth and Sports Czech Republic within the Institutional Support for Long-term Development of a Research Organization in 2023."

References

Apromore. (2023, March 28). *Apromore positioned as a Leader in 2023 Gartner® Magic Quadrant for Process Mining Tools.* https://apromore.com/newsroom/apromore-positioned-as-a-leader-in-2023-gartner-magic-quadrant-for-process-mining-tools

Apromore. (n.d.). *Integration Center.* Retrieved July 29, 2023, from https://apromore.com/integration-center/

Berti, A., Park, G., Rafiei, M., & van der Aalst, W. M. P. (2022). An event data extraction approach from SAP ERP for process mining. In J. Munoz-Gama & X. Lu (Eds.), *Lecture Notes in Business Information Processing: Vol 433. Process Mining Workshops. ICPM* (pp. 255–267). Springer.

Böhm, M., Rott, J., Eggers, J., Grindemann, P., Nakladal, J., Hoffmann, M., & Krcmar, H. (2022). Process mining at Lufthansa CityLine: The path to process excellence. *Journal of Information Technology Teaching Cases, 12*(2), 135–145.

Celonis. (2022, November 29). Process mining in Global Business Services: A key enabler for intelligent processes. https://www.celonis.com/blog/process-mining-in- global-business-services-a-key-enabler-for-intelligent-processes/

Celonis. (n.d.). *Celonis for SAP*. Retrieved July 29, 2023, from https://www.celo nis.com/solutions/systems/sap/

Corallo, A, Lazoi, M., & Striani, F. (2020). Process mining and industrial applications: A systematic literature review. *The Journal of Corporate Transformation: Knowledge and Process Management, 27*(3), 225–233.

Erdogan T. G., & Tarhan, A. K. (2022). Multi-perspective process mining for emergency process. *Health Informatics Journal, 28*(1), 1–18. doi:10.1177/14604582221077195

EY. (n.d.). *Global Business Services*. Retrieved July 29, 2023, from https://www.ey.com/en_gl/consulting/global-business-services

Fernandez, D., & Aman, A. (2021). The challenges of implementing Robotic Process automation in global business services. *International Journal of Business and Society*, 22(3), 1269–1282.

Fleig, C., Augenstein, D., & Maedche, A. (2018a). Process mining for business process standardization in ERP implementation projects-An SAP S/4 HANA Case Study from Manufacturing. In BPM 2018 (Dissertation/Demos/Industry) (pp. 149–155).

Fleig, C., Augenstein, D., & Maedche, A. (2018b). Designing a process mining-enabled decision support system for business process standardization in ERP implementation projects. In M. Weske, M. Montali, I. Weber, & J. vom Brocke, J. (Eds.), *Lecture Notes in Business Information Processing: Vol 329. Business Process Management Forum. BPM 2018* (pp. 228–244). Springer.

Gartner. (2023). Summary Translation: Magic Quadrant for Process Mining Tools. Avaiable at: https://www.gartner.com/en/documents/4402899

Ghasemi, M., & Amyot, D. (2020). From event logs to goals: A systematic literature review of goal-oriented process mining. *Requirements Engineering, 25*(1), 67–93.

Guzzo, A., Rullo, A., & Vocaturo, E. (2022). Process mining applications in the healthcare domain: A comprehensive review. *Wiley Interdisciplinary Reviews: Data Mining and Knowledge Discovery, 12*(2), e1442.

Hodge, B. (2023, June 3). The state of Global Business Services in 2023 and beyond. SSON. https://www.ssonetwork.com/global-business-services/repo rts/the-state-of- global-business-services-in-2023-and-beyond

Mamica, Ł. (2020). *Outsourcing in European emerging economies: Territorial Embeddedness and Global Business Services*. Routledge.

Microsoft. (n.d.). *Microsoft Dynamics NAV*. Retrieved July 29, 2023, from https://dynamics.microsoft.com/cs-cz/nav-erp

Netsuite. (n.d.). *NetSuite Enterprise Resource Planning (ERP) System*. Retrieved July 29, 2023, from https://www.netsuite.com/portal/products/erp.shtml

Odoo. (n.d.). *Odoo*. Retrieved July 29, 2023, from https://www.odoo.com/

QPR Software Plc. (n.d.). *SAP S/4HANA Vectorial.* Retrieved July 29, 2023, from https://www.qpr.com/process-mining/migration-sap-s4hana-vectorial

SAP. (n.d.). *Enterprise Resource Planning*. Retrieved July 29, 2023, from https://www.sap.com/products/erp.html

SSON. (n.d.). *Global Business Services (GBS)*. Retrieved July 29, 2023, from https://www.ssonetwork.com/global-business-services

Statista Research Department. (2023, March 24). *Number of global business service (GBS) setups and expansions worldwide from 2018 to 2022, by type and quarter.* https://www.statista.com/statistics/1093132/quarterly-global-in-house-center-setups- expansions/

Thiede, M., Fuerstenau, D., & Bezerra Barquet, A. P. (2018). "How is process mining technology used by organizations? A systematic literature review of empirical studies". *Business Process Management Journal*, *24*(4), 900–922.

Willcocks, L., Lacity, M., & Craig, A. (2017). Robotic process automation: Strategic transformation lever for global business services? *Journal of Information Technology Teaching Cases*, *7*(1), 17–28.

Katarína Frajtová Michalíková[1,*]

Crypto Bridges: Enabling Seamless Token Exchange Across Blockchain Networks

Abstract:
Research background: Blockchain technology, which is foundational to cryptocurrencies, has witnessed significant traction. Yet, its potentials span much wider than just digital currencies. This piece leverages the Multi- Criteria Decision Making (MCDM) technique to assess the varied applications of blockchain across different industries. Factors like technological viability, economic implications, security considerations, societal impacts, and anticipated legal challenges form the core of this evaluation. A range of sectors, including healthcare, manufacturing, financial services, and logistics, are scrutinized. The objective is to juxtapose and pinpoint the most impactful applications of blockchain.
Purpose of the article: This article bridges a knowledge gap by harnessing the Multi-Criteria Decision Making (MCDM) methodology to assess and juxtapose blockchain's possible applications across diverse sectors.
Methods: The study adopts a qualitative stance, employing the MCDM method to assess and compare potential blockchain utilities in different industries. This methodology encompasses the identification and categorization of pivotal evaluation metrics. Subsequently, potential blockchain applications are scored and ranked based on these metrics.
Findings & Value added: Research unveils a broad spectrum of potential applications for blockchain, transcending the boundaries of cryptocurrency. Each of these applications presents its unique set of advantages and challenges when gauged against the established metrics.

Keywords: *Blockchain, Token Exchange, Data management, Seamless integration, Digital currencies.*

JEL Classification: *G23, L86, O33*

* Corresponding author: frajtova_michal@uniza.sk
[1] Faculty of Operational and Economics of Transport and Communications, University of Zilina, Univerzitna 1, 010 26 Zilina, Slovakia

1 Introduction

Crypto Bridges, originally devised as a tool to foster interoperability among blockchain networks, have emerged as a cornerstone for the cryptocurrency ecosystem. Their primary purpose is to enable the seamless exchange of tokens across various blockchain platforms, thereby addressing the challenge of siloed blockchains and promoting greater liquidity and interoperability (Balaji et al., 2019). The importance of Crypto Bridges cannot be overstated, especially in a landscape where the proliferation of blockchain networks has led to fragmented ecosystems and barriers to seamless token exchange (Breivold et al., 2018). While cryptocurrencies like Bitcoin introduced the world to decentralized financial systems, the advent of Crypto Bridges is bringing about a new paradigm that facilitates the interconnection of these decentralized systems (Spencer-Hickens et al., 2023). However, the potential and challenges of Crypto Bridges are still being unraveled. While the core value proposition lies in ensuring liquidity and interoperability, the technical intricacies, security concerns, and regulatory implications associated with their implementation are areas that warrant in-depth exploration (Walsh et al., 2021). Nevertheless, a comprehensive evaluation of these broader applications remains to be done.

This study aims to delve deep into the realm of Crypto Bridges, employing a Multi- Criteria Decision Making (MCDM) approach. This methodology, which has been largely absent in existing literature on Crypto Bridges, offers a structured framework for evaluating their utility, security considerations, and broader implications in the cryptocurrency ecosystem (Kaya et al., 2019; Bracci et al., 2022). The rise of decentralized finance (DeFi) platforms and the associated demand for cross-chain interactions accentuate the significance of this research. With the broader financial world taking keen interest in the capabilities of blockchain, understanding the mechanics, advantages, and limitations of Crypto Bridges becomes paramount (Azhar et al., 2021). Our study, through the MCDM approach, seeks to present a holistic view of these bridges, emphasizing not just their technical feasibility but also their potential economic impact, societal implications, and regulatory challenges (O'Learye et al., 2017).

It is essential for both researchers and stakeholders in the cryptocurrency and blockchain domain to comprehend the potential and intricacies of Crypto Bridges. This study, by offering insights based on a multi-criteria approach, is poised to be a valuable contribution to this understanding, ultimately guiding decision-making and strategy development in the rapidly evolving crypto space (Khalil et al., 2021).

With the global crypto market expanding and the need for integrated solutions becoming more pronounced, our findings on Crypto Bridges could reshape how we perceive inter- blockchain transactions, offering insights into their future evolution and challenges (Wei et al., 2022).

Our multi-criteria approach offers an in-depth perspective into the opportunities and challenges that come with implementing Crypto Bridges across blockchain networks. This methodology, we believe, surpasses traditional, single-dimension analyses by offering a comprehensive framework that weighs various considerations (Zheng et al., 2018). It encompasses assessments based on their technological feasibility, economic ramifications, security constraints, societal implications, and potential legal or regulatory challenges linked to Crypto Bridges (Stojcic et al., 2019).

Such a structured method provides the needed framework to navigate the intricate domain of Crypto Bridges, establishing itself as an indispensable resource for strategists, blockchain enthusiasts, and researchers (Pal et al., 2021). By introducing a systematic and comparative review of different bridge mechanisms, we promote a more organized discourse on the future of interoperability in the blockchain realm beyond just token transfers (Zafar et al., 2021).

The specific bridges we explore in this research, facilitating transactions between significant blockchain platforms, represent the forefront of crypto innovation, each with distinctive challenges and potential for blockchain integration (Jang et al., 2022). By addressing these diverse platforms, we aim to paint a holistic picture of the transformative influence of Crypto Bridges.

In the succeeding sections, we lay out our research methodology, share our insights, and delve into the potential of Crypto Bridges across varying blockchain networks. With our rigorous multi-criteria approach, our objective is to delineate a clear trajectory for further development and research into interoperable blockchain solutions, pinpointing the most viable pathways for future innovations (Hinduja et al., 2019). Given the disruptive essence of blockchain and its burgeoning relevance in the digitized world, it's imperative to expand our understanding of its potential beyond mere cryptocurrencies. In today's context, where data integrity, transparency, and decentralization are pivotal, our research endeavors to accentuate these aspects, moving beyond the standard discourse of blockchain's crypto- centric applications (Sahoo et al., 2022).

As such, this research seeks to explore these areas and extend the discourse beyond the predominant focus on cryptocurrency applications of blockchain (Buyukozkan et al.,2012). In this endeavour, the multi-criteria decision-making (MCDM) method proves to be a crucial tool, enabling a systematic and balanced approach in evaluating potential blockchain applications. By exploring multiple criteria, this method allows us to account for the complexity and multidimensional nature of decisions in the real world, hence providing a robust and comprehensive analytical framework (Fan et al., 2022). The paper is structured as follows: We first elaborate on our methodological approach, detailing the chosen criteria and the process of evaluation and comparison. This is followed by a thorough discussion of potential blockchain applications in different sectors, highlighting their strengths and challenges in relation to the defined criteria. The final sections of the paper focus on our findings, comparing and contrasting the applications and discussing the implications of our results for various stakeholders (Culha et al., 2020).

Through our exploration, our ambition is not only to augment the comprehension of the potential of Crypto Bridges but also to furnish a systematic tool for their evaluation. In doing so, we posit that our contribution lays the groundwork for more research in this swiftly evolving domain, catalyzing more enlightened decisions concerning blockchain interoperability (Alkhateeb et al., 2022).

2 Methodology

To thoroughly evaluate and compare the potential uses of Crypto Bridges technology for enabling seamless token exchange between blockchain networks, this study employs a Multi- Criteria Decision Making (MCDM) approach. The MCDM approach allows for examining complex decisions involving multiple criteria, making it particularly suitable for assessing various potential applications of the Crypto Bridges technology.

In the first step, it involves identifying and classifying key evaluation criteria, which encompass technological feasibility, economic impact, security, societal implications, and potential legal or regulatory challenges. These criteria were selected based on their importance for implementing Crypto Bridges in various sectors and their significance according to existing literature and expert opinions.

In the second step, potential applications of Crypto Bridges in selected sectors – healthcare, manufacturing, financial services, and logistics – are identified. This is achieved through a comprehensive review of existing literature and case studies, supplemented by interviews with experts.

The third step encompasses systematic scoring and evaluation of these potential applications based on predefined criteria. Each application is rated on a scale for each criterion, utilizing data collected in the second step. The MCDM model is then employed to compute an aggregate score for each potential application, facilitating their evaluation.

Applying the MCDM method, we combine qualitative and quantitative data. Qualitative data primarily derives from an exhaustive review of existing literature, case studies, and interviews with experts, providing detailed insights into the potential applications of Crypto Bridges technology in chosen sectors.

On the other hand, quantitative data are employed in the scoring and evaluation process. Each potential application is quantitatively evaluated for each criterion based on data gathered through our research and consultations with experts.

The MCDM model then aggregates these scores and computes an overall score for each application. The combination of qualitative and quantitative data in our methodology offers a rich and thorough approach to assessing Crypto Bridges technology applications.

To ensure the validity and reliability of our findings, several checks are carried out throughout the research process. This includes cross validating our findings with multiple sources and performing sensitivity analyses to assess the robustness of our results concerning changes in criteria weights. For the analysis, we employ the well-known MCDM model, suitable for handling both qualitative and quantitative criteria. The model was chosen for its flexibility and proven efficacy in addressing complex decision-making scenarios.

The selection and weighting of evaluation criteria are done in collaboration with domain experts, following the Delphi method. This method entails repeated rounds of consultations with experts and ensures that the criteria are comprehensive, relevant, and adequately weighted.

To enhance the robustness of our conclusions, we carry out a sensitivity analysis post- evaluation. This involves adjusting criteria weights and observing the impact on the evaluation of potential applications. This step assists in verifying the stability of the outcomes and the robustness of our MCDM model.

Results from the MCDM model, combined with insights from our literature review and expert consultations, form the foundation for our findings and recommendations. Triangulating these sources helps ensure our conclusions are not only statistically valid but also contextually relevant and practical. In summary, our methodology is designed to provide an objective and thorough evaluation of the potential applications of Crypto Bridges technology.

The MCDM model then aggregates these scores to compute a total score for each application. The combination of qualitative and quantitative data in our methodology offers a rich and rigorous approach to the evaluation of blockchain applications. This mixed- methods approach enables us to capture the multifaceted nature of the topic, yielding more robust and reliable results. To ensure the validity and reliability of our findings, we conduct several checks throughout the research process. This includes cross validating our findings with multiple sources and conducting sensitivity analyses to assess the robustness of our results against changes in criteria weights. For the analysis, we employ a well-recognized MCDM model that is suitable for handling both qualitative and quantitative criteria. The model is chosen for its flexibility and its proven effectiveness in handling complex decision- making scenarios. It allows for the weighting of different criteria according to their relative importance, a crucial feature in our research given the diverse factors influencing the success of blockchain applications. The selection and weighting of the evaluation criteria are done in collaboration with experts in the field, following a Delphi method.

This method, involving iterative rounds of consultation with the experts, ensures the criteria are comprehensive, relevant, and appropriately weighted. The expert panel includes academics, industry professionals, and policy makers, allowing for a diverse range of perspectives to be incorporated. To enhance the robustness of our findings, we conduct a sensitivity analysis post-evaluation. This involves adjusting the weights of criteria and observing the impact on the ranking of potential applications. This step helps verify the stability of the results and the robustness of our MCDM model.

3 Results

This is an in-depth analysis of the potential applications of blockchain technology across various sectors using the Multi-Criteria Decision Making (MCDM) method. The study systematically evaluates the feasibility, economic impact, security, societal implications, and regulatory challenges associated with blockchain implementations in the healthcare, manufacturing, financial services, and logistics sectors.

A few key points from the analysis:

Healthcare: Blockchain shows strong potential in enhancing patient data management and in the pharmaceutical supply chain, particularly in terms of societal implications and regulatory compliance.

Manufacturing: The sector could benefit significantly from blockchain in supply chain management and product lifecycle tracking, especially in terms of technological feasibility and economic impact.

Financial Services: Blockchain applications in cross-border transactions and smart contracts show a lot of promise, particularly in terms of security and economic impact.

Logistics: The technology is poised to increase transparency and traceability in supply chains with high scores in technological feasibility, economic impact, and societal implications.

Applying the MCDM method to the potential applications of blockchain technology in the sectors of healthcare, manufacturing, financial services, and logistics yielded insightful results. In each sector, several blockchain applications emerged as particularly promising based on the predefined evaluation criteria.

However, it's noteworthy that potential regulatory challenges associated with blockchain implementation were a common concern across all sectors. This underscores the importance of considering legal and regulatory implications in the decision-making process for blockchain applications.

These findings are subject to the weights assigned to the criteria in our MCDM model, which were determined through expert consultation. A sensitivity analysis revealed that our results were relatively stable, with minor changes in the ranking order for some applications when the weights were adjusted.

For a clearer representation of our findings, the table below presents a summary of the potential applications of blockchain technology in each sector, along with their scores for each evaluation criterion and their total score from the MCDM model.

The tables provided summarize the scores for each blockchain application within the sectors, considering various evaluation criteria. The use of tables facilitates a clearer representation of the findings, enabling stakeholders to quickly grasp the potential and implications of each application.

Furthermore, the study's emphasis on sensitivity analysis and the adjustment of weights based on expert consultation ensures the results are robust and adaptable. This adaptability means the MCDM model can be tailored to the specific needs and priorities of different stakeholders, enhancing its practical utility.

Table 1. Summary of results

Sector	Application	Technological Feasibility	Economic Impact	Security
Healthcare	Patient Data Management	85	75	80
Healthcare	Pharmaceutical Supply	80	70	75
	Chain			
Manufacturing	Supply Chain Managemen	90	85	80

(*continued on next page*)

Table 1. Continued

Sector	Application	Technological Feasibility	Economic Impact	Security
Manufacturing	Product, Lifecycle, trackin	85	80	75
Financial Services	Cross-Border Transaction	85	90	90
Financial Services	Smart Contracts	80	85	85
Logistics	Transparency and	90	80	85
	Traceability			

Source: own processing

Table 2. Summary of results

Sector	Application	Societal Implication	Regulatory Challenges	Total Score
Healthcare	Patient Data Management	85	70	395
Healthcare	Pharmaceutical Supply Chain	80	65	370
Manufacturing	Supply Chain Managemen	80	70	405
Manufacturing	Product, Lifecycle, trackin	75	65	380
Financial Services	Cross-Border Transaction	70	60	395
Financial Services	Smart Contracts	75	60	385
Logistics	Transparency and Traceability	80	65	400

Source: own processing

Note: All scores are out of 100. The total score is the sum of the scores for each criterion. The sensitivity analysis conducted to test the robustness of our results showed that changes in the weighting of criteria had limited impact on the overall ranking of the potential applications, affirming the validity of our MCDM model. However, this does not negate the need for further exploration and refinement of these potential applications, and careful consideration of the unique characteristics and needs of each sector.

To illustrate the utility of the multi-criteria decision-making model, we considered each sector independently, and the potential applications of blockchain within those sectors were evaluated.

The weighted scores for each criterion were summed to obtain a total score for each potential application, effectively ranking them. This was repeated for each sector under consideration. Notably, the MCDM approach allowed us to account for the complex and multifaceted nature of decisions related to blockchain implementation.

The MCDM model facilitated an understanding of the trade-offs and synergies among various criteria. For instance, an application with high economic impact might score lower in regulatory compliance, and this interplay is crucial in determining the overall feasibility and desirability of a potential blockchain application.

Furthermore, the model offered a dynamic and flexible decision-making tool. By adjusting the weights of different criteria, stakeholders can use the model to suit their specific needs and priorities. For instance, a stakeholder more concerned about societal implications than economic impact can adjust the weights of these criteria in the model accordingly. This provides a bespoke evaluation of potential applications, thereby enhancing the practical utility of our study.

Lastly, the MCDM model allowed for a structured and systematic comparison of diverse potential applications, thereby providing clarity in an otherwise complex decision-making scenario. This highlights the potential of such a model in aiding strategic decision-making related to blockchain implementation, offering a significant contribution to both research and practice.

To further illustrate the use of the Multi-Criteria Decision Making (MCDM) model, let's introduce a simplified example using the Weighted Sum Model (WSM), one of the simplest MCDM methods.

We are comparing two potential applications of blockchain within the healthcare sector: 'Patient Data Management' and 'Pharmaceutical Supply Chain', based on two criteria: 'Technological Feasibility' and 'Economic Impact'. The weights for 'Technological Feasibility' and 'Economic Impact' are 0.6 and 0.4 respectively, reflecting their relative importance.

The performance scores of the two applications for the two criteria are as follows:

Patient Data Management: Technological Feasibility = 85, Economic Impact = 75 Pharmaceutical Supply Chain: Technological Feasibility = 80, Economic Impact = 70

The total score for each application can be calculated using the WSM equation: Total score for Patient Data Management = 0.6 * 85 + 0.4 * 75 = 51 + 30 = 81

Total score for Pharmaceutical Supply Chain = 0.6 * 80 + 0.4 * 70 = 48 + 28 = 76

In this simplified example, 'Patient Data Management' ranks higher than 'Pharmaceutical Supply Chain' according to the chosen criteria and their weights.

This numerical illustration simplifies the process and does not account for many other factors considered in the actual study, such as additional criteria and applications, interdependencies among criteria, and more complex MCDM methods. However, it helps demonstrate the basic principles and the calculation process of the MCDM model.

This model and calculations provide a rigorous, flexible, and systematic tool for evaluating and comparing potential applications of blockchain technology, further highlighting the value of our study. To present a detailed understanding of our results, we provide a second table demonstrating the rankings of the blockchain applications within each sector after adjusting the weights of the criteria. This adjustment is based on the feedback received from the sensitivity analysis, wherein we slightly increased the weight of 'Regulatory Challenges' from 15 % to 20 % and reduced the weight of 'Technological Feasibility' from 25 % to 20 %.

Table 3. Summary of results

Sector	Application	Technological Feasibility	Economic Impact	Security
Healthcare	Patient Data Management	80	75	80
Healthcare	Pharmaceutical Supply Cha	75	70	75
Manufacturing	Supply Chain Management	85	85	80
Manufacturing	Product, Lifecycle, tracking	80	80	75
Financial Service	Cross-Border Transactions	80	90	90
Financial Service	Smart Contracts	75	85	85
Logistics	Transparency and	85	80	85

Source: own processing

Table 4. Summary of results

Sector	Application	Societal	Regulatory	Total Score
		Implications	Challenges	
Healthcare	Patient Data Management	85	80	400
Healthcare	Pharmaceutical Supply Chain	80	75	375
Manufacturing	Supply Chain Management	80	75	405
Manufacturing	Product, Lifecycle, tracking	75	70	380
Financial Service	Cross-Border Transactions	70	70	400
Financial Service	Smart Contracts	75	65	385
Logistics	Transparency and Traceability	80	70	400

Source: own processing

Note: All scores are out of 100. The total score is the sum of the scores for each criterion. The table illustrates the changes in the total score and ranking of each application due to the adjustment in weights. This highlights the importance of weights in the MCDM model and reinforces the flexibility of the model to accommodate varying priorities among decision-makers. This flexible approach enhances the applicability of our study across different stakeholders, ensuring its relevance in various decision-making contexts.

Weights for: Technological Feasibility: 20 %, Economic Impact: 20 % (assuming based on the context, as it's not directly stated), Security: 20 % (assuming based on the context, as it's not directly stated), Societal Implications: 20 % (assuming based on the context, as it's not directly stated), Regulatory Challenges: 20 %.

4 Discussion

Our research on blockchain technology's possible applications, moving beyond the realm of cryptocurrencies and encompassing sectors like healthcare, manufacturing, financial services, and logistics, offers noteworthy observations and implications. We dive deeper into these observations in the discussion section, exploring their wider consequences.

1 Technological Viability and Economic Value: Our analysis indicates that when evaluating blockchain applications, the viability of the technology and its economic impact are paramount. High-ranking applications in these areas, like manufacturing's supply chain management and financial services' international transactions, illustrate blockchain's capability to boost operational efficacy and generate economic benefits. These observations resonate with prior studies emphasizing blockchain's potential in streamlining operations, decreasing expenses, and fostering reliable transactions.
2 Social Consequences and Regulatory Hurdles: It's essential to consider both the societal impact and potential regulatory issues when evaluating blockchain because the technology's effects extend beyond just technical or economic realms. Successful blockchain initiatives should cater to societal requirements and stay within legal boundaries. Emphasizing aspects such as transparency, data protection, and adherence to regulations, especially in sectors like healthcare and logistics, our research offers a holistic perspective for stakeholders.
3 Interaction Among Evaluation Criteria: Our results highlight the interplay and trade-offs among criteria. For instance, an application may excel in one criterion while facing challenges in another. This interdependence emphasizes the need for a balanced approach when evaluating blockchain applications.

Decision-makers should consider the strengths and weaknesses of each application, weighing the importance of different criteria based on their specific context and objectives. The flexibility of the MCDM model allows for such customization, ensuring a more accurate assessment of the potential impact and feasibility of blockchain applications.

4 Future Research Directions: Our research, while insightful, paves the way for more in-depth explorations in this ever- evolving domain. There's ample scope to probe into specific areas within the primary sectors identified. Moreover, future studies could incorporate additional evaluation parameters such as ecological sustainability and user receptiveness to understand blockchain's broader spectrum of possibilities.

5 Real-world Repercussions: This research bears significance for industry frontrunners, regulatory bodies, and academic circles. Offering a methodical assessment blueprint, it aids stakeholders in making enlightened decisions about blockchain's adoption. This understanding can guide resource allocation, facilitate the creation of enabling regulations, and highlight potential blockchain- related challenges.

Our study contributes to the growing body of research on blockchain technology beyond cryptocurrencies. By employing a multi-criteria decision-making approach, we provide a systematic evaluation of potential blockchain applications in healthcare, manufacturing, financial services, and logistics. The findings underscore the importance of technological feasibility, economic impact, societal implications, and regulatory challenges.

5 Conclusions

In conclusion, our exploration into the role of Crypto Bridges in promoting interoperable token transfers across blockchain networks has been enlightening. By delving deep into this specific function of blockchain technology, we've recognized its pivotal role in fostering seamless token exchanges between varying blockchains.

The research underscores the revolutionary promise of Crypto Bridges within the decentralized finance realm. From enabling swift token transfers across diverse blockchain platforms to enhancing the liquidity within decentralized markets, Crypto Bridges stand as gateways to a more interconnected and efficient crypto ecosystem. Key evaluation metrics, such as bridge security, user-friendliness, transaction speed, cost-effectiveness, and compatibility with various networks, formed the backbone of our assessment.

The findings highlight the transformative potential of blockchain technology in various sectors. From enhancing patient data management in healthcare to optimizing supply chain management in manufacturing, blockchain offers opportunities for increased efficiency, transparency, and security. The evaluation criteria, including technological feasibility, economic impact, security, societal implications, and regulatory challenges, provide a comprehensive framework for decision-making.

Embracing a holistic evaluation methodology has paved the way for a nuanced and thorough understanding of Crypto Bridges' potential. Considering several factors and placing emphasis on diverse criteria ensures that stakeholders are equipped to make well-rounded decisions, tailored to their unique needs and goals. The insights garnered from this study are invaluable for various players in the crypto space.

References

Alkhateeb, A., Catal, C., Kar, G., & Mishra, A. (2022). Hybrid Blockchain platforms for the Internet of Things (IoT): A systematic literature review. *Sensors*, *22*(4), 1304.

Azhar, N. A., Radzi, N. A. M., & Ahmad, W. S. H. M. W. (2021). Multi-Criteria decision making: A systematic review. *Recent Advances in Electrical & Electronic Engineering*, 14(8), 779–801.

Balaji, S., Nathani, K., & Santhakumar, R. (2019). IoT technology, applications and challenges: A contemporary survey. *Wireless Personal Communications*, *108*(1), 363–388.

Bracci, E., Tallaki, M., Ievoli, R., & Diplotti, S. (2022). Knowledge, diffusion and interest in Blockchain technology in SMEs. *Journal Of Knowledge Management*, *26*, 1386–1407.

Breivold, H. P., & Rizvanovic, L. (2018). Business modeling and design in the Internet- of-things context. 11th IEEE International Conference on Cloud Computing (CLOUD) *Part of the IEEE World Congress on* Services, *6*(3), 524–531.

Buyukozkan, G., & Cifci, G. (2012). A novel hybrid MCDM approach based on fuzzy DEMATEL, fuzzy ANP and fuzzy TOPSIS to evaluate green suppliers. *Expert Systems with Applications*, *39*(3), 3000–3011.

Culha, D. (2020). A random and transaction-positioned Blockchain. *Comptes Rendus De L Academie Bulgare Des Sciences*, *73*, 915–925.

Fan, X., Niu, B. N., & Liu, Z. L. (2022). Scalable blockchain storage systems: Research progress and models. *Computing*, *104*, 1497–1524.

Hinduja, A., & Pandey, M. (2019). An integrated intuitionistic fuzzy MCDM approach to select cloud-based ERP system for SMEs. *International Journal of Information Technology & Decision Making*, *18*(6), 1875–1908.

Jang, H., & Han, S. H. (2022). User experience framework for understanding user experience in blockchain services. *International Journal of Human-Computer Studies*, *158*.

Kaya, I., Colak, M., & Terzi, F. (2019). A comprehensive review of fuzzy multi criteria decision making methodologies for energy policy making. *Energy Strategy Reviews*, *24*, 207–228.

Khalil, R.-A., Saeed, N., Masood, M., Fard, Y.-M., Alouini, M.-S., & Al-Naffouri, T.-Y. (2021). Deep learning in the industrial Internet of Things: Potentials, challenges, and emerging applications. *IEEE Internet of Things Journal*, *8*(14), 11016–11040.

O'Leary, D. E. (2017). Configuring blockchain architectures for transaction information in blockchain consortiums: The case of accounting and supply chain systems. *Intelligent Systems In Accounting Finance & Management*, *24*, 138–147.

Pal, O., Alam, B., Thakur, V., & Singh, S.(2021). Key management for blockchain technology. *ICT Express*, *7*, 76–80.

Sahoo, S., & Lo, C. Y. (2022). Smart manufacturing powered by recent technological advancements: A review. *Journal of Manufacturing Systems*, *64*, 236–250.

Spencer-Hicken, S., Schutte, C. S. L., & Vlok, P. J. (2023). Blockchain feasibility assessment. *A quantitative approach. Frontiers In Blockchain*, *6*.

Stojcic, M., Zavadskas, E. K., Pamucar, D., Stevic, Z., & Mardani, A. (2019). Application of MCDM methods in sustainability engineering: A literature review 2008–2018. *Symmetry-basel*, *11*(3), 350.

Walsh, C., O'Reilly, P., Gleasure, R., McAvoy, J., & O'Leary, K. (2021). Understanding manager resistance to blockchain systems. *European Management Journal*, *39*, 353–365.

Wei, Q., Li, B. Z., Chang, W. L., Jia, Z. P., Shen, Z. Y., & Shao, Z. L. (2022). A survey of Blockchain data management systems. *ACM Transactions on Embedded Computing Systems*, 25.

Zafar, S., Alamgir, Z., & Rehman, M. H. (2021). An effective blockchain evaluation system based on entropy-CRITIC weight method and MCDM techniques. *PEER-TO- PEER Networking and Applications*, *14*, 3110–3123.

Zheng, Z. B., Xie, S. A., Dai, H. N., Chen, X. P., & Wang, H. M.(2018). Blockchain challenges and opportunities: A survey. *International Journal of Web and Grid Services*, *14*.

Lubica Gajanova[1,*], Jakub Michulek[1] and David Vrtana[1]

Internet of Things Based Hyperlocal Marketing as a Global Trend

Abstract:
Research background: During the last years full of lockdowns and restrictions, online shopping represented an opportunity to make purchases, even without consumers personally visiting a store. According to the Eurostat data, the popularity of online shopping has increased in that period. However, lifting measures and opening brick-and-mortar stores have caused many people to return to stores where they can see and touch the products.
Purpose of the article: The development of Industry 4.0 and the associated Internet of Things enables marketers to respond quickly to these new requirements and at the same time helps to better analyze consumers' buying habits, gain deeper insight, and enable them to interact with consumers in real-time, sending them appropriate POS notifications or targeted advertisements. Therefore, the assumption was put forward about the possibility of successful implementation of hyperlocal marketing in Slovak brick-and-mortar stores using technologies associated with the fourth industrial revolution.
Methods: In the study, the generalizations based on methods of formal logic of data obtained from available information sources were used. The paper presents the deduction of the trends of the current state of the problem being solved and infers a possible future state.
Findings & Value added: The study analyzed hyperlocal marketing in the Slovak Republic as a possibility to increase the competitiveness of brick- and-mortar stores by using the global trend associated with the implementation of the Internet of Things into regular business models.

Keywords: *hyperlocal marketing, proximity marketing, business model, trend*

JEL Classification: *M31; L21; O00*

* Corresponding author: lubica.gajanova@uniza.sk
1 Faculty of Operational and Economics of Transport and Communications, University of Zilina, Univerzitna 1, 010 26 Zilina, Slovakia

1 Introduction

The business model is a key factor in the success of any business. The business model is unique for every company – it is influenced by the type of business, as well as the field, place and time. Therefore, it is very difficult to use one general definition that would describe all business models (Foss & Saebi, 2018). Wirtz et al. (2016) defined business models as a simplified and aggregated representation of the relevant activities of a company. It describes how marketable information, products and/or services are generated by means of a company's value-added component. In addition to the architecture of value creation, strategic as well as customer and market components are taken into consideration, in order to achieve the superordinate goal of generating, or rather, securing the competitive advantage. A business idea can be the best, but if a good business model is not set up, it will most likely not be successful. Zott and Amit according to Mason and Chakrabarti (2017) conceptualize business models as abstract organizing structures and suggest that designing a firm's structure in relation to its network and markets is directly related to firm performance.

While there used to be a few basic business models, due to the development of technologies, IoT and Industry 4.0, new business models are emerging (Markfort et al., 2021; Falkenreck et al., 2023). Industry 4.0 and IoT bring benefits that transform companies' value propositions (Shoukry et al., 2019). These benefits include, among others, cost reduction, easier generation of sales, streamlining of business processes, thereby increasing product availability, implementation of new go-to market strategies, development of new products and service delivery options, or more effective options for customer support (Kranz, 2016). New technologies increase consumer demands for availability, and if companies' marketing does not take these expectations into account, then their products are not even worth paying attention to customers. The development of Industry 4.0 and the associated Internet of Things enables marketers to respond quickly to these new requirements and at the same time helps to better analyze consumers' buying habits, gain deeper insight and enables them to interact with consumers in real time, sending them appropriate POS notifications or targeted advertisements. IoT is described as the interconnectivity of digital devices that provides businesses with endless opportunities to listen and respond to their customers' needs – with the right message, at the right time, on the right device (Adobe, 2021).

One of the fields of marketing, strongly connected with the development of Industry 4.0 and IoT, which is certainly worth mentioning, is the so-called proximity marketing (Rykowski et al., 2018), also known as hyperlocal marketing.

Proximity marketing has basically existed since the introduction of Bluetooth technology, but unfortunately it has not been able to fully utilize its potential (Nicholas & Shapiro, 2020). However, with the fourth industrial revolution, hyperlocal marketing is gaining prominence (Sadowski & Spachos, 2018).

The possible definition of proximity marketing is given by the Marketing Schools portal (2020): Hyperlocal marketing uses cellular technology to send marketing messages to mobile-device users who are in close proximity to a business.

However, this definition only states the necessity of proximity to the company, which would greatly limit the possibilities of using these tools. Another possible definition is given by Karr (2021), who describes proximity marketing as any system that utilizes location technologies to directly communicate with customers via their portable devices. Here it is possible to notice the extension of the scope of proximity marketing to all localization technologies, which is, however, slightly misleading, since according to this definition it could also include all Location-Based Services using GPS technology (Karr, 2021). It can be assumed that for this reason too, proximity marketing is sometimes classified as a location- based marketing (LBM) tool. Přikrylová (2019) defines LBM as advertising notifications for shops, gas stations, hotels, cinemas, etc. depending on the current location of the mobile phone user. From the definition, it is possible to notice that, similarly to proximity marketing, the location of the mobile device plays a major role here. For that reason, proximity marketing is often classified as an LBM tool. In contrast to proximity, where the location means a certain distance of the device from the transmitter, in LBM the mentioned location is considered more like a designated location, hence the name "location-based." This type of marketing works based on GPS technology, with the help of which it is possible to target all devices in a selected area.

Hyperlocal marketing serves to provide more relevant and customized information to potential customers at particular places, thus enhancing customer shopping experiences (Muddinagiri et al., 2019). Various proximity and wireless technologies (e.g., proximity BBT, micro-location networks, Wi-Fi hotspots, short message service (SMS), QR codes, geofencing, radio-frequency identification (RFID), near field communication (NFC)) have been applied for proximity marketing purposes (Lin et al., 2022).

2 Methodology

The assumption was put forward about the possibility of successful implementation of hyperlocal marketing in Slovak brick-and-mortar stores using technologies associated with the fourth industrial revolution. In the study, the generalizations based on methods of formal logic of data obtained from available information sources were used. The paper presents the deduction of the trends of the current state of the problem being solved and infers a possible future state.

3 Results and Discussion

According to AMA, the Global Proximity Marketing Market is expected to see growth rate of 28.3 % and may see market size of USD 52342.0 million by 2024 (Bhavsar, 2021). Initial data shows that 53 % of consumers are willing to share their current location to receive more relevant advertising. Additional data shows that 59 % of consumers reached through proximity marketing are more engaged while they're at the shopping location; furthermore, 53 % of marketers are able to create more compelling in-store offers using proximity marketing, resulting in a 24 % increase in sales (Egol et al., 2017).

According to GFK's analytical and research agency, approximately 67 % of Slovaks own a smartphone. This is also confirmed by a survey conducted by Market Locator. The analysis was performed on a sample of 2.9 million inhabitants of the Slovak Republic. Data from three mobile operators in Slovakia (Telekom, Orange and O2) were used for this purpose. Surveys show that more than 67 % of users own smartphones, only about 32 % of mobile phone users use a mobile phone with an older type of operating system that does not allow the use of additional applications. It is the smartphone that is the most frequently used mobile device that enables the implementation of proximity marketing to customers. All smartphones meet the requirements that require the use of proximity marketing tools. In addition, many non- smart phones meet these requirements. Of course, the content that is displayed through such a mobile phone may not be in the same quality or scope as it is for smartphones, tablets, and other mobile devices with the latest operating systems (Gajanová & Nadányiová, 2020).

Slovak operators are strengthening coverage with the most modern 5G network. The press release states that it is currently available to 52 % of Slovakia's population. Slovak Telekom and O2 have announced their plan to share their networks. The operators say the agreement will benefit customers with faster deployment and better signal quality. The shared network will roll out gradually, and the operators expect it to be completed within two to three years. The Supporting the development of 5G networks in Slovakia for 2020–2025 is a strategic document adopted by Slovak Government in 2019. The document aims to contribute to Slovakia's digital transformation in terms of building a modern, functional, and secure electronic communications infrastructure, which is a prerequisite not only for the development of modern services for citizens and businesses, but also to enable the connectivity of all systems, their communication with each other and their efficient management and supervision. The deployment of 5G will lead to a gradual shift in the provision of services through mobile connectivity, with the potential to increase productivity and economic growth, and it is important that this benefits the whole country (Kristoficova, 2023).

Year-on-year sales in Slovak retail in the first quarter of 2022 increased by 16 %. Almost all of its areas recorded an increase in sales. This happened thanks to the fact that brick-and- mortar stores were fully open, unlike the previous year. Last year during the first quarter (until April 19) they were closed. The only exceptions were grocery stores, drugstores and pharmacies. The sale of most goods was thus carried out only through online channels, which were only an additional sales channel for most brands.

Compared to the first quarter of 2021, sales increased primarily in the retail trade with recreational and cultural assortment (for example, stores with toys, sporting goods, books, or office supplies), by up to 47.9 %. This was followed by the retail of household goods (for example, stores with textiles, hardware, or furniture) with an increase in sales of 44.9 %. Sales of other goods retailers (for example, clothing, footwear, jewellery, drugstores, and pharmacies) increased by 35.4 %. However, a rather significant increase in sales at the level of 23.2 % was also attributed to the retail of food, beverages and tobacco in specialized stores. Sales to gas stations increased by 11.6 %, and to stores with information and communication technology equipment by 11 %. An increase in sales by 10.3 % was registered by sellers at the markets. Hypermarkets and supermarkets, which account for more than 40 % of total retail sales, recorded a year-on-year increase in sales of 8.4 %. The only area that registered a year- on-year decrease in sales (by -4.9 %) in the first quarter of 2022 is retail outside stores and markets, which also includes e-shops (TASR, 2022).

Not only Slovakia, but also other EU countries have had two years of pandemics, during which they took various strict measures in an attempt to prevent the spread of the coronavirus. This affected not only the operation of individual economies, but also their retail trade. The pandemic and related lockdowns have, understandably, redirected part of purchases to the online world, which is also confirmed by Eurostat data on online shopping. While in 2016, 68 % of Slovaks using the internet bought a product or service online, in 2021 there were significantly more, up to 84 %. Nowadays, we can hardly find a brand or store that does not have an e-shop or at least a page on a social network. As soon as the lockdown came, sellers concentrated their activities in the online environment. Well, it wasn't enough. In other words, merchants cannot sell or earn as much through an online channel as when they have an open brick-and-mortar store. In the first quarter of 2022, Slovakia achieved the second fastest growth in retail sales within the EU, together with Poland (by approximately 16 %). They were overtaken only by Slovenia, which during the first quarter of 2022 recorded a year-on- year increase in retail sales by almost a quarter.

It was thus confirmed that for a large group of consumers contact with the seller is still key. They want to see, feel, try, and talk about the product before buying it. They want to have the purchased goods available immediately, and for many, shopping is a form of relaxation or experience. Obviously, online shopping has its important place in the shopping scheme. However, as it turns out, in the long run it is ideal in combination with classic shopping in brick-and-mortar stores. E-shops have therefore not replaced physical stores, but serve as their complement (FinReport.Sk, 2022).

From the results above we can say that addressing consumers of the Slovak Republic through proximity marketing is feasible.

4 Conclusion

The retail landscape has been under intense pressure for several years. The assumption was put forward about the possibility of successful implementation of hyperlocal marketing in Slovak brick-and-mortar stores using technologies associated with the fourth industrial revolution. More than half of the Slovak population owns a smartphone, the most widely used device for the implementation of proximity marketing, which represents a considerable potential for success for businesses. Already 52 % of Slovakia's population can use the fastest 5G network. All types of retail that use brick-and-mortar stores as their main sales channel saw a year-on-year increase in sales in the first quarter of 2022. On the contrary, retail trade outside stores and the market, which includes stores focused exclusively or mainly on online shopping, was the only one to experience a decrease in sales, and therefore failed to repeat the turnover from the beginning of 2021. Regarding generalizations based on methods of formal logic of data obtained from available information sources we expressed the assumption of success and validity of the hyperlocal marketing application in the specific conditions of the Slovak Republic.

Acknowledgments

The contribution is a partial output of scientific project 1/0409/23 Forensic marketing as a platform of objective empirical support for managerial decision-making processes.

References

Adobe (2021). *The Definitive Guide to Marketing Automation*. https://www.marketo.com/definitive-guides/marketing-automation/

Egol, M., Schweiger, R., Baber, Z., & Grenis, W. (2017). *Proximity marketing offers a comprehensive strategy to engage consumer*. Pwc. https://www.strategyand.pwc.com/gx/en/insights/archive/the-missing-link/the-missing- link.pdf

Falkenreck, C., Leszczyński, G., & Zieliński, M. (2023). What drives the successful launch of IoT-related business models? *Journal of Business & Industrial Marketing, 38*(13), 180–194.

Foss, N. J., & Saebi, T. (2018). Business models and business model innovation: Between wicked and paradigmatic problems. *Long Range Planning, 51*(1), 9–21.

Gajanová, Ľ., & Nadányiová, M. (2020). Reshaping of the retail environment due to internet as a global competitor. *SHS Web of Conferences*.

Kranz, M. (2016). *Building the internet of things: Implement New Business Models, Disrupt Competitors, Transform Your Industry*. John Wiley & Sons.

Lin, M. Y., Nguyen, T. T., Cheng, E. Y., Le, A. N. H., & Cheng, J. M. S. (2022). Proximity marketing and Bluetooth beacon technology: A dynamic mechanism leading to relationship program receptiveness. *Journal of Business Research, 141*, 151–162.

Markfort, L., Arzt, A., Kögler, P., Jung, S., Gebauer, H., Haugk, S., Leyh, C., & Wortmann, F. (2021). Patterns of business model innovation for advancing IoT platforms. *Journal of Service Management, 33*(1), 70–96.

Mason, K., & Chakrabarti, R. (2017). The role of proximity in business model design: Making business models work for those at the bottom of the pyramid. *Industrial Marketing Management, 61*, 67–80.

Muddinagiri, R., Ambavane, S., & Bayas, S. (2019). "Self-Hosted Kubernetes: Deploying Docker Containers Locally With Minikube," *2019 International Conference on Innovative Trends and Advances in Engineering and Technology (ICITAET)*, Shegoaon, India, 2019, pp. 239-243, doi: 10.1109/ICITAET47105.2019.9170208.

Nicholas, G., & Shapiro, A. (2020). Failed hybrids: The death and life of Bluetooth proximity marketing. *Mobile Media and Communication, 9*(3), 465–487.

Přikrylová, J. (2019). *Moderní marketingová komunikace*. Grada.

Rykowski, J., Chojnacki, T., & Strykowski, S. (2018). In-Store proximity marketing by means of IoT devices. *IFIP advances in information and communication technology* (pp. 164–174).

Sadowski, S., & Spachos, P. (2018). RSSI-Based indoor localization with the Internet of Things. *IEEE Access, 6*, 30149–30161.

Shoukry, A. M., Khader, J. A., & Gani, S. (2019). Improving business process and functionality using IoT based E3-value business model. *Electronic Markets, 31*(1), 17–26.

Wirtz, B. W., Pistoia, A., Ullrich, S., & Göttel, V. (2016). Business Models: Origin, development and future research perspectives. *Long Range Planning, 49*(1), 36–54.

Marketing Schools. (2020, November 25). *Proximity marketing*. https://www.marketing- schools.org/types-of-marketing/proximity-marketing/#section-5

Karr, D. (2021, February 5). *Proximity Marketing: What is it? What types?* Martech Zone. https://martech.zone/what-is-proximity-marketing/

Bhavsar, N. (2021, February 25). *According to AMA, the Global Proximity Marketing Market is expected to see growth rate of 28.3% and may see market size of USD 52342.0 Million by 2024*. www.linkedin.com. https://www.linkedin.com/pulse/according-ama- global-proximity-marketing-market-expected-bhavsar/

FinReport.Sk. (2022, March 6). *Obchody sa v prvom štvrťroku nadýchli, ich tržby medziročne vzrástlio 16%, klesajúlene-shopy*. www.finreport.sk. https://www.finreport.sk/podnikanie/obchody-sa-v-prvom-stvrtroku-nadychli-ich-trzby-medzirocne-vzrastli-o-16-klesaju-len-e-shopy/?host=f140e72ccbe24ee9208d0bb777698bc3

TASR. (2022, May 24). *Maloobchod mal v 1. kvartáli vyššie tržby pre otvorené kamenné obchody*. TERAZ.sk. https://www.teraz.sk/najnovsie/maloobchod-mal-v-1-kvartali- vyssie-t/635642-clanok.html

Kristoficova, L. (2023, August 15). *Slovakia – Supporting the development of 5G networks inSlovakiafor2020–2025*.https://digital-skills-jobs.europa.eu/en/actions/national-initiatives/national-strategies/slovakia-supporting- development-5g-networks

Martina Hedvičáková[1,*]

Globalization's Impact on Capital-Labor Substitution: Dynamic Model

Abstract:
Research background: Due to rapidly changing market conditions and increasing global and local competition, companies have to look for new ways to reduce their costs and increase profits. Nowadays, there is also an emphasis on high production quality, small series production adapted to the changing needs of customers, and the shortest possible delivery time. All of these variables are putting pressure on manufacturers to find new ways to succeed in an increasingly competitive environment. One possibility is to use the possibilities of Industry 4.0 and replace human work with new modern technologies.
Purpose of the article: Due to the global market environment, it is necessary to look for new ways to succeed in this competitive environment. Investments in new technologies are one of the ways to strengthen your position in the market and increase your competitive advantage. Also, the price of human labor is constantly increasing, there may not be enough of it on the market, and for this reason, investments in technology and robotics are very beneficial in the long term.
Methods: Using dynamic modeling in the Stella Professional software, the substitution between capital and labor will be modeled under the influence of Industry 4.0.
Findings & Value added: New technologies are necessary for the further development and competitiveness of the company. By replacing human labor with new technologies, lower costs, higher labor productivity, and quality production can be achieved, which are the three most important points in the current market. Dynamic modeling is a suitable tool and facilitates the understanding of these processes.

Keywords: *unemployment, forecast, gross domestic product*

JEL Classification: *E24; J24; O14*

---

* Corresponding author: martina.hedvicakova@uhk.cz

1 University of Hradec Kralove, Faculty of Informatics and Management, Rokitanskeho 62, 500 03 Hradec Kralove, Czech Republic

1 Introduction

Computer-assisted machines, robotics, and artificial intelligence (AI) have already entered many industries and automated several parts of the manufacturing process. However, there is still widespread disagreement regarding the conceptualization and modeling of the automation process itself (Acemoglu & Restrepo, 2018a).

In today's rapidly changing market environment, which is increasingly influenced by both global and local competition, companies must seek innovative strategies to optimize their costs and increase their profits. The conclusion is the emphasis on achieving high production quality, the ability to respond to the changing needs of customers through small series production, and the minimization of time data (just in time). This dynamic is putting pressure on manufacturers to discover new ways to thrive in an ever-tightening competitive environment.

One of the key approaches to achieving success in such a competitive environment is to take advantage of the opportunities offered by the Industry 4.0 initiative, also called the fourth industrial revolution. Industry 4.0 and the requirements of the present time include replacing human work with modern technologies or robots and automation of production. If you want companies to survive in a globally competitive environment, robotization and automation are inevitable (Hedvičáková & Král, 2021).

Since the market is subject to the influence of the global environment, it is necessary to look for new strategies to achieve a competitive advantage. Investments in new technologies represent one of the ways to gain a leading position in the market or to become a market leader and gain a competitive advantage. It is also necessary to consider the increasing cost of human labor and, above all, the availability of workers in the market at the moment. The Czech Republic has long had one of the lowest unemployment rates among European Union countries. The unemployment rate is below the natural rate of unemployment, which increases the cost of human labor but also complicates the acquisition of quality workers. For these reasons, investments in technology and robotization are economically inevitable in the long term for competitive reasons (Hedvičáková, 2022).

New technologies are necessary for the further development and maintenance of the company's competitiveness. By replacing work with modern technologies, lower costs, higher labor productivity and the currently necessary high quality of production can be achieved. These factors are crucial in the market environment for success and maintaining a competitive advantage. It can be stated (Ma et al., 2022) that robots are a powerful means of addressing labor shortages and productivity inefficiencies.

Industry 4.0 and related investments in modern technologies are essential for companies for their long-term growth and maintaining competitiveness in a dynamic and competitive environment.

Five broad categories of technologies (ICT, Robots, Innovation, TFP-style, Other) can be distinguished that have an impact on employment (Hötte et al., 2023). There are also new studies (Aghion et al., 2022; Hötte et al., 2023; Ma et al., 2022) that emphasize the positive effects of technology on employment. Other research (Qiu et al., 2020) emphasizes that interaction with automation technologies brings a positive effect on the financial leverage of companies. This effect is more pronounced in cases where firms face higher labor costs, perform routine tasks more intensively, face high layoff costs, have a higher proportion of minimum wage workers, and are unionized. On the contrary, other authors (Calvino & Virgillito, 2018) critically assess the role of technical changes in shaping employment dynamics at different levels of aggregation.

Other factors that may influence the faster adoption of new technologies are the negative effects of an aging population on economic growth, either due to lower labor force participation or the productivity of older workers. However, the research (Acemoglu & Restrepo, 2017) did not confirm this negative relationship but found that countries that experience faster aging have grown more in recent decades. They believe this finding could reflect faster adoption of automation technologies in countries experiencing more significant demographic change.

In the static version, where capital is fixed and technology is exogenous, automation reduces employment and the labor share and may even reduce wages, creating the opposite effects in creating new tasks. On the contrary, new models (Acemoglu & Restrepo, 2018b) endogenize the accumulation of capital and the direction of research toward automation and the creation of new tasks.

2 Methodology and the Goals of the Paper

Both primary and secondary data were used for the analysis of the replacement of human labor with capital. For this paper, a sample of companies in the manufacturing industry in the Czech Republic was selected. These firms provided information on their production processes, technologies used, employment, and payback period. This information was used to build models of the capital-labor substitution.

In parallel with the analysis of the primary data, the analysis of the secondary data was carried out. These were needed from, for example, the International Federation of Robotics (IFR), Eurostat, Czech Statistical Office, and relevant studies. This secondary data provided a general context regarding employment, productivity, and technological developments in the manufacturing industry.

Subsequently, the results of the analysis of primary and secondary data were combined and it was possible to identify general variables and dependencies in the process of capital- labor substitution in the context of Industry 4.0. Subsequently, a capital-labor substitution model was created using dynamic modeling in Stella Professional. The last step was the final analysis and interpretation of the identified trends and results, which included an evaluation of the degree and consequences of the substitution between capital and labor.

The article aims to use dynamic modeling in the Stella Professional software to model the substitution between capital and human labor under the influence of Industry 4.0.

Dynamic modeling in Stella is a method dedicated to exploring the interactions and relationships between different variables over time. The basic elements of dynamic modeling in Stella are flows, links, and stocks. The most important elements are:

Flows: Flows are rates of change that represent how something changes or moves over time. These can be physical flows (for example, a changing number of employees) or abstract flows (for example, wage consideration). Fluxes are fundamental elements of dynamic models because they capture how the amount of something changes over time.

Links: Links are connections between different elements of the model that determine how one element affects another. Links can be direct (one element affects another directly) or indirect (interaction between elements takes place through other variables). Bindings are important for modeling the relationships and dynamics between different parts of a system.

Stock: The rectangle represents stock, which is the amount of something that accumulates or stores over time. Resources can be physical (such as the amount of working population) or abstract (such as the amount of capital). Inventory is a key element because it captures the state of the system at a point in time.

Dynamic models in Stella use these elements to describe how the state of a system changes over time and what relationships and interactions affect that state. Models can be used to simulate and analyze system behavior under different conditions and to test different scenarios (Saeed, 2021). This method is useful in studying complex and dynamic systems, such as economic processes or environmental models.

3 Results

Dynamic modeling was chosen as a suitable tool that facilitates the understanding of the processes of replacement of human work by new technologies. Dynamic modeling helps to visualize and simulate different scenarios, allowing a deeper understanding of how these processes play out over the years. This enables businesses to make informed decisions, optimize resource allocation, and remain agile in a rapidly evolving technological and competitive environment.

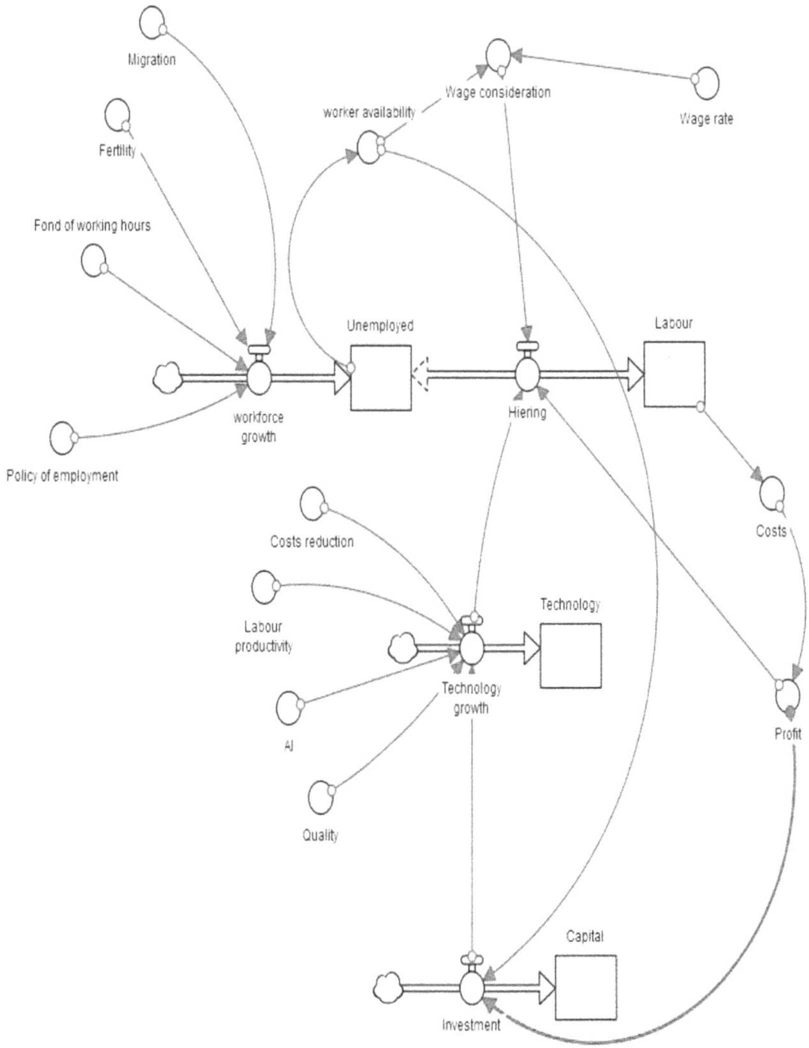

Figure 1. Links between capital and labor substitution in Stella. Source: own processing.
Source: own processing (2023)

Figure 1 illustrates the dynamic modeling of the substitution between capital and labor in the Stella Professional software. Complex relationships between key factors are shown here. The first of them is Unemployment, which depends on the growth of the labor force. Labor force growth is influenced by various parameters such as employment policies, working hours, birth rate, and migration. People's willingness to work is another important factor that affects unemployment. This willingness to work is sensitive to the level of wage rates and other economic factors. When wages are high enough and enough workers are available in the market, human labor is hired into production processes.

The transformation of unemployed individuals into workers (Labor) is a consequence of the fulfillment of certain conditions, including suitable wage rates and a sufficient number of workers. Profit growth also plays a role. If profits are sufficient, it may not be necessary to invest in technology, leading to further recruitment into the labor market.

However, if profits are insufficient or the labor market lacks sufficient workers, firms must invest in technology. These investments increase quality, an increase in labor productivity, and a reduction in the costs of the production process.

Artificial intelligence (AI) may be a key element of technological growth. Artificial intelligence can positively affect all aspects of the economy and the labor market, from automating routine tasks to creating new job opportunities in AI-related fields.

Dynamic modeling in sw Stella Professional helps to better understand and plan processes related to capital-labor substitution in the economic context.

4 Discussion

The study (Acemoglu & Restrepo, 2019) points out that the increase in the employment rate over the past three decades in the US can be explained by the following factors: the main factor has been an accelerated trend of displacement of workers, which means that technological innovation and automation have significantly reduced the need for human labor, especially in the manufacturing sector. This has led to a reduction in job opportunities and low employee growth. Other important factors were the weaker effects of the economic recovery. The economy after the recession did not have such dynamic growth as the period before, which means an increase in new jobs. This is also related to the comparison of slower labor productivity growth with previous decades. The consequence of this is that the economy does not achieve such an increase in labor productivity, which may limit the need for additional employees. The result was an impact on the labor market and its dynamics. The study (Acemoglu & Restrepo, 2019) further highlights that automation results in a continuous reduction in labor's share of value-added and can potentially lead to a reduction in labor demand, even as it increases productivity. However, these impacts of automation are offset by the creation of new tasks and areas in which human labor has a comparative advantage. In another study, the same authors (Acemoglu & Restrepo, 2020) warn that AI will evolve towards further automation, but this could lead to the promise of the "right" kind of AI with better economic and social outcomes. Another study (Korinek & Stiglitz, 2021) points out that technological advances in AI need to be managed to complement work and increase productivity.

5 Conclusion

To promote sustained growth and maintain a competitive advantage in today's fast-paced global environment, the integration of new technologies is becoming essential for every company. Embracing these innovations and replacing human labor with cutting-edge technology (robots) can bring several benefits, with the main factors in the current market environment being:

- cost reduction – with the adoption of new technologies, costs are significantly reduced. Automated systems and advanced machines can operate efficiently and consistently, minimizing operating costs associated with labor, training, and/or errors. This cost efficiency not only enables higher profitability but also provides room for investment in further technological advancement.
- increasing labor productivity using modern technologies. Machines and automated processes can perform tasks at a speed and accuracy that surpasses human capabilities. This increased productivity translates into faster production cycles, increased output, and the ability to quickly meet evolving customer demands.
- the quality of production increases by integrating new technologies. Automation and advanced machinery can ensure consistency and accuracy in manufacturing processes, reducing the likelihood of defects or errors. The result is higher quality products that meet or exceed customer expectations, ultimately increasing company reputation and customer loyalty (Hedvičáková, 2022).

Technological change occurs when the quantity and/or quality of inputs or outputs changes (Hötte et al., 2023; Ruttan, 1959; Saviotti & Pyka, 2013). This means that new technologies can bring changes to production processes, allowing firms to produce the same products with less labor or raw materials. Changes in technology can also be reflected in output, where new technologies allow firms to bring new products to market (Hötte et al., 2023) and technological changes are inevitable for economic growth.

The conclusion of the article provides a reflection on the inductive theory, which advances the perspective on the future of the workforce in both developed and developing countries. The study (Wadley, 2021) emphasizes that the changes are not confined solely to the immediate relationship between capital and labor but extend to industrial and market organization, the global geo-economic order, and the worldwide population. Furthermore, it highlights the ongoing evolution of the digital revolution, altering the occupational structure in the market, automating tasks through new technologies, and responding to the growing influence of artificial intelligence. This dynamic has a significant impact on consumer demand and requires constant attention and adaptation from the workforce and business structures (Chen et al., 2022).

Acknowledgments

"The work was supported by the internal project 'SPEV – Economic Impacts under the Industry 4.0 / Society 5.0 Concept,' 2023, University of Hradec Králové, Faculty of Informatics and Management, Czech Republic. The authors are grateful to the student Zdeněk Novák, who collaborated on feedback on the overall concept and editing of the article."

References

Acemoglu, D., & Restrepo, P. (2017). Secular stagnation? The effect of aging on economic growth in the age of automation. *American Economic Review, 107*(5), 174–179.

Acemoglu, D., & Restrepo, P. (2018a). Modeling automation. *AEA Papers and Proceedings, 108*, 48–53.

Acemoglu, D., & Restrepo, P. (2018b). The race between man and machine: Implications of technology for growth, factor shares, and employment. *American Economic Review, 108*(6), 1488–1542.

Acemoglu, D., & Restrepo, P. (2019). Automation and new tasks: How technology displaces and reinstates labor. *Journal of Economic Perspectives, 33*(2), 3–30.

Acemoglu, D., & Restrepo, P. (2020). The wrong kind of AI? Artificial intelligence and the future of labour demand. *Cambridge Journal of Regions, Economy and Society, 13*(1), 25–35.

Aghion, P., Celine, A., Bunel, S., & Jaravel, X. (2022). The effects of automation on labor demand: A survey of the recent literature. *CEPR Discussion Paper No. DP16868*, 2022. https://ssrn.com/abstract=4026751

Calvino, F., & Virgillito, M. E. (2018). The innovation-employment Nexus: A critical survey of theory and empirics. *Journal of Economic Surveys, 32*(1), 83–117.

Hedvičáková, M. (2022). Capital-Labor Substitution and Economic Efficiency in the Context of Industry 4.0 (J. Maci, P. Maresova, K. Firlej, & I. Soukal, Ed.; s. 243–250).

Hedvičáková, M., & Král, M. (2021). Performance evaluation framework under the influence of Industry 4.0: The case of the Czech Manufacturing Industry. *E+M Ekonomie a Management, 24*(1), Art. 1.

Hötte, K., Somers, M., & Theodorakopoulos, A. (2023). Technology and jobs: A systematic literature review. *Technological Forecasting and Social Change, 194*, 122750.

Chen, N., Sun, D., & Chen, J. (2022). Digital transformation, labour share, and industrial heterogeneity. *Journal of Innovation & Knowledge, 7*(2), 100173.

Korinek, A., & Stiglitz, J. E. (2021). Covid-19 driven advances in automation and artificial intelligence risk exacerbating economic inequality. *BMJ*, n367.

Ma, X., Mao, C., & Liu, G. (2022). Can robots replace human beings? – Assessment on the developmental potential of construction robot. *Journal of Building Engineering, 56*, 104727.

Qiu, J., Wan, C., & Wang, Y. (2020). Automatability and capital structure. *SSRN Electronic Journal.*

Ruttan, V. W. (1959). Usher and Schumpeter on invention, innovation, and technological change. *The Quarterly Journal of Economics, 73*(4), 596.

Saeed, K. (2021). Limits to growth concepts in classical economics. In R. Y. Cavana, B. C. Dangerfield, O. V. Pavlov, M. J. Radzicki, & I. D. Wheat (Ed.), *Feedback economics* (s. 217–246). Springer International Publishing.

Saviotti, P. P., & Pyka, A. (2013). The co-evolution of innovation, demand and growth. *Economics of Innovation and New Technology, 22*(5), 461–482.

Wadley, D. (2021). Technology, capital substitution and labor dynamics: Global workforce disruption in the 21st century? *Futures, 132*, 102802.

Zaneta Karazijiene[1,*], and Migle Eleonora Cernikovaite[2]

Assessment of Innovation Factors in Lithuanian Small and Medium-sized Agricultural Enterprises

Abstract:
Research background: Today, innovation is becoming not only a source of competitive advantage for agriculture but also a crucial prerequisite for survival. Most of the innovations mentioned in the literature focus on the production of agricultural products but it is also necessary to apply innovations aimed at the storage and maintenance of the products already produced. Agricultural innovativeness is of comprehensive benefit to the state, and it is therefore important to assess the degree of innovativeness of Lithuanian small and medium-sized agricultural enterprises and the factors that promote it.
Purpose of the article: The main aim of this paper is to assess the factors influencing the innovativeness of Lithuanian agriculture.
Methods: To fulfill the aim of the paper, the methods of comparative analysis of scientific literature, questionnaire survey (quantitative research), descriptive statistics, correlation, and factor analysis were used.
Findings & Value added: The results of the study showed that both the environmental and economic aspects of innovation are important for small and medium farmers. Only some of the innovations identified in the theoretical part do not have any interest among farmers at all (e.g., the current relevance of participation in block systems). Most organizational innovations also receive minimal interest. Young farmers were found to be less likely to innovate and more constrained by various barriers to innovation.

Keywords: *agriculture, agricultural innovation, innovation types, innovation implementation, sustainability*

JEL Classification: *Q10; Q16; Q55; Q56*

* Corresponding author: zkarazijiene@mruni.eu
[1] Mykolas Romeris University, Faculty of Public Governance and Business, Ateities str. 20, 08303 Vilnius, Lithuania
[2] Vilnius Gediminas Technical University, Faculty of Creative Industries, Trakų str. 1, 01132 Vilnius, Lithuania

1 Introduction

The literature on agricultural innovation has focused on the development and application of technological innovations. More and more farms are trying to equip themselves with technologies such as sensors, batteries, drones, and meteorological information transmitters (Lopez-Morales et al., 2020). Goh (2021) identifies the following types of technological innovations in modern agriculture: biotechnology; information and communication technologies (ICT); data analysis tools; Internet of things (IoT) equipment and applications; robots and other automation solutions; and blockchain.

Technological innovations (especially ICT) have led to the development of the concept of precision farming. Precision farming has the dual objectives of increasing productivity and reducing ecological damage. The concepts of precision farming and digital farming are said to overlap and complement each other. Van Es and Woodard (2017) argue that today's agricultural innovation trend is more accurately defined as digital farming rather than precision farming, as many of the tools used to improve performance are based on digital technologies. Digital innovation enables optimized, personalized, highly connected, data- driven and real-time management.

It can be noted that most of the innovations mentioned in the literature are focused on the production of agricultural products, but that innovations for the storage and maintenance of the products already produced are also necessary. Digitized solutions allow farmers to extend the shelf-life of produce, monitor freshness and quality information, and increase security and convenience (Bickauske et al., 2020). At the same time, innovative storage systems help to reduce the problem of wastage of unsold produce (Sira & Pukala, 2020).

According to Vidickiene et al. (2013), agricultural improvement should not be limited to technological innovations. Organisational innovations, which include the introduction of new methods of marketing, logistics, accounting, and work organisation, are equally relevant in agriculture. Goh (2021) points out that digital innovations can lead to better access to financial resources and easier access to new markets.

In view of environmental concerns, farmers are also advised to apply eco-innovation, i.e., to find ways to shorten supply chains and to market their produce in nearby (local) markets. According to Sira and Pukala (2020), one way to improve the financial sustainability of agriculture is to create a direct link between the producer and the consumer and to cut out the middlemen. Such a solution increases the consumer's trust in the farmer's products. At the same time, it can increase sales and the farmer's share of profits.

Goh (2021) also argues in support of the benefits of digitising farms that creating opportunities for direct sales to consumers eliminates intermediaries who do not add any value to the farm. Blakeney (2022) argues that farmers need to apply modern marketing innovations to market their products themselves. Using digital technologies, farmers can carry out e-commerce themselves. The direct marketing of agricultural products without intermediaries is particularly relevant for small farmers. By creating more added value, farmers are adopting new business models, becoming not only growers, but also producers, offering their own food, cosmetics, etc. to the market.

In summary, the literature analysis shows that innovations in agriculture can be divided into three main groups: product innovations, technological process innovations and organisational innovations (see Table 1).

Innovativeness within an agricultural company is determined by human resources, financial resources, knowledge and technology, organisational structure and management. External factors can strengthen or weaken the potential of a company's existing capabilities. External factors include political factors, the science and research system, infrastructure factors, legal factors and market factors.

External factors include political factors, the science and research system, infrastructure factors, legal factors and market factors.

Table 1. Types of agricultural innovation.

AGRICULTURAL INNOVATION		
Product innovation New and improved products	**Technological process innovation** Precision farming Renewable energy Collection of economic data Information management and solutions Automation and robotics Smart storage and processing	**Organizational innovation** Quality management Marketing solutions Participation in block systems Direct sales to consumers Participation in research activities

Source: compiled by Ministry of Agriculture (2021), Vidickiene et al. (2013), Goh (2021), Van Es and Woodard (2017), Sira and Pukala (2020), Kamilaris et al. (2021)

According to Bickauskas et al. (2020), technologies such as mobile applications, social networks, precision farming and remote sensing systems are not new to the agricultural sector, but technological advances have already reached a new level, where information management is based on Big Data analysis, block chain systems, machine learning, artificial intelligence, robotics, and autonomous control systems. It is assumed that the gap between innovative and lagging farms is widening with the acceleration of technological progress. Companies that are late adopters of digital innovations risk being left behind in the digital supply chain. This threat leads to the need to look at economic, financial, social and other factors that encourage farms to go beyond long- established, simple and resource-efficient innovations and keep up with the latest trends.

Private agriculture under-invests in areas that are important for agricultural development and do not generate direct commercial benefits, such as the environment, food security and nutrition. The economic and financial determinants of agricultural innovativeness will be analyzed below

Due to the high demand for investment, developed economies tend to have higher levels of innovation. In addition, a country's economic development helps to keep investment in innovation constant (Rawat, 2020).

While economic development is an important precondition for innovation, even in economically strong countries, small farms lack the resources needed to apply cutting-edge innovation (Maziliauskas et al., 2018; Peillon & Dubrue, 2019; Van Es & Woodard, 2017; Schuh et al., 2017). Maziliauskas et al. (2018) add that the financial capacity of farms to innovate is further constrained by rising operating costs. Rising operating costs do not leave profits that can be reinvested in innovation. Various financing mechanisms are used to address the financial constraints of agriculture. It is in the interest of the State to encourage the development of innovation, as its success has a positive impact on the economic growth of the country.

Although financial resources are one of the most commonly highlighted constraints to innovation, according to Peillon and Dubruc (2019), companies often tend to have misconceptions about the complexity and costs of innovation. This leads to the assumption that farmers lack information as much as financial resources. The issue of farmers' awareness is closely linked to the social and institutional determinants of innovativeness.

Given that innovation promotion mechanisms are publicly funded, institutional factors are determined by the political context. The political environment for innovation includes the tax system, laws and political relations with other countries. According to Blakeney (2022), agricultural challenges posed by population growth, the threat of food insecurity, environmental degradation and climate change have led many governments to target investments in science, technology and innovation. Fostering innovation in the country's regions reduces the socio-economic divide compared to the country's major cities. These actions are a prerequisite for economic growth not only for individual countries but also for Europe as a whole (Sund et al., 2018). According to Daniteviciene

(2022), investments in agricultural innovation in government programmes are the most common example of engagement in agriculture, but equally relevant are the regulation of tax policies to facilitate investment in innovation development and the protection of intellectual property rights to increase incentives for private firms to conduct private agricultural research. Meanwhile, the stagnation of innovative activity is due to legislative factors such as slow development of the legislative framework or its inadequacy to adapt to local business conditions (Krusinskas & Benetyte, 2014).

It is notable that rural development programmes focus on technological innovation. Particular importance has been given to the development of infrastructure for alternative energy sources (wind, solar, biogas, etc.). According to Melnikiene and Vidickiene (2019), insufficient attention is paid to non-technological innovations. With the rise of the sharing economy concept, networking and servitisation in agribusiness models, few initiatives have been supported in Lithuania to innovate in these models. It is believed that the success of innovation strategy innovation in Lithuania will be determined by the introduction of managerial, marketing and social innovations in agriculture.

One of the most researched factors determining the level of innovativeness of a farm is its size. Small farms are less likely to innovate (Mwagi & Kariuki, 2015; Ramanauskas & Kirstukas, 2009). Small farms are particularly lacking in human resources. The ideas generated, their development, shaping and implementation depend directly on humans (Labarthe et al., 2021). Human resource management cannot be limited to finding and selecting the best professionals (Ma & Yu, 2021). Innovative companies need to manage their human resources, which, according to Jewell et al. (2020), includes investing in employees, fostering loyalty, setting long-term goals and allocating tangible and intangible resources.

Mwagi and Kariuki (2015) also point out that agricultural innovativeness is determined by engagement with farmers' social structures (communities). Some of the determinants of farm innovativeness are related to the characteristics of their owners. According to Olum et al. (2017), education is the most important farmer characteristic that determines the propensity to innovate. Farmers with higher education are more likely to innovate. Another determinant of innovativeness is the age of farmers. Olum et al. (2017), after structuring the results of studies on the determinants of farmers' innovativeness, point out that many studies have found a relationship between innovativeness and age, with younger farmers being more likely to innovate.

In summary, agricultural innovation is driven by the growing demand for innovation – growing consumer needs, environmental requirements and competitiveness. However, the innovativeness of farms (especially small farms) is constrained by a number of factors, which can be divided into several groups: innovation-related factors, farm- related factors, economic and financial factors, social and institutional factors. It can be seen that many of the different factors of innovativeness are closely intertwined and are conditioned by the socio-economic structure of a country. This makes it difficult to increase the level of agricultural innovation, as direct incentives such as financial incentives and advisory mechanisms are not enough.

2 Methods

The quantitative part of the research methodology is implemented through a questionnaire survey of small and medium-sized farmers. A questionnaire is a formalised questionnaire designed to collect the required information from the intended group of. Given that the object of this study is the promotion of innovation in small and medium-sized farms, a questionnaire is the most convenient way to collect a large array of quantitative information to find out the prevailing barriers to innovation in small and medium-sized farms in Lithuania and the desired additional incentives. The questionnaire consists of four thematic blocks: (1) innovation experience; (2) the need for innovation in agriculture (Identifying what factors motivate farmers to innovate. The answer options are based on Bickauske et al. (2020), Sira and Pukala (2020), Goh (2021), Van Es and Woodard (2017), Kamilaris et al. (2021), etc.); (3) Barriers to and encouragement of innovation (answer options based on Ashari et al. (2020), Maziliauskas et al. (2018), Van Es and Woodard (2017), Schuh et al. (2017), Melnikiene and Vidickiene (2019)); (4) Sociodemographic issues.

Study sample. According to the Ministry of Agriculture of Lithuania, there are 80.9 thousand small and medium-sized farms in Lithuania in 2021, so the formula for large populations is used to calculate the sample (Gaizauskaite & Mikene, 2014):

$$n = t^2 p(1-p) / \Delta^2 \tag{1}$$

where n is sample size; t is the confidence level; p is the distribution coefficient; Δ is sampling error.

The formula is applied with a 5 % ($\Delta = 0.05$) margin of error and a 95 % confidence level ($t = 1.96$). The coefficient of distribution of the unknown is therefore the value where p(1-p) takes the highest value ($p = 0.5$) (Gaizauskaite & Mikene, 2014). After calculating the sample according to the above formula, it was found that the minimum number of respondents should be 384 in order to carry out a survey with a margin of error of 5 %. However, once the threshold of 336 questionnaires was reached, the completion of new questionnaires stopped, resulting in a revised reliability of 5.3 %.

The questionnaire was almost evenly split in terms of the size of the farm. 50.9 % of the respondents have a farm of less than 10 ha and 49.1 % have a farm of more than 10 ha. The highest proportion of respondents was between 26 and 35 years of age (45.2 %). Respondents aged 36–45 also made up a large proportion of the participants (33.3 %). Respondents aged 45–55 made up 9.2 % of the participants. Respondents aged over 55 accounted for 6.3 % of the participants. The youngest farmers were the least represented in the survey, with farmers under 25 years of age accounting for 6 % of the survey participants.

In terms of education, the largest share of the survey participants were farmers with a university degree (45.5 %). 29.5 % of the respondents have a non-university degree, 13.7 % have a vocational degree and 11.3 % have a secondary education.

The study was carried out between 1 October and 9 November 2023. The questionnaire was distributed in two ways – electronically and physically. The electronic questionnaire will be distributed through social networking groups and online farmer forums. The physical distribution of the questionnaires was carried out through the District Farmers' Associations. The data from the physical questionnaires collected are fed into a common data package together with the data from the electronically distributed questionnaires. Descriptive statistics, correlation and factor analysis were used for statistical analysis of the data.

Research ethics. The principles of freedom, anonymity, privacy and confidentiality were respected during the survey. The interview questionnaire was designed to make the questions easy to understand, but not straightforward and primitive, to reflect the content of the problem, and to avoid wasting the respondents' time by answering irrelevant or insignificant questions.

3 Results and Discussions

The first questionnaire survey was designed to find out what proportion of respondents had innovated on their farm. It turned out that the proportion of farmers who had innovated was lower than the survey respondents' 44.3 %. As many as 55.7 % of the respondents did not introduce any innovation during this period.

Innovation trends on respondents' farms were assessed from a number of perspectives, comparing innovation performance by farm size, farm type, farmer education and age. It showed that innovation was more frequent among owners of larger farms. In the group of farms up to 10 ha, 37.4 % of respondents had innovated (62.6 % had not). In the group of owners of farms larger than 10 ha, slightly more than half of the respondents (51.5 %) had innovated (48.5 % had not). The analysis in terms of education showed that only 13.2 % of respondents with secondary education had implemented innovations (86.8 % had not). Thus, respondents with the lowest level of education were the least likely to innovate. The cross- analysis shows that farmers with non-university higher education are the most likely to innovate. In total, 64.6 % of farmers with non-university higher education innovated (35.4 % did not).

The survey also disproves the common perception that young farmers are the most likely to innovate. It is the youngest group of farmers who are the least likely to innovate. Only 29.7 % of farmers under 35 years of age have innovated on their farm (70.3 % have not). Farmers aged between 36 and 45 were the most likely to innovate on their farms. In total, 70.5 % of respondents in this age group had introduced an innovation on their farm (29.5 % had not). In the group of farmers aged over 45, the proportion of respondents who had innovated was 41.2 % (60.8 % had not). However, these results do not invalidate the claim that young farmers have a high potential for innovation. Innovation is also dependent on opportunities.

Respondents were asked about recent innovations on their farms. The question was open- ended, so respondents' answers were analyzed through content analysis. The categories of responses correspond to the typology of agricultural innovation developed in the theoretical part of the paper, distinguishing between product, process and organisational innovations. The theoretical analysis revealed that process innovation is the most focused area in the scientific literature. The results of the questionnaire survey show that this type of innovation is also the most popular among the farmers who participated in the study. In total, process innovations were mentioned 115 times in the respondents' answers. Innovations for on-farm data collection and analysis (sensors, drones, etc.) are particularly popular, with 11.9 % of respondents having implemented them. Innovations in renewable energy (6.8 %), precision farming (4.2 %), tillage techniques (3 %), warehousing, logistics and field machinery (2.7 % each) were also popular (see Table 2).

In order to analyze the barriers to innovation on respondents' farms, farmers were asked how they themselves perceived their previous innovation experience. It was found that the majority of respondents had a positive perception of their experience of innovation (54.70 %), 16.30 % of respondents said they had a negative perception of their experience and a surprisingly high proportion of respondents (29 %) either had no opinion on the matter or had never innovated.

A comparison of the experience ratings of the different groups of respondents shows that there is a particular difference in the experience of innovation between owners of farms larger and smaller than 10 ha. Farmers with more than 10 ha were more than twice as likely to rate their innovation experience positively (64.7 %). In the group of owners of farms smaller than 10 ha, only 24.2 % of respondents were positive about their innovation experience. The results suggest that innovation is more difficult for smallholders in particular.

Table 2. Innovations used by respondents' farms in the last 24 months.

Category	Subcategory	Mentioned times	Percentage of total respondents
Process innovation	Farm data collection and analysis (sensors, drones, statistical data analysis, geolocation)	40	11.9 %
	Renewable energy (solar, wind, etc.)	23	6.8 %
	Precision farming (fertiliser, water requirements, soil testing)	14	4.2 %
	Cultivation methods (conservation tillage, direct drilling)	10	3.0 %
	Modernization of warehousing and logistics	9	2.7 %
	Modernization of outdoor machinery	9	2.7 %
	Methods of processing products	6	1.8 %
	Automation of livestock feeding	2	0.6 %
	Protection against rodents, erosion, etc.	2	0.6 %
	Total: 115		
Product innovation	Biotechnology (new vaccines, fertilisers)	12	3.0 %
	New products	8	1.5 %
	New services (wine tasting, rural tourism)	2	0.6 %
	Total: 22		
Organizational innovation	Quality management	7	2.1 %
	Direct sales	6	1.8 %
	Marketing (logo, brand)	4	1.2 %
	Accounting automation	2	0.6 %
	Staff motivation system	1	0.3 %
	Eco certificates	1	0.3 %
	Participation in the knowledge creation system	1	0.3 %
	Total: 22		

Source: compiled by authors

Looking at the objectives of innovation in Lithuanian agriculture, it has become clear that farmers have different innovation objectives. Respondents could choose more than one objective in response to the question, but the majority of respondents chose only one objective of most relevance to them. The results show that there is no dominant innovation objective. The least important motivation for farmers to innovate is to reduce costs, with only 12.5 % of respondents identifying this as an important objective, although theoretical analysis has highlighted the problem of rising costs of farming (see Figure 1).

Farmers are also keen on the environmental aspect of innovation, with 21.4 % of respondents indicating that sustainability is one of the most important objectives when innovating.

The questionnaire survey also sought to find out whether innovating farmers perceive innovation as an important part of their farming activities. Farmers were asked whether they would recommend innovation to other farms. The majority of innovating farmers indicated that they would recommend innovation to other farms (47.3 %). Only 5.7 % of respondents would not recommend innovation. A further 47 % said they had no opinion on the matter or had never innovated themselves.

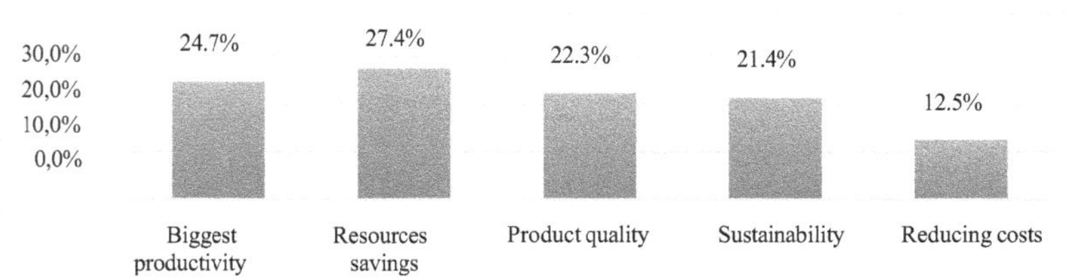

Figure 1. Farmers' top innovation objectives.
Source: compiled by authors

The analysis of the questionnaire survey also shows that the predominant attitude among respondents is one of commitment to future innovation, with a total of 67.9 % of respondents indicating that they intend to innovate in the future. Only 2.1 % of respondents do not intend to innovate in agriculture. Of particular relevance in the context of this study is the proportion of farmers who are hesitant to innovate, with a total of 28.3 % of respondents indicating that they are not sure whether they will innovate in agriculture in the future.

Respondents to the questionnaire also revealed which agricultural innovations are most relevant to them. It showed that the innovations of most interest to the farmers who took part in the survey were those related to automation and robotics (50.6 %), renewable energy (45.2 %) and precision farming (41.7 %). Thus, technological process innovations dominate among the most relevant innovations (see Figure 2).

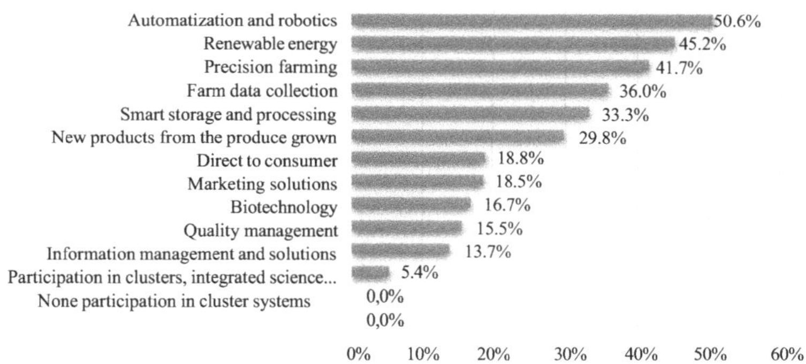

Figure 2. Innovations most relevant to respondents.

Source: compiled by authors

It is worth noting that there were no respondents who indicated that they were not interested in any innovation, although 2.7 % of respondents in the previous question stated that they had no intention to innovate. It should be noted that in this question respondents could choose more than one answer option. It is estimated that on average one respondent chose 3 relevant innovations in response to the question.

Having established the respondents' attitudes towards agricultural innovation, the next step is to analyze the barriers to innovation and the incentives for innovation. Participants were asked to rate, on a 5-point scale, the factors limiting innovation in their agriculture. The dominant barrier to innovation in agriculture was found to be limited financial possibilities (4.34 points). The second most important factor is also related to the financial aspect of innovation, i.e., the complexity of support schemes (3.96 points) (Table 3).

Table 3. Innovations used by respondents' farms in the last 24 months.

	Average	Asymp. Sig. (2-sided)
Limited financial possibilities	4.34	0.045
Complicated support schemes	3.96	0.005
Lack of knowledge/available information on innovation	3.55	0.133
Lack of innovation-savvy professionals	3.53	0.034
Increasing farming risks	3.24	0.048
Lack of time to take an interest in innovation	3.16	0.075
Lack of legislation on innovation	3.16	0.233
Shortage of agricultural professionals	3.12	0.048
Concerns about cybersecurity	2.63	0.133
Critical evaluation of innovation among staff	2.51	0.068
Negative past experience with innovation	2.30	0.048

Source: compiled by authors

The results show that not all of the factors limiting innovation in agriculture discussed in the theoretical part of the study are really significant. The vast majority of respondents were found to be more likely to innovate if additional incentives were provided. Overall, 90.5 % of respondents indicated that additional measures/incentives could encourage more innovation in their agriculture. Only 7.1% of respondents would not be encouraged by any additional measures/incentives. 2.4 % of respondents had no opinion on this issue. This shows that there is a need to promote innovation in small and medium-sized agriculture.

Table 4. Values of innovation drivers.

	Average	Asym.Sig. (2-sided)
Clearer innovation support scheme	4.13	0.050
More tangible and measurable benefits of innovation	4.07	0.023
More information on innovation in Lithuanian	4.04	0.048
Positive experience of other agricultural innovations	3.93	0.133
Increased competence of innovation professionals in agriculture	3.87	0.068
Opportunities to share innovation experiences with other farms	3.83	0.133
Personalized innovation advice	3.82	0.039
More frequent/easier access to workshops/training on innovation	3.82	0.075
Improving your digital literacy	3.27	0.233
Improved foreign language skills	3.21	0.048

Source: compiled by authors

Respondents ranked on a 5-point scale the innovations that could have the biggest impact on their decision to increase their adoption of agricultural innovations. Table 4 shows the calculated means of the estimates and the reliability value (p-level) complex support schemes. The assessment of the incentives to innovate also differs between the two groups (see Table 5).

Table 5. Barriers to agricultural innovation and the need to promote innovation in relation to farm size.

	Up to 10 ha	**More than 10 ha**
Assessing the constraints to innovation		
Limited financial possibilities	4.17	4.52
Complicated support schemes	3.71	4.21
Lack of knowledge/available information on innovation	3.38	3.73
Critical evaluation of innovation among staff	2.36	2.67
Lack of time to take an interest in innovation	3.04	3.28
Lack of innovation-savvy professionals	3.08	3.99
Shortage of agricultural professionals	2.64	3.64
Concerns about cybersecurity	2.44	2.82
Increasing farming risks	2.70	3.79
Lack of legislation on innovation	2.94	3.39
Negative past experience with innovation	2.03	2.59
Measuring incentives to innovate		
Clearer innovation support scheme	4.42	3.82
Personalized innovation advice	3.91	3.73
Opportunities to share innovation experiences with other farms	3.67	4.00
Positive experience of other agricultural innovations	3.94	3.93
More tangible and measurable benefits of innovation	3.89	4.24
More frequent/easier access to workshops/training on innovation	4.08	3.54
Increased competence of innovation professionals in agriculture	4.02	3.71
Improving your digital literacy	3.34	3.21
Improved foreign language skills	3.40	3.02
More information on innovation in Lithuanian	4.07	4.00

Source: compiled by authors

Smaller farm owners would value additional incentives such as clearer innovation support schemes (4.42 points), more frequent training and seminars (4.08 points), greater competence of innovation specialists in agriculture (4.02 points), better digital literacy (3.34 points), better foreign language skills (3.40 points). Although owners of larger farms are more likely to acknowledge the influence of factors limiting innovation, they are more sceptical about the impact on their innovativeness of measures aimed at addressing these factors. Larger farm owners are more likely than small farm owners to value the more tangible and measurable benefits of innovation (4.24 points) and the opportunity to share innovation experience with other farms (4 points). Both groups of respondents significantly value the need for information in Lithuanian (owners of farms up to 10 ha – 4.07 points, owners of farms larger than 10 ha – 4 points).

It was also decided to analyze separately the differences in the perceptions of farmers who intend to innovate and those who are hesitant to innovate in the future, in terms of barriers and incentives to innovation. It turned out that for the group of farmers hesitant to innovate, the increasing risk of farming (3.98 points) and the lack of legislation on innovation (3.74 points) were significantly more important factors. Despite these differences, in both groups, the most significant factors limiting innovation are limited financial possibilities and complicated support schemes (4.3 for those who intend to innovate and 4.27 for those who are hesitant to innovate).

The theoretical analysis revealed that farmers' awareness is one of the key prerequisites for agricultural innovativeness, so it was also important to find out how the system of seminars/training for farmers functions and how it could be improved. It was found that the majority of respondents had never used the opportunity to participate in a seminar or training related to innovation (61 %). Only 39 % of respondents had attended such workshops at least once.

The majority of respondents would like to receive training and seminars on advanced agricultural techniques (33 %) and financial support solutions (31.8 %). Other training and seminar topics do not seem to be as relevant for farmers. 14.3 % of farmers would like to learn more about organic farming solutions, 12.2 % would like to learn more about digitization of agriculture and 11 % would like to learn more about marketing and e-commerce opportunities. It should be noted that respondents could choose more than one answer option, but the majority of farmers in the survey indicated only one relevant training/seminar topic.

In summary, there is a need for additional incentives for innovation in small and medium- sized agriculture. Although there are agricultural innovation measures, training and seminars on innovation in Lithuania, the existing measures are considered insufficient. The vast majority of farmers indicated that additional incentives would encourage more innovation on their farms. The most important barrier to innovation on farms is the limited financial possibilities. However, there are other significant constraints, the expression of which depends on the characteristics of the farm (size, type of farm, owner's education, age, innovation experience).

4 Conclusions

The survey showed that less than half of the small and medium-sized farmers surveyed (44.3 %) were innovating, even though innovation in agriculture is now seen as a necessity and an ongoing process. Despite the fact that a lower proportion of respondents have innovated in the last period, the majority of farmers have a positive attitude towards innovation. Positive attitudes towards innovation are reflected both in the intention of many to innovate in the future and in the propensity to recommend innovation to other farmers.

The results also showed that both the environmental and economic aspects of innovation are important to farmers. The greatest interest shown by farmers is in process innovation, as shown by the analysis of the innovations implemented by respondents and the most relevant innovations highlighted. Only some of the innovations identified in the theoretical part do not have any interest among respondents at all – no respondent in the study indicated that they are currently interested in participating in blockchain systems, even though the scientific literature identifies this innovation as an opportunity to improve the management of information from the producer to the end-user, and to increase the transparency and reliability of agricultural activity. Most organisational innovations have also received minimal attention, although some, such as marketing solutions and direct selling opportunities, are of particular interest to small and medium-sized farms as a way of improving the financial sustainability of agriculture, increasing sales and the farm's share of profits by eliminating non-value-creating intermediaries. It is also worth noting that organisational innovations generally require less investment and are therefore more accessible to small and medium- sized farms. However, the farmers surveyed are most interested in one of the most investment-intensive areas of innovation – robotics and automation.

The results of the study confirmed the observations of many researchers (Peillon and Dubrue, 2019, cited in Bickauske et al., 2020; Van Es & Woodard, 2017; Schuh et al., 2017) that the dominant factor limiting innovativeness is the financial constraint. It should be noted that the impact of financial constraints on the ability to innovate is particularly significant for farmers aged under 35. Young farmers were found to be less likely to innovate and more constrained by various barriers to innovation, such as lack of knowledge/available information on innovation, lack of time to be interested in innovation, lack of specialists with knowledge of innovation, lack of specialists with knowledge of farming. The most desired incentives for farmers to innovate are clearer innovation schemes, more information on innovation in English, more tangible and measurable benefits of innovation.

The dissemination of good practice is important in promoting innovation in small and medium-sized agriculture. Farmer organisations (associations and cooperatives) should be used to improve the dissemination of innovation practices. The dissemination of knowledge, information on innovation and good practice is also limited by the low involvement of farmers in educational activities. 61 % of respondents have never participated in any training/seminars related to innovation.

References

Ashari, N. F. N., Saliem, H. P., Maulana, M., Ariningsih, E., & Septanti, K. S. (2020). The determinants of sustainable agricultural technology adoption. *Forum penelitian Agro Ekonomi, 38*(1), 1.

Bickauske, D., Sermuksnyte-Alesiuniene, K., & Simanaviciene, Z. (2020). Skaitmenines transformacijos issuuiai zemes ukio sektoriuje. *Visuomenes saugumas ir viesoji tvarka*, 24, 45–56.

Blakeney, M. (2022). Agricultural innovation and Sustainable Development. *Sustainability, 14*(5), 2698.

Danileviciene, S. (2022). Zemes ukio produktyvumo vertinimo teoriniai modeliai. *19- osios jaunųju mokslininku konferencijos straipsniu rinkinys*, 314–318.

Gaizauskaite, I., & Mikene, S. (2014). *Socialiniu tyrimo metodai: apklausa.* Vilnius: Mykolo Romerio universitetas.

Goh, L. (2021). *How AgriTech Is Transforming Traditional Agriculture in Emerging Markets "Think Big, Act Fast, Start Small".* https://www.brookings.edu/wp-content/uploads/2021/12/Chapter-Seven_Breakthrough.pdf

Jewell, D. O., Jewell, S. F., & Kaufman, B. E. (2020). Designing and implementing high-performance work systems: Insights from consulting practice for academic researchers. *Human Resource Management Review, 32*(1).

Kamilaris, A., Cole, I., & Prenafeta-Bondu, F. X. (2021). Blockchain in agriculture. *Food Technology Disruptions*, 247–284.

Krusinskas, R., & Benetyte, R. (2014). Inovacijos įmonės veiklos kontekste: teorinis aspektas. *Science and Studies of Accounting and Finance: Problems and Perspectives, 9*(1), 77–82.

Labarthe, P., Coleno, F., Enjalbert, J., Fugeray-Scarbel, A., Hannachi, M., & Lemarie, S. (2021). Exploration, exploitation and environmental innovation in agriculture. The case of variety mixture in France and Denmark. *Technological Forecasting and Social Change, 172*, 1210–1228.

Lopez-Morales, J. A., Martinez, J. A., & Skarmeta, A. F. (2020). Digital transformation of agriculture through the use of an interoperable platform. *Sensors, 20*(4), 1153.

Ma, B., & Yu, D. (2021). Research on the influence of R&D human resources on innovation capability – Empirical research on GEM-listed enterprises of China. *Managerial and Decision Economics, 42*(3), 751–761.

Maziliauskas, A., Baranauskiene, J., & Pakeltiene, R. (2018). Factors of effectiveness of European innovation partnership in agriculture. *Management Theory and Studies for Rural Business and Infrastructure Development, 40*(2), 216–231.

Melnikiene, R., & Vidickiene, D. (2019). Lietuvos zemes ukio politikos vertinimas remiantis kokybines strukturos analizes metodu. *Viesoji politika ir administravimas, 18*(1), 52–67.

Ministry of Agriculture. (2021). *Zemes ukio ziniu ir inovaciju sistemos 2023–2027 m. Koncepcinis modelis.* https://zum.lrv.lt/uploads/zum/documents/files/ZUZIS%20koncepcija%202021%2005%202 .pdf

Mwagi, M., & Kariuki, S. (2015). Factors determining adoption of new agricultural technology by smallholder farmers in developing countries. *Journal of Economics and Sustainable Development, 6*(5), 208–218.

Olum, S., Gellynck, X., Ongeng. D., & De Steur, H. (2017). Farmers' adoption of agricultural innovations: A systematic review on willingness to pay studies. *Outlook on Agriculture, 49*(3), 187–203.

Peillon, S., & Dubruc, N. (2019). Barriers to digital servitization in French manufacturing SMEs. *Procedia CIRP, 83*, 146–150.

Ramanauskas, J., & Kirstukas, J. (2009). Inovaciju pletra modernizuojant ukininku ukį. *Vadybos mokslas ir studijos – kaimo verslu ir jų infrastrukturos pletrai, 18*(3).

Rawat, S. (2020). Global volatility of public agricultural R&D expenditure. *Advances in Food Security and Sustainability, 5*, 119–143.

Schuh, G., Vogt, F., Lau, F., & Bickendorf, P. (2017). Concept of innovation transfer from corporate incubators. *2017 Portland International Conference on Management of Engineering and Technology (PICMET)*, 1–11.

Sira, E., & Pukala, R. (2020). Management of agriculture innovations: Role in economic development. *Marketing and Management of Innovations, 2*, 154–168.

Sund, K. J., Galavan, R. J., & Brusoni, S. (2018). *Cognition and innovation: A framework and invitation to explore*. Bingley: Emerald.

Van Es, H., & Woodard, J. (2017). *Innovation in agriculture and food system in digital age*. https://www.wipo.int/edocs/pubdocs/en/wipo_pub_gii_2017-chapter4.pdf

Vidickiene, D., Melnikiene, R., & Gedminaite-Raudone, Z. (2013). Inovaciju diegimo Lietuvos ukininku ukiuose motyvai ir barjerai. *Management Theory and Studies for Rural Business and Infrastructure Development, 35*(1), 140–149.

Peter Krajcovic[1,*]

The Use of Artificial Intelligence in the Marketing Communications of Micro-enterprises

Abstract:
Research background: Artificial intelligence has brought fundamental changes to many fields, including marketing and marketing communications. In this field, we can even talk about significant changes that can affect the entire process of building a communication strategy.
Purpose of the article: Academic studies indicate that there are several barriers to the adoption of artificial intelligence in business processes, including marketing and marketing communications in the small and medium-sized enterprise environment. Only a limited number of studies address the issue of AI implementation in micro-enterprises. The aim of the paper is to find out the current state of awareness and the use of artificial intelligence in marketing and marketing communication of micro- enterprises in Slovakia.
Methods: The survey was conducted on a sample of 78 micro-enterprises. Data collection took place in the period from September 25 to October 8, 2023. The method of selecting respondents was random, conditional only on the number of employes.
Findings & Value added: More than 60 % of companies have come across the term artificial intelligence. Almost 30 % of companies have come across the term but do not know exactly what it means and how it is used. Artificial intelligence has been used by 37 %, but outside of business activities. No company is using AI for marketing or marketing communications. However, in more than 30 % of cases, entrepreneurs said they did not know what benefits artificial intelligence could bring them. Lack of experience and knowledge are among the most common and biggest barriers to adopting artificial intelligence tools.

Keywords: *artificial Intelligence, micro-enterprises, marketing, marketing communications*

JEL Classification: *M30; M31; M39*

* Corresponding author: peter.krajcovic@ucm.sk

1 University of Ss. Cyril and Methodius in Trnava, Faculty of Mass Media Communication, Nam. J. Herdu 2, 917 01 Trnava, Slovakia

1 Introduction

The use of artificial intelligence is an important and topical aspect of business development and innovation. This applies to large and medium-sized enterprises as well as small and micro-enterprises. Corporate communication is also becoming important from the point of view of development and innovation, both internally and externally. The use of artificial intelligence (AI) in small and micro enterprises is an equally important aspect of modern business. AI offers these businesses new opportunities for automation, efficiency and competitiveness. Not all enterprises, especially in the small and micro enterprise segment, have been able to effectively implement artificial intelligence tools in their management processes, including the process of creating a communication strategy.

According to the European Business Survey on the Use of Technologies Based on Artificial Intelligence (European Commission, 2020), 78 % of companies say they know what the term Artificial Intelligence is, while only 7 % do not know and 15 % are unsure. At a more granular level, awareness of specific AI technologies is consistently high, ranging from 87 % for anomaly detection to 96 % of companies aware of autonomous machines. Awareness of AI is clearly not a major barrier to AI adoption in Europe, except for a small cohort of enterprises. Looking at Europe as a whole, businesses tend to fall into one of two camps: 'adopters' (42 %), who are currently using at least one AI technology, and 'non-adopters' (40 %), who are not currently using AI and do not intend to use any of the AI technologies (at least in the next two years). The remaining 18 % of organisations represent a significant proportion that plan to adopt AI in the next two years, despite not currently using AI solutions in their organisation. The intensity of adoption also shows encouraging signs, with a quarter (25 %) of organisations using at least two AI technologies.

Vlacic et al. (2021) point out that a growing body of research on intelligent systems/artificial intelligence (AI) in marketing has shown that AI is capable of imitating humans and performing activities in an 'intelligent' manner. As a result of the growing interest in AI among marketing researchers and practitioners, we can expect to see more research focused on the possibilities of using AI, as well as a deeper understanding of the principles of its operation in marketing and marketing communication.

According to Dimitrieska et al. (2018), in the coming years, companies can expect a greater impact of AI through smarter search, smarter advertising, more sophisticated content delivery, reliance on bots and continuous learning. Fraud and data breach prevention, sentiment analysis, image and speech recognition, sales forecasting, language recognition, predictive customer service and customer segmentation will also be challenges.

This paper analyses the use of artificial intelligence tools in marketing communications. It examines the degree of use of these tools in the conditions of micro-enterprises in Slovakia, compares the current situation with foreign countries and gives recommendations for the use of artificial intelligence in the process of creating a communication strategy.

1.1 Theoretical Starting Points and Analysis of the Current State

Several academic papers and studies have been devoted to the issues and possibilities of using artificial intelligence in the business environment. Most of them focus on understanding how AI affects companies and how these companies can use AI to improve their operations. In the literature, we can find several important directions related to the use of artificial intelligence.

Brynjolfsson and McAfee (2015) discuss the impact of artificial intelligence on the labour market and businesses, including small and micro enterprises. Davenport (2018) provides examples of the successful use of artificial intelligence in business and highlights its benefits for small businesses. Bartik et al. (2020) investigate how small and micro enterprises use technology, including artificial intelligence, to adapt to new conditions during the COVID- 19 pandemic. Casadesus-Masanell and Zhu (2013) look at the use of artificial intelligence in new business models for small businesses. Elliott (2019) provides an overview of the opportunities and challenges of implementing artificial intelligence in small and micro enterprises.

Wirtz et al. (2016) describe different business models that can be applied in small businesses using artificial intelligence. Hitt et al. (2018) examine how small businesses use ERP systems with integrated artificial intelligence to increase their efficiency. A study by Chen and Xie (2011) looks at the use of sentiment analysis and machine learning to analyze online reviews for small businesses. Popovic et al. (2018) focus on the use of AI for personalized advertising. Their study shows that AI can help micro and small businesses to create personalized advertising based on customer data. This increases the effectiveness of advertising campaigns. Rialti et al (2017) look at predictive analytics for marketing, which helps small businesses predict customer behavior and adapt their marketing campaigns based on these predictions. The ethical and legal aspects of AI in marketing are addressed by Singhapakdi et al. (2019). This topic mainly includes issues of personal data protection and transparency. Finally, the implementation of AI in small businesses is addressed by Iansiti and Lakhani (2017).

2 Methods

The topic of using artificial intelligence in micro and small business marketing communications is important because it shows how small businesses can use AI to improve their marketing activities and interactions with customers.

2.1 Use of Artificial Intelligence in Marketing and Marketing Communications

De Bruyn et al (2020) predict that AI will fall short of its promise in many marketing areas if we do not solve the challenges of tacit knowledge transfer between AI models and marketing organisations.

Artificial intelligence in marketing helps to track and predict consumers' next purchase decisions and improve their purchase decisions. According to Dimitrieska et al. (2018), the power of AI is reflected in three core elements: big data, machine learning and powerful solutions. These elements make it possible to collect and segment a large amount of data with minimal effort, understand and draw logical conclusions from this data, as well as predict consumption trends, track and analyze consumer purchasing behavior and its future development.

According to Vlacic et al. (2021), AI is becoming increasingly important from a strategic point of view in marketing. Companies such as Google, Rare Carat, Spotify and Under Armor are among the growing list of companies that improve their performance by adopting AI- based platforms (such as Microsoft Cognitive Services, Amazon Lex, Google Assistant or IBM Watson). This approach increases their interaction with customers across marketing channels and improves market forecasting and automation.

According to a Tractica research report (2020), AI is recognised as the most influential technology for business, with an expected growth from $10.1 billion in 2018 to $126 billion by 2025. The results of a survey of business leaders by MIT Technology Review (n.d.) show that the priority area for the application of AI is sales and marketing, with 24 % of US companies already using AI and 60 % expecting to use it by 2022.

The importance of applying AI in marketing has also been outlined in several academic studies, such as Davenport et al. (2020) and Kumar et al. (2023). Current research also focuses on determining the impact of AI on marketing. Shaik (2023), in a study that involved semi-structured interviews with 15 marketing professionals from several Indian companies, highlights the elements that influence the integration of AI in marketing, the benefits and barriers of integrating AI in marketing, as well as the company's marketing strategy before and after AI, ethical considerations, and the use of AI in the marketing industry. The study suggests the integration of AI into marketing tasks to improve business performance and, as a result, achieve profitability and competitive advantage. This study also contributes to strategic marketing research by identifying research gaps that bridge strategic marketing practice and AI research in a systematic and consistent manner.

A study by Bhalerao et al. (2022) focuses on understanding the limitations and benefits of AI adoption in SMEs. According to the authors, if SMEs do not adopt available technologies, they may lose their competitive position. The authors also explored issues related to the challenges and benefits of AI adoption in SMEs. They found that factors such as technical competence, human resources in the field of AI, financial situation, size of the organisation and awareness of the benefits of AI influence the adoption and use of artificial intelligence.

A study by Bunte et al. (2021) found that lack of expertise, start-up costs and time investment, infrastructure, resources, experience and company size are significant challenges in implementing AI in SMEs. Marketing solutions based on artificial intelligence are changing the game for many small and medium-sized businesses around the world. Artificial intelligence enables business decision-makers to identify and understand customer buying behavior, enabling SME marketers to formulate appropriate strategies that match their target customers.

3 Results and Discussions

Several studies have shown that there are several barriers to the adoption and implementation of AI in business processes, including marketing and marketing communications, in the SME environment. However, only a limited number of studies have addressed the issue of AI implementation in micro-enterprises.

3.1 The Use of Artificial Intelligence in the Conditions of Micro-enterprises in Slovak Republic

Therefore, we conducted our own empirical study and survey among a sample of 78 micro- enterprises in the Slovak Republic. The aim was to find out the current state of awareness and use of AI in marketing and marketing communication.

The survey was conducted in the form of an electronic questionnaire. The basic file consisted of a database of small and micro enterprises with a maximum number of 9 employees processed by the author of the article.

The research questions were as follows:

RQ1: To what extent have entrepreneurs in micro enterprises encountered the concept of artificial intelligence?
RQ2: To what extent do micro-entrepreneurs use artificial intelligence tools?
RQ3: What are the most common barriers perceived by micro-entrepreneurs when implementing artificial intelligence tools?

The results of the survey showed that more than 60 % of enterprises have encountered the term artificial intelligence. Almost 30 % of enterprises have come across the term but do not know exactly what it means and how it is used. Figure 1 shows more detailed results.

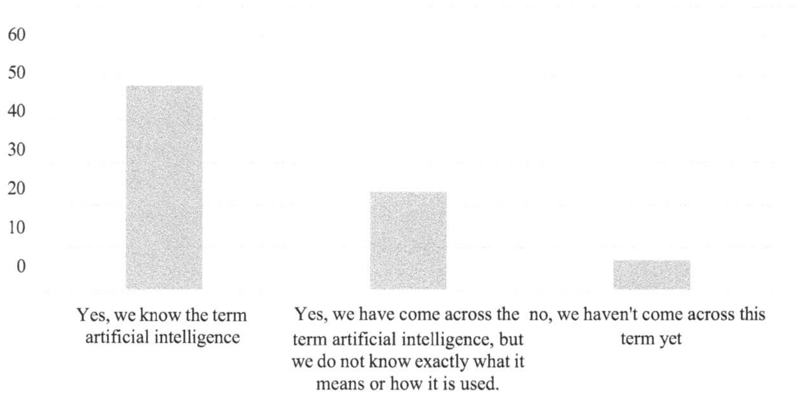

Figure 1. Level of awareness of artificial intelligence in the micro-enterprise environment in Slovakia.

Source: own processing

In the next part, we looked at whether entrepreneurs in micro enterprises used artificial intelligence. Artificial intelligence was used by 37 %, but it was used outside the business activity. Only 16 entrepreneurs used AI in their business. About 46 % of entrepreneurs have not used AI at all. Figure 2 shows the results.

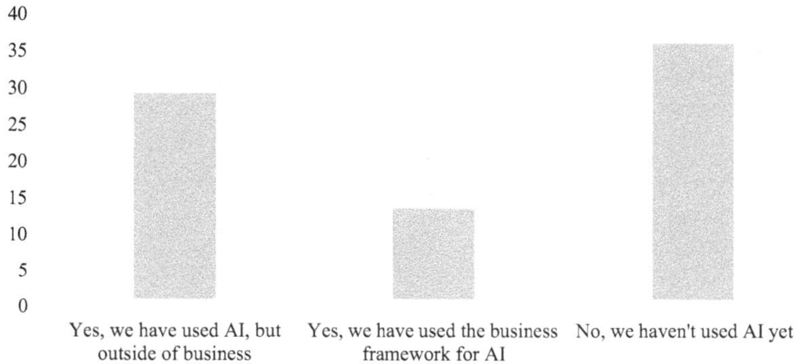

Figure 2. The use of artificial intelligence in the environment of micro-enterprises in Slovakia.

Source: own processing

When it comes to the use of artificial intelligence for marketing and marketing communications, the results are even more surprising. No company regularly uses AI for marketing or marketing communications. Around 10 % of companies have used it during testing. As many as 60 % of companies said that they had not used AI in this way at all, and almost 30 % said that they had no plans to use it for this purpose. The reason for this is a lack of knowledge about how AI could help entrepreneurs in the area of marketing and marketing communication. Figure 3 shows the results.

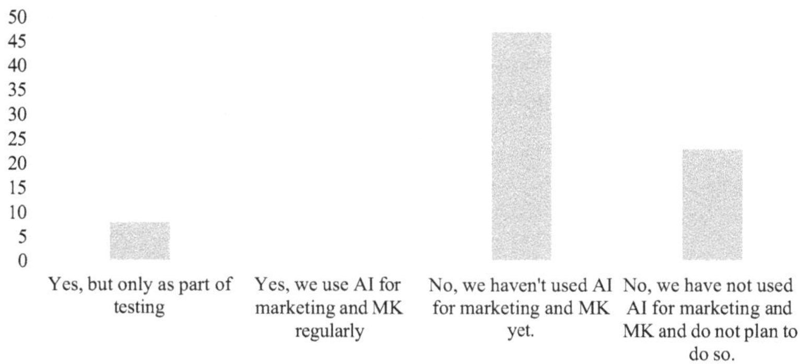

Figure 3. Using Artificial Intelligence for Marketing and Marketing Communication in Micro Enterprises in Slovakia.

Source: own processing

From the point of view of the benefits that artificial intelligence brings to companies, entrepreneurs cited simplifying and speeding up work as the biggest benefits. However, in more than 30 % of cases, entrepreneurs said they did not know what benefits artificial intelligence could bring them, and in almost 9 % of cases, they said that AI did not bring any benefits. The results indicate a low level of experience in using AI tools, but also a low level of awareness of the possibilities of using them. Figure 4 shows the results.

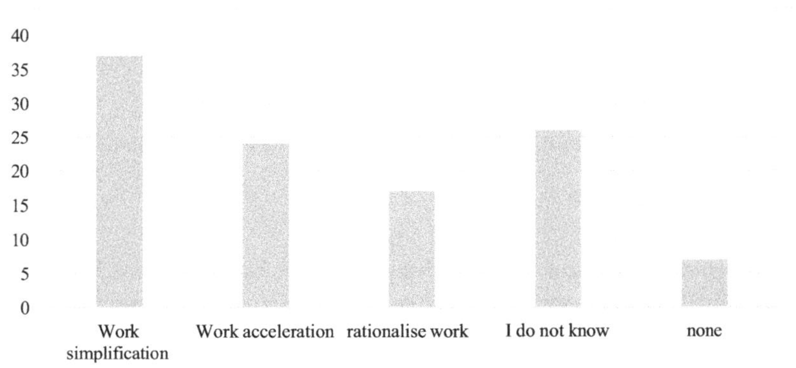

Figure 4. Advantages of using artificial intelligence in marketing and marketing communication in micro-enterprises in Slovakia, according to entrepreneurs.
Source: own processing

Finally, we examined the barriers to the use of artificial intelligence in the micro-enterprise environment. Using a 5-point scale, entrepreneurs rated the severity of each of the six barriers. Figure 5 shows the results.

Figure 5. Barriers to the use of artificial intelligence in the micro-enterprise environment (expressed as averages on a 5-point scale, where 1 = least impact, 5 = greatest impact).

Source: own processing

4 Conclusions

Artificial Intelligence has significantly changed and is changing our daily activities, including business activities. Companies that have already been able to implement and fully utilize artificial intelligence tools are reaping the benefits in terms of increased efficiency and effectiveness of individual business activities. However, from the point of view of the structure of business entities, these are mostly large companies that have extensive experience in implementing various online platforms and tools. In the case of small and medium-sized enterprises, it is mostly limited experience with the use of artificial intelligence and a number of identified barriers that prevent more intensive use of artificial intelligence tools. It is mainly small companies that have the least experience with the use of AI.

According to data from the Slovak Business Agency, small and medium-sized enterprises accounted for 99.9 % of the total number of business entities in 2020. These businesses provided employment opportunities for almost 75 % of the active workforce and participated in more than 50 % of gross production and value added (SBA, 2020).

At the same time, SMEs are an important source of new innovations and technologies, creating a competitive environment and supporting economic growth.

The implementation of artificial intelligence tools can make these attributes even more effective.

However, micro enterprises also have a significant presence on the market in terms of the number of units. These are mainly family-owned or very small enterprises with a maximum of 9 employees and an annual turnover of less than 2,000,000 euros. These enterprises are often characterized by a limited technical and technological infrastructure and a delayed introduction of technological innovations. This also applies to the implementation of artificial intelligence tools.

The results of our own survey show that more than 60 % of companies have come across the term artificial intelligence. Almost 30 % of companies have come across the term but do not know exactly what it means and how it is used. Artificial intelligence has been used by 37 %, but outside of business operations. No company is using AI for marketing or marketing communications. However, in more than 30 % of cases, entrepreneurs said they did not know what benefits artificial intelligence could bring them. Lack of experience and knowledge are among the most common and biggest barriers to adopting artificial intelligence tools.

These findings highlight the need to raise awareness and train micro-entrepreneurs in the use of AI tools. Artificial intelligence tools can significantly help these entrepreneurs to achieve better results not only in process automation, but also in marketing communication. With the help of AI, they can create advertising messages, write creative texts for social networks, personalise communications or carry out predictive analysis, activities for which many micro-enterprises do not have sufficient human or financial capacity.

Being a pilot survey, the study and survey results have several limits and limitations. The first is the limited number of respondents, as well as the duration of the survey. Another is the implementation of research in exclusively the conditions of the Slovak Republic. Nevertheless, the study and the results of the empirical investigation bring interesting results, which will be the subject of further research questions, as well as further research in order to confirm or reject current state of using and implementing the artificial intelligence in micro enterprises.

Acknowledgments

The article is a result of the scientific project APVV-22-0469 entitled "Roadmap of a digital platform providing AI (Artificial Intelligence) automation of decision-making processes in the field of communication strategy."

References

Bartik, A. W., Bertrand, M., Cullen, Z. B., Glaeser, E. L., Luca, M., & Stanton, C. T. (2020). *How are small businesses adjusting to COVID-19? Early evidence from a survey*. National Bureau of Economic Research.

Bhalerao, K., Kumar, A., Kumar, A., & Pujari, P. (2022). A study of barriers and benefits of artificial intelligence adoption in small and medium enterprise. *Academy of Marketing Studies Journal*, *26*, 1–6.

Brynjolfsson, E., & McAfee, A. (2015). The second machine age: Work, progress, and prosperity in a time of brilliant technologies. *Choice Reviews Online*, *52*(06), 52–3201.

Bunte, et al. (2021). A study of barriers and benefits of artificial intelligence adoption in small and medium enterprise. *Academy of Marketing Studies Journal*, *26*(1), 1–6.

Casadesus-Masanell, R., & Zhu, F. (2013). Business model innovation and competitive imitation: The case of sponsor-based business models. *Strategic Management Journal*, *34*(4), 464–482.

Davenport, T. H., & Ronanki, R. (2018). Artificial intelligence for the real world. In *Harvard Business Review*, *96*(1), 108–116.

Davenport, T., Guha, A., Grewal, D., & Bressgott, T. (2020). How artificial intelligence will change the future of marketing. *Journal of the Academy of Marketing Science*, *48*(1), 24–42.

De Bruyn, A., Viswanathan, V., Beh, Y. S., Brock, J. K.-U., & Von Wangenheim, F. (2020). Artificial intelligence and marketing: Pitfalls and opportunities. *Journal of Interactive Marketing*, *51*(1), 91–105.

Dimitrieska, S., Stankovska, A., & Efremova, T. (2018). Artificial intelligence and marketing. *Entrepreneurship*, *6*(2), 298–304.

Elliott, M. (2019). Artificial intelligence: Implications for business strategy. *Strategy & Leadership*, *47*(1), 9–16.

European Commission. (2020). *European Enterprise Survey on the Use of Technologies Basedon Artificial Intelligence*. https://www.ipsos.com/sites/default/files/ct/publication/documents/2020-09/european-enterprise-survey-and-ai-executive-summary.pdf

Hitt, L. M., Wu, D. J., & Zhou, X. (2018). Investment in enterprise resource planning: Business impact and productivity measures. *MIS Quarterly*, *42*(2), 549–566.

Chen, Y., & Xie, J. (2011). Online consumer review: Word-of-mouth as a new element of marketing communication mix. *Management Science*, *57*(1), 193–212.

Iansiti, M., & Lakhani, K. (2017). *The truth about Blockchain. Harvard Business Review*, 1–11.https://enterprisersproject.com/sites/default/files/the_truth_about_blockchain.pdf

Kumar, Y., Koul, A., Singla, R., & Ijaz, M. F. (2023). Artificial intelligence in disease diagnosis: A systematic literature review, synthesizing framework, and future research agenda. *Journal of Ambient Intelligence and Humanized Computing*.

MIT Technology Review. (n.d.). Articles by MIT Technology Review Insights | MIT Technology Review. https://www.technologyreview.com/author/mit-technology- review-insights/

Popovic, A., Hackney, R., & Tassabehji, R. (2018). The impact of artificial intelligence in marketing. *Journal of Business Research*, *98*(2), 261–276.

Rialti, R., Marzi, G., & Ciappei, C. (2017). Big Data and dynamic capabilities: A bibliometric analysis and systematic literature review. *Management Decision*, *57*(2), 2052–2068.

SBA. (2020). *Mala a stredne podnikanie v cislach*. https://www.sbagency.sk/male-a- stredne-podnikanie-v-bratislavskom-samospravnom-kraji-v-roku-2020

Shaik, M. (2023). Impact of artificial intelligence on marketing. *East Asian Journal of Multidisciplinary Research*, *2*(3), 993–1004.

Singhapakdi, A., Yu, G. B., & Thongpapanl, N. (2019). *Ethics in marketing: International cases and perspectives*. Routledge.

Tractica Research Report. (2020). *Artificial Intelligence for telecommunications applications*. https://omdia.tech.informa.com/topic-pages/artificial-intelligence

Vlacic, B., Corbo, L., Costa, S., & Dabic, M. (2021). The evolving role of artificial intelligence in marketing: A review and research agenda. *Journal of Business Research*, *128*, 187–203.

Wirtz, B. W., et al. (2016). Business models: Origin, development and future research perspectives. *Long Range Planning*, *49*(1), 36–54.

Pavol Kral[1,*], and Katarina Janoskova[1]

An Overview of the Key Benefits and Threats of Digital Marketing

Abstract:
Research background: In today's company context, digital marketing is critical since it provides cost-effective, targeted, and quantifiable ways for connecting with and engaging a worldwide audience. Organizations that embrace digital marketing are better positioned for success as customer behavior shifts online.
Purpose of the article: The purpose of the paper is to point out the key characteristics of digital marketing (benefits and threats) and to define basic attributes that allow answering strategic questions for the future application of digital marketing tools in business practice, identify new possibilities of applying digital marketing, and find suitable support formats. These attributes will be defined based on knowledge of the theoretical background, analysis of scientific literature and studies, and evaluation of successful projects.
Methods: An analysis of the available scientific literature, including electronic sources, with a subsequent synthesis of the acquired knowledge will be applied for the factual theoretical definition of a solved problem. The ambition of the authors is to use theoretical knowledge, results of systematic research, experience, and publication activity outputs to create an informative scientific platform dedicated to digital marketing and its implementation in company practice. There were several suitable methods of scientific research (formal logic methods: analysis, synthesis, deduction, induction, comparison, and abstraction).
Findings & Value added: The results will enable business practices to understand the essence of digital marketing, get to know this environment and the current trend, and create a suitable platform for planning successful digital marketing projects. There is a potential for paper and research outputs to be applied in management practice at the national or global level.

Keywords: *digital marketing, digital technologies, marketing strategies, competition*

JEL Classification: *M31; M37; M39*

* Corresponding author: pavol.kral@fpedas.uniza.sk
1 University of Zilina, Faculty of Operation and Economics of Transport and Communication, Department of Economics, Univerzitna 8215/1, 010 16 Zilina, Slovak Republic

1 Introduction

Digital marketing is a multidimensional field that includes a variety of online techniques and tactics for promoting products, services, brands, or ideas to a specific audience. The impact of digital media on how businesses communicate, market their products and services, and build consumer connections is expanding. Digital marketing has evolved significantly from conventional means of advertising and promotion with the emergence of the internet, social media, and mobile technology. Around the start of the twenty-first century, digital marketing began to acquire importance and use, coinciding with the emergence and development of the internet and digital technology. While certain digital marketing approaches and technologies may be traced back to previous decades, the genuine birth of digital marketing as a unique and major discipline happened in the last two decades.

Digital marketing is a complex ecosystem of tools, technology, and practices that impact how businesses and brands connect with the rest of the world. Its importance to modern businesses cannot be overstated, therefore knowing its principles, evolution, and current trends is critical. In turn, this paper helps to a deeper knowledge of how digital marketing influences the modern corporate environment today and in the future.

2 Methods

Consumers might think and act differently as ICT advances and high-speed internet becomes more widely available. For starters, customers are shifting their ways of communication to instant messaging and aesthetically driven smartphone apps like Instagram. Second, customers are expecting greater involvement in value co-creation, making customer engagement and empowerment critical to economic sustainability (Acar & Puntoni, 2016; Jaakkola & Alexander, 2014). The business sector is experiencing the effects of technology advancements, and many entrepreneurs are using digital marketing to sell their products (Gaol & Ichsan, 2022; Hoffman et al., 2022). Digital marketing has changed the way businesses manage and engage with their consumers and society throughout the world. It is quickly becoming a critical and important tool for addressing the remaining issues in the field of marketing. At the same time, sustainability has emerged as one of the most significant concerns for businesses since the turn of the century, particularly for marketers (Jones et al., 2008; Diez-Martin et al., 2019). The global adoption of the internet continues to rise, with digital becoming an increasingly essential source of competitive advantage in both B2C and

B2B marketing. Much emphasis has been placed on the amazing benefits that digital marketing brings, with less emphasis placed on the genuine obstacles that businesses face when going digital (Leeflang et al., 2014; Sujanska & Nadanyiova 2022). In the future, IoT technology has the potential to improve digital marketing (Badica & Mituca, 2021). As a result, technology have put tremendous pressure on businesses to adjust their practices to the different modern mechanisms that exist. As a result, digital marketing has become a crucial instrument for competing in the market, serving as an effective way of reaching out to potential customers (Campos et al., 2021).

Digital marketing is a profitable industry, with yearly revenue exceeding USD 200 billion and inter-annual growth over 20 %. A critical issue in digital marketing is the development of effective marketing investment plans across many channels and campaigns (Leguina et al., 2020). In Slovakia, a significant increase in spending on digital advertising was recorded in 2021. According to estimates, when compared to spending on other media types, online became the strongest advertising medium for the first time (Gajanova & Michulek, 2023). The digital advertising sector is consolidating and getting increasingly competitive. As a result of technical innovation, which enhances the dynamic of the environment and raises the expectations imposed on online operations, online marketing is a constantly growing subject.

Internet marketing, like offline marketing, adapts to the current situation by adapting classic marketing ideas to the online world (Chong et al., 2017).

The essence of digital marketing is proven to be the personification of business operations in the "seller-buyer" system. It is established the model of advanced marketing communication, and it represents the distinctiveness of progressive technologies in digital marketing communications, the possibilities and benefits of online communication, and marketing goals in online activities. It is highlighted that in the presence of the benefits of new technologies, it is necessary to remember that a communication campaign should use both digital and conventional means (Oklander & Oklander, 2017).

The share of digital marketing from total marketing spending is increasing fast year by year (Leeflang et al., 2014). Digital marketing helps to increase online purchases and hence sales of items in all categories such as apparel, accessories, technological gadgets, and so on. As the use of social media grows in popularity, digital marketing becomes increasingly important in reaching out to the target demographic. After doing a thorough research of consumer interests and determining the target population, marketing advertising may be disseminated through digital marketing. This aids in obtaining a high conversion rate from leads produced by such adverts. Inbound marketing and content marketing are relatively new ideas (Erdmann & Ponzoa, 2021). Digital marketing offers a promising future for long- term product or service sustainability in today's technology market, with all of its advantages and disadvantages (Desai, 2019). Digital marketing is related to the most recent technological advancements – a move from digital marketing to intelligent marketing through the application of artificial intelligence, which has begun to capture more and more sectors (Dumitriu & Popescu, 2020).

3 Results and Discussion

For most businesses and organizations, digital marketing is an essential component of their marketing plans. In today's digital age, digital marketing provides numerous advantages to businesses and organizations. These advantages add to its popularity and general acceptance. With the growing relevance of the internet, mobile technology, and social media, digital marketing is evolving into a sophisticated and effective instrument for meeting marketing objectives and engaging with target consumers. Here are the main qualities and benefits of digital marketing:

- **Cost-Effective:** Digital marketing is often more cost-effective than traditional marketing channels like print or TV advertising. It allows businesses to reach a large audience with smaller budgets, making it accessible to startups and small businesses. Digital marketing seamlessly integrates with e-commerce platforms, enabling direct online sales and a streamlined shopping experience.
- **Easy Testing and Experimentation:** Digital marketing allows businesses to test different strategies, messages, and creative elements quickly. This helps in identifying what resonates best with the audience and refining marketing campaigns accordingly.
- **Global Reach:** Digital marketing enables businesses to reach a global audience. With the internet's worldwide reach, you can target customers not only locally but also nationally and internationally.
- **Immediate Results:** Some digital marketing tactics, such as pay-per-click (PPC) advertising, can generate immediate results. This can be beneficial for promotions or events that require rapid response. Digital channels provide convenient ways to collect customer feedback and conduct surveys, allowing businesses to gather insights for improvement. PPC and display advertising campaigns can be easily scaled up or down based on budget and performance. Digital marketing allows marketers to see accurate results in real time (Desai, 2019).

- **Integration with Offline Marketing:** Digital marketing can seamlessly integrate with traditional marketing efforts. For example, you can use QR codes in print materials to drive online engagement.
- **Measurable Results:** Digital marketing provides detailed analytics and data tracking tools, allowing businesses to measure the performance of their campaigns in real-time. Marketers can track metrics like website traffic, conversion rates, click-through rates, and more, helping them make data-driven decisions. Digital marketing tools enable businesses to monitor and analyze competitors' online activities, helping them stay ahead in the market.
- **Global Collaboration:** Digital marketing enables businesses to collaborate with partners, influencers, or customers worldwide, breaking down geographical barriers.
- **Multi-Channel Marketing:** Digital marketing allows for multi-channel campaigns that span various platforms and touchpoints, ensuring a consistent message across the customer journey.
- **Targeted Advertising:** Digital marketing offers precise targeting options. Businesses can tailor their marketing efforts to specific demographics, interests, and behaviors, ensuring that their messages reach the most relevant audience.
- **Personalization:** Digital marketing enables personalized marketing messages. Marketers can use data to create personalized content and offers, enhancing the customer experience and increasing engagement.
- **Immediate Impact:** Digital marketing campaigns can be launched quickly, reaching the audience within minutes. This agility is especially beneficial for time-sensitive promotions or responding to market changes.
- **Interactivity:** Digital marketing allows for two-way communication between businesses and customers. Social media, email marketing, and interactive content engage customers and encourage feedback and interaction. Social media and live chat features enable real-time engagement with customers, building relationships and trust. Dynamic content can be customized based on user behavior and preferences, increasing relevance.
- **Flexibility:** Digital marketing campaigns can be adjusted and optimized in real-time. If a campaign isn't performing as expected, marketers can make immediate changes to improve results. Online chat, social media, and email provide efficient channels for customer support, resolving queries and issues promptly.
- **Content Syndication:** Digital content can be easily syndicated and shared across various platforms, increasing its reach and potential for virality.

- Predictive Analytics: Advanced analytics tools and machine learning can be used in digital marketing to predict customer behavior, allowing for proactive marketing strategies.
- **Improved Conversion Rates:** Digital marketing often leads to higher conversion rates compared to traditional marketing. Targeted messaging and effective call-to-actions can drive more prospects to take desired actions, such as making a purchase or signing up for a newsletter.
- **Enhanced Brand Awareness:** Consistent online presence through digital marketing channels helps build and strengthen brand awareness. Social media, content marketing, and search engine optimization (SEO) all contribute to a brand's online visibility. Consistent and valuable digital content can establish a brand's authority in its industry and position it as a thought leader.
- **Engagement and Interaction:** Digital marketing channels facilitate direct engagement with customers through social media comments, reviews, and messages. This interaction can help build trust and customer loyalty.
- **Level Playing Field:** Digital marketing provides an equal opportunity for businesses of all sizes to compete in the online space. Smaller businesses can effectively compete with larger ones by implementing effective digital marketing strategies.
- **Scalability:** Digital marketing strategies can be scaled up or down to match the needs and budget of the business. This scalability is particularly valuable for businesses with fluctuating demands.
- **Enhanced Customer Insights:** Digital marketing tools and platforms offer in-depth insights into customer behavior, preferences, and demographics, helping businesses refine their targeting strategies.
- **Continuous Improvement:** Digital marketing allows for ongoing optimization. Marketers can analyze performance data and make adjustments to improve campaigns over time, ensuring long-term success.
- **Access to Mobile Audiences:** As mobile device usage continues to grow, digital marketing allows businesses to target consumers on smartphones and tablets, reaching them where they spend a significant amount of their online time.

Overall, digital marketing provides organizations with a dynamic and successful approach to engage with their target audience, promote their products or services, and fulfill their marketing goals in an efficient and quantifiable manner. These benefits show digital marketing's flexibility, adaptability, and efficacy in the digital realm.

Digital marketing provides tremendous potential for firms, but it also introduces new dangers and obstacles. Businesses must be aware of these hazards and take proactive measures to mitigate them. Here are some of the most typical digital marketing threats:

- **Cybersecurity Risks:** Digital marketing often involves collecting and storing customer data. The threat of data breaches, hacking, and other cybersecurity issues can result in the exposure of sensitive customer information and damage to a brand's reputation.
- **Privacy Concerns:** As digital marketing relies on collecting and using customer data, there are concerns about violating consumer privacy and regulations like GDPR (General Data Protection Regulation). Non-compliance with data protection laws can lead to legal consequences and reputational damage.
- **Ad Fraud:** Advertisers may fall victim to ad fraud, where fake clicks, impressions, or conversions are generated to inflate advertising costs without delivering real results. This can result in wasted ad spend and skewed performance metrics.
- **Platform Dependency:** Relying too heavily on a single digital marketing platform (e.g., Google Ads or Facebook Ads) can be risky. Changes in algorithms, policies, or account suspensions on these platforms can disrupt marketing efforts and impact ROI.
- **Online Reputation Management:** Negative online reviews, comments, or social media mentions can harm a brand's reputation. Monitoring and managing online reputation is crucial to address potential threats to brand image. Due to the prevalence of fake news and fraudulent websites, consumers may be sceptical of online ads and content.
- **Competitive Pressure:** The digital landscape is highly competitive. Rivals can quickly adapt to your digital marketing strategies or outspend you in advertising, making it challenging to maintain a competitive edge. In some industries, digital marketing competition is intense, making it challenging to stand out.
- **Technological Advances:** Rapid changes in digital technologies and marketing trends require businesses to continually update their strategies and tools. Falling behind in digital advancements can result in reduced effectiveness and competitiveness. Digital marketing technologies and trends evolve rapidly, necessitating continuous learning and adaptation.
- **Information Overload:** Consumers are inundated with digital content and advertisements. Cutting through the noise and capturing the audience's attention is becoming increasingly challenging.
- **Ad Blockers:** Many internet users employ ad-blocking software, which can limit the reach of digital advertising efforts and reduce ad visibility.

- **Content Quality:** Poorly executed content marketing can harm a brand's credibility. Creating high-quality, engaging content is essential for digital marketing success.
- **Creativity Fatigue:** Continuously creating content and creative campaigns can be mentally draining and lead to creative burnout.
- **Budget Constraints:** Effective digital marketing often requires a substantial budget for advertising, tools, and personnel. Limited resources can constrain marketing efforts and impact results.
- **Measuring ROI:** Accurately measuring the return on investment (ROI) for digital marketing efforts can be challenging. Inaccurate metrics can lead to poor decision-making.

Businesses should invest in robust cybersecurity measures, adhere to data protection regulations, diversify their digital marketing strategies, stay informed about industry trends, and prioritize delivering value to customers through quality content and personalized experiences to mitigate these threats. Furthermore, ongoing monitoring and adaption of digital marketing tactics are required to successfully meet developing risks.

4 Conclusions

The future of digital marketing will be determined by a variety of elements and developments in technology, customer behavior, and legislation. Data and artificial intelligence will be increasingly used by digital marketers to improve content and ad personalisation. To improve client experiences, they will strive to offer relevant and precisely focused messaging. Video content will continue to reign supreme. Consumers will be engaged through live broadcasts, social media videos, and interactive videos, which will be deemed successful communication methods. Consumers will increasingly demand greater control over their personal data and greater transparency from marketers about how they manage their data. Growing privacy protection laws (GDPR) will have an impact on how marketers obtain and use personal data. Marketers' marketing practices may need to be more careful and open. Social media will continue to be an important digital marketing medium, although popular platforms and consumer tastes may shift. Marketers will need to be adaptable to these changes.

It is clear that digital marketing has the ability to adapt and develop in response to changing technology and shifting customer behavior. Hyper-personalization, the dominance of video content, the continued expansion of mobile marketing, and the use of new technologies like as Augmented Reality (AR) and Virtual Reality (VR) are key aspects determining the future of digital marketing.

These patterns suggest that the future of digital marketing will be dynamic, with marketers' capacity to adapt to new technology, laws, and customer preferences being critical. To win in the continuously changing digital marketing world, businesses must be imaginative and adaptable. Automation and artificial intelligence play critical roles in increasing the efficiency of marketing initiatives, while transparency and social responsibility are becoming more prominent. To succeed in the future digital marketing landscape, businesses must nurture creativity, adaptability, and a dedication to providing value to their consumers. Digital marketing will remain a dynamic discipline in which successful businesses negotiate changing difficulties and grab new possibilities, eventually offering customers with relevant and meaningful experiences. Despite the ever-changing world of privacy legislation and consumer preferences, digital marketing remains an essential tool for interacting with consumers and accomplishing corporate goals.

Acknowledgment

The contribution is an output of the project VEGA 1/0409/23 Forensic marketing as a platform of objective empirical support for managerial decision-making processes.

References

Acar, O. A., & Puntoni, S. (2016). Customer empowerment in the digital age. *Journal of Advertising Research*, *56*(1), 4–8.

Badica, A., & Mituca, M. (2021). IOT-Enhanced Digital Marketing conceptual framework. *Broad Research in Artificial Intelligence Neuroscience*, *12*(4), 509–531.

Campos, A. C., De Rezende, D. C., Leme, P. R., De Brito, M. J., & Antonialli, L. M. (2021). Marketing Digital em Tempos de Crise. *Revista Gestão E Desenvolvimento*, *18*(3), 102–130.

Chong, A. Y. L., Ch'ng, E., Liu, M. J., & Li, B. (2017). Predicting consumer product demands via Big Data: The roles of online promotional marketing and online reviews. *International Journal of Production Research*, *55*(17), 5142–5156.

Desai, V. (2019). Digital marketing: A review. *International Journal of Trend in Scientific Research and Development*, *5*(5), 196–200.

Diez-Martin, F., Blanco-Gonzalez, A., & Prado-Roman, C. (2019). Research challenges in Digital Marketing: Sustainability. *Sustainability*, *11*(10), 2839.

Dumitriu, D., & Popescu, M. A. (2020). Artificial Intelligence solutions for Digital Marketing. *13th International Conference Interdisciplinarity in Engineering. Procedia Manufacturing*, *46*, 630–636.

Erdmann, A., & Ponzoa, J. M. (2021). Digital inbound marketing: Measuring the economic performance of grocery e-commerce in Europe and the USA. *Technological Forecasting and Social Change*, *162*, 120373.

Gajanova, L., & Michulek, J. (2023). Digital Marketing in the context of consumer behaviour in the ICT Industry: The case study of the Slovak Republic. *Virtual Economics*, *6*(1), 7–18.

Gaol, J. L., & Ichsan, R. N. (2022). Traditional market management model based on Digital Marketing. *General Management*, *23*(191), 228–233.

Hoffman, D. L., Moreau, C. P., Stremersch, S., & Wedel, M. (2022). The rise of new technologies in marketing: A framework and outlook. *Journal of Marketing*, *86*(1), 1–6.

Jaakkola, E., & Alexander, M. (2014). The role of customer engagement behavior in value co-creation: A service system perspective. *Journal of Service Research*, *17*(3), 247–261.

Jones, P., Clarke-Hill, C., Comfort, D., & Hillier, D. (2008). Marketing and sustainability. *Marketing Intelligence and Planning*, *26*(2), 123–130.

Leeflang, P. S., Verhoef, P. C., Dahlstrom, P., & Freundt, T. (2014). Challenges and solutions for marketing in a digital era. *European Management Journal*, *32*(1), 1–12.

Leguina, J. R., Rumin, A. C., & Rumin, R. C. (2020). Digital Marketing attribution: Understanding the user path. *Electronics*, *9*(11), 1822.

Oklander, M., & Oklander, T. (2017). Segmentation and communication in Digital Marketing. *Marketing and Management of Innovations, 3*, 69–78.

Sujanska, L., & Nadanyiova, M. (2022). Online marketing communication as a key tool to capture the attention of Generation Z. *Ekonomicko-manazerske spektrum*, *16*(2), 81–90.

Michal Kubovics[1,*], and Anna Zauskova[1]

Global Use of Artificial Intelligence for Predicting and Working with

Abstract:
Research background: Artificial intelligence has hit the contemporary world globally. The changes are far-reaching. The digital environment and social media in particular are no exception.
Purpose of the article: The present research paper focuses on the application of Artificial Intelligence (AI) in the context of groundswell monitoring and prediction in a digital environment. The paper presents a developed methodological approach that combines machine learning (ML) with a dataset containing big data for more accurate groundswell predictions.
Methods: The methods include a detailed literature review, production, and testing of the experimental system developed in the paper, which showed that the proposed AI has the potential to achieve high accuracy in predicting groundswell effects, which can improve monitoring and contribute to system design and a more effective response to changes in the digital environment.
Findings & Value added: The results may be applicable to autonomous platforms and the automation of the detection of adverse effects that may arise on social networks. Thus, based on the results of the analysis of marketing communication in the digital environment, businesses in a global environment can respond more quickly and successfully to the changing environment and thus ensure a positive impact of communication. Thus, the present paper helps in the advancement of artificial intelligence and marketing communication in the global digital environment and allows for a better understanding and resolution of situations in practical and theoretical terms.

Keywords: *artificial intelligence, groundswell monitoring, machine learning, marketing communication in digital environment*

JEL Classification: *M3; M30; B31*

---

* Corresponding author: michal.kubovics@ucm.sk
[1] University of Ss. Cyril and Methodius in Trnava, Faculty of Mass Media Communication, Department of Marketing Communication, Namestie J. Herdu 2, 917 01 Trnava, Slovakia

1 Introduction

The importance of Artificial Intelligence (AI) technology has increased in the field of prediction and collaboration with the development of the aforementioned systems when advances have been made and AI has become a mass popularized topic (Oc et al., 2023). In the same way, the marketing environment has been experiencing a social media boom for several years, which has been implemented in people's lives (Ozdemir et al., 2020). As a result of the above, the currently mentioned environment provides new approaches to supervising and managing a wide range of aspects of people's behavior on social media, and systems could currently include the ability to predict the groundswell and intervene in users' behavior.

1.1 The Groundswell

The groundswell is a common phenomenon in the field of marketing communications in relation to social media. The essence of the phenomenon is that users engage in generating discussion in the form of content contributing on various online platforms. This particular phenomenon tends to gain momentum in the form of shares and reach due to the widespread popularity, influx and active participation of the online community. The groundswell can pose a challenge for brands and organizations. Businesses should aim to intervene in the debate to activate cultivated participation in online discussions, encourage content creation for social media platforms, and provide opportunities for users to collaborate and express their positive opinions. In doing so, it is important for businesses to ensure that users create constructive communities and transform the impact of the groundswell into a positive emotional charge (Svec et al., 2021). The groundswell can directly or indirectly affect reputational or even economic aspects of a company (Bezakova et al., 2021). Within social networks, different target groups may interact with the groundswell in different ways (Cabyova & Hudakova, 2022). Nevertheless, it is clear that the groundswell should be managed with the help of a social media manager (Madlenak, 2020). In conclusion, monitoring on different social media is very important, which can translate into a timely response and successful management of the situation (Nagyova & Bednarik, 2022).

1.2 Artificial Intelligence and Machine Learning in Marketing Communication

Artificial intelligence and its global application in marketing communication has recently achieved great popularity (Ma & Sun, 2020). With the availability, there has also been a faster development and application across all components of marketing communications (Syam & Sharma, 2018). In doing so, machine learning is significant, which involves input in the form of textual, visual or audio content, which is then analyzed using the collected data and evaluated based on clustering or categorization. Statistical forecasting is also currently being used. A basic overview was provided by Kushwaha and Badhera (2023) who defined the major gaps in applied AI research in relation to marketing and the need to apply it. Malthouse and Copulsky (2023) demonstrated the impact of AI and machine learning on advertising and marketing communications, which takes into account a set of variables affecting the effectiveness of AI in marketing, involving algorithms, customer data, digital environment, digital content and information technology. In the context of marketing communications, it is possible to build on the exploration of Mo and Yang (2022), who directly identify the potential of machine learning prediction. In doing so, it can be applied to any piece of content because machine learning enables learning based on a dataset. It is important to include a target audience because the diversity of user behavior can directly influence AI outputs (Moradi & Dass, 2022).

The primary objective of the present paper is to thoroughly review and analyze the current state of the theoretical framework for the use of artificial intelligence in marketing communication fields with respect to the groundswell. The investigation will be carried out by thoroughly analyzing the theoretical foundations and conducting an in-depth analysis of the potential capabilities that can be achieved through the use of AI tools in the digital environment. The ultimate outcome of this study is to identify and develop specific components of the methodological approach that, when combined, can form a cohesive and harmonious symbiosis, resulting in a comprehensive and well-optimized system. As a result of the aforementioned investigation, a set of research questions and hypotheses have been formulated that specifically relate to the application of artificial intelligence in the field of marketing communications.

The previous theoretical background led to the research question and hypothesis:

RQ1: How can the integration of artificial intelligence (AI) and machine learning (ML) facilitate the anticipation of groundswell effects in digital environment and enhance the monitoring and management of their impact?

H1: A methodological approach to research that concentrates on the integration of artificial intelligence (AI) and machine learning (ML) within an experimental framework allows for the identification of groundswell in a digital setting with an error rate that is lower than 10 % when compared to a social media manager.

2 Methods

The paper includes a comprehensive review using qualitative and quantitative scientific procedures. The theoretical framework includes qualitative methods, specifically focusing on analysis, synthesis, induction, deduction and comparison. In the qualitative research design, the main focus is on the examination of texts authored by eminent scholars. The key search terms used to retrieve these materials were defined as "artificial intelligence," "use of artificial intelligence in marketing," "application of artificial intelligence in social media marketing," and "integration of artificial intelligence in social media marketing communications." The primary sources of scholarly papers are reputable academic journals as well as conference proceedings, literary works, and online resources.

The creation of the methodological procedure was carried out on the basis of the collected results, the subsequent research and definition of the basic features of the methodological procedure was carried out, then the experimental verification of the methodological model was defined. Experimental verification of the methodological procedure was applied with the help of programming language, programming libraries and server due to which an applied scientific output in the form of a functional system for groundswell analysis was created.

Verification of the methodological procedure was carried out after the system was created with the help of a social media manager from the practice on a sample of one hundred comments, when the system marked which comments can and cannot trigger the groundswell and in the same way the social media manager marked which comments can and cannot trigger the groundswell, then the error rate of the system was calculated according to the methodological procedure.

3 Results

Based on the theoretical background, important findings emerged. The proposition and impetus for the elaboration of the methodological system is that the modern marketing environment, with both scientific and practical spheres, places immense importance on understanding and communicating effectively with recipients on social networks in order to achieve the goals of the organization. With the rise of technology, digitization has brought a huge amount of customer data, especially in the form of online reviews, discussion posts and social media interactions. Yet the sheer volume and unorganized nature of this textual information presents a significant challenge. It is essential to use advanced technologies and methodologies to gain actionable insights and improve marketing strategies. The research question "How can the combination of artificial intelligence (AI), machine learning (ML) make predictions of groundswell effects in digital environments and contribute to better monitoring and more effective management of groundswell impact?" is contained in the following methodological approach:

3.1 Machine Learning Methodology in the Context of the Groundswell

The process starts with accurately identifying the target audience, which involves segmenting them based on demographic, psychographic and behavioral characteristics, and selecting the content that the target audience contributes in the form of content on or off the business's social media profiles. Once the audience and content are defined, a key step is comprehensive pre-processing, data analysis, and selection of specific content for analysis.

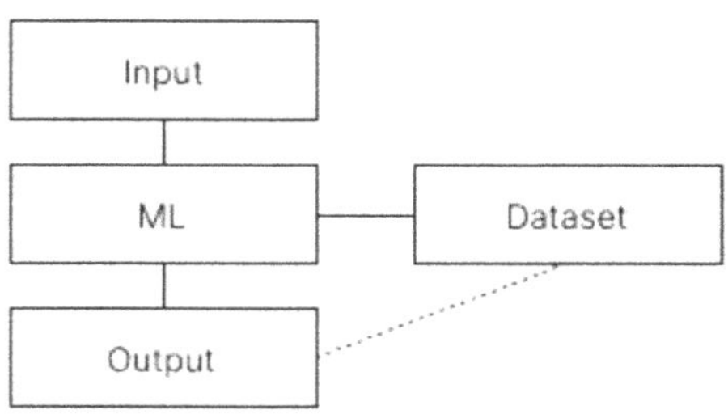

Figure 1. A machine learning methodology in the context of the groundswell.
Source: own processing (2023)

Data processing follows. The data is usually extracted into a CSV file. The content of the data file is the previous step. The data includes key information such as comments or customer reviews. In order to extract useful insights from this unstructured textual data, a preprocessing stage is necessary.

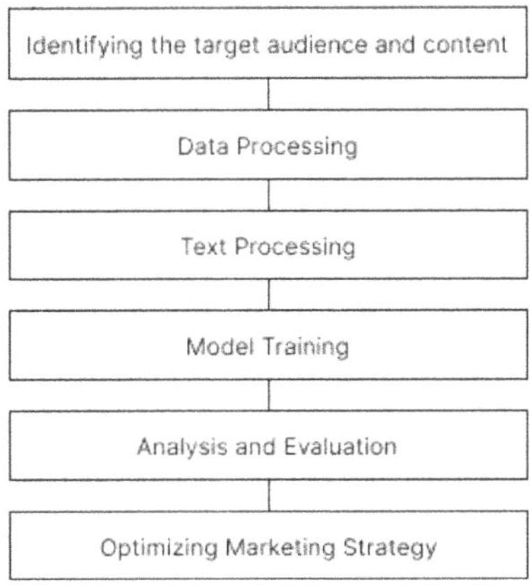

Figure 2. Methodological procedure of the input processing system.
Source: own processing (2023)

The application of methodologies in natural language processing, which encompasses processes such as tokenization, named entity recognition, sentiment analysis, and part-of- speech tagging, significantly enhances the comprehension of textual content. The aforementioned phase may consist of various tasks, such as tokenization, stemming, stop- word elimination, and vectorization. Tokenization effectively disassembles text into smaller units known as tokens, while sentiment analysis efficiently gauges the emotional tone conveyed in communication. These tools facilitate the interpretation of sentiments and opinions expressed in customer comments.

Training the predictive model is crucial in this methodological procedure. Approaches such as Support Vector Machines (SVMs), Random Forest, or neural networks can be employed for the purpose of binary or multiclass classification in order to precisely anticipate whether a provided comment is probable to generate a pessimistic or optimistic reaction.

Outcome assessment. The performance of the trained model is displayed via visualization or text to the user, or further analysis, inclusion in the user typology, etc. is possible.

The optimization of marketing strategies is based on model predictions and results. Outputs can be further generated to match the expected responses of the target audience. This includes adapting advertising campaigns or adjusting communication strategies to mitigate potential negative impacts identified through the analysis.

3.2 Creation of the Experimental System According to the Methodological Procedure

Based on the above methodological procedure, an experimental system was further implemented and programmed using the PHP-ML library. From the PHP-ML library, the classification module was selected and from it the SVC system, which stands for support vector classification. Furthermore, it was important and necessary to create a suitable dataset that could be applied and incorporated into the programming system. The dataset contained one hundred comments that tied to the groundswell and one hundred comments that tied to common comments that do not or should not trigger the groundswell.

Figure 3. Sample dataset of the system.
Source: own processing (2023)

Subsequently, an input was programmed into the system where users can write comments or copy them directly from social networks. The system learned through the dataset to classify comments as either able to trigger a groundswell or unable to trigger a groundswell. The following figure contains a visualization of the complete prototype system in test mode.

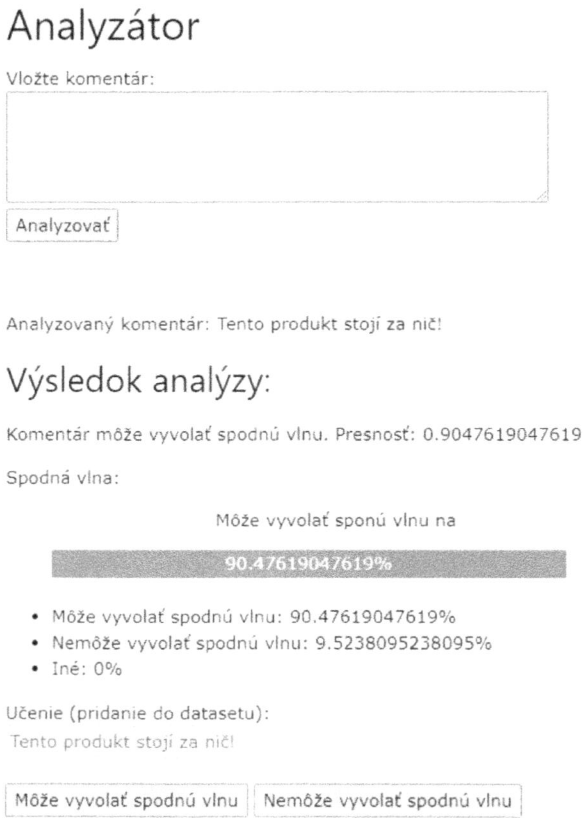

Figure 4. Example of the system according to the methodological procedure.
Source: own processing (2023)

The system contained an input at the top where you could write or paste a comment from the clipboard. Next came the analyze button. When the user pressed the button, the analyzed comment and the result of the analysis were displayed. Then, the next section displayed whether or not the comment could trigger a groundswell and the accuracy with which the statistical system inferred the statement. The next section visualized in more detail the percent probability that it may or may not trigger a groundswell. The visualization was also included in the test mode, with percentages and individual percentages for items can trigger a groundswell, cannot trigger a groundswell, and other. A system for future learning was also included, that is, whether a given comment was closer to the can trigger a groundswell option or the can't trigger a groundswell option. A particular button, when pressed, included the comment in the dataset.

3.3 Verification of the Designed Experimental System According to the Methodological Procedure

Verification of the proposed system according to the methodological procedure was carried out based on the analysis of comments from social networks. One hundred comments were randomly selected and individually added to the system and the analyzed results from it were entered into a spreadsheet. Similarly, the said comments were submitted to the social media manager who evaluated the individual comments with the understanding that whether or not there may be a groundswell. The result of the experiment was in the percentage of correct responses or the percentage of system errors relative to the social media manager. The percentage of error rate of the system relative to the designated social media manager was less than <5 %, which we rate very positively. The above system has been verified and hence we can hypothesize H1 "A research methodological approach focusing on the combination of artificial intelligence (AI), machine learning (ML) in an experimental system enables the determination of groundswell in a digital environment with an error rate below 10 % relative to a social media manager." Confirm.

4 Discussion and Conclusions

The objective was achieved, as well as the definition of a methodological procedure that would meet the current trends in the field of marketing communication in the relationship with the groundswell. Verification was also fulfilled, i.e., first an experimental prototype was built that met the requirements of the methodological procedure and then it was verified with the help of an A-test involving the manager and the tested prototype. Gubela et al. (2022), defined methodological procedures in relationship marketing communication with a wide range of variables that they can influence. The aforementioned exploration included a proposition that led to the definition and implementation of the present methodological procedure. The author's present investigation complements that of Basri (2020), where an artificial intelligence system with the AISMM module can be supplemented with an additional module that relates to the investigation of marketing communication in the context of the groundswell. Similarly, the study by Mameli et al. (2022), which focused on the fashion segment, can be enriched with other segments by our investigation and broadly applied to social media, of any business entity. This is one of the fundamental findings that the present study makes possible. Further exploration is just from Volkmar et al. (2022), where they have defined, the variables that were equally a proposition and that is the analysis of customer behavior. The presented model, respecting the user outcomes, segments on the target groups and thus completes the strategy and implementation, which has been taken into account in the model. The present investigation connects to a large extent to previous investigations, thus complementing the theoretical and practical level in the scientific category of applied marketing communication.

Acknowledgments

The research was supported by the Scientific Grant Agency of the Ministry of Education, Science, Research and Sport of the Slovak Republic and the Slovak Academy of Sciences (VEGA, No. 1/0458/21) under the project entitled "Management of the 'groundswell' concept by business entities in promotion of environmentally-friendly products in times of technology interference."

References

Basri, W. (2020). Examining the impact of artificial intelligence (Ai)-assisted social media marketing on the performance of small and medium enterprises: Toward effective business management in the Saudi Arabian context. *International Journal of Computational Intelligence Systems*, *13*(1), 142–152.

Bezakova, Z., Madlenak, A., & Svec, M. (2021). Security risks of sharing content based on minors by their family members on social media in times of technology interference. *Media Literacy and Academic Research*, *4*(1), 53–69.

Cabyova, L., & Hudakova, V. (2022). Social media use and adolescents' levels of advertising literacy. *Media Literacy and Academic Research*, *5*(2), 147–163.

Gubela, R. M., Lessmann, S., & Stocker, B. (2022). Multiple treatment modeling for target marketing campaigns: A large-scale benchmark study. *Information Systems Frontiers*.

Kushwaha, P. S., & Badhera, U. (2023). Artificial intelligence and machine learning in marketing: A bibliometric review. *Pacific Business Review International*, *15*(5), 55–66.

Ma, L., & Sun, B. (2020). Machine learning and AI in marketing – Connecting computing power to human insights. *International Journal of Research in Marketing*, *37*(3), 481–504.

Malthouse, E., & Copulsky, J. (2023). Artificial intelligence ecosystems for marketing communications. *International Journal of Advertising*, *42*(1), 128–140.

Mameli, M., Paolanti, M., Pietrini, R., Pazzaglia, G., Frontoni, E., & Zingaretti, P. (2022). Deep learning approaches for fashion knowledge extraction from social media: A review. *IEEE Access*, *10*, 1545–1576.

Mo, L., & Yang, L. (2022). Research on application effective evaluation of artificial intelligence technology in marketing communication. *Security and Communication Networks*, *2022*, 1–8.

Moradi, M., & Dass, M. (2022). Applications of artificial intelligence in B2B marketing: Challenges and future directions. *Industrial Marketing Management*, *107*, 300–314.

Nagyova, N., & Bednarik, J. (2022). Position of corporate social responsibility in a corporate design. *European Journal of Media, Art and Photography*, *10*(2), 110–119.

Oc, Y., Plangger, K., Sands, S., Campbell, C. L., & Pitt, L. (2023). Luxury is what you say: Analyzing electronic word-of-mouth marketing of luxury products using artificial intelligence and machine learning. *Psychology & Marketing*, *40*(9), 1704–1719.

Ozdemir, O., Batar, M., & Isık, A. H. (2020). Churn analysis with machine learning classification algorithms in python. *Artificial Intelligence and Applied Mathematics in Engineering Problems*, 43, 844–852.

Svec, M., Madlenak, A., Bezakova, Z., & Horecky, J. (2021). Possibilities and limitations of communication of special purpose civic associations-The case of internal communication of a trade union active in a company influenced by the groundswell concept. *Communication Today*, *12*(2), 32–44.

Syam, N., & Sharma, A. (2018). Waiting for a sales renaissance in the fourth industrial revolution: Machine learning and artificial intelligence in sales research and practice. *Industrial Marketing Management*, *69*, 135–146.

Volkmar, G., Fischer, P. M., & Reinecke, S. (2022). Artificial Intelligence and machine learning: Exploring drivers, barriers, and future developments in marketing management. *Journal of Business Research*, *149*, 599–614.

Madlenak, A. (2020). Social media as an opportunity for s-commerce development at the time of covid-19 pandemic. *Marketing Identity: COVID- 2.0*, 397–404.

Matus Madlenak[1,*], and Katarina Kampova[1]

Global Indicators Affecting Cyber Security in Slovak Republic

Abstract:
Research background: Organizations are threatened by various types of cyber-attacks that can have a negative impact on their cyber security and cause financial losses or disrupt system functionality. Consequently, organizations have initiated the implementation of security measures aimed at mitigating the risk of cyber-attacks. At the national level in the Slovak Republic, organizations such as CSIRT.SK have been established. CSIRT.SK collects data and publishes statistics on cyber-attacks that have been reported and recorded in their information system. Statistics of this kind can be used in researching trends in cyber-attacks and the indicators influencing their occurrence.
Purpose of the article: This article will analyze these statistics and examine the influence of global events on the frequency of cyber-attacks. The technological advancements and globalization of today introduce new cyber security challenges and it is therefore necessary to understand how these global indicators contribute to shaping the cyber security environment. Understanding these factors is key to improving security measures, incident response and overall cyber security management in today's complex and ever-changing cyber environment.
Methods: For the purposes of this article, the analysis of available statistics from CSIRT.sk will be used. Other methods used are synthesis, induction, deduction and comparison.
Findings & Value added: Analysis of cyber security incident statistics shows that global events influence the occurrence of cyber security incidents. These global events are indicators that a higher risk of phishing attacks or other security incidents may be approaching.

Keywords: *phishing, cyber-attack, cyber security, indicators*

JEL Classification: *F52, H55, H56*

1 Introduction

Cyber security is becoming an increasingly important issue in today's digital age (Wang et al., 2014). The Slovak Republic is no exception and must face a growing

* Corresponding author: matus.madlenak@uniza.sk
1 University of Zilina, Faculty of Security Engineering, Univerzitna 1, 010 26 Zilina, Slovakia

number of cyber security incidents (Soltes et al., 2023). This article focuses on the examination of global events that affect cyber security, which is related to the occurrence of cyber security incidents in the Slovak Republic. This article will also include: a description of the process by which cyber security incidents are reported, highlighting the frequency of cyber security incidents in the Slovak Republic and description of cyber security incidents. To prove that global indicators influence the occurrence of cyber security incidents it is necessary to map the global events over time and compare them with the frequency of cyber security incidents. This data can provide proof that the presence of global incidents is an indicator that may be influencing cyber security in the country (Lallie et al., 2021).

1.1 Cyber-attacks in Slovak Republic

The Slovak Republic, like other countries, is threatened by various cyber-attacks. cyber- attacks include various forms of incidents in the digital environment that aim to attack, damage or steal sensitive information, breach network security or otherwise damage cyber infrastructure (Liang et al., 2019). These threats can come from many different actors, including states that are trying to spy on, sabotage or interfere with others' cyber systems, as well as from criminal groups or hacktivists who have own goals and motivations (Solms & Niekerk, 2013).

1.1.1 Incident Reporting

In the Slovak Republic, the sectors involved can report a security incident to the competent authorities, which are CSIRT.SK or SK CERT. Incidents are reported via a form or via email communication. In the case of email communication, it is recommended to encrypt the communication with a PGP key. For the purpose of this article, the way in which incidents are reported on the CSIRT.SK portal will be described. CSIRT.SK (2023) defines the rules and information that must be included when reporting an incident, which are:

The following rules must be observed when reporting an incident:

- provide a contact email address,
- provide a clear description of the incident,
- when describing the incident, provide as much information as possible that could help in the analysis of the incident.

Useful details that may assist in resolving the incident include: Information about the person in the organization reporting the incident, Information about the incident and Information about the affected devices and impacts.

Information about the person in the organization reporting the incident:

- job title,
- organization name,
- type of organization,
- other organizations involved.

Information about the incident:

- start time of the incident (if known),
- time and way of discovery,
- status of the incident (ongoing – yes/no/don't know),
- identification of exploited vulnerabilities (yes/no/don't know),
- what security measures have been taken,
- a detailed description – the process of the incident, the type of attack, the direction of the attack,
- security measures and their potential exploitation,
- in case of spam, virus, phishing, specific email messages, files or URLs should be sent,
- and in the case of a DoS attack, time stamps, time zone, source and destination IP (or MAC) addresses and ports, protocol type (TCP, UDP, ICMP, etc.) and, if possible, a sample of captured packets (by using WireShark) should be sent.

Information about the affected devices and impacts:

- device type and function IP address, hostname, protocol and ports to which the attack was directed,
- description of the device hardware,
- operating system (type, version),
- affected software or files,
- identification of the criticality of the device and its impact on business continuity,
- the status of the device ("in-service/out-of-service"),
- contact person which have access to the device,
- and presence of non-public information on the device (yes/no).

Once a cyber security incident is reported, CSIRT.SK can perform reactive services to resolve and troubleshoot the incident, provide support and coordinate incident resolution.

1.1.2 Statistics of Cyber Attack

CSIRT.SK records statistics on cyber security incidents, based on which it can be shown that phishing attacks are currently the most common among all known threats in the cyber environment. While the numbers of phishing attacks were lower in the past, there has been a rapid increase in recent times. From this data, it can be concluded that in 2019, 265 incidents of phishing attacks were recorded, but in 2020, this number has more than doubled to 548. In the following years, the number of reported phishing attacks outnumbered the number of other reported cyber security incidents. In fact, as many as 554 phishing attacks were reported last year (CSIRT.SK, 2022). The statistics of cyber security incidents are shown in Figure 1.

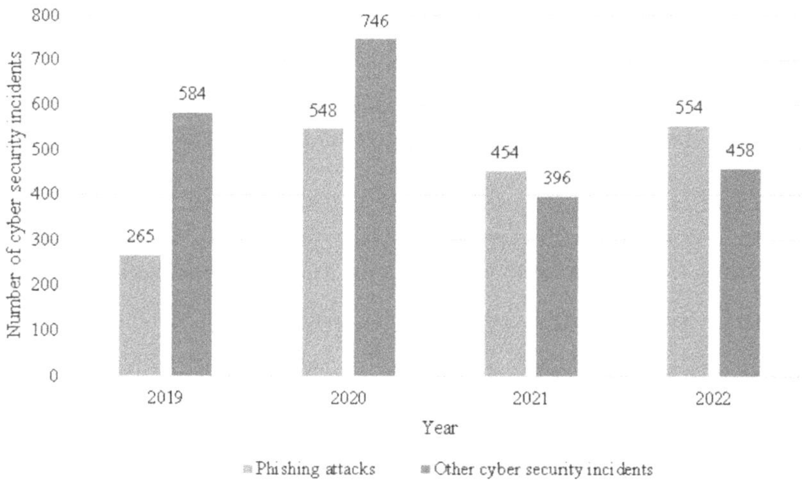

Figure 1. Statistics of phishing attacks and other cyber security incidents.
Source: CSIRT.SK (2022)

Based on the fact that phishing attacks are the most common type of cyber security incident, in this article we will categorize these incidents into: phishing attacks and other cyber security incidents (CSIRT.SK, 2022).

1.1.3 Phishing Attacks

Phishing attack is a cyber-attack that uses social engineering techniques to trick people into revealing sensitive information such as login credentials, financial data or personal information (Sahingoz et al., 2019). These attacks often involve fraudulent emails, websites or messages that pose as legitimate entities and create a false sense of trust and urgency. The attackers' aim is to manipulate the user into taking actions such as: voluntarily giving away personal information, clicking on malicious links or downloading malware (Wu et al., 2020). There are many types of phishing attacks, some more and some less sophisticated.

Common types of phishing attacks include for example: email phishing (Park & Rayz, 2018), spear phishing (Pande & Voditel, 2017) or pharming (Li & Chu, 2015). While there are many types of phishing attacks, all phishing attacks are characterized by specific significant features that can be used to detect them.

1.1.4 Other Cyber Security Incidents

Other cyber security incidents involve malicious activities and techniques designed to compromise the Confidentiality, Integrity, and Availability of systems (Gundz & Das, 2018). For the purposes of this article, all incidents except phishing attacks that are listed in CSIRT.SK's data will be considered as "other cyber security incidents." CSIRT.SK (2022) categorizes cyber security incidents as:

- botnet,
- DoS, DDoS,
- unauthorized access to information/information leakage,
- unauthorized modification of information,
- spam,
- scam,
- attempted breach,
- intrusion into the system,
- malicious code,
- vulnerability,
- other.

Some of these attacks are often more sophisticated than phishing attacks and can cause more significant damage to organisations' systems or cause higher financial losses (Solms & Niekerk, 2013). However, according to CSIRT.SK statistics, these cyber security incidents are in the minority, which is why they are defined in this article as "other cyber security incidents" (CSIRT.SK, 2022).

2 Methodology

The aim of the article is to investigate if global events affect the occurrence of cyber security incidents, which ultimately affects cyber security in the territory of the Slovak Republic.

Firstly, it was necessary to obtain theoretical knowledge about possible cyber-attacks and the way of reporting cyber-attacks in the Slovak Republic. It was also necessary to obtain relevant statistical data about reported cyber security incidents. This data was analyzed in terms of the frequency of cyber-attacks in specific years.

The final part of the paper focuses on the analytical investigation and comparison of the frequency of cyber security incidents in relation to global events by which the Slovak Republic was also affected. T This way it can be determined if global events are indicators that affect cyber security in Slovak Republic.

3 Results

First, it was necessary to map the events that affected not only the Slovak Republic, but the whole world. One of these events was the COVID-19 pandemic, which started to occur globally in 2019, but the first case of COVID-19 in the Slovak Republic was recorded in the first quarter of 2020. This event definitely had a significant impact not only on the Slovak Republic, but also on the whole world. The COVID-19 pandemic, caused by the SARS-CoV- 2 coronavirus, has become a global health crisis with widespread social, economic, security and political implications (Soltes et al., 2021). Therefore, the COVID-19 pandemic was definitely one of the most significant events in modern history, and its consequences will continue to be felt in various spheres of life in Slovakia and in the world.

Another event that has affected the social, economic, security and political spheres in the world, including the Slovak Republic, is the conflict between the Russian Federation and Ukraine. This military conflict in Ukraine, which started as early as 2014, escalated and gained global attention only in the first quarter of 2022. This event has an impact on states around the world, including Slovakia. The conflict between the Russian Federation and Ukraine therefore remains a significant issue in the international context and its impact and consequences for Slovakia and the world will continue to be felt in the future.

To clearly represent these events over time, a timeline was created that shows these events in each quarter of the years. This timeline is necessary to evaluate if global indicators have an impact on the occurrence of phishing and other cyber security incidents. The timeline is shown in Figure 2.

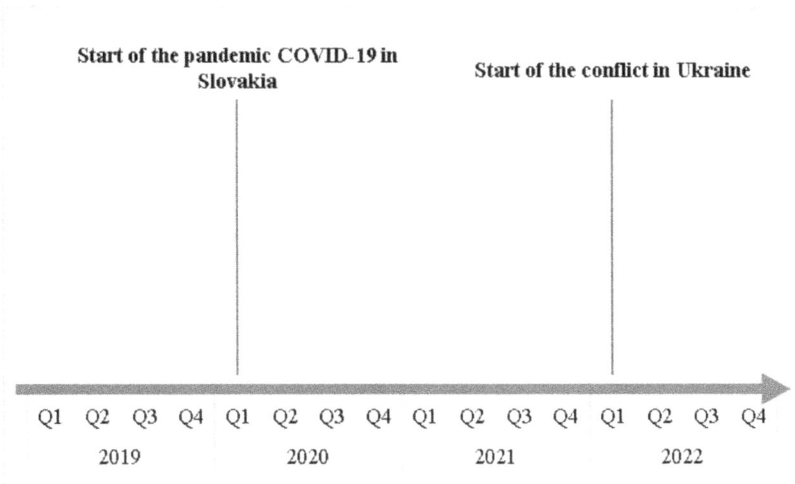

Figure 2. Global events timeline.
Source: Ryngach (2023)

To investigate if global indicators affect the occurrence of cyber-attacks, data from CSIRT.SK for the years 2019 to 2022 will be used. The data has been processed and split into individual quarters for each year. Based on this split and knowledge about when global events occurred, it can be examined if there was an increased occurrence of cyber-attacks in each time period. According to the timeline in Figure X, it is evident that the investigated global events occurred in the first quarter (Q1) of 2020 and the first quarter (Q1) of 2022.

The first thing that will be investigated is if global indicators have influenced the frequency of phishing attacks. Based on the filtering cyber-attacks data from CSIRT.SK, it is possible to track the frequency of reported phishing attacks in each quarter. Phishing attacks reach the highest frequency of reports in 2020 and 2022, as can be seen in Figure 3. The highest frequency in 2020 was in Q1, where the number of reported phishing attacks increased by 110 reports compared to the previous quarter. Another interesting finding is that the number of reported phishing attacks never dropped to the same level as it was in 2019. The second highest frequency of reported phishing attacks in 2022 was in Q1, where phishing attacks increased by 56 compared to the previous quarter.

The highest numbers of phishing attacks were reported in the quarters where global events such as the covid-19 pandemic and the conflict in Ukraine were occurring. Therefore, it can be assumed that these global indicators have influenced the occurrence of phishing attacks in the Slovak Republic.

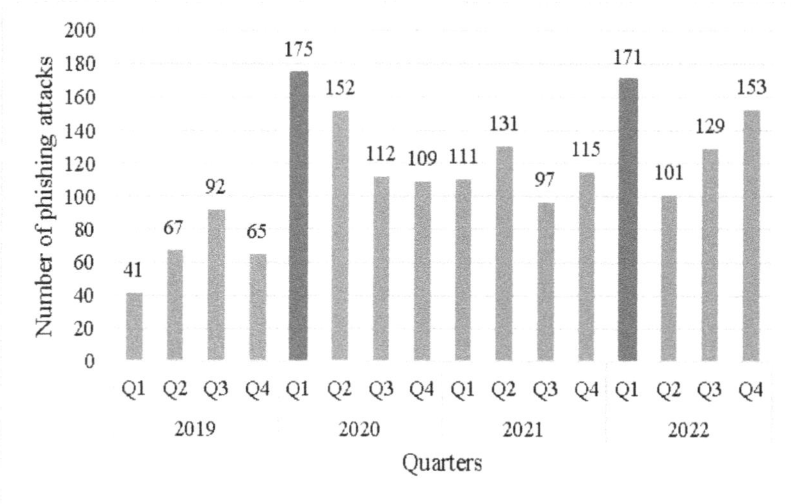

Figure 3. Phishing attack statistic.
Source: CSIRT.SK (2022)

Next, it will be investigated if global indicators have influenced the frequency of other cyber security incidents. By filtering other cyber security incidents in the CSIRT.SK data, it is possible to track the frequency of their reporting. As can be seen in Figure 4, other cyber security incidents reach their highest reporting frequency in 2020 and 2022. The highest frequency in 2020 was in Q1, in which the number of other security incidents increased by 173 reports compared to the previous quarter. It is also interesting to note that the number of these reports decreased significantly during 2020. The second highest number of reports of other security incidents was in Q1 2022, where they increased by 55 compared to the previous quarter.

The highest frequencies of reports of other security incidents were recorded in quarters where global events such as the covid-19 pandemic and the conflict in Ukraine occurred. Therefore, it can be assumed that these global indicators have influenced the occurrence of other security incidents in the Slovak Republic in some way.

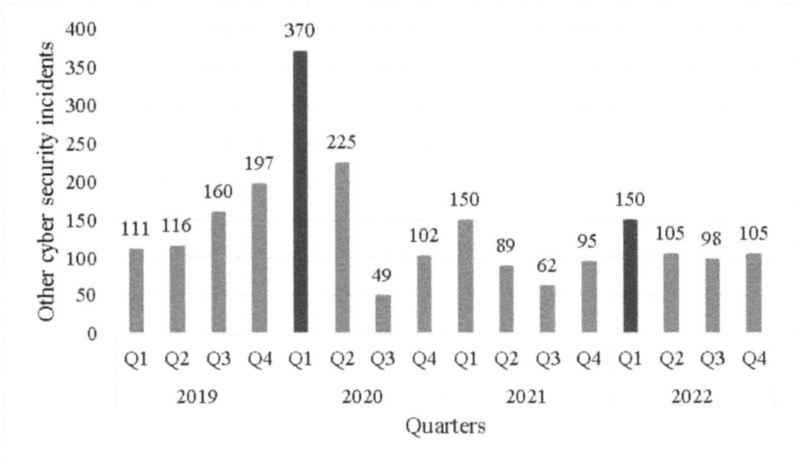

Figure 4. Other cyber security incident statistics.
Source: CSIRT.SK (2022)

It is important to highlight the trends in cyber-attacks over time. Phishing attacks, as shown in Figure 5, have a mostly increasing trend and can be expected to grow in the future. On the other hand, other security incidents have a decreasing trend and it can be assumed that their occurrence will decrease or stagnate with the passage of time.

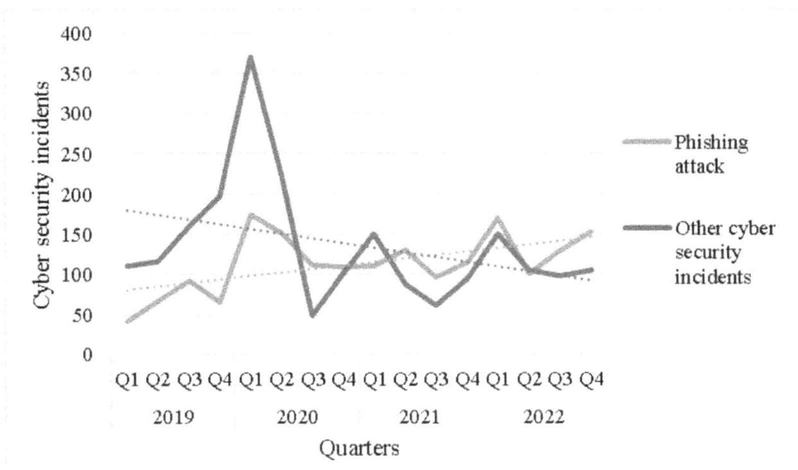

Figure 5. Trends of phishing attack and other cyber security incidents.
Source: CSIRT.SK (2022)

The CSIRT.SK statistics provide relevant data to investigate the correlation between the frequency of cyber-attacks and global indicators. This investigation revealed a higher occurrence of cyber security incidents in quarters where global events occurred.

4 Discussion

Global indicators such as the COVID-19 pandemic and the conflict in Ukraine are having a significant impact on cyber security and on the increase in phishing attacks. These events create ideal conditions for cyber attackers to exploit the chaos and uncertainty that often prevails during these global crises. During the COVID-19 pandemic, the world moved online, where more people worked, learned and communicated. This massive move online created a huge space for cyber-attacks. Attackers were able to misuse the confusion surrounding the pandemic and the urgency of information regarding protection from COVID-19 to create fake websites and phishing campaigns that enticed people to provide their sensitive data. It was during the approach of the COVID-19 virus (Q1 – 2020) that an increased occurrence of phishing attack reports was detected. Therefore, it can be concluded that the COVID-19 pandemic had some impact on the occurrence of phishing attacks and other security incidents. The conflict in Ukraine, which began in 2022, has contributed to the rise in phishing attacks and other security incidents. In a military crisis, attackers are trying to take advantage of geopolitical instability and public fears. For example, they may try to spread fake news or attachments containing malware through email messages. The fear and increased attention to the conflict may make people more inclined to click on suspicious links or download attachments, which opens the door for attackers. During start of the conflict in Ukraine (Q1–2022), an increased occurrence of phishing and other security incidents was detected. Therefore, it can be concluded that the conflict in Ukraine has had some impact on the occurrence of phishing attacks and other security incidents.

Statistics confirm the rise of phishing attacks and other security incidents during these global events. Therefore, organisations and individuals must be careful about the security of their online communications and invest in solutions that can protect them from these cyber threats. It is essential to stay alert and informed about current events in the world, as these global indicators can significantly affect the level of cyber security.

Acknowledgments

This paper was supported by project KEGA 031ŽU-4/2022 Creation of original study materials and a university textbook in the field of criminology.

References

CSIRT.SK. (2022). *Incident statistics.* Ministry of Investment, Regional Development and Informatization of the Slovak Republic. https://www.csirt.gov.sk/index.html? csrt=16999763538465700465

CSIRT.SK. (2023). *Report an incident.* Ministry of Investment, Regional Development and Informatization of the Slovak Republic. https://www.csirt.gov.sk/nahlasit- incident.html?csrt=16999763538465700465

Gunduz, M. Z., & Das, R. (2018). Analysis of cyber-attacks on smart grid applications. *2018 International Conference on Artificial Intelligence and Data Processing (IDAP)*, 1–5.

Lallie, H., Shepherd, L., Nurse, J., Erola, A., Epiphaniou, G., Maple, C., & Bellekens, X. (2021). Cyber security in the age of COVID-19: A timeline and analysis of cyber- crime and cyber-attacks during the pandemic. *Computers & Security, 105.*

Li, Y., & Chu, S. (2015). A pharming attack hybrid detection model based on IP addresses and web content. *Optik, 126*(2), 234–239.

Liang, G., Weller, S. R., Luo, F., Zhao, J., & Dong, Z. Y. (2019). Distributed blockchain- based data protection framework for modern power systems against Cyber Attacks. *IEEE Transactions on Smart Grid, 10*(3), 3162–3173.

Pande, D., & Voditel, P. (2017). Spear Phishing: Diagnosing attack paradigm. *2017 International Conference on Wireless Communications, Signal Processing and Networking (WiSPNET)*, 2720–2724.

Park, G., & Rayz, J. (2018). Ontological detection of Phishing Emails. *2018 IEEE International Conference on Systems, Man, and Cybernetics (SMC)*, 2858–2863.

Ryngach, N. O. (2023). The mortality from external causes: Impact of the COVID-19 pandemic and the war in Ukraine. *Statistics of Ukraine, 100*(1), 140–153.

Sahingoz, O., Buber, E., Demir, O., & Diri,B. (2019). Machine learning based phishing detection from URLs. *Expert Systems with Applications, 117*, 345–357.

Solms, R., & Niekerk, J. (2013). From information security to cyber security. *Computers & Security, 38*, 97–102.

Soltes, V., & Durica, J. (2021). Impacts of the covid-19 pandemic on education funding in Slovakia. *14th annual International Conference of Education, Research and Innovation,* 9729–9734.

Soltes, V., Adamova, V., & Hubocan, S. (2023). Effectiveness of peer-to-peer crime prevention program in the field of education about internet security. *15th International Conference on Education and New Learning Technologies,* 7836–7841.

Wang, Y., Chao, L., & Cheng, N. (2014). Internet security protection in personal sensitive information. *2014 Tenth International Conference on Computational Intelligence and Security*, 628–632.

Wu, J. et al. (2020). Who are the Phishers? Phishing scam detection on Ethereum via network embedding. *IEEE Transactions on Systems, Man, and Cybernetics: Systems, 52*(2), 1156–1166.

Adam Madlenak[1,*], and Marek Svec[2]

Expression Restrictions on the Global Social Networks as a Barrier to the Implementation of the Concept of Groundswell in Promotion of Eco-products

Abstract:
Research background: The advancement of the digital landscape and global social media platforms has expanded the scope for individuals to voice their thoughts and disseminate ideas without restraint. Freedom of expression has evolved into a fundamental instrument for self- representation, even during instances where individuals may perceive others' opinions as disagreeable or as a direct intrusion on their right to privacy. Likewise, such expressions can also be perceived in relation to corporate entities involved in commercial undertakings. Within this framework, the right to privacy encompasses safeguarding the positive reputation of these enterprises.
Purpose of the article: This paper aims to establish the parameters of freedom of speech and expression within the online sphere, drawing from established jurisprudence both at home and abroad. Furthermore, it endeavors to ascertain the legal framework governing interferences with individuals' privacy.
Methods: In pursuit of the designated objective of this paper, the authors employed scientific research methodologies that naturally facilitated the exploration of issues pertaining to the identification of problem areas concerning intrusions into the privacy of individuals, as well as within the bounds of permissible dissemination of negative expressions. Predominantly, they harnessed analytical, inductive, deductive, and comparative research methods.
Findings & Value added: The significance of this paper can be found in its systematic structuring and translation of court-derived conclusions into the set of rules relevant for

* Corresponding author: adam.madlenak@ucm.sk
1 University of Ss. Cyril and Methodius in Trnava, Faculty of Mass Media Communication, Department of Marketing Communication, Námestie J. Herdu 2, 917 01 Trnava, Slovakia
2 Matej Bel University in Banská Bystrica, Faculty of Law, Department of Civil and Labor Law, Komenského 20, 974 01 Banská Bystrica, Slovakia

overseeing expressions on social media platforms of businesses endorsing environmentally-conscious products.

Keywords: *digital media, social networks, right to privacy, freedom of expression, communication*

JEL Classification: *K36; M31; M54*

1 Introduction

The concept of the right to privacy undeniably falls under the category of fundamental human rights and freedoms that should receive the utmost attention from the government due to their potential impact on the human dignity of individuals involved. This is precisely why legal protection for private and family life, commonly referred to as privacy, is enshrined in some of the most significant legal frameworks in the Slovak Republic, such as the Constitution of the Slovak Republic and the Civil Code. Furthermore, international agreements also extend this legal safeguard. However, there exists a certain tension between the right to freedom of expression and the right to privacy (Iemets et al., 2020), with the latter ensuring individuals the opportunity to voice their opinions on various social or legal matters. Consequently, the scope of freedom of expression encompasses a wide array of thoughts, viewpoints, declarations, or observations, which, by their very nature, can sometimes be perceived as negative, discomforting, or intrusive by those affected (Bedi, 2009). However, adopting a similar perspective, these expressions can also be viewed concerning legal entities or civic organizations engaged in activities with potential commercial aspects, such as the promotion of eco-friendly products. Here, the freedom of expression exercised by their clientele or stakeholders often leads to assessments of their operations, organizational structure, or their representatives (Pacalajova & Kubinec, 2021). In this context, it appears that the right to privacy undergoes a certain transformation, taking the shape of the right to safeguard the reputation or good name of these enterprises (as an integral component of personal rights). This is also reflected in the protection of the reputation of the services or eco-friendly products these businesses introduce or offer within the competitive economic landscape. Given the substantial shifts in our social landscape, marked by a shift from conventional offline interactions to a digital-centric environment, potential adverse manifestations of freedom of expression can primarily be observed in the online sphere. These manifestations may manifest as negative reviews on various online platforms or through comments and expressions on social media platforms, whether by individuals or legal entities.

However, what seems to be conspicuously lacking, to a certain degree, is a heightened awareness of personal responsibility for the messages conveyed by both natural individuals and legal entities who currently invoke the safeguard of freedom of expression. This void in awareness becomes particularly apparent when the entity that becomes the target of their expressions begins to demand the protection of their human dignity (Vives & Morales, 2021). The subjective perception of the boundaries of freedom of expression on the part of these individuals often translates into an unbridled presentation of their views and commentary on specific events and situations (Doyle & Bagaric, 2005). They perceive and judge these situations solely from their perspective, often neglecting to consider the objective facts related to the subject matter of their conveyed messages. The outcome is a one-sided expression of opinion or attitude, frequently characterized by a negative or defamatory tone. Such expressions may not necessarily be the result of an objective thought process but instead represent an emotionally charged personal expression, devoid of minimal evaluation regarding the societal or personal consequences and repercussions it may entail.

The same principle holds true when the subject of a subjective 'assessment' is a specific eco-product or service, which the individual making the evaluation might not have personally experienced or used (Kupec, 2021). Nevertheless, their assessment could yield negative outcomes when perceived by others. It is crucial to acknowledge that while the online environment and social networks, as prominent manifestations of it, have ushered in a significant transformation in the rapidity and efficacy of information dissemination, they have concurrently paved the way for the proliferation of inaccurate or unverified information and messages, which bear a strong potential for encroachment upon fundamental human rights and freedoms, as well as the legally protected interests of both natural and legal entities (Mills, 2022). We must also recognize the inherent nature of the groundswell as an online tool for sharing experiential knowledge and fostering connections, often without the necessity for the involvement of the subjects affected – the very entities that form the subjects of the pertinent information. This dynamic has forged an uncontrolled and unstoppable information ecosystem, in which anyone can participate and contribute to its formation and expansion.

Legislation and judicial rulings have explicitly defined the criteria for establishing liability concerning expressions, even when such expressions do not fall within the broad interpretation of freedom of speech (Zulova, 2020a). When applying the proportionality test, they have set substantive legal conditions that prioritize the right to safeguard private and family life, as well as the right to protect the reputation and standing of a legal entity (including its products and services), over the right to freedom of speech and the ability to articulate oneself in a particular manner and content (Alvear, 2014). According to the standpoint of the Supreme Court of the Slovak Republic, the right to privacy encompasses a natural person's prerogative to autonomously decide whether and to what extent personal aspects of their private life should be disclosed or disseminated to others. The violation of the right to privacy occurs not only in cases of unauthorized acquisition of information pertaining to an individual's private life but also in instances of unauthorized dissemination of said information.[1]

Expressions made by specific individuals or entities, particularly those conveyed through social media platforms, exert an immediate and direct influence on an individual's privacy. Consequently, the legal framework governing this matter possesses an unmistakably interdisciplinary nature. This applies regardless of whether these expressions, for example, were shared on personal social media accounts or presented within official public profiles on professional social networks (Marsoof, 2011). The Constitutional Court of the Czech Republic has offered insights into the character of Facebook, highlighting that "it does not possess a strictly private or public status. Its nature largely hinges on the preferences of specific users, as they configure their privacy settings within their profiles and potentially within individual posts." The Court categorizes communication restricted to one user, with no visibility or interference from other users, as inherently private (as detailed in paragraph 39 of the Constitutional Court's Decision dated October 30, 2014, file reg. no. III 844/13). Legally speaking, the crucial assessment centers on the expressions and statements originating from the source of information, particularly if they carry harmful or defamatory implications. The pivotal element lies in whether this information was conveyed to another individual via a private channel or shared within a private social media network. The latter may grant other users of the network access to the communicated information, potentially leading to a discernible intrusion into the privacy of another individual, especially within a group comprising numerous social network users.

2 Methods

This scientific paper endeavors to examine the judicial approaches taken when assessing the collision between freedom of expression and the right to privacy,

1 Decision of the Supreme Court of the Slovak Republic dated February 18, 2010, file reg. no. 3 Cdo 137/2008.

particularly within the online domain. It is based on a critical legal analysis of judicial rulings from national and European judicial authorities. Subsequently, it aims to deduce specific principles to guide the formulation of relevant regulations and the potential legal safeguarding of both individuals and businesses operating in competitive economic markets. The core focus of this scholarly exploration lies in identifying pertinent legal tools and their prospective legislative framework. Such a framework should be capable of providing effective legal protection, whether it pertains to preserving a good reputation or safeguarding eco-products and services. Notably, this pertains to situations wherein other entities, potentially competitors, engage in unauthorized criticism via social networks, websites, or even pose as 'fictional' customers reacting to purchased eco-products (Strbova, 2016). The analysis places particular emphasis on examining legal judgments rendered by courts, as they hold the unique capacity to delineate the boundaries and constraints of freedom of expression. This is especially relevant given the somewhat vaguely formulated legal provisions pertaining to fundamental human rights and freedoms, as enshrined in Chapter 2 of the Constitution of the Slovak Republic and the general provisions of the Civil Code. To reach the goal, the authors employ an integrative methodological approach. By leveraging select qualitative and logical-cognitive methods, this approach aims to provide a thorough and systematic examination of the chosen subject matter. This is conducted with the expectation of encountering various legislative adjustments along the way. In addition to conducting an in-depth critical analysis, which centers on the existing national and European regulations geared toward shaping future legislation, cognitive processes such as induction, deduction, comparison, and synthesis are also utilized. These cognitive operations are intended to further the advancement of scientific knowledge, stimulate discussion, and facilitate the eventual formulation of conclusions. The authors have drawn from both domestic and international professional literature as sources of factual information. While the content of these sources has, to a large extent, contributed to addressing the scientific inquiries at hand – questions that form the core of this scientific work. Furthermore, attention has been directed towards knowledge disseminated through monographs and peer-reviewed journal publications, all of which are cataloged within internationally recognized bibliographic databases.

3 Results and Discussion

Freedom of speech and freedom of expression are classified within the realm of second- generation basic human rights and freedoms. Its legal safeguard is delineated in Article 26 of the Constitution of the Slovak Republic, as well as in Article 10 of the Convention on Fundamental Human Rights and Freedoms, to which the Slovak Republic is a signatory. These provisions do not confer unrestricted freedom of expression; instead, their interpretation hinges on three criteria that circumscribe the scope of this right. The first criterion stipulates that any restriction must be authorized by law, while the second and third criteria outline the prerequisites that must be satisfied for such restrictions to be permissible. These prerequisites *include "necessity in a democratic society" and "the overarching goal of safeguarding the rights and freedoms of others, state security, public order, public health, and moral values"* (Drgonec, 2012). Nevertheless, it's crucial to acknowledge that freedom of speech, as constitutionally assured, does have its limits. The constitutionally enshrined right to voice one's opinions encounters constraints in terms of content, especially when these constraints involve the rights enumerated in Article 19 of the Slovak Republic's Constitution. The clash between these rights is evident, for instance, in the application of Section 11 and subsequent sections of the Civil Code in tandem with the implementation of civil protections for personal rights. Similarly, it arises in the utilization of Section 19b, paragraph 3, of the Civil Code concerning the safeguarding of the reputation of a legal entity. In such instances, the obligation of the judiciary is to interpret individual legal provisions primarily through the lens of the purpose and significance behind safeguarding constitutionally guaranteed rights and freedoms. When freedom of expression is at odds with the right to personal protection, it is imperative to ensure that, under the specific circumstances of the case, neither of these rights is unjustly favored over the other. A case-specific assessment must invariably delve into the degree or intensity of the alleged encroachment on the fundamental right to personal protection, particularly in the context of freedom of expression and the right to access information, while taking into account the imperative of proportionality in the exercise of these rights.[2]

Section 11 of the Civil Code outlines the protected personal rights, while Section 13 of the Civil Code goes on to furnish examples of forms and methods that an aggrieved natural person may select to safeguard their rights. As specified in Section 13, paragraph 1, of the Civil Code, a natural person possesses the entitlement to request suitable redress. The term 'suitable' implies that the redress should align with the nature of the infringement, the personal

2 Decision of the Regional Court in Bratislava dated December 20, 2022, file reg. no. 5Co/146/2021.

domain impacted, and the specific circumstances and repercussions of the infringement. Notably, the Civil Code refrains from stipulating the degree of 'suitability' required. In court practice, typically, in cases involving the mildest forms of defamatory infringements (provided all criteria for incurring liability for personal rights infringement are met), an apology is deemed appropriate. Section 13, paragraph 2, of the Civil Code correlates the 'severity' of the harm or the 'significant diminishment of dignity' with situations wherein non- material redress, as per Section 13, paragraph 1, of the Civil Code, appears to be insufficient.[3]

Personal rights can be encroached upon through spoken or written words, images, or any other action of a disparaging, demeaning, disgraceful, or disreputable nature (Marmor, 2015). When assessing the appropriateness of specific statements, it is crucial, foremost, to differentiate whether the statement constitutes a statement of fact or an evaluative judgment (critique). This differentiation is essential because the criteria governing the acceptability of each of these categories vary. Factual claims are grounded in verifiable facts, representing an objectively existing reality that can be confirmed through evidence, making the veracity of the claim demonstrable. Conversely, an evaluative judgment reflects the subjective viewpoint of its author, who adopts a particular stance on the given fact by evaluating it in terms of accuracy and acceptability based on their own (subjective) standards.[4] Factual statements are inherently objective and subject to verification; they represent statements of specific, empirically demonstrable facts. In contrast, evaluative judgments always carry a subjective nature, as they reflect the opinions of the individuals expressing these judgments. While the existence of factual statements can be substantiated through evidence, the same requirement does not apply to evaluative judgments regarding the verification of their truth. Evaluative judgments tend to interpret reality with varying degrees of freedom, with objective and non-objective criticism serving as manifestations of evaluative judgments rather than objective critiques. In certain contentious scenarios, hybrid statements may emerge, blending elements of both factual statements and evaluative judgments. The evaluation of such statements necessitates consideration within a broader context, with the overall tone of the discourse playing a decisive role.

---

3 Decision of the Regional Court in Bratislava dated January 25, 2023, file reg. no. 7Co/25/2019.

4 Decision of the Regional Court in Bratislava dated March 29, 2023, file reg. no. 7Co/4/2021.

Concerning the realm of freedom of expression, evaluative judgments receive heightened protection compared to factual statements (statements of fact); an evaluative judgment's acceptability requires merely a reasonable foundation.[5] Moreover, it becomes imperative to draw a clear distinction between criticism and unwarranted intrusion. The distinguishing factor hinges upon the critical components of truth, credibility, objectivity, and the underlying intent driving a particular expression. Legal safeguards come into play solely when the criticized statement is fundamentally untrue or grossly misrepresents the facts. Criticism remains well-founded if it remains within the confines of substantial criticism (rooted in factual accuracy and conclusions derived from them that substantiate these facts) and adheres to appropriateness in both substance and presentation.[6] For criticism to be deemed permissible or well-founded, it necessitates a substantive, specific approach that aligns with the requisites of both content and presentation, without straying from the essential parameters essential for its intended purpose. Factual criticism implies commencing from genuine and accurate sources and subsequently deriving relevant evaluative judgments based on these sources. Statements or viewpoints whose outcomes cannot be logically inferred from the factual details elucidated within the described event cannot be classified as criticism.[7]

Legal entities are endowed with the privilege to uphold their untarnished image from the moment of their establishment. The positive repute of a legal entity is contingent upon the manner in which it conducts itself in the realm of business relationships and is established based on the experiences encountered by its business associates, patrons, or other affiliated entities.[8] Employee criticism directed at the employer is not inherently impermissible. The European Court of Human Rights (ECtHR) underlined that employment relationships should be rooted in mutual trust, without necessitating absolute loyalty from the employee to the employer. The court emphasized that certain expressions, while permissible under certain conditions, may not be deemed appropriate within the sphere of labor relations. To illustrate, the court found that the use of highly offensive or derogatory language in a workplace context warranted severe repercussions,

5 Decision of the Regional Court in Banská Bystrica from January 19, 2023, file reg. no. 11Co/1/2022.

6 Decision of the Supreme Court of the Slovak Republic R 103/1967.

7 Decision of the Supreme Court of the Slovak Republic, file reg. no 3 Cdo 61/2000.

8 Decision of the Supreme Court of the Czech Republic dated March 18, 2008, file reg. no 30 Cdo 1385/2006.

including the termination of the employment relationship.[9] The legal framework governing the protection of the right to privacy, which can be encroached upon through active or passive actions such as expressing oneself on social media or sharing related information, unequivocally supports the permissibility of holding the responsible natural person accountable for such interference (Arneson, 2000). Subsequently, what becomes significant is ascertaining the legal status of said individual, leading to the aforementioned accumulation of liability relationships, and eventually culminating in the imposition of appropriate sanctions under the relevant legal framework (comprising civil law, labor law, or civil regulations). By examining actual cases, various scenarios come to light, including online expressions that directly or indirectly infringe upon the personal rights or reputation of an employer or are directed towards other employees within the same organization. Furthermore, expert opinions from beyond these defined circles have also highlighted instances where online expressions encroach upon the rights of customers or business partners, encompassing the personal rights of individuals or the reputation of legal entities (Pfisterer, 2019). Speech that is deemed inappropriate concerning an employer's clients, customers, or business partners ultimately impacts the employer as well (e.g., contract losses), potentially constituting an indirect violation of their personal rights or good reputation. Therefore, when evaluating the specific consequences of expressions on social networks by natural or legal persons (encompassing not only the dissemination of incorrect or false information but also activities often categorized as hate speech, trolling, or the spread of hoaxes), it is essential to consistently establish the relationship between the originator of the information and the affected entity about which the information is shared. Subsequently, the relevant legal framework for ascribing responsibility to the information's source must be applied. In its decision-making role, the European Court of Human Rights upholds that freedom of expression extends to civil law and employment relations (Madrid, 2016), not only for employees in the public sector but also those in private law employment relationships.

Full provisions for the safeguarding of personal rights within legal relationships are contained within the Civil Code, specifically under Article 11 of the Civil Code. To successfully assert a legal claim by an individual in cases of personal rights infringement or the need to protect one's personality, it is not necessary for

9 Decision of the Grand Chamber of the European Court of Human Rights dated September 12, 2011. Palomo Sanchez and others v. Spain, complaint no. 28955/06, no. 28957/06, no. 28959/06 and no. 28964/06.

adverse consequences to result in physical harm to the person or for the person to incur specific material losses due to such interference. The Civil Code does not mandate the wrongdoer's culpability for an unlawful act infringing upon the right to protect one's personality. Even establishing that the subject of such interference acted under a misconception cannot absolve responsibility. The quantification of remedies available to an employee in cases of unauthorized intrusion into their privacy can be ascertained from the provisions set forth in Section 13 of the Civil Code: (a) negative action (the right to demand the cessation of unauthorized interference), (b) restitution action (the right to demand the removal of the consequences of unauthorized interventions) and (c) satisfactory action (the right to provide adequate satisfaction). The Civil Code also provides individuals whose right to privacy has been unlawfully infringed upon with the entitlement to monetary compensation for non-material harm. This entitlement may be claimed particularly if an individual's standing or social respectability has been significantly diminished. The Civil Code refrains from explicitly defining what constitutes a significant reduction in dignity or social respectability. The overarching prerequisites for the emergence of liability encompass the presence of an intervention that objectively carries the potential to cause non-material harm, encompassing the violation or jeopardization of a natural person's physical and moral integrity. This intervention must be unauthorized, and a causal link must exist between the aforementioned prerequisites.

Concerning the concept of monetary compensation for non-material harm according to Section 13, par. 2 of the Civil Code, it's essential to emphasize that it serves a fundamentally equivalent purpose to adequate satisfaction as defined in Article 127 of the Constitution of the Slovak Republic and just satisfaction in line with Article 41 of the Convention. The prerequisite for granting financial compensation is non-material harm, which has the potential to substantially diminish a citizen's dignity or their standing in society. In most instances, discerning the precise repercussions of an intrusion on the right to the protection of personality proves to be highly challenging and, given the unique nature of the subject matter at hand, essentially unattainable. The guiding criterion for determining the appropriateness of granting financial compensation is found in the legal perspective of the Constitutional Court of the Slovak Republic, wherein such compensation is primarily considered in cases where the infringement of a fundamental right or freedom is irreparable. This implies that there exists no avenue for rescinding the decision or measure or achieving restoration.[10] Unless the non-material harm

---

10 The decision of the Constitutional Court of the Slovak Republic on January 21, 2003, file reg. no. I ÚS 15/02.

inflicted upon a natural person can be alleviated through one of the forms of moral satisfaction as outlined in Section 13, par. 1 of the Civil Code, it is imperative to select a suitable and simultaneously effective means in the given context. The application of Section 13, par. 2 of the Civil Code (linked to considerations of the 'severity' of the infringement and the 'significant diminishment of dignity') only comes into play when moral satisfaction (Section 13 par. 1 of the Civil Code) proves to be inadequate. The aforementioned formulations adequately rationalize and clarify why the initial court rightfully imposed an obligation on the defendant to offer an apology to the plaintiff in accordance with Section 13, par. 1 of the Civil Code. Furthermore, they elucidate why the defendant was not subjected to penalties as stipulated in Section 13, par. 2 of the Civil Code (a matter also raised by the plaintiff but not subject to appellate review).[11]

In cases of necessity, we must place the compensation awarded for damages within the broader framework of the concept of freedom of expression, a cornerstone of democratic societies (Diggelmann & Cleis, 2014). This principle, subject to limitations articulated in Article 10, paragraph 2 of the Convention, encompasses not only information or ideas that find favor, pose no harm, or elicit indifference but also extends to information or ideas that may offend, shock, or disturb. Freedom of speech, as outlined in Article 10, is circumscribed by specific exceptions that necessitate a narrow interpretation, with each restriction compellingly substantiated. These principles carry significant weight, particularly in the realm of publishing. While the press must operate within the boundaries established, including those safeguarding state security and upholding the authority of the judiciary, it remains an essential conduit for the dissemination of information and ideas, with the public retaining an equal entitlement to receive them. To think otherwise would diminish the press's role as a vigilant guardian of the public interest. The adjective 'necessary,' as mentioned in Article 10, paragraph 2 of the Convention, inherently implies the presence of an immediate requirement. According to the jurisprudence of the ECtHR, Article 10, paragraph 2 of the Convention should be construed in a manner where the exercise of the right to freedom of expression may incur penalties (including the imposition of an obligation to provide monetary compensation for non-material damage under Section 13, paragraph 2 of the Civil Code) solely contingent upon the substantiated existence of an immediate necessity for such a penalty. Exceptions to the right to freedom of expression

11 Decision of the Regional Court in Bratislava dated January 25, 2023, file reg. no. 7Co/ 25/2019.

must undergo a stringent interpretation, and the imperative need for any limitation must be convincingly established.[12]

In proceedings aimed at safeguarding personal rights, when it comes to awarding monetary compensation for non-material harm, the plaintiff bears the onus of proof. They are required to substantiate (shoulder the burden of proving their assertion) that moral satisfaction alone is inadequate due to an unauthorized intrusion into their personal rights, particularly when such an intrusion has significantly undermined their personal dignity or standing in society. In the established jurisprudence of the Supreme Court of the Slovak Republic, it has been consistently emphasized that assessing the extent to which this intrusion has eroded an individual's dignity or societal reputation should commence by examining the subsequent responses elicited within the individual's family, professional, or other pertinent environments. This yardstick must be established through the presentation and evaluation of these responses. Only in cases where there exists compelling evidence indicating reactions indicative of a substantial decline in personal dignity or societal esteem, in line with Section 13 of the Civil Code, may an individual, under extraordinary circumstances, be eligible for supplementary monetary compensation for non-pecuniary harm.[13] In instances of encroachments upon the right to privacy, it's worth noting that a significant decline in personal dignity or societal regard isn't the sole pivotal aspect to gauge the gravity of harm inflicted upon an individual's protected rights. When privacy has been breached, it shouldn't be incumbent upon the affected individual to establish that the unauthorized intrusion bore defamatory consequences, leading to a diminishment of their standing and dignity within society.[14] When considering compensation for non-monetary harm, it is crucial to refrain from bestowing disproportionate or overly substantial amounts that might lead to undue enrichment. This approach is essential to prevent any devaluation of compensations granted for infringements on other fundamental rights, as enshrined in the Constitution of the Slovak Republic, including those concerning health or even the preservation of life.[15]

---

12 Finding of the Constitutional Court of the Slovak Republic, file reg. no. II. ÚS 326/09.

13 Decision of the Supreme Court of the Slovak Republic, file reg. no. 4Cdo 15/2003.

14 Decision of the Supreme Court of the Slovak Republic dated February 18, 2010, file reg. no. 3 Cdo 137/2008.

15 Decision of the Supreme Court of the Slovak Republic dated April 28, 1998, file reg. no.1 Cdo 89/97

4 Conclusion

The increasing dominance of the digital sphere, at the expense of traditional 'offline' connections, has facilitated the rise of extreme or unacceptable beliefs that are incompatible with the values of a democratic society (De Terwangne, 2012). Such beliefs are frequently accompanied by offensive language and a deliberate intent to encroach upon an individual's personal life, particularly those at the receiving end of this expression, or to undermine the reputation of a product or service associated with the person's unfavorable sentiments. In many cases, this harm is the result of deliberate actions aimed at gaining a competitive advantage in a fiercely contested economic market. Across all the scenarios outlined, a shared factor is the lack of awareness regarding the minimal level of accountability and the potential repercussions. These consequences may bear relevance within the realms of civil, commercial, or criminal law. Furthermore, in cases involving an employment relationship, they may extend into the domain of labor law (Duff & Johnson, 1983), particularly when the source of unverified or inaccurate information concerning the subject is an individual currently engaged in an employment relationship with the company or the product associated with the dissemination of such information. Legal precedent has laid down relatively explicit guidelines for assessing the acceptability of such critique or expression, with a primary emphasis on the factual veracity of these ideas and the objectivity of the claims. The constraints on expression and the entitlement to non-pecuniary damage compensation in instances where the requisite legal prerequisites for the permissibility of intrusions into the privacy of natural or legal persons are not met have been carefully outlined through the extensive case law produced by national and European judicial authorities. The decision to assert their right to privacy protection ultimately rests with the affected entities (Zulova, 2020b). Nonetheless, the legislative framework in this regard remains relatively unambiguous.

Acknowledgments

The research was supported by the Scientific Grant Agency of the Ministry of Education, Science, Research and Sport of the Slovak Republic and the Slovak Academy of Sciences (VEGA, No. 1/0458/21) under the project entitled *"Management of the 'groundswell' concept by business entities in promotion of environmentally-friendly products in times of technology interference."*

References

Alvear, M. N. (2014). The right to communicate: Conflicts surrounding freedom of expression in contemporary societies. *Chasqui: Revista Latinoamericana de Comunicación*, *126*, 126–127.

Arneson, R. J. (2000). Egalitarian justice versus the right to privacy? *Social Philosophy & Policy*, *17*(2), 91–119.

Bedi, S. (2009). *Rejecting rights*. Cambridge University Press.

De Terwangne, C. (2012). Internet privacy and the right to be forgotten/right to oblivion. *IDP-Internet Law and Politics*, *13*(1), 53–66.

Diggelmann, O., & Cleis, M. N. (2014). How the right to privacy became a human right. *Human Rights Law Review*, *14*(3), 441–458.

Doyle, C., & Bagaric, M. (2005). The right to privacy: Appealing, but flawed. *International Journal of Human Rights*, *9*(1), 3–36.

Drgonec, J. (2012). *Constitution of the Slovak Republic: Commentary* (3rd ed.). Heureka.

Duff, K. J., & Johnson, E. T. (1983). A renewed employee rights to privacy. *Labor Law Journal*, *34*(12), 747–762.

Iemets, L. O., Pyshna, A. H., & Hridina, K. V. (2020). Right to freedom of expression in conditions of information technologies development. *Revista Genero & Direito*, *9*(4), 1030–1045.

Kupec, V. (2021). The role of SoLoMo marketing and media in the communication of eco-innovations. *Communication Today*, *12*(1), 184–185.

Madrid, R. B. (2016). Constitutional right to privacy and its conflict with the intellectual rights. *Propiedad Intelectual*, *19*(1), 136–158.

Marmor, A. (2015). What is the right to privacy? *Philosophy & Public Affairs*, *43*(1), 3–26.

Marsoof, A. (2011). Online social networking and the right to privacy: The conflicting rights of privacy and expression. *International Journal of Law and Information Technology*, *19*(2), 110–132.

Mills, K. (2022). Consent and the right to privacy. *Journal of Applied Philosophy*, *39*(4), 721–735.

Pacalajova, N., & Kubinec, M. (2021). Statutory bar on the right to exercise a mortgage under the conditions applicable in the Slovak Republic and comparison with the legal regulation of the Czech Republic. *Danube: Law, Economics and Social Issues Review*, *12*(3), 224–238.

Pfisterer, V. M. (2019). The right to privacy – A fundamental right in search of its identity: Uncovering the CJEU's flawed concept of the right to privacy. *German Law Journal*, *20*(5), 722–733.

Strbova, E. (2016). Consumer involvement and motivation in attending socially oriented marketing. *European Journal of Science and Theology*, *12*(2), 191–201.

Vives, L. D., & Morales, D. J. G. (2021). The liberal foundation of the right to privacy. *Revista Boliviana de Derecho*, *32*(1), 70–94.

Zulova, J. (2020a). Functionality of conjunctions as a factor obfuscating comprehension of legal texts (demonstrated on examples from the Slovak Labor code). *The Lawyer Quarterly: International Journal for Legal Research*, *10*(4), 393–401.

Zulova, J. (2020b). Service of documents in the context of employment during employee quarantine. *Central European Journal of Labour Law and Personnel Management: International Scientific Journal*, *3*(1), 77–88.

Branislav Micieta[1,*], Vladimira Binasova[1,*], Martin Krajcovic[1], Beata Furmannova[1], Gabriela Gabajova[1], and Marta Kasajova[1]

The Model of an Automated Warehouse

Abstract:
Research background: The paper deals with the multifunctional kit is a robust training model that simulates and demonstrates warehouse automation in the world's most advanced enterprises.
Purpose of the article: Programming takes place in the Siemens TIA Portal software, which is then loaded into a Programmable Logic Automator which is interconnected with the source Siemens SITOP PSU100S. The main objective of the paper was to provide an overview of the current state-of- the-art in automated manufacturing and to create an example of an automated warehouse that can be used in teaching as an ideal simulation and demonstration model for training and industrial automation.
Methods: SIEMENS TIA Portal (Totally Integrated Automation) gives the possibility to write a program for control elements such as PLCs but also HMI panels, essentially integrating all design processes for automation in 1 software. Historically this has been divided into 2 non-core software but today TIA Portal allows programming of PLCs, HMI panels but also different peripherals. This makes the work easier but mostly saves time and money in the programming stations or different industrial machines.
Findings & Value added: The automated warehouse model example offers the opportunity to continue to develop and extend the model and create an experimental manufacturing system in a selected laboratory.

Keywords: *Automated warehouse, software, PLC Automated warehouse, software, PLC*

JEL Classification: *L19; A14; B16*

1 Introduction

Warehouse decision-makers face some genuine hurdles in moving toward the widespread adoption of automation and robotics. But the reasons for

---

* Corresponding author: vladimira.binasova@fstroj.uniza.sk
1 University of Zilina, Department of Industrial Engineering, Univerzitna 1, 010 26 Zilina, Slovakia

automating – as well as the benefits – make it well worth the investment. Automation is essential for a company to remain competitive and viable, which is why the global warehouse automation market is projected to expand to $69 billion by 2025 (Tank, 2023).

This paper presents a multifunctional training model designed to emulate and showcase warehouse automation within the realm of the world's most advanced enterprises. The core of this model lies in its capability to simulate and demonstrate various facets of warehouse automation, providing an immersive learning experience.

The programming of this model is accomplished through the utilization of Siemens TIA Portal software, a leading platform in industrial automation. The programmed logic is then seamlessly transferred into a Programmable Logic Automator, which forms the automation control center. This control center is intricately connected to a reliable power source, the Siemens SITOP PSU100S, ensuring stable and uninterrupted operation.

The primary objective of this paper is two-fold. Firstly, it aims to offer a comprehensive overview of the contemporary landscape of automated manufacturing. By exploring the latest technologies, trends, and applications in the field, the paper provides valuable insights into the state-of-the-art practices.

Secondly, this paper endeavors to contribute to the realm of industrial automation education by creating a tangible example of an automated warehouse. This warehouse serves as an ideal simulation and demonstration model for training purposes. Its hands-on, practical approach makes it a valuable tool for both students and professionals seeking to enhance their understanding of industrial automation.

In essence, this multifunctional training model not only embodies the cutting-edge advancements in warehouse automation but also serves as a pivotal resource for educators and learners alike, fostering knowledge dissemination and practical skill development in the domain of industrial automation.

The main objective of this paper was to provide an overview of the current state of the art in automated manufacturing and to create an example of an automated warehouse that can be used in Department of Industrial Engineering training, simulation, and demonstration model for training and industrial automation. The automated warehouse model example offers the opportunity to continue developing and extending the model and creating an experimental manufacturing system in a selected laboratory at the

Department of Industrial Engineering, Faculty of Mechanical Engineering, at University of Zilina.

The vision of Industry 4.0 (Grznar et al., 2019, Grznar et al., 2021) is to achieve a highly automated and autonomous manufacturing environment in which decision-making processes are provided by a variety of technologies that rely on the collection and subsequent analysis of input data performed in real time. (Filipova et al., 2021). Newly explored technologies can often transform entire industries (Krajcovic et al., 2021a; Dulina et al., 2021). The expansion of the engineering industry increasingly requires the use of state-of-the-art technologies in the field of production to achieve significant labour productivity and optimisation of the production in question (Krajcovic et al., 2022). At the same time, with the increase in higher demands on the products or services produced, there is a need to speed up the production process as much as possible, but at a cost, that maximizes the quality of the product. This is why automation is also being used. (Lee et al., 2022; Marschall et al., 2022)

The efficiency of production is constantly conditioned by the work of pre-production components (construction, technology, design) (Krajcovic et al., 2021b; Antoniuk et al., 2021). The role of the engineer is to analyze the already used, but also newly created working procedures (Leng et al., 2021), to discover the best method to perform the work (optimal working method). The best working method is generally considered to be is the one in which the cost of performance is minimised as much as possible. An effort is to make each work operation as short and simple as possible, so that it can be more easily learnt and at the same time require a minimum of human effort to perform. (Lee & Jeong, 2021).

2 Methods

As an example, a Programmable Automated Warehouse Model was created (Figure 1). This multifunctional kit from Fischertechnik (Fischertechnik, 2023) is a complete, stable training model that is used to simulate and demonstrate warehouse automation in the world's most advanced companies. A transfer/transport station with conveyor belt, a shelf stacker (3-axis robot) for stacking and retrieving special workpiece carriers, storage rack with nine storage slots.

Figure 1a. Transport station with conveyor belt.
Source: Fischertechnik (2023)

The procedure for running the automated model:

- Acquisition of the kit and subsequent repair of components that have been damaged repairing the components damaged during transport.
- Installing the Siemens TIA Portal software to verify the functionality individual components.
- Connecting the power supply to the network.
- Connect the commissioned power supply to the PLC.
- Interconnect the PLC to the kit, via the circuit board with the change relay direction of rotation of the motors.
- Checking the wiring and subsequent rewiring to make the individual components work correctly.
- Familiarization with the programming language, the individual parts of the block programming.
- Programming a particular part of the model, using individual inputs and outputs.
- Loading a given program into a Programmable Logic Automata. Subsequently running the program and monitoring the individual components in motion.
- Redesign/Improvement of programmed block.
- Printed circuit board with relay.
- Connecting the PLC to the kit and the power supply.

In order to be able to work with the automated warehouse model further it is it is necessary to connect it with a PLC Programmable logic controller (Programmable logic automaton) + Siemens SITOP PSU100S 24 V/5 A power supply for mounting rail (DIN rail) 24 V/DC 5 A 120 W. A programmable logic controller or PLC can be described as a relatively small industrial computer used to control a variety of industrial processes. The control takes place in real time. A PLC is also typical in that the program that controls it is loaded in cycles, unlike everyday computers, PLCs are designed to be directly integrated into the manufacturing process and because of this have customized peripherals. Such computers have a standardized construction, according to the IEC-1131-(x) standard. In terms of design, PLCs can be divided into the following groups:

- compact,
- modular.

The compact PLC has a fixed and immutable structure that cannot be modified or extended. Everything that the PLC needs to function, such as the CPU and other input/output peripherals, is combined in one unit. A modular PLC is a PLC that can be modified or expanded. Such a design allows almost unlimited modification of the input-output peripherals. The program processed by the PLC is mostly subject to the IEC 1131–3 standard, which defines programming languages such as:

- Instruction List IL,
- Structured Text ST,
- Contact Diagram Language (Ladder Diagram LD),
- Function Block Diagram (FBD) (Girman, 2015).

Connection to PLC control: The model has a relay to change the direction of rotation of the motors. All inputs and outputs can be connected to a jack connector (26-pin, 2.54 mm pitch) or to serial terminals with socket clamps. The Simatic S7–1200 Basic Controller PLC product is shown in Figure 2. This product is described as The Simatic S7–1200 Siemens PLC Basic Controller is a high-performance system with a compact and space-saving design. This CPU PLC has 2 integrated analog inputs, 6 integrated digital inputs and 4 integrated digital transistor outputs. It comes with integrated IO and communication interfaces to meet the highest industrial requirements. This is also made possible by a range of powerful integrated technology features that make this controller an integral part of a complete automation solution. The controller is at the heart of a new offering for simple but high-precision automation tasks.

Figure 1b. PLC Simatic S7-1200.
Source: Own processing (2023)

It is the ideal choice when it comes to performing automation tasks for a range of applications in the low to medium power range with maximum flexibility and efficiency.

Thanks to standardized remote control protocols, you can connect the controller directly to your control to your control centre without any programming. The Siemens SITOP PSU100S 24 V/5 A DIN rail mount power supply 24 V/DC 5 A 120 W.

The SITOP smart power supply is one-third smaller but has more power is one of the narrowest DIN rail power supplies and has excellent overload behavior. Even high loads can be switched on without problems. Rated outputs of 120 % consistently make the power supplies the most reliable of their kind. Numerous certifications facilitate universal and worldwide use as well as use in potentially explosive areas. Overview of benefits:

- Rounded power range from 60 to 960 W for universal use.
- Compact design from 32.5 to 150 mm wide for small mounting area.
- Easy DIN rail mounting. Extra power: 150 % of rated power for 5 seconds as reliable protection against

- Overload protection – for trouble-free switching of DC/DC converters, motors and loads with high surge currents. More power through sustained 120 % of rated output up to 45°C.
- Large output voltage adjustment range up to 28 V, easily accessible from the front by potentiometer.
- Parallel connection to increase power output is possible. Input voltage 120 V (85 – 132 V) / 230 V (170 – 264 V).

3 Results

SIEMENS TIA Portal (Totally Integrated Automation) gives the possibility to write a program for control elements such as PLCs but also HMI panels, essentially integrating all design processes for automation in 1 software. Historically this has been divided into 2 non- core software but today TIA Portal allows programming of PLCs, HMI panels but also different peripherals. This makes the work easier but mostly saves time and money in the programming stations or different industrial machines.

Programming takes place in the Siemens TIA Portal program, as the 1200 series module is used in the work, moreover, the TIA Portal is used not only for programming PLCs, HMI panels but also various other peripherals provided by Siemens. Therefore, it can be defined in 2 big groups namely PLC programming and programming resp. Animation of the HMI interface for the user. The TIA Portal program has these two groups integrated in one program and hence it makes the job of the programmer easier. Since some projects may involve many inputs, outputs or different variables that may not only be input / output but also in a version processed internally by the PLC processor.

PLC programming is carried out in the following way and that is that the programmer has to clarify the subsequent sequence of steps that lead to the solution of the problem and when the next step should occur. Subsequently, the task, i.e., if it is complex and large, has to be divided into smaller subgroups and chronologically these subgroups have to be set up in such a way that they are correct. We can make such a division by assigning all the action members to one group but in principle, the division is a matter of the programmer and his habits.

The program is uploaded to the PLC via the TIAPORTAL program (TIA Portal V17) as follows. It is necessary to select the PLC in my case (PLC_1 [CPU 1214C DC/DC/Rly]), right click and select the option (Download to device) and then (Hardware and software). The next step is to check if the program has been loaded correctly, you need to mark Go online in the top bar and check if there are green balls everywhere in the (Project tree). This indicates whether the program in the PLC matches the program that is currently loaded in TIAPORTAL. If the color orange is present, this indicates that the block at which the orange ball is located is different. If the ball happens to be red, an error has occurred, but this condition usually only occurs on the physical PLC.

4 Discussions

In recent years, the emergence of new industrial technologies has been visible (Burganova et al., 2020). These necessarily include cobots capable of working alongside humans. In many cases, manufacturing companies, to innovate and be competitive, turn to such robots. The number of successful implementations is still low despite this huge interest. One of the reasons for this may be precisely the lack of a methodology for implementing cooperating robots in holonic manufacturing systems.

It is the combination of different technologies that is considered from the point of view of automation advanced companies as a key. A combination of robotic tools based on rules and diversity of artificial intelligence capable of understanding, learning and making decisions, will soon become common practice for the majority of respondents (85 %).

To successfully integrate intelligent automation, it is necessary that you company she realized its necessity. The process begins with the conscious selection of goals based on individual possibilities of the company. From the defined achievable goals, subsequently a realistic strategy will do. However, the Deloitte survey shows that only a quarter of respondents developed the necessary before introducing intelligent process automation company-wide strategy. The Deloitte survey proves that organizations have made significant progress in the new world of advanced intelligent automation. However, he also points out that the introduction of processes does not guarantee added value. Those who see the greatest benefits in automation, are involved in company-wide transformation, in the creation of a strategy with regarding people and with a view to the future.

5 Conclusion

The work focused on new trends in the field of automated production. Automation nowadays is an essential part of a mature enterprise on an international level. The introduction includes a study dealing with the current state of automation in the world, and then the advantages and disadvantages of automation are mentioned, with the advantages outweighing the disadvantages.

The third chapter provides a graphical representation of the importance of mechanization and automation, followed by an example of automation technology on a programmable model of an automated warehouse, along with the various points of how I went about running the model. The programming is done in the Siemens TIA Portal software, which is then uploaded to the Programmable Logic Automat or, which is interconnected with the Siemens SITOP PSU100S power supply. The main objective of the paper was to provide an overview of the current state of the art in automated manufacturing and to create an example of an automated warehouse that can be used in teaching in the Department of Industrial Engineering as a training, simulation, and demonstration model for training and industrial automation. The automated warehouse model example offers the opportunity to continue to develop and extend the model and create an experimental manufacturing system in a selected laboratory.

Acknowledgments

This work was supported by the VEGA 1/0524/22.
This work was supported by the VEGA 1/0248/21.

References

Antoniuk, I., Svitek, R., Krajcovic, M., & Furmannova, B. (2021). Methodology of design and optimization of internal logistics in the concept of Industry 4.0. *Transportation Research Procedia, 55*, 503–509.

Burganova, N., Grznar, P., & Mozol, S. (2020). Design of logistics system in production, In Technologie, procesy i systemy produkcyjne. Bielsko-Biala: Wydawnictwo naukowe Akademii techniczno-humanistycznej w Bielsku-Białej, ISBN 978-83-66249-56-1, 11–18.

Dulina, L., Gola, A., Gaso, M., Horvathova, B., Bigosova, E., Barbusova, M., & Kyncl, J. (2021). Influence of various types of office desk chair for dynamizing the operation assessed by Raster Stereography. *Applied Sciences*, *11*(11), 4910.

Filipova, I., Dulina, L., Bigosova, E., & Plinta, D. (2021). Modern possibilities of patient transport aids. *Transportation Research Procedia*, *55*, 510–517.

Fischertechnik. (2023). *AutomatedHigh-Bay Warehouse*. https://www.fischertechnik.de/en/service/elearning/simulating/automatisierteshochregallager24v2020.

Girman, M. (2015). PLC programming according to the standard IEC 1131–1, https://qip-journal.eu/files/2000/1/girman/girman.html

Grznar, P., Gregor, M., Mozol, S., Krajcovic, M., Dulina, L., Gaso, M., & Major, M. (2019). A system to determine the optimal work-in-progress inventory stored in interoperation manufacturing buffers. *Sustainability*. Basel: Multidisciplinary Digital Publishing Institute, *11*(14).

Grznar, P., Krajcovic, M., Gola, A., Dulina, L., Furmannova, B., Mozol, S., Plinta, D., Burganova, N., Danilczuk, W., & Svitek, R. (2021). The use of a genetic algorithm for sorting warehouse optimisation. *Processes*. *9*(7).

Krajcovic, M., Furmannova, B., Grznar, P., Furmann, R., Plinta, D., Svitek, R., & Antoniuk, I. (2021a). System of parametric modelling and assessing the production staff utilisation as a basis for aggregate production planning. *Applied Sciences,* 11(19).

Krajcovic, M., Gabajova, G., Matys, M., Furmannova, B., & Dulina, L. (2022). Virtual reality as an immersive teaching aid to enhance the connection between education and practice. *Sustainability*, *14*(15), 9580.

Krajcovic, M., Gabajova, G., Matys, M., Grznar, P., Dulina, L., & Kohar, R. (2021b). 3D interactive learning environment as a tool for knowledge transfer and retention. *Sustainability*, *13*, 7916.

Lee, H., Hong, J., & Jeong, J. (2022). MARL-Based dual reward model on segmented actions for multiple mobile robots in automated warehouse environment. *Applied Sciences*, *12*(9), 4703.

Lee, H., & Jeong, J. (2021). Mobile robot path optimization technique based on reinforcement learning algorithm in warehouse environment. *Applied sciences*, *11*(3), 1209.

Leng, J., Yan, D., Liu, Q., Zhang, H., Zhao, G., Wei, L., & Chen, X. (2021). Digital twin- driven joint optimisation of packing and storage assignment in large-scale automated high-rise warehouse product-service system. *International Journal of Computer Integrated Manufacturing*, *34*(7–8), 783–800.

Marschall, M., Gregor, M., Durica, L., Vavrik, V., Bielik, T., Grznar, P., & Mozol, S. (2022). Defining the number of mobile robotic systems needed for reconfiguration of modular manufacturing systems via simulation. *Machines 2022*, *10*, 316.

Tank, T. (2023). *Warehouse Automation: The Drivers, the Barriers, and the Trends for 2023*. Supply chain brain. https://www.supplychainbrain.com/blogs/1-think-tank/post/37669-warehouse-automation-the-drivers-the-barriers-and-the-trends-for- 2023

Renata Miklencicova[1,*]

How Global Aspects Affect the Groundswell in the Context of Online Communication and Shopping Environment

Abstract:

Research background: Globalization in the digital environment has opened up space for new interactive ways of communication and ways of buying the groundswell. The changes are manifested mainly in the application of artificial intelligence, online stream shopping on various social platforms, or live e-commerce and other options that make many business processes applicable in various strategic areas more efficient. As a result of the pandemic COVID-19, the largest social network has offered a way to support small and medium-sized companies that can offer their products, e.g., via Facebook Shop or online shopping stream to potential customers.

Purpose of the article: The aim of the scientific contribution will be to point out the use of the way of shopping and motivational appeals of the sellers themselves, who implement their sales on social networks through a video live stream. During the comparison, we will assess the various attributes used by the investigated companies for interactive communication with the groundswell. We will also focus on the feedback and reactions of the groundswell during the purchase process itself.

Methods: Analytical, deductive and comparative research methods were used to fulfill the purpose of the contribution. Research studies dealing with the solved issue by various authors are also part of the submitted contribution.

Findings & Value added: The benefit of the post is to point out the possibilities and the use of video live stream when buying groundswell from online sellers on social networks.

Keywords: *globalization, online retailers, groundswell, streaming platforms, social networks*

JEL Classification: *M15; M31; O35*

* Corresponding author: renata.miklencicova@ucm.sk

1 University of Ss. Cyril and Methodius in Trnava, Faculty of Mass Media Communication, Department of Marketing Communication, Námestie J. Herdu 2, 917 01 Trnava, Slovakia

1 Introduction

Globalization in the digital environment has opened up space for new interactive ways of communication and shopping by users of social networks, creating the groundswell. These changes are mainly manifested in the application of artificial intelligence, online shopping stream on various social platforms, or live e-commerce and other options that speed up and make many processes applicable in various strategic areas more efficient (Jong et al., 2022). The Covid-19 pandemic has brought an increase in productivity, potential customers, and a sufficiently wide audience of followers for online stores in particular. Online sellers adapted their business model to this situation and thus opened their "online doors" to new technologies and business opportunities. Thanks to this, sellers can innovate and automate their sales processes, whether in the form of artificial intelligence, online shopping on various social platforms (Wang et al., 2022).

Shopping through various digital platforms is turbulently advancing the behavior, perception and communication of companies with the groundswell. Authors define groundswell as a social trend where people use technology to achieve what they need from each other, but also towards society. Three trends that directly affect the groundswell are people who are interested in communicating, interactive online technologies and the online economy (Madhavi & Akbar, 2011).

2 Methods

Many studies show that the Covid-19 pandemic has brought many advantages to companies in the online space, e.g., in the form of a wide audience of potential new customers (Moon et al., 2021). The pandemic and the crisis have generally encouraged the development and adaptation of new technologies in the field of digital shopping. Innovative online business models bring companies a reduction in operating costs, mainly through investments in automation but also the use of artificial intelligence elements. The combination of live shopping technologies, e-commerce technologies, social networking technologies and the aspect of creating a sense of fun, give space to followers to make their purchases in an innovative, yet largely interactive way (Pang et al., 2021). Through livestream shopping, companies obtain, in addition to profit, a large volume of data about their online customers, their shopping preferences, their attitudes, which is very important for the groundswell, and their interactions with the companies themselves. Also, based on the information obtained, they can transform their attention to the improvement of supply chains (Hayashi & Abe, 2015).The implementation of various types of applications brings increased comfort in the field of communication between several parties, such as between employees, suppliers, distribution companies, but especially in two-way communication between the company and the online audience. One way to engage and engage an online audience is livestream shopping, which combines live streaming with various features of social streaming platforms (Wang et al., 2022). This method allows customers to directly communicate with the seller in the form of asking different types of questions, in addition to shopping. What is much more important brings them experience and the possibility of interactivity on social networks. Online sellers focus on communication with a wide audience, but at the same time adapts it and respond to the individual needs of each of the following customers. Livestream shopping brings customers experience and interactivity on social networks. This way of shopping and promoting your products on social networks is changing the whole process and way of selling and communicating with the groundswell. The main participants in this sales process include: product providers, live streaming sellers, media streaming platforms and consumers (Cheng et al., 2022). The constant development of internet and media technologies has supported the realization of livestream sales not only in China, but also in Slovakia (Sun et al., 2019).

Sellers who carry out livestream shopping with the groundswell use different platforms:

- Shoppable social media platforms – Facebook, Instagram and TikTok.
- Specialized trading platforms and applications.
- Separately hosted shopping platforms.

For the purposes of the post, we will focus on the Facebook platform. In 2020, Facebook launched a platform that enabled sales through livestream, specifically to sellers who are affected by the global health crisis Covid-19. Companies could not offer to sell their products in the traditional mode, because their operations had to be closed for security reasons. As a result, they were forced to look for new and innovative ways to get closer to their consumers. It was in this context that Facebook launched a platform that allowed companies to set up their online stores accessible through Facebook and Instagram. This interface can be used by sellers to connect with customers. Livestream shopping, in addition to live video content, ensures two-way communication and the possibility for the target audience to easily make their purchase (Wongkitrungrueng et al., 2020).

Livestream trading takes place through various platforms, where either the seller himself or the influencer can promote products live to their target audience (Zhu et al., 2021). During a direct sale, the follower joins the stream, where they can follow not only the seller, but also the reactions and comments of other followers. They can also ask questions related to the presented products, but also ask for a more detailed version of the products, functions, product quality, product size, etc. In addition to these features, the audience can chat with other followers to get feedback and opinions (Ma, 2021). The audience interacts with the stream in real time with likes and reactions, which greatly helps to build and strengthen relationships with social media users, the groundswell. Many companies in such a sales method also use cooperation with influencers, who provide various benefits to motivate the online audience to make the purchase itself. Livestream shopping doesn't just expand online shopping, but its main advantages are that they provide excitement, support spontaneous purchases, and connect the customer with the brand itself. Livestream shopping, in addition to live video content, ensures two-way communication and the possibility for the target audience to easily make their purchase. Livestream sales provide us with two dimensions of value to the target audience and experiential and practical value. Experiential value brings or it is related to the visual and interactive nature of the product, but it is also largely related to the entertainment that the customer feels during the live broadcast. And the practical value brings various motivational incentives such as discounts, saving money. But it also saves time for the groundswell (Cheng et al., 2022).

Based on the above, we can deduce the advantages of livestream shopping for sellers and customers (Gao et al., 2021). Benefits of livestream shopping for merchants include:

- Increase in attractiveness – Marketers often use cooperation with influencers to increase their appeal. The main advantage is that the audience can ask the influencer real-time questions about the product being demonstrated.
- Building relationships between audiences – this way of selling allows merchants to establish deeper relationships with the audience itself, especially through interactions, which brings an increase in sales. They also try to foster a sense of community and trust with followers, which is a very important aspect of live shopping.
- Speeding up the purchasing process – Live shopping is fun, brings a certain kind of experience to the audience and also attracts the attention of potential buyers. Shortened consideration time and increased engagement results in higher sales for the merchant.
- Incentive discounts during the live broadcast – Sellers use various discounts with which they want to make the purchase itself more efficient, such as: discounts, discount coupons, etc.

- Livestream data – in addition to achieving conversion with the groundswell, marketers also focus their attention on obtaining important data about their target audience. This mainly concerns data about their purchasing behavior during the broadcast, who participated in the live broadcast, what types of questions users asked during the broadcast, etc.
- Video archive of the live stream – Sellers offer video archives even after the end of the live broadcast itself, in which the groundswell can watch either previous livestream sales, interactivity and audience communication.

The advantages of livestream shopping include (Pang et al., 2021):

- Greater interactivity – The interactive involvement of the audience in the communication during livestream shopping allows you to leave comments in real time.
- Sufficient information about the products offered and the discounts provided – directly during the livestream shopping, the audience has the product itself available to them, various types of actions to motivate them to make the purchase itself.
- Motivation to purchase through various discounts – for example, options for various discounts, one-time and time-limited discount coupons, etc. Live streaming experiences and discounts are more compelling in the eyes of the target audience because they help bring sales closer to the customer in an engaging and human way.
- Unlimited time spent in livestream shopping – Customers can spend several minutes or even hours in this type of shopping. Throughout the broadcast, the audience is motivated to complete the purchase. Interaction, original product variations, live product testing on a specific person, questions and answers from the audience can help the groundswell to make a decision faster.
- Faster purchase decisions – Shopping during live streaming breaks down any barriers when making a purchase decision. Shopping even after the end of the transfer itself – after the end of the transmission itself, the video from the livestream shopping has another way of use, in the form of a video that the audience can view the product portfolio that the seller offered during the transmission. They can also view questions and reviews from customers even after the end of the transmission.

As mentioned in the post, with live streaming, companies can reach a very wide audience in a short time, which consists of both potential and current customers. As a result of the Covid-19 pandemic, many companies had to look for new, interactive ways to get closer to their customers. It is livestream shopping that brings many benefits to the users themselves, especially in interactive two-way communication, creating live video content, by increasing the engagement of the groundswell (Bharadwaj et al., 2021; Tesarova et al., 2022). Live broadcasts with the functions of social and streaming platforms bring the possibility of interactivity right during the sales process, which represents for digital sellers the use of a wide range of followers and at the same time allows them to individually adapt their communication and sales tactics, motivational appeals directed to the groundswell (Jiang et al., 2022).

3 Results and Discussion

For the purposes of the presented article, only partial results of the conducted survey are used, which was aimed at a mutual comparison of several companies that use live streaming for communication and primarily for selling their products and services to their followers, i.e., the groundswell. The partial goals were to clarify what factors motivate and to what extent they influence the purchasing behavior of the target audience in livestream broadcasts. For comparison, two companies that offer their products via live streaming during the period January-June 2022 are selected.

The first company belongs to the textile and fashion industry, which focuses its sales on clothes, dresses, and also has accessories for its followers in its product portfolio. He has been conducting livestream sales on the Facebook platform since September 2021, where he has 17,000 active followers. They communicate much less frequently through their Instagram account, where they have 900 followers and only 28 posts published. The sale is carried out on a regular basis on the Facebook page, where the profile is followed by approximately 23,000 followers and they have reached 35,000 views of the live stream broadcasts. With such a broadcast, they reach about 2,000 shares and the interactivity with the audience is really high, they have about 2,500 comments and 1,500 likes from followers. The visual treatment of livestream videos can be largely cheesy to some audience types, they use a lot of gold and flashy elements. Content processing is friendly, but also largely noisy and sometimes chaotic. In addition to live broadcasts, they also archive their broadcasts in the form of a video archive, where customers can view the sale itself and audience comments even after a certain period. There are also reviews from followers about purchased goods, where not only comments but also photos of satisfied customers are attached. They speak to their followers on a regular basis every day, either in the form of posts or live broadcasts themselves. The live broadcast lasts approximately 3–5 hours and starts regularly at 19:00 during the working week. Also, on a daily basis, they provide various posts focused on the product offer itself, comments to their followers. Part of their livestream transmissions is the implementation of various competitions aimed at followers, which are intended to motivate even greater interactivity of the groundswell. During the live broadcast, they have approximately 50 likes from their followers during the competitions. The company also tries to support the activity of its customers on the Facebook page, where it regularly interacts with them, thereby involving them to a much greater extent in the entire company's activities. They try to direct their communication to customers in the form of sales support and thus motivate the audience to shop. Among these motivational incentives, the company uses various gifts for purchases, financial rewards for purchased products worth up to €50, they offer various rewards for sharing, free shipping, etc. With this form of sales support, they not only motivate a large following, but also build the trust and loyalty of their customers in this way. Followers' satisfaction is also reflected in their numerous positive comments.

The second compared company also offers its activities in the clothing and textile industry. It offers women's, men's and children's goods through livestream sales. It communicates with his audience through his Facebook and Instagram profiles. They also support their online community by collaborating with various influencers. Through this cooperation, the company receives tags from influencers on stories in their accounts, where they comment on the quality and execution of the company's products. Based on the Instagram account, the company has 1,160,000 active followers. They have this account active and linked to their e-shop, where they also use Instagram shopping. Stories with stories are available 24 hours a day, where the target audience can view the photos at any time. The photos are clear and divided into individual product groups that they offer. The frequency of views for the monitored month was 8000 views and 200 likes. They have been using their Facebook account for livestream sales since December 2021. They have approximately 26,000 followers on their Facebook profile and have reached 30,000 live stream views. The frequency of posts is often 3 times a day, whether through photos, reviews from customers, or videos. On their profile, they have a link to automatic replies, which are redirected to a messenger chat, where the customer can communicate with the seller. The visual and content processing of livestream transmissions is uniform, friendly, representative, supporting interactivity with the target audience. Also, the posts have a single identity. As for the actual communication with the target audience, the company informs about its livestream broadcasts in advance. The sale is on a regular basis, 2 days a week, starting at 6:00 p.m. The audience is informed about the live stream itself through posts announcing when the live broadcast will begin. The seller also states the conditions of purchase here. The purchase process takes place during the live broadcast, where the followers write their order directly in the comment, after it is confirmed by the seller, he writes his contact information in the message. The company sends the purchased products via a courier company or, if interested, the customer can pick up the goods in person in a physical store. During live streams, the company records the largest interactions of about 1,000 comments, 8,000 views and about 270 shares. This researched company also uses various motivational incentives to support sales, such as discounts for the next purchase, free shipping and gifts. The Company does not use any contests to encourage interaction with its audience.

Table 1. Comparison of competing companies implemented livestream shopping.

Companies	Social networks	Frequency of livestream sales	Sales Support
Company 1	Facebook Instagram	5 days a week – always at 7 p.m	Gifts for purchase, financial rewards for purchase, rewards for sharing, free shipping, contests
Company 2	Facebook Instagram	2 days a week – always at 6 p.m	Discounts and gifts for purchase, free shipping.

Source: author

Based on the comparison of these two competing companies that use live stream sales to reach their target audience, we can observe that the first company conducts a live stream regularly every working day, while the second company offers its products through live broadcasts 2 days a week. Both companies use different motivational incentives to approach the audience as effectively as possible and motivate them to make further purchases. It is in the form of various discounts, financial benefits, gifts, free shipping, contests and rewards for sharing, etc. The second compared company uses discounts, gifts for purchases, free shipping and, in addition, cooperation with influencers as motivational factors. An interesting criterion for comparison is also the visual and content processing of livestream transmissions. The first company presents itself very energetic and noisy. In contrast, the other company has a uniform, friendly and representative style directed at the target audience. We can see the difference in the interactivity during the transfer. The first company – when streaming reaches about 2,000 shares and interactivity with the audience is about 2,500 comments and 1,500 likes from followers. The other company sees interactions of about 1,000 comments, 8,000 views and about 270 shares during live streams. Based on these data, we can conclude that the interactivity with the groundswell is very large in both cases. We can consider this kind of interactivity with the audience as a constantly developing trend with great potential. The very process of such sales uses a two-way interactive way to encourage the audience to follow and then to buy from selected companies.

4 Conclusion

We can consider live streaming shopping as a new trend by which companies motivate the interactivity of the groundswell, specifically through the live transmission itself on streaming media. We can see the essence of such a sale in two ways, namely in the live sale itself, the essence of which is social commerce, building a community between the company and the audience in a live broadcast, attracting followers and building two-way interactive communication. The second look is directed directly at the audience. The motivation of the audience to watch livestream sales consists not only in satisfying their needs in the form of a completed purchase, but another stimulating factor is the building of a community, the ability to watch and respond to the comments of other viewers in a live broadcast. The turbulent development of e-commerce in China and the global Covid – 19 pandemic have brought space for the application of new ways, methods and business models for the realization of sales with a target audience. The combination of live broadcasting with the functions of social and streaming platforms bring the possibility of interactivity directly during the sales process, which represents for digital sellers the use of a wide range of followers and at the same time allows them to individually adapt their communication and business tactics, motivational appeals directed to the target audience.

Acknowledgments

The research was supported by the Scientific Grant Agency of the Ministry of Education, Science, Research and Sport of the Slovak Republic and the Slovak Academy of Sciences (VEGA, No. 1/0458/21) under the project entitled "Management of the 'groundswell' concept by business entities in promotion of environmentally-friendly products in times of technology interference."

References

Bharadwaj, N., Ballings, M., Naik, P. A., Moore, M., & Arat, M. M. (2021). A new livestream retail analytics framework to assess the sales impact of emotional displays. *Journal of Marketing, 86.*

Gao, X. Y., Xu, S. Y., Tayyaab, S. M. U., & Li, Q. (2021). How the live streaming commerce viewers process the persuasive message: An ELM perspective and the moderating effect of mindfulness. *Electronic Commerce Research and Applications, 49.*

Hayashi, Y., & Abe, A. (2015). Chance for conversation activation on shopping activities. *Procedia Computer Science, 60.*

Cheng, H. N., Huang, Y. T., & Huang, J. S. (2022). The application of DEMATEL-ANP in Livestream E-Commerce based on the research of consumers' shopping motivation. *Scientific Programming,* 2022.

Jiang, Z., Wang, H. Z., Xue, J. L., & Zhai, T. Q. (2022). Propelling consumer engagement via entrepreneurs' live streaming? *Frontiers in Psychology, 13* .

Jong, D., Tseng, Y., & Wang, T. (2022). Accessing the influence of user relationship bonds on continuance intention in livestream E-Commerce. *Sustainability, 14.*

Ma, Y. Y. (2021). To shop or not: Understanding Chinese consumers' live-stream shopping intentions from the perspectives of uses and gratifications, perceived network size, perceptions of digital celebrities, and shopping orientations. *Telematics and Informatics, 59.*

Madhavi, C. V., & Akbar, M. (2011). Groundswell effect part I: A new concept emerging in the world of social networks. *Strategic Change – Briefings in Entrepreneurial Finance, 20.*

Moon, J., Choe, Y., & Song, H. (2021). Determinants of consumers' online/offline shopping behaviours during the COVID-19 pandemic. *International Journal of Environmental Research and Public Health, 18.*

Pang, Q. W., Meng, H. Y., Fang, M. J., Xing, J. J., & Yao, J. G. (2021). Social distancing, health concerns, and digitally empowered consumption behavior under COVID-19: A study on livestream shopping technology. *Frontiers in Public Health, 9.*

Sun, Y., Shao, X., Li, X. T., Guo, Y., & Nie, K. (2019). How live streaming influences purchase intentions in social commerce: An IT affordance perspective. *Electronic Commerce Research and Applications, 37.*

Tesarova, E. N., Krizanova, A., Kubjatkova, A., & Michulek, J. (2022). Digital transformation of enterprises and post-pandemic Sustainable Developmental Goals. *Sustainable Development and Innovation of Digital Enterprises for Living with COVID-19.* Singapore: Springer Nature Singapore.

Wang, W., Huang, M. X., Zheng, S. Y., Lin, L. T., & Wang, L. (2022). The impact of broadcasters on consumer's intention to follow livestream brand community. *Frontiers in Psychology, 12.*

Wongkitrungrueng, A., Dehouche, N., & Assarut, N. (2020). Live streaming commerce from the sellers' perspective: Implications for online relationship marketing. *Journal of Marketing Management, 36.*

Zhu, L. J., Li, H. Y., Nie, K., & Gu, C. M. (2021). How do anchors' characteristics influence consumers' behavioural intention in livestream shopping? A moderated chain- mediation explanatory model. *Frontiers in Psychology, 12.*

Marek Nagy[1,*]

The Impact of Industry 4.0 on Employment in Slovakia

Abstract:
Research background: From the perspective of the globalisation of value chains, we selected this topic for a more in-depth examination of the relationship between employment and the most recent Industry 4.0 trends. This complication signifies a fundamental shift for society, particularly for countries such as Slovakia, which is a manufacturing powerhouse with a vast number of pertinent employees.
Purpose of the article: The purpose of this paper is to identify and evaluate the impact of Industry 4.0 on employment in the Slovak Republic, as well as its current and prospective development. Additionally, identify the vulnerable and strong aspects of this complex issue.
Methods: In order to evaluate employment, statistical index analysis techniques are employed, allowing one to determine whether employment has increased or decreased. To analyze the development, the method of forecasting was used.
Findings & Value added: The added value of the work can be measured by the relevance of its subject matter to global and national issues that are vital to the country's population. The proper integration of digitization trends and Industry 4.0 will substantially contribute to the development of intelligent populations and professions. Not only the working population of the country, but also the entire nation, must be able to adapt quickly and appropriately to this trend.

Keywords: *globalization, Industry 4.0, employment, digitization, industry*

JEL Classification: *A11; C10; O32*

1 Introduction

Everyone is conversant with the concept of employment, as is the concept of employment, which is of vital importance. Employment encompasses not only employment in and of itself, but also employment policy and the labour market.

* Corresponding author: marek.nagy@stud.uniza.sk
1 University of Zilina, Faculty of Operation and Economics of Transport and Communications, Univerzitna 1, 010 26 Zilina, Slovakia

Today's world is swift and constantly evolving. Each of us will eventually begin using a variety of emerging technological conveniences. Not only in our residences, but also in our workplaces. Everywhere we labour, whether in the office or in production, we encounter technological enhancements and efficiencies. Industry 4.0, the fourth industrial revolution, has become increasingly prominent in recent years. This revolution will bring about changes not only in the industrial sector, but throughout the entire region. In addition to industry, it impacts security, education, science, and research, as well as our way of life. However, the introduction of the fourth industrial revolution can be observed specifically in industrial production. Programmable robotics and devices are primarily used for heavy labour in large manufacturing plants, such as automobile plants (Su et al., 2022).

The labour market is a crucial aspect of the company's operations. Individuals, vendors of their work, employers, and the government attend. From the perspective of the individual, work is a source of income, self-fulfilment, and social status. For the employer, it is essential to have a sufficient supply of work on the market that is of sufficient quality to ensure problem-free production. The state enters the labour market not only as an employer but also as a creator and enforcer of market norms (Hodder, 2020; Krizanova and Michulek, 2022).

As stated previously, the purpose of this article is to estimate, identify, and assess the effects of Industry 4.0 on employment in the Slovak Republic. The work also provides a comprehensive overview of the relevant literature and fundamental concepts. Employment is a subject that is frequently discussed, but its connection to Industry 4.0 is a less-discussed topic, so its effect on employment is even less understood, if not unknown. The purpose of this article is to provide responses to the aforementioned queries.

2 Literature Review

Employment can be defined as the participation of the labour force in the process of producing new products, commodities, or services. It is a crucial indicator for assessing the efficacy of economies and their respective regions. Its monitoring is justified by the significance of the human factor and its significant impact on the growth of every economy. Employment is also related to the economic activity of the human factor; consequently, it is essential to examine the population in terms of its economic activity (Filippi et al., 2023). On the labour market, the supply of labour is implemented in the same manner as the demand for labour. The functioning of the labour market depends on the economic model employed by the economy. It relates to all economic and social processes that occur during a specified time period. The labour market therefore functions as a component of the overall market system (Teshabaeva & Kodirova, 2023; Gajdosikova et al., 2022).

Both absolute and relative measures of employment are available. The quantity in its entirety is the number of employees. This is the number of residents who are employed. The rate of unemployment is a relative indicator (Fana et al., 2020; Valaskova et al., 2022). The employment rate indicates what proportion of the population of working age is employed. Basic macroeconomic indicators include the following: *Rate of economic activity* – expresses the proportion of the population of productive and post-productive age that is economically active; *Employment* – the population's participation in the labour process; measured by the number of employees and the employment rate; *Employment rate* – the proportion of the population aged 15–64 that is employed, expressed as a percentage (De Stefano et al., 2021).

Like every other nation, the Slovak Republic desires to attain complete employment. Full employment occurs when all individuals are willing and able to work for a certain real wage. There is no such thing as unlimited employment. Full employment does not imply that all economically active residents are employed. Full employment is the employment level that corresponds to the natural unemployment rate and the condition of the economy at the level of potential output. Employment policy is the targeted regulation of employment by the government and employers, with the objective of reducing the unemployment rate and guaranteeing unemployment assistance. (Majid, 2020). As part of the employment policy, the labour market policy is a system of support and assistance for the integration of citizens into the labour market. Labour market policy is divided into the following categories: 1. passive labour market policy; 2. a vigorous employment market policy (Kolade & Owoseni, 2022).

Historically, passive labour market policy is an ancient type of labour market policy. In the 1920s, development began. It does not resolve the situation's consequences; it merely mitigates them. By passive labour market policy, we mean, for instance, unemployment benefits, material need benefits, and early old-age pensions (Gallacher & Hossain, 2020).

Active labour market policy is a relatively recent development in the history of labour market policy. In the 1970s, development began. Active labour market policy is a collection of programmes aimed at increasing unemployed people's access to the labour market and employment, as well as the labour market's efficiency (Dottori, 2021; Lăzăroiu et al., 2021a). The active policy's objectives include, for instance, bolstering the positive and negative motivation of workers receiving unemployment benefits to enhance employment opportunities by enhancing the skills of the unemployed (Ballestar et al., 2021).

Utilizing the applicability of *Act No. 5/2004* on Employment Services, as amended, active labour market measures are implemented. According to this law, active labour market policy measures are divided into two categories: (a) support for enhancing the employability of job seekers and job candidates; and (b) support for employment, job creation, and job maintenance (Arestis et al., 2020; Ljungholm, 2021). Employment policy is a collection of measures that fosters equilibrium on the labour market and efficient utilization of labour force. It is a component of the social policy intended to prevent unemployment and eliminate labour market rigidity. The state is the primary creator of employment policy. The difficult objective of employment policy is to strike a balance between supply and demand for labour force, productive use of labour resources, and protection of the employment rights of citizens (Zhong et al., 2021; Lăzăroiu et al., 2021b).

Since this work focuses predominantly on the effects of Industry 4.0, it is necessary to describe its fundamental characteristics and connections. Internet and wholly autonomous, self-configurable networks are the propelling force behind Industry 4.0 (Clayton & Kral, 2021). It also encompasses Internet technologies that have been incorporated into various industrial production sectors. Skare et al. (2021) emphasize the need to communicate through both virtual and corporeal information. The concept of digitization is central to Industry 4.0 and is applied to horizontally integrated processes that are described in terms of their values and flow. This connection suggests the notion of "digitization." According to Ruttimann and Stockli (2016), it is crucial to substantially increase the need to implement interconnected technologies in order to accomplish full connectivity. Vuong and Mansori (2021) have a comprehensive understanding of Industry 4.0, i.e., they consider the endeavours of the entire industry to adapt to this phenomenon. Industry 4.0 is described by Lawrence and Durana (2021) as the transformation of production into an entirely automated process. This is accomplished by developing intricate global networks, the core of which is the interconnection of production facilities with cyber-physical CPS systems. These systems are the foundation for "smart factories" (Galbraith & Podhorska, 2021; Konecny et al., 2021).

Johnson and Nica (2021) discuss the ability of data to generate value while emphasizing the singularity and significance of specific technologies.

3 Methods

Index analysis, a statistical method, will be utilized in the work for the calculation and subsequent evaluation of employment growth. With the aid of the calculation, an analysis of the employment rate for 2007–2019 is also provided.

Basic index – it is an index with a constant premise of the initial – base period values. Variables: I – growth factor; y_t – the value of the indicator in the current period; y_0 – value of the indicator in the base period.

$$i = \frac{y_t}{y_0} \tag{1}$$

Where:

I – growth factor;
y_t – the value of the indicator in the current period;
y_0 – value of the indicator in the base period.

Chain index – it is an index with a floating basis and values from the immediately preceding period as its basis.

$$Growth\ rate = \frac{y_t}{y_0} \cdot 100 = l \cdot 100(\%) \tag{2}$$

$$Rate\ of\ increase = \frac{y_t - y_0}{y_0} \cdot 100 = (l-1) \cdot 100(\%) \tag{3}$$

Where:

I – growth factor;
y_t – the value of the indicator in the current period;
y_0 – value of the indicator in the base period.

In general, a prognosis is a scientifically supported forecast that determines the likelihood of further development or the probable future of a particular phenomenon. Using the function of forecast sheets in the data pane, we constructed our forecasts using the Excel programme.

3.1 Presuppositions and Anticipations

First assumption – authors presume that employment will diminish, for example in the field of industrial production where low-skilled workers predominate. These employed individuals can be progressively supplanted by machines and automata, which are introduced gradually into production.

Second assumption – authors presume that the level of employment will remain the same, but that employees who work in industrial production, such as belt production, will be displaced by employees responsible for repairing, maintaining, and programming machines and robots.

The Internet portal of the Statistical Office of the Slovak Republic was utilized to gather accurate data on employment, the subject of this paper.

Table 1. Employment in the Slovak Republic, in millions, from 2007 to 2019.

2007	2008	2009	2010	2011	2012	2013	2014	2015	2016	2017	2018	2019
2.36	2.43	2.37	2.32	2.32	2.33	2.33	2.36	2.42	2.50	2.53	2.57	2.58

Source: author's compilation according to SUSR (2023)

In Table 1, the number of employed individuals in the Slovak Republic is displayed. The data ranges from 2007 to 2019 and is presented in millions. It can be seen that employment in the Slovak Republic is rising gradually and has been rising annually. In the most recent year for which data is available, 2,583,636 persons were employed in the Slovak Republic.

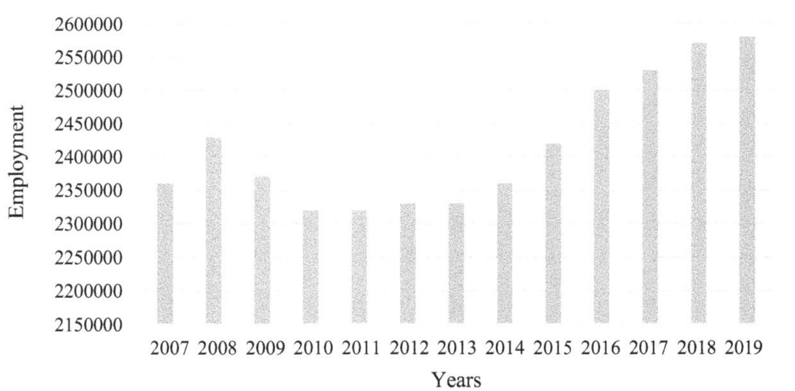

Figure 1. Two-pillar scheme of the production system of the Toyota company.
Source: author's compilation according to SUSR (2023)

Figure 1 depicts employment in the Slovak Republic from 2007 to 2019 with greater clarity. 2011 was the year with the lowest employment rate, and 2019 will be the year with the highest employment rate. From 2008 to 2012, the employment rate declined, and then began to rise. The subsequent section of the work focuses on the specific calculation of the chosen indices as well as the previously mentioned analysis of future development.

4 Results

This section contains the results of chain index calculations as well as an analysis of the employment outlook in the Slovak Republic.

Table 2. Employment growth rate in the Slovak Republic in %.

2007	2008	2009	2010	2011	2012	2013	2014	2015	2016	2017	2018	2019
X	103.24	97.21	97.21	99.91	100.59	100.01	101.45	102.58	102.81	101.55	101.42	100.66

Source: author's compilation according to SUSR (2023)

Using the chain index, we determined the percentage growth of employment in the Slovak Republic. Compared to 2007, employment increased by 3.24 % in 2008. This was also the largest employment increase. In 2009, when compared to 2008, employment decreased by 6.14 %, the most of any year since the Great Depression. Multiple studies (Teshabaeva and Kodirova, 2023; Majid, 2020) indicate that the majority of long-term employees in the Slovak Republic are between the ages of 35 and 39, 40 and 44, 45 and 49, and 50 and 54. These individuals are of productive age. People who continue to work past age 55 are in the post-productive age. In 2019, 77.5 % of 55–59-year-olds were employed, 37 % of 60–64-year-olds were employed, and 4.6 % of 65-plus-year-olds were employed.

However, only a small percentage of secondary education pupils, ages 15 to 19, are employed. Over 65-year-olds, or pensioners, have the lowest employment rate. Nonetheless, the number of working retirees in the Slovak Republic grows annually.

Through this analysis, we determined how many individuals are employed in the Slovak Republic and in which age groups. The work then classifies employment into eleven categories based on economic activities. The following are: 1. agriculture, forestry, and fisheries; 2. industry as a whole; 3. industrial production; 4. construction industry; 5. wholesale and retail; repair of motor vehicles and motorcycles; transport and storage; accommodation and catering services; and wholesale and retail; 6. communication and information, administrative services; 7. financial and insurance activities; 8. real estate- related activities; 9. professional, scientific, and technical activities; 10. public administration, mandatory social security, defence, education, healthcare, and social assistance; 11. art, amusement, and recreation; additional activities.

Table 3. Employment by economic activity in the Slovak Republic in thousands from 2007 to 2019.

	1.	2.	3.	4.	5.	6.	7.	8.	9.	10.	11.
2007	82.8	573.3	516.5	165.6	569.5	48.2	38.0	22.1	176.0	445.4	56.1
2008	81.8	591.7	537.8	181.0	590.5	51.0	41.1	19.7	181.8	448.8	59.3
2009	77.6	530.9	479.6	187.5	591.0	52.4	41.4	19.6	189.6	450.1	63.4
2010	73.1	511.8	461.6	183.8	581.6	50.2	40.1	21.6	190.2	454.0	63.4
2011	73.0	529.7	479.8	177.3	592.2	55.5	40.6	24.0	198.6	453.7	63.8
2012	70.6	524.8	476.5	171.8	594.0	54.7	41.8	24.4	214.3	449.6	63.5
2013	73.9	518.0	469.5	166.5	588.6	57.0	42.4	22.9	210.0	448.7	64.1
2014	72.4	527.2	479.1	164.1	599.5	59.3	43.9	22.4	210.4	457.6	66.3
2015	73.4	537.9	490.7	163.2	604.0	60.9	45.7	22.6	228.5	463.8	67.2
2016	72.5	556.1	508.9	165.8	610.7	64.2	46.4	25.4	239.2	469.1	71.5
2017	72.3	576.2	528.8	169.7	621.6	67.1	45.9	27.3	241.9	474.6	75.6
2018	72.2	586.4	537.8	173.7	632.8	71.0	46.6	28.9	253.3	478.8	76.4
2019	73.3	584.4	536.8	181.8	632.9	74.0	46.9	28.2	264.8	486.6	77.2

Source: author's compilation according to SUSR (2023)

In Table 3, economic activities are divided into eleven columns, representing the industries in which Slovak Republic citizens are employed. In the longer time horizon, 2007–2019, the largest number of people are employed in wholesale and retail; repair of motor vehicles and motorcycles; transport and storage; accommodation and catering services (column 5), followed by industry as a whole (column 2), industrial production (column 3) and public administration, defence, compulsory social security, education, healthcare, and social assistance (column 10). Fewest individuals are employed in economic sectors such as financial insurance activities (column 7), agriculture, forestry, and fisheries (column 1), and arts, entertainment, recreation, and other activities (column 11). During the examined years, employment increased most in wholesale and retail trade, automobile and motorcycle repair, transportation and storage, lodging and food services, and transportation and storage. In contrast, employment decreased in the agriculture, forestry, and fishery sectors during the review period. In the last three years, i.e., 2017, 2018, and 2019, there has been a modest increase in employment within the real estate industry. Since the Slovak Republic dominates industrial production, it makes sense to focus on this sector. Therefore, the task also incorporates a projection of employment growth in industrial production through 2025.

Table 4. Forecast of employment growth in industrial production through 2025.

Years	Values	Prognosis	Lower confidence limit	Upper confidence limit
2007	516446			
2008	537783			
2009	479617			
2010	461458			
2011	479849			
2012	476495			
2013	469496			
2014	479094			
2015	490670			
2016	508899			
2017	528786			
2018	537824			
2019	536755	536755	536755	536755
2020		553600	504591	602608
2021		559432	490159	628705
2022		565264	464327	666202
2023		571097	430502	711691
2024		576929	390569	763289
2025		582761	345540	819983

Source: author's compilation

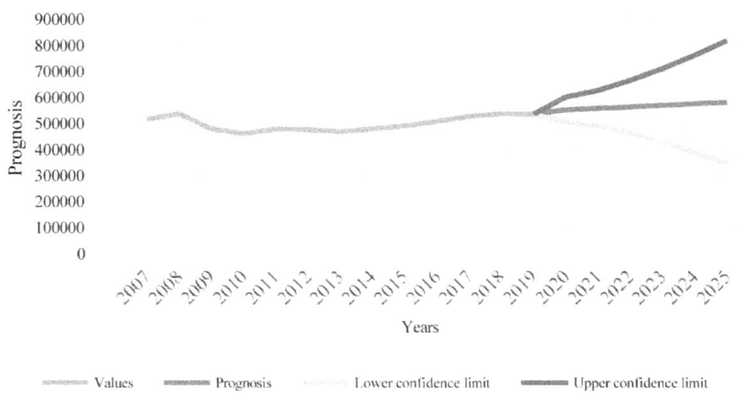

Figure 2. Forecast of employment growth in industrial production through 2025.
Source: author's compilation

If employment conditions in this economic sector remained the same through 2025 as they were through 2019, employment projections for the industrial production sector would improve. By 2025, more than 582,000 people will be employed in industrial production, which is nearly 50,000 more than in 2019. However, it is currently conceivable to incline towards the numbers in the fourth column, which represent the lower limit of reliability. Thus, it is reasonable to infer that industrial production employment will decrease to approximately 345,000 by 2025.

Industry 4.0 focuses primarily on industry and industrial production as such. Therefore, we also made a forecast for the evolution of industrial production employment. The number of individuals employed in industrial production exceeds 500,000. Given the present state of affairs, we can presume that the majority of those who work in this industry will be laid off. Therefore, we can follow the yellow line on the graph, which represents the lower limit of reliability. As shown by the red line in the graph, if the situation in the Slovak Republic were to continue as it has until 2019, employment in industrial production would develop positively and rise marginally until 2025.

5 Discussion

Industry 4.0 aims to provide "competitive products from a nimble, sustainable, and loss-free value stream" Industry 4.0 definitions state that "by connecting people, machines, objects, and systems, it is possible to achieve an increase in flexibility, robustness, and optimal deployment of resources," which is precisely what is meant by "value stream without losses," which is also discussed in the vision of BPS (Bosch Production System) (Zhong et al., 2021). Industry 4.0 can therefore be viewed as a collection of digitization tools that support lean manufacturing system visions – attaining agile, sustainable, and loss-free value flows. Inaccurate monitoring of the quantity of material supplied to the production line and frequent alterations to the production schedule are violations of the pull principle. In recent years, employment in the Slovak Republic has gone through several phases that have shaped its current state. In terms of the veracity of its development, it is uncertain when and in what direction this formulation will continue to evolve. The Slovak population has a tremendous amount of potential in terms of their knowledge, determination, and desire to learn new and contemporary concepts (Vuong & Mansori, 2021). Therefore, it is necessary to state that new industrial revolutions should not be feared; rather, they should be greeted with understanding and compassion for future generations. It is evident that certain occupations will vanish entirely within the next few years, but it is up to us to continue advancing and learning new, modern technologies that digitization can provide. It is not only about money, but also about the future and well-being of humanity as a whole. Due to the imperfect nature of technology, individuals must continue to devote a substantial portion of their working hours to production (Johnson & Nica, 2021). They must continue basing their decisions on their own observations and conversations with other production team members. However, the technologies of Industry 4.0 will be of great assistance in gaining an objective perspective and obtaining accurate, relevant data that will allow for improved and quicker decision- making and the creation of new employment opportunities.

6 Conclusions

The only remaining step is to evaluate the findings based on the accumulated and arranged data. Considering the reviewed years, it is evident that employment is heavily influenced by international and domestic events. The Slovak Republic is no exception; the past few years have been a test for the population and the country as a whole, during which the country's future direction has been demonstrated and determined. The COVID-19 crisis was predominantly responsible for the development of the "home office," which altered the employment landscape in the Slovak Republic. It is debatable whether this transition is positive or negative, but it is inconceivable without technological advancement and innovation. According to the prognosis, a large number of jobs will be eliminated, but a large number of new positions will be created. Therefore, it is necessary to swiftly and accurately adapt to these changes within the context of the connection between digitization and Industry 4.0 and reach a new level of mental adjustment of the population, which the young of today must already be guided towards. This is the only method to accomplish the innovativeness of the population and the country as a whole, where value addition and an innovative mindset will prevail. It is not a vision, but rather a necessity, so that the nation does not lag behind its neighbors in the European Union. The added value of this work is derived from the theoretical processing of current sources for the solved problem and their connection. Occasionally, if at all, this interconnectedness can be observed. The study's findings can be used as an overview and as a guide for potential residents and employees regarding what to prioritise and what to de-emphasize in the future, if only because of the increasing digitalization and the need to implement it in a variety of production processes. The limitations of the study indicate that the research is conducted on a smaller sample size and with fewer sources, but after appropriate evaluation, it only pertains to the Slovak Republic. For the future, it can be viewed as a challenge to conduct an analysis on multiple countries and to compare them to one another, particularly the V4 countries, as they represent a kind of whole and share nearly the same history and other factors. In addition, a broader spectrum of industries and populations will contribute to a more comprehensive and nuanced understanding of this complex.

Acknowledgments

This research was financially supported by the Slovak Research and Development Agency – VEGA 1/0121/20: Research of transfer pricing system as a tool to measure the performance of national and multinational companies in the context of earnings management in conditions of the Slovak Republic and V4 countries.

References

Arestis, P., Ferreiro, J., & Gómez, C. (2020). Quality of employment and employment protection. Effects of employment protection on temporary and permanent employment. *Structural Change and Economic Dynamics, 53*, 180–188.

Ballestar, M. T., Camina, E., Díaz-Chao, Á., & Torrent-Sellens, J. (2021). Productivity and employment effects of digital complementarities. *Journal of Innovation & Knowledge, 6*(3), 177–190.

Clayton, E., & Kral, P. (2021). Autonomous driving algorithms and behaviors, sensing and computing technologies, and connected vehicle data in smart transportation networks. *Contemporary Readings in Law and Social Justice, 13*(1), 9–22.

De Stefano, V., Durri, I., Stylogiannis, C., & Wouters, M. (2021). *Platform work and the employment relationship (No. 27)*. ILO Working Paper.

Dottori, D. (2021). Robots and employment: Evidence from Italy. *Economia Politica, 38*(2), 739–795.

Fana, M., Torrejón Pérez, S., & Fernández-Macías, E. (2020). Employment impact of Covid-19 crisis: From short term effects to long terms prospects. *Journal of Industrial and Business Economics, 47*, 391–410.

Filippi, E., Bannò, M., & Trento, S. (2023). Automation technologies and their impact on employment: A review, synthesis and future research agenda. *Technological Forecasting and Social Change, 191*.

Gajdosikova, D., Valaskova, K., Kliestik, T., & Machova, V. (2022). COVID-19 pandemic and its impact on challenges in the construction sector: A case study of Slovak Enterprises. *Mathematics, 10*(17), 31–30.

Galbraith, A., & Podhorska, I. (2021). Artificial Intelligence data-driven Internet of Things systems, robotic wireless sensor networks, and sustainable organizational performance in cyber-physical smart manufacturing. *Economics, Management, and Financial Markets, 16*(4), 56–69.

Gallacher, G., & Hossain, I. (2020). Remote work and employment dynamics under COVID-19: Evidence from Canada. *Canadian Public Policy, 46*(S1), 44–54.

Hodder, A. (2020). New technology, work and employment in the era of COVID-19: Reflecting on legacies of research. *New Technology, Work and Employment, 35*(3), 262–275.

Johnson, E., & Nica, E. (2021). Connected vehicle technologies, autonomous driving perception algorithms, and smart sustainable urban mobility behaviours in networked transport systems. *Contemporary Readings in Law and Social Justice, 12*(13), 37–50.

Kolade, O., & Owoseni, A. (2022). Employment 5.0: The work of the future and the future of work. *Technology in Society*.

Konecny, V., Barnett, C., & Poliak, M. (2021). Sensing and computing technologies, intelligent vehicular networks, and Big Data-driven algorithmic decision-making in smart sustainable urbanism. *Contemporary Readings in Law and Social Justice, 13*(1), 30–39.

Krizanova, A., & Michulek, J. (2022). Does corporate culture and leadership influence employee work performance? Evidence from the Slovak Republic, *Ekonomicko- manazerske spektrum*, 16(2), 37–48.

Lawrence, J., & Durana, P. (2021). Artificial Intelligence-driven Big Data analytics, predictive maintenance systems, and Internet of Things-based real-time production logistics in sustainable Industry 4.0 wireless networks. *Journal of Self-Governance and Management Economics, 9*(4), 62–75.

Lăzăroiu, G., Kliestik, T., & Novak, A. (2021a). Internet of Things smart devices, industrial Artificial Intelligence, and real-time sensor networks in sustainable cyber- physical production systems, *Journal of Self-Governance and Management Economics*, *9*(1), 20–30.

Lăzăroiu, G., Mihăilă, R., & Braniște, L. (2021b). The language of COVID-19 vaccine hesitancy and public health misinformation: Distrust, unwillingness, and uncertainty. *Review of Contemporary Philosophy, 20*, 117–127.

Ljungholm, D. P. (2021). COVID-19 threat perceptions and vaccine hesitancy: Safety and efficacy concerns. *Analysis and Metaphysics, 20*, 50–61.

Majid, M. A. (2020). Renewable energy for sustainable development in India: Current status, future prospects, challenges, employment, and investment opportunities. *Energy, Sustainability and Society, 10*(1), 1–36.

Ruttimann, B. G., & Stockli, M. T. (2016). Lean and Industry 4.0 – Twins, partners, or contenders? A due clarification regarding the supposed clash of two production systems. *Journal of Science Service and Management, 9*(6), 485–500.

Skare, M., Gil-Alana, L. A., Claudio-Quiroga, G., & Pržiklas Družeta, R. (2021). Income inequality in China 1952–2017: Persistence and main determinants. *Oeconomia Copernic. 1*(12), 863–888.

Su, C. W., Yuan, X., Umar, M., & Lobonţ, O. R. (2022). Does technological innovation bring destruction or creation to the labor market? *Technology in Society, 68*(2).

SUSR. (2023, June 12). *Miera zamestnanosti vo veku 15–64 podľa vzdelania a pohlavia ročné údaje*. DataCube. https://datacube.statistics.sk/#!/view/sk/VBD_SLOVSTAT/pr2020rs/v_pr2020rs_00_00_00_sk

Teshabaeva, O. N., & Kodirova, R. A. (2023). Analysis of methods for further development of the labor market to ensure employment in the Digital Economy. *Best Journal of Innovation in Science, Research and Development, 2*(4), 74–78.

Valaskova, K., Gajdosikova, D., & Pavic Kramaric, T. (2022). How important is the business environment for the performance of enterprises? Case study of selected European Countries. *Central European Business Review, 11*(4), 85–110.

Vuong, T. K., & Mansori, S. (2021). An analysis of the effects of the fourth industrial revolution on Vietnamese Enterprises. *Management Dynamics in the Knowledge Economy, 3*(9), 447–459.

Zhong, R., Xu, X., Klotz, E., & Newman, S. T. (2021). Intelligent manufacturing in the context of Industry 4.0: A review. *Engineering. 3*(5), 616–630.

Eva Nahalkova Tesarova[1,*], and Anna Krizanova[1]

Globalization of Trade in the Context of the Retail Sector: A Bibliometric Analysis

Abstract:
Research background: The present brings with it the expansion of retail companies, which face globalization trends, whose main impulse is growth. The global retail industry is characterized by maturity and high competitiveness in developed countries complemented by emerging economies of the world that are instrumental in driving market growth. We operate in a global economy where businesses and consumers know no borders. Retailers are increasingly taking advantage of this opportunity to extend their brand beyond the web and existing stores, set up shop in new markets around the world and offer consumers an "in-store" experience to improve shopper loyalty. However, the successful implementation of global store expansion today requires strict adherence to local regulations to ensure the highest levels of efficiency, safety and security.
Purpose of the article: The aim of the article is to measure and quantitatively analyze documents communicating scientific knowledge on the subject matter.
Methods: We will achieve the goal of the paper by using the bibliometric analysis of papers on the topic of globalization in retail using the visualization tool VosViewer. Articles from the Web of Science database were used as input data in this analysis.
Findings & Value added: The results of the study provide a literary and theoretical overview of the investigated issue. The contribution also includes the creation and visualization of network maps showing the connection between keywords, countries and the most cited research publications of more than 5,000 articles dealing with the topic of globalization in retail over the past five years.

Keywords: *globalization, e-commerce, retail, impact*

JEL Classification: *M31; F60; L81*

* Corresponding author: eva.tesarova@stud.uniza.sk

1 University of Zilina, Faculty of Operation and Economics of Transport and Communications, Univerzitna 1, 010 26 Zilina, Slovakia

1 Introduction

According to most authors, globalization has a significant impact on economic, social and political aspects within all countries of the world, either through trade, capital flows or technology transfer. Along with the globalization process and trade exchange that industry has developed, natural resources have become an irreplaceable material base for all production and consumption activities. There is a close relationship between economic development, trade, urbanization and the use of natural resources. Therefore, there has been an escalation of consumption, and thus production to meet demand, which has a direct impact on the environment (Shao et al., 2021). Over the years, this process has been influenced by developments and advances in various fields, from ICT to transportation, which fosters a growing interdependence between marketing activities and other business operations such as management, logistics, accounting, and the like (Surugiu & Surugiu, 2015). For more than two decades, retail has been one of the fastest growing sectors of the economy. It is becoming more and more international. The position of retail and its transformation should continue to be dramatic especially in situations where retailers in developed countries begin to focus on finding opportunities outside their local, regional and national markets towards developing countries in order to maintain potential future company sales and project growth. We can look at retail as an industry with a new perspective and face brought to it by globalization precisely to meet the problems, changing tastes and needs of consumers (Balaji, 2014). Adaptability within the external operating environment, which is characterized by a high degree of participation of individual regions or countries at the level of economic, informational, commercial and sociocultural globalization, is the main key to achieving the competitiveness of the company. It is necessary to take into account globalization and its effects, primarily from the point of view of the extent and pace of its progress, about which there is an assumption of its irreversibility. We can talk about globalization as a phenomenon with elements of logic, objectivity and clarity, which cannot be limited. It is a transnational trend that strengthens economic competition, facilitates communication in solving international social problems, and is even an expanding element of the size of the network society and its development (Ramazanov et al., 2021). Globalization in the retail sector, which is also associated with online shopping and the redevelopment of cities, has caused, for example, markets to be pushed to the outskirts of cities. At the same time, it is the marketplaces that are referred to as authentic places of consumption, where residents and tourists look for experiences (González, 2020). In times of demographic change and globalization, the integration of older and rural structures can be essential to penetrate diverse and underdeveloped consumer segments (Piroth et al., 2020). According to a study by Adebayo et al. (2023), globalization in conjunction with political responses can reduce ecological damage in groupings of countries such as the BRICS states. Consumer globalization is a fundamentally new stage of modern economic development. The Internet and digital technologies are becoming key drivers of consumer globalization. The obtained results allow us to conclude that consumers in countries with high per capita income and higher prevalence and availability of Internet technologies are more globalized. At the same time, the results make it possible to talk with confidence about the beginning of a new stage of economic globalization, which will be determined by new technologies and consumer networks (Kheyfets & Yu, 2022). The globalization of retail is not clearly understood and defined. This term mainly refers to the following three interconnected phenomena: 1. the fact that "major retailers operating in developed markets enter markets in countries at different levels of economic development," 2. the fact that "the supply chain, which is the backbone of retailers' operations, is becoming increasingly global in scope," 3. "diffusion of retail innovations in different parts of the world" (Marchevská et al., 2021). The current development of the modern European business market can be characterized as development based on the principle of concentration and globalization. In this context, in recent years there has been an increase in the average sales area of retail units, a decrease in the number of entities on the market, an expansion of large-scale sales units, both food and non-food. The share of hypermarkets and large-scale supermarkets, as well as discount stores, is growing. The development of the retail market in Slovakia follows similar trends as in the rest of Europe, but it lags behind the European trade market by several years. Manufacturers and traders actively cooperate with the aim of making communication and distribution of manufactured goods more efficient. Large business networks put pressure on suppliers through their strict selection and requirements for product range, quality, low price and synchronization of logistics. Such relations cause concentration and globalization pressures in the production-supplier sphere as well. In accordance with consumer and regional differentiation and the development of consumer perception, behavior and needs, the spectrum of retail concepts and multifunctional centers is expanding (Mitríková, 2011).

2 Methods

Bibliometric analysis is a popular and rigorous method for examining and analyzing large amounts of scientific data. (Donthu et al., 2021). It is widely known that bibliometric indicators have become one of the most common tools of common practice in the management of evaluation research. (Szomszor et al., 2021). Among other things, bibliometric methodologies are considered useful as decision-support tools for setting research priorities, monitoring the development of science and technology, or appreciating scientific excellence. Due to their versatility, these methods have expressly expanded beyond the field of information and library science, from where they were initiated (Zuccala, 2016). Bibliometrics refers to the application of mathematical and statistical methods to books and other forms of written communication. On the other hand, scientometrics refers to all quantitative aspects of science and scientific research. According to these definitions, the overlap between metrics becomes apparent in the creation and analysis of academic literature, which is the written representation of academic output (Mejia et al., 2021). We perform bibliometric analysis using the VOSviewer tool, which is a software tool for creating and visualizing bibliometric networks. Visualization has proven to be an effective approach for analyzing a wide range of bibliometric networks, from networks of citation relationships between publications or journals to networks of co-authorship between researchers or co- occurrence networks between keywords (Majerova et al., 2021). VOSviewer also offers a text mining function that can be used to construct and visualize co-occurrence networks of important terms extracted from a large body of scientific literature. The input data that we will work with in this software program are more than 5,000 scientific articles published in the scientific database Web of Science.

3 Results

Due to the increased rate of publication of scientific research contributions on various topics from various fields, the correct choice of works whose main feature is value is significant, and this is why bibliometric analysis is used pointed out this fact in the presented article, we focus on bibliometric analysis in the context of the globalization of retail (Van Eck & Waltman, 2017). We also subjected the records extracted from the WOS database to an analysis of the co-occurrence of the most used keywords related to the topic in question. We performed this analysis in the VOS Viewer program, and the output in the form of a network visualization can be seen in Figure 1. Figure 1 presents a network visualization of the interconnection of keywords related to the topic of globalization of retail, which were most used in this context in the analyzed records extracted from the WOS database. The first step was the collection of data from a database with more than 5,000 scientific publications, which we then subjected to analysis using the VOSviewer tool. The size of the circle represents the weights, and the larger the circle, the higher the weight of that keyword. The color of the circles determines the cluster to which the keyword belongs. Individual links are links between items. By default, up to 1000 strongest links can be displayed. The distance between the circles expresses the connection of the keywords in terms of correlation links, and the closer these lines are, the stronger the relationship of the keywords (Hallinger & Wang, 2020). In the mentioned bibliometric map, we can see that globalization in retail is indirectly included in all created clusters. These are: 1. trust (red); 2. impact (green); 3. e-commerce (blue); 4. logistics (yellow) and 5. supply chain (purple).

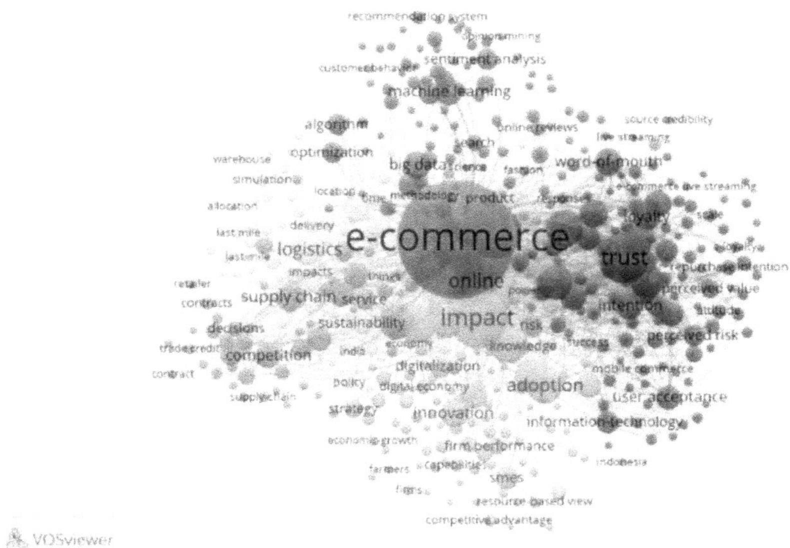

Figure 1. Bibliometric analysis according key words.
Source: Database WOS (2023)

Figure 2 records a visualization of the item density represented by the countries in which the relevant research papers were published. Due to this, it can be concluded that authors from countries such as China, India and Germany have mostly devoted themselves to the topic of globalization of retailing during the selected period.

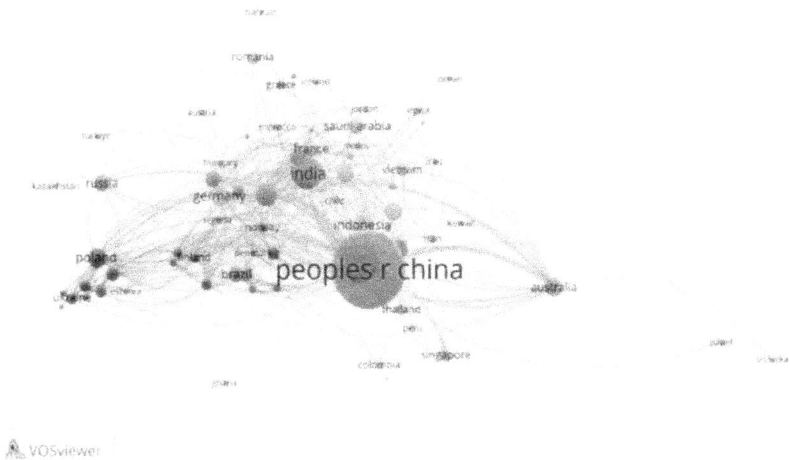

Figure 2. Bibliometric analysis according to countries.
Source: Database WOS (2023)

As part of the bibliometric analysis, we also focused on specific publications of specific authors and the corresponding number of citations, which we considered to be a determinant of the importance and significance of specific articles recorded in the WOS database for the monitored period. In Figure 3, you can see which authors and to what extent, according to the density of publication activity recorded in the WOS database, addressed the topic of globalization in retail, and in which year their publication was the most significant according to the number of citations. The most cited publication (131 citations) is the article entitled "A blockchain-based framework of cross-border e-commerce supply chain," in which the authors Liu and Li (2020) discuss blockchain technology as a new tool to solve the traceability problem of products in supply chain management. This research focuses on the cross-border e-commerce context to propose a blockchain-based framework and develop a set of corresponding techniques and methods to achieve traceable products and transactions in supply chain management. A general blockchain-based product traceability framework is being introduced. This framework is based on the context of a cross-border e-commerce supply chain, which includes a series of blockchain-based models, including a multi-chain structure model, a data management model, and a block structure model. The second author with the largest number of citations (128) is Dannenberg et al. (2020), Digital Transition by COVID-19 Pandemic? The

German Food Online Retail. The study shows the general boom in grocery and the disproportionately high growth of online grocery and identifies the drivers and restraining factors. While COVID-19 has opened a window of opportunity, results of research indicate little shift from grocery to e-commerce. This finding can be explained by a sudden and temporary constellation at the level of the socio-technical regime during the pandemic. The third most cited contribution from the scientific community was "Managing the effectiveness of e-commerce platforms in a pandemic" (with 118 citations). Given the severe impacts of the COVID-19 pandemic on business activities, this study presents a systematic framework to examine the impact of perceived effectiveness of e-commerce platforms (PEEP) on consumer perceived economic benefits in predicting sustainable consumption (Tran, 2021).

Figure 3. Bibliometric analysis according to citations,
Source: Database WOS (2023)

4 Discussion

One of the processes accelerating globalization is digitization (Wassan et al., 2022). It is this that is transforming retail exchanges in many ways and in various aspects of exchange, including communication, transactions and distribution. Among other things, it changes the nature of retail offers, when the differences between products and services are partially erased, creating a real offer and price. Retail settings are also changing, such as the space for retail sales and actors involved in retail (Hagberg et al., 2016). Globalization brings with it various situations to which retail is largely exposed and constantly influenced. Offline retailers have faced countless challenges since the advent of e-commerce. The intensity of these challenges has increased as consumers have become accustomed to shopping online. This comfort with online shopping has been skipped several times during the pandemic. Some of the changes in consumer behavior brought about by the pandemic are likely to persist. E-commerce is a very dynamic industry that responds quickly and flexibly to new technologies, which is inevitably reflected in supply and logistics processes (Gauri et al., 2021). E-commerce is a common part of life today. People are increasingly using this form of trading, which is easier, more convenient and, in some cases, cheaper for many. So far, the biggest disadvantage seems to be the unavailability of the Internet for all residents in relation to price and availability. However, the development of information technology is still progressive and it is only a matter of time when more and more people will use the Internet and all the benefits it brings. The future of e-commerce should be in favor of online customers, whether through offer, availability or ease of ordering. The perception of e- commerce and its importance in the current and future period is indisputable. For businesses in the global economy, they are also trying to increase their sales through business strategies that include the creation and use of e-commerce. E-commerce is the best marketing tool a business could ever have, thanks to customized SEO that a website can use to gain worldwide exposure while targeting the right audience while optimizing the marketing budget. E- commerce allows businesses to increase profitability with less risk and cost, e-commerce is digital and allows products to be stored directly in a warehouse with automated inventory available immediately after an order is completed. Lower costs allow businesses to be more competitive by reducing their operating costs, which leads to a significant increase in revenue margin and at the same time an expansion of market share, given that e-commerce, in addition to reducing costs and increasing available capital for larger investments, increases the visibility of businesses against competitors. Fluctuations not only from a health point of view, but also from a political-economic point of view can be behind the development of this scientific field.

5 Conclusion

The retail sector has gone through major changes over the past three decades. These changes have been made possible by advances in information and communications technology that have enabled new business models, communication tools, technologies, and supply chain practices to emerge and shape the behavior of actors across the retail value chain. For example, from its initial incarnation as only a separate, albeit small, channel in the retail and marketing mix, e-commerce is now a critical part of a firm's multi- and omnichannel strategy (Hanninen et al., 2021). From a business perspective, the Internet has significantly changed the retail landscape over the past few decades. At the same time, the demand for the use of the Internet, which is a common practice in everyday activities, has increased. Especially in recent years, there is a higher demand for digital technologies in terms of the availability of new developments in digital technologies and platforms. In addition, the dominance of online channels in many sectors has led to a large number of retailers and firms adopting multi- channel strategies (Thaichon et al., 2022). Globalization refers to the growing interdependence of countries resulting from the increasing integration of trade, finance, people and ideas into one global market. International trade and cross-border investment flows are the main elements of this global integration. Freedom of trade is the best economic strategy for all nations of the world. No single nation has the natural resources, infrastructure and human capital in sufficient quantity and quality to achieve the standard of living to which developed nations have become accustomed and to which developing nations aspire. So we trade. The main economic benefits of free trade arise from the differences between trading partners, which allow each country to compete in the global market according to its basic economic strengths (Dzaleva, 2009). Thanks to the dynamism that characterizes retail, we can expect that this sector of the economy will once again face the challenges that accompany a global society.

Acknowledgment

The contribution is the output of VEGA 1/0409/23 Forensic marketing as a platform of objective empirical support for managerial decision-making processes.

References

Adebayo, T. S., Samour, A., Alola, A. A., Abbas, S., & Aga, M. (2023). The potency of natural resources and trade globalisation in the ecological sustainability target for the BRICS economies. *Heliyon, 9*(5).

Balaji, R. (2014). Retail management in India-a global perspective of the challenges and opportunities. *Indian Journal of Science and Technology, 7*(2), 1–4.

Dannenberg, P., Fuchs, M., Riedler, T., & Wiedemann, C. (2020). Digital transition by COVID-19 pandemic? The German food online retail. *Tijdschrift voor Economische en Sociale Geografie, 111*(3), 543–560.

Donthu, N., Kumar, S., Mukherjee, D., Pandey, N., & Lim, W. M. (2021). How to conduct a bibliometric analysis: An overview and guidelines. *Journal of business research, 133*, 285–296.

Dzaleva, T. (2009). *Globalization, trade and business.* Core. https://core.ac.uk/down load/pdf/35331351.pdf

Gauri, D. K., Jindal, R. P., Ratchford, B., Fox, E., Bhatnagar, A., Pandey, A., & Howerton, E. (2021). Evolution of retail formats: Past, present, and future. *Journal of Retailing, 97*(1), 42–61.

González, S. (2020). Contested marketplaces: Retail spaces at the global urban margins. *Progress in Human Geography, 44*(5), 877–897.

Hagberg, J., Sundstrom, M., & Egels-Zanden, N. (2016). The digitalization of retailing: An exploratory framework. *International Journal of Retail & Distribution Management, 44*(7), 694–712.

Hallinger, P., & Wang, R. (2020). Analyzing the intellectual structure of research on simulation-based learning in management education, 1960–2019: A bibliometric review. *International Journal of Management Education. 18*(3), 100418.

Hanninen, M., Kwan, S. K., & Mitronen, L. (2021). From the store to omnichannel retail: Looking back over three decades of research. *The International Review of Retail, Distribution and Consumer Research, 31*(1), 1–35.

Kheyfets, A. B., & Yu, C. V. (2022). Consumer involvement in the globalisation of trade: Case of the European Union. *Ekonomika regiona, 18*(2), 413–422.

Liu, Z., & Li, Z. (2020). A Blockchain-Based framework of cross-border E-commerce supply chain. *International Journal of Information Management, 52*, 102059.

Majerova, J., Gajanova, L., & Nadanyiova, M. (2021). A bibliometric analysis of branding trends: Does irrationality really matter?. Globalization and its socio-economic consequences 2021, Slovak Republic, Rajecke Teplice. *19* .

Marchevská, M., Kozarova, I., & Mitrikova, J. (2021). Globalizacia Maloobchodu vo Svetovom Meradle a na Slovensku. *Young Science/Mlada Veda, 9*(3).

Mejia, C., Wu, M., Zhang, Y., & Kajikawa, Y. (2021). Exploring topics in bibliometric research through citation networks and semantic analysis. *Frontiers in Research Metrics and Analytics, 6*, 742311.

Mitríkova, J. (2011). Vplyv globalizacie maloobchodu na nakupne spravanie sa zakaznikov a ich akceptaciu velkoplosnych predajni. *Folia Geographica, 17*(52), 255–273.

Piroth, P., Ruger-Muck, E., & Bruwer, J. (2020). Digitalisation in grocery retailing in Germany: An exploratory study. *The International Review of Retail, Distribution and Consumer Research, 30*(5), 479–497.

Ramdazanov, I. A., Panasenko, S. V., Cheglov, V. P., Krasilnikova, E. A. E., & Nikishin, A. F. (2021). Retail transformation under the influence of digitalisation and technology development in the context of globalisation. *Journal of Open Innovation: Technology, Market, and Complexity, 7*(1), 49.

Shao, J., Tillaguango, B., Alvarado, R., Ochoa-Moreno, S., & Alvarado-Espejo, J. (2021). Environmental impact of the shadow economy, globalisation, trade and market size: Evidence using linear and non-linear methods. *Sustainability, 13*(12), 6539.

Surugiu, M. R., & Surugiu, C. (2015). International trade, globalization and economic interdependence between European countries: Implications for businesses and marketing framework. *Procedia Economics and Finance, 32*, 131–138.

Szomszor, M., Adams, J., Fry, R., Gebert, C., Pendlebury, D. A., Potter, R. W., & Rogers, G. (2021). Interpreting bibliometric data. *Frontiers in Research Metrics and Analytics, 30*(5).

Thaichon, P., Phau, I., & Weaven, S. (2022). Moving from multi-channel to Omni-channel retailing: Special issue introduction. *Journal of Retailing and Consumer Services, 65*, 102311.

Tran, L. T. T. (2021). Managing the effectiveness of e-commerce platforms in a pandemic. *Journal of Retailing and Consumer Services, 58*, 102287.

Van Eck, J. N., & Waltman, L. 2017. Citation-based clustering of publications using CitNetExplorer and VOSviewer. *Scientometrics. 111*(2), 1053–1070.

Wassan, S., Gulati, K., Ghosh, A., Mammani, B. S., Tabbassum, S., & Mohiddin, M. K. (2022). Impact of digitalization on retailers and its future trends. *Materials Today: Proceedings, 51*, 803–809.

Zuccala, A. (2016). Inciting the metric oriented humanist: Teaching bibliometrics in a faculty of humanities. *Education for Information, 32*(2), 149–164.

Elvira Nica[1,*], Gheorghe H. Popescu[2], and George Lăzăroiu[3*]

Generative Artificial Intelligence in the Workplace: Job Automation and Augmentation, Labor Devaluation and Replacement, and Increased Productivity and Profitability

Abstract:

Research background: The aim of this systematic review is to clarify how generative artificial intelligence can assess workforce motivation and commitment, shaping organizational productivity and retention, improving content operations, and streamlining operational workflows.

Purpose of the article: Our findings and analyses indicate that generative artificial intelligence-driven organizational systems, performance management and knowledge sharing practices, and talent development procedures in terms of attraction and retention enable employee collaboration, involvement, and turnover through career development, reducing unreasonable workload.

Methods: Throughout July 2023, a quantitative literature review of outstanding databases such as the Web of Science, Scopus, and ProQuest was carried out, with search terms including "job automation and augmentation," "labor devaluation and replacement," and "increased productivity and profitability," with inspecting research published in 2023 and selecting 25 eligible articles. Dimensions and VOSviewer were employed as data visualization tools for bibliometric mapping and layout algorithms. PRISMA was the reporting quality assessment tool, while AMSTAR, AXIS, Dedoose, Distiller SR, ROBIS, and SRDR were the methodological quality assessment tools.

---

* Corresponding author: phd_lazaroiu@yahoo.com

1 The Bucharest University of Economic Studies, Department of Economics, Piața Romană 6, 010374, Bucharest, Romania

2 "Dimitrie Cantemir" Christian University, Department of Economics, Splaiul Unirii 176, 040042, Bucharest, Romania

3 Spiru Haret University, Department of Economics, Fabricii 46G, 060821, Bucharest, Romania

Findings & Value added: Generative artificial intelligence-based effective organizational practices transform human capital development and derived knowledge, skills, and expertise into competitive advantage, and lead to productive workplace, employee loyalty and satisfaction, talent attraction and retention, and low attrition by articulating positive work environments.

Keywords: *generative artificial intelligence, job automation and augmentation, labor devaluation and replacement, increased productivity and profitability*

JEL Classification: *E42; J33; O14*

1 Introduction

Generative artificial intelligence systems can boost productivity and career growth, build meaningful connections, and enhance organizational performance through employee onboarding, interaction, socialization, and training, while resulting in job destruction, replacement, creation, and loss. Generative artificial intelligence tools can augment employee productivity, fostering supportive work environments in virtual meetings and remote work in the metaverse while prioritizing operational workflows and value propositions through industrialized machine learning operations and natural language processing systems. Generative artificial intelligence algorithms further massive productivity gains, increase employee engagement and product development, and achieve optimal performance, while leading to mass job displacement and staff attrition reduction by use of self-service option automation, human worker augmentation, and algorithmic decision-making processes.

2 Conceptual Framework and Literature Review

Generative artificial intelligence technologies configure labour market automation and industrialization processes (Agrawal et al., 2023; Fosso Wamba et al., 2023; Pan et al., 2023; Zhu et al., 2023), measurable organizational goals, and product and service development by integrating people analytics, automated employment decision tools, and learning management systems (Bouschery et al., 2023; Ko et al., 2023; Ritala et al., 2023), and thus building value-creating institutional and digital analytics capabilities. Generative artificial intelligence systems articulate employee value proposition, engagement, innovation, and creativity, building psychosocial working conditions, functional capabilities, performance appraisals, and organizational outcomes in the changing organizational landscape and data. Generative artificial intelligence tools assist leadership development and behaviors and non-standard hiring processes, building foundational skills and high-priority capabilities and achieving breakthrough organizational performance (Bilgram & Laarmann, 2023; Jin et al., 2023; Que et al., 2023) through deep learning-based computer vision algorithms (Branikas et al., 2023; Lee & Park, 2023; Sun et al., 2023), spatial computing technologies (Budhwar et al., 2023; Lee et al., 2023; Wörsdörfer, 2023), and collaborative robots. Staffing practices, talent and performance management, and flexible work arrangements can unlock growth in equitable workplace cultures by harnessing generative artificial intelligence algorithms (Chou & Lee, 2023; Li & Zhao, 2023; Zhang et al., 2023), edge computing services, and haptic devices, across business process performance (Chun et al., 2023; Liu et al., 2023; Zhong et al., 2023) and capabilities. Generative artificial intelligence technologies are instrumental in changing workplace demands, human capital, decision, and performance management, employee training, workplace perks, appraisal processes, institutional capability building, talent attraction and retention, and career development (Agrawal, 2023; Guliyev, 2023; Park et al., 2023), reducing labor costs and pressures, driving operational efficiencies, and building a scalable workforce. Generative artificial intelligence systems can streamline business processes, complete job tasks, provide staff with adaptive learning experiences, increase organizational productivity and effectiveness, foster creative repeatable processes and collaboration, bolster productivity, and reduce workflow burdens.

3 Methodology

Throughout July 2023, a quantitative literature review of outstanding databases such as the Web of Science, Scopus, and ProQuest was carried out, with search terms including "job automation and augmentation," "labor devaluation and replacement," and "increased productivity and profitability," with inspecting research published in 2023 and selecting 25 eligible articles. Dimensions and VOSviewer were employed as data visualization tools for bibliometric mapping and layout algorithms. PRISMA was the reporting quality assessment tool, while AMSTAR, AXIS, Dedoose, Distiller SR, ROBIS, and SRDR were the methodological quality assessment tools (Figures 1–5).

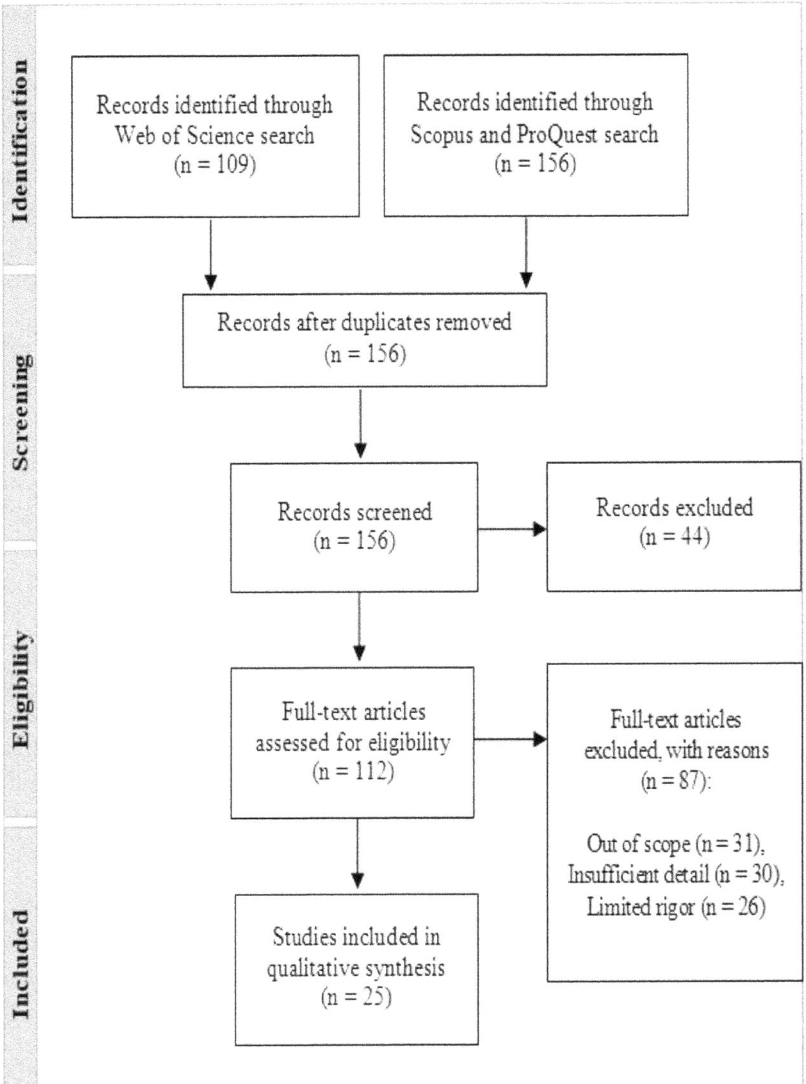

Figure 1. PRISMA flow diagram describing the search results and screening.
Source: authors

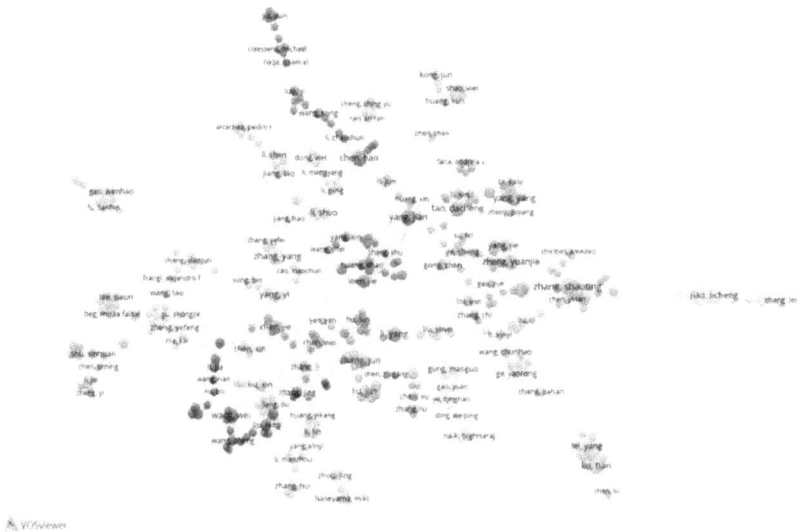

Figure 2. VOSviewer mapping of generative artificial intelligence in the workplace in terms of job automation and augmentation, labor devaluation and replacement, and increased productivity and profitability regarding co-authorship.
Source: authors

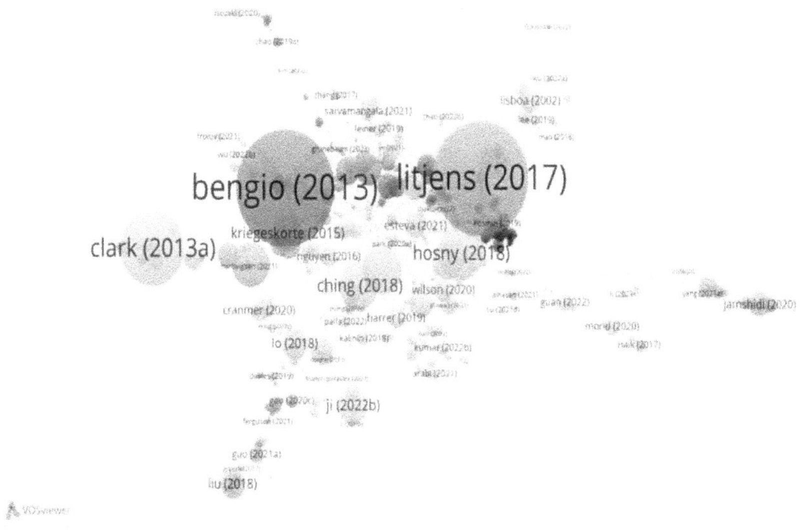

Figure 3. VOSviewer mapping of generative artificial intelligence in the workplace in terms of job automation and augmentation, labor devaluation and replacement, and increased productivity and profitability regarding citation.
Source: authors

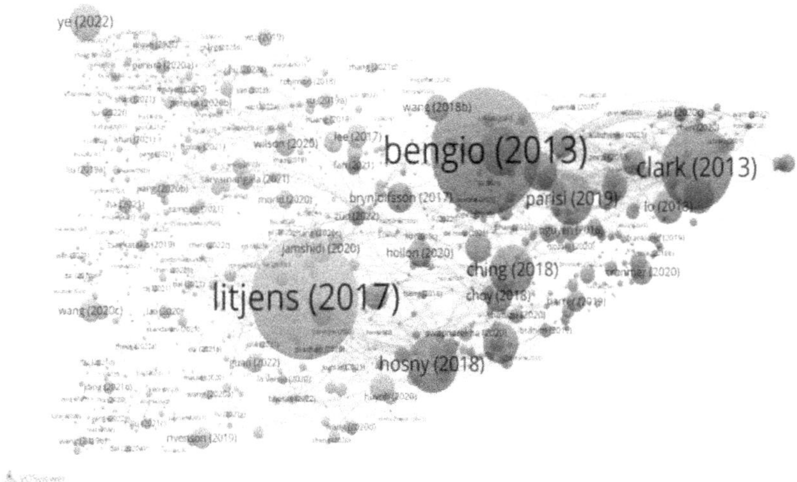

Figure 4. VOSviewer mapping of generative artificial intelligence in the workplace in terms of job automation and augmentation, labor devaluation and replacement, and increased productivity and profitability regarding bibliographic coupling.

Source: authors

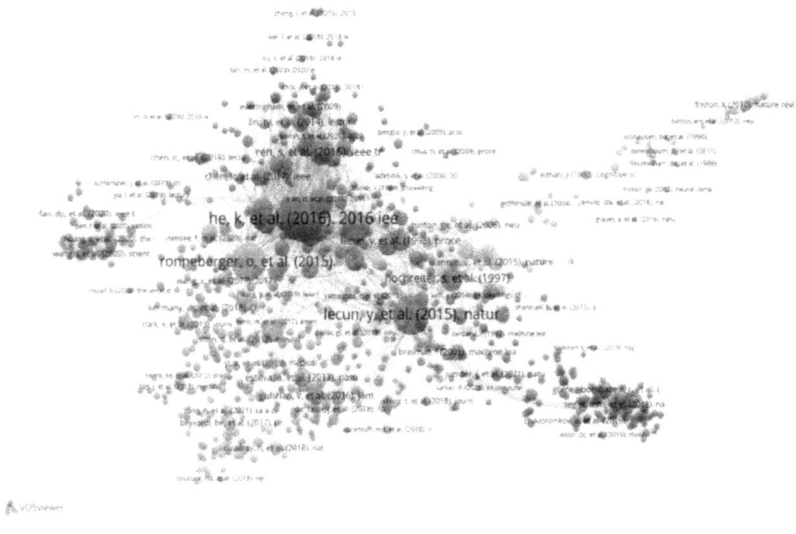

Figure 5. VOSviewer mapping of generative artificial intelligence in the workplace in terms of job automation and augmentation, labor devaluation and replacement, and increased productivity and profitability regarding co-citation.

Source: authors

4 Results and Discussion

Generative artificial intelligence tools improve employee sentiment, engagement, and retention through event processing, image recognition and classification, pattern recognition, and object detection tools, being decisive in skilled labor attracting and training, crowdsourced decisions, and workforce development. Generative artificial intelligence algorithms can assess workforce motivation and commitment, organizational performance practices, and employee value proposition, shaping creative talent markets, employee autonomy and creativity, socioeconomic mobility, and demand forecasting and data-driven decisions. Generative artificial intelligence technologies articulate the labor force participation rate, talent acquisition and management, shifting employment needs, and workplace upskilling and productivity improvements, creating organizational value, building resilient and engaged personnel, and optimizing workforce retention. Generative artificial intelligence systems can streamline efficiency, create business value, improve employee engagement and commitment, and boost productivity through synthetically created content, growth analytics, distributed neural network and self-learning systems, demand forecasting and planning tools, and smart workflows.

Generative artificial intelligence tools can boost robust job and productivity growth, career progression, organizational commitment, and workplace relationship management, leading to sustained productivity improvements through ambient Internet of Things sensing devices, workplace collaboration software and automation, business intelligence tools, and virtual reality training technologies. Generative artificial intelligence algorithms can assist organizations in achieving a competitive advantage through performance management processes and systems, boosting employee engagement and labor productivity growth, enabling staff reskilling and making employment decisions, and developing resilient personnel. Generative artificial intelligence technologies can configure long-term talent pipelines and changing workforce needs, creative jobs, meaningful work, employee expectations and productivity, sustained organizational operations, and career development, maximizing performance outcomes and continual staff training. Employee effectiveness, productivity, attraction, well-being, reskilling, retraining, development, recruitment, retention, satisfaction, engagement, commitment, and performance can develop on generative artificial intelligence tools that may lead to workforce reductions and qualified skilled labor increase.

5 Conclusions and Implications

Generative artificial intelligence can assess workforce motivation and commitment, shaping organizational productivity and retention, improving content operations, and streamlining operational workflows. Generative artificial intelligence-driven organizational systems, performance management and knowledge sharing practices, and talent development procedures in terms of attraction and retention enable employee collaboration, involvement, and turnover through career development, reducing unreasonable workload. Generative artificial intelligence-based effective organizational practices transform human capital development and derived knowledge, skills, and expertise into competitive advantage, and lead to productive workplace, employee loyalty and satisfaction, talent attraction and retention, and low attrition by articulating positive work environments. Generative artificial intelligence systems can positively impact job skills, employee retention and reskilling, workplace productivity, competitive talent pools, product development teams, talent management, and predictive workflows by use of task automation and collaboration tools.

References

Agrawal, A., Gans, J. S., & Goldfarb, A. (2023). Do we want less automation? *Science*, *381*, 155–158.

Agrawal, K. P. (2023). Towards adoption of generative AI in organizational settings. *Journal of Computer Information Systems.*

Bilgram, V., & Laarmann, F. (2023). Accelerating innovation with generative AI: AI-Augmented digital prototyping and innovation methods. *IEEE Engineering Management Review*, *51*(2), 18–25.

Bouschery, S. G., Blazevic, V., & Piller, F. T. (2023). Augmenting human innovation teams with Artificial Intelligence: Exploring transformer-based language models. *Journal of Product Innovation Management*, *40*(2), 139–153.

Branikas, E., Murray, P., & West, G. (2023). A novel data augmentation method for improved visual crack detection using generative adversarial networks. *IEEE Access*, *11*, 22051–22059.

Budhwar, P., Chowdhury, S., Wood, G., Aguinis, H., Bamber, G. J., & Beltran, J. R., et al. (2023). Human resource management in the age of generative artificial intelligence: Perspectives and research directions on ChatGPT. *Human Resource Management Journal.*

Chou, C.-B., & Lee, C.-H. (2023). Generative Neural Network-Based Online Domain Adaptation (GNN-ODA) approach for incomplete target domain data. *IEEE Transactions on Instrumentation and Measurement*, *72*, 3508110.

Chun, P. J., Suzuki, M., & Kato, Y. (2023). Iterative application of generative adversarial networks for improved buried pipe detection from images obtained by ground-penetrating radar. *Computer-Aided Civil and Infrastructure Engineering*.

Fosso Wamba, S., Queiroz, M. M., Chiappetta Jabbour, C. S., & Shi, C. V. (2023). Are both generative AI and ChatGPT game changers for 21st-Century operations and supply chain excellence? *International Journal of Production Economics*, *265*, 109015.

Guliyev, H. (2023). Artificial intelligence and unemployment in high-tech developed countries: New insights from dynamic panel data model. *Research in Globalization*, *7*, 100140.

Jin, K.-H., Kang, K.-S., Shin, B.-K., Kwon, J.-H., Jang, S.-J., & Kim, Y.-B., et al. (2023). Development of robust detector using the weather deep generative model for outdoor monitoring system. *Expert Systems with Applications*, *234*, 120984.

Ko, J., Ennemoser, B., Yoo, W., Yan, W., & Clayton, M. J. (2023). Architectural spatial layout planning using artificial intelligence. *Automation in Construction*, *154*, 105019.

Lee, J., & Park, J. (2023). AI as "Another I": Journey map of working with artificial intelligence from AI-phobia to AI-preparedness. *Organizational Dynamics*, *52*(3), 100994.

Lee, J. A., Park, J., Choi, Y. T., Kim, R. E., Jung, J., & Lee, S., et al. (2023). Influence of tensile properties on hole expansion ratio investigated using a generative adversarial imputation network with explainable artificial intelligence. *Journal of Materials Science*, *58*, 4780–4794.

Li, S., & Zhao, X. (2023). High-resolution concrete damage image synthesis using conditional generative adversarial network. *Automation in Construction*, *147*, 104739.

Liu, P., Qi, H., Liu, J., Feng, L., Li, D., & Guo, J. (2023). Automated clash resolution for reinforcement steel design in precast concrete wall panels via generative adversarial network and reinforcement learning. *Advanced Engineering Informatics*, *58*, 102131.

Pan, Y., Zhang, Y., Wang, X., Gao, X. X., & Hou, Z. (2023). Low-cost livestock sorting information management system based on deep learning. *Artificial Intelligence in Agriculture*, *9*, 110–126.

Park, N. H., Manica, M., Born, J., Hedrick, J. L., Erdmann, T., & Zubarev, D. Y., et al. (2023). Artificial intelligence driven design of catalysts and materials for ring opening polymerization using a domain-specific language. *Nature Communications*, *14*, 3686.

Que, Y., Dai, Y., Ji, X., Kwan Leung, A., Chen, Z., & Jiang, Z., et al. (2023). Automatic classification of asphalt pavement cracks using a novel integrated generative adversarial networks and improved VGG model. *Engineering Structures*, *277*, 115406.

Ritala, P., Ruokonen, M., & Ramaul, L. (2023). Transforming boundaries: How does ChatGPT change knowledge work? *Journal of Business Strategy*.

Sun, K., Wang, W., Cheng, R., Liang, Y., Xie, H., & Wang, J., et al. (2023). Evolutionary generative design of supercritical airfoils: An automated approach driven by small data. *Complex & Intelligent Systems*.

Wörsdörfer, M. (2023). The E.U.'s artificial intelligence act: An ordoliberal assessment. *AI Ethics*.

Zhang, Y., He, R., Ai, B., Yang, M., Chen, R., & Wang, C., et al. (2023). Generative adversarial networks based digital twin channel modeling for intelligent communication networks. *China Communications*, *20*(8), 32–43.

Zhong, J., Huyan, J., Zhang, W., Cheng, H., Zhang, J., & Tong, Z., et al. (2023). A deeper generative adversarial network for grooved cement concrete pavement crack detection, *Engineering Applications of Artificial Intelligence*, *119*, 105808.

Zhu, X., Lou, Y., Zhao, J., Gao, W., & Deng, H. (2023). Generative non-autoregressive unsupervised keyphrase extraction with neural topic modeling. *Engineering Applications of Artificial Intelligence*, *120*, 105934.

Jan Panus[1,*], and Petr Dolejs[1]

Augmented Reality Application for Mobile Devices

Abstract:
Research background: This paper explores and compares the possibilities of creating augmented reality applications for mobile devices. In today's globalized world, we encounter many areas where augmented reality is appropriate and even used. For example, augmented reality assists schools in teaching or can be used in the analysis of ubiquitous reality.
Purpose of the article: The aim of this paper is to bring new perspectives on the possibilities of creating applications that use augmented reality for various purposes. The paper will describe these purposes and uses of augmented reality with a view to expanding it within the current globalized world. The possibilities where augmented reality can be used are many and not just in the video game industry where it is directly offered.
Methods: The methods used in this paper are mainly observation and surveys of existing papers. A functional application has also been created using selected libraries and therefore it will be possible to compare this application with other libraries that are currently being used extensively.
Findings & Value added: The development of augmented reality applications is quite widespread nowadays, yet it faces many problems. It is also true that there is an ever-increasing number of possibilities for the use of these applications. There is also an ever-increasing number of different libraries and SDKs for creating such applications. The contribution of this paper is then to compare the different libraries and another contribution is to find out how such applications can be used and especially created.

Keywords: *augmented reality, mobile devices, programming*

JEL Classification: *C61; C63; D83*

* Corresponding author: jan.panus@upce.cz
1 University of Pardubice, Faculty of Electrical Engineering and Informatics, náměstí Čs. Legií 565, 530 02 Pardubice, Czech republic

1 Introduction

Augmented Reality (AR) is a technology that allows you to embed digital content into real environments in real time. While Virtual Reality (VR) creates a whole new environment, in AR users see a real-world environment with added digital objects and models (Azuma, 1997).

It is about enriching the real world by adding digital elements, sounds or other sensory stimuli. Companies can use this technology to promote their products and services, but also to launch new marketing campaigns. The commercial sector has also used AR to improve the product shopping experience. Companies in this area have incorporated AR into their catalogues, allowing them to focus a reference image in the catalogue and display the relevant product as a 3D model (Luebbers et al., 2019). The technology can also be used when purchasing furniture, allowing the user to insert a virtual desk into their room.

In the current era, digital real estate is a very growing market. This can lead to misunderstandings of each of them.

Types of digital realities:

- Augmented Reality (AR) – Created to insert digital objects into the real world with limited interaction (Carmigniani & Furht, 2011).
- Virtual reality (VR) – Through a headset and headset, it can completely isolate the user from the real world, while using accessories to make them feel in a completely different reality (LaValle, 2023; Zheng et al., 1998).
- Mixed reality (MR) – This is a combination of AR and VR elements that allows interaction between the user, digital content and the real world (Luebbers et al., 2019; Speicher et al., 2019).
- Extended reality (XR) – Encompasses technologies that enhance our senses, including AR, VR and MR (Andrews et al., 2019; Cardenas-Robledo et al., 2022).

AR continues to grow and offer an immersive experience for all its users. The most common forms of AR include use with smart glasses or a camera (mobile device, tablet), where all devices make use of the five major components of AR:

- Artificial Intelligence – The vast majority of AR solutions require artificial intelligence to process information (Devagiri et al., 2022; Sahu et al., 2021).
- AR software – Appropriate tools and applications are needed to access and work with AR(Nee et al., 2012).
- Processing – It is necessary to have sufficient computing power to process the necessary information.

- Viewport – To display content, it is necessary to have a sufficiently high quality viewport (mobile device, tablet).
- Sensors – To properly synchronize the real and digital worlds, sensors are needed to capture information and send it to software for processing (Limbu et al., 2018).

AR can be very useful in a work environment. It enables effective training of new employees as well as training of current ones. With AR we can improve the quality of training and education materials.

Many work sectors are already using AR:

- Production – AR can provide very accurate workflows, plus allow trainers to give immediate feedback to the trainee (Friedrich et al., 2002).
- Healthcare – AR makes healthcare practice risk-free and can provide accurate, practical and safe instructions for surgery or information about the body's anatomy and body systems (Ferrari et al., 2019).
- Army – AR assists in a military environment in combat training by aircraft.
- Automobiles – Using AR, all the components of a vehicle can be explored and broken down into their individual parts for a better understanding of the component(Fründ et al., 2005).

2 Methods

A mobile application was designed and developed for the Android operating system that will work with AR and demonstrate the capabilities of this technology. The application will be divided into four AR parts, each of which will demonstrate one of the functionalities offered by ARCore.

In the first part, called AR Marker, the app focuses on recognizing a marker that the user selects directly from the device and then inserts the selected model into the scene. The next part of the app is AR Face, which allows facial recognition and the addition of digital content, which can be a moustache or glasses. In these two parts, the application provides the ability to create a configuration from the current models in the scene, which is then uploaded to the server. This configuration can later be applied back to the scene, adding all the models defined in the configuration with the corresponding position, rotation and size. The following section, called AR Area, allows the user to add 3D models to the area after the horizontal surfaces have been detected. The last section for working with AR is called AR Video. This part works with marker recognition in the same way as AR Marker. However, unlike the AR Marker, it does not insert 3D models into the scene, but after the marker is recognized, a user- defined video starts playing on the scene.

There is also a non-AR part of the app. This section called Options allows the user to set the IP address of the server and check its availability. It is also possible to download all 3D models, configurations and videos from the server and save them to the device. At the same time, this section allows us to view the models stored on the server or directly on the device to see how they will look in the scene.

The mobile app also works offline. To do this, all models and videos must first be downloaded to the device, after which it is possible to work without internet access. When you try to upload the configuration in offline mode, it is not uploaded to the server, but is saved locally.

A Windows app has also been created for the mobile app, which allows us to adjust the size and rotation of individual models. This application will not be discussed in detail as it is only an add-on to the mobile application.

In the mobile app, digital content is inserted into the scene in the form of 3D models. A 3D model is a mathematical representation of an object in three dimensions. These models are used to represent real world objects and their use can be found in 3D printing, VR and AR, computer games and other industries.

The 3D model is made up of vertices that, when connected by edges, form a mesh. This mesh forms the core of the whole model. The individual vertices can change their position in space and thus change the overall shape of the 3D model. Most often, a 3D model is created based on primitive shapes, which include cube, cylinder or sphere.

It is also common to create animations for the models themselves. In this case, it is necessary to create the 3D model very carefully, as unexpected states could occur when the model moves.

Models can have their colour, light work and other surface characteristics defined using a program called a shader. Without the use of a shader, these characteristics can be defined using multiple files in the form of 2D images.

The mobile application is working with 3D models in GLB format. GLB stands for GL Transmission Format Binary File and is suitable for AR and VR. The format was created in 2015 as a binary format to glTF format. GLB is a binary format, while glTF is a JSON text file based format. At the same time, the GLB format is made up of only one file that contains all the components. These components include textures, animations, material, and the overall model hierarchy. glTF is also only one file, but it needs external files to function properly. These are typically files containing textures, but can also be shaders or animations(Tóth et al., 2021).

The structure of the glTF file contains the model folder itself, and inside there are several files: scene.bin, scene.gltf, license.txt and the textures themselves

3D models can be efficiently worked with in standard graphical programs such as 3ds Max, Maya or Blender. In these programs it is possible to work with a wide range of formats including FBX, OBJ or STL. Besides the dedicated programs, it is also possible to work with models in the Unity engine, which is used in this paper.

3 Results

Functional requirements are features that the developer implements in the application. These requirements describe how the entire system can behave under certain conditions. They can be seen in the final version of a given system or application, and the user can implement these functions.

Table 1. Functional requirements of the application.

ID	Request
F1	The system will recognize horizontal surfaces in the surrounding area
F2	The system will recognise the face
F3	The system will recognize predefined tags
F4	The system will be able to add digital content (models, videos) to recognized objects (surfaces, faces, markers)
F5	The system will be able to download models from the server
F6	The system will be able to upload model configurations to the server
F7	The system will be able to manipulate models (movement, rotation, resizing)
F8	The system will be able to set up tags and videos directly from the device
F9	The system will be able to cache selected data
F10	The system will be able to set the server address
F11	The system will be able to test the connection to the server

Source: Author's research

Table 2. Non-functional application requirements.

ID	Request
N1	The system will be programmed in C# programming language.
N2	The system will be developed using the Unity engine.
N3	The system will use GLB models.
N4	The system will work on devices running Android 7.0 or higher that support ARCore
N5	The system will use AR Foundation and ARCore to work with augmented reality.
N6	The system will be able to work online and offline

Source: Author's research

Non-functional requirements specify system properties that are not related to individual functions. They specify qualitative factors that the system must meet and were agreed upon before the project started. These requirements are most often determined by developers, software architects or technical teamleaders.

For this work, it is necessary to create a server on which the data will be stored. The server will store 3D models, individual configurations of these models and videos. It will only be possible to upload and download data, for this reason we just need to create a very simple server. For this purpose, the XAMPP package was chosen, which includes an Apache HTTP server and allows working with MariaDB, PHP and Perl.

Apache is open-source software that is free to use and runs on approximately 40 % of websites worldwide. It allows site owners to make their sites available to other users. The software was developed and continues to be maintained by the Apache Software Foundation, which released the first version in 1995.

Apache is software that runs on a physical server, and its main purpose is to establish a connection between the web browser and the physical server. For this application, it is sufficient for the server to be a computer.

After a simple installation of the XAMPP package on a computer, it is necessary to make configuration adjustments to make the server accessible via a mobile device. This is done by editing the httpd.conf configuration file, which can be opened using the Config button. To access the server using a mobile device, the computer on which the server is mediated needs to be on the same Wifi network as the mobile device.

To work with 3D models in GLB format, you need to import these models into the application. One way to do this is to use a Github project from Siccity called GLTFUtility. This project focuses on ease of use and simplicity, and makes it very easy to import models into an application using a single line of code.

GameObject model = Importer. LoadFromFile(Path.Combine(Application. persistentDataPath,folder, name));

The project also offers importing models asynchronously or directly from an array of bytes, and should be able to export GLB models in the future.

The project also handles a number of components that allow us to convert a GLB format model into a GameObject that we can work with in Unity. These components include working with static meshes, normals, tangents, vertex colors, materials, textures or cameras. To work properly, the selected shaders must be inserted into a specific part of the project, so that they will always be part of the build. Add the shaders to the *Project Settings/Graphics/Always Included Shaders* section. The necessary shaders to insert can be found in *GLTFUtility/*

Materials/Built-in. These are *Standard-Metallic-Blend, Standard- Metallic, Standard-Specular-Blend and Standard-Specular*. You also need to insert a shader from the *glTFast* package called *glTFPbrMetallicRoughness* into this section.

4 Discussion and Conclusion

The AR Magic mobile app for Android devices shows the possibilities of using augmented reality in indoor environments. This app focuses on showing the main functionalities offered by ARCore technology, which include brand recognition, facial recognition and horizontal surface recognition. With the ability to embed models on recognized marks and horizontal surfaces, this application can be used for educational purposes which solved (Wu et al., 2013) or in (Lee, 2012). In this area, the application is suitable for primary schools where students can explore models of body organs in detail. For high school students with a technical background, the app could be used to display the necessary components, which would be more beneficial than a traditional 2D picture in a book. The app could also find its use in museums (Ding, 2017), where it could function as an interactive guide that would display an informative video or model with information about the selected exhibit after recognizing the marker.

The application would offer a greater number of uses once selected functionalities are added. In the future, it would be possible to add animations (Hou et al., 2013) to individual models, which could greatly simplify the explanation of the functions of the body organs. Animation support would also make it easier to describe historical events, which could be battles or other important events. In future development, we could also add the ability to define and then display a caption for each model.

It would also be possible to direct AR Magic to a specific purpose. There is the possibility of using it alongside the Edison learning robot (Linder & Maes, 2010), which can drive on a black line or react to light. The application could be extended so that when a target position is reached, a selected model would appear to indicate successful completion of the robot's task. This would provide children with visual confirmation that the robot has been successfully programmed and could encourage further interest in learning in this area.

Based on these studies, it is possible to state that the issues investigated in this paper are appropriate in many areas, thus supporting the results obtained in this paper. Augmented Reality has potential applications in many areas, not only those mentioned above.

References

Andrews, C., Southworth, M. K., Silva, J. N., & Silva, J. R. (2019). Extended reality in medical practice. *Current Treatment Options in Cardiovascular Medicine, 21*, 1–12.

Azuma, R. T. (1997). A survey of augmented reality. *Presence: Teleoperators & Virtual Environments, 6*(4), 355–385.

Cardenas-Robledo, L. A., Hernández-Uribe, Ó., Reta, C., & Cantoral-Ceballos, J. A. (2022). Extended reality applications in industry 4.0.-A systematic literature review. *Telematics and Informatics*, 101863.

Carmigniani, J., & Furht, B. (2011). Augmented reality: An overview. *Handbook of augmented reality*, 3–46.

Devagiri, J. S., Paheding, S., Niyaz, Q., Yang, X., & Smith, S. (2022). Augmented reality and Artificial Intelligence in industry: Trends, tools, and future challenges. *Expert Systems with Applications*, 118002.

Ding, M. (2017). Augmented reality in museums. *Museums & augmented reality–A collection of essays from the arts management and technology laboratory*, 1–15.

Ferrari, V., Klinker, G., & Cutolo, F. (2019). Augmented reality in healthcare. *Journal of Healthcare Engineering.*

Friedrich, W., Jahn, D., & Schmidt, L. (2002). ARVIKA-Augmented Reality for Development, Production and Service. *International Symposium on Mixed and Augmented Reality ISMAR, Germany, 2.*

Fründ, J., Gausemeier, J., Matysczok, C., & Radkowski, R. (2005). Using augmented reality technology to support the automobile development. *Computer Supported Cooperative Work in Design I: 8th International Conference, CSCWD 2004, China*, 289–298.

Hou, L., Wang, X., Bernold, L., & Love, P. E. (2013). Using animated augmented reality to cognitively guide assembly. *Journal of Computing in Civil Engineering, 27*(5), 439–451.

LaValle, S. M. (2023). *Virtual reality.* Cambridge University Press.

Lee, K. (2012). Augmented reality in education and training. *TechTrends, 56*, 13–21.

Limbu, B. H., Jarodzka, H., Klemke, R., & Specht, M. (2018). Using sensors and augmented reality to train apprentices using recorded expert performance: A systematic literature review. *Educational Research Review, 25*, 1–22.

Linder, N., & Maes, P. (2010). LuminAR: Portable robotic augmented reality interface design and prototype. *Adjunct proceedings of the 23nd annual ACM symposium on User interface software and technology, USA*, 395–396.

Luebbers, M. B., Brooks, C., Kim, M. J., Szafir, D., & Hayes, B. (2019). Augmented reality interface for constrained learning from demonstration. *Proceedings of the 2nd International Workshop on Virtual, Augmented and Mixed Reality for HRI (VAM-HRI), Korea.*

Nee, A. Y., Ong, S., Chryssolouris, G., & Mourtzis, D. (2012). Augmented reality applications in design and manufacturing. *CIRP Annals*, *61*(2), 657–679.

Sahu, C. K., Young, C., & Rai, R. (2021). Artificial intelligence (AI) in augmented reality (AR)-assisted manufacturing applications: A review. *International Journal of Production Research*, *59*(16), 4903–4959.

Speicher, M., Hall, B. D., & Nebeling, M. (2019). What is mixed reality? *Proceedings of the 2019 CHI conference on human factors in computing systems, United Kingdom*, 1–15.

Tóth, R., Zichar, M., & Hoffmann, M. (2021). Improving and measuring spatial skills with augmented reality and gamification. ICGG 2020-Proceedings of the 19th International Conference on Geometry and Graphics, Brazil, 755–764.

Wu, H.-K., Lee, S. W.-Y., Chang, H.-Y., & Liang, J.-C. (2013). Current status, opportunities and challenges of augmented reality in education. *Computers & Education*, *62*, 41–49.

Zheng, J., Chan, K., & Gibson, I. (1998). Virtual reality. *IEEE Potentials*, *17*(2), 20–23.

Lucia Sujanska[1,*], and Pavol Kral[1]

Online Marketing's Impact on Customers in the Globalization Era

Abstract:
Research background: The Internet offers a large number of opportunities through which businesses can attract new potential customers, increase awareness of their products and brand, and communicate with their customers, which significantly helps in establishing good relationships and building loyal groups of consumers. These aspects help companies to achieve corporate goals, which are primarily the economic stability and prosperity of the company. Online marketing is one of the powerful and effective tools that can provide businesses with new opportunities to reach potential customers. It is therefore essential for businesses to know how to implement and use elements of online marketing in their activities. Due to the influence of innovations and new technological procedures, online marketing has a great potential for continuous expansion in the future, which will provide companies with new opportunities to improve their financial indicators.
Purpose of the article: The main aim of the article is to determine the impact of the online marketing and its tools on customers in Slovak Republic.
Methods: For the purpose of data processing, general scientific methods were used, and mathematical-statistical methods and statistical hypothesis testing were used to evaluate the data obtained on the basis of the conducted survey.
Findings & Value added: The benefits of using online marketing are formulated, based on the analysis of the theoretical basis of the solved problem and on the results obtained from the conducted questionnaire survey.

Keywords: *online marketing, marketing communication, digital advertising*

JEL Classification: *M30; M31; F60*

---

* Corresponding author: sujanska2@stud.uniza.sk
1 University of Zilina, Faculty of Operation and Economics of Transport and Communications, Univerzitna 1, 010 26 Zilina, Slovakia

1 Introduction

With the advent of new technologies and the Internet, new methods have developed through which people can communicate with each other, share their thoughts, opinions, and digital content across the globe. As the dominant technology and medium of the past two decades, the Internet has had a significant impact on how society evolves. Since 2000, the global rate of Internet penetration has increased by 1100 % (Orzan et al., 2020). In the same way, the marketing environment began to take shape, up to the form in which we know it today. The number of Internet users is increasing every day, and the Internet thus constantly brings new opportunities for businesses to reach a wide range of people, which motivates businesses to use the online environment to promote their products. According to Statista (2023) in Slovak Republic the internet penetration rate in 2022 was 90,65 %, which offers large base of potential consumers that company can reach with their online marketing communication. Regardless of the nature of their marketing efforts, more and more businesses and organizations have begun to realize and profit from the benefits that the Internet environment can provide them. Many businesses are already trying to follow trends in this area, and despite the high competition in this area, it is desirable that businesses use at least basic tools for online promotion and communication in their marketing activities.

2 Literature Review

The origins of online marketing can be traced back to year 1978, when Gary Thuerk delivered the first promotional emails to 320 recipients (Oetjen, 2019). For online marketing $522.5 billion worldwide was spent in 2021 and online marketing spending is expected to increase to $626.86 billion by the end of the year 2023 (Statista, 2023). Online marketing can be characterized as a method by which the desired marketing goals can be achieved through the Internet. Similar to classic marketing, it includes a number of activities that are associated with influencing, persuading and maintaining relationships with customers (Janouch, 2020). Product, Price, Place, and Promotion are the four Ps that make up the marketing mix in general. While in online marketing the Promotion is associated with advertising, branding, and public relations, the Place stands for social networks, websites, or mobile applications, to mention a few (Harvey & An, 2018). Search engines, social networks, various advertising systems and measurement tools are some of the multiple communication channels that characterize the specificity of digital marketing. The most common indicators for evaluating the effectiveness of online marketing activities include the visibility of an Internet resource in communication channels, such as search engines, social networks, and websites (Krstic, 2019).

In order for online marketing to work properly and bring results, it is important that it targets the right group of people. With the help of properly targeted marketing, the company can identify groups of people who have the same characteristics and the same needs and desires as those that the company decides to satisfy (Sanchez & Bernabeu, 2021). At the heart of well-targeted marketing is segmentation, which divides potential customers into segments using demographic data, geographic data, socioeconomic data, and psychological data. The company will choose the segments it wants to target, and this will decide the procedure for other marketing activities. It is important for a company to set goals that it wants to achieve through online marketing. Through online marketing business can try to strength brand awareness. Brand and reputation management is key to the success of any business. Many consumers prefer to buy products from brands they know and trust, rather than products from brands they have never encountered. In today's highly competitive market, the brand is the best and strongest way to distinguish substitute products and differentiate yourself from the competition. Business can also try to boost sales and the profit from sales with online marketing (Liao & Tsai, 2021).

If a business wants to use online marketing in its operations, it is essential for it to have a comprehensive understanding of the advantages and potential disadvantages of this approach. Based on this information, businesses can then make decisions that are in line with their goals and market dynamics. The main advantages of online marketing include fast and easy reaching of target customers. A business can reach a target segment of customers almost instantly with paid advertising and over time the website can reach a large number of potential customers, thanks to the website's search engine ranking (Hajarian et al., 2021). Through online marketing, companies can easily connect with people from all over the world and thus acquire new customers, expand their business, and operate on the global market. This means that companies now have easy access to a global audience regardless of where they are based, and online marketing helps businesses become part of the larger global economy. Nowadays, when the world is becoming more and more connected and many people buy things from other countries, it's getting still more important (Murad et al., 2018).

Despite the fact that online marketing undoubtedly has many advantages, it is necessary to realize that, like any business strategy, it also has its weaknesses. Knowing and understanding these potential drawbacks of online marketing is necessary so that businesses can effectively navigate the digital environment and reduce potentially negative effects. Access to an audience from all over the world also means strong global competition. The goal of every company is to get as many customers as possible, and millions of businesses use online marketing for this purpose. Businesses must therefore be very original and innovative in order to differentiate themselves from the competition. Another disadvantage for businesses can be the age-limited range of the audience. Older age groups of users do not use the Internet to a large extent or at all. If the company sell goods or offers services, the target segment of which is the older age group of customers, online marketing can be less effective compared to classic tools of marketing communication (Tabuena et al., 2022).

In the modern business world, online marketing offers many tools that businesses can use to boost their business. One of the older but still popular online marketing tools is email marketing. The main goal of email marketing is to enable businesses to communicate with customers, building relationships and interacting with customers in real time. Email marketing serves not only to promote goods and services, but also to guide and motivate customers to use company websites (Civelek et al., 2020). Despite the current popularity of social media, many people still prefer to receive news about businesses via email (Camilleri, 2018). Email marketing is characterized by low costs, therefore it is very effective in terms of return on investment (ROI). The effectiveness of email marketing can be increased in various ways. Sahni et al. (2018) found that the probability that the recipient will read an email increase by 20 % if the email is personalized. For this purpose, the company may, for example, add the recipient's name to the email subject. Many companies also use websites for promoting and selling their products online.

In order to be effective and reach the largest audience as possible it is important to build well-functioning website. The main reason any business should have a website is to showcase the business, increase awareness of the business and help attract potential customers. Websites are used to support marketing activities such as sales, product promotion and customer support (Blazheska et al., 2022). To improve the position of the website in the search engine with the so-called organic or unpaid searches are served by SEO – search engine optimization. When searching on the Internet, the user starts from keywords that are the subject of his interest. Subsequently, large amounts of websites appear in the search engine, and the most relevant ones are at the top. SEO is responsible for this search (Matta et al.,2020). Another online marketing tool is social media marketing. Companies can use social networks such as Instagram or Facebook to present their site, communicate with their customers and promote their products and services to potential customers. This can help the company improve brand awareness and boost product sales (Smith et al., 2016). Social media marketing can take many forms including influencer marketing, viral marketing, and video marketing. Social networks can provide companies with various benefits, as they can use them to publish their content online to a wide audience. The primary objective is to influence consumers and entice them to buy their products or services (Hajarian et al., 2021). Social media marketing is closely related to influencer marketing, which is another type of online marketing. Influencers can be characterized as online users who promote products or brands to their audience, where an influencer is usually a popular person, including celebrities and athletes, who have a high number of followers on social media. They can be considered as online social network celebrities (Jin & Muqaddam, 2019).

3 Methods

The main aim of the article is to determine the impact of the online marketing and its tools on customers in Slovak Republic. Theoretical background is also included. Scientific studies, statistical databases, and published professional papers were significant sources of secondary data. For the purpose of data processing, general scientific methods were used, and mathematical-statistical methods and statistical hypothesis testing were used to evaluate the data obtained on the basis of the conducted survey. In order to determine the impact of online marketing and its tools on Slovak consumers a questionnaire survey was conducted. Utilizing the Sample Size Calculator, a tool included in Creative Research Systems' survey software, the sample size was established. In order to get results that precisely reflect the target population and prevent survey data from being distorted it is necessary to determine number of respondents that need to be interviewed. With a 95 % confidence level, the confidence interval was determined at 5 %. This indicates that a 5 % margin of error is allowed for the questionnaire survey. The base file consists of population data for the Slovak Republic, particular people who are 18 years and older. The minimum sample of respondents required for the survey is therefore 384 respondents and total of 401 respondents took part in the survey. The survey was conducted in the form of a questionnaire and was conducted in the period from May 2023 to July 2022 within the Slovak Republic. The quantitative evaluation technique was used to process the data collected from the questionnaire survey.

To achieve the main aim of the article research hypotheses are formulated:

- ***Hypothesis 1***: More than 50 % of Slovak consumers buy products from online stores at least three times a month.

- *Hypothesis 2*: More than 50 % of Slovak consumers bought product based on promotional email that they received.
- *Hypothesis 3*: More than 50 % of Slovak consumers have ever made a purchase as a result of seeing online advertisement.

We used regularly used approach - one-tailed testing to determine the test statistic for hypotheses 1 - 3, with significance level determined at 0.05 (Lombardi & Hurlbert 2009; Ruxton & Neuhauser, 2010).

4 Results

A total of 401 respondents filled the questionnaire, from which 56 % (225) were women and 44 % (176) was men. According to the findings of a questionnaire survey 83 % (333) respondents ever bought a product form online store as a result of seeing an online advertisement. Respondents were most likely to buy a clothes 41 % (164), electronics 27 % (108) and cosmetics 13 % (52). When it comes to frequency most respondents buy products online on average at least three times a month 35 % (141), once a month 23 % (92), at least five times a month shop online 21 % (84) respondents, more than five times a month 9 % (36) respondents and 12 % (48) respondents don't shop online at all. More than a half - 63 % (253) respondents are following their favourite brands on the social media, mostly on Instagram 66 % (167), 18 % (45) on Facebook and 12 % (31) on Tiktok. One of the new tools of online marketing are influencers therefore we also investigated if respondents trust them and to what degree. We found out that 11 % (44) respondents fully trust influencers, 31 % (124) have average trust in influencers, 19 % (77) trust influencers a little and 39 % (156) respondents don't trust influencers at all. When buying a product 69 % (277) respondents actively seek online reviews before making a purchase. Most respondents 58 % (233) don't read promotional emails that they receive, 37 % (148) respondents read it occasionally and 5 % (20) read it frequently. Based on promotional emails 21 % (84) of respondents ever bought product promoted in this email and 79 % (317) respondents don't.

To verify the statistical hypotheses 1 - 3, we used the method testing a single proportion. Results of verification these statistical hypotheses are shown in Table 1.

Significance level α was determined at 0.05. The test criteria were calculated according to:

$$U_{(x)} = \frac{p - \pi_0}{\sqrt{\frac{\pi_0 \cdot (1 - \pi_0)}{n}}} \tag{1}$$

By using the tables of the normalized normal distribution, we find the critical value for the right-tailed test (2) for hypotheses 1 – 3.

$$T > z_{2\alpha} \tag{2}$$

Table 1. Verification of statistical hypotheses.

Calculation of the sample proportion: $p = \frac{m}{n}$	**Satisfaction of the condition** $n * \pi_0 \ (1 - \pi_0) > 9$	**Test criteria**	**Critical field**	**Inequality**	**Acceptance or rejection of the hypothesis**
Hypothesis 1: H_0: 50 % of Slovak consumers have ever made a purchase as a result of seeing online advertisement. H_1: More than 50 % of Slovak consumers have ever made a purchase as a result of seeing online advertisement.					
p = 0.83	97,5 > 9	13.216	1.645	13.216>1.645	H_0 rejected
Hypothesis 2: H_0: 50 % of Slovak consumers buy products from online stores at least three times a month. H_1: More than 50 % of Slovak consumers buy products from online stores at least three times a month.					
p = 0.65	97,5 > 9	6.007	1.645	6.007>1.645	H_0 rejected
Hypothesis 3: H_0: 50 % of Slovak consumers didn't bought product based on promotional email that they received. H_1: More than 50 % of Slovak consumers didn't bought product based on promotional email that they received.					
p = 0.79	97.5> 9	11.61	1.645	11.61 >1.645	H_0 rejected

Source: own processing

Table 1 shows, that in hypotheses 1 – 3 the inequality applies, so we reject the hypothesis H0, and accept the alternative hypothesis H1.

5 Discussion

Based on the findings of the study we found out that online marketing can be effective tool for promoting business and product, and that it can influence buying behavior of consumers.

Online advertisements are low-cost but effective method to capture attention of potential customers. Also, good availability and growth of Internet users provides businesses large base of customers that they can reach to and persuade with their advertisements. However Wei at al. (2020) found out consumers often fear that their personal data will be stolen, so they avoid online shopping. In spite of earlier research suggesting that consumers found pop- up advertising invasive (Dreze & Hussherr, 2003), personalized advertisements in the study of Wei et al. (2020) did not substantially increase the perception of intrusion compared to non-targeted ads, but instead produced more positive reactions. Today more and more people are shopping online. Online stores offer large selection of products, from which they can choose in the comfort of their homes at any time of the day. Based on the results of survey we found out that majority of Slovak consumers shop online at least three times a month, which proves that Slovak consumers use online shopping relatively often. But for effectively attract these customers, company must know how to choose right online marketing tools for its goals. Companies can choose from new tools such as influencer marketing or more traditional tools like email marketing. Online marketing has benefits but also difficulties, so it is necessary to align used tools with company goals. As Santos (2020) pointed out business can also use social media as their marketing platform, companies do not need to only sell through their own websites, because they can simply reach customers utilizing internet connection and engage in two-way dialogue at their own speed. But according to Hofacker and Belanche (2016) some customers are still hesitant to make online purchases because they want to physically inspect the goods or services and determine if it meet their needs.

6 Conclusions

It is clear from the provided data and past studies that online marketing is effective marketing communication tool and is becoming still more important for businesses in order to be able to promote their products and brands and succeed in the highly competitive Internet environment. The use of online marketing can help a business achieve its set business goals by reaching a large number of people who use the Internet on a daily basis. If businesses can build effective online marketing communication, they can increase awareness of their brand and thus contribute to creating a good relationship with customers, which leads to increased sales, based on which the economic profit of businesses also increases. Most of Slovak consumers shop in online stores at least three times a month, so online marketing has potential to reach many consumers. In our study we also proved that online advertisements are effective and can persuade customers to buy thing, that is advertised. In order to reach as many consumers as possible it is necessary for this advertisement to be personalized and tailored to customer's needs. This can be done based on previous purchases and searching history of consumers. However, some customers are still hesitant to buy products online because they are afraid of quality of product, therefore many customers are actively seeking online reviews of products to minimalize the potential risk that online shopping represents for them. For a company it is important to know benefits and potential disadvantages of various marketing tools. Online marketing is also evolving, which means that new trends in this area still arises. One of these trends are influencers. Majority of our respondents trust to recommendation of influencers, but to different degree. This can be influenced by the character and price of product they are recommending. If the price is lower, to consumers it represents lower risk, so they can be more willing to accept the recommendation of influencer. On the other hand, when it comes to more expensive products like electronics it represents higher risk of potential loss, so the power of influencers as online marketing tool can be lower here. Company therefore must know to adapt chosen tools not only to protentional customers but also to the character of the product. A big advantage for businesses, mainly in Slovak republic, where the most businesses are small and medium sized enterprises, is that online marketing communication tools are mostly less expensive than traditional offline marketing tools and lead to a return on investment. The Internet is constantly improving and bringing new opportunities for promotion, so businesses should follow the trends in online communication in order to attract consumers. Therefore, it is extremely important for businesses to understand the importance and power of online marketing and strive to promote their business and products as effectively as possible.

Acknowledgments

The contribution is a partial output of scientific project 1/0409/23 Forensic marketing as a platform of objective empirical support for managerial decision-making processes.

References

Blazheska, D., Ristovska, N., & Gramatnikovski, S. (2022). The impact of websites and social media marketing on the efficiency of e-commerce. *UTMS Journal of Economics, 13*(2).

Camilleri, M. A. (2018). The SMEs' technology acceptance of digital media for stakeholder engagement. *Journal of Small Business and Enterprise Development, 26*(4), 504–521.

Civelek, M., Gajdka, K., Svetlik, J, & Vavrecka, V. (2020). Differences in the usage of online marketing and social media tools: Evidence from Czech, Slovakian and Hungarian SMEs. Equilibrium. *Quarterly Journal of Economics and Economic Policy, 15*(3), 537–563.

Dreze, X., & Hussherr, F. (2003). Internet advertising: Is anybody watching? *Journal of Interactive Marketing, 17*(4), 8–23.

Hajarian, M., Camilleri, M. A., Díaz, P., & Aedo, I. (2021). A taxonomy of online marketing methods. *Strategic corporate communication in the digital age*. (pp. 235–250). Emerald Publishing Limited.

Harvey, K. E., & An, Y. (2018). Marketing and mobile: Increasing integration. *Mobile Commerce: Concepts, Methodologies, Tools, and Applications* (pp. 299–327).

Hofacker, C. F., & Belanche, D. (2016). Eight social media challenges for marketing managers. *Spanish Journal of Marketing, 20*(2), 73–80.

Janouch, V. (2020). *Internetový marketing*. Computer Press.

Jin, S. V., & Muqaddam, A. (2019). Product placement 2.0: Do brands need influencers, or do influencers need brands?. *Journal of Brand Management, 26*, 1–16.

Krstic, N. (2019). The relationship between website management and search engine optimization. *Megatrend revija, 16*(2), 155–168.

Liao, H., & Tsai, S. B. (2021). Research on the B2C online marketing effect based on the LS-SVM algorithm and multimodel fusion. *Mathematical Problems in Engineering*, 1– 11.

Lombardi, C. M., & Hurlbert, S. H. (2009). Misprescription and misuse of one-tailed tests. *Australian Ecology, 34*(4), 447–468.

Matta, H., Gupta, R., & Agarwal, S. (2020). Search Engine optimization in digital marketing: Present scenario and future scope. *2020 International Conference on Intelligent Engineering and Management*, (530–534).

Murad, S. A., Murad, D. F., Wandanaya, A. B., & Fernando, E. (2018, July). Critical success factor online service quality in online marketing: A systematic literature review. *2018 10th International Conference on Information Technology and Electrical Engineering*. (pp. 158–163).

Oetjen, J. (2019). Using artificial intelligence in the fight against spam. *Network Security*, 2019*(7)*, 17–19.

Orzan, M. C., Burlacu, S., Florescu, M. S., Orzan, O. A., & Macovei, O. I. (2020). The effects of online marketing on financial performance in the textile industry. *Industria Textila, 71*(3), 288–293.

Ruxton, G. D., & Neuhäuser, M. (2010). When should we use one-tailed hypothesis testing? Methods in Ecology and Evolution, 1(2), 114–117. https://doi.org/10.1111/j.2041-210x.2010.00014.x

Sahni, N. S., Wheeler, S. C., & Chintagunta, P. (2018). Personalization in email marketing: The role of noninformative advertising content. *Marketing Science, 37*(2), 236–258.

Sanchez, D. G., & Bernabeu, M. A. (2021). The Smart scenario and its derivatives in the online marketing strategy of tourist destinations. The case of the Valencian Region. *Investigaciones Refionales – Journal of Regional Research. 15*(3), 537–563.

Santos, K. E. S. (2020). Online marketing: Benefits and difficulties to online business sellers. *International Journal of Advanced Engineering Research and Science, 7*(3).

Smith, D., Hernández-García, Á., Agudo Peregrina, Á. F., & Hair Jr, J. F. (2016). Social network marketing: A segmentation approach to understanding purchase intention. *Proceedings of the 7th 2016 International Conference on Social Media and Society* (20).

Statsista. (2023, August 21). *Share of households with internet access in Slovakia from 2009 to 2022.* Statista. https://www.statista.com/statistics/377764/household-internet- access-in-slovakia/

Statsista. (2023, August 21). *Digital advertising spending worldwide from 2021 to 2026.* Statista. https://www.statista.com/statistics/237974/online-advertising-spending- worldwide/

Tabuena, A. C., Necio, S. M. L., Macaspac, K. K., Bernardo, M. P. E., Domingo, D. I., & De Leon, P. D. M. (2022). A literature review on Digital Marketing strategies and its impact on online business sellers during the COVID-19 crisis. *Asian Journal of Management, Entrepreneurship and Social Science, 2*(01), 141–153.

Wei, L., Kang, J., & Schmierbach, M. (2020). Memory at play: Personalizing online advertisements based on consumers' autobiographical memory. *Journal of Promotion Management, 26*(3), 322–349.

Simona Scepkova[1,*]

Narcissistic Ghosting and Its Global Significance in the Context of the Emergence of Groundswell Communication on Social Media

Abstract:
Research background: The worldwide increase in the use of global social media has prompted academia to research its impact on mental and social well-being. As various statistical arguments and previous research studies confirm, that the number of social media users has been steadily increasing over the years, there is an accelerating need to approach the study of social media also in terms of the psychological implications of the new phenomenon of "groundswell communication" on the individual and society.
Purpose of the article: The aim of this study is to explore the global link between the "groundswell effect" in social media communication and narcissistic ghosting, examining the different forms and consequences of this phenomenon on platforms such as Steam, Metacritic and X (Twitter). Specifically, we will analyze the complex relationship between communication paradigms and narcissistic ghosting, examining its occurrence and implications across different communication channels.
Methods: The study examines the association between social media communication and narcissistic ghosting using different methodologies – analysis of official statistics data, data collection, sentiment analysis and data comparison.
Findings & Value added: In this paper, we investigate the phenomenon of narcissistic ghosting and its impact on user sentiment. We illustrate the significant impact of brand-related communication on customer sentiment by analyzing an example of a selected game "Overwatch 2." We outline how the lack of direct communication with the audience can lead to long-term negative sentiment after a crisis situation has occurred. Sentiment analysis on selected platforms (Metacritic, X (Twitter), Steam) reveals the global context of sentiment communication.

Keywords: *global significance ghosting, groundswell, narcissistic ghosting, sentiment analyze, social media platforms*

JEL Classification: *M15; M31; O31; P36; Z33*

---

* Corresponding author: scepkova1@ucm.sk

1 University of Ss. Cyril and Methodius in Trnava, Námestie Jozefa Herdu 2, 917 01 Trnava, Slovakia

1 Introduction

The use of social media has increased significantly in recent years. This argument can be supported by the statistical finding that the number of active social media users worldwide reached approximately 4.9 billion users in 2023 (Datareportal, 2023). According to DataReportal, in 2023, the average internet user will spend 2 hours and 31 minutes per day on social media. This is a 2 % increase from last year's figures and this figure is set to rise, making these channels another key tool for businesses (Datareportal, 2023). Although social media platforms bring many benefits to their users, concerns have been raised about the potential adverse effects of frequent activity on social media (Müller et al., 2016), particularly on mental and social well-being. As a result of the growing interest in social media, there is an increase in fuelling addiction, anxiety, social isolation or FOMO (Alutaybi et al., 2020). Our paper addresses the issue of social media use (PSMU) and its relationship to psychiatric disorders, in the context of the popular phenomenon of the groundswell effect, which, based on our previous research, is observed mainly in social media settings (Zaušková & Ščepková, 2022), according to many research papers there are positive correlations between intensive Facebook use and symptoms of key psychiatric disorders, such as anxiety, depressive symptoms, body image dissatisfaction and eating disorders (McCrae et al., 2017; Anderson & Hamilton, 2023). Excessive social use is related to an individual's emotional intelligence and can lead to atypical behaviors that are significant for addiction. In extreme cases, this addiction manifests with symptoms and consequences that are traditionally associated with substance addictions, such as the potential to be conspicuous, mood changes, tolerance, or the emergence of conflict situations that can lead to periodic relapses. In the present paper, we aim to investigate three current issues – social media communication, the groundswell effect, and the popular trend of narcissistic ghosting, which we predict is influencing consumers' shopping patterns.

1.1 Definition of the Term "narcissistic ghosting"

While social media platforms provide many advantages to their users, apprehensions have been voiced regarding the potentially harmful ramifications of prolonged engagement with these platforms, notably with regard to mental and social well-being (Sundararajan, 2019). A comprehensive review of 65 studies conducted by Frost and Rickwood (2017) has disclosed affirmative associations between intensive Facebook (FB) utilization and manifestations of pivotal psychiatric disorders, such as anxiety, depressive symptoms, body image dissatisfaction, and eating disorders. Particular emphasis was placed on theoretical speculations that social media is an ideal environment for achieving narcissistic goals. In fact, various attributes of SNSs appear to be ideal tools for displaying grandiosity and gaining desired attention (Reich & Maglio, 2020). This means that narcissists can become addicted to the unique communication environment that social media offers because it helps fulfil their self-enhancement needs. Previous studies examining the association between narcissistic traits and PSMU have shown opposite findings or at least inconsistent results.

The term "narcissistic ghosting" is a combination of two – narcissistic and ghosting. According to Merriam-Webster dictionary, the definition of ghosting is: *"the act or practice of abruptly cutting off all contact with someone (such as a former romantic partner) usually without explanation by no longer accepting or responding to phone calls, instant messages, etc."* (2023). Fanti et al. (2023) wrote that ghosting can be carried out via platforms mediated by technology. Mostly, ghosting is discussed in the romantic relationships context (LeFebvre et al., 2019), but it is important to understand, that any human relationship, whether personal or business, may be subject to it. Narcissistic ghosting occurs when the contact is cut off abruptly without explanation by a person who shares narcissistic personality traits (Drescher, 2023). Another example of ghosting we want to mention that is connected to our research is the one in consumer-brand relations. It becomes more and more common for a brand to "ghost" its customers for a while, ignoring the issue and pretending there is none. It is important to note, that in such cases brands may still have some contact with the customer, but ignore the issues that customers want to be solved. We also suppose, that when a brand just tries to ignore a certain topic of conversation, it may be considered an act of ghosting.

1.2 The Concept of Groundswell Communication and Basics of Sentiment Analysis

In digital space, the meaning of discourse lies not only in its substance but also in the complex mechanisms underpinning the recognition and interpretation of the text content. This stealthy form of communication, often referred to as "groundswell" (Zaušková & Ščepková, 2022), can exert profound outcomes on the perception and reputation of entities, be they institutions, products, or services (Ho-Dac et al., 2013). Its capacity to influence collective opinions and concurrently frame the image of subjects constitutes a phenomenon for profound exploration. This variant of communication has been gaining momentum due to the shift in user behavior and engagement patterns, as inhabitants of the online environment evolve into active content creators, enthusiastically expressing their opinions and sharing experiential narratives.

This paper seeks to clarify the usefulness of sentiment analysis as an instrument for identifying the underlying perspectives inherent in the paradigm of groundswell communication in the digital world. Through a careful study of the meaning of emotion contained in the text contributions and comments of users via social media platforms and discussion forums, our goal is to gain a more nuanced understanding of the complex interaction between assertive behavior, emotional content and the dissemination of groundswell communication. Groundswell communication encompasses the intricate network of interactions within virtual communities, wherein users actively participate in content generation and the dissemination of their perspectives regarding particular themes, subjects, or topics of discourse.

In the present scientific study, sentiment analysis can be interpreted as contextual "text mining" that identifies and extracts subjective information in the source file with the intention of helping subjects understand the social sentiment of their brand, products or services in the process of monitoring conversations taking place online (Vitman et al., 2023). Sentiment text analysis also involves extracting information related to the opinions, feelings and even emotions that authors of texts (comments or posts on social networks, blogs, video blogs or public discussions) convey publicly to other people. Sentiment can be threefold – positive, negative or neutral. The extraction of the dataset of opinions, which we refer to as the "opinion dataset," is made possible through Natural Language Processing (NLP), which is supported by Machine Learning (ML) and Artificial Intelligence (AI) tagging definitions that help us determine the stance of the author of a comment, post or opinion published through posts, related to a given topic, based on the existing set of texts (Zucco et al., 2020). Different transform-based language models have recently achieved significant results that have been captured in many NLP tasks, including BERT (Bidirectional Encoder Representations from Transformers) or RoBERTa (Robustly Optimized BERT Pre-training Approach), ALBERT (A Lite BERT For Self -Supervised Language Learning) and GPT (Huang & Rust, 2022).

2 Methodology

The main objective of this research is to understand the relationship between groundswell communication and narcissistic ghosting, particularly in a global context. The study seeks to explore the impact of narcissistic ghosting, its variations and their global significance concerning the emergence of groundswell communication on prominent social media platforms, including Steam, Metacritic and X (Twitter). In order to fulfil the main objective, we aim to research the sentiment of comments and reviews not only from different platforms but also from different time periods to understand the development of sentiment values in connection to the occurrence of the narcissistic ghosting variation.

A number of scientific methods were applied – in particular, structured analysis and description of facts, as well as the method of synthesis, inductive and deductive methods or logical procedures, which were necessary for the purpose of examining the given research problem and fulfilling the tentative aim. In order to achieve the main objective of the paper, it was firstly necessary to create a comprehensive literature review (these were mainly articles published in WoS) containing the necessary theoretical assumptions of the problem addressed. The methodology of the paper is systematic, comparative and applies a logical analysis of the factors determining a representative result set. In the present paper, the author focuses on assessing the impact of narcissistic ghosting and its global significance in the context of the emergence of groundswell communication on selected social media. The analysis we apply to draw the final findings of this study is based on the consideration of 100 comments from each platform, with Steam, Metacritic and X (Twitter) being the selected platforms from which we collected and analyzed comments and reviews.

The primary tool we used conducts sentiment analysis by quantifying a sentiment score indicative of the holistic affective and emotional attributes within the input text. The sentiment score operates on a numerical scale spanning from -100 to +100, where a value of -100 signifies a profoundly negative or gravely serious emotional tone, while a score of +100 denotes an exceedingly positive or highly enthusiastic emotional tone. Sentiment analysis is predicated on computational linguistics and text mining techniques, which are employed to autonomously discern the prevailing sentiment or affective characteristics inherent within the subject text under scrutiny (NelSenso.Net., n.d.). The second Sentiment Analyzer was meticulously trained through the utilization of a comprehensive dataset encompassing in excess of 8,000 textual samples derived from both written texts and transcripts of spoken dialogues, catalogued within the American National Corpus (ANC) (Soper, 2023).

The result of the work will be the confirmation or refutation of two basic assumptions:

(a) *Sentiment analysis scores vary significantly across different social media platforms (Steam, Metacritic, and X (Twitter)) in the context of discussions related to narcissistic ghosting.*
(b) *Sentiments expressed in discussions related to narcissistic ghosting on social media have undergone cultural and temporal shifts, with variations in sentiment scores observed over time and across different cultural contexts.*

Methodology for Scientific Premise a: analyze 100 comments from each of the three platforms, Steam, Metacritic, and X (Twitter), using the sentiment analysis tool. Compare the sentiment scores to identify platform-specific variations and trends.

Methodology for Scientific Premise b: collect comments from Steam, Metacritic, and X (Twitter) over different time periods and conduct sentiment analysis. Additionally, stratify the data by keywords usage and analyze the sentiment scores to identify platform-specific shifts.

3 Results

3.1 Brand Ghosting Variation and Customers' Response

To show the global character of impact ghosting may have on a groundswell communication surrounding the brand, in our research we are aiming to research an example of a big international company and include different social media channels to understand the sentiment surrounding ghosting activities. It is important to note that in our example we won't be talking about the classic interpretation of interpersonal ghosting, but about what we can consider a variation of ghosting when brands try to dodge talking about certain topics. We also can see traits of narcissistic behavior when the brand tries to dodge the topics consumers want to know about. The example we want to analyze is from the game "Overwatch 2" from Activision Blizzard. The product was released on October 4, 2022, as a free-to-play game on PC and consoles with a few big changes from the first part. The game's monetization model was changed, making it almost impossible to earn in-game rewards just by playing. Originally, the main USP of Overwatch 2 was supposed to be its PvE (Player versus Environment) single-player content, however, at the time of release it wasn't ready, so the game was released without it.

On May 16th, 2023, Blizzard released one of its "Developers update" videos, where the news about PvE content in its originally planned form being scraped completely were communicated. And even the way they did it felt like some variation of ghosting, because, instead of making an official statement, or apology about the fact, they just talked about it for a few minutes after 40 minutes of video, which not many people were watching. After receiving a negative reaction from the community, Blizzard posted a statement with the reaction, however, they didn't really address the problem the community was trying to tell them, mainly that they were tolerating more than 3 years without major updates to getting promised PvE, but now they won't get neither.

3.2 Consumers' Sentiment Research

As a subject for our research, three platforms where people engage in groundswell communication were selected – Metacritic, Steam and X (formerly Twitter). Metacritic is the platform where customers' and critics' reviews are shared, Steam is the largest digital game store available in Europe, and X is the social network where people share their thoughts. Such an approach was selected in order to prove or disapprove of the "global" factor of groundswell communication when ghosting or its variations occur. Since the above- mentioned video was released on May 16th of 2023, we aim to analyze reviews on Metacritic and commentaries from X from this date until the end of May 2023 in order to understand, which impact did it have on consumers' immediate groundswell communication. The game was released on Steam only on the 10th of August 2023, approximately 3 months later than the news about PvE occurred. That is why, when analysing Steam reviews we would analyze the most relevant ones from August and September.

Starting with the reviews from Metacritic, it is fair to mention, that, since the game was released in November 2022, there were a lot of negative reviews even before the above- mentioned incident. However, the number of reviews was declining, and in April of 2023, only 17 new ones were written. It is only on the 16th of May that we may see a drastic increase in the number of new reviews, the vast majority of which were negative. In order to understand which topics were talked about the most and which sentiment was applied in those reviews, we conducted an analysis of 100 reviews posted in the time period from 16th to 30th May of 2023. To analyze those reviews, firstly we used a tool called Netlytic, which provided us with a list of keywords and frequency of their usage. A total of 1 109 keywords were identified and on the word cloud below we placed the most used ones. Among the negative keywords that were mentioned more often than others were: promised, cash, dead, canceled, killed, worst, bad, scrapped, cancelled, and money. As we may see, the words were mainly associated with the occasions we mentioned earlier. We also may state, that 99 out of 100 reviews we took into analysis were negative, and 1 was neutral.

To understand the sentiment of text in those reviews we used two services – Tonetizer by Nelsenso and Sentiment Analyzer by Dr. Daniel Soper, methodology of which we wrote about previously. According to SWAS Sentiment analysis, general sentiment had a numerical value of -0.49, meaning that the general sentiment of the text was neutral. The second sentiment analysis we conducted gave us a value of -1.8, which corresponds with the first analysis. The average value from both analyses was -1.145 (neutral). It may seem strange that with 99 % of negative commentaries, the sentiment of the messages was neutral, so we researched it additionally to find the possible reasons why. When reading through the reviews, we noticed that many of them were written about their long-term experience with the game, including a lot of good experiences with the previous version and disappointment in a new one, which most probably affected the results. Also, it is worth mentioning that certain swear words were censored, and therefore unrecognizable for the tools. Last but not least, a certain part of the audience was writing sarcastic messages or just making jokes about the game, which may not be recognizable by the tools automatically. Those points are valid for all analyses present in this paper, however, the results provided are still valid.

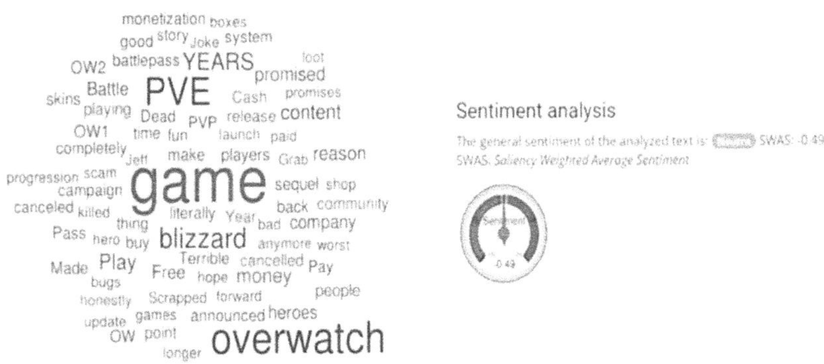

Figure 1. Word Cloud from 100 reviews and Sentiment analysis by Tonetizer – Metacritic reviews May 2023.

Source: own processing

To keep it chronologically correct, the next platform we wanted to research was X (Twitter). In this case, we analyzed 100 comments shared by the community under the post from the 16th of May 2023 about the video where changes to the promised PvE content were communicated. One more thing we need to note is that on X there is no censorship of swear words, so the texts this time were not influenced by the platform. Among the keywords, PvE was mentioned the most, in the negative context were used words like: shit, disappointed, killed, waited, sad, money, paid, stopped, and promised. The numerical value from Tonetizer was -3.09, the second test on the other hand provided a value of 1.5. The average value from both analyses was -0.795 (neutral). We may state that the values between the groundswell communication on two platforms in the second half of May 2023 were very similar, from both, the style of communication and sentiment of the messages. The difference in numerical values can be described as the sampling error. Also, since the swear words were not censored on this channel, their presence could've influenced results from Tonetizer. Since the results among the channels are very similar, we may state that an occasion of a situation like the one that happened with Overwatch 2, and lack of communication during such situations have a global impact on groundswell communication among various channels and audiences.

Figure 2. Word Cloud from 100 comments and Sentiment analysis by Tonetizer – X (Twitter) comments May 2023.

Source: own processing

To prove our point even further, we bring an analysis of the third channel – Steam. Steam, unlike the previous two platforms, is the place where people buy and play games. It is a giant platform, and reviews play a crucial role in the sales of many games. Overall, Overwatch 2 has 203,129 reviews on Steam as of late October 2023, and 89 % of them are negative. Again we selected 100 comments for a detailed analysis, and among the negative keywords this time were: predatory, removed, deleted, negative, greed, uninstall, bad, promised, and worse. However, we may notice a slight shift in focus from the topic of PvE to monetization. Overall, 96 out of 100 comments were marked "not recommend." Sentiment analysis from Tonetizer this time showed a value of -4.51, even more negative than the one from X. It is important to note, that in Steam swear words were censored with hearts. The second sentiment analytics tool showed a result of 5.9. At this point, it has become evident that the algorithms between the two services are different and clearly interpret the same text in two different ways. The average value from both analyses was 0.695 (neutral). The average value corresponds with the results from two other services, proving the idea of global influence on groundswell further basis. On Steam it was apparent that much more sarcasm, jokes, and inappropriate reviews were posted, possibly showing the approach of a slightly different target audience that is using the service.

Figure 3. Word Cloud from 100 reviews and Sentiment analysis by Tonetizer – Steam Reviews August 2023.

Source: own processing

These examples proved that a single event of miscommunication, or lack of communication may have a global impact on brands' groundswell communication. This inquiry encompassed an in-depth scrutiny of groundswell communication spanning three diverse platforms: Metacritic, X, and Steam. The findings manifest the profound, widespread, and global ramifications arising from a form of brand disengagement, particularly when it involves the sudden termination of promised content.

4 Discussion

4.1 Discussion of the Results and Their Implications for the Management of Groundswell Communication

The outcomes of this paper hold substantial ramifications for brand management within the phenomenon of groundswell communication. The Overwatch 2 case serves as an example, clarifying the profound influence of brand-related communication on customer sentiment. Firstly, the research emphasizes the importance of clear and timely communication with the customer community. In the case of Overwatch 2, the sudden cancellation of promised content and the complete lack of communication for several years prior led to a surge in negative sentiment, making customers feel abandoned. Secondly, analyzing sentiment across various platforms, such as Metacritic, X, and Steam, reveals how interconnected groundswell communication is. What happens on one platform can quickly affect sentiment on others, emphasizing the need for a comprehensive approach to customer engagement. This leads us to the conclusion that companies should closely monitor sentiment across different channels and adjust their communication strategies accordingly. It is also important to understand the pros and cons of sentiment analysis tools. While these tools offer valuable insights, it's essential to note that their results can vary based on the algorithms and text characteristics, just like we saw in our research.

Comparing the results of our paper to other scientific studies, Pace et al. (2017) discovered that social media may worsen the consequences of a crisis, which corresponds with the results of our research. Mishra and Sharma (2019) found that positive groundswell communication by dedicated customers may help a brand mediate the crisis' influence, once again underlining the importance of groundswell communication for the brand today. Finally, Nadeau et al. (2020) analyzed several case studies and stated that ignoring an issue by the brand did not provide good outcomes, but worse results than other approaches a brand may use while in a crisis situation. Those results also correspond with the outcome of our paper, underlining the globality of groundswell communication.

4.2 An Evaluation of the Benefits and Limitations of Sentiment Analysis Tools in the Context of the Groundswell

Sentiment analysis tools, as employed in this research, afford a spectrum of advantages and limitations when applied to the study of groundswell communication. Among the benefits of sentiment analysis, based on the information we discovered in our research are:

- Efficiency: Sentiment analysis tools serve as a prompt and efficient mechanism to assess the prevailing sentiment within a substantial corpus of textual data.
- Consistency: Uniformity leaves the potential for dependable cross-platform and longitudinal comparisons. Still, it is important to research which algorithm is used by a certain tool to provide the most accurate results.
- Keyword Identification: Many sentiment analysis tools possess the capability to recognize and accentuate keywords that contribute to the overall sentiment score.

On the contrary, the limitations include:

- Contextual Understanding: Even though the models are constantly evolving, so does the language, and certain phrases may be unknown to the sentiment tool.
- Censorship and Vulgar Language: Certain platforms, exemplified by Steam, may impose censorship on profanity and inappropriate language, thereby influencing the results of sentiment analysis.
- Long-term vs. Short-term Sentiment: Sentiment analysis, conventionally, provides a composite sentiment score, devoid of distinctions between long-term customer sentiment and short-term responses to specific events.

These tools should be used with an awareness of their benefits and limitations to enhance our understanding of customer sentiment in the digital landscape. However, the very existence of such tools opens a vast space for further research and a better understanding of the phenomenon of groundswell communication.

5 Conclusion

This research underscores the critical role of sentiment analysis in the realm of effective communication management. The importance of sentiment analysis can be summarized in the following key points:

1. It provides a scalable approach to understanding customer sentiment. By efficiently evaluating extensive sets of textual data, sentiment analysis enables organizations to grasp the collective sentiment exhibited by their customer base.
2. Sentiment analysis offers a means to track sentiment evolution over time. This temporal aspect is particularly beneficial for brand managers to adapt their strategies in response to evolving customer sentiment.
3. Sentiment analysis tools are crucial in gaining insights into diverse online platforms. Sentiment analysis enables organizations to comprehend how

customer sentiment varies across these platforms, aiding in platform-specific communication strategies.

The field of text sentiment analysis holds potential for further research of brand communication, groundswell interaction and customer reviews with a possible extension of research with multimodal analysis, emotion detection and management strategies. By integrating theoretical knowledge and evidence-based practices, brands can foster more robust relationships with their online communities and navigate the challenges of narcissistic ghosting with greater efficacy. This fusion of theory and practice is a necessity in the digital age, where the online community have a significant influence on brand perception and success.

Acknowledgments

Scientific Paper was elaborated within the framework of the project VEGA No. 1/0458/21 under the title "Management of the 'groundswell' concept by business entities in promotion of environmentally-friendly products in times of technology interference."

References

Alutaybi, A., Al-Thani, D., McAlaney, J., & Ali, R. (2020). Combating Fear of Missing Out (FoMO) on social media: The FOMO-R method. *International Journal of Environmental Research and Public Health, 17*(17), 6128.

Anderson, S., & Hamilton, K. (2023). Consumer-driven memorialization. *Journal of Consumer Research.*

DataReportal – Global Digital Insights. (2023, September 12). *Global Social Media Statistics.* DataReportal. https://datareportal.com/social-media-users

Drescher, A. (2023, October 9). *What is narcissistic ghosting and how to deal with it.* Simply Psychology. https://www.simplypsychology.org/narcissistic-ghosting.html

Fanti, E., Di Sarno, M., & Di Pierro, R. (2023). Dating in a digital world: The role of pathological personality traits in psychological reactions to direct and ambiguous rejection. *Personality and Individual Differences, 215,* (112397).

Frost, R., & Rickwood, D. (2017). A systematic review of the mental health outcomes associated with Facebook use. *Computers in Human Behavior, 76,* 576–600.

Ho-Dac, N. N., Carson, S. J., & Moore, W. L. (2013). The effects of positive and negative online customer reviews: Do brand strength and category maturity matter?. *Journal of marketing, 77(6),* 37–53.

Huang, M.-H., & Rust, R. T. (2022). A framework for collaborative artificial intelligence in marketing. *Journal of Retailing, 98*(2), 209–223.

LeFebvre, L. E., Allen, M., Rasner, R. D., Garstad, S., Wilms, A., & Parrish, C. (2019). Ghosting in emerging Adults' romantic relationships: The digital dissolution disappearance strategy. *Imagination, Cognition and Personality, 39*(2), 125–150.

McCrae, N., Gettings, S., & Purssell, E. (2017). Social media and depressive symptoms in childhood and adolescence: A systematic review. *Adolescent Research Review, 2*(4), 315–330.

Merriam-Webster. (n.d.). (2023, October 29). *Ghosting*. Merriam-Webster.com dictionary. https://www.merriam-webster.com/dictionary/ghosting

Mishra, M., & Sharma, R. W. (2019). Brand crisis-sentiment analysis of user-generated comments about @Maggi on Facebook. *Corporate Reputation Review, 22(2)*, 48–60. https://doi.org/10.1057/s41299-018-0057-4

Müller, K., Dreier, M., Beutel, M. E., Duven, E., Giralt, S., & Wölfling, K. (2016). A hidden type of internet addiction? Intense and addictive use of social networking sites in adolescents. *Computers in Human Behavior, 55*, 172–177.

Nadeau, J., Rutter, R., & Lettice, F. (2020). Social media responses and brand personality in product and moral harm crises: Why waste a good crisis? *Journal of Marketing Management, 36*(11–12), 1031–1054. https://doi.org/10.1080/0267257x.2020.1764080

NelSenso.Net. (n.d.). *Online sentimentanalys App: Tonetizer*. https://www.nelsenso.net/sv/tonetizer.aspx

Pace, S., Balboni, B., & Gistri, G. (2017). The effects of social media on brand attitude and WOM during a brand crisis: Evidences from the Barilla case. *Journal of Marketing Communications, 23*(2), 135–148. https://doi.org/10.1080/13527266.2014.966478

Reich, T., & Maglio, S. J. (2020). Featuring mistakes: The persuasive impact of purchase mistakes in online reviews. *Journal of Marketing, 84*(1), 52–65.

Soper, D. (n.d.). *Free Sentiment Analyzer*. https://www.danielsoper.com/sentimentanalysis/default.aspx

Sundararajan, A. (2019). Commentary: The Twilight of brand and consumerism? Digital trust, cultural meaning, and the quest for connection in the sharing economy. *Journal of Marketing, 83*(5), 32–35.

Vitman, O., Kostiuk, Y., Sidorov, G., & Gelbukh, A. (2023). Sarcasm detection framework using context, emotion and sentiment features. *Expert Systems with Applications, 234*, 121068.

Zaušková, A., & Ščepková, S. (2022). *Groundswell: The cornerstone of interactive communication on social media*. Wolters Kluwer Hungary Kft.

Zucco, C., Calabrese, B., Agapito, G., Guzzi, P. H., & Cannataro, M. (2020). Sentiment analysis for mining texts and social networks data: Methods and tools. *WIREs Data Mining and Knowledge Discovery, 10*(1), e1333.

Janka Taborecka[1,*], Lubos Elexa[1], Michal Budinsky[1] and Miroslava Moncolova[1]

The Impact of Business Size on Adoption of Facial Biometric Technologies

Abstract:
Research background: This research offers valuable insights to businesses considering the adoption of facial biometric technology into their processes. It emphasizes the significance of business size as a relevant segmentation criterion in the marketing strategy of companies developing facial biometric technologies and launching them on the market.
Purpose of the article: The main aim of the research was to investigate the relationship between business size and distinctive aspects of business buying behavior regarding facial biometric technologies. We assume that larger businesses, with greater number of resources and existing infrastructure, may have an advantage in terms of easier implementation of biometric technology.
Methods: A questionnaire survey as a method of data collection was conducted on the sample of 521 companies. For the data analysis, Spearman correlation coefficients was used. We expected that the size of the business, measured by average annual revenues, is significantly related to various aspects of business buying behavior.
Findings & Value added: Firstly, we found out that higher average annual revenues are associated with increased innovativeness of businesses. Secondly, larger businesses perceive greater value from the implementation of facial biometric technology and perceived technology usefulness. Finally, it was revealed that larger businesses require a more complex solution. However, the study did not find a statistically significant relationship between business size and purchase intention. These findings suggest that while larger businesses perceive biometric technologies as more attractive in terms of innovativeness, added value, usefulness, and complexity, purchase intention is not significantly influenced by business size.

Keywords: *facial biometric technologies, adoption process, business size, business buying behavior, innovations*

JEL Classification: *M10; O30; O14*

---

* Corresponding author: janka.taborecka@umb.sk
1 Matej Bel University in Banska Bystrica, Faculty of Economics, Tajovskeho 10, 975 90, Banska Bystrica, Slovakia

1 Introduction

The past few decades demonstrated an urgent need of a reliable person recognition system as the safety concerns have risen to unprecedented levels after numerous security breaches around the world such as terrorism or cyber-attacks. Combined with the recent technological advancements, a new phenomenon, biometric technologies, started proliferating all areas of life starting from international border crossing to welfare benefit disbursement to online commerce concluding with financial services or retail sector. Due to the advent of computers, we can now swiftly and effectively authenticate human identities by relying on distinctive physiological or behavioral traits, irrespective of the quantity of individuals involved. Additionally, the identity can be linked to any kind of personal data available in an associated database.

Companies developing biometric technologies should study carefully how their potential customers perceive biometric technologies adoption, who these customers are, with which characteristics, from which industries, or to what extend they are willing to adopt them within their processes. Firm size seems to be a significant factor in innovative business model success (Gonzalez-Benito et al., 2016) and sustainability of innovation (Farooq et al., 2021). The size affects innovation specifically in case of exogenous shock, like was the COVID-19 (Assefa et al., 2022). According to Vaona and Pianta (2008) the role of small firms is more relevant where entry costs are lower and niche markets exist, although the forms of interaction between firms of different sizes (from subcontracting to licensing and to collaborative innovation) influence the final result and have different application in case of product and process innovation. For the large companies, empirical evidence shows product innovations result in an overall larger share of new products in total sales, relative to existing products in which process innovations are rooted (Fang et al., 2021). Small companies are less devoted to incremental innovation, multidimensional combinations, have more disadvantages and perform less heterogeneous research activities (Choi and Lee, 2018). While corresponding research of opinions and perceptions from consumer and business perspective has been extensive in other, mainly Western and Asian, countries, the investigations of the Slovak market are rather limited so far.

1.1 Definition and Types of Biometric Technologies

The ability to identify a person has always been essential for human society. People typically use physical characteristics such as face and voice combined with other contextual information such as location for this purpose. These unique attributes related to an individual represent their identity (Jain & Ross, 2015). The explosive growth of population along with rising mobility in the modern world created an urge to develop a sophisticated system to manage identities of people (Jain & Ross, 2011). Therefore, the history of the actual science of establishing personal identities named biometrics dates back further than one might initially expect. The term origins in Greek words 'bios' meaning life, and 'metrikos' meaning measure (Zhang et al., 2018). Individual characteristics through which an individual can be recognized, include, but are not limited to fingerprints, hand and palm geometry, facial mapping, iris and retina scans, voice identification, signature and writing style, and gait (Clodfelter, 2010). Some authors categorize these attributes into primary (hard) biometric traits and secondary (soft) biometric traits (Chen & Fondeur, 2015; Sinha, 2019). In the literature, these terms can be found: 'biometrics', 'biometric technologies' and 'biometric systems.' According to Jain and Ross (2015), biometrics is "the science of establishing the identity of a person based on the physical (e.g., fingerprints, face, hand geometry, and iris) or behavioral (e.g., gait, signature, and keyboard dynamics) attributes associated with an individual." The term "biometric technology" emphasizes the technique and/or the technology behind the science of determining one's identity, i.e., biometrics. Whereas a "biometric system" is used to capture and evaluate the biometric trait of a person by means of appropriately designed sensors. Nevertheless, the terms biometrics and biometric technologies are being used interchangeably.

1.2 Practical Applications and Adoption of Biometric Technologies

In the past few decades, the boom in use of biometric technologies brought numerous new options. In the United States, an Elementary School at Park Avenue has gone so far that the students need to undergo an eye scan for the school doors to open. The Disney World introduced fingerprints as an identification tool for one-time tickets as well as season pass holders, and casinos in Las Vegas use facial recognition in order to detect scam artists (Clodfelter, 2010). In our modern, technology-driven society where everything is connected and mobile devices are inevitable part of human lives, it's becoming crucial to confidently confirm a person's identity. The increased security concerns of the last few decades and significant developments regarding communication, networking and mobility necessitated a trustworthy user authentication system. The appeal of biometrics lies both in its convenience and its reliability.

To fully grasp the potential and scope of biometrics, we should look at the global market value that has reached USD 27 billion in 2020 and with an average growth rate of 15.2 % projected for the upcoming years, it is anticipated to reach USD 62 billion in 2026, with Northern America still being the largest market (Mordor Intelligence, 2022). The growth can be attributed to (cyber-) terrorist activities, and rising identity and sensitive data thefts raising concerns about national security. The worldwide pandemic combined with new consumer behavior patterns will also contribute to accelerated implementation. Additionally, growth will be driven geographically in expanding regions such as Asia-Pacific, with particularly China being at the forefront of the worldwide digital payment revolution, as well as by means of biometric innovations like the multi-model systems or contact-free scanning. The multi- model recognition employs different features (face, eye, fingerprints, etc.) during identity verification. This enhances reliability, speed and precision in large-scale system together with flexibility and improved control for the user. Contact-free fingerprint scanning reflects on the requirements of consumers to deliver more hygienic and safe biometrics health-wise in the light of the recent pandemic. Companies plan to take advantage of the perfectly available devices that most people dispose of, i.e., smartphones. Developing reliable software that will be able to process fingerprint images taken by the high-quality cameras of modern smartphones will path an easy and considerably inexpensive way for private as well public institutions to transition to this new technology (White, 2022).

The range of biometrics applications is rather vast; however, they can be categorized into three general areas, i.e., commercial, government and forensic use. Commercial use, we are interested in our research, presents seemingly endless opportunities limited solely by vague legal restrictions, consumer acceptance and convenience for both parties – enterprises and customers (Jain and Ross, 2011). Generally, De Keyser et al. (2021) highlighted six activities where businesses can take advantage of biometrics adoption: (a) consumer intelligence, (b) marketing mix customization and personalization, (c) customer journey automation, (d) security reinforcement, (e) personal health and well-being enhancement, and (f) human resources recruitment and management. Biometric technologies have been a tool for gaining access to (secure) premises of private companies and its use for access to files or computers is not uncommon in large corporate structures. Similarly, to how attendance of employees is recorded by means of fingerprint scanners, operating cash registers in retail could be simplified in the future (Clodfelter, 2010).

Furthermore, biometrics can serve as a payment method and as a registration tool in travel and hospitality services. In healthcare, biometrics such as DNA enabled genetic testing for commercial purposes, e.g., ancestry tracing, and for medical purposes, e.g., detecting medical conditions or health predispositions.

Smart bracelets and other devices can provide exceptional insights for healthcare practitioners based on heart rate, body temperature, activity and sleep pattern. The automotive industry uses facial characteristics and eye movement to monitor whether drivers are alert or tired and/or distracted. Fingerprint scanning serves as a substitute to a key when unlocking the new Hyundai models and turning on the ignition and unique heartbeat rhythm can also help authenticate a driver's identity and detect fatigue or increased stress level. Yet another example of biometrics application in practice are retail sales and e-commerce. Retailers have deployed facial recognition to identify VIP customers as well as known shoplifters, body movement and facial characteristics to monitor customer behavior and movement in the stores (e.g., time spent, gender, age, mood, etc.), fingerprint scanning to facilitate access (for instance, Disney World registers up to 100,000 visitors daily) and various types of biometrics can also enable providing personalized offers based on past orders and favourite options, and biometric payments. Sales are very closely related to market research and researchers dispose of a whole new range of possibilities thanks to biometrics and neuroscience in terms of collecting market intelligence. These new technologies allow them to predict individual behavior in a much more reliable manner based on examination of brain activity, heart rate, eye movement, etc. Also financial services and the banking industry changes due to IT innovations exhibit an extraordinary potential in regard to biometrics (De Keyser et al., 2021).

2 Research Methodology

The main aim of the paper was: "To investigate the relationship between business size and distinctive aspects of business buying behavior regarding facial biometric technologies." We assume that larger businesses, with greater number of resources and existing infrastructure, may have an advantage in terms of easier implementation of biometric technology. Our research question was **RQ1: Which type of businesses in terms of their size are more prone to adopt biometric technologies?** And the corresponding main hypothesis was formulated as: **H1: We assume that there is a relationship between size of business and distinctive aspects of business buying behaviour.**

Since the business buying behaviour is a rather broad term, we have formulated five additional hypotheses to cover different areas:

H1a: We assume that there is a positive relationship between size of business and business *level of innovativeness*, therefore bigger business, higher innovativeness of business.

H1b: We assume that there is a positive relationship between size of business and *perceived added value*, therefore bigger business, higher added value perception.
H1c: We assume that there is a positive relationship between size of business and *perceived technology usefulness*, therefore bigger business, higher usefulness perception.
H1d: We assume that there is a positive relationship between size of business and *level of complexity implementation,* therefore bigger business, more complex solution required.
H1e: We assume that there is a positive relationship between size of business and *purchase intention*, therefore bigger business, higher purchase intention.

2.1 Methods

Prior to realizing the main quantitative research phase, we initially conducted a qualitative inquiry as an exploratory means of data acquisition. The primary objectives of this qualitative phase were to gain qualitative insights, reveal prevailing opinions, expectations, and practical experiences via an in-depth interview with the Chief Executive Officer (CEO) of the company specializing in the development of biometric solutions for the commercial sector, and a series of six semi-structured interviews with CEOs of companies varying in size and spanning diverse industries within Slovakia. These selected interviewees were considered potential end users or customers of biometric solutions. Following the qualitative exploration, a questionnaire survey was used as the principal methodological approach. The questionnaire's design was crafted to unveil the latent market potential of facial biometric technology. The findings presented herein reflect partial outcomes of this survey. The comprehensibility and effectiveness of the questionnaire were ascertained through a pilot study. Subsequently, the final iteration of the questionnaire was prepared and disseminated. The distribution strategy encompassed face-to-face interactions, complemented by an online distribution utilizing the contact database via the analytical portal known as "Index Podnikateľa." This comprehensive data collection initiative took place during the closing months of 2019 and the outset of 2020. Upon acquiring the dataset, we initially employed basic descriptive statistics to gain a holistic overview of the collected information. Then, we investigated deeper the relationships formulated within our hypotheses and their empirical validation. To accomplish this, we leveraged statistical methodologies and tests, employing the SPSS, which included the utilization of the Binomial test and Wilcoxon Signed rank test.

2.1 Representativeness of the Sample

Within classification of our research sample, we used the criteria of European Union (Table 1), which are created by three main aspects – annual turnover, number of employees and balance sheet total. Results were analyzed just for SME businesses, as utilization of new technologies in micro-enterprises is questionable. In the pursuit of our research objectives, we deliberately chose businesses with a workforce of a minimum of 10 employees.

Table 1. Classification of SME's.

Category	Number of employees	Annual turnover in mil. of Euros	Balance sheet total in mil. of Euros
Micro enterprises	0–9	to 2	to 2
Small enterprises	10–49	to 10	to 10
Medium enterprises	50–249	to 50	to 43
Large enterprises	more than 250	from 50	from 43

Source: Commission recommendation 2003/361/EC (2003)

This strategic choice stemmed from the revelation, during our interviews, that the potential for the adoption of this technology in micro-businesses was exceedingly limited. Adoption of new technologies in micro-enterprises was also reviewed by Barba-Sánchez et al. (2007), where they identified several constraints and challenges these businesses face. In general, the smaller the enterprise, the bigger challenges open, because in many cases micro- enterprises such as self-employed, fast-food corner shops or the other ones do not use IT technology for their business activity (except for little accounting activities). Therefore, challenges are categorized into six groups – attitude, context, capabilities, resources, operations and access. Within their study, they identified that implementation of new technologies can bring a benefit to these organizations, but its adoption is not easy, and benefits are not guaranteed. From this reason, many micro-enterprises rather chose not to implement new technologies because of high initial costs, poor added value or low usability, due to much smaller amount of customer base on which this technology could be applied within their business. Therefore, we decided to focus only on small, medium and large businesses, as they abound with greater resources, have tendency to invest into high-end and sophisticated technologies and potential of biometric technology implementation is much higher.

Our final research sample was comprised of 521 companies actively operating within Slovakia. To ensure the robustness of our findings and the generalizability of our results to the broader population of companies, we established two criteria for representativeness: the size of the businesses and the distribution of businesses across various districts in Slovakia. Research sample was assigned by combination of deliberate, quota sampling based on predetermined characters. To validate the representativeness of our research sample, we employed the Chi-square goodness of fit test within the statistical software IBM SPSS 19.0. The results of this test are shown in Tables 2 and 3. Based on the outcomes of the Chi-square goodness of fit test, we confidently affirm that our research sample aligns with the broader population of companies in Slovakia in terms of both workforce size and regional distribution.

Table 2. Chi-square Goodness of Fit Test for Number of Employees.

Number of Employees	
Chi-square	0.014[a]
Df	2
Asymp. Sig.	0.993

Source: own processing, SPSS output

Table 3. Chi-square Goodness of Fit Test for Region.

Region	
Chi-square	0.100[a]
Df	7
Asymp. Sig.	1.000

Source: own processing, SPSS output

3 Results and Discussion

The initial section of the questionnaire was devoted to uncovering business attitudes and inclinations toward the adoption of facial biometric technology. Our findings, supported by the subsequent testing, revealed that approximately half of the surveyed businesses exhibited some degree of interest in incorporating this technology into their operations. This interest manifested in three distinct categories: those intrigued by basic applications, those exploring the advanced capabilities of facial biometric technology, and a third group displaying enthusiasm for comprehensive integration of facial biometric technology across all facets of their business processes (Budinsky & Taborecka-Petrovicova, 2021).

Then we looked closer on perception of various business types (by number of employees and annual revenues), regarding added value of biometric technologies. We found out that in case of large businesses (more than 250 employees) only 17.65 % of them perceive very low added value of the implementation of this technology. Compared to the small businesses (10–49 employees), where this option was selected by 29.78 % of businesses or by medium businesses (50–249 employees), where it represented 20.88 % of respondents. We found out also differences in usefulness perception based on annual average revenues of businesses. Our results shown that from businesses with revenues between 11 and 50 million €, 34.67 % consider it as useful, while businesses with revenues over 50 million € see it even more positive – up to 40 % of them consider it useful.

It is important to note that for the following hypotheses testing we decided to use categorization of business size according to the average annual revenues since no statistically significant relationships have been found within categorization according to the number of employees. There is a rationale underlying this fact, since facial biometric technology is perceived as a relatively high initial investment, therefore average annual revenues of business appear as more relevant classification criterion for this relationship.

Firstly, we examined hypothesis **H_{1a}**, where we expected *positive relationship between size of business and business level of innovativeness.* Based on results of statistical tests, we found out statistically significant relationship between these variables with indirect low dependence (Spearman's rho = -0.197), as well as p-value (0.00) is lower than Alpha (0.01). Thus, according to the different formulation of questions and statements, we can say that *with increased average annual revenues, businesses reach higher level of innovativeness* and we accept hypothesis H_{1a}.

Secondly, we tested hypothesis **H_{1b}**, where we expected *positive relationship between size of business and perceived added value.* Results of statistical tests showed us that, there is statistically significant relationship between these two variables, while indirect low dependence (Spearman's rho = -0.131) was proved, as p-value (0.003) is lower than Alpha (0.01). Hence, according to the different formulation of questions and statements we can say that, *with increased average annual revenues, businesses perceive higher added value from implementation of facial biometric technology,* and we accept hypothesis H_{1b}.

Thirdly, we evaluated hypothesis **H_{1c}**, where we expected *positive relationship between size of business and perceived technology usefulness.* Based on results of statistical tests, we found out statistically significant relationship between these variables with indirect low dependence (Spearman's rho = -0.133), as well as p-value (0.00) is lower than Alpha (0.01). Thus, according to the different formulation of questions and statements we can say that, *with increased average annual* *revenues, higher usefulness of facial biometric technology is perceived among business*, and we accept hypothesis H1c.

Further, we examined partial hypothesis **H1d**, where we expected *positive relationship between size of business and level of complexity implementation*. Results of statistical tests showed us that, there is statistically significant relationship between these two variables, while direct low dependence (Spearman's rho = 0.160) was proved, as well as p-value (0.00) is lower than Alpha (0.01). Hence, we can say that *businesses with higher average annual revenues require more complex level of implementation of facial biometric technology*. Hypothesis H1d, was confirmed.

Finally, we tested last partial hypothesis **H1e**, where we expected *positive relationship between size of business and purchase intention*. According to the results of statistical tests, we found out that relationship between these variables was not confirmed, as well as p-value (0.748) is no lower than Alpha (0.05). Thus, we can say that *there is no statistically significant relationship between average annual revenues and business purchase intention*. It means we do not accept hypothesis H1e.

Table 4. Overview of Statistical Verification of Hypotheses.

Hypotheses	Result	p- value	Spearman's rho
H_1: We assume that there is a relationship between size of business and distinctive aspects of customer behaviour.	**confirmed**	-	-
H_{1a}: We assume that there is a positive relationship between size of business and **business level of innovativeness**, therefore bigger business, higher innovativeness of business.	**confirmed**	0.00	-0.197
H^{1b}: We assume that there is a positive relationship between size of business and **perceived added value**, therefore bigger business, higher added value perception.	**confirmed**	0.003	-0.131
H_{1c}: We assume that there is a positive relationship between size of business and **perceived technology usefulness**, therefore bigger business, higher usefulness perception.	**confirmed**	0.00	-0.133
H_{1d}: We assume that there is a positive relationship between size of business and **level of complexity implementation**, therefore bigger business, more complex solution required.	**confirmed**	0.00	0.160
H_{1e}: We assume that there is a positive relationship between size of business and **purchase intention**, therefore bigger business, higher purchase intention.	**rejected**	0.748	-

Source: Own processing

To sum it up, we can conclude that hypothesis **H1** can be confirmed, since 4 from 5 partial hypotheses were accepted. We proved that *there is a statistically significant dependence between size of business (based on average annual revenues) and distinctive aspects of consumer behaviour*. It means that *businesses with higher average annual revenues perceive this technology as more attractive through perspective of higher level of innovativeness, higher added value from technology implementation, higher usefulness of technology implementation and higher level of complexity of technology implementation*. On the other hand, *relationship between size of business and purchase intention was not approved*. It is important to mention that due to the value of Spearman's rho that is below 0.2, we talk about very low dependence between selected variables. Therefore, investigation of this relationships requires closer attention in future research.

4 Conclusions

From marketing point of view, these findings are indicating that companies developing biometric technologies should define their potential target market customers as "*more innovative, rather larger companies in terms of higher average annual revenues*" where there will be higher probability to accept and adopt this technology. Within our more complex research, we also revealed that *retail and service industry* are more interested in implementation of facial biometric technology, specifically in *marketing or sales area* in comparison with other business sector (Taborecka-Petrovicova et al., 2023). We can perceive these domains as relatively "emerging" areas for the implementation of biometrics, especially within the context of Slovakia. Historically, and even today, their primary applications have predominantly revolved around security identification and human resources functions. So, we can claim that the new potential of implementation can be seen e.g., in big retailers (with sufficient financial resources) that are regionally concentrated mainly in Bratislava region that is characterized by the highest purchase power of customers because of the highest average salaries, higher number of tourists and visitors from home and abroad…etc. For example, revenues of retailers from Bratislava region represent on average almost half of whole retail market (48 % in 2016). On the other hand, the lowest part of a cake belongs to the region of Košice, where only 5.3 % of total retail revenues were generated. Proportion of remaining regions oscillated between 7 up to 8.6 %, while the biggest growth in revenues was recorded in a Banská Bystrica region, represented by increase of 3.4 % (Glasova, 2016).

Within development of retail industry in Slovakia, increased pressure on higher standards, modern design or necessity of improved services forced them to perform better. As well as they took over trends from western countries, they realized importance of in-store communication within their stores. Nowadays, not only leaflets, ads in magazines or any traditional form is utilized. Everything what can be used, is deployed in order to attract customers and to increased sales. Especially in case of in-store activities that are significantly cheaper compared to the traditional TV ads (Turzo, 2018). Retailers realized that their stores are not just a place of making purchase, but it's a place of experience. From this reason, they revealed importance of digital technologies and their necessity, because customers want to utilize the time spent in a store efficiently, comfortably and with new experiences. This challenges retailers, about how to utilize available technologies in order to satisfy customer. Other issue is how to help also other companies that are willing and ready to implement biometric technologies into their processes. Company size does not seem to be very relevant in case of business support and financing of innovation given to Slovak companies. Budget size and target area of implementation remain more significant, moreover, many priorities are strongly interconnected in support programs. Another fact is that the number of open or planned calls is huge, and they are sometimes confusing as to the source and management (Operational programs, post-pandemic Recovery and Resilience Plan, Just Transition Fund, etc.) but provides opportunities for all stakeholders, like academia, business and public sector including their triple/quadruple/quintuple interactions. Biometric or other innovative activities may find financial coverage through the support of both internationalization (cooperation in research and development, Horizon Europe participation) or on national level. Several technological priorities (digital transformation, green transformation, intelligent growth, decarbonization, excellent science and many others), including innovation and digital vouchers are suitable for initial stages of entrepreneurship and even for smaller budgets.

Acknowledgments

The research was realized within the project VEGA 1/0290/22 "Regional investment aid as a determinant of the development of companies and regions in the Slovak Republic" and project VEGA No. 1/0036/21 "Determinants of eco-innovation activities of enterprises in the context of changes in the external economic environment."

References

Assefa, D. Z., Colovic, A., & Misganaw, B. A. (2022). Firm size, firm age and business model innovation in response to a crisis: Evidence from 12 countries. *International Journal of Innovation Management*, *26*(07), 1–26.

Barba-Sánchez, V., del Pilar Martínez-Ruiz, M., Jiménez-Zarco, A. I. (2007). Drivers, Benefits and Challenges of ICT Adoption by Small and Medium Sized Enterprises (SMEs): A Literature Review. *Problems and Perspectives in Management*, Volume 5, Issue 1, 104-115.

Budinsky, M., & Taborecka-Petrovicova, J. (2021). Examination of business interest in level of complexity of facial biometric technology implementation in Slovakia. In *Advances in Longitudinal Data Methods in Applied Economic Research: 2020 International Conference on Applied Economics (ICOAE)* (pp. 135–146). Springer International Publishing.

Clodfelter, R. (2010). Biometric technology in retailing: Will consumers accept fingerprint authentication? *Journal of Retailing and Consumer Services*, *17*(3), 181–188.

De Keyser, Arne; Bart, Yakov; Gu, Xian; Liu, Stephanie Q.; Robinson, Stacey G., & Kannan, P. K. (2021). Opportunities and challenges of using biometrics for business: Developing a research agenda, *Journal of Business Research, 136,* 52–62.

Chen, Y., & Fondeur J. C. (2015). Biometric algorithms. In: *Encyclopedia of Biometrics*. Boston, MA: Springer.

Choi, J., & Lee, J. (2018). Firm size and compositions of R&D expenditures: Evidence from a panel of R&D performing manufacturing firms. *Industry and Innovation*, *25*(5), 459–481.

Fang, X., Paez, N. R., & Zeng, B. (2021). The nonlinear effects of firm size on innovation: An empirical investigation. *Economics of Innovation and New Technology*, *30*(1), 48–65.

Farooq, R., Vij, S., & Kaur, J. (2021). Innovation orientation and its relationship with business performance: Moderating role of firm size. *Measuring Business Excellence*, *25*(3), 328–345.

Glasova, J. (2016, October 12). *Kde sa na Slovensku vlani najviac nakupovalo*?. Retail magazine. http://www.retailmagazin.sk/jana-glasova/1294-kde-sa-na- slovensku-vlani-najviac-nakupovalo

Gonzalez-Benito, O., Munoz-Gallego, P. A., & Garcia-Zamora, E. (2016). Role of collaboration in innovation success: Differences for large and small businesses. *Journal of Business Economics and Management*, *17*(4), 645–662.

Jain, A., & Ross, A. (2011). *Introduction to biometrics*. New York: Springer.

Jain, A., & Ross, A. (2015). *Encyclopedia of biometrics*. Boston, MA: Springer.

Mordor Intelligence. (2022). Global Biometrics Market – Growth, Trends, COVID- 19 Impact, And Forecasts (2022 – 2027). Hyderabad, India.

Sinha, G. R. (2019). *Advances in biometrics*. Springer.

Taborecka-Petrovicova, J., Budinsky, M., & Sipulova, M. (2023). Implementation of facial biometric technologies: A business perspective. In Tsounis, N. & Vlachvei, A. (Eds.), *Advances in Empirical Economic Research*. Springer Proceedings in Business and Economics. Springer.

Turzo, J. (2018, October 12). *Sedem skutočností, ktoré ovplyvnili retail na Slovensku*. Retail magazin. http://www.retailmagazin.sk/obchodnik/maloobchod/3 608-7-skutocnosti-ktore-ovplyvnili-retail-na-slovensku

Vaona, A., & Pianta, M. (2008). Firm size and innovation in European manufacturing. *Small Business Economics*, *30*(3), 283–299.

White, C. (2022, October 12). *Biometrics and digital identity: 5 bold predictions for 2022*. Biometric Update. https://www.biometricupdate.com/202201/biometrics- and-digital-identity-5-bold-predictions-for-2022

Zhang, D., Lu, G., & Zhang, L. (2018). *Advanced biometrics*. Springer.

Irina Tulyakova[1,*], Victor Dengov[1], and Anton Aksenov[1]

Peculiarities of State Regulation of Food Retail in St. Petersburg and Medium-term Prospects for Its Development

Abstract:
Research background: The problems and prospects for the development of trade in food products in the world's major metropolitan areas, including St. Petersburg, have been the area of scientific interests of the authors of the article for many years.
Purpose of the article: With global shifts in world markets due to various causes, food trade has undergone significant changes around the world. Among the consequences of these changes, one should single out the accelerated growth in food prices. In an attempt to contain cost-push inflation, countries resort, among other things, to measures of state regulation of food markets. Taking into account the place and role of the food market in St. Petersburg, we have set the task to analyze the features of its state regulation and, on this basis, anticipate the medium-term prospects for its development.
Methods: Generalizations of the research are based on the processing and systematization of data obtained from available information sources. By analyzing the statistics, the authors were able to deduce the trends of the current moment and determine the prospects.
Findings & Value added: An analysis of expert research and the macroeconomic situation in the country made it possible to identify the main trends in the development of food retail in St. Petersburg in the medium term.

Keywords: *food networks, pricing policy, virtual reality in e-commerce, marketplaces*

JEL Classification: *C43; D12; D21; D43*

1 Introduction

Having originated in the United States at the turn of the 19th–20th centuries, the format of retail chains has spread throughout the world, and the first retail chains in Russia appeared at the end of the 20th – beginning of the 21st century.

* Corresponding author: i.tulyakova@spbu.ru
1 St. Petersburg State University, Faculty of Economics, 7/9 Universitetskaya nab., St. Petersburg, 199034 Russia

COVID-19 has had a global impact on retail across the globe. Retailers have had to prove themselves in the area of corporate social responsibility (CSR) like never before (Kadekova et al., 2020). Merchants were forced on the one hand, to adapt to massive changes in consumer behavior patterns (Sheth, 2020), and on the other hand, to offer buyers their new consumption business models. An example is the model of the so-called "sharing economy," the essence of which is the collective use of various consumer goods on a lease or exchange basis. Thanks to it, a new culture of consumption was formed, which changed the attitude towards property (Hollowell et al., 2019). Another example is the exponential expansion of e-commerce (Stefko et al., 2019; Dsouza & Sharma, 2020).

Various aspects of the state and prospects for the development of food retail in St. Petersburg have long been the sphere of scientific interests of the authors of the article. Over the years, we were interested in the level of concentration and competition in the food market, the pricing policy of the main players (Dengov et al., 2016; Maksimov et al., 2016), a comparative analysis of the food markets in Moscow and St. Petersburg (Gregova et al., 2018), pricing strategies of food retail chains in the face of global competition and the place of their private labels in this struggle (Tulyakova et al., 2020; Gregova et al., 2020).

2 Subject and Basis of the Study and Methodology

In our article, we conducted a study of the regulatory impact of the state on the food trade in St. Petersburg and identified new trends in its development during the pandemic period and the period of adaptation to anti-Russian sanctions. We had to determine what changes had already taken place and what more should be expected. The factual and statistical basis for the study was information obtained from official open sources, such as retail.ru, infoline.spb.ru, rbc.ru, gov.spb.ru, etc. During the study, we used the methods of statistical and system analysis. The preliminary hypothesis was that despite the objective difficulties, this sector of the economy has quite successfully adapted to the new circumstances.

3 Results and Discussion

A feature of Russian retail trade networks has become the presence of different formats in terms of scale, penetration and turnover – federal and local, or regional networks. The development of trade in the format of "chains" in the region, the growth of competition between federal and regional chains contribute to curbing price increases and motivate retail chains to improve the quality of service. At the same time, it must be taken into account that the promotion of retail chains should be consistent with the normal conditions for the functioning of small businesses, which also perform important social and economic functions.

3.1 Peculiarities of State Regulation of Food Retail in St. Petersburg

The main normative act regulating the activities of food retail in St. Petersburg is the law "On State Regulation of Trading Activities in St. Petersburg." Since 2014, within the framework of the state program "Development of Entrepreneurship and the Consumer Market of St. Petersburg," the subprogram "Development of wholesale and retail trade, public catering, consumer services and the sphere of funeral services" has been implemented The main tasks of the subprogram:

- ensuring a balanced development and deployment of infrastructure for wholesale and retail trade, public catering, consumer services and funeral services in St. Petersburg;
- creation of conditions for increasing demand for goods of Russian manufacturers and increasing the economic accessibility of goods and services for the population of the city.

Program indicators and results are shown in Table 1.

Table 1. Subprogramme indicators and results.

Indicator name	Target value for 2021	Actual value for 2021
Retail trade turnover, billion rubles	1 602,2	1 875,4
Index of physical volume of retail trade turnover in comparable prices, %	102,0	115,0
Turnover of public catering per capita, thousand rubles	13,8	18,9

Source: SPb IAC (2022)

The turnover of network retailers exceeded the figures planned for 2021. And this despite the fact that the consumer market of the city was under the influence of anti-COVID legislative restrictions. At the same time, the trade turnover of retail food chains amounted to 1,875.4 billion rubles, which is 15 % more than in 2020.

The annual report "On the state and development of the competitive environment in the markets of goods, works and services in St. Petersburg" of the Committee for Industrial Policy, Innovation and Trade of the Government of

St. Petersburg monitors the level of competition by industry, customer satisfaction, and the state of the market in the reporting period. Thus, the city authorities are developing the basis for administrative and regulatory measures in various sectors. The 2021 report assesses the level of competition in the retail market as "high," with the share of the private sector over 80 %. In addition, much attention is paid to assessing the quality of goods and services in retail chains. For this purpose, social networks and instant messengers are monitored. In St. Petersburg, information on checking the quality of food products sold in chains is very popular, and the city government monitors this information (Table 2).

Table 2. Information on compliance with the quality of products in the retail chains of St. Petersburg (by groups in the VKontakte network).

Community name	Link	Number of subscribers as of 10.10.2021	The number of reviews for low-quality goods from 01.01.2021 to 10.10.2021
Blacklist Peter	hhtps://vk.com/stoplistspb	52727	85
Protection of consumer rights	hhtps://vk.com/spbpotrebitel	10693	7
Overheard in DIXY	hhtps://vk.com/dixi_ru	4474	1
Protecting the rights of citizens in SPb	hhtps://vk.com/czpgspb	2461	4
Public control	hhtps://vk.com/club85554982	1600	38
Overdue patrol	hhtps://vk.com/prosrokspb	667	20

Source: Administration of St. Petersburg (2022)

On March 1, 2022, retailers signed a voluntary agreement to limit the markup to 5 % on certain socially important food products. The mandatory list includes products from the categories of dairy products, bakery products, vegetables, sugar. Retail chains must choose specific names themselves. There were 276 such goods in Magnit's assortment, 150 each in Pyaterochka and Perekrestok. At the same time, private labels do not fall under these restrictions. As the experts emphasize, "the margin cap option is more flexible than last year's agreements on fixing wholesale and retail prices for sugar and sunflower oil, and is also more adequate to the current unstable conditions. The intensification of inflationary processes and the impossibility of state regulation of prices will stimulate the expansion of the practice of such agreements for other positions and categories as well" (Polukhin, 2022).

In general, the trend of opening discount stores is currently developing in St. Petersburg. For example, antimonopoly restrictions that are aimed at containing the X5 Group chain are not an obstacle to the development of Chizhik stores of the same chain, since the chain has the right to reformat outlets within the allowed market share of the city. This allowed the chain to open 163 new outlets in July-August 2022.

In contrast to retail in Europe and the USA, in Russia, the participation of the state in the FMCG industry is obvious. For example, since 2018, VTB has been the largest co-owner of Magnit. At the same time, the bank remains a key financial partner of the network: it issues Magnit debit cards, and also launched a payment service with expanded functionality Magnit Pay. Both Magnit and Lenta have said they will finance takeover deals with their own funds and unused credit line balances. At the same time, both companies borrow mainly from state- owned banks – VTB and Sberbank (Prostakov, 2021).

To a certain extent, this became the basis of the development model, the desire for which was declared by the management of X5 Group:

1. Commitment to the goals of sustainable development in unity with society and the state.
2. Implementation of ESG principles in corporate culture, purchasing activities and social responsibility programs. ESG stands for environmental, social and governance indicators of sustainable development at different levels – from small companies to corporations and countries. In the past few years, with the growing understanding of the environmental and social pressures of today, the principles of ESG have become popular and have reached the level of public awareness of their importance.

   ESG data tends to reflect non-financial factors in overall performance that have traditionally been missing from financial analysis: an organization's energy and water management, waste generation, employee rights and working conditions, and more traditional measures of organizational accountability and transparency. The ESG brings together and systematizes almost everything that reflects how an organization works in society and the environment, and whether that mode of operation is sustainable and responsible.
3. Digital transformation as the basis for making "managerial decisions based on big data and artificial intelligence" (Lvov, 2020).

These trends, proclaimed by the state, affect the business models of Russian retail. The influence of the state on the activities of food retail is also associated with forced regulatory activities in the situation of sanctions restrictions. This regulation includes the permission of parallel imports. With regard to federal networks, it concerns the supply of household chemicals, hygiene products and cosmetics. The state accepts the risks of claims from the right holders, but this does not negate the special legal control and expertise on the part of the largest players in the FMCG industry: "in order to defend your right from any claims, it is important that the import by the entrepreneur is carried out in accordance with the legislation in force at the time import" (RGRU, 2022).

In a situation of rising logistics costs and sanctions for regional retail, the issue of competition with federal networks is especially acute. Under these conditions, the business model that is traditional for regional retail trade is relevant – convenience stores and mobile trade under the brands of retail chains as a guarantor of product quality and a loyal pricing policy.

At the same time, it is natural to increase the share of domestic retail due to the withdrawal of foreign producers and retail chains from the market. Thus, a certain retail business model is also formed, which takes into account, for example, the former name of the retail chain, to which consumer loyalty of customers has formed.

Thus, the situation on the commodity food market is developing in the context of restrictive measures, a decrease in the growth of the purchasing power of the population, but also an increase in revenue. The restrictions imposed by the regulator relate to sanitary measures, pricing policy, quality of goods and services. Due to the fact that the opening of large retail outlets for networks has become less relevant, antitrust restrictions are not so sharp. Retail chains can redistribute the format of stores within the available volumes of retail space, and now this is happening in favor of discounters.

3.2 Trends in the Development of Retail in the Medium-long Term in St. Petersburg

Retail development trends depend both on the strategies of retailers and on the macroeconomic situation. In the first case, they are usually formed by large federal players, in the second case, regional representatives of the FMCG industry and the state are actively involved.

The influence of large federal players must be taken into account because their influence on network trading is only increasing. And this is a global trend: "a high degree of concentration of the retail market is typical for Germany – the 5 largest retail operators control 65 % of the market share, Great Britain – 4 networks occupy more than 70 %, France – 5 largest networks control 85 %,

Denmark – 2 leading networks share between represents 60 % of the market" (Belova and Verona, 2021). In Russia, the consolidation of the FMCG industry is lower, but it shows a steady trend (Figure 1).

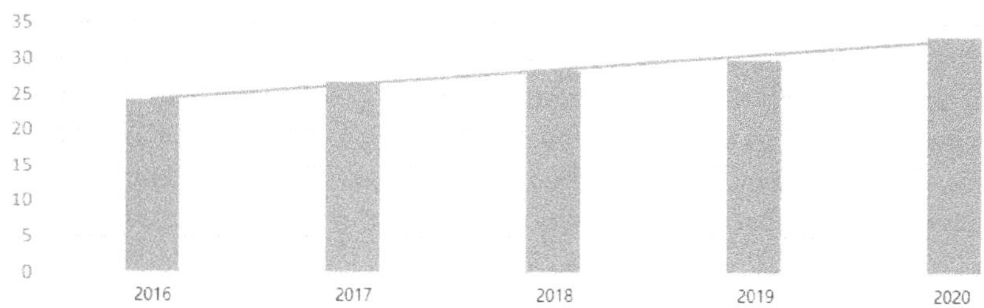

Figure 1. Share of TOP-10 largest federal food retail chains, %.
Source: compiled by the authors based on Belova and Verona (2021)

One of the trends reflecting the relationship between the economic development of retail and the social responsibility of business is the compliance of retail strategies with the national development goals of the country. The strategic programs of federal retail chains are being brought into line with such government objectives as maintaining the health of the population, a comfortable environment for life and effective entrepreneurship.

For example, X5 Group sets an example in this regard by implementing the social projects "Kindness Basket," "Safety Island," "Healthy Habits Route," developing "green marketing." In addition, the retailer's management set the task of organizing an infrastructure for the collection of secondary raw materials and packaging, reducing greenhouse gas emissions by 10 % by 2023, increasing by 355 the volume of products that are recycled instead of disposed of (Lvov, 2020).

An analysis of expert research and the macroeconomic situation on the market allows us to identify the following trends in the development of retail in the medium-long term for St. Petersburg:

- development of a delivery service for federal and regional retailers, which will focus not only on the product range, but also on non-grocery items from the SKU of the outlet;
- development of private label assortment not only for federal, but also for regional players, including discounters;
- maintaining a high level of product quality at "hard discounters" that enter the market of St. Petersburg, including the development of private labels of the middle price category, which will be sold only in retail outlets of the city;

- the growth of the "green" economy and marketing, the allocation of a "green shelf" in all federal chains with the prospect of developing individual retail outlets under the auspices of large retailers;
- digitalization of trade: active development of online stores, joint marketplaces, digital service zones and mobile applications. In addition, "the development of category management, as well as the digital sphere and e-commerce, remain the priorities of retail trade. Innovative technologies are the present and future of Russian trade, in which assortment forecasting, depending on external factors, the opening of new stores from geo-forecasting, personalization of purchases is already becoming a reality today." (Belova & Verona, 2021).

Retailers in St. Petersburg can contribute to the development of another trend, which was revealed as a result of a change in the assortment matrix of retail chains due to sanctions and disrupted supply chains: the introduction of mid-priced delicatessen products into the assortment. Such goods include alcohol, chocolate, fish and meat delicacies, and high-quality cheeses. There are manufacturers in St. Petersburg who are able to produce such products, and retail chains have experience in opening and maintaining retail shelves with such an assortment that will be especially in demand on the eve of the holidays.

That is, it is necessary to develop a special promotional and pricing strategy that will combine the following elements: the opportunity for the mass buyer to purchase everyday goods (milk, bread, eggs, groceries) using promotions and discounts, and products of the "holiday" assortment or delicacies at affordable prices. prices and in sufficient range.

The experience of Perekrestok and VkusVill revealed another trend in the work of retail chains: the demand for dark stores and partner delivery. In this regard, the unification of dark stores, retailers' delivery departments and partner services will become relevant. Magnit is currently working on this trend by teaming up with the iGooods delivery service. IGooods has developed logistics centers in St. Petersburg, the range of which includes at least 10,000 SKUs. Darkstore itself forms the assortment matrix, but it can also include exclusive brands of retailers, including private labels. If IGooods and retail chains enter into partnership agreements, the range of the service will reach 22,000 items. As Magnit's experience shows, partnership with the service allows "to make delivery from a retail network even more convenient and attractive for users who prefer to make large purchases of products, but at the same time spend a little time on the whole process" (Sorokin, 2022).

This experience gives impetus to another trend – the development of e-commerce services, and it is under the brand of a retailer. This can be either your own delivery service or affiliate programs, for example, with Yandex.Food, Samokat. However, in the case of a private label or an original assortment, such as VkusVill, delivery with its own brand will help maintain the loyalty of customers who are used to the assortment of a particular retailer and choose it. Particular attention should also be paid to the development of STM. In October 2022, according to Lenta, in St. Petersburg, the share of private labels in total sales was from 16 % to 20 %, although retailers expected a maximum of 15.4 %. In this regard, the formation of special centers for the development and analysis of private labels for retail grocery chains is relevant.

As an experiment, Lenta launched the Product Lab marketing project in St. Petersburg hypermarkets, a special test center where experts from among regular customers will test and taste new private label chains. For participating in testing, experts receive bonuses on the Lenta loyalty card. Thus, two tasks are solved at once: customer loyalty is maintained, which encourages them to make purchases in the stores of the network, and actual testing of private labels that have not yet been put into circulation is carried out.

The peculiarity of the development of private labels lies in the fact that in different regions there are different consumer preferences. For example, manufacturers know that Petersburgers prefer creme brulee ice cream and instant coffee, but drink little non-alcoholic beer. Thus, the private label put on the shelf of a city retailer must take into account these consumer preferences and traditions.

As part of the development of private labels, it is important to adhere to the following trends:

- develop private labels not only in the lower price segment, but also in the middle and premium segments;
- to develop category management aimed at SMT and regional producers;
- timely test, update or replace private labels on the shelf, focusing on the fact that in the most popular segments the actual or potential share of private labels should be at least 16–20 %. Within the framework of the city program for the development of the concept of the "15- minute city," retail development trends are also being formed (Dom.RF, 2021). According to Romir, the structure of retail trade over the past 5 years has changed from a decrease in preference for traditional hypermarkets (from 34 % to 29 %) to an increase in preferences for "hard" discounters (from 1 % to 4 %), online shopping (from 3 % to 6 %) and convenience stores (from 12 % to 19 %).

Based on this, a trend is gaining momentum in St. Petersburg, when traditional hypermarkets begin to open outlets that are not typical for them. For example, in 2021, O'KEY announced that it intends to develop the convenience store format, which is insufficient in St. Petersburg and has great potential. Analysts believe that a few smaller stores can generate more customer traffic. In the summer of 2021, the chain filed an application with Rospatent for the registration of the O'KEY Daily trademark, which will be intended for this type of outlets (Zaitseva, 2021).

Experts emphasize that this format in St. Petersburg will be in great demand in places of new development in already inhabited areas. For example, in the Petrogradsky, Kalininsky, Moskovsky, Vyborgsky districts of St. Petersburg, where new housing is being introduced, and there are quite few territories for opening hypermarkets with all the infrastructure. At the same time, there are enough premises on the real estate market with an area of less than 300 sq.m, which are just right for the convenience store format. If hypermarkets do not master the new format, they risk losing customers.

This format is already being actively developed by Azbuka Vkusa, which opens retail outlets called AB Daily in new buildings in the Petrogradsky District, but there are still few of them and clearly not enough. Also, as part of the 15-minute city concept, Lenta opens new retail outlets. The popularity of hypermarkets is falling, they occupy an area of at least 5,500 square meters and cannot be located in densely populated new buildings. Therefore, Lenta is launching the SuperLenta format on the first floors of residential buildings or in small detached premises.

At the same time, the retailer does not intend to develop net discounters, emphasizing that they are looking for a model that could then be safely scaled up, being sure that it will be able to recoup the shareholders' investments… We are rather trying to find an economy store option that would be suitable for our current client in the current economic situation and at the same time could enjoy most of the synergies that can be obtained by being part of the "big" Lenta (Retail.Ru., 2022).

Another trend that has become familiar and the relevance of which is not disputed, but it can undergo certain transformations. We are talking about the digitalization of the network business. Since the beginning of the pandemic, the growth of online commerce has shown at least 6 % per year. The cumulative increase in network retail until 2024 is planned to be 4.4 trillion rubles, with a total income of 23.3 trillion rubles.

The total volume of e-commerce and the place of network retail in it is shown in Figure 2.

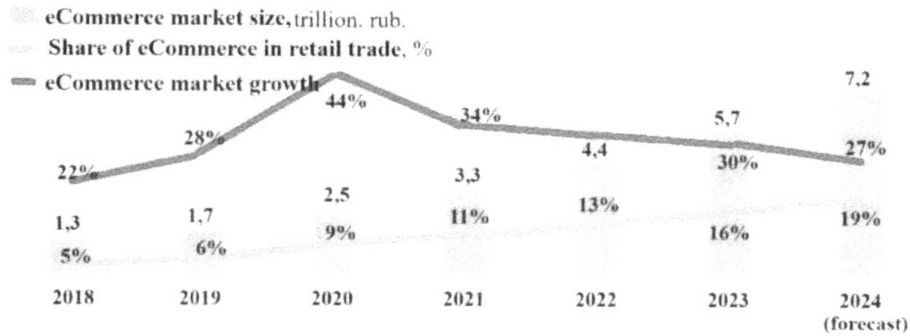

Figure 2. The growth of e-commerce and the share of online retail in the trend, %.
Source: EDIWEB (2021)

The following current trends that St. Petersburg specialists are working on can be distinguished:

- the introduction of virtual reality (VR) in e-commerce can increase online commerce by 17 %. These technologies contribute to the so-called "risk-free trading," when you can make a more informed purchase decision;
- automation of purchases and analysis of consumer demand, updated in mobile offers. Now this technology is implemented in VkusVilla applications and in the future it will be extended to the activities of other retailers;
- analysis of the authenticity of the marking "Honest Sign" using a smartphone. The technology is implemented by Perekrestok and is attractive to other large retailers;
- creation of own marketplaces. X5 Group followed this path, having created the "For the future" marketplace and setting a certain trend.

4 Conclusions

As the analysis showed, the trends in the development of retail in St. Petersburg are similar to the all-Russian trends (and international ones too). But in St. Petersburg, they have a higher potential for development, as the city has better financial and human resources than most other regions of the country.

Statistical analysis also showed that there was no reduction in the volume of food retail. Food is the last thing people will save on. The rise in food prices was held back by agreements between retailers, rather high competition among sellers, and the regulatory influence of the state. Due to sanctions and the withdrawal of some Western chains from the Russian market, the share of domestic retail chains naturally increased. At the same time, competition between retailers of different levels has intensified – from federal and regional chains to small and medium-sized businesses.

There was an active change in business models in food retail, taking into account the principles of ESG, the need for digital transformation and the use of artificial intelligence. The development of retail in the medium-long term in St. Petersburg will manifest such trends as: the further development of home delivery services, the development of the range of private labels not only among federal, but also regional players, including discounters, support at a high level of product quality at hard discounters, the growth of the green economy and marketing, the allocation of the green shelf in all federal networks, the digitalization of trade: the active development of online stores, joint marketplaces, digital service zones and mobile applications and e-commerce.

In order to improve the anti-crisis state policy in the sphere of regulation of regional retail, it is necessary to make scientifically based decisions, in connection with which the work reflected new approaches to the innovative development of retail and proposed a model of anti-crisis management of regional retail in the context of the consequences of the pandemic.

References

Administration of St. Petersburg. (2022, September 29). *Doklad o sostoianii i razvitii konkurentnoi sredy na rynkakh tovarov, rabot i uslug v Sankt-Peterburge*. Plan. https://plan.fas.gov.ru/media/ckeditor/uploads/2022/09/29/2021_.pdf

Belova, L. A., & Verona, L. I. (2021). Modern trends in Russian retail. *Natural and humanitarian Studies, 33*(1), 42–46.

Dengov, V. V., Gregova, E., & Maksimov, A. V. (2016). Globalization in the field of food retail St. Petersburg: Analysis of the price policy. *Proceedings of the 16th International Scientific Con-ference on Globalization and its Socio-Economic Consequences,* 362–374.

Dom, R. F. (2021, February 3). *Standart kompleksnogo razvitiia territorii*. Dom-rf. https://дом.рф/urban/standards/printsipy-kompleksnogo-razvitiya-territoriy/

Dsouza, D., & Sharma, D. (2020). Online food delivery portals during Covid-19 times: An analysis of changing consumer behavior and expectations. *International Journal of Innovation Science, 13*, 218–232.

EDIWEB. (2021, May 27). *Riteil budushchego: tekhnologii, kotorye meniaiut rynok uzhe seichas*. Ediweb. https://ediweb.com/ru-ru/media/blog/retail-future?ysclid=lp6tf3c2n77919 11608

Gregova, E., Dengov, V., & Tulyakova, I. (2018). Global trends in Russian retail: A comparison of the market of St. Petersburg and Moscow. *Proceedings of the 18th International Scientific Conference on Globalization and its Socio-Economic Consequences*, 1079–1086.

Gregova, E., Dengov, V., Tulyakova, I., & Mustafaev, A. (2020). Private label as a global trend of food networks for pricing policy optimization (case study of St. Petersburg). *SHS Web of Conferences. Collection of Materials of the 19th International scientific conference, 74,* 04007.

Hollowell, J. C., Rowland, Z., Kliestik, T., Kliestikova, J., & Dengov, V. V. (2019). Customer loyalty in the sharing economy platforms: How digital personal reputation and feedback systems facilitate interaction and trust between strangers. *Journal of Self-Governance and Management Economics, 7*(1), 13–18.

Kadekova, Z., Savov, R., Kosiciarova, I., & Valaskova, K. (2020). CSR activities and their impact on brand value in food enterprises in Slovakia based on foreign participation. *Sustainability, 12*(12), 4856.

Lvov, V. (2020, November 11). *Krupneishii riteiler strany – o modeli upravleniya biznesom dlya ustoichivogo razvitiya.* RGRU. https://rg.ru/2020/11/10/krupnejshij-ritejler-strany-o-modeli-upravleniia-biznesom-dlia-ustojchivogo-razvitiia.htm

Maksimov, A. V., Dengov, V. V., & Tulyakova, I. R. (2016). Globalization in the field of food retail St.Petersburg: Concentration and competition. *Proceedings of the 16th International Scientific Conference on Globalization and its Socio-Economic Consequences,* 1277–1286.

Polukhin, A. (2022, March 1). *Ede otmerili natsenki.* Kommersant.Ru. https://www.kommersant.ru/doc/5238646

Prostakov, G. (2021, May 21). *Sliyaniya v produktovom riteile usilivayut rol gosudarstva v sektore.* Vedomosti.Ru. https://www.vedomosti.ru/opinion/articles/2021/05/21/870676

Retail.Ru. (2022, November 3). *«Magnit» i igooods zapustili dostavku produktov.* Retail.ru. https://www.retail.ru/news/oborot-wildberries-vpervye-prevysil-1-trln-rub-3-noyabrya-2022-222099/

RGRU. (2022, June 17). *Interviu s Viktorom Evtukhovym, zamestitelem ministra promyshlennosti i torgovli.* Rg-ru. https://rg.ru/video/2022/06/17/interviu-s-viktorom-evtuhovym-zamestitelem-ministra-promyshlennosti-i-torgovli.html?ysclid=lp6vls025o6773 36538

Sheth, J. (2020). Impact of Covid-19 on consumer behavior: Will the old habits return or die? *Journal of Business, 117*, 280–283.

Sorokin, V. (2022, September 27). *My khotim postroit effektivnuyu model malenkogo magazine.* Retail.Ru. https://www.retail.ru/interviews/vladimir-sorokin-lenta-my- khotim-postroit-effektivnuyu-model-malenkogo-magazina/

SPb IAC. (2022, July 4). *Sostoianie potrebitelskogo rynka Sankt-Peterburga v 2021*. Gov-spb. https://www.gov.spb.ru/static/writable/documents/2022/04/07/.pdf.

Stefko, R., Bacik, R., Fedorko, R., Olearova, M., & Rigelsky, M. (2019). Analysis of consumer preferences related to the use of digital devices in the e-commerce dimension. *Journal of Entrepreneurship and Sustainability*, *7*, 25–33.

Tulyakova, I., Gregova, E., Dengov, V., & Mustafaev, A. (2020). Improvement of retail pricing strategies in food distribution networks in terms of global competition (St. Petersburg's example). *SHS Web of Conferences. Collection of Materials of the 19th International scientific conference, 74,* 06030.

Zaitseva, D. (2021, July 2). *Poblizhe k domu: krupnomu reteileru prochat novyi format*. DP.Ru. https://www.dp.ru/a/2021/07/02/I_snitsja_nam_OKej_u_doma

Anna Zausková[1], and Michal Kubovics[1,*]

Bibliographic Mapping of the Global Groundswell in the Context of Social Media

Abstract:
Research background: In line with the continuous globalization and dynamic development of social media, the phenomenon of the groundswell is emerging in communication studies. Reflecting the evolution of interpersonal communication and information dissemination, it has gained the attention of the academic world.
Purpose of the article: The present scholarly paper is devoted to a comprehensive exploration of the theoretical framework of the phenomenon of the groundswell and its key aspects within social media by means of bibliographic mapping. The aim is to identify, categorize and analyze relevant sources published to date that address the groundswell as a significant factor in digital communication.
Methods: A mixed research design is applied in the groundswell analysis, combining a systematic literature review and a detailed bibliographic mapping, subsequently visualized for clarity. Initially, identification of keywords related to the problem area is carried out. Subsequently, WoS database tools are used to identify sources. Based on the identified connections, thematic categories and broader areas. Based on the above, visualization through VOSviewer.
Findings & Value added: The results of this analysis provide a detailed insight into the current state of the topic under study in the form of the groundswell within social media. Not only areas that have already been explored are defined, but also potentially unexplored aspects and directions for further research efforts. In this way, the paper sheds deeper light on the theoretical context of the groundswell and provides useful information for researchers and a wider audience of interested readers.

Keywords: *Groundswell, Social Media Community, Bibliographic Mapping in Communication Studies, Thematic Categories in Groundswell Research*

JEL Classification: *M3; M30; B31*

* Corresponding author: michal.kubovics@ucm.sk
1 University of Ss. Cyril and Methodius in Trnava, Faculty of Mass Media Communication, Department of Marketing Communication, Namestie J. Herdu 2, 917 01 Trnava, Slovakia

1 Introduction

Together, social media create an environment in which interacting users occur, with the possibility of creating a bottom-up ripple effect. Different social media platforms reinforce this. Messages, comments, and discussions can thus spread rapidly among a large number of users, resulting in potential social, cultural, or political influence and impact. For users, social media provides an effective tool for communicating, connecting with each other, distributing content, or activating them to take action. In doing so, they can easily achieve their goal once activated. The creation of communities and the intensification of communication on social networks are prerequisites for this. Businesses and individuals should be vigilant and focused on reacting quickly and monitoring the groundswell. In this way, the negative impact of the ripple effect can be avoided, and the polarisation can be shifted in a positive direction towards the business entity.

In terms of impact on different segments, the bottoming effect has been addressed by a number of authors, among them Freeman (2015), who defined the possibilities of bottoming in different areas such as health-focused discourse, healthy lifestyles, and public health communities. The investigation was extended by Freeman and colleagues (2015) with the finding that paid campaigns to influence the community in favour of the groundswell have been shown to be functional and have a high potential for success. Similarly, the groundswell in the political sphere in the context of ecology (global warming) has been well observed and measurable (Chiluwa & Ifukor, 2015). This was followed up by Leon et al. (2021), where they defined evidence of the functionality of influencing public opinion and changing perceptions as positive in relation to the climate crisis.

In terms of focusing on users and their behaviour, the above-mentioned facts have been addressed by Jabbar et al. (2022). The authors defined that users' engagement with the groundswell can lead to frustration, discomfort, tension, and hostility. On the other hand, if it is a positive groundswell, the user may also feel positive because the groundswell includes community support, user interconnectedness, and self-expression (Braghieri et al., 2022). Within the economic segment, it is possible to talk about a global revolution in marketing communication, especially in the area of the groundswell. The groundswell can be inherently created or moderated by small, medium, and large enterprises. With the help of a positive groundswell, it is possible to achieve product and service promotion, business-to-business collaboration, or even influence the expansion of the user base (Kennedy et al., 2022).

Another part is the possible potential for promoting brand identity and engaging potential consumers, ultimately increasing sales (Lim et al., 2017). The origins of the groundswell phenomenon have been explored by Mills (2012) and referred to the predecessor of the term as viral marketing. Another segment where it is possible to talk about groundswell linkages is education. The potential of the groundswell in education may just be in clarifying doubts or creating collaboration (Jayakumar & Tamilselvan, 2018). It is also important to mention the research conducted by Li et al. (2022) that looked at crowdfunding. Where philanthropy is concerned, the groundswell is the effect that is observable if the outreach or campaign becomes extremely widespread with a high impact. The community thus takes care of advocacy and dissemination of philanthropic information. Li et al. added a comparison with classical digital marketing or digital marketing channels, and the effectiveness of the groundswell in the context of social networks was enormous. On the other hand, e-Wom, which is the essence of the groundswell, is an inherent element in the groundswell (Bernardino et al., 2021).

A comprehensive examination has revealed that it is crucial to closely monitor and capture adverse groundswell. Simultaneously, it is of utmost importance to prioritize the numerous opportunities that social media offer. Conversely, it is also exceedingly essential to establish measures that will result in the elimination of the unfavorable undertone and redirect it towards the positive undertone. In this manner, a business can foster a positive perception and enhance its standing, consequently leading to economic progress via increased consumer acquisitions.

The primary aim of the present paper is to thoroughly examine and analyze the current state of the theoretical framework of the groundswell in the context of social media. The ultimate outcome of the present study is to identify and create a bibliographic mapping that will cover the authors' activity to date and identify explored and unexplored places in the scholarly apparatus. As a result of the aforementioned investigation, a set of research questions and hypotheses have been formulated.

Research topic:

The groundswell in the context of social media.

The research question and hypothesis emerged from the previous theoretical background:

VO1: What is the state of coverage of particular topics and authors in relation to the groundswell on social media?

H1: The occurrence of the groundswell in the Web of Science database is represented by more than 100 occurrences and the issue is covered in the marketing communications segment with more than 10 papers.

2 Methods

Qualitative and quantitative approaches are used in the methodology. A well-defined research framework that is consistent with the desired research objective is a prerequisite. Qualitatively, the emphasis is on the analysis of textual data from reputable sources, especially scientific journals with rigorous review processes. In addition, conference papers are included in conference proceedings. In addition, scholarly texts in various forms, whether in print or online, are used.

The study uses quantitative methods to analyze the results obtained from the Web of Science database. More specifically, the keyword "groundswell" was examined in the context of social media. In the results section of the paper, specific numerical indicators are provided regarding the number of works within a particular category, which can greatly help future research, especially in terms of categorization and exploration of other relevant sources. A subsequent criterion involves the distribution of works based on the years in which they were written, allowing for an examination of the periods during which the most works were produced by the authors.

By conducting a comprehensive analysis over the entire timeframe, it is possible to determine whether a topic is currently experiencing growth, stability or stagnation. The analysis is further extended to identify keywords within the network diagram. Using visualization, keywords with a frequency of three or more than three can be identified. The related keywords that accompany the central keyword "groundswell" are known as VOSViewer. Similarly, the present paper discusses the topic areas associated with the keyword. Also, the three core areas (clusters) with the most frequent coverage and the accompanying keywords are defined.

3 Results

The following results define the answer to the research question "What is the state of coverage of each topic and author in relation to the groundswell on social media?" The first analysis focuses on defining the authors who covered a given topic in the Web of Science database of papers. Anonymous has the highest number of occurrences, followed by Bezáková with 3 and Madlenak with the same number of 3. The other results are in smaller numbers, namely 2 and 1.

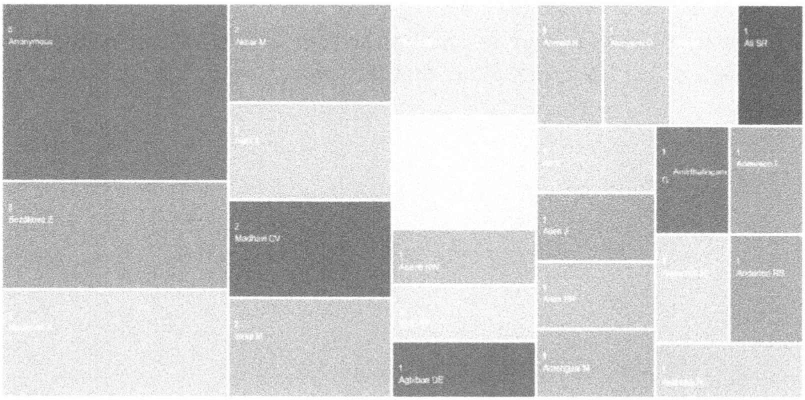

Figure 1. Authors' contributions.
Source: own processing

The following analysis has defined which country has the highest number of contributions, in particular the USA with 123 and Australia with 43, next in order is England with 39 and Canada with 18, the rest of the results are below 10.

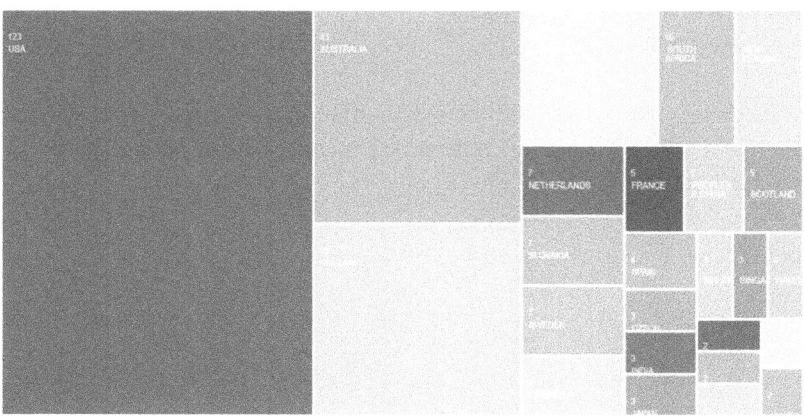

Figure 2. Country of origin of contributions.
Source: own processing

The following analysis focuses on the year of publication of the papers. This analysis has highlighted the current state of the art in addressing the issue. For the year 2020, the highest frequency is 27, followed by 2019 with 22. The next place is occupied by 2011 with 17 and 2021 with the same number of 17. The year 2022 has a count of 15, and the year 2023 is ranked as high as 11 with a count of 12. The result shows that the subject is currently in decline and stagnant.

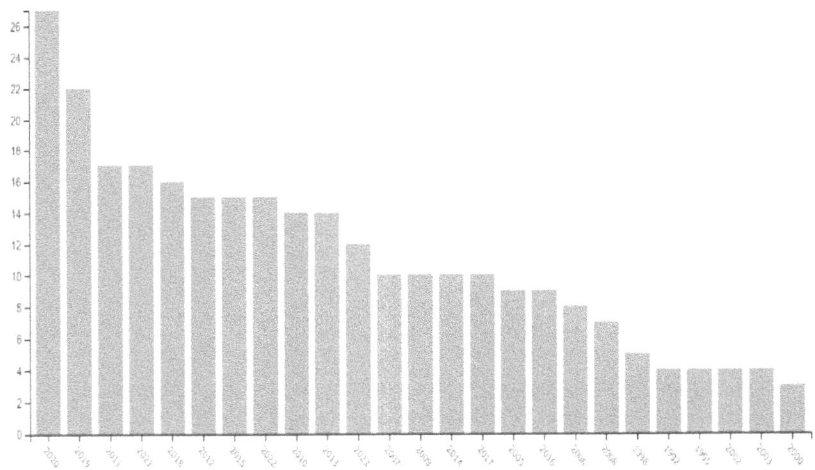

Figure 3. Year of publication of papers.

Source: own processing

The following analysis yielded the finding that journal papers were the most numerous (208), followed by conference papers (28), and book chapters (14) ranked fourth.

Figure 4. Location of contributions.

Source: own processing

The following analysis includes the different segments covered by the contributions, with business economics in first place with 31, law in second place with 30 and communications in third place with 19. This is followed by social sciences with 18 and environmental sciences with 17.

Figure 5. Segments of contributions.

Source: own processing

Further analysis is focused on individual keywords using WoS Viewer. Of the analyzed posts, the most focus is on social networking, groundswell, politics and law, and others.

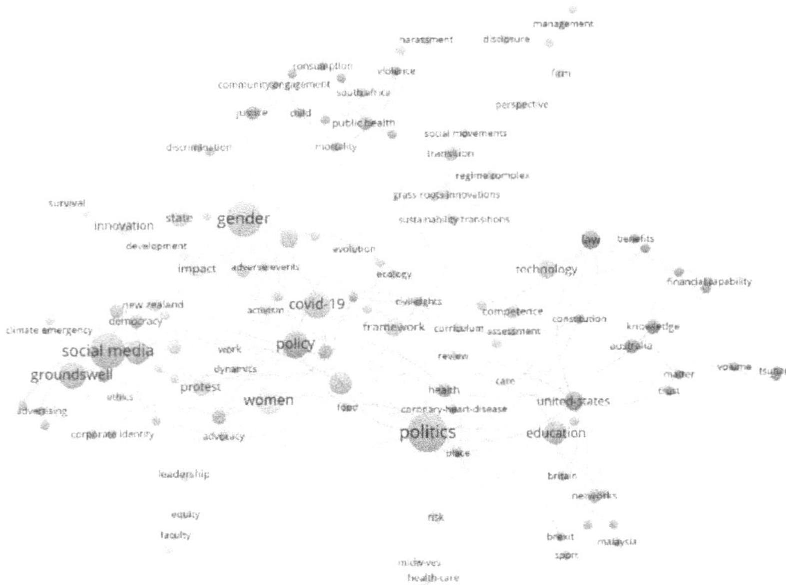

Figure 6. Keyword analysis using WoS Viewer.

Source: own processing

Deeper analysis revealed individual keyword clusters. The most dominant areas are communication and law, ecology and innovation.

Table 1. Keyword clustering.

Communication and law	Ecology	Innovations
advertising	assessment	development
advocacy	biodiversity	impact
childrens	competence curriculum	innovation
communication	ecology	organizations
corporate identity	evolution	survival
democracy	framework	systems

Table 1. Continued

Communication and law	Ecology	Innovations
design	intensity	
groundswell	student	
information	support	
marketing communication		
media		
privacy		
rights		
social media		

Source: own processing

In conclusion, we can confirm that the issue of groundwater is mainly addressed in the context of its management and analysis, with a focus on business entities in the context of ecology and legal aspects. In particular, technological interference and the digital environment. The given hypothesis "The occurrence of the groundswell in the Web of Science database is represented by more than 100 occurrences, and the given issue is covered with more than 10 papers in the marketing communication segment." is confirmed, there are 297 results in the database, of which 19 are focused on communication.

4 Discussion and Conclusions

The given objectives have been met. The bibliographic mapping revealed important findings; the coverage of the groundswell extends to the legal framework, where the authors add important factors (Bezakova et al., 2021; Svec et al., 2021). Similarly, a portion of the papers is devoted to environmental exposures during COVID-19 (Bezáková & Tomová, 2020). An important insight that was found during the bibliographic mapping is the focus on different target groups that may respond in different ways (Cabyova & Hudakova, 2022). This opens up space for further exploration and analysis of unique, homogeneous target groups. General definitions and the origins of the term have been defined by Washington (2012) and Fyfe (2009). It is also important to note the impact on business entities in the form of changing reputation and perception in the complex category of corporate identity (Nagyová & Bednarik, 2022). In the same way, B2B or B2C-oriented business in the digital environment offers a vast area for exploration (Madlenak, 2020). In the space of segments such as tourism, there are uncovered areas, which are also defined by Dredge et al. (2015) and Sigala (2014) in education.

The scope for further exploration is extensive, and the topic offers further avenues for investigation. The present review has grasped the issue and provided important answers to the current state of the art.

Acknowledgments

The research was supported by the Scientific Grant Agency of the Ministry of Education, Science, Research and Sport of the Slovak Republic and the Slovak Academy of Sciences (VEGA, No. 1/0458/21) under the project entitled "Management of the 'groundswell' concept by business entities in promotion of environmentally-friendly products in times of technology interference."

References

Bernardino, S., Santos, J. F., & Oliveira, S. (2021). The impact of social media and E-Wom on the success of reward-based crowdfunding campaigns. *Cuadernos De Gestión,* 35–48.

Bezakova, Z., & Tomova, M. (2020). Online marketing communication of restaurants in context of Covid-19 pandemic. *Marketing Identity: Covid-2.0,* 22–31.

Bezakova, Z., Madlenak, A., & Svec, M. (2021). Security risks of sharing content based on minors by their family members on social media in times of technology interference. *Media Literacy and Academic Research, 4*(1), 53–69.

Braghieri, L., Levy, R., & Makarin, A. (2022). Social media and mental health. *American Economic Review, 112*(11), 3660–3693.

Cabyova, Ľ., & Hudakova, V. (2022). Social media use and adolescents' levels of advertising literacy. *Media Literacy and Academic Research, 5*(2), 147–163.

Chiluwa, I., & Ifukor, P. (2015). 'War Against Our Children': Stance and evaluation in #BringBackOurGirlscampaign Discourse on Twitter and Facebook. *Discourse & Society, 26*(3), 267–296.

Dredge, D., Airey, D. W., & Gross, M. J. (Eds.). (2015). *The Routledge handbook of tourism and hospitality education.* Routledge.

Freeman, B., Potente, S., Rock, V., & McIver, J. (2015). Social media campaigns that make a difference: What can public health learn from the corporate sector and other social change marketers? *Public Health Research & Practice, 25*(2), e2521517.

Fyfe, T. (2009). Groundswell: Winning in a world transformed by social technologies. *Global Media Journal – Canadian Edition, 2*(1), 181–183.

Jabbar, J., Dharmarajan, S., Raveendranathan, R. P., Syamkumar, D., & Jasseer, A. (2022). Influence of social media on adolescent mental health. *International Journal of English Literature and Social Sciences, 7*(1).

Jayakumar, R., & Tamilselvan, N. (2018). Pros and Cons of using social media for educational purposes by Higher Secondary Students – A case study of the Study School, Puducherry. *International Journal of Library and Information Science, 7*(1).

Kennedy, E. D., Horky, A., & Kaufmann, E. (2022). Ties that bind: Leveraging horizontal and vertical ties within an entrepreneurial community in cross-promotional social media marketing. *Journal of Research in Marketing and Entrepreneurship, 25*(2), 310–327.

Leon, B., Bourk, M., Finkler, W., Boykoff, M., & Davis, L. S. (2021). Strategies for climate change communication through social media: Objectives, approach, and interaction. *Media International Australia, 188*(1), 112–127.

Li, B., Hou, F., Guan, Z., & Chong, A. Y. (2022). The use of social media for a better world: Roles of social experience, empathy and personal impulsiveness in charitable crowdfunding. *Information Technology and People. 36*(6), 2587–2610.

Lim, X., Aifa Rozaini bt Mohd Radzol, Cheah, J., & Wong, M. W. (2017). The impact of social media influencers on purchase intention and the mediation effect of customer attitude. *Asian Journal of Business Research, 7*(2), 19–36.

Madlenak, A. (2020). Social media as an opportunity for s-commerce development at the time of covid-19 pandemic. *Marketing Identity, 8*(1), 397–404.

Mills, A. J. (2012). Virality in social media: The SPIN framework. *Journal of Public Affairs, 12*(2), 162–169.

Nagyova, N., & Bednarik, J. (2022). Position of corporate social responsibility in a corporate design. *European Journal of Media, Art and Photography, 10*(2), 110–119.

Sigala, M. (2014). A co-creation approach for exploiting social media and redesigning (e-) learning in tourism and hospitality education. *The Routledge handbook of tourism and hospitality education*, 440.

Svec, M., Madlenak, A., Bezakova, Z., & Horecky, J. (2021). Possibilities and limitations of communication of special purpose civic associations-The case of internal communication of a trade union active in a company influenced by the groundswell concept. *Communication Today, 12*(2), 32–44.

Washington, L. (2012). Groundswell: Winning in a world transformed by social technologies. *Media International Australia, 142*, 184–185.

Armen Altunyan[1], and Tatiana Kotcofana[1,*]

Financial Security of the National Economy in the New Reality

Abstract:
Research background: In the modern conditions, there is a systemic crisis of capitalism: the competition in the economic sphere is replaced by the monopolization on a global scale; the monetary unit of a separate country, initially performing the function of a reserve currency, is used as an instrument of political pressure and competition, the principle of inviolability of the institution of private property is abandoned.
Purpose of the article: The main purpose of this article is to analyze the problems faced by developing countries (for example, Russia) in the modern economic model, and ways to solve these problems.
Methods: To conduct the study, we used official statistics data, the analysis of which allowed us to determine the degree of mutual influence of key parameters of economic development.
Findings & Value added: The medium-term economic policy may be the structural and technological restructuring of the Russian economy based on the domestic market and the entry into stable rates of sovereign economic growth by 2025. The goal of such a policy is to build a self-sufficient economy capable of providing itself with 90 % of everything necessary and limiting imports to 10 % of GDP. Before the isolation of Russia due to political events, this share ranged from 20 % to 30 %. In general, the state policy in the field of financial security should include a single balanced set of measures aimed at ensuring the stability of the financial system, preventing capital outflow, and rational use of financial resources.

Keywords: *economy policy, model of the economy, finance system, financial security*

JEL Classification: *E52; E612; E62*

1 Introduction

The Western model of economic development with a focus on the development of the financial sector, a high level of usage with a low level of production has

---

* Corresponding author: t.kotsofana@spbu.ru
1 Saint-Petersburg State University, Faculty of Economics, Department of Economics and Economical Policy, Universitetskaya emb., 7–9, 199034, Saint-Petersburg, Russia

turned the economy of the golden billion into a destabilizing factor of the world economy. In May – June 2020, the president of the World Economic Forum, Klaus Schwab, proclaimed the "Great Reset," the main goal of which is the conversion from the current capitalism to the so-called inclusive supranational world capitalism, which hides a new neocolonial order (Katasonov, 2021).

In the conditions of modern realities, there is a systemic crunch of capitalism: perfect competition in the economic sphere is replaced by the monopolization of power at a global scale, the monetary unit of a separate country, initially performing the function of a reserve currency, is used as an instrument of political pressure and competition, the principle of inviolability of the institution of private property is abandoned.

In the conditions of scientific and technological progress boost and changing the structure of the economy of developed countries, when the service sector, significantly outpacing material production, ensures the predominance of the sphere of circulation and the building of an economy model focused on the consumption process. As a result, the parity between labor and capital is changing, and forms of capital are developing, due to the separation of the financial sector of the economy and its infiltration into the service sector. The modern economy, with its glaring inequality in the distribution of income and wealth, has gone down the wrong path. While some withdraw value and pump out wealth from national economies, others act as resource providers and wealth creators, but they do not receive anything from this wealth. The current development model, which encourages "rent seekers" rather than genuine "wealth creators," encourages the desire to generate income not by producing something new, but by setting margins above the competitive environment and undermining competition. Rent-oriented activity is aimed at taking value from the creators. The financial sector has diversified enormously, and its total volume has increased significantly. He acts as a rentier – value taker and he is interested in short – term income. «For large banks and speculative funds, the satisfaction of private interests is increasingly at odds with the common good and interests of the economy» (Rampini & Viswanathan, 2018). It is especially true for such a segment as asset management, which has become one of the fundamental characteristics of modern capitalism. The capital accumulated in excess, outstripping the necessary volume for the reproduction cycle corresponding to a certain level of technological development, strive for self-growth and the development of new spheres, using non-economic factors: a decrease in the norms of morality and behavior, the granting of greater freedoms, a pandemic, local wars.

The problem today is not just the size of the financial sector and its advantage over the non-financial sector, but its impact on significant segments of the economy that have become financialized. Financial markets simply distribute the income generated by activities in other areas, and do not add anything to this income. The financial sector no longer performs the function of optimal placement of capital and risks and contributes to the further development of "casino finance." Due to these circumstances, the economy ceases to play its role and contribute to public welth (Bernards, 2019; Bresser-Pereira, 2019). According to the study (Van Velthoven et al., 2019) income inequality caused by finance (financial development, financial liberalization and banking crises) is associated with a greater redistribution of income than inequality caused by other factors. Meanwhile, the increasing social stratification of society and economic inequality are considered by many leading economists as one of the major global threats not only to economic development, but also to the world community as a whole. (Nordhaus & Romer, 2019; Piketty et al., 2019; Stiglitz, 2015; Sen, 2015)

Since 2008, the global financial system has solved any problems with additional money issuance and the build-up of state debt, which did not solve the accumulated structural problems, but created new ones. The debts of developed countries such as the USA, Italy, France, Japan exceeded 100 % of GDP. They can be serviced only at zero rates. The rise in inflation in these countries has increased the price of new borrowings and led to a tightening of monetary policy, which carries the potential for global destruction of the world economy with a slide into financial disaster.

The current world order in the conditions of financial disarrais is particularly painful for countries whose financial markets are among the developing ones. Small unrest at world markets leads to capital escape into a "quiet" dollar harbor, which destroys their currency systems and causes inflation. We observed such a script in the conditions of the world crises of 1998, 2008, when a massive outflow of capital from Russia led to panic on the currency and stock exchange, increased ruble inflation, suppressed real investments, which led to a drop in real income of the population and an increase in unemployment.

2 Research Methods

The methodological basis of the research is the dialectical materialistic and concrete historical method. At the same time, the dialectical-materialistic approach is the initial principle of research. As applied to this study, this means that, on the one hand, the dialectical method allows to know the essence and causes of the processes considered in the most adequate reflection of their dynamic integrity, on the other hand, any theoretical research should be supported by historical practice and statistical data. In this regard the empirical basis of the analysis is statistical materials and specific economic and statistical studies.

3 Results and Discussions

Thirty years of integration into the global financial system, which can reasonably be called the offshoring of the Russian economy, is over. However, after Russia's exit from the global financial web, our economic system and the economy as a whole are being reformatted. In the context of the worsening geopolitical situation, an important task of the government for increasing its financial security is to ensure an effective system of prevention of threats and risks of financial losses, stabilization of the national economy and the formation of the potential for financial support of economic growth.

The issue of financial security of the government is extensive and multifaceted. The financial security of the government is based on effectively functioning of financial and credit systems of the country, the condition of which can be evaluated through a set of measures and indicators of budgetary, tax, currency, monetary, debt, investment security, security of insurance and stock markets.

Budget security is the state of the government's solvency, taking into account the balance of income and expenses of budgets of all levels, as well as their effectivity of use. Indicators of budget security are the size of the budget; the level of redistribution of GDP through the budget; the size of the budget shortage and methods of its financing, the ratio of the shortage (surplus) of the consolidated budget to GDP, the scale of budget financing, the share of transfers from the state budget to GDP, the coefficient of budget provision of the population.

Tax security is a condition in which the volume of optimal and effective tax revenues that meet the interests of the government, corporations and households is ensured. Tax security indicators – tax collection indicator, quality indicator of fulfillment of tax obligations, tax burden, turnover ratio of tax arrears, rate of concealment (understatement) of taxes, rate of effectiveness of on-site tax audits, the rate of identified bugs while filling out tax returns.

In the conditions of the new reality, the main characteristic of budget security should be an acceptable size of the budget shortage. Before the well-known events, the most important postulate of budget policy was a balanced budget. Additional oil and gas revenues under the budget rule were accumulated in special sovereign funds, being converted into reserve currencies of unfriendly countries. In the current conditions, such a design is no longer acceptable and there is a need to switch to shortage budget financing. At the same time, the shortage should serve as a development budget aimed at stimulating the structural adjustment of the economy. The size of the shortage should be regulated taking into account the possibilities of domestic, market, non-emission financing. The federal budget shortage in 2022 amounted to 3.3 trillion rubles. or 2.3 % of GDP, it is one of the lowest among the G7 countries. In 2023–2025, it is planned to have a federal budget shortage of 2.0 % of GDP in 2023, 1.4 % of GDP in 2024, and up to 0.7 % of GDP in 2025. The budget mechanism is turned off from the organization of the new growth model, although the threshold value of the budget shortcoming to GDP can reach no more than 4 %.

As a positive thing, from the point of view of Russia's internal development in the new conditions, it is possible to indicate a reduction in the dependence of the budget on oil and gas income. The reduction in oil and gas revenues relative to GDP from 8.0 % in 2022 to 5.0 % of GDP by 2025 is due to the projected gradual decline in oil prices and total oil production. The predicted increase in non-oil and gas income is due to an increase in the receipts of the main internal additional income as a result of the adjustment of taxation of certain sectors of the economy and the implementation of measures taken to improve administration and increase collectability. The share of non-oil and gas income in federal budget income will grow from 57.9 % in 2022 to 69.7 % in 2025 (Ministry of Finance of the Russian Federation, 2023).

Debt security of the government – the level of government internal and external debt, taking into account the cost of its maintenance. Indicators of the debt security of the government expressing the stability of the country's financial system to internal and external threats; while ensuring the comparative independence of the government and the ability of the country to service the public debt without threatening its sovereignty – the ratio of total state debt to GDP, the ratio of external state debt to GDP, the ratio of domestic state debt to GDP, the ratio of domestic debt to tax revenues, the ratio of state external debt at the end of the year to the annual volume of exports, the ratio of state external debt service costs to the annual volume of exports of goods and services, the share of service costs and repayment of the state debt in the total amount of federal budget expenses.

According to the Bank of Russia, the external debt of the Russian Federation on January 1st, 2023 amounted to 381.8 billion US dollars, having decreased by 100.4 billion US dollars since the beginning of the year (Bank of Russia). The decrease in the indicator is largely caused by a decrease in the external debt of other sectors on loans. The total amount of Russia's internal and external state debt by the end of 2022 is 22.8 trillion rubles, or about 15 % of GDP, being one of the lowest in the world (see Table 1), and its service costs for January-December 2022 totaled 1.33 trillion rubles, or about 4 % of all federal budget expenses. The threshold value of the ratio of external debt to GDP is not more than 25 %.

The currency security of the government is considered from the position of the provision of the government with the necessary foreign exchange funds to fulfill the country's international obligations, the accumulation of foreign exchange reserves to maintain the stability of the national monetary unit and create conditions for the development of exports, the receipt of foreign investments. Measures of currency security is the ratio of the volume of gold and foreign exchange reserves to GDP, the rate of change of the index of the official exchange rate of the national currency to the US dollar, the ratio of the volume of deposits in foreign currency to the total volume of deposits (the level of dollarization and euroization).

In the spring of 2022, in order to support the foreign exchange market, the Bank of Russia, together with the Government, introduced currency restrictions: there was a standard for the mandatory sale of export foreign exchange earnings (initially at 80 %, from May 24 it was lowered to 50 %, and from June 10 it was canceled), as well as measures aimed at curbing capital outflow, the foreign exchange instruments of their foreign trade settlements were restructured. Russia, which found itself under sanctions, transferred trade to national currencies with China, and after it with other friendly countries. Also formal gas trade for rubles with Europe. As a result, according to the Bank of Russia, the share of "unfriendly" currencies in export settlements fell from 87 % at the beginning of last year to 48 % at the end. The share of the Russian ruble in export payments increased from 12 % to 34 %, the share of the dollar decreased from 56 % to 34 %. And in general, the share of the ruble and the currencies of friendly countries, mainly yuan, exceeded half in December last year, accounting 52 % of export settlements and 54 % of import transfers.

Table 1. The ratio of state debt to GDP in some developed and developing countries.

Country	**Debt / GDP (average for 5 years), %**	**Debt / GDP (2020), %**	**Debt / GDP (2021), %**
Germany	64,9	68,9	70,3
USA	110,8	127,1	132,8
China	55,5	66,8	69,6
Saudi Arabia	20,9	32,4	31,0
Russia	15,2	19,3	18,1
India	74,4	89,6	86,6
Mexico	55,6	60,6	60,5
Brazil	86,8	98,9	98,4
South Africa	60,1	77,1	80,8

Source: Tabah et al. (2021)

After the gold reserves of Russia were frozen, the general global trend was to reduce the share of the dollar in international settlements and create preconditions for the emergence of small trade unions using other currencies instead of the dollar. In terms of de-dollarization, two different processes are going on in parallel: the rejection of dollars in gold reserves and the rejection of the dollar as a means in the payment system. So, according to the IMF, from 1999 to 2022, the dollar's share in gold and foreign exchange reserves decreased from 71 % to 47 % (Koroleva, 2023). Against this background, the share of the euro in the reserves of world central banks has grown slightly – from 18 % in 2000 to 20 % today. That means that alternative currencies, not euros, will be able to compete with the dollar. The share of gold in the reserves of the world's central banks is also growing, it is now 13.9 %. The yuan's share in international reserves today is only 2.88 %, but it is constantly growing. The share of the dollar in international payments, according to SWIFT, is today 41.89 %. The share of the euro is 36.34 %. That is about 25 % of cross-border payments are already carried out in alternative currencies.

In August 2023, a large BRICS summit was held, which was joined by Latin America, Saudi Arabia, among others, the largest economies in the world. The share of BRICS countries in world GDP by PPP has increased from 15 % to 31 % over the past 30 years, and the share of G7 countries has decreased from almost 44 % to 31 %. And in 2019, the BRICS, with a share of 31.5 % of global GDP, beat the G7 by 30.7 % (The BRICS Summit, 2023). The decline in the economic potential of developed countries, the increase in the share of settlements in national currencies and the growing volume of US government debt cause a desire to create a fairer payment system and slowly move away from dollar dependence. Instead of the dollar, perhaps the BRICS will eventually use its own currency, backed by gold and other goods.

Under the conditions of sanctions, not all companies have the opportunity to conduct foreign exchange transactions abroad, and therefore the Central Bank does not force exporters to repatriate foreign exchange earnings, which is partly a forced measure. Therefore, part of the money should somehow remain outside of Russia. But in a broad sense, this is one of the constituents of capital outflow. Capital outflow – according to various estimates for 2022 amounted to 220–230 billion, which looks excessive (Prime, 2023). Moreover, net exports have a retarding effect on economic dynamics. It raises question why the withdrawal of funds abroad for citizens remains to be 10 thousand dollars per month. Immediately, the government complains about the lack of long money and tries to attract citizens to the stock market by various measures. Rich Russians have opened accounts in foreign banks over the past year and have withdrawn $64 billion there. It makes no sense to prohibit the withdrawal of money – but we can adjust the rules and volumes. For some reason, it is believed that as soon as ruble assets become attractive, everything will happen by itself. But this attraction must be created. To begin with, without letting the ruble be weakened.

Monetary security is the state of the monetary system in which the stability of the national monetary unit is achieved, the availability of credit resources, and the level of inflation that ensures economic growth and improving the welfare of citizens. Indicators – the level of monetization of economies, the share of cash in GDP, the rate of inflation per year, money supply growth, the capital adequacy ratio of banks, the ratio of total funds of the banking system to GDP, the ratio of banks' equity to GDP, the return on equity of banks, the return on funds of banks, the share of non-residents in the total funds of the banking system.

The Russian banking system is already less connected to the global financial system and is less exposed to the exposure shown by Western banks, whose risks have arisen due to long periods of low, near-zero rates. In the conditions of the most acute geopolitical crisis, the formation of available financial resources for import substitution becomes an issue of national security.

For many years, the banking system did not perform the function of redistributing money and provided only current activities, but not long-term ones. We observed a concentration of finance in a narrow segment of the banking sector. But for the current stage of economic development, long-term loans are required by increasing own funds and attracting long-term liabilities. The total volume of credits into the economy to GDP (non-financial organizations and individuals) in 2022 reached 56.3 % (see Table 2), although the threshold value of the share of credits into the economy in % to GDP is not less than 50 %.

Table 2. Main indicators of the Russian banking sector in 2017–2022.

Year Indicator	2017	2018	2019	2020	2021	2022
Bank assets to GDP in %	92,5	90,8	88,4	96,9	92,1	87,8
The share of credits to the economy in % to GDP	45,6	46,5	47,0	60,6	58,8	56,3
The share of credits in the assets of banks in %	49,1	51,3	53,2	62,5	63,8	64,1
The profit of the banking sector in billion of rubles	789,6	1344,8	2036,0	1909,7	2363,0	212,6

Source: The Central Bank (2023)

An important feature of the degree of availability of money is the dynamics of the money supply in the measurement of the M2 aggregate. In 12 years, since 2011, the M2 monetary aggregate has grown from 21 trillion to 82 trillion rubles at a rate of 12 % per annum in nominal terms, while for most of this period the real money supply has practically not grown. And in 2021 and 2022, the nominal growth rate of M2 was 14 and 24 %, respectively, and the real growth rate was 7 and 12 %. The coefficient of monetization of the economy for 2022 was 54 %, the threshold value of the level of monetization of the economy is at least 50 % (see Table 3).

Table 3. Money supply M2 to GDP (coefficient of monetization of the economy).

Year	Money supply billion 0 f rubles (M2)	Nominal GDP billion of rubles	Monetary base billion of rubles MV	The level of monetization (M2/GDP)	Money Multiplier (M2/MV)
2014	31 615,7	79 030,0	9139,8	0,4	3,46
2015	35 179,7	83 087,0	8745,9	0,423	4,02
2016	38 418,0	85 616,0	9076,1	0,448	4,23
2017	42 442,2	91 843,0	9854,1	0,462	4,31
2018	47 109,3	103 861,0	10 646,9	0,453	4,42
2019	51 660,3	109 241,0	10 979,7	0,472	4,71
2020	58 652,1	107 658,0	13 826,3	0,544	4,24
2021	66 252,9	135 294,0	14 608,2	0,489	4,53
2022	82 388,0	153 435,0	16 454,7	0,536	5,00

Source: The Central Bank (2023)

By the end of 2022, inflation in Russia was 11.94 % after 8.39 % in 2021. Inflation in 2022 was the highest since 2015, when it was 12.9 %. According to the medium-term forecast of the Central Bank itself, inflation in 2023 will be 5–7 %, and in 2024 it will return to 4 %. Although the threshold value of the inflation rate is not more than 6 %, achieving the inflation target at the expense of the interests of the population and the real sector of the economy may later lead to the opposite consequences. A decrease in the rate of inflation due to monetary compression does not lead to an increase in investment activity, but to its decrease. That's why, it is very important for the Central Bank to maintain a fine line between stimulating economic growth and preventing an increase of inflation. It is necessary to expand and reduce the cost of lending without fear of accelerating inflation. The contraction of the money supply in real terms has always led to a drop in GDP.

In conditions of investment hunger, with falling consumer demand, the real sector is able to accumulate money issues without pressure on the currency and consumer markets. And it is high time for the Bank of Russia to follow the path of most developed countries, where government and central banks provide regular support to their economy as financial injections and the provision of government guarantees. (Ruščáková, 2015). At the same time, they see deflation, not inflation, as the main threat to the stability of their economy (Jarý, 2015). And this is completely substantiated, since an important indicator for the economy is not inflation, but real interest rates for the non-financial sector and the volume of lending to the non-financial sector (Domashcenko, 2016), which grows in proportion to the money supply. There are studies proving that the correlation between inflation and economic growth is not significant, especially in the long term (Bhaduri, 2015). As for the dependence between the growth rate of the money supply and the rate of consumer inflation, it should be noted here that the growth of the money supply, on the contrary, causes a decrease in consumer inflation (Altunyan, 2015). And here we can agree with Bresser-Pereira (2020) in fact that "Money is an endogenous variable that does not cause but just validates a going inflation."

Of course, during the process of increasing the amount of money in circulation in general and as capital in particular, the risks of excessive accumulation of surplus value and the growth of monetary inflation should be taken into account. Taking into account the peculiarities of the current moment, on the one hand, the need for industrialization, investment in infrastructure and socially significant sectors of the economy, on the other hand, minimizing the risks of excessive accumulation of surplus value and growth of monetary inflation, and the possibility of growth of the M2 aggregate, the introduction of a digital currency of the Central Bank is widely discussed. The idea of using the digital ruble should correlate its potential – money as a measure of value and money as financial capital – with the requirements of the socio-economic development of the country.

The use of the Central Bank directly transforms state monetary capital into productive capital, bypassing the expensive stage of borrowing private financial capital and excessive accumulation with expanded reproduction. The digital ruble should become the government financial capital for investments on a planned project basis in strategic sectors of the economy.

Investment security is ensured by establishing a level of investment sufficient to meet the current needs of the economy in capital investments in terms of volume and structure Indicators of investment security – the ratio of investments in fixed capital to GDP, the ratio of the growth rate of investments in fixed capital to GDP growth, the growth rate of investments in total budget expenditures, the share of foreign direct investment to GDP, the share of innovative products sold in total industrial output, the share of research expenditures into GDP, the depreciation rate of fixed funds, the coefficient of renewal of fixed funds.

Investments in fixed assets in Russia in 2022 increased by 4.6 %. In 2021, investment's growth was 8.6 %. Good indicators in the dynamics of investments in 2022 were the result of a sharp restriction on the import of investment equipment. This set the task of import substitution for Russian companies, the urgent solution of which required additional investments. This has become especially topical for the branches of the military-industrial complex. If we fully use the tools of project financing, we can increase investments and finance the main projects of technological sovereignty.

The sources of investment have changed a little compared to 2021. The main share is the companies' own funds (56.3 % in 2022 against 59.4 % a year earlier). All budget funds amounted to 17.8 % (15.1 % a year earlier). In the structure of investments, foreign sources took less than 3 % in 2021. Degree The degree of depreciation of fixed assets in our country for 2022 was 40.5 %, the threshold value is not more than 35 %. The investment outlook looks extremely uncertain. Despite the surge in investment activity in 2022, its further prospects do not seem encouraging. The main barriers hindering business development are the unavailability of financial resources, insufficient infrastructure development, weak protection of entrepreneurs and excessive dominance of state-owned companies and institutions. At the moment, investments account for only about 20 % of GDP. The threshold value of the ratio of investments in fixed funds to GDP is not less than 30 %. Under these conditions, investments in fixed funds are not capable of becoming a driver of rapid economic growth, although there are all prerequisites for their development in 2023: there are those who are ready to invest, there are areas -projects for investment, there are also internal resources, savings of citizens (Kaigorodova et al. showed in their study (2018) that in Russia there is a tendency to increase the amount of money left outside the sphere of consumption or investment), and there is a good reason – ensuring technological sovereignty.

Financial security of the insurance market is the level of provision of insurance companies with sufficient resources that allow them to cover insurance claims of customers and at the same time continue to function effectively. Indicators of financial security of the insurance market, characterizing the state of development of the insurance market are – its financial performance, and the effectiveness of its activities – the level of insurance infiltration, the level of insurance payments, the share of premiums owned by non-resident reinsurers, the share of participation of foreign investments in the authorized capital of Russian insurance companies.

So, the average values for the period 2007–2018 of the share of insurance premiums (without life insurance) to GDP in % in twelve economically developed countries turned out to be higher than 2.2 % (Japan – 2.26 %), while the maximum level is in the Netherlands (8.70 %). In eight developing countries (some of them claim the status of a developed economy today), this indicator ranged from 0.74 % (India) to 1.85 % (United Arab Emirates), that is, it turned out to be below the level of 2.0 %. In Russia in 2021, this indicator was 1,38 %.

The financial security of the stock market should be considered as the financial security of the government and corporate securities market. Financial security indicators of the stock market are – the share of capitalization in GDP, the proportion of the M2 aggregate to capitalization, the share of non-residents in the government securities market.

The capitalization of the Russian stock market in connection to GDP decreased from 41.7 % in 2021 to 31.6 % in 2022. In the USA, the capitalization of the stock market is 174 % of GDP, in Canada it is 140.9 % of GDP, in the Netherlands the capitalization is 134 % of GDP, in France it is 102 %, in China it is only about two-thirds of GDP 64.4 %, the comparatively low level of capitalization of the stock market in Germany is only 44 % of GDP. The level of the indicator between countries differs depending on which markets country has access to, how their stock and financial markets are arranged, what type of business prevails, how the growth of the economy is financed.

The volume of gross national savings in recent years has been about 30 % of GDP, and gross savings – about 22 %. This gap represents a resource for long-term investments and the potential to increase the capitalization of the stock market. On February 1, 2023, there were 22.8 trillion rubles in deposits of individuals and 12.8 trillion rubles in bank accounts. These are the funds that, in theory, can be attracted to the stock market. Although deposit rates are negative today, the population prefers the relative reliability of deposits to the instability of the stock market.

As a part of the program of supporting the financial sovereignty in the country, it is planned to create new investment opportunities, including individual investment accounts (IIS) of a new type, for which tax benefits will be applied – both in the form of a deduction for the entire amount deposited, and in the form of exemption of income from personal income tax, but it will be possible to use these benefits only in in the event that funds are put on the IC for five years or more, a long – term savings program, which will be insured for up to 2.8 million rubles – twice as much as at bank deposits. It is planned to extend a tax deduction to citizens' contributions: according to preliminary information, if a citizen pays up to 400 thousand rubles a year, the personal income tax refund will amount to 52 thousand, according to the AIS.

A typical feature of the earlier macroeconomic policy was the withdrawal of resources from the Russian economy in the form of capital outflow and the formation of various funds for a "rainy day." The urgent need for changes in the financial sector has led to the fact that over the past year the Russian financial authorities have done more for the development of the country's domestic financial sector than in a decade. Determining the directions of implementation of the new economic policy, it seems important to build a two-circuit model of economic management based on the compatibility of the planned system and private interest. On the one hand, there is a mobilization, administrative and command economy aimed at ensuring its stability in the face of external challenges and priority support for strategic industries. On the other hand, it is a market economy, where private business would deal with the problems of saturation of the domestic market due to import substitution.

4 Conclusion

The medium-term goal of economic policy may be the structural and technological restructuring of the Russian economy based on the domestic market and reaching stable rates of sovereign economic growth by 2025, building a self-sufficient economy capable of 90 % providing itself with everything necessary and only 10 % of imports relative to GDP. Before the well-known events, this share ranged from 20 % to 30 %.

In general, the state policy in the field of financial security should include a single balanced set of measures aimed at ensuring the stability of the financial system, preventing capital outflow, and rational use of financial resources.

References

Altunyan, A. G. (2015). Priorities of monetary policy in the context of national interests. *Vestnik of Saint-Peterburg University. Ser.5: Economics, 1*, (103–115).

Bank of Russia. (2023). Balance of payments, international investment position and external debt of the Russian Federation in January – June 2023. https://cbr.ru/statistics/macro_itm/svs/p_balance / (accessed: 05/20/2023)

Bernards, N. (2019). The poverty of fintech? Psychometrics, credit infrastructures, and the limits of financialization. *Review of International Political Economy*, *26*(5), 815–838.

Bhaduri, S. (2015). Revisiting the growth-inflation Nexus: A wavelet analysis. *Economic Notes*, *45*(1), 79–89.

Bresser-Pereira, L. C. (2019). Secular stagnation, low growth, and financial instability. *International Journal of Political Economy*, *48*(1), 21–40.

Bresser-Pereira, L. C. (2020). Financing COVID-19, inflation and the Fiscal Constraint. *Forum For Social Economics*, *49*(3), 241–256.

Domashchenko, D. (2016). Correlation between economic growth, oil prices and the level of monetization of economy in oil and gas exporting countries: Challenges for Russia. *Economic and Social Changes: Facts, Trends, Forecast*, *43*(1), 96–107.

Jarý, C. (2015). Globalization and deflation. *Globalization and Its Socio-Economic Consequences 2015* (pp. 265–273).

Kaigorodova, G. N., Mustafina, A. A., Alyakina, D. P., Pyrkova, G. Kh., & Abduzalimov, I. R. (2018). Peculiarities of forming the savings by the Russian Population in modern conditions. *Revista San Gregorio*, *25*, 21–27.

Katasonov, V. Y. U. (2021). *CHitaya SHvaba. Inklyuzivnyj kapitalizm i velikaya perezagruzka. Otkrytyj zagovor protiv chelovechestva*. M., Knizhnyy mir.

Koroleva, A. (2023, April 28). Gud-Bay, Amerika! Discred.ru. https://www.discred.ru/2023/04/28/gud-baj-amerika / (accessed: 05/19/2023)

Ministry of Finance of the Russian Federation. (2023). Execution of the federal budget and budgets of the budgetary system of the Russian Federation. Access mode: minfin.gov.ru/ru /

Nordhaus, W., & Romer, P. (2019). The Sveriges Riksbank prize in economic sciences in memory of Alfred Nobel. *Scandinavian Journal of Economics*, *121*(11), 857–858.

Piketty, T., Yang, L., & Zucman, G. (2019). Capital accumulation, private property, and rising inequality in China. *American Economic Review*, *109*(7), 2469–2496.

Prime. (2023, February 10) The expert commented on the scale of capital outflow from Russia https://1prime.ru/finance/20230210/839772117.html

Rampini, A. A., & Viswanathan, S. (2018). Financial intermediary capital. *Review of Economic Studies*, *85*(4), 1937–197.

Ruščáková, A. (2015). The European sovereign debt crisis: The result of the financial globalisation and of the system failures of global economic and political order. *Globalization and Its Socio-Economic Consequences* (617–626).

Sen, A. (2015). The idea of justice: A response. *Philosophy & Social Criticism*, *41*(1), 77–88.

Stiglitz, J. (2015). The origins of inequality, and policies to contain it. *National Tax Journal*, *68*(2), 425–448.

Tabah, A., Procudin, A., & Podrugina, A. (2021). The Russian public debt market: Is there life under sanctions during the pandemic. *Expert*. https://raexpert.ru/researches/public_debt_2021 / (accessed: 05/21/2023)

The BRICS Summit. (2023, April 18). Bloomberg calculated that the BRICS "left the West behind" in the growth of economies. RBC. https://www.rbc.ru/economics/18/04/2023/643ddd2d9a7947e6c741245c

The Central Bank of the Russian Federation. (2023). Annual reports of the Bank of Russia. [electronic resource]. URL: https://cbr.ru/about_br/publ/god (accessed: 05/21/2023)

Van Velthoven, A., De Haan, J., & Sturm, J. E. (2019). Finance, income inequality and income redistribution. *Applied Economics Letters*, *26*(14), 1202–1209.

Asadula Asadulaev[1], Vladimir Urazgaliev[1,*], Andrey Agashin[1], and Galina Menshikova[1]

Global Trends in the World Gas Market in Conditions of Turbulence and High Uncertainty: Price Convergence and Changes in the Structure of Demand

Abstract:
Research background: At present, changes are taking place in the world gas market that affect both consumer countries and countries-suppliers of this energy resource. In a situation of high instability and non-stationarity of gas prices, their unpredictability, an unprecedented increase in prices, as in August 2022 at the Dutch TTF hub to €323.9 per 1 MWh, there was a divergence in prices for world gas markets, despite continued convergence until 2020. These changes affected a number of regional markets, especially countries with market prices, as well as the global gas market as a whole.
Purpose of the article: Consider the processes of convergence of prices and demand for gas in different regions of the world depending on price models, identify the causes of convergence or divergence in the world gas markets and assess the prospects.
Methods: Analysis of time series stationarity, study of cointegration of natural gas prices in different regions of the world, factor analysis.
Findings & Value added: The article contains a time series analysis of natural gas price patterns before and after 2021, the main trends in import volumes by region depending on price patterns, and the impact of reduced natural gas price convergence on the global natural gas market as a whole.

Keywords: *world gas market, gas prices, price convergence, gas imports*

JEL Classification: *C32; F63; Q41*

---

* Corresponding author: uvsh54@yandex.ru
1 St. Petersburg State University, Faculty of Economics, 7/9 Universitetskaya nab., St. Petersburg, 199034 Russia

1 Introduction

In the pre-crisis period of 2020, there was a steady trend towards the universal integration of global natural gas markets, which manifested itself in the convergence of world prices for natural gas and LNG for various regions of the world. In the process of globalization, liberalization and expansion of spot trade in natural gas up to 2020, there was a tendency to decrease the rate of variation in natural gas prices from 43 % to almost 33 % in 2005–2020 for countries where the prevailing mechanism of pricing for natural gas is the market mechanism or the so-called "liberal" pricing. For countries engaged in natural gas pricing, mainly with reference to the price of crude oil and petroleum products under the OPE pricing mechanism, the dispersion in the same period turned out to be less and was at the level of 25–30 %, which indicated a low variation in natural gas prices in this group of countries. These trends persisted until recently and indicated a convergence of prices in various regions of the world against the background of an increase in LNG supplies.

After the energy crisis of 2021–2022, which affected many European countries, there were changes in the global natural gas markets – the convergence of prices in the global natural gas market for countries with a competitive market pricing mechanism, GOG "Gas-on-Gas" has sharply decreased, with a relatively stable convergence of natural gas prices in countries with pricing by the OPE "Oil Price Escalation" mechanism with reference to the price of oil and petroleum products. Against the background of an unprecedented increase in gas prices in August 2022 at the Dutch TTF hub to 323.9 euros per 1 MWh, the price discrepancy intensified, against the background of turbulence in spot gas prices and high uncertainty about the future regarding the dynamics of the latter, the convergence of natural gas prices was replaced by divergence and new global energy trends.

2 Materials and Methods

The research on the integration of global natural gas markets, including the analysis of the dynamics of natural gas prices before and after the energy crisis of 2021–2022, has been devoted to the work of many researchers (Urazgaliev & Titkov, 2018; Novikov et al., 2021). For example, some of them (Novikov et al., 2021) point to the relative independence of the gas markets in Europe, Asia, and the USA, with a possible convergence of prices against the background of their growth after the 2020 pandemic. It is impossible not to deny the existing contradictions arising in the emerging natural gas market in the global world, including those related to the transportation of natural gas and the existing gas transportation infrastructure, against the background of the geopolitical struggle for increasing LNG supplies from the United States to the EU (Urazgaliev & Titkov, 2018; Filimonova et al., 2022).

According to a number of researchers, the global energy crisis of 2021–2022 led to the need to save "blue fuel" for various sectors of industry and for the population of a number of countries, and its shortage, for example, in Germany, led to a reduction in natural gas consumption in the second half of 2022 by 23 % compared to the baseline level (Ruhnau et al., 2023). However, the decline in natural gas supplies from Russia was not the only and not the main factor that influenced the energy crisis in the EU countries. This process was primarily due to the key role of the ultra-liberal pricing mechanism and spot trading, which led to an unprecedented increase in gas prices and their stochastic nature or unsteadiness against the background of demand for natural gas and its limited supply in the EU. Despite the fact that during 1980–2020. the dynamics of prices for natural gas, as well as for many other types of energy resources, maintained a trend-stationary character (Landajo, 2021), already today it is becoming obvious that there has been an increase in the number of factors affecting price dynamics, such as the transformation of existing pricing models and the transition to competitive pricing, and the strengthening of the seasonal component in the analysis of the stationarity of time series.

In these conditions, the unpredictability and increased dispersion of prices at European gas hubs and the idea of overcoming the uncertainty of the future dynamics of natural gas prices using various modern forecasting methods, for example, predicting the volatility of natural gas prices in a cloud of uncertainty, received the most attention (Chen et al., 2023). So, even after the COVID-2019 crisis, global uncertainty has significantly increased (Chen et al., 2023), and in the current period, the need to achieve carbon neutrality, including overcoming uncertainty in the oil supply and demand markets, which is closely related to natural gas markets and its prices, global uncertainty has become an independent subject of research, including in relation to the study of specific regional energy markets and natural gas markets. In the context of this uncertainty, forecasting spot gas prices is one of the most important issues requiring the most modern methods of solutions (Mouchtaris et al., 2021; Pei et al., 2023).

In our opinion, in the conditions of the current uncertainty, the convergence of natural gas prices may be due to their relative stability and predictability, as well as the immutability of their dispersion over time, which is the basis of such a concept as stationarity. Presumably, it is the non-stationary nature of the price dynamics of natural gas that can cause prices to diverge in different regions, while their stationarity leads to relatively less dispersion and a low coefficient of variation. In addition, in our opinion, the convergence of prices can be considered not only as a decrease in price variation in individual regions, but also as a convergence of prices in their absolute value.

3 Results and Discussion

Let's turn to the data presented in the report of the International Gas Union (IGU), which provides analytics on more than 100 global natural gas markets based on a database for 14 years. To assess the convergence of regional markets, the coefficient of variation (in %) (International Gas Union, 2022) is used, the higher the level of the indicator, the lower the convergence of prices in the studied markets, that is, there is a divergence, and vice versa. The coefficient of variation is calculated as the ratio of the standard deviation of the indicator to the average value (Jaworski et al., 2018) using the following formula:

$$CV = \frac{\sigma^{gas}_{price}}{\overline{x}_{price}} \quad (1)$$

where:

σ^{gas}_{price} standard deviation of natural gas prices;

$\overline{x}_{price}$ unweighted average price of natural gas by gas markets.

As a result of a significant decrease in average world prices for natural gas, implemented both by the GOG and OPE pricing mechanism, in 2012–2016 from 7.2–7.3 \$/MMBTU to 4.2–4.3 \$/MMBTU, the a significant decrease in their dispersion and the coefficient of variation as a whole from 68–69 % to 48–49 %, however The variation in natural gas prices remained high, and the sample was heterogeneous.

In addition, for countries with predominantly market pricing mechanisms (GOG, OPE, BIM), as well as regions connected by an integrated natural gas market and more able to carry out physical imports of natural gas, the convergence of prices was more noticeable.

It is important to note that the price convergence for various natural gas markets was more noticeable until 2020 for countries with OPE gas pricing linked to the price of oil and petroleum products than for countries with GOG pricing. After the crisis of 2020 and at the beginning of the energy crisis of 2021–2022, a new round appeared in the dynamics of prices at European gas hubs, which led to a divergence in natural gas prices and a high variation in world gas prices, implemented by the GOG mechanism (Figure 1).

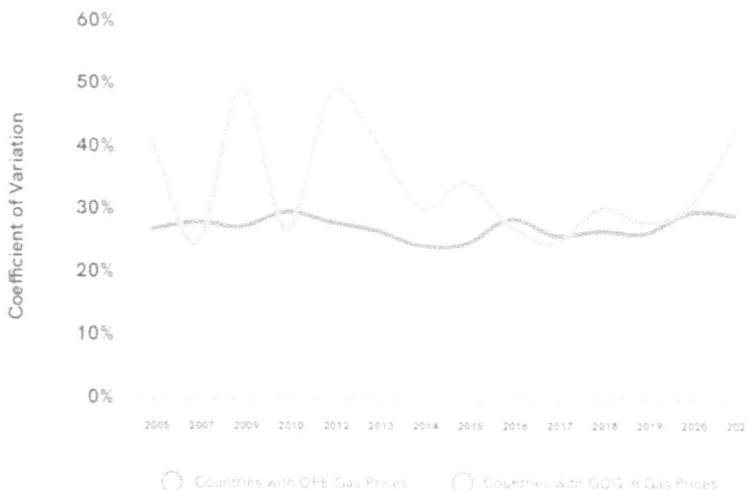

Figure 1. Price Convergence for OPE and GOG Prices.
Source: International Gas Union, 2022

With relatively stable dynamics of contract prices linked to the price of oil and petroleum products, the dynamics of prices at gas hubs in Europe demonstrated a high degree of uncertainty and unpredictability, was non-stationary. Despite this fact, price convergence in European countries remained higher (Figure 2), which is primarily related to the integrated gas market of the EU countries. The coefficient of variation in prices for natural gas sold under market pricing mechanisms for EU countries in 2021 turned out to be less than 25 %, while for all other countries in the same year (including EU countries), the indicator was about 45–46 % and indicated a high degree of variation, hence the divergence of world oil prices natural gas.

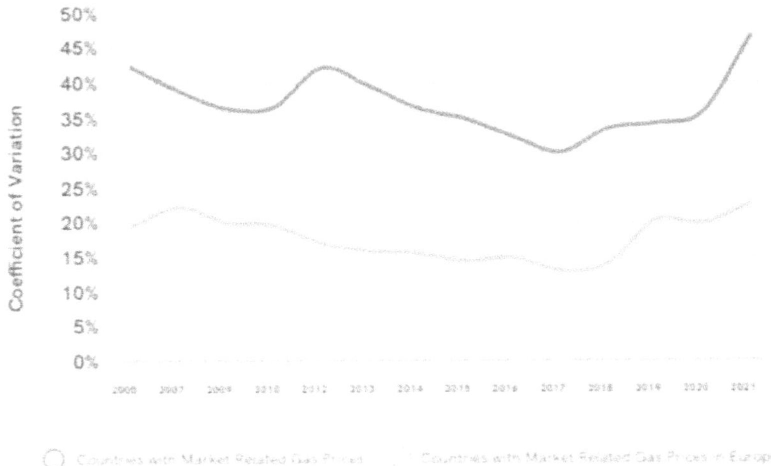

Figure 2. Price Convergence for Europe in 2005–2021.
Source: International Gas Union, 2022

Thus, despite the increased volatility of futures at the NBP hub in the UK, TTF in the Netherlands, the European gas market retained the convergence property, even under the condition of mutual non-stationarity of prices at these hubs, their linear combination presumably remained stationary due to the cointegration and coincidence of the general trend of these time series (Engle & Granger, 1987). Consequently, the stationary dynamics of natural gas prices may be characterized by less dispersion. If the price dynamics is unpredictable, then due to the property of co-integration of temporary prices for natural gas, it is possible to achieve their joint stationarity, which is possible thanks to the integrated natural gas market that has developed in the EU. The convergence of prices was also manifested in the relationship between electricity and natural gas prices on European markets during the energy crisis of 2021–2022. (Uribe et al., 2022).

Discussion of the problem of high natural gas prices during the energy crisis of 2021–2022 is conducted by various authors (Kotek et al., 2023). Thus, to solve this problem in the EU, the implementation of the fifth PCI package adopted by the European Commission in November 2021 was undertaken, which was aimed at significantly reducing prices in the EU, especially in the eastern member states, most of which largely depend on a single source of natural gas supplies (Kotek et al., 2023). Among these packages, the majority, about 67 out of 98 key projects, are related to electricity transmission and storage projects in Western Europe, Central-Eastern and Southern Europe, as well as in the Baltic States as part of their energy system interconnection projects, including 20 projects aimed at creating a new EU gas infrastructure (Enerdata, 2021).

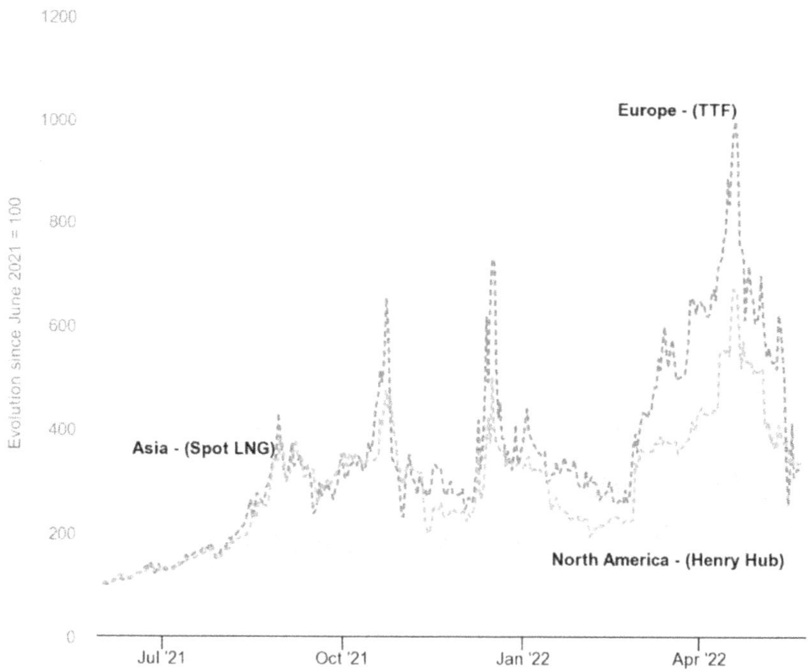

Figure 3. Evolution of key regional natural gas prices, June 2021–October 2022.
Source: IEA, 2022

In 2022, the EU adopted a Joint Gas Procurement Mechanism when gas prices in Asia reached a record high. Also in December 2022, the EU Energy Council adopted a temporary market correction mechanism to reduce excessive price volatility at European gas hubs. This mechanism provides for a ceiling limit on gas prices in the amount of the base price of LNG plus 35 euros/MWh and is activated if gas prices for a month in advance for three consecutive days exceed 180 euros/MWh and the gas hub price TTF price for a month in advance by 35 euros/MWh is higher than the price of LNG on the world market during the same three days (IEA, 2023).

Indeed, in order to overcome the increased volatility of natural gas prices, it is necessary to search for new effective mechanisms and methods of regulating natural gas pricing, and it is desirable that these mechanisms be coordinated with each other in order to achieve single market integration (Uribe et al., 2022).

Convergence of prices is possible not only within individual regions, but also for the emerging global natural gas market in the process of universal integration and globalization. Let's take a look at the dynamics of natural gas prices after the global energy crisis in such key regions as Asia, Europe and North America (Figure 3).

After prices on the Dutch TTF jumped more than 8.9 times on August 26, 2022, compared to June 2021, a trend towards convergence of prices and their even greater divergence became noticeable. Thus, until August 2022, the European natural gas market had a closer price relationship with the Asian market and similar dynamics in gas prices (Figure 3), compared to the relatively isolated North American gas market. After the sharp increase in gas prices, the dynamics of prices for spot Asian gas and European TTF remained similar, but the discrepancy in absolute prices or interregional divergence became noticeable. By the end of 2022, the convergence of gas prices had become noticeable again after the attempts of the EU Energy Council to stabilize the dynamics of natural gas prices in conditions of high uncertainty. In turn, energy regulation can be considered a kind of strategic influence tool (Boute, 2022), which affects not only the convergence of world gas prices, but also the processes of forming a single gas market.

4 Conclusion

The analysis presented in the paper of the dynamics of time series for natural gas for various regions in the period before and after the energy crisis of 2021 indicates a decrease in the convergence of world prices for natural gas or the reverse trend – divergence. At the same time, the dynamics of prices for natural gas sold under the OPE mechanism with reference to the price of oil and petroleum products remained less volatile in comparison with prices for gas sold under the GOG mechanism, which is due to their greater exposure to market mechanisms during the energy crisis.

Despite the fact that Europe turned out to be the region most exposed to the energy crisis, price convergence in this region turned out to be higher, and price variation was not so significant (the coefficient of variation was less than 25 %), due to the formed single natural gas market.

The energy crisis of 2021–2022 showed an increase in the divergence of world gas prices, which is an obstacle to the formation of a global natural gas market. Divergence of gas prices leads to a separation of interests in the creation of a unified gas infrastructure.

In the future, it is possible to return to intraregional convergence, however, with a greater level of price divergence between individual regions, if effective mechanisms for controlling natural gas prices are not adopted, which could strengthen the processes of formation of the global natural gas market and ensure its sustainable functioning.

References

Boute, A. (2022). Shaping the Eurasian Gas Market: The geopolitics of energy market regulation. *Geopolitics,28*(5), 2042–2073.

Chen, J., Xiao, Z., Bai, J., & Guo, (2023). Predicting volatility in natural gas under a cloud of uncertainties. *Resources Policy, 82*(C), Article 103436.

Enerdata. (2021, November). *European Commission adopts 5th list of energy Projects of Common Interest.* https://www.enerdata.net/publications/daily-energy-news/european-commission-adopts-5th-list-energy-projects-common-interest.html

Engle, R. F., & Granger, C. W. J. (1987). Co-integration and error correction: Representation, estimation and testing. *Econometrica, 55*(2), 251–276.

Filimonova, I. V., Komarova, A. V., Sharma, R., & Novikov, A. Y. (2022). Transformation of international liquefied natural gas markets: New trade routes. *Energy Reports, 8*, 675–682.

IEA. (2023, November). Gas Market Report, Q1-2023. https://www.iea.org/reports/gas-market-report-q1-2023

IEA. (2022, October). Global Energy Crisis. https://www.iea.org/topics/global-energy-crisis

International Gas Union. (2022, October). Wholesale Price Report 2022 https://www.igu.org/resources/2022-wholesale-price-report

Jaworski, A., Kuszewski, H., Ustrzycki, A., Balawender, K., Lejda, K., & Woś, P. (2018). Analysis of the repeatability of the exhaust pollutants emission research results for cold and hot starts under controlled driving cycle conditions. *Environmental Science and Pollution Research, 25*(18), 17862–17877.

Kotek, P., Selei, A., Toth, B., & Felsmann, B. (2023). What can the EU do to address the high natural gas prices? *Energy Policy, 173*, Article 113312.

Landajo, M., Presno, M. J., & González, P. F. (2021). Stationarity in the prices of energy commodities. A nonparametric approach. *Energies*, *14*(11), Article 3324.

Mouchtaris, D., Sofianos, E., Gogas, P., & Papadimitriou, Th. (2021). Forecasting natural gas spot prices with machine learning. *Energies*, *14*(18), Article 5782.

Novikov, A., Urazgaliev, V., & Titkov, M. (2021). Prospects for the formation of a global natural gas market: Price analysis of European, Asian, American Gas Markets. *SHS Web of Conferences*, *92*, Article 07044.

Pei, Y., Huang, C.-J., Shen, Y., & Wang, M. A. (2023). Novel model for spot price forecast of natural gas based on temporal convolutional network. *Energies*, *16*(5), Article 2321.

Ruhnau, O., Stiewe, C., Müßel, J., & Hirth, L. (2023). Natural gas savings in Germany during the 2022 energy crisis. *Nature Energy*, *8*(6), 621–628.

Urazgaliev, V. Sh., & Titkov M. V. (2018). A gas component of energy security of Russia. *St Petersburg University Journal of Economic Studies*, *34*(2), 179–216.

Uribe, J., Mosquera-López, S., & Arenas, O. (2022). Assessing the relationship between electricity and natural gas prices in European markets in times of distress. *Energy Policy*, *166*, Article 113018.

Ovidiu Andrei Cristian Buzoianu[1,*], Oana Camelia Iacob (Pargaru)[2], Ion Pargaru[2], Radu Alexandru Chiotan[3], and Irina Elena Petrescu[1]

The Electricity Crisis in the Context of Globalization

Abstract:
Research background: The energy sector is a key sector for the national economy of any contemporary state, which is in close interdependence with other branches of the economy. The energy crisis leads to the stagnation of the economy, and the change in macroeconomic indicators.
Purpose of the article: The present paper proposes to present the most important theoretical and practical aspects of the energy crisis in the context of globalization, through an analysis of the European Union level, but also at the regional level – Romania.
Methods: Mix research technique has been used. While qualitative research entails in-depth literature readings and reports, quantitative analysis entails presenting data via graphs and tables.
Findings & Value added: Following these researches, the economic, social and ecological impact was found, determined on the one hand by the depletion of resources at the global level, and on the other hand, by the war in Ukraine and the directly proportional increase in prices. Globalization has determined a more careful management of new energies, an interstate exchange of ideas, as well as the creation of economic and environmental policies, aimed at solving the energy crisis at the European and, of course, global level. The article adds value through the analysis carried out at the European and Romanian level and through the interpretation of statistical data..

Keywords: *electricity, energy, European Union, globalization*

JEL Classification: *013; P18; Q42*

* Corresponding author: ovidiu.buzoianu@man.ase.ro
1 Bucharest University of Economic Studies, Romana Square 6, Bucharest, Romania
2 Polytechnic University, Splaiul Independenței 313, Bucharest, Romania
3 Carol Davila UMF, Boulevard of Sanitary Heroes 8, Bucharest, Romania

1 Introduction

Human society cannot continue its life without electricity, without light in the house, without refrigerators, elevators or technological equipment (Hoppe & De Vries, 2019). The war in Ukraine brings to the fore a series of problems that, until now, Europeans did not even think about. The risk of experiencing significant power outages in the dead of winter is one of them (Zakeri et al., 2022).

It does not necessarily have to be a major energy supply crisis (Rădulescu et al., 2023). Recent events, as well as history, have shown us that a major power failure can also occur due to an act of sabotage, but also due to calamities (Bodislav et al., 2020). Despite the apocalyptic scenarios that often circulate in the public eye, no one can know if or when Europe will actually experience an energy crisis so acute that it leads to rationing or power cuts (Connolly et al., 2016).

All the incidents that are taking place worldwide feed an old fear, we can be left not only without electricity, but also without internet connections. (Mudakkar et al., 2013). In addition to electrical cables, the largest digital superhighway passes through the waters of the seas: almost all Internet traffic travels through 400 fiber optic pipes that add up to 1.3 million kilometers (Johansson et al., 2019). The size of a garden hose, through these cables pass not only the data sent by the population, but, for example, also those transmitted by the financial markets (Chowdhury et al., 2019). And much of it is in international waters, making it harder for governments to protect (Burlacu et al., 2020).

Electricity is of vital importance for the economic and social development of the contemporary world, the consumption of electricity being indispensable for all sectors of activity (Argyrou et al., 2018). The introduction of modern technologies (mechanization, robotization, automation) cannot be achieved without electricity (Angheluta et al., 2019). The increase in the level of material and spiritual life of the world population (Bodislav et al., 2021), of the level of civilization, be it urban or rural, is closely linked to electricity, production and consumption in the field becoming an indicator of the appreciation of the stage of economic – social development and the standard of living (Trinomics, 2020).

Electricity has a number of qualities (Cantarero, 2020):

- It is convertible into other forms of primary energy (light, mechanical, thermal, chemical).
- It is easily transported over long distances with minimal losses.
- It is non-polluting.

2 Methodology

Mix research technique has been used. While qualitative research entails in-depth literature readings and reports, quantitative analysis entails presenting data via graphs and tables.

The development of the article on the research topic that we have proposed involves the use of the main research methods, specific to the field of economic sciences and not only. Thus, among the main scientific research methods for the elaboration of the paper, we can mention: the comparison method

With the help of deduction and induction methods, it was possible to argue the necessity of the energy policy, as well as the positive role played by this community space. Starting from concrete examples, from the results, it was possible to extrapolate some arguments in favor of new energy implementation strategies based on alternative, non-polluting resources. Through the deductive method, arguments were brought to justify the Energy Policy. I used the analysis method on this article, when I examined the different aspects in the targeted field, seen as the basic policy, respectively the implementation of this policy in European states.

3 Results and Discussion

3.1 The Electricity Crisis at the Level of the European Union

In the natural gas market, Europe has the largest imbalance: it consumes 14.2 % of world production, but produces only 5.7 % of it. So it remains the biggest importer. Reducing dependence on Russian gas remains a distant wish. For several years, it appeared that the Old Continent was on the right track – imports of liquefied natural gas, the advance of renewable resources and the opening of new high-capacity gas pipelines to ensure flows from the Caspian Basin had the potential to put Europe at ease from the Kremlin's games. So many commercial contracts with Gazprom were terminated or reduced.

The deficits were successfully covered on the international exchanges, being small quantitie (Sarbu et al., 2021). Now, the lack of stable contracts with the only supplier that can consistently ensure high volumes- Gazprom- leaves European states vulnerable to increasingly high international quotations.

Now, the Russian president is giving assurances that he will not use natural gas as a weapon in his ideological disputes with the European Union and that he will make available to the EU bloc exactly the amount they demand and need.

Analysts warn, however, that the moment is a crossroads in EU-Russia relations: the signing of new medium- or long-term contracts would bring Europe out of winter and stabilize prices, but would again give unwanted power to the Kremlin- and that for many years. So far, the Kremlin has pointed out that the lack of these stable contracts makes negotiations difficult and keeps prices high.

Europe's energy crisis deepens as Russia further curbs natural gas exports, forcing governments to spend billions to protect businesses and consumers from rising bills as the region looks ever closer to a recession (Diaconu et al., 2019).

The reference price of natural gas in Europe (Dutch Title Transfer Facility) increased by about 28 %, reaching 275 euros per megawatt hour. Benchmark natural gas futures fell 2.5 %.

Russia has shut down all natural gas flows to Europe via the Nord Stream 1 pipeline, adding a new risk factor to the already crowded mix weighing on the markets. Russian energy company Gazprom has halted flows through the vital Nord Stream 1 pipeline indefinitely, claiming it had found an oil leak in a turbine. Some states are being forced to take quick action, bracing for significant spending to try to limit the impact on consumers.

For example, the German government announced an aid package of 65 billion euros to help households and companies cope with accelerating inflation. Germany, Europe's largest economy, is particularly dependent on Russian gas exports to power its homes and heavy industry, the initiative brings the total amount of the government support package to 95 billion euros, equivalent to about 2.5 % of Germany's GDP.

Earlier, Germany, which has been trying to reduce its heavy reliance on Russian gas, pledged to cut the value-added tax on natural gas from 19 % to 7 % by the end of March 2024. The state approved two aid packages totaling 30 billion euros to help its citizens with rising energy prices this year. The German government will offer all taxpayers a one-off payment of €300 to pay their energy bills.

In Romania, the government has implemented a scheme of capping gas and electricity bills for households and other users, up to certain monthly consumption levels, and compensating energy suppliers for the difference. The scheme will be in place until March 2023. Although the scheme was initially estimated to cost €3 billion, analysts now expect it to exceed the €10 billion mark.

The commission will propose a price cap for Russian gas, a mandatory target for reducing peak-hour electricity consumption, a cap on the revenue of companies that do not produce electricity with natural gas, a "solidarity contribution" from fossil fuel companies, which have posted record profit levels, and aid for utility companies facing liquidity problems.

3.2 Causes of the Electrical Energy Crisis at the Level of the European Union

The energy crisis manifests itself in the European Union through the lack of energy because the production capacities do not have raw materials, which leads to an increase in prices (Fitó et al., 2021). The market is poorly organized, even if the model proved valid in peacetime. In the current situation when Russia started a warm war against Ukraine and an energy war against the EU, it is demonstrated that the adopted model is no longer reliable for such a critical situation.

The main cause that destabilized the world energy market is the reckless war launched by Russia against Ukraine, and solving the energy crisis can only be achieved by respecting three basic principles: cooperation, investment and solidarity.

In addition to the geopolitical factor, there is a mix of continental events that led to the current reality:

- Very low nuclear availability in France (Electricite de France recently lowered its 2023 production guidance to 300–330 TWh and is now experiencing cooling issues affecting the already low level of availability for 2022.)
- Historically low levels of hydropower storage from Scandinavia to the Iberian Peninsula (given widespread drought conditions.)
- Closures of thermal power plants in Western Europe (in the case of old technology coal, nuclear and gas plants.)
- Fuel supply logistics driven by a combination of very low water levels in the Rhine (eg impact on coal delivery to German power stations) and logistical issues driven by the conflict in Russia.
- Periods of low levels of wind and solar production.

3.3 The Effects of the Electrical Energy Crisis

There are many effects of the electricity crisis at the level of the European Union, but one of the most important is that some of the largest consumers of electricity reduce their production because the increase in electricity prices leads to an increase in production costs and would affect companies from a financial point of view as well as from a competitive perspective (Profiroiu et al., 2020). Industries in Europe's largest economy are suffering a major impact, the list of industries reducing production is growing (Oskouei et al., 2020). The food and beverage industry, the chemical industry and even oil processing are on the list of sectors affected by the energy crisis.

For example, the Alvance Company, the largest aluminum producer, reduced its production by 4 % as the outages of several nuclear power plants led to an increase in electricity prices in France. Nyrstar, the zinc producer owned by commodities trader Trafigura, said it would shut a 150,000-tons-a-year smelter in Auby, France after Christmas due to record electricity prices.

Poland's largest chemical company, Grupa Azoty, has stopped producing some of its key products and cut ammonia production due to record gas prices. In France, new orders fell this month in both services and manufacturing.

In these moments of balance for the European Union, we are forced to make drastic savings in what it means to use electricity. Excessively high costs have a negative impact on households and companies (Osman et al., 2022).

The situation in Germany is particularly difficult: the country's dependence on Russian gas makes it vulnerable as it desperately seeks alternative methods of supply. The state is considering restarting coal plants and could extend the life of remaining nuclear plants, but at the same time it is also urging gas conservation. Industries in Europe's largest economy are suffering a major impact.

As Europe's largest economy, the combination of industrial exposure and energy-intensive industries could have a significant impact on Germany as the crisis continues.

3.4 Measures to Overcome the Crisis

Through the Versailles Declaration, agreed in March 2022, EU leaders of the 27 member states agreed to phase out the EU's dependence on Russian fossil fuels as soon as possible.

At the end of May, the European Council agreed on a ban on almost 90 % of all oil imports from Russia until the end of 2022, with a temporary exception for pipeline crude. The European Council urged the Council to finalize and adopt without delay the sixth sanctions package, which will include this ban.

Given the different energy mixes, conditions and circumstances of EU Member States, EU leaders have called for:

- further diversification of energy supply sources and routes;
- accelerating the use of renewable energy sources;
- further improvement of energy efficiency;
- improving the interconnections between the gas and electricity networks.

In early June, the Council adopted the sixth package of sanctions against Russia, which includes the ban on oil imports agreed by EU leaders in May 2022.

Towards the end of this month, referring to the Versailles Declaration, EU leaders reiterated the invitation to the Commission to explore together with international partners ways to limit the increase in energy prices, including the feasibility of introducing temporary price ceilings.

In the context of the use of gases as a weapon by Russia, the European Council invited the Commission to urgently continue efforts to ensure the supply of energy at affordable prices.

Three major measures are highlighted in order to reduce the enormous costs of electricity bills, as follows:

1 Reduction of electricity consumption;
   a. Voluntary measures to reduce overall electricity use by 10 % in the EU by the end of March 2023;
   b. The obligation of EU countries to reduce consumption by at least 5 % during peak hours;
   c. States choose their mitigation measures.
      i. **Expected result**
         (1) Maintaining stocks of fuel and gas used for the production of electricity;
         (2) Positive price effect.

2 **Capping the income of electricity producers;**

3 **Introduction of a solidarity contribution from fossil fuel companies;**
   a. The contribution should come from the profits of companies that have increased by more than 20 % compared to the average profits of the last 4 years;
   b. This targets companies in the oil, coal and refinery sectors;
   c. Revenues can be collected by EU member states and will be distributed to families and businesses.

The European Parliament also approved the EU budget targeting the energy crisis. New energy sources and renewable energy, as well as support for SMEs affected by the cost of energy, a package of 535 million euros was proposed above the draft budget. The European Commission is proposing that member states buy gas together in order to cope with high energy prices and ensure security of supply.

The increase in the prices of energy resources creates a chain reaction on the prices of all goods and services, while the disposable income of the majority of the population remains intact. In a short time the population will realize that they are getting poorer every day. Increasing population polarization, widening the gap between the rich and the poor can lead to mass unrest (Davi-Arderius & Schittekatte, 2023).

In order not to admit this, and to keep the loyalty of the electorate, some member countries of the European Union began to promote policies to support the vulnerable. France has announced that it will grant a donation of 100 euros each to more than 5.8 million low-income families.

Europe took the path of the green economy, the nuclear power plants, the power stations, which operated on the basis of coal, were closed. In addition, two months without wind in northwestern Europe prevented wind power from being produced, which also caused a shortage of natural gas (Battle et al., 2022).

The created situation proves that in the near future the 100 % transition to the green economy is not feasible. Fossil resources still cannot be replaced, in the volume necessary for the national economy and the population, with renewable energy sources (Radulescu et al., 2020; Khan & Anwar, 2022).

The inefficient management of the energy sector propagated the energy crisis, therefore, to improve the situation, coal-fired power plants were put into operation, which inevitably leads to increased carbon dioxide emissions, and to an increase in the price of coal (Cambini et al., 2020).

3.5 The Effects of the Electrical Energy Crisis in Romania

Statistics from the last year show the efforts that Romania has made in order to protect its consumers and the business environment in the face of the increase in electricity. This effort cost 3 % of GDP, about 6.9 billion euros.

Rising prices for energy resources affect both producers and consumers. First of all, the energy component in the cost structure of manufactured products and services increases, which inevitably leads to a decrease in the competitiveness of goods on the foreign and domestic market

Table 1. The impact of the electricity crisis.

The impact of the electricity crisis	
On the national economy	**On society**
• Increase in the prices of goods and services • Inflation • Decreasing the competitiveness of goods at the internal and external level • Increase in the number of bankruptcies • Increasing the unemployment rate • GDP decrease • Increasing the trade balance deficit • Increasing the current account deficit of the balance of payments	• Reducing the solvency of the population • Increasing the Gini coefficient (economic inequality of the population) • Increase in the absolute poverty rate • Decrease in the well-being of the population

Source: own processing

The energy crisis led to the closure of many companies, or to the shortening of working hours, so that many people lost their jobs thus increasing the unemployment rate (Jamasb & Sen, 2022).

It can be seen that, in January, when the war was making its presence felt more and more acutely, the number of unemployed people was 234.072, 8.648 more than in September, when the war calmed down.

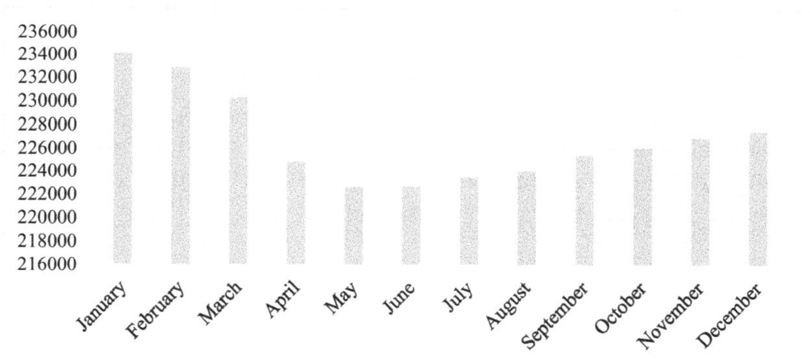

Figure 1. Total compensated/non-compensated unemployed in Romania, 2022.
Source: INSS (2022)

4 Conclusion

Energy prices hit record highs in 2022, particularly as a result of Russia's unjustified invasion of Ukraine and its use of gas supplies as a weapon of war.

The wholesale price of electricity on the EU internal market is directly linked to the price of gas, which is mostly imported. Russia's deliberate cut in gas supplies is the main cause of the recent spike in gas prices in the EU, which has had an impact on the price of electricity produced in gas-fired power plants and affected electricity prices in general.

Energy prices are expected to continue to remain high in the EU in the coming months as it takes time to replace gas supplies from Russia with EU sources of supply. EU countries have therefore adopted an emergency regulation to tackle the issue of high energy prices and help the citizens and businesses most affected by the energy crisis.

The energy crisis manifests itself in the European Union through the lack of energy because the production capacities do not have raw materials, which leads to an increase in prices. The market is poorly organized, even if the model proved valid in peacetime. In the current situation when Russia started a warm war against Ukraine and an energy war against the EU, it is demonstrated that the adopted model is no longer reliable for such a critical situation.

There can be no doubt that environmental issues and global warming are issues that need to be considered, only after academic researchers and energy industry professionals are asked, with moderate listening to environmental activists.

Another problem with the European energy market (gas and electricity) would be that it is not fully regulated. This market was financialized by a few companies and investment funds that imposed their own rules.

Thus, with the introduction of the energy futures market, the amounts and quantities of energy negotiated on this market far exceeded the amounts and quantities on the spot market, where the purpose of the transactions is the exchange of goods of actual energy consumed.

Acknowledgments

Thanks to the team for their help in writing this article. I would like to express my deep gratitude to my colleagues for their continuous encouragement, critical analysis of this article and guidance.

References

Angheluta, S. P., Burlacu, S., Diaconu, A., & Curea, C. S. (2019). The energy from renewable sources in the European Union: Achieving the goals. *European Journal of Sustainable Development, 8*(5), 57–65.

Argyrou, M. C., Christodoulides, P., & Kalogirou, S. A. (2018). Energy storage for electricity generation and related processes: Technologies appraisal and grid scale applications. *Renewable & Sustainable Energy Reviews, 94*, 804–821.

Cantarero, M. V. (2020). Of renewable energy, energy democracy, and sustainable development: A roadmap to accelerate the energy transition in developing countries. *Energy Research & Social Science, 70*, Article 101716.

Battle, C., Schittakate, T., & Knittel, C. (2022). Power price crisis in the EU: Unveiling current policy responses and proposing a balanced regulatory remedy. https://energy.mit.edu/publication/power-price-crisis-in-the-eu-unveiling-current-policy-responses-and-proposing-a-balanced-regulatory-remedy/

Bodislav, D. A., Burlacu, S., Rădulescu, C. V., & Gombos, S. P. (2021). Using a hybid economic indicator (BADEM) to evaluate the retail sector (R5N) and consumption. *7th BASIQ International Conference on New Trends in Sustainable Business and Consumption* (pp. 34–42).

Bodislav, D. A., Radulescu, C. V., Bran, F., & Burlacu, S. (2020). Public policy in the areas of environment and energy. In V. Dinu (Eds.), *6th BASIQ International Conference on New Trends in Sustainable Business and Consumption* (pp. 228–235).

Burlacu, S., Vasilache, P. C., Velicu, E. R., Curea, Ș. C., & Margina, O. (2020). Management of water resources at global level. In A. M. Dima (Eds.), *Proceedings of the International Conference on Economics and Social Sciences* (pp. 998–1009). Sciendo.

Cambini, C., Congiu, R., Jamasb, T., Llorca, M., & Soroush, G. (2020). Energy systems integration: Implications for public policy. *Energy Policy*, *143*, August, 111609.

Chowdhury, M. S. R., Azad, A. K., Karim, Md. R., Naser, J., & Bhuiyan, A. A. (2019). Reduction of GHG emissions by utilizing biomass co-fring in a swirl-stabilized furnace. *Renew Energy*, *143*, 1201–1209.

Connolly, D., Lund, H., & Mathiesen, B. V. (2016). Smart Energy Europe: The technical and economic impact of one potential 100% renewable energy scenario for the European Union. *Renewable & Sustainable Energy Reviews*, *60*, 1634–1653.

Davi-Arderius, D., & Schittekatte, T. (2023). Environmental impacts of redispatching in decarbonizing electricity systems: A Spanish case study. *Copenhagen Business School Working Paper, 01-2023CSEI(2023-01)*.

Diaconu, A., Popescu, M. L., Burlacu, S., & Buzoianu, O. (2019), Strategic options for the development of renewable energy in the context of globalization. In I. Popa, C. Dobrin, & C. N. Ciocoiu (Eds.), *Proceedings of the international management conference: Management strategies for High Performance* (pp. 1022–1029).

Fitó, J., Dimri, N., & Ramousse, J. (2021). Competitiveness of renewable energies for heat production in individual housing: A multicriteria assessment in a low-carbon energy market. *Energy Build*, *242*, Article 110971.

Hoppe, T., & De Vries, G. (2019). Social innovation and the energy transition. *Sustainability*, *11*(1), Article 141.

Jamasb, T., & Sen, A. (2022). The new energy state: A review of offshore governance regimes for renewables as natural resources. *Copenhagen Business School Working Paper, 2022-02(2022-05)*.

Johansson, I., Mardan, N., Cornelis, E., Kimura, O., & Thollander, P. (2019). Designing policies and programmes for improved energy efficiency in industrial SMEs. *Energies*, *12*(7), Article 1338.

Khan, M. T. I., & Anwar, S. (2022). Natural disasters and foreign exchange reserves: The role of renewable energy and human capital. *Renewable Energy, 192*, 838–848.

Mudakkar, S. R., Zaman, K., Khan, M. M., & Ahmad, M. (2013). Energy for economic growth, industrialization, environment and natural resources: Living with just enough. *Renewable & Sustainable Energy Reviews, 25*, 580–595.

Oskouei, M. Z., Mohammadi-Ivatloo, B., Abapour, M., Ahmadian, A., & Piran, Md. J. (2020). A novel economic structure to improve the energy label in smart residential buildings under energy efciency programs. *Journal of Cleaner Production, 260*, Article 121059.

Osman, A. I., Chen, L. Yang, M. Y., Msigwa, G., Farghali, M., Fawzy, S., Rooney, D. W., & Yap, P. S. (2022). Cost, environmental impact, and resilience of renewable energy under a changing climate: A review. *Environmental Chemistry Letters*.

Profiroiu, C. M., Rădulescu, C. V., & Burlacu, S. (2020). The challenges of Smart City in the context of globalization and the health crisis. *Proceedings of Administration and Public Management International Conference, 16*(1), 4–11.

Rădulescu, C. V., Bodislav, D. A., Burlacu, S., Bran, F., & Karimova, L. (2020). Econometric model for forecasting oil production in OECD member states. *In E3S Web of Conferences, 159*, Article 02005.

Rădulescu, C. V., Gâf-Deac, I. I., Bran, F., Mănescu, C. O., Bodislav, D. A., & Burlacu, S. (2023). The mix of resources, security and sustainability of the energy complex in Romania in the European Context. *The Amfiteatru Economic, 25*(63), 447–447.

Sarbu, R., Alpopi, C., Burlacu, S., & Diaconu, S. (2021). Sustainable urban development in the context of globalization and the health crisis caused by the covid-19 pandemic. *SHS Web of conferences, 92*, Article 01043.

Trinomics. (2020). *Energy Costs, Taxes and the Impact of Government Interventions on Investments, Final Report Network Costs, Trinomics by the Directorate-General for Energy*. https://data.europa.eu/doi/10.2833/827631

Zakeri, B. et al. (2022). Pandemic, war, and global energy transitions. *Energies, 15*(17), Article 6114.

Raluca Florentina Cretu[1,*], Florin Dobre[1], Catalin Octavian Mănescu[1], Carol Cristina Gombos[1], and Radu Florin Chiotan[2]

Population Dynamics and Food Security in Europe in the Context of Globalization

Abstract:
Research background: Health protection is the primary objective of all EU rules and standards for agriculture, animal husbandry and the food industry. European legislation covers both the entire food production and processing chain in the EU, as well as imported and exported goods. By population dynamics is meant all the changes that determine the population number, the structure and the spread of the population of a territory, in a certain time interval, as a result of births, deaths, immigrations and emigrations.
Purpose of the article: This article aims to analyze, using various quantitative or qualitative methods, the current situation in terms of population dynamics and the way in which, under the action of globalization, certain directions appear regarding food security at the level of the EU states.
Methods: Mix research technique has been used. While qualitative research entails in-depth literature readings and reports, quantitative analysis entails presenting data via graphs and tables.
Findings & Value added: Food insecurity has increased worldwide since 2016. Against the background of rising commodity prices worldwide last year and this year, Russia's war against Ukraine and the use of food as a weapon of war had a strong impact on food markets. The current study can represent a first step in creating viable and sustainable solutions at the population level, at the level of adequate resource management, so that food security is not deficient on large areas.

Keywords: *food, globalization, population, resources*

JEL Classification: *P42;Q56*

* Corresponding author: carmen-valentina.radulescu@eam.ase.ro
1 Bucharest University of Economic Studies, Romană Square, no. 1, district 1, Bucharest, Romania
2 Valahia University of Târgovişte, 13 Aleea Sinaia Street, 130004, Targoviste, Romania

1 Introduction

Population dynamics means all the changes that determine the no. population, the structure and distribution of the population of a territory, in a certain period of time, as a result of births, deaths, immigrations and emigrations (Seaman et al., 2014; Radulescu et al., 2018; Profiroiu et al., 2020).

The global population reached 8 billion people on November 15, 2022, considered a milestone in human development (Al-Saidi, 2023). The achievement of this unprecedented number is due to the gradual increase in human life expectancy, thanks to the improvement of the public health system at the global level, modern nutrition, the increase in the degree of hygiene and education (Burlacu, Stoica et al., 2022; Radulescu, Bran et al., 2020).

While the global population took 12 years to grow from 7 to 8 billion, it will take about 15 years, until 2037, for the planet's population to reach 9 billion, a sign that the overall growth rate of of the global population is slowing due to the increase in comfort, individualism, emancipation from traditions and living standards (Mediafax).

The latest UN projections show that the world's population could grow to around 8.5 billion in 2030 and 9.7 billion in 2050, before peaking at around 10.4 billion in the 2080s. The population is expected to remain at this level until 2100.

On January 1, 2021, 447.0 million people lived in the European Union. The most populous EU member state was Germany (83.2 million, 19 % of the EU total), followed by France (67.4 million, 15 %), Italy (59.3 million, 13 %), Spain (47.4 million, 11 %) and Poland (37.8 million, 9 %). In total, the population of these five Member States represented two thirds of the EU population. At the other end of the range, the least populated EU member states were Malta (500 thousand people, which corresponds to 0.1 % of the EU total), Luxembourg (600 thousand, 0.1 %) and Cyprus (900 thousand, 0.2 %).

Between 2001 and 2020, the EU's population grew from 429 million to 447 million, an increase of 4 %. Seventeen Member States recorded population increases during this period, while the other ten recorded decreases. Increases were recorded in Luxembourg, Malta.

2 Methods

The methodology adopted was a mixed one, combining qualitative and quantitative methods to provide an exhaustive perspective on the subject. The qualitative part of the research involved an analysis of specialized literature and relevant reports, with the aim of understanding the theoretical and practical context of population dynamics and food security within the European Union. This analysis focused on the interpretation and analysis of descriptive data, thus contributing to the theoretical grounding of the study.

In parallel, the quantitative part of the research included the presentation and interpretation of statistical data through graphs and tables. The data used in this section came from various statistical databases of the European Union, reports of international organizations and specialized studies. This method aimed to illustrate current and emerging trends in population dynamics and food security, thus providing a solid empirical basis for further analysis.

Data analysis was carried out through statistical and interpretive methods, with the aim of identifying significant patterns and correlations between the studied variables. This analysis was crucial to determine the impact of globalization factors on food security, in the context of European population dynamics. The results of qualitative and quantitative research were then integrated to form a holistic understanding of the subject, contributing to a deeper analysis of how globalization factors influence food security within the European Union, taking into account demographic changes.

3 Results

3.1 Demography of Europe

Demographic statistics are among the most popular data that Eurostat produces and are important for almost all policy areas (Aktürk & Lerski, 2021).The pandemic has reiterated how important it is that our policies resonate with people and protect them (Sarbu et al., 2021). What sets this new Eurostat publication apart is its simple and interactive way of bringing information about European demography to our citizens.

The population in the EU is aging, and this can be seen through a number of different statistical indicators: the evolution of the share of the elderly population, the old-age dependency ratio and the median age, to give a few examples (Burlacu, Oancea et al., 2020). Looking at the share of people aged 65 and over in the total population, Italy (23 %), Greece, Finland Portugal, Germany and Bulgaria (all 22 %) had the highest shares, while Ireland (14 %) and Luxembourg (15 %) had the lowest shares. The share of people aged 80 and over increased in all Member States between 2001 and 2020, except in Sweden, where it remained constant (5 %). In some Member States, this share has doubled in Lithuania and Croatia from 2 % in 2001 to 6 % in 2020, in Romania, Bulgaria and Slovenia from 2 % to 5 %.

As for young people, the highest shares of under-20s in the total population were seen in Ireland (27 %), France (24 %) and Sweden (23 %), while the lowest percentages were recorded in Malta, Italy and Germany (all 18 %). In the period 2001–2020, a decrease in the share of young people could be observed in all member states.

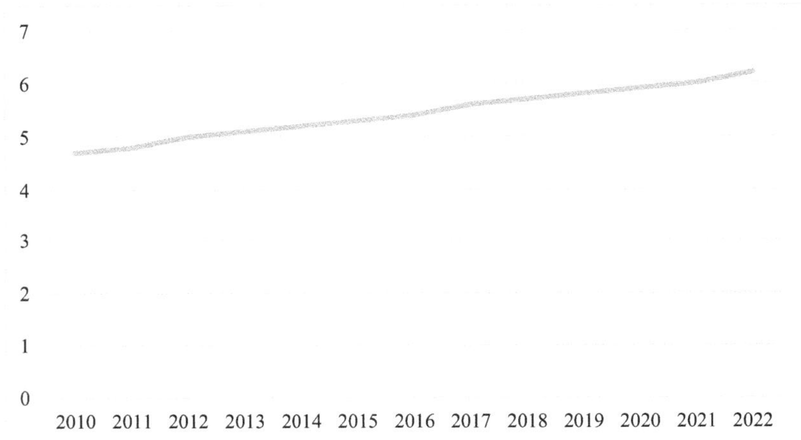

Figure 1. Share of population aged 80 and over, 2010–2022.
Source: Eurostat (2022a)

3.2 Demographic Changes – Trends

In 2021, life expectancy at birth increased to 78.2 years for men and 83.7 for women. This increase is expected to continue: men born in 2070 will live 86 years and women 90.

In 2018, the average number of births per woman was 1.55, and their average age at birth was 31.3.

By 2070, 30.3 % of the population is projected to be 65 years or older (compared to 20.3 % in 2019) and 13.2 % is projected to be 80 or older (compared to 5.8 % in 2019);

Across the EU as a whole, the composition of our households is changing- two-parent households with children are being joined by households made up of people living alone, lone parents or couples without children. Some choose to move or live abroad, but the size of these flows is volatile and can change quickly. Europe's share of the world's population is shrinking and by 2070 it will represent just under 4 % of the world's population.

3.2.1 Overpopulation

In demography, the term overpopulation refers to a state in which the total population in a given region far exceeds the carrying capacity of that region. Although this term refers to the ratio of population to available surface area, the ratio of population to accessible resources should not be ignored either.

The overpopulation of the planet is mainly attributed to the fact that people nowadays live longer and have a higher birth rate. In some cases, the overpopulation of a region is the result of mass migration.

The consequences of global overpopulation are diverse. First of all, it is worth mentioning the accelerated destruction of available natural resources and, above all, the consumption of resources that do not allow their cyclical recovery. This is what we mean when we say "we consume the natural resources of future generations. In other words, we consume more than the Earth can produce. This involves the destruction of the natural means of producing resources (Crippa et al., 2022). When the population grows the first and greatest risk is related to the resources consumed, many of which are non-renewable. From deforestation, to illegal fishing or hunting, mining, to a possible food crisis, all are effects that destroy the natural ecosystem, the balance that ultimately ensures our life.

Overpopulation is a threat to the survival of mankind, and if this cannot be controlled, then the effects will be one that will destroy the environment, which is the equivalent of life. Moreover, there is the risk of a food crisis, which will lead to big problems in all areas of life (Martin-Shields & Stojetz, 2019).

Analysts explain that education brings in some parts of the world an unprecedented decision: to give up having children. This is not because people think so far, about overpopulation, but in highly developed countries people feel the need to develop professionally, thereby giving up their family (Flies et al., 2018). We are currently dealing with an extreme situation: while the birth rate is skyrocketing in developing countries, in states that have already reached a high level of education the birth rate is falling. Today's statistics still show the fact that the balance tends towards an unprecedented increase in the population (Fanzo et al., 2018).

To improve the efficiency of human activities, it is necessary to carry out research and development processes. They enable the development of new technologies that will later have applications in the various fields that influence well-being on the planet. In this way, it is an area that cannot go unnoticed. When it comes to providing solutions to global overpopulation, it takes more time than solutions that reduce consumption in the short term (Fanelli, 2019).

3.2.2 Overcrowding

The overcrowding rate is defined as the percentage of the population living in an overcrowded dwelling, and a person is considered to live in an overcrowded house if it does not have a minimum number of rooms available equal to one room per couple in the household, a room for each person aged 18 or over, one room per pair of single persons of the same sex between 12 and 17 years; one room for each person between the ages of 12 and 17, who is not included in the previous category; a room for a pair of children under 12 years old (Hasegawa et al., 2018).

Romania is the country with the highest rate of housing overcrowding in the European Union (48.4 %), followed by Latvia with 43.2 % of the country's population, Bulgaria (42.5 %), Croatia (41.1 %) , Poland (40.7 %), Hungary (40.4 %) and Slovakia (37.9 %), and around one in four citizens of Greece (28.7 %), Italy (27.8 %) and Lithuania (23.7 %).

At the opposite end of the scale, the lowest overcrowding rates were recorded in Cyprus (2.4 %), Malta (2.9 %), Ireland (3.2 %), Belgium (3.7 %), the Jos (4.0 %) and Spain 5.4 %. Overpopulation was also a problem for less than 10 % of the population in Finland (6.6 %), Germany (7.2 %), France (7.7 %), the United Kingdom (8.0 %) and Luxembourg (8.1 %).

In the European Union (EU), 16.6 % of the population lived in overcrowded housing in 2016, which means that they did not have the number of rooms appropriate to the size of the household. On the other hand, more than one in three people (34.8 %) in the EU lived in under-occupied housing, meaning that housing was considered too large, in terms of excessive spaces and especially bedrooms, for the needs of the occupant's household (Eurostat, 2018).

3.3 The Ratio of Wealth to Poverty

Although the income and wealth gap between the rich and the poor has grown in the European Union over the last decades, the EU bloc is still a world leader in combating inequality, say economic analysts (Benevolenza & DeRigne, 2019).

The internationally accepted Gini coefficient formula to measure the disproportion in the distribution of income and wealth places the European Union as a whole in one of the best positions worldwide.

In 2020, the European Union registered a value of this coefficient of 31, on a scale from 0 to 100, an increasing value illustrating a higher level of inequality. But the score obtained by the EU states taken separately differs a lot between them, the average being negatively influenced by some Eastern states as well.

Bulgaria registers the highest level of economic inequality, with a Gini coefficient of 40, according to Eurostat data. It is followed by Lithuania and Latvia, then by Spain, Portugal and Greece, followed by Romania with a coefficient of 33.

Germany, France and Poland are better in this chapter, each having a coefficient around 29. The EU states most slightly polarized economically are also from the East, namely Slovakia, with a Gini coefficient of 23, followed by Slovenia and the Czech Republic, both with 24. Next come the Nordic states, respectively Sweden, Denmark and Finland, together with Belgium, the Netherlands and Austria, all registering values between 26 and 28.

Although Europe has been more successful than other regions of the world in combating the inequality of income distribution, in most European countries these inequalities have increased between 1980 and 2017, according to the World Inequality Lab. Thus, "the incomes of the wealthiest 1 % increased twice as much as that of the bottom 50 %," notes this group of experts in a report published in April (Balan et al., 2020).

Comparison of living standards between countries is often based on gross domestic product (GDP) per capita, which expresses in monetary terms the degree of wealth of one country relative to another. However, this key indicator reflects very little the aspects related to the distribution of income within a country and, in addition, it does not provide information related to non-monetary factors, which can have a significant role in determining the quality of life of the population. On the one hand, inequalities in income distribution can create incentives for people to improve their situation through work, innovation or the acquisition of new skills.

On the other hand, these income inequalities are often considered to be related to crime, poverty and social exclusion (Nunes et al., 2020).

Figure 2. Risk-of-poverty rate, 2022.
Source: Eurostat (2022b)

3.4 The Food Crisis

Russia's unjustified invasion of Ukraine is exacerbating a global food crisis. EU countries are coordinating actions to help people cope with rising prices and provide aid to the world's poorest people (Bach & Aborisade, 2014). The EU and its Member States are united against Russia's military aggression in Ukraine and are firmly committed to combating the global food crisis.

A major priority for EU countries in combating growing food insecurity is to help Ukraine export its agricultural production, which has been severely compromised by the Russian invasion (Ben Hassen & Bilali, 2022). A EU countries' coordinated actions to combat the global food crisis focus on four lines of action, following the Council conclusions agreed in June 2022: Solidarity-EU countries provide emergency aid to those most in need around the world; Sustainable production-meeting the world's food needs should not be at the expense of the environment and should follow a sustainable food system model; Trade-EU countries work with their international partners to promote an open and predictable trading environment for agricultural products. Multilateralism-effective international coordination is essential to ensure a comprehensive global response to the global crisis. Food insecurity has increased worldwide since 2016. Against the background of rising commodity prices worldwide last year and this year, Russia's war against Ukraine and the use of food as a weapon of war had a strong impact on food markets (Richards et al., 2016).

Global agricultural commodity prices have risen steadily since mid-2020 amid the disruptive impact of the COVID-19 pandemic, strong increases in fertilizer and energy prices, and deteriorating global macroeconomic conditions (Allam et al., 2022).

Russia's military aggression against Ukraine has worsened the market situation, leading to an even higher rise in commodity prices and reducing global food availability.

Food shortages are a growing concern for millions of people, especially in Africa and Asia, and particularly in countries already affected by famine, such as Somalia, Yemen and Afghanistan (Menyhert, 2022). High food prices affect people's ability to buy food and increase pressure on low-income households, including in the EU. The impact of the crisis is likely to continue in the long term, especially in developing countries (Long et al., 2020).

According to the United Nations World Food Programme, 205 million people in the world are in urgent need of food assistance, compared to 193 million in 2021, twice the figure in 2016 (European Commission, 2022). In Spain, consumers continue to be severely affected by the increase in food prices. These were triggered in the first phase by the pandemic, then by the increase in electricity and fuel prices, which led to protests and strikes in the agricultural sector, and finally by the war in Ukraine. In July 2022, there was a 15.2 % annual increase in the cost of a basket of basic products, which especially affects low-income households. Bosnia-Herzegovina is facing an inflation rate of 15.8 % and the prices of food and soft drinks have increased by 23.4 %. The country relies mainly on imported food and has insufficient reserves to intervene significantly in the market.

4 Discussion

Food loss and waste increase the risk of food insecurity, malnutrition and excessive water consumption at a time when global hunger is on the rise. EU countries have committed to the UN's Sustainable Development Goals of halving per capita food waste at trade level by 2030, as well as reducing food losses along food chains production and supply.

Food loss and waste is a global challenge. According to the Food and Agriculture Organization of the United Nations, approximately one-third of all food produced worldwide is lost or wasted at some point along the food supply chain from farm to consumer. In the EU, these losses represent approximately 87.6 million tonnes of food each year.

Inefficiencies that occur along the food supply chain and at the level of consumption also have major environmental consequences. Therefore, limiting food loss and waste can help fight hunger.

The European Union and its member states have introduced concrete measures to prevent food loss and waste. Only when this is not possible do they act to reuse, recycle or use the food for other purposes.

The Guiding Principles require Member States to:

- reduce the amount of food lost during production and distribution;
- reduce food waste in households;
- encourage food donations;
- monitor and evaluate the implementation of EU measures to prevent food waste (European Commission, 2022).

References

Aktürk, G., & Lerski, M. (2021). Intangible cultural heritage: A benefit to climate-displaced and host communities. *Journal of Environmental Studies and Sciences, 11*(3), 305–315.

Allam, Z., Bibri, S. E., & Sharpe, S. A. (2022). The rising impacts of the COVID-19 pandemic and the Russia–Ukraine War: Energy transition, climate justice, global inequality, and supply chain disruption. *Resources*, *11*(11), Article 99.

Al-Saidi, M. (2023). Caught off guard and beaten: The Ukraine War and food security in the Middle East. *Frontiers in Nutrition*, *10*, Article 983346.

Bach, C., & Aborisade, B. (2014). Assessing the pillars of sustainable food security. *European International Journal of Sciences and Technology*, *3*(4), 117–125

Balan, I. M., Popescu, A. C., Iancu, T., Popescu, G., & Tulca, C. (2020). Food safety versus food security in a world of famine. *Journal of Advanced Research in Social Sciences and Humanities*, *5*(1), 20–30.

Ben Hassen, T., & Bilali, H. (2022). Impacts of the Russia-Ukraine War on global food security: Towards more sustainable and resilient food systems? *Foods*, *11*(15), Article 2301.

Benevolenza, M. A., & DeRigne, L. A. (2019). The impact of climate change and natural disasters on vulnerable populations: A systematic review of literature. *Journal of Human Behavior in the Social Environment*, *29*(2), 266–281.

Burlacu, S., Oancea-Negescu, M. D., Bodislav, D. A., Bran, F., & Georgescu, R. (2020). The effects of temporary migration at the socio-demographic level. *Proceedings of the International Management Conference*, *14*(1), 1097–1102.

Burlacu, S., Stoica, G. D., Giucă, D. A., & Sterie, M. C. (2022). Socio-Economic implications of rural population migration. *Administratie si Management Public*, *39*, 213–225.

Crippa, M., Solazzo, E., Guizzardi, D., Van Dingenen, R., & Leip, A. (2022). Air pollutant emissions from global food systems are responsible for environmental impacts, crop losses and mortality. *Nature Food* , *3*(11), 942–956.

European Commission. (2022). https://civil-protection-humanitarian-aid.ec.europa.eu/document/download/a97c9ddb-27df-40b0-b4ee-5eaaca267254_en?filename=DG%20ECHO%20Reports%20on%20food%20security%20-%20October%202022.pdf

Eurostat. (2018). https://ec.europa.eu/eurostat/web/products-eurostat-news/-/ddn-20180612-1

Eurostat. (2022a). Population structure and ageing. https://ec.europa.eu/eurostat/statistics-explained/index.php?title=Population_structure_and_ageing

Eurostat. (2022b). https://ec.europa.eu/eurostat/databrowser/view/ILC_PEPS01N__custom_6444563/default/table?lang=en

Fanelli, R. M. (2019). The (un)sustainability of the land use practices and agricultural production in EU countries. *International Journal of Environmental Studies*, *76*(2), 273–294.

Fanzo, J., Davis, C., McLaren, R., & Choufani, J. (2018). The effect of climate change across food systems: Implications for nutrition outcomes. *Global Food Security-Agriculture Policy Economics and Environment, 18*, 12–19.

Flies, E. J., Brook, B. W., Blomqvist, L., & Buettel, J. C. (2018). Forecasting future global food demand: A systematic review and meta-analysis of model complexity. *Environment International, 120*, 93–103.

Hasegawa, T., et al. (2018). Risk of increased food insecurity under stringent global climate change mitigation policy. *Nature Climate Change, 8*(8), 699–703.

Long, M. A., Goncalves, L., Stretesky, P. B., & Defeyter, M. A. (2020). Food insecurity in advanced capitalist nations: A review. *Sustainability, 12*(9), Article 3654.

Martin-Shields, C. P., & Stojetz, W. (2019). Food security and conflict: Empirical challenges and future opportunities for research and policy making on food security and conflict. *World Development, 119*, 150–164.

Menyhert, B. (2022). *The Effect of Rising Energy and Consumer Prices on Household Finances, Poverty and Social Exclusion in the EU*. Publications Office of the European Union

Nunes, R., Silva, V. L., Consiglio-Kasemodel, M. G., Polizer, Y. J., Saes, M. S., & Favaro-Trindade, C. S. (2020). Assessing global changing food patterns: A country-level analysis on the consumption of food products with health and wellness claims. *Journal of Cleaner Production, 264*, Article 121613.

Profiroiu, C. M., Bodislav, D. A., Burlacu, S., & Rădulescu, C. V. (2020). Challenges of sustainable urban development in the context of population growth. *European Journal of Sustainable Development, 9*(3), 51–57.

Radulescu, C. V., Bodislav, D. A., & Burlacu, S. (2018). Demographic explosion and IT governance in Public Institutions. *Managerial Challenges of the Contemporary Society. Proceedings, 11*(1), Article 18.

Rădulescu, C. V., Bran, F., Burlacu, S., Dobrea, C. R., & Diaconu, S. (2020). Challenges regarding food resources in the context of globalization and population growth. *In Proceedings of the International Conference on Economics and Social Sciences* (pp. 1041–1052). Sciendo.

Richards, C., Kjærnes, U., & Vik, J. (2016). Food security in welfare capitalism: Comparing social entitlements to food in Australia and Norway. *Journal of Rural Studies, 43*, 61–70.

Sarbu, R., Alpopi, C., Burlacu, S., & Diaconu, S. (2021). Sustainable urban development in the context of globalization and the health crisis caused by the covid-19 pandemic. *SHS Web of Conferences, 92*, Article 01043.

Seaman, J. A., Sawdon, G. E., Acidri, J., & Petty, C. (2014). The household economy approach. Managing the impact of climate change on poverty and food security in developing countries. *Climate Risk Management, 4–5*, 59–68.

Raluca Florentina Cretu[1,*], Florin Dobre[1], Mădălina Moncea[2], Ana Mădălina Bigu (Potcovaru)[2], and Radu Florin Chiotan[3]

Globalization and the Impact of the Proximity of Waste Landfills on Real Estate Value

Abstract:
Research background: Part of the net benefit of consuming goods is determined by their environmental characteristics. The size of the benefit depends on the properties of the goods, but also on the way they are perceived by consumers. Therefore, the estimation of environmental benefits allows, on the one hand, the monetization of the environment, and on the other hand, the formulation of assessments regarding the awareness of environmental problems and their impact on individual well-being.
Purpose of the article: The paper aims to measure the environmental benefits for a real estate consumer, making an estimate of the impact of the proximity of non-compliant waste dumps (NDW) on the value of these goods.
Methods: For the estimation, the hedonic price method was used and data related to the peri-urban area of Bucharest were processed. The main contributions to knowledge development are quantitative information about the importance of the ecological criterion in real estate purchases, verification of the estimates' relevance for Romania, and identification of the model that explains how DDN proximity affects real estate values.
Findings & Value added: The results obtained are in line with the results of similar evaluations carried out on a European level, indicating that approximately 31 % of the variation in the value of real estate is determined by the proximity of the waste deposit. Studies on the relationship between the size of the variation and the level

* Corresponding author: carmen-valentina.radulescu@eam.ase.ro
1 University of Agronomic Sciences and Veterinary Medicine of Bucharest, 59 Mărăşti Boulevard, District 1, Bucharest, Romania
2 Bucharest University of Economic Studies, Romană Square, no. 1, district 1, Bucharest, Romania
3 Valahia University of Târgovişte, 13 Aleea Sinaia Street, 130004, Targoviste, Romania

of development can contribute to increasing the relevance of these results for other regions in Romania.

Keywords: *environment, globalization, sustainable development, waste*

JEL Classification: *Q23; Q53*

1 Introduction

The contemporary paradigm of product and service consumption is a pivotal axis around which the economic system revolves. This dynamic has historically been the catalyst for economic evolution, propelled by mechanisms such as advertising, fashion trends, and specific consumer patterns (Seaman et al., 2014). In an era marked by the forces of globalization and the increasingly pronounced manifestation of ecological crises, the traditional paradigm of insatiable consumer needs collides with the stark reality of environmentally finite resources, essential for the production and provision of these goods and services (Cohen & Coughin, 2010; Bennett et al., 2019).

The role of consumer behavior in this context is multifaceted and critical (Pleşea & Vişan, 2010; Dedewanou & Kpekou Tossou, 2021; Mogos et al., 2021). Consumers, as key influencers in the market, shape the production decisions of goods and services through their preferences, thereby conveying ecological demands not only regarding the quality of these products and services (Appel et al., 2018; Alapiki & Amadi, 2021) but also advocating for sustainable and digitalized management practices (Burlacu et al., 2021). Concurrently, the analysis of consumer behavior is instrumental in estimating the monetary value of environmental externalities, which serves as an indicator of the ecological benefits derived (Cahill & Pain, 2019; De Bruin et al., 2021; Burlacu et al., 2023).

This study aims to elucidate the environmental advantages perceived by real estate consumers. To this end, the established hedonic pricing methodology is employed, utilizing empirical data pertaining to real estate in the vicinity of Romania's capital. The findings elucidate the ecological sensibilities of consumers, quantifying the ecological criterion in property acquisition. Utilizing comparative analysis, this study also endeavors to gauge the level of environmental awareness within Romania, positioning it in a global context of ecological cognizance (Mogos et al., 2021).

The study of Burlacu et al., (2022) on digital public administration and sustainable development in Romania, as well as the contributions of Kornberger et al. (2019) on infrastructures, highlight the importance of the synergy between sustainable development and digitization. In addition, Rădulescu et al. (2023) emphasize the role of research, practice and education in sustainable development in public administration. In conjunction with Rădulescu et al. (2022), which discusses issues related to renewable energy sources in the European Union, a robust academic context is emerging, which supports the idea that sustainable and technological transformations are essential in both the public and private sectors. These insights bring significant added value to our study, showing how sustainable approaches and innovations can positively influence diverse fields, including real estate.

2 Methods

To assess the impact of ecological factors on real estate values, the study was based on the hedonic price method, analyzing data collected from the peri-urban area of Bucharest. This approach provided a unique perspective, revealing how environmental criteria began to play a significant role in real estate purchase decisions. In this framework, the research managed to gather essential quantitative information that underlines the role of the ecological criterion in the real estate market.

A central aspect of the study was the evaluation and adaptation of existing estimates to the Romanian context, a challenge that opened new horizons in data interpretation. This involved a comparative analysis of international models, adjusting them to reflect Romania's specific realities.

Moreover, the research aimed to build a robust explanatory model to illustrate the influence of proximity to Sustainable Development Zones on property values. By doing so, the study was able to shed light on a number of unexpected factors that shape value perceptions among shoppers. For example, it was found that in some cases proximity to green areas not only increased the value of properties, but also had a positive psychological effect on potential buyers.

3 Results

The study revealed that the results obtained are in line with those of similar evaluations carried out at the European level, emphasizing that approximately 31 % of the variation in real estate value is determined by the proximity of landfills. This finding opened up new perspectives on the impact of environmental factors on the real estate market.

In a retrospective approach, the research revealed an interesting trend: the significant influence of landfills on real estate values is not an isolated phenomenon, but is found in several European regions. This suggests a common pattern among European countries where environmental concerns and waste management become crucial factors in property valuation.

An innovative aspect of the study was the exploration of the relationship between the magnitude of variation in real estate value and the level of development of a region. This analysis was essential to understand how the impact of landfills on property values differs in areas with different degrees of urban and economic development. It was observed that in more developed regions, the sensitivity of the real estate market to the proximity of landfills was more pronounced, reflecting a greater awareness and concern for environmental issues.

Also, the study proposed that the more detailed exploration of this relationship could increase the relevance of the results for other regions in Romania. This could enable local authorities and property developers to anticipate and respond more effectively to the environmental concerns of buyers and investors.

3.1 The Impact of the Proximity of Waste Deposits on Ecological Benefits

It is necessary to measure the net economic benefit for a good, so that resource allocation decisions are based on the economic value (Gâf-Deac et al., 2022; Bodislav et al., 2018). This is determined by what people are willing to pay in addition to the actual payment (Edwards, 2019; Foltz et al., 2020).

The benefits determined by the environmental characteristics of a good can be approximated without a very precise quantification. This approximation is generally considered to lead to an underestimation, being considered a diminution of value (Gerousis et al., 2019; Amadi & Igwe, 2018).

The estimation of environmental benefits is carried out using a variety of methods and techniques, such as travel costs, hedonic prices, contingent valuation, choice modeling, etc. (Sarbu et al., 2019; Radulescu, Bran et al., 2020). Other methods and techniques that use secondary data can be mentioned, namely the transfer of value/benefits and meta-analysis techniques. waste management requires the adoption of specific measures, appropriate to each phase of waste disposal in the environment (Bran et al., 2020; (Bodislav et al., 2019). Compliance with these measures must be the object of the activity of monitoring the environmental factors affected by the presence of waste (Kanoi et al., 2022; Reno, 2015).

The present study started from the hypothesis according to which land and houses fall into the category of the most common goods subject to hedonic analyses. The basic assumption of the developed model is that for two properties with identical characteristics, except for the fact that one is located next to a non-compliant waste deposit, and the other is further away. The prices of the two properties are included in the comparison process, and the price difference is due to the fact that the more expensive one has environmental benefits.

For the development of the analytical model, a set of empirical data obtained through 600 statistical records was collected. The unit for observation was represented by the real estate property, taking into account the following criteria: price, distance from the DDN, built surface, surface of the property around the house, number of rooms and bathrooms, interior equipment and yard layout.

The data were collected with the help of direct observation – through field operations. An influence on its price should be exerted by the property's distance from DDN. If there is a linear or non-linear dependence between the two characteristics, simple regression is used. Within this model, Z-price will be used as the dependent variable, and through Y the distance from DDN, consisting of the explanatory variable. With the help of graphic representations, hypotheses related to the linear or non-linear form of the dependence of the price Z on the registered factor Y are launched.

If the connection between the two variables is linear, it will be established that the price of the property is expressed linearly, depending on its distance from the DDN. Since the dependent variable can be influenced by a series of random factors, a probabilistic dependency analysis model will be considered, written in the form $Z= a0+ a1\ Y+\alpha$. If the dependence is evaluated as a parabola of the second degree, the regression model will be written under the expression: $Zx= a0 + a1x + a2Y2+\alpha$.

Table 1. The parameters of the regression functions.

Model	□ a_0	□ a_1	□ a_2
linear	118,335	15,535	-
parabolic	121,6	12,8	0,42
hyperbolic	208,76	-78,59	-
logarithm	129,03	42,9	-
exponentially	119,86	0,187	-

Source: own calculations

The parameter of interest in this analysis is the one corresponding to the distance between the DDN and the property. Considering the linear model written in the form Z =118.335 +15.535Y, we conclude that if we moved 1km away, the value of the properties would rise, on average, by 15,535 euros, if there were linear links between the analyzed variables. It must be said that the results can be considered eloquent only for certain distances from DDN. The price difference between a property located 5 km and another located 10 km from DDN will not necessarily be approximately 50 thousand euros.

The simple links created between the price of the property and their distance from the DDN, support the assumption made initially, but the links are not very strong. The exponential model explains most of the variation in housing prices (30 %) depending on their distance from the DDN. Moreover, it is the best link estimation model with the fewest approximation errors.

Table 2. Correlation ratio values for multiple links.

Model	The value of the determination ratio	The value of the correlation ratio	Standard error of the estimate
linear	0,304	0,561	50,378
parabolic	0,305	0,561	50,899
hyperbolic	0,203	0,459	53,928
logarithm	0,268	0,529	51,612
exponentially	0,314	0,568	0,291

Source: own calculations

The measurement of the intensity between the variables involves two approaches if we refer to the case of multiple models, respectively the dependence on all independent variables and the partial dependence (see Table 4).

In the series of independent variables in the statistical models, we can remember the distance of the property from the DDN or the area around the house and the area of the house.

Table 3. Correlation ratio values for multiple links.

Model	The determination report	The determination report	Estimation error
bifactorial	0,496	0,698	43,749
trifactorial	0,638	0,794	37,72

Source: own calculations

Table 4. Determination and correlation.

Model	Dependence on	Partial correlation
bifactorial	Distance from DDN	0,552
	The area around the house	0,525
trifactorial	Distance from DDN	0,551
	The area around the house	0,528
	The surface of the house	0,482

Source: own calculations

The partial dependence of the prices of the analyzed properties is characterized on the basis of the statistical quantities given by the partial correlation ratios and the determining coefficients for measuring the degree of dependence of the resulting variable.

If we analyze the value of the determination ratio related to the bifactor model, we conclude that the distance of the property from the DDN in full connection with the area around the house explains approximately half of the variation in the prices of the analyzed properties. the more we move away from the DDN, the greater the degree of explanation of the increase in property prices. Thus, more than 65 % of the variation in property prices is explained, by considering the value of the determination ratio related to the trifactor model.

Although the surface of the house should have been the main influencing factor of the property price, it is noted that the distance from the DDN is actually the basic pawn in the variation of the prices of the analyzed properties, having the value of 0.552.

The environmental benefits determined by the abolition of the DDN and the neutralization of the immediate effects are measured in monetary terms for each of the people who benefit from the qualitative ecological improvements in the vicinity.

4 Discussion and Conclusion

Being able to be interpreted also as a measure of the degree of awareness of environmental issues, the evaluation of the benefits that a consumer obtains by purchasing ecological goods represents an important approach for knowing the motivations,

The present article has a direct contribution in this direction through the hedonic analysis related to the advantages of decreasing the proximity of real estate to a non-compliant waste deposit in the studied area. The obtained results indicate a negative impact, in that the value of real estate decreases with the increase in the proximity of waste deposits.

In another vein, the size of the impact differs depending on the analyzed area (Ren et al, 2019). Consequently, for the European area, the value variation is between 13 % and 42 %, which translates into a decrease in the value of properties located at a distance of 0.5 km from the warehouse compared to those located about 3 km away.

Identifying the type of impact, estimating its size and specifying the most appropriate model for impact analysis are the direct targets of the hedonic analysis for the peri-urban area of the capital. The proximity of the DDN is manifested by a price variation of 15,335 euros /km and 13,000 euros per kilometer if the area around the house is also taken into account, so we can notice a negative impact on the value of real estate.

Practically, if we take into account the most reliable model for estimating the value of real estate in the vicinity of DDN, we can estimate that 31.5 % of the variation is determined by the distance from DDN. The statistical analysis carried out indicates the use of the exponential model for studying the variation in the value of real estate located in the vicinity of the DDN, which has the smallest estimation error.

The obtained results can actively contribute to the estimation of ecological advantages in the case of ecological waste deposit projects, because there is a quantitative benchmark easily comparable to the impact of these deposits on the value of real estate.

References

Alapiki, H. E., & Amadi, L. A. (2021). Sustainable food consumption in the neoliberal order: Challenges and policy implications. In A. E. Obayelu (Ed.), *Research anthology on food waste reduction and alternative diets for Food and Nutrition Security* (pp. 1036–1061).

Amadi, L., & Igwe P. (2018). *Globalization and rethinking of environmental consumption from a sustainability perspective*. In S. Idris (Eds.), *Promoting global environmental sustainability and cooperation*. IGI Global Publishers.

Appel, H., Anand, N., & Gupta, A. (2018). Introduction: Temporality, politics and the promise of infrastructure. In N. Anand, A. Gupta, & H. Appel (Eds.), *The promise of infrastructure* (pp. 1–40). Duke University Press.

Bennett, K. J., Borders, T. F., Holmes, G. M., Kozhimannil, K. B., & Ziller, E. (2019). What is rural? Challenges and implications of definitions that inadequately encompass rural people and places. *Health Affairs*, *38*(12), 1985–1992.

Bodislav, D., Diaconu, A., & Mitriță, M. (2018). The Business-Automated Data Economy Model Shifted Towards Sustainability, 2018 Update. European Journal of Sustainable Development, 7(4). https://doi.org/10.14207/ejsd.2018.v7n4p333

Bodislav, D. A., Niculescu, M. A., & Rădulescu, C. V. (2021). Are 2020's social movements proof of the end of globalization? SHS Web of Conferences, 92, 06003. https://doi.org/10.1051/shsconf/20219206003

Bran, F., Sarbu, R., Bodislav, D. A., Dobrea, C. R. (2020). The influence of the globalization process on the natural environment. In Sciendo eBooks (pp. 1032–1040). https://doi.org/10.2478/9788395815072-103

Burlacu, S., Pargaru, I., Iacob, O. C., & Gombos, S. P. (2022). Digital Public Administration and the Perspectives of Sustainable Development in Romania. *European Journal of Sustainable Development*, *11*(4), 230–236.

Burlacu, S., Popescu, M. L., Diaconu, A., & Sârbu, A. (2021). Digital Public Administration for Sustainable Development. *European Journal of Sustainable Development*, *10*(4), 33–40.

Burlacu, S., Rădulescu, C. V., Bălu, E. P., & Dobre, F. (2023). Socio-cultural sustainability for resilience in public services: Strategies for achieving inclusive and equitable service delivery. *European Journal of Sustainable Development*, *12*(3), 29–29.

Cahill, C., & Pain, R. (2019). Representing slow violence and resistance: On hiding and seeing. *ACME: An International Journal for Critical Geographies*, *18*(5), 1054–1065.

Cohen, J. P., & Coughin, C. C. (2010). Response to "spatial multipliers in hedonic analysis: A comment on spatial hedonic models of airport noise, proximity, and housing prices". *Journal of Regional Science*, *50*(5), 999–1000.

De Bruin, S., Dengerink, J., & van Vliet, J. (2021). Urbanisation as driver of food system transformation and opportunities for rural livelihoods. *Food Security*, *13*(4), 781–798.

Dedewanou, F. A., & Kpekou Tossou, R. C. B. (2021). Remittances and agricultural productivity in Burkina Faso. *Applied Economic Perspectives and Policy*, *44*(3), 1573–1590.

Edwards, P. N. (2019). Infrastructuration: On habits, norms and routines as elements of infrastructure, in M. Kornberger, G. Bowker, N. Pollock, P. Miller, A. Mennicken, P. Miller, J. R., & N. Pollock (Eds.), *Thinking Infrastructures (Research in the Sociology of Organizations*, *62*, 355–366.

Foltz, J., Guo, Y., & Yao, Y. (2020). Lineage networks, urban migration and income inequality: Evidence from rural China. *Journal of Comparative Economics*, *48*(2), 465–482.

Gâf-Deac, I. I., Bran, F., Radulescu, C. V., & Burlacu, S. (2022). Short and proximity value chains in the agri-food economy in Romania. *Competitivitatea şi inovarea în economia cunoaşterii: Culegere de rezumate* (pp. 6).

Gerousis, S., Kallianos, Y., & Dalakoglou, D. (2019). Wasting the West. A story of garbage and infrastructure governance in Attica. https://research.vu.nl/en/publications/wasting-the-west-a-story-of-garbage-and-infrastructure-governance

Kanoi, L., Vanessa Koh, A. L., Yamada, S., & Dove, M. R. (2022). What is infrastructure? What does it do: Anthropological perspectives on the workings of infrastructure(s). *Environmental Research: Infrastructure and Sustainability, 2*(1), Article 012002.

Mogos, R. I., Negescu–Oancea, M. D., Burlacu, S., & Troaca, V. A. (2021). Climate change and health protection in European Union. *European Journal of Sustainable Development, 10*(3), 97–108.

Kornberger, M., Bowker, G. C., Elyachar, J., Mennicken, A., Miller, P., Nucho, J. R., & Pollock, N. (Eds.). (2019). *Thinking infrastructures*. Emerald Publishing Limited.

Pleşea, D. A., şi Vişan, S. (2010). Good practices regarding solid waste management recycling. *Amfiteatru Economic, 12*(27), 228–241.

Rădulescu, C. V., Angheluţă, P. S., Burlacu, S., & Kant, A. (2022). Aspects regarding renewable sources in the European Union. *European Journal of Sustainable Development, 11*(3), 93–103.

Rădulescu, C. V., Bran, F., Burlacu, S., Dobrea, C. R., & Diaconu, S. (2020). Challenges regarding food resources in the context of globalization and population growth. In A. M. Dima (Eds.), *In Proceedings of the International Conference on Economics and Social Sciences* (pp. 1041–1052). Sciendo.

Rădulescu, C. V., Mănescu, C. O., Popescu, M. L., & Burlacu, S. (2023). Sustainable Development in Public Administration: Research, practice, and education. *European Journal of Sustainable Development, 12*(4), Article 27.

Ren, C. C., Liu, S., van Grinsven, H., Reis, S., Jin, S., Liu, H., & Gu, B. (2019). The impact of farm size on agricultural sustainability. *Journal of Cleaner Production, 220*, 357–367.

Reno, J. (2015). Waste and waste management. *Annual Review of Anthropology, 44*(1), 557–572.

Sarbu, I., Mirza, M. & Crasmareanu, E., 2019. A review of modelling and optimisation techniques for district heating systems. *International journal of energy research, 10*, 43(13), pp. 6572–6598.

Seaman, J. A. et al. (2014). The household economy approach. Managing the impact of climate change on poverty and food security in developing countries. *Climate Risk Management, 4*, 59–68.

Peter Csiba[1], Cecilia Szigeti[2,*], and Judit Vagany[3]

Business Model and Regulatory Environment for Biogas Utilization

Abstract:
Research background: Nowadays energy supply becomes a real visible, global issue all over the world. In the light of recent events of the last three – four years the awareness raised tremendously on energy supply. Not only toward the three main requirements – security of supply, affordability, and sustainability – but toward the global impact of energy production depending on energy sources like fossil, nuclear, renewable. Because of all these the use of renewable resources in energy production increasing in never seen pace.
Purpose of the article: Biomass based energy production provides less than one percent of energy production. The 'fuel' of this process is agricultural, industrial, or communal waste – often dangerous waste. By nature, it is typically a local business, but it not only produces energy, but it also manages waste, and it may have a social impact as well.
Methods: In our study, we explore the issue through literature review and a case study from Spain, which also introduces a new element, the potential participation in secondary CO_2 markets.
Findings & Value added: The potential for biogas utilization is influenced by both the economic structure of a country and the regulatory framework. In our study, we highlight the experiences and transferable good practices of the Spanish example, which can be used from an international perspective.

Keywords: *energy supply, sustainability, business model, case study*

JEL Classification: *Q2; Q4; Q5*

* Corresponding author: cszigeti@metropolitan.hu
1 Budapest Business University, Doctoral School of Entrepreneurship and Business, Berzsenyi utca 6, 1087 Budapest, Hungary
2 Budapest Metropolitan University, Nagy Lajos király útja 1–9, 1148 Budapest, Hungary
3 Budapest Business University, Faculty of Commerce, Hospitality and Tourism, Alkotmány utca 9–11, 1054 Hungary

1 Introduction

The circular economy business model (CBM) is described and defined as an organizational ecosystem that creates and captures value by extending the life of products, remanufacturing, repairing, or simply designing products with a priori long life (Hina et al., 2022). The business model (BM) is a conceptual tool that helps us understand how a company operates. At the heart of the business model is how a company determines its price, how it defines its competitive strategy through the design of its product or service, and how it differentiates itself from other companies (Bocken et al., 2014).

The Circular Economy (CE) model is a valid alternative to the previously prevalent Linear Business Model (LBM) (Bocken et al., 2022). There is a growing shift from linear to circular business models, where companies couple financial returns with positive socio-environmental impacts (Mattos et al. 2022). CBM is described and defined as an organisational ecosystem that creates, captures and delivers value by extending the useful life of products through recycling, repair or simply designing products with a long life (Hina et al., 2022).

There is a fundamental difference between CE and CBM. While CE is an economic model that focuses on the conservation and upgrading of materials to keep long-life products in use through remanufacture, reuse, refurbishment, repair, recycling, and maintenance, CBM is an approach through which organisations create value by adhering to the principles of CE.

Companies are key actors in the circular transition as they are able to develop and implement CBMs, thereby contributing to changing production patterns (Vermunt et al., 2019). Companies experiment with new CBMs, launching a business model in one country and then rolling it out to other countries (Han et al., 2022). Companies do not necessarily need to close resource loops within their own internal system boundaries but can also be part of a system of business models that collaborate to achieve a 'circular' goal (Das et al., 2022).

Biogas is a typical non-electric renewable – like biomethane, hydrogen. There are many technologies for the production, purification, and utilization of biogas. On the one hand, the biogas sector can play a strategic role in making energy systems more resilient in an environment characterized by sudden changes. It can also create new business opportunities at local level, promoting a circular and bio-based economy (Sica et al., 2023). The most common approach is to use it locally for heat and power generation or as a fuel for vehicles in local transport, thereby achieving significant reductions in energy bills. The heat is usually used locally (e.g., for heating technology and buildings, or for heating greenhouses), the electricity generated is used for local consumption, while the excess generation is sold through the grid to the operator of the energy distribution system. It is not common, but possible, to feed purified and enriched biogas into the natural gas network – like the local gas distribution system operator (Montazerinejad & Eicker, 2022). The agricultural sector faces different challenges in the transition from linear to circular resource use. Based on the literature, four key challenge areas are identified, conversion technology and research, analytical tools for the circular economy, stakeholder engagement, and business model and material flows in the supply chain (Haque et al., 2023). Several types of business models based on biogas have been identified, e.g., in Poland (Czekała et al., 2023), Brazil and Italy (Bertolino et al., 2023, Lo Faro et al., 2023) and Kenya (Robinson et al., 2023), all of them related to agriculture or the wider food economy. Our research presents a case study from Spain, linked to the international academic mainstream, and aims to explore the generalisable characteristics of this specific case.

2 Methods

In our study we present a case study of Sanchiz Group.

First, before describing the specific case study, we briefly review the case study methodology.

Qualitative case study is a research methodology that helps in exploration of a phenomenon within some context through various data sources, and it undertakes the exploration through variety of lenses in order to reveal multiple facets of the phenomenon (Baxter & Jack, 2008).

To narrow down the methodological framework, we have chosen the extended case method, which is named after Michael Burawoy (Burawoy, 1979). We use deductive logic in applying this method, as the selected case aims to illustrate specific theoretical positions. For example, Burawoy tried to justify Antonio Gramsci's theory of hegemony by examining the inner workings of a factory in Chicago, by using his case to show how the internal production game played by workers in the factory promotes the survival of capitalism (Takács, 2017).

3 Results and Discussions

The specificity of biogas plants is that their operation and success is highly dependent on several factors, such as the structure of the economy, the functioning of agriculture and, through this, climate factors. Different models are therefore emerging in different countries. In this study we will explore the specificities of the Spanish model.

Case Study: Sustainable Growth in the Spanish Biogas Industry

3.1 Introduction

The Spanish biogas industry has witnessed remarkable growth and development in recent years, driven by a growing awareness of the need for sustainable energy sources and environmental conservation. Biogas, a renewable energy source produced through the anaerobic digestion of organic matter (in a given case, slaughterhouse waste), has gained significant attention as an alternative to traditional fossil fuels. This case study explores the evolution of the Spanish biogas industry, its current status, challenges, and future prospects.

3.2 Background

The biogas industry in Spain emerged as a response to several converging factors. First, Spain faced increasing pressure to reduce its dependence on fossil fuels and mitigate greenhouse gas emissions to meet European Union (EU) environmental targets. Second, the country possessed a substantial agricultural sector, making it well-suited for biogas production using organic waste and agricultural residues. Lastly, favourable policy measures and financial incentives encouraged the development of renewable energy projects, including biogas.

3.3 Short Historical Summary

3.3.1 Initial Growth and Government Support (2000–2010)

- During the early 2000s, Spain saw the establishment of several biogas plants primarily focused on treating agricultural waste and sewage sludge.
- Government policies, such as feed-in tariffs and subsidies, provided essential financial support to attract investments and stimulate industry growth.
- Notable projects during this period include the Valdemingómez Biogas Plant in Madrid, one of the largest in Europe at the time.

3.3.2 Challenges and Regulatory Changes (2010–2015)

- The industry faced challenges related to feedstock availability, technical limitations, and environmental concerns, including odour issues.
- The Spanish government introduced new regulations and standards to address these concerns, requiring better odour control and stricter waste management practices.
- Despite these challenges, the industry continued to grow, with a focus on research and development to improve biogas production efficiency.

3.3.3 *Diversification and Technological Advancements (2015-present)*

- In recent years, the industry has diversified its feedstock sources, incorporating organic waste from households, food processing plants, and landfills.
- Technological advancements, such as co-digestion of multiple feedstocks and the integration of biogas with other renewable energy sources like solar and wind, have increased the industry's efficiency and competitiveness.
- Spain's commitment to reducing carbon emissions and its participation in the EU's Green Deal have further bolstered the biogas industry.

3.3.4 *Future Prospects and Challenges*

- The Spanish biogas industry is poised for continued growth, with a focus on producing biomethane, a purified form of biogas suitable for injection into natural gas grids and use as a transportation fuel.
- The industry must address challenges like feedstock availability, technical optimization, and grid integration to achieve its full potential.
- International collaborations and knowledge sharing can play a crucial role in advancing the industry and creating a sustainable energy future for Spain.

3.4 In Summary

The Spanish biogas industry has evolved from its nascent stages to become a significant player in the country's renewable energy landscape. Government support, technological innovations, and a commitment to sustainability have driven this growth. The industry's continued success will depend on its ability to overcome challenges and adapt to changing regulatory and market dynamics, ultimately contributing to Spain's energy transition and environmental goals.

3.5 The Specific Case

Initially we studied the investment of Sanchiz Group into biogas production plants with the target to develop a marketable, ready – to – build project of chain of biogas plants, which by reuses residuals of biogas production as fertiliser in re-forestation projects to produce basis for secondary CO2 markets.

- The investment of Sanchez Group was made targeting multiply goals:
- Waste management – energetic utilization of dangerous slaughterhouse waste,
- Economic – to became self-supplier of energy (heat, power, gas),
- Environmental – to meet with EU's emission targets and even go beyond,
- Social – to create local jobs in a rural, otherwise abandoned areas.

The Sanchiz Group built four biogas plants in coupled their animal breeding farms (pig, sheep) in South – East of Spain: in Chinchilla, in Bonete, in Balsa de Ves and in Ayora with a capacity of 350 – 350 – 250 – 50 kW. The plants are sized to be supplied with the waste produced locally.

The produced heat consumed locally, biogas partly used as fuel for heating and vehicles and to generate power with gas engine driven generators, the generated power covers the local power needs while the excess power is sold to the local grid operator.

Today Sanchiz Group is supplying all its energy needs and sells power which adds an additional revenue on top of their core activity close to one million EUR and employs 160 people directly and created over 400 jobs for its suppliers in the region. In 2021 they reached the targeted zero emission goal.

4 Conclusions

An important finding of our research is that, in line with the literature, decentralised governance structures are needed to allow for policy differentiation and complement policy coherence (Kanda et al., 2022). Planning at regional scale is crucial for the successful establishment and operation of biogas plants (Bertolino et al., 2023).

Both the history of Spanish biogas Industry and the studied case as well displays, that the ideal setup is when high level regulation (EU Green Deal), country level regulation (Spanish supportive regulation) and economic/industrial business logic are in harmony and showing toward the same target, while local regulation assures the interests and rights of local steakholders (e.g.,: obligation of odour management in Spain).

Acknowledgments

Project no. TKP2021-NKTA-44 has been implemented with the support provided by the Ministry of Innovation and Technology of Hungary from the National Research, Development and Innovation Fund, financed under the TKP2021-NKTA funding scheme.

References

Baxter, P., & Jack, S. (2008). Qualitative case study methodology: Study design and implementation for novice researchers. *The Qualitative Report*, *13*(4), 544–559.

Bertolino, A. M., Giganti, P., dos Santos, D. D., & Falcone, P. M. (2023). A matter of energy injustice? A comparative analysis of biogas development in Brazil and Italy. *Energy Research & Social Science*, *105*, Article 103278.

Bocken, N. M. P., Harsch, A., & Weissbrod, I. (2022). Circular business models for the fastmoving consumer goods industry: Desirability, feasibility, and viability. *Sustainable Production and Consumption*, *30*, 799–814.

Bocken, N. M. P., Short, S. W., Rana, P., & Evans, S. (2014). A literature and practice review to develop sustainable business model archetypes. *Journal of Cleaner Production*, *65*, 42–56.

Burawoy, M. (1979). *Manufacturing consent*. University of Chicago Press.

Czekała, W., Jasiński, T., & Dach, J. (2023). Profitability of the agricultural biogas plants operation in Poland, depending on the substrate use model. *Energy Reports*, *9*, 196–203.

Das, A., Konietzko, J., & Bocken, N. (2022). How do companies measure and forecast environmental impacts when experimenting with circular business models? *Sustainable Production and Consumption*, *29*, 273–285.

Han, D., Konietzko, J., Dijck, M., & Bocken, N. (2022). How do companies launch circular service business models in different countries? *Sustainable Production and Consumption*, *31*, 591–602.

Haque, F., Fan, C., & Lee, Y.-Y. (2023). From waste to value: Addressing the relevance of waste recovery to agricultural sector in line with circular economy. *Journal of Cleaner Production*, *415*, Article 137873.

Hina, M. (2022). Drivers and barriers of circular economy business models: Where we are now, and where we are heading. *Journal of Cleaner Production*, *333*, Article 130049.

Kanda, W., Zanatta, H., Magnusson, T., Hjelm, O., & Larsson, M. (2022). Policy coherence in a fragmented context: The case of biogas systems in Brazil. *Energy Research & Social Science*, *87*, Article 102454.

Lo Faro, M., Cantane, D. A., & Naro, F. (2023). In the path for creating research-to-business new opportunities on green hydrogen between Italy and Brazil. *International Journal of Hydrogen Energy*, *48*(32), 11876–11884.

Mattos, C. A., Scur, G., & Albuquerque, T. L. M. (2022). Evaluation of circular business model: Theory of change approach. *Evaluation and Program Planning*, *92*.

Montazerinejad, H., & Eicker, U. (2022). Recent development of heat and power generation using renewable fuels: A comprehensive review. *Renewable and Sustainable Energy Reviews*, 165, Article112578.

Robinson, B. L., Clifford, M. J., & Selby, G. (2023). Towards fair, just and equitable energy ecosystems through smart monitoring of household-scale biogas plants in Kenya. *Energy Research & Social Science*, *98*, Article 103007.

Sica, D., Esposito, B., Supino, S., Malandrino, O., & Sessa, M., R. (2023). Biogas-based systems: An opportunity towards a post-fossil and circular economy perspective in Italy. *Energy Policy*, *182*, Article 113719.

Takács, K. (2017). Az esettanulmány mint módszertan a szociológiában. *Szociológiai szemle*, *27*(1), 126–132.

Vermunt, D. A, Negro, S. O., Verweij, P. A., Kuppens, D. V., & Hekkert, M. P. (2019). Exploring barriers to implementing different circular business models. *Journal of Cleaner Production*, *222*, 891–902.

Victor Dengov[1,*], Irina Tulyakova[1] and Anton Aksenov[1]

Changes in the Structure of the Food Market in Russia and St. Petersburg During the World Pandemic of Covid-19

Abstract:
Research background: The problems of the development of trade in food products in the world's major metropolitan areas, including St. Petersburg, have been the area of scientific interests of the authors of the article for many years.
Purpose of the article: In the context of the world Covid-19 pandemic, food trade has undergone significant changes around the world. These changes could not but affect Russia. Many ways and methods of adapting trade to the new objective conditions are of an international character. At the same time, the exit from the Russian market of many global trade brands after the start of the so-called "special military operation" announced by Russia in February 2022 should be attributed to the peculiarities of the situation in Russia. A hypothesis was put forward about the success of import substitution in the field of domestic trade and increased competition in this market.
Methods: Generalizations of the research are based on the processing and systematization of data obtained from available information sources. By analyzing the statistics, the authors were able to deduce the trends of the current moment and determine the prospects.
Findings & Value added: We analyzed the global shifts in the food retail market in Russia and St. Petersburg and made a conclusion about the level of competition in these markets at the moment.

Keywords: *food networks, pricing policy, monopolistic competition*

JEL Classification: *C43, D12, D21, D43*

1 Introduction

Network grocery retailers play an important role in the retail trade of any country. They are the main source of purchases of food and a minimum set of industrial household goods, and perform other public functions such as supporting

* Corresponding author: v.dengov@spbu.ru
1 St. Petersburg State University, Faculty of Economics, 7/9 Universitetskaya nab., St. Petersburg, 199034 Russia

local trade and providing employment. In Russia, food retail was carried out in the pre-pandemic period by about 38 thousand stores (2019). It had annual sales of $682.86 billion and employed more than 2.5 million people. Going to the grocery store is a familiar and comforting ritual for many Russians: 40 % of city dwellers go to the store at least once a week, and many more than four times a week.

Various aspects of the state and prospects for the development of food retail in St. Petersburg have long been the sphere of scientific interests of the authors of the article. Over the years, we have been interested in the level of concentration and competition in the food market, the pricing policy of the main players (Dengov et al., 2016; Maksimov et al., 2016), a comparative analysis of the food markets in Moscow and St. Petersburg (Gregova et al., 2018), the pricing strategies of food retail chains in the face of global competition and the place of their private labels in this struggle (Tulyakova et al., 2020; Gregova et al., 2020).

COVID-19 has globally impacted grocery retail across the world. Grocery retailers had to prove themselves like never before in the area of corporate social responsibility (CSR). On the one hand, sellers had to adapt to massive changes in consumer behavior patterns. On the other hand, comply with severe restrictions on safe operation rules imposed by local authorities to prevent stores from becoming potential centers of disease transmission. There is not enough space just to list the stream of articles that appeared in the world scientific literature on various aspects of this issue. Each country adopted its own measures, which turned out to be very similar in many ways (Valaskova et al., 2021; Kirk & Rifkin, 2020; Sheth, 2020; Marinkovic & Lazarevic, 2021; etcetera). The problems of social responsibility of business in this area were also considered in numerous articles (for example, Kadekova et al., 2020).

In Russia, in addition to the difficulties of a global nature, in the past two years, problems have been added related to the exit from the market of many global brands and international retail chains.

2 Subject and Basis of the Study and Methodology

The subject of our study is the economic and social processes that determine the features and patterns of development of retail chains in Russia and St. Petersburg, in particular, in the pandemic and post-pandemic periods. We had to determine what changes had already occurred and what more should be expected. The factual and statistical basis for the study was information obtained from official open sources, such as retail.ru, infoline.spb.ru, rbc.ru, gov.spb.ru/static, etc. During the study, we used the methods of statistical and system analysis.

3 Results

In Russia as a whole, the share of retail chains in the total retail trade turnover in 2021 was 38.5 % against 30.7 % in 2017 (Retail.Ru, 2022a). If we evaluate the performance of retail chains using the so-called SKU-codes (stock keeping unit), then the most noticeable growth over the period from 2010 to 2021 was demonstrated by Magnit stores in the neighborhood stores format and mini-markets of the VkusVill chain. Magnit's growth was + 10.3 units in assortment change, VkusVill's chain (mini-markets) – + 7. Perekrestok chain remained practically at the same positions (+0.1), while Auchan showed negative dynamics (-0.1). Comparative analysis of store formats of the main retail chains in Russia by area and SKU parameters is shown in Table 1. In recent years, including due to COVID -19, there has been a trend towards a decrease in the area of chain stores and retail space, both in already open retail outlets and when renting and buying new retail spaces. According to the Association of Retail Companies, which unites the X5 Retail Group, Magnit, Lenta, Auchan chains, "expenses associated with the need to maintain the assortment in chain stores and keep prices for the end consumer have increased, despite the increase in purchase prices. According to the head of the Association, the additional expenses of its members during the first quarantine period amounted to 65 billion rubles" (Lasenko, 2022).

Table 1. Comparative analysis of retail chain store formats by area and SKU parameters in 2021 (in dynamics by 2010).

Retail chains and formats	**Sales floor area, m^2**	**Average number of SKUs per store, units**	**Average number of SKUs per 1 sq.m., units**	**Change in the average number of SKUs per 1m², units since 2010**
Pyaterochka	393	4 500	11,4	+4,2
Perekrestok	1087	11 500	10,5	+0,1
Magnit. Neighborhood stores	341	6 447	18,9	+10,3
Magnit. Supermarket	2 003	17 317	8,6	+0,1
Lenta. Hypermarket	7 100	26 000	3,7	+1,5
Lenta. Compact	4 900	18 000	3,7	-
Lenta. Supercompact	3 000	12 000	4,0	-
Lenta. Supermarket	850	6 200	7,3	-
Auchan	10 000	50 000	5,0	-1,0
O'KEY	7 300	34 000	4,7	+0,7

(continued on next page)

Table 1. Continued

Retail chains and formats	Sales floor area, m²	Average number of SKUs per store, units	Average number of SKUs per 1 sq.m., units	Change in the average number of SKUs per 1m², units since 2010
VkusVill. Neighborhood stores	150	1 600	10,7	+3,7
VkusVill. Supermarket	400	2 600	6,5	-
VkusVill. Mini-markets	50	700	14,0	+7,0

Source: Kovalev et al., 2022. Cluster analysis of food retailers in Russia. *Manager, 13* (2), 74 – 75.

From the point of view of market capacity and the population development index, the most promising regions for the development of grocery retail chains are considered to be mainly large regions of the central, northwestern and southern parts of Russia.

In the country as a whole, the ranking of leaders and outsiders in terms of the share of chain retail in total retail trade looked as follows in 2021 (Table 2):

Table 2. Share of chains in retail trade turnover by regions of Russia, 2021 (in %).

"Leaders"	Share of chains - in retail, %	"Outsiders"	Share of chains in retail, %
St. Petersburg	59,60	Magadan Region	18,5
Leningrad region	58,50	Transbaikal	16,1
Moscow region	57,50	North Ossetia Alania	14,80
Kemerovo region	50,60	Sakhalin region	13,80
Republic of Mari El	49,30	Republic of Sakha (Yakutia)	12,70
Kaluga region	48,40	Buryatia	11,40
Tomsk region	47,80	Kabardino-Balkaria	8,40
Novosibirsk region	47,80	Ingushetia	3,30
Kaliningrad regio	47,00	Chechnya	2,20
Murmansk region	46,50	Dagestan	1,30

Source: https://datalens.yandex/qfv15a0hhidok?state=75cc7c38160.

In 2022, Russian grocery retail faced new challenges: changing the assortment due to the lack of familiar imported products, disrupting supply chains, and changing consumer preferences. However, in the summer of 2022, sales in the grocery segment showed a positive trend after several months of falling sales. However, as the analytics show, this dynamics is relative, since inflation largely affects revenue volumes. This led to the following phenomena – a decrease in real demand against the backdrop of inflation, a redistribution of the consumer basket in favor of cheaper or promotional goods, a change in the assortment matrix of retail chains, the introduction of a large number of private labels and the withdrawal of a number of goods. According to NielsenIQ agency estimates, 13 thousand new products arrived on the shelves of retail chains, but the delisting affected 14.5 thousand items. Representation of the average SKU on the shelf decreased by 7 % and, above all, due to the disappearance of many brands (Nielseniq.Com, 2022). New SKUs are determined by the presence of sales in the current week and the absence of sales in the previous week. The increase in the share of private labels in monetary terms amounted to 1.8 %, the increase in the share of the assortment – 1.4 %. However, the share of active SKUs in May-July 2022 decreased by 2.3 % compared to the same period in 2021. In general, in retail, 62 % of FMCG categories reduce their assortment.

As for the rating of retail chains, an analysis of the industry base for the two hundred largest FMCG retail chains at the end of 2021 showed that Lenta became the leader in revenue. In the Lenta-hypermarket format, revenue grew by 4.4 % and amounted to about 425 billion rubles. New hypermarkets have been opened, but 3 "old" ones have also been closed. The total retail space of the network increased by 20 thousand m2 (Infoline.Spb.Ru., 2023).

Auchan Retail's revenue has finally begun to grow due to the introduction of a large number of private labels and the revision of the assortment, as well as the opening of an online delivery channel. In the Moscow region, 4 Auchan and Auchan City hypermarkets were closed, the area of 1 hypermarket was reduced. As a result, the total sales area decreased by 34,000 sq.m. The number of METRO AG stores in Russia has not changed. The main focus of the network is on the development of online sales, especially in the regions, and the development of franchising. The O'KEY chain opened a new hypermarket in Moscow, at the beginning of 2022 it acquired 4 hypermarkets from X5 Group in the Moscow region (trading area 15,000 sq. m).

According to the results of the 1st quarter of 2022, there was a rotation in the TOP-10 grocery chains in Russia: the hypermarkets of the O'KEY chain moved to 8th place, leaving behind the VkusVill chain. The latter's revenue increased by 39 % over the year and amounted to about 50 billion rubles per year. O'KEY, in turn, showed an overall growth of 9.3 %, and discounters of this network called "Yes!" – by 57.6 % (Retail.Ru, 2022b).

The fastest growing network in the regions was the Svetofor network – it moved from 10th place in the TOP rating to 5th place with a 45 % increase in revenue compared to 2020. In 2021, Svetofor opened 1,134 new retail outlets, outperforming Magnit due to the volume of retail space. In fact, "Svetofor" is the federal leader in the "hard dietscounter" format.

In 2022, federal chains continued to expand into the Urals. Magnit acquired a holding, which includes the regional trading network Megamart. Magnit has 904 stores in the region, mostly in the convenience store format. When renaming the stores of the purchased network in those settlements where the share of Magnit is above 25 %, Megamart stores will operate under the old name. In general, in 2021, about 250 federal chain stores appeared in the region: Magnit opened 80 stores, Pyaterochka – 72, Monetka – 47, Verny – 15 (Rg.Ru, 2022). In general, over the past five years, the regional chains Piknik, Zvezdny, and Wright have left the FMCG market in the Ural region, and the Elisey chain has closed more than 50 % of retail outlets. In the overall structure of the Urals Federal District, federal networks occupy 54 % of the market, regional networks – 12 %, local – 34 %. The regional network Zhiznmart is popular; 33 stores have been opened in Yekaterinburg that sell only locally produced goods.

In the first quarter of 2022, X5 Group reorganized the Perekrestok store regional development department. In this regard, the opening of new stores planned for 2022 in the Volga Federal District was suspended. The following federal networks are most active in this region: Magnit, Auchan, Metro, and Lenta. Of the three regional networks, only one remained.

The regional trading network "Radezh" sells its stores in the Volga region and the Rostov region, part of the stores were bought by "Magnit," for which "Radezh" was a real competitor. In Volgograd, the MAN chain also closed, which first changed owners from local to Moscow, and then went bankrupt. The trade mark and retail space are also for sale. The regional network "Pokupochka," which has more than 300 stores, is still quite active, managed to set up logistics and replace federal brands that have fallen out with local goods. The chain takes 9th place in the rating of trading enterprises in the Volga region in 2021 (Novostivolgograda.Ru, 2022).

In 2021, a new large regional alliance "Eastern Union" appeared in Siberia and the Far East, which included the companies Krasny Yar, Slata, Samberi. The holding creates a centralized system of logistics, marketing and promotion management, creation of private labels, category management, online trading, etc. The holding also plans to "organize hubs for trunk deliveries and distribution centers of the last mile, which will allow rebuilding the supply chain on the scale of the Siberian and Far Eastern federal districts, increasing market share and becoming a major customer for suppliers comparable to the main federal networks" (Rbc.Ru, 2022a).

In Eastern Siberia, chain stores of the discounter format have been developing most actively over the past few years. The largest regional players operate under the "KhlebSol," "Khoroshiy," and "Baton" brands. KhlebSol is part of the Slata company (Retail.Ru, 2022a). From 2014 to the present, more than 280 outlets have been opened in three regions – the Irkutsk region, Transbaikalia and Buryatia. The area of each store is at least 280 sq.m., the assortment includes at least 1300 SKUs, plus 200 SKUs of seasonal goods. Private label is represented by goods with "Ptichka" and is approaching 20 % of the total turnover.

Discounters "Khoroshiy" are part of the regional network "Commander." The first discounter was opened in 2014 in Kemerovo, now there are 215 of them. The geography of distribution of discounters "Khoroshiy": Krasnoyarsk Territory, Kemerovo Region, Tyva, Khakassia, Irkutsk Region. The average area of retail outlets is 300 – 350 sq.m. and about 3000 SKUs. There are private labels under the brands "Our leader," "K," "I'll take it!." The Krasny Yar company opens the Baton discounter, the largest geography of distribution is the Krasnoyarsk Territory, there are stores in Khakassia and Tuva, a total of 170 stores. The average area of retail outlets is 350 – 380 sq.m. and about 1800 SKUs.

Thus, regional retailers actually dictate a certain model of the FMCG market. According to experts, regardless of the dynamics of the recovery of the industry, all players will have to reconsider their sales strategy. It will be necessary to adapt the assortment matrix, change the pricing and promotional policy, adapt to the new consumer model aimed at saving.

If we consider the structure of food retail in Russia in territorial terms, then among the leaders in terms of the share of retail chains in the total turnover of retail sales, we will definitely see St. Petersburg. The total share of food retail in the St. Petersburg market, according to the FAS Office for St. Petersburg, is almost 90 %. The shares of the main food retailers are shown in Table 3.

The consumer market of St. Petersburg began to transform during the pandemic period, but serious structural changes began in the first quarter of 2022. They were provoked by a change in the model of consumer behavior associated with the start of a special military operation and the imposition of sanctions against the Russian Federation.

Table 3. Shares of major business entities in the food retail market in St. Petersburg in 2019–2020, (in % of total sales).

Trading network	2019	2020
X5 Retail Group (Pyaterochka, Perekrestok, Karusel)	27,37	31,75
Lenta	13,30	17,55
O'KEY	9,94	10,12
Trade House Intertorg (Family,Spar,Idea)	10,0	market exit
Dixy	6,95	7,42
Magnit	5,76	7,24
METRO AG	2,42	2,21
Auchan	1,43	1,15
Prisma	1,55	1,49
Land	0,91	0.9
Verny	1,30	1,47
7 steps (Trading House "Progress")	2,10	3,07
Real	1,0	1.0
Season	0,7	0,7
Rang	0,80	0,85
Plovdiv	0,7	1,0
Azbuka Vkusa	0,63	0,76
The total share of large retail chains	86,86	87,78

Source: https://spb.fas.gov.ru/news/11258.

According to the St. Petersburg Analytical Center, retail trade turnover during this period increased by 8 % compared to the same period in 2021 (Figure 1).

Figure 1. Retail trade turnover in St. Petersburg, 2021 – 2022 (billion rubles).

Source: https://www.gov.spb.ru/static/writable/documents/2022/08/15/AC2022.pdf.

These changes were manifested in the fact that new players appeared, and some retail chains lost their positions. Researchers believe that the key event was the departure of the NGO Trade House Intertorg, as a result of which not only convenient and profitable retail space was released, but also the market share in the industry.

In 2021, Magnit actively opened new stores: 38 units of the Magnit Cosmetic format, 59 convenience stores, 1 discounter and a test Magnit City at Pulkovo Airport. VkusVill opened 37 new stores, 8 dark stores (night delivery of goods). Lenta stopped opening hypermarket stores, and in 2021 opened 58 Mini stores and 34 "SuperLenta" supermarkets in St. Petersburg and the Leningrad Region. X5 Group continued the policy of closing Karusel hypermarkets. According to the company's management, "the market share of X5 Group reached 28.9 % in 2020 and for the third year in a row exceeded the maximum allowable limit in St. Petersburg (up to 25 %). The company cannot buy and rent new premises for shops during the year – this is prohibited by the Federal Antimonopoly Service. Openings in St. Petersburg are possible only through the transfer of points"(Rbc. Ru, 2022b).

As of April 2022, the leader in food retail in St. Petersburg is the Magnit chain, which has 1,109 stores. The chains Red and White (450 outlets), Dixy (441) and Pyaterochka (416) are far behind the leader. Then come Lenta (150 outlets) and VkusVill (130). Less than 100 outlets at Perekrestok (83) and O'KEY chain (24). If we consider the situation in the city as a whole, then, as Zaitseva (2022) notes, "the total number of FMCG retail stores in St. Petersburg and the Leningrad Region increased by 18.3 % over the year, taking into account closed outlets. At the same time, in January-November, the turnover of retail trade in food products, including drinks and tobacco products, in St. Petersburg increased by 9.5 % in actual prices. But taking into account the growth in prices for the year by about 9 %, in physical terms, sales increased slightly."

At the same time, many retail chains have taken a wait-and-see attitude in planning and opening new outlets, since any new project requires guarantees, and the current situation is not conducive to this. Since spring 2022, despite the planned market penetration strategy, not a single new X5 Group store (Pyaterochka and Perekrestok), Magnit and VkusVill has been opened. Market experts emphasize that "the opening of new outlets today is the result of transactions initiated before February 24, 2022." (Dmitrieva & Zaitseva, 2022).

Another feature of the development of food retail in St. Petersburg was the active transition of traditional retail to online. For example, X5 Group reported that in 2021 sales at retail outlets grew by 10.1 %, reaching 2.1 trillion rubles, while online sales of the retailer grew by 140 % (X5 Group.Ru, 2023). During the same time, Lenta's traditional retail chain grew by 88 %, while the online sales segment grew by 208 % (Zaitseva, 2022).

The next growth opportunity for the largest food retail players in St. Petersburg is manifested in the development of the discounter format. The concept of developing discounters appeared in the chains even before the pandemic. For example, as part of X5 Retail Group's recovery from the crisis, the "hard" discounter format was given maximum autonomy to quickly respond to changes in local demand. In July-September 2021, the company opened 163 "Chizhik" stores, the discounter's revenue in Q3 2021 increased 13 times. Discounters Da!, owned by O'KEY, brought in revenue of RUB 13.4 billion, up 54.8 % year-on-year, although the total revenue of O'KEY hypermarkets fell 1.2 % due to closing of shopping centers. There are also 6 "My Price" discounters in St. Petersburg, which belong to the Magnit chain. In September 2022, plans were announced to open the GOST network in the city, where only domestic products manufactured in accordance with GOST (Rbc.Ru, 2022b) will be sold. This is a new format in which there will be no intermediaries between manufacturers and sellers. The stores themselves will be small: counter format with an assortment of about 200 items. The second federal network in the format of a "hard discounter" called "Dobrotsen" also plans to open in 2023 and is currently actively looking for space for retail outlets.

In our opinion, when assessing the opportunities for growth and development of the largest retail chains, the opinion of buyers is also important. The point of sale is not always chosen by proximity to the house, pricing policy or convenience and accessibility. An important factor is the general perception of the outlet, cleanliness, assortment, culture of behavior and service of sales personnel, as well as the optimal combination of qualities that are important for the consumer.

We conducted a study of the largest grocery chains in St. Petersburg based on data from the Yandex-Maps service, where you can get information on reviews and visits to various outlets. Considered from January to September 2022 based on 70,000 user reviews. The following networks were taken for analysis: O'KEY, Lenta, Perekrestok, Auchan, VkusVill, Azbuka Vkusa, Pyaterochka, Magnit, Karusel, Verny and Dixy.

For comparison, not only large retail chains were deliberately taken, but also mid-level chains, since in relation to them, buyers can trace certain trends in the development of grocery retail and consumer attitudes towards them. The average assessment of grocery chains by buyers is shown in Figure 2.

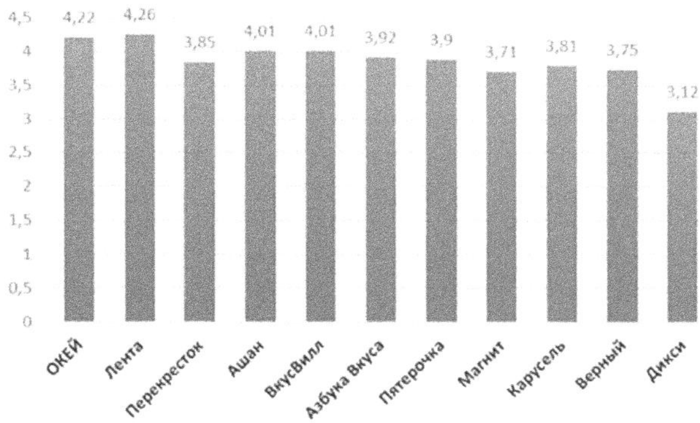

Figure 2. Comparison of retail outlets of food chains in St. Petersburg according to the overall assessment of Yandex-Maps visitors.

Source: Compiled by the authors

Residents of St. Petersburg give the highest rating to the outlets of the Lenta (4.26) and O'KEY (4.22) chains, Dixy (3.12) is the outsider. Estimates of other networks fluctuate in the range of 4.01 – 3.71. In addition, based on customer reviews on the Yandex-Maps service, it is possible to generate ratings by infrastructure and product categories. The infrastructure includes the convenience of the location of the outlet, the need and possibility of parking, the relevance and attractiveness of promotions, the culture of behavior and staff service, queues, cleanliness in sales areas, the relevance of the assortment, and the general pricing policy. The rating of retail chains by infrastructure category is shown in Figure 3.

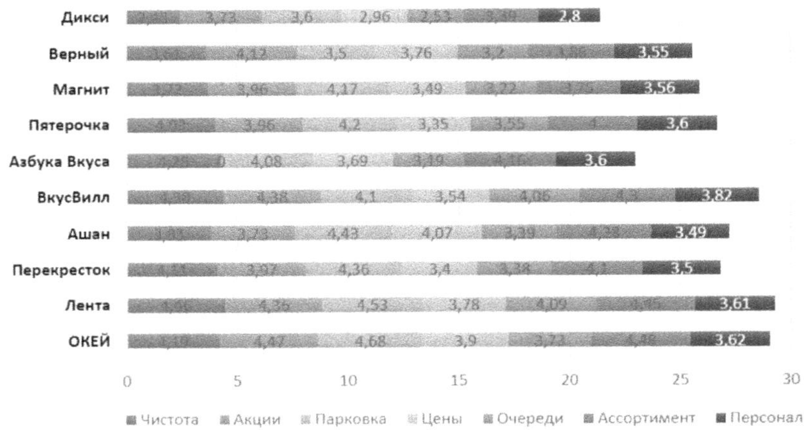

Figure 3. Rating of retail chains in St. Petersburg in terms of infrastructure according to Yandex- Maps visitors.

Source: Compiled by the authors

It is obvious that in the category "Cleanliness and order in the trading floor" stores of the Dixy chain are in the lowest position (2.43). At the same time, VkusVill stores, which are traditionally located in small and cramped premises, have a rating of 4.38, only Lenta is higher with a rating of 4.46. The leaders in promotions and bonus programs (4.47), in terms of convenience of location (4.68) are the O'KEY chain (4.47). The most attractive prices for buyers are in the Auchan network (4.07), the smallest queues are in Lenta (4.09), the most attractive assortment is in Lenta and O'KEY, and the most polite staff – in VkusVille (3.82).

The rating of retail chains in St. Petersburg in terms of assortment and quality, according to Yandex-Maps visitors, is shown in Figure 4.

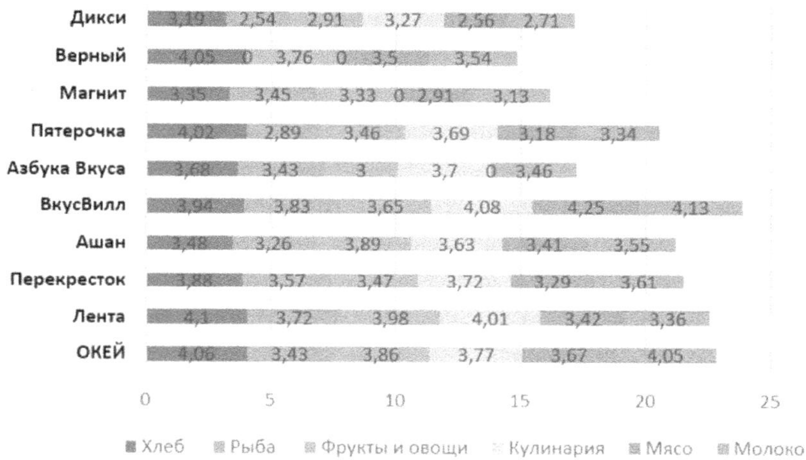

Figure 4. Rating of retail chains in St. Petersburg in terms of assortment and quality according to Yandex-Maps visitors.

Source: Compiled by the authors

The leaders in the assortment of bakery products and pastries (4.1), fruits and vegetables (3.98) are Lenta chain stores, in terms of the assortment of fish and seafood (4.83), culinary (4.08), meat (4. 25) and milk (4.13) – VkusVill. Such a gap between the VkusVill grocery retailer and the leading industry players in terms of the key assortment indicates the right choice of the chain concept: reliance on local suppliers and low price of joining the chain.

In general, at the end of 2021, St. Petersburg ranks 4th in the rating of Russian regions in terms of retail trade dynamics in retail chains. The change in turnover gave an increase of 18.6 % compared to the same period last year. The retail trade turnover in the second half of 2021 per city resident amounted to 160.8 thousand rubles, and the share in the all-Russian turnover was 4.8 % (Ria.Ru, 2022).

Thus, the current growth and development opportunities for the largest food retail players in St. Petersburg can be assessed as quite high. Despite the decline in the purchasing power of the population, the level of revenue of retail chains did not fall, although it was redistributed. However, large retailers should monitor trends in the FMCG industry and respond to them in a timely manner. In 2021, the city's consumer market was under the influence of anti-COVID legislative restrictions. At the same time, the trade turnover of retail food chains amounted to 1,875.4 billion rubles, which is 15 % more than in 2020.

The annual report of the Committee for Industrial Policy, Innovation and Trade of the Government of St. Petersburg monitors the level of competition by industry, customer satisfaction, market conditions in the reporting period. In the report for 2021, the level of competition in the retail market is assessed as "high," the share of the private sector in them is more than 80 % (Gov.Spb. Ru, 2023).

In contrast to retail in Europe and the United States, in Russia, the participation of the state in the FMCG industry is noticeable. For example, since 2018, VTB Bank has been the largest co-owner of Magnit. He is a key financial partner of the network: he issues Magnit debit cards, and also launched a payment service with advanced functionality Magnit Pay. Both Magnit and Lenta have said they will finance takeover deals with their own funds and unused credit line balances. At the same time, both companies borrow mainly from state-owned banks – VTB and Sberbank (Prostakov, 2021).

To a certain extent, this became the basis of the development business model, the desire for which was declared by the management of X5 Group. The essence of the model is commitment to the goals of sustainable development in unity with society and the state and the introduction of ESG principles into corporate culture, procurement activities and social responsibility programs. In the past few years, with the growing understanding of the environmental and social pressures of today, the principles of ESG have become popular and have reached the level of public awareness of their importance.

ESG data typically reflects non-financial factors in overall performance that have traditionally been missing from financial analysis: an organization's energy and water management, waste generation, employee rights and working conditions, and more traditional measures of organizational accountability and transparency. An important element of the model is digital transformation as the basis for making managerial decisions based on big data and artificial intelligence.

The influence of the state on the activities of food retail is also associated with forced regulatory activities in the situation of sanctions restrictions. This regulation includes the permission of parallel imports. With regard to the FMCG industry, we are talking about the supply of household chemicals, hygiene products and cosmetics.

In a situation of rising logistics costs and sanctions for regional retail, the issue of competition with federal networks is especially acute. In these conditions, the business model that is traditional for regional retail trade is relevant – convenience stores, semi-stationary and mobile trade under the brands of retail chains as a guarantor of product quality and a loyal pricing policy. At the same time, it is natural to increase the share of domestic retail due to the withdrawal of foreign producers and retail chains from the market. At the same time, a certain retail business model is formed, which takes into account, for example, the former name of the retail chain, to which consumer loyalty of customers has formed.

4 Conclusions

Based on the study, the following conclusions can be drawn:

1. The retail chain in Russia has shown resilience in difficult economic conditions: it was able to adapt first to the conditions of anti-pandemic restrictions, then to the conditions of sanctions and the withdrawal of foreign manufacturers and suppliers. Consumers have demonstrated that they are not ready to abandon such a retail format as hypermarkets, supermarkets and convenience stores.
2. St. Petersburg continues to maintain its leading position in the volume of network retail trade in the country. Anti-pandemic restrictions lasted longer in the city than in other regions, they have not been completely canceled so far. However, in the period 2021–2022, there were no closures of chain stores in the city for economic reasons. Urban retail both sets the tone for new trends in the development of network trade, and follows in line with the all-Russian ones. Among such trends are the opening of discounters, e-commerce, the development of the convenience store format and a wide range of private labels in different price categories.
3. The situation on the commodity food market is developing in the context of restrictive measures, a decrease in the purchasing power of the population, but also an increase in revenue. The restrictions imposed by the regulator relate to sanitary measures, pricing policy, quality of goods and services. Due to the fact that the opening of large retail outlets for networks has become less relevant, antitrust restrictions are not so sharp. Retail chains can redistribute the format of stores within the available volumes of retail space, and now this is happening in favor of discounters.

References

Dengov,V. V., Gregova, E., & Maksimov, A. V. (2016). Globalization in the field of food retail St. Petersburg: Analysis of the price policy. *Proceedings of the 16th International Scientific Con-ference on Globalization and its Socio-Economic Consequences,* Part I. Zilina, Slovakia, pp. 362–374. WOS:000393253800046

Dmitrieva, D., & Zaitseva, D. (2022). Without sudden movements: Stores stopped looking for space for new outlets. *Delovoy Petersburg.*

Gov.Spb.Ru. (2023, May 23). https://www.gov.spb.ru/gov/otrasl/c_industrial_and_trade/ standart-razvitiya-konkurencii-v-sankt-peterburge/doklady-o-sostoyanii-i-razvitii-konkurentnoj-sredy-na-tovarnyh-rynkah-/.

Gregova, E., Dengov, V., & Tulyakova, I. (2018). Global trends in Russian retail: A comparison of the market of St. Petersburg and Moscow. *Proceedings of the 18th International Scientific Conference on Globalization and its Socio-Economic Consequences,* PTS I-VI, Žilina, Slovakia, pp. 1079–1086. WOS:000681676300140

Gregova, E., Dengov, V., Tulyakova, I., & Mustafaev, A. (2020). Private label as a global trend of food networks for pricing policy optimization (case study of St. Petersburg). *SHS Web of Conferences. Collection of Materials of the 19th International scientific conference. University of Zilina, SR, 74,* 04007.

Hina, M., Chauhan, C., Kaur, P., Kraus, S., & Dhir, A. (2021). Drivers and barriers of circular economy business models: Where we are now, and where we are heading. Journal of Cleaner Production, 333, 130049. https://doi.org/10.1016/j.jclepro.2021.130049

Infoline.Spb.Ru. (2023, May 23). https://infoline.spb.ru/upload/iblock/ce6/ce6ac3027ff5f0071caefab127cbcb95.pdf.

Kadekova, Z., Savov, R., Kosiciarova, I., & Valaskova, K. (2020). CSR activities and their impact on brand value in food enterprises in Slovakia based on foreign participation. *Sustainability, 12*(12) Article 4856.

Kirk, C. P., & Rifkin, L. S. (2020). I'll trade you diamonds for toilet paper: Consumer reacting, coping and adapting behaviours in the Covid-19 pandemic. *Journal of Business Research, 117*(2), 124–131.

Kovalev, V.E., Novikova, K.V., Antineskul, E.A. (2022). Cluster analysis of food retailers inRussia. *Manager, 13* (2), 74–75.

Lasenko, D. V. (2022). Russian retail during the pandemic. *In situ, 1*, 21–25.

Maksimov, A. V., Dengov, V. V., & Tulyakova, I. R. (2016). Globalization in the field of food retail St.Petersburg: Concentration and competition, *Proceedings of the 16th International Scientific Conference on Globalization and its Socio-Economic Consequences,* Part I–V. Zilina, Slovakia, pp. 1277–1286. WOS:000393253800158

Marinkovic, V., & Lazarevic, J. (2021). Eating habits and consumer food shopping behavior during the Covid-19 virus pandemic: Insights from Serbia. *British Food Journal.*

Nielseniq.Com. (2022, May 23). https://nielseniq.com/global/ru/insights/analysis/2022/kak-izmenilsya-fmcg-rynok-v-2022/.

Novostivolgograda.Ru. (2022, May 23). https://novostivolgograda.ru/news/2022-04-28/torgovye-seti-rvutsya-spravitsya-li-volgogradskiy-riteyl-s-novymi-vyzovami-1566810.

Prostakov G. (2021, May 21). *Mergers in grocery retail strengthen the role of the state in the sector.* Vedomosti. https://www.vedomosti.ru/opinion/articles/2021/05/21/870676-sliyaniya-produktovom.

Rbc.Ru. (2022a). https://www.rbc.ru/spb_sz/19/09/2022/632870989a794757d4e41852

Rbc.Ru. (2022b). https://www.rbc.ru/spb_sz/20/09/2022/6329caa29a794746e5e52736

Retail.Ru (2022a) https://www.retail.ru/rbc/pressreleases/vkusvill-potesnil-set-o-key-v-reytinge-fmcg-ot-infoline-po-itogam-i-kvartala-2022-goda/

Retail.Ru (2022b) https://www.retail.ru/photoreports/diskauntery-sibiri-kak-oni-ustroeny-i-chem-otlichayutsya-drug-ot-druga/

Rg.Ru. (2022, May 23). https://rg.ru/2022/01/12/reg-urfo/federalnye-torgovye-seti-prodolzhat-v-2022-godu-ekspansiiu-na-ural.html.

Ria.Ru. (2022, May 23). https://ria.ru/20210830/torgovlya-1747765752.html.

Sheth, J. (2020). Impact of Covid-19 on consumer behavior: Will the old habits return or die? *Journal of Business Research, 117*, 280–283.

Tulyakova, I., Gregova, E., Dengov,V., & Mustafaev A. (2020). Improvement of retail pricing strategies in food distribution networks in terms of global competition (St. Petersburg's example). *SHS Web of Conferences. Collection of Materials of the 19th International scientific conference. University of Zilina, SR, 74*, 06030.

Valaskova, K., Durana, P., & Adamko, P. (2021). Changes in consumers' purchase patterns as a consequence of the COVID-19 pandemic. *Mathematics, 9*(15), Article 1788.

X5 Group.Ru. (2023, May 23). https://www.x5.ru/ru/investors/annual-reports/

Zaitseva, D. (2022). A good year for online: Retail chains in St. Petersburg predicted rapid growth. *Delovoy Petersburg.*

Mihai Dinu[1,*], Ioan I. Gâf-Deac[2], Cătălin Octavian Mănescu[2], Romeo Cătălin Crețu[4] and Carina Ilinca Gombos[5]

Economic Globalization and the Environment: Strategies for Sustainable Development in the Age of Global Connectivity

Abstract:
Research background: The contemporary world is marked by rapid globalization, increasing interconnection of economies, and growing concern for the environment. A need for sustainable development practices that align with global economic growth is paramount. The research background thus encompasses an in-depth analysis of the impact of economic globalization on environmental sustainability, as well as the integration of policies that foster both.
Purpose of the article: This article aims to explore the intersection between economic globalization and environmental stewardship, identifying the challenges and opportunities that arise from this nexus. By understanding how these domains interact, the article proposes coherent strategies to advance sustainable development without hampering economic growth.
Methods: The research was based on a qualitative approach. To understand the topic in depth, we used case studies and interviews with experts in the field. The analyzes performed were mainly thematic comparisons and content analyses, which helped to identify and interpret relevant trends and patterns.
Findings & Value added: The findings reveal a complex relationship between globalization and environmental protection, where economic growth can either exacerbate or alleviate

* Corresponding author: carmen-valentina.radulescu@eam.ase.ro
1 Bucharest University of Economic Studies, Associate Professor Ph.D, Romania
2 Ec./Technical Science, Sci. Research., INCE C. Kiritescu / Romanian Academy, Senior Lecturer, PhD. Romania
3 Bucharest University of Economic Studies, Associate Professor Ph.D, Romania
4 Professor, PhD., University of Agronomic Sciences and Veterinary Medicine of Bucharest
5 Ministry of the Environment, Waters, Forests

environmental challenges, depending on implemented policies. Strategies for creating synergy between economic advancement and environmental sustainability are identified.

Keywords: *environment, globalization, sustainable development, strategies*

JEL Classification: *Q23; Q53*

1 Introduction

In a world where economic boundaries are blurring and global connectivity is becoming the norm, the debate on the relationship between economic globalization and the environment is becoming essential (Gawor, 2008). Our research sheds light on a complex subject that influences the future of the planet and the quality of life of its population. As flows of capital, goods and services cross national borders at unprecedented speed, the impact of this globalization process on natural resources and biodiversity is becoming a topic of great interest (Murali & Alamar, 2008; Rădulescu & Burlacu, 2019; Rădulescu et al., 2020).

History has shown us that, on numerous occasions, rapid economic development has come at the expense of the environment. Forests have been cleared, mineral resources depleted, and fragile ecosystems disrupted, all in the name of progress and economic growth. However, in the era of global connectivity in which we live, we also have the unique opportunity to learn from the mistakes of the past and to develop strategies that integrate both the objectives of economic development and those of environmental protection.

This article aims to analyze the dynamics between globalization and environmental change, highlighting both the challenges and opportunities that arise. By examining cases and studies over time, we will identify appropriate strategies for navigating an era of economic interdependence while ensuring a sustainable future for generations to come.

Literature review: Linkages between globalization, environmental policies, and sustainable development.

Conceptualizing globalization in the context of the environment: The foundations of the interaction of globalization with the environment, as postulated by Alpopi et al. (2018), emphasize the dual role of globalization, both as a catalyst for environmental challenges and as a channel for the diffusion of environmental technologies and practices. Rondinelli (2007) further enriches this perspective by highlighting the potential of transnational corporations in incorporating sustainable practices, thus reframing the often-perceived antagonism between corporate actions and sustainable agendas.

The link between environmental policies and globalization: There is an unmistakable confluence between environmental policies and the forces of globalization. Bodislav et al. (2019, 2020) provide a complex analysis of the evolution of environmental policies, especially in the Romanian context, illustrating how these policies try to achieve a balance between development imperatives and environmental conservation. Bran et al. (2020) further extends this narrative by juxtaposing environmental risks within the larger scheme of globalization, drawing a compelling case for proactive policy interventions.

Technological innovations: a double-edged sword:The digital domain of globalization, as elucidated by Burlacu and colleagues (2018, 2019, 2022), emphasizes a transformative influence on socio-economic paradigms. While the digital age has led to unprecedented efficiencies, Popescu et al. (2021) warn of its unintended consequences, as evidenced by heightened vulnerabilities during the COVID-19 pandemic. This links to Ashford and Hall (2011), who argue for a conscientious integration of technology, based on sustainable principles, into the fabric of globalization.

Urbanization, health crises and globalization: The modern challenges of urbanization in a globalized world are closely related to the dynamics of health. Burlacu et al. (2021) and Sarbu et al. (2021) present a compelling narrative about the demands of sustainable urban development in the context of health crises. Their analysis is further complemented by Profiroiu et al. (2020), who research the concept of "Smart Cities," emphasizing the need for these cities to be resilient and adaptable in the face of global disruptions.

Reconceptualizing sustainable development: The tapestry of sustainable development woven with threads of globalization has been meticulously unraveled by several scholars. Norouzi and Ataei (2021), Bakari (2013) and Romano (2000) all criticize traditional paradigms of development, advocating a reconceptualization that truly imbibes sustainable principles. Dhiman (2023) and Ciulli and Kolk (2023) then turn this discussion towards business practices, emphasizing the symbiotic relationship between sustainable enterprises and global viability.

Synthesis: Synthesizing the rich tapestry of literature, one discerns a complex interplay between globalization, environmental imperatives, and the general ethos of sustainable development. The complexity of these dynamics, from policy frameworks to technological innovations and urban challenges, underscores the multifaceted nature of sustainable development in a globalized era (Blewitt, 2012). Collective scholarship offers not only a diagnostic lens but also prescriptive insights, paving the way for a harmonious coexistence of development and sustainability.

2 Methodology

In researching the relationship between globalization and the environment, we chose to use a qualitative method. This decision came in response to the complexity and depth of the problem, where mere quantitative data would not have been sufficient. To begin with, we analyzed several case studies, each reflecting a specific situation or region, to understand the impact of globalization on the environment. We have selected the cases based on specific criteria so that we have a complete picture of the global situation. Next, we interviewed experts in the field, people who had experience and knowledge in the global economy and environmental protection. Through these interviews, we wanted to better understand the challenges facing the world and identify possible solutions. In parallel, we analyzed various documents, from policies and international agreements to sustainability reports, to see how globalization and the environment are reflected in them. After gathering all this information, we conducted a thematic analysis. This involved grouping and organizing information into major themes to identify patterns and trends. Finally, to ensure that our results were robust, we compared information from different sources and identified commonalities and differences.

We were aware of possible limitations of our research, such as subjective interpretations or the fact that some case studies might have unique characteristics. Through this approach we have tried to gain a clear and detailed perspective on the relationship between globalization and the environment.

3 Results and Discussion

The research unveiled a nuanced relationship between globalization and environmental protection. It was discerned that, contingent upon the contextual backdrop and the policies in place, economic growth can variably impact the environment. Specifically, there are scenarios where rapid economic development can intensify environmental challenges, while in other situations, with the right policies, it can lead to innovative solutions that mitigate environmental concerns.

Based on the literature reviewed, policies centered around ecological preservation can play a pivotal role in how globalization affects the environment (Byrne et al., 2006). Echoing this, our study has spotlighted strategies that establish synergies between economic advancement and environmental sustainability, such as the embrace of green technologies or the institution of efficient resource management systems (Wheelen et al., 2023).

Our research crafted a comprehensive framework for decision-makers that offers guidance to industry leaders and scholars on aligning globalization endeavors with sustainable development objectives. Furthermore, the study underscores the significance of an integrative approach where economic and ecological elements converge for a more sustainable future. An illustrative point is the necessity for enhanced international cooperation to ensure that the benefits of globalization are equitably distributed while minimizing its environmental footprint.

Table 1. Detailed analysis of the relationship between ecological policies and the impact of globalization.

Factors	Positive Impact	Negative Impact	Proposed Strategies
Green Technologies	Enhanced energy efficiency leading to reduced carbon footprints.	Initial high costs can strain economies.	Wider adoption and fostering innovation. Subsidies for R&D.
Resource Management	Sustainable use conserves resources for future generations.	Over-extraction can lead to resource depletion.	Implement efficiency measures & promote fair redistribution.
International Cooperation	Shared best practices can benefit multiple nations.	Disparities in commitments can hamper collective objectives.	Strengthen global partnerships & harmonize policies.
Waste Reduction Initiatives	Decreased environmental pollution.	Economies heavily reliant on consumerism may resist change.	Global awareness campaigns & incentivize recycling industries.
Biodiversity Conservation	Maintenance of ecosystem balance and services.	Global trade can introduce invasive species.	Establish international reserves & control trade in endangered species.
Economic Incentives for Sustainability	Businesses align with sustainability for economic benefits.	Short-term profits may overshadow long-term sustainability.	Introduce tax breaks for sustainable practices & penalties for non-compliance.
Education and Awareness	Informed populations can push for sustainable policies.	Misinformation can hinder ecological progress.	Global educational campaigns & integration of ecology in curricula.

Source: Author's contribution

This table provides a deeper dive into the relationship between globalization and ecological policies, focusing on the identified factors. Each factor is evaluated for its potential positive and negative impacts, followed by proposed strategies to optimize benefits and mitigate drawbacks.

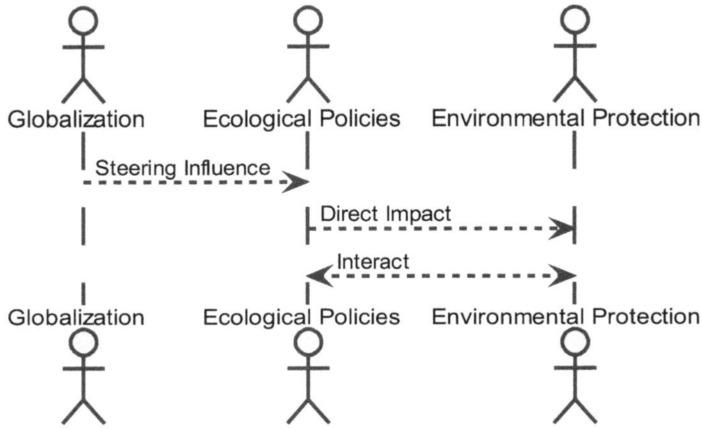

Figure 1. Diagram illustrating the interplay between globalization, ecological policies, and environmental protection.
Source: Author's contribution

This diagram showcases how ecological policies can steer the direction and influence of globalization on the surrounding environment.

Table 2. Globalization & environmental protection: analysis and recommendations.

Aspect	Identified Cause	Observed Impact	Recommendations	Potential Limitations
Carbon Emissions	Rapid industrialization in emerging economies	Increase in global greenhouse gas emissions	International standards on emissions; promotion of clean energy	Differences in national priorities; cost of green technologies
Biodiversity Loss	Global trade leading to habitat destruction	Decline in species richness and ecosystems	Strengthened global policies on land use; promote sustainable agriculture	Economic interests of certain industries; policy enforcement issues

Table 2. Continued

Aspect	Identified Cause	Observed Impact	Recommendations	Potential Limitations
Water Pollution	Global industries discharging waste	Decline in freshwater quality	Implementation of strict wastewater treatment standards globally	Initial financial implications; feasibility in underdeveloped regions
Resource Depletion	Unsustainable extraction due to high demand	Scarcity of critical resources	Promotion of circular economy; improved global resource management practices	Economic growth vs. sustainable practices; technological limitations
Waste Accumula-tion	Global consumerism & production	Increased land and ocean pollution	Global adoption of zero-waste policies; promotion of recycling	Cultural differences in consumption; infrastructural challenges

Source: Author's contribution

This table provides a more granular view, dissecting specific environmental challenges arising due to globalization. For each challenge, the underlying cause is identified, followed by the observed impact, actionable recommendations, and the potential limitations or challenges in implementing those recommendations. Such a framework can be instrumental for policy-makers and industry leaders in making informed decisions.

5 Conclusion

In the context of an increasingly globalizing world, the relationship between sustainable development and economic progress has become central to academic and policy discussions. This research has highlighted a complex relationship between environmental policies and the impact of globalization, providing a deep understanding of how these areas intersect.

The results indicate that globalization, in the absence of appropriate policies, can accelerate environmental problems. However, when properly directed through sound environmental policies, globalization can become an ally in environmental protection and conservation. Green technologies, efficient resource management and international cooperation are proving to be essential in shaping a globalization framework that promotes sustainability.

The tables and diagram presented above highlight the interactions and potential strategies that can be adopted to ensure that globalization and environmental protection go hand in hand. It is evident that a multidisciplinary and collaborative approach is essential to ensure a sustainable future in the context of a globalized world.

To progress towards a more sustainable future, it is crucial that policy makers, industry leaders and researchers embrace an integrated vision, where economic development and environmental protection are seen not as separate entities, but as interconnected parts of the same system. We thus consider that this research can be integrated into the mainstream of knowledge by offering a balanced and comprehensive perspective on the challenges and opportunities at the intersection of globalization and ecology.

References

Alpopi, C., Burlacu, S., & Iovițu, M. (2018). Procesul de globalizare şi politicile ecologice. In: *Competitivitatea şi Inovarea în Economia Cunoaşterii. Vol.2, 28–29 septembrie 2018, Chişinău, Republica Moldova: Departamentul Editorial-Poligrafic al ASEM, 2018, pp.* 317–324. ISBN 978-9975-75-931-1.

Ashford, N. A., & Hall, R. P. (2011). *Technology, globalization, and sustainable development: Transforming the industrial state.* Yale University Press.

Bakari, M. E. K. (2013). Globalization and sustainable development: False twins?. *New Global Studies, 7*(3), 23–56.

Blewitt, J. (2012). *Understanding sustainable development.* Routledge.

Bodislav, A. D., Rădulescu, C. V., Moise, D., & Burlacu, S. (2019). Environmental policy in the Romanian public sector. *The Bucharest University of Economic Studies Publishing House, 312.*

Bodislav, D. A., Radulescu, C. V., Bran, F., & Burlacu, S. (2020). Public policy in the areas of environment and energy. In *6th BASIQ International Conference on New Trends in Sustainable Business and Consumption* (pp. 228–235).

Bran, F., Rădulescu, C. V., Bodislav, D. A., & Burlacu, S. (2020). Environmental risks in the context of globalization. *Economic Convergence in European Union,* 350–356.

Burlacu, S., Curea, Ș. C., Popescu, L. M., & Stăncioiu, F. (2019). Electronic governance versus Open Government in the Globalization Era. *Collaborative Research for Excellence in Economics and Social Sciences,* 55.

Burlacu, S., Diaconu, A., Mocanu, V., & Gombos, S. P. (2022). The effects of digital globalization on economics and society. 8th BASIQ International Conference on New Trends in Sustainable Business and Consumption. Graz, Austria, 25–27 May 2022. Bucharest: ASE, 95–100. https://conference.ase.ro/wp-content/uploads/2022/06/22011_Final.pdf

Burlacu, S., Gutu, C., & Matei, F. O. (2018). Globalization-Pros and Cons. *Quality-Access to Success, 19.*

Burlacu, S., Patarlageanu, S. R., Diaconu, A., & Ciobanu, G. (2021). E-government in the era of globalization and the health crisis caused by the covid-19 pandemic, between standards and innovation. *Les Ulis: EDP Sciences.* doi:http://dx.doi.org/10.1051/shsconf/20219208004

Byrne, J., Glover, L., & Alrøe, H. F. (2006). Globalization and sustainable development: A political ecology strategy to realize ecological justice. In *Global development of organic agriculture: Challenges and prospects* (pp. 49–74). Wallingford UK: CABI Publishing.

Ciulli, F., & Kolk, A. (2023). International Business, digital technologies and sustainable development: Connecting the dots. *Journal of World Business, 58*(4), 101445.

Dhiman, S. (Ed.). (2023). *Sustainable development and environmental stewardship: Global initiatives towards engaged sustainability.* Cham: Springer International Publishing.

Gawor, L. (2008). Globalization and its alternatives: Antiglobalism, alterglobalism and the idea of sustainable development. *Sustainable Development, 16*(2), 126–134.

Murali, N., & Alamar, K. (2008). Globalization, the environment and sustainable development. In *Taylor & Francis eBooks* (pp. 13–19). https://doi.org/10.1201/9780203881255.ch2

Norouzi, N., & Ataei, E. (2021). Globalization and sustainable development. *International Journal of Innovative Research in Humanities, 1*, 69.

Popescu, M. L., Gombos, S. P., Burlacu, S., & Mair, A. (2021). The impact of the COVID-19 pandemic on digital globalization. In *SHS Web of Conferences* (Vol. 129, p. 06008). EDP Sciences.

Profiroiu, C. M., Rădulescu, C. V., & Burlacu, S. (2020). The challenges of Smart City in the context of globalization and the health crisis. In *Proceedings of Administration and Public Management International Conference* (Vol. 16, No. 1, pp. 4–11). Research Centre in Public Administration and Public Services, Bucharest, Romania.

Rădulescu, C. V., & Burlacu, S. (2019). Human pressure on air quality in Bucharest. *Competitiveness of Agro-Food & Environmental Economy.*

Rădulescu, C. V., Bran, F., Burlacu, S., Dobrea, C. R., & Diaconu, S. (2020). Challenges regarding food resources in the context of globalization and population growth. *In Proceedings of the International Conference on Economics and Social Sciences* (pp. 1041–1052). Sciendo.

Romano, P. (2000). Sustainable development: A strategy that reflects the effects of globalization on the international power structure. *Houston Journal of International Law*, *23*, 91.

Rondinelli, D. A. (2007). Globalization of sustainable development: Principles and practices in transnational corporations. *Multinational Business Review*, *15*(1), 1–24.

Sarbu, R., Alpopi, C., Burlacu, S., & Diaconu, S. (2021). Sustainable urban development in the context of globalization and the health crisis caused by the covid-19 pandemic. *Les Ulis: EDP Sciences.* doi:http://dx.doi.org/10.1051/shsconf/20219201043

Wheelen, T. L., Hunger, J. D., Hoffman, A. N., & Bamford, C. E. (2023). *Strategic management and business policy: Globalization, innovation, and sustainability.* Pearson.

Ján Dvorsky[1,*], Renata Skypalova[2], and Zora Petrakova[3]

Attitudes of Owners on the Corporate Social Responsibility on the SMEs Segment V4 Countries – Gender View

Abstract:
Research background: Corporate social responsibility (CSR) is a valuable tool of a better management of enterprises for the benefit of the whole society. Small- and medium-sized enterprises (SMEs) have been facing this challenge for a shorter time than large enterprises. Owners' characteristics as is gender, age, level of education, time in business can also play important role in this context..
Purpose of the article: Aim of the article is comparison the attitudes of owners of SMEs on the corporate social responsibility according to the gender.
Methods: The questionnaire fulfill 1090 owners or top managers of small and medium-sized enterprises in the business environment of the Visegrad Group. Case study was realized in the years 2022/2023. The statistical methods as is correlation analysis and analysis of dependences were used on the evaluation of the statistical hypotheses. The hypotheses were evaluated with using IBM SPSS Statistics vs. 28.
Findings & Value added: The are no important differences between man and women on the perception of CSR concept and their implementation in the SMEs segment V4 countries. Authors findings and consequences are important for better understanding of support the national agencies and institutions which help the segment of small and medium-sized in the areas as is a education, prevention and future in business.

Keywords: *corporate social responsibility, owners, gender, small and medium-sized enterprises, V4 countries*

JEL Classification: *D90; G30; L21; L25; L25*

---

* Corresponding author: jan.dvorsky@uniza.sk
1 University of Zilina, Faculty of Operation and Economics of Transport and Communications, Department of Economics, Univerzitna 1, 010 26 Zilina, Slovakia
2 Ambis College, Department of Economics and Management, Lindnerova 575/1, 180 00 Prague 8 – Liben, Czech Republic
3 Slovak University of Technology, Faculty of Civil Engineering, Institute for Forensic Engineering, Vazovova 5, 812 43 Bratislava, Slovakia

1 Introduction

Corporate social responsibility is a concept that reflects business reactions to the expectations and needs of diverse stakeholders including individuals, society, and the environment (Agyemang & Ansong, 2017). CSR has become a important point of sustainability (e.g., sustainable development of SMEs), and its concept has received higher attention from researchers and practitioners (Le, 2022; Martínez-Martínez, 2017).

From the point of view of CSR in SMEs, it is the employees who create a competitive advantage. In order for the employee to create a competitive advantage for the company, he should be satisfied and motivated in his work. This statement is also proven by the research of the authors Doh et al. (2015), who investigated how organizational culture affects internal corporate social responsibility activities and the impact of these activities on employee happiness levels. The authors found that an internal social responsibility policy has a positive effect on the work-life balance of employees (Belas et al., 2021). At the same time, the authors report that an internal corporate social responsibility policy on employees has a significant positive impact on employee happiness and helps engage in more innovative work ideas. It could therefore be said that a strategically designed internal corporate social responsibility policy can have a significant positive impact on an employee's work-life balance, and this can ultimately help increase employee satisfaction. More importantly, satisfied employees may have innovative ideas for business development (Nazir et al., 2021; Glavas, 2016).

In this article, the approach of SMEs to selected aspects of the CSR concept is evaluated, while the subject of empirical research is the quantification of differences in the perception of CSR in terms of the gender of owners/managers.

The structure of the post is as follows. The first part presents the results of studies that deal with the impact of CSR on financial performance, competitiveness and employee care in the SME segment. In the next chapter, the aim of the research is presented, methodology and data that were obtained on the basis of empirical research in the V4 countries. The next chapter presents the detailed results of the empirical research. At the end, the basic results are presented in an aggregated form. This research is original in that we present the attitudes of entrepreneurs in the SME segment to selected aspects of the CSR concept.

1.1 Literature Background

The concept of CSR has escalated in importance to become a fundamental pillar for any company intending to become a competitive agent in the current market

(Nagy et al., 2022; Tao et al., 2018). According to Bahta et al. (2021), CSR seeks to reduce the company's negative impact on the environment by voluntarily improving social and environmental standards.

Nowadays, companies all around the world are becoming more and more interested in implementing CSR strategies with the aim of generating competitive advantages and establishing a constructive relation with stakeholders (Cera et al., 2022; Bahta et al., 2021). One of the main objectives of the CSR is to build a constructive relation with customers (Adams & Funk, 2012). It has not only become a marketing goal but a significant factor to generate competitive advantage (Adams & Ferreira, 2009; Okoye, 2012).

A research carried out by Ahmad et al. (2022) established a relationship between CSR and improvements related to customers through a variable named relational improvements. According to the authors, the commitments with the customers have a positive effect on the firm's performance.

Moreover, an investigation developed by Pfajfar et al. (2022) studied the impact of CSR on customer loyalty and found a positive relationship expressed mainly in economic and legal effects. Other authors demonstrated that the perceptions of customer-centric CSR strategies positively and consistently impact satisfaction and repurchase behaviors.

The global economic environment represents a variety of risks for companies and CSR policies can be a key element in a firm's risk management strategy (Prochazkova & Micak, 2023; Sikyr et al., 2023). According to Godfrey (2005), a firm's prior CSR engagement can lead to an insurance-like protection in the context of corporate financial distress by reducing potential sources of business risk. In the same line, Platonova et al. (2018) developed a research framework using social and environmental ratings from the MSCI ESG database as a substitute for CSR and found that a SD increase of CSR investment decreases the likelihood of bankruptcy in approximately 28.5 %.

Moreover, Sial et al. (2018) concluded that companies developing a strong CSR strategy are more likely to have earning warnings before negative announcements than companies with weak CSR strategies. These warnings can represent an important tool that may help predict and avoid a possible crisis.

2 Methodology

Aim of the article is comparison the attitudes of owners of SMEs on the corporate social responsibility according to the gender.

2.1 Data Collection

The empirical research, which was aimed at finding out the attitudes of SMEs in the field of CSR, was carried out in the countries in December 2022 and January 2023. The data collection was carried out by the renowned external company MNFORCE using "Computer Assisted Web Interviewing" (CAWI Research Method) according to a questionnaire created by research team. The respondent could answer the statements by choosing one of the following answers: I completely agree, I agree, I have no opinion, I disagree and I completely disagree.

Based on defined requirements by the research team, the MNFORCE agency ensured an adequate structure of respondents in terms of size (the number of micro-enterprises and small and medium-sized enterprises corresponded to the structure of these enterprises in individual economies) and representativeness of the research. The selection of respondents was carried out using the method of random selection from the agency's professional database.

2.2 Variables

Authors defined the following statements in the questionnaire:

- Corporate Social Responsibility statements (CSRS)
- CSRS1: The concept of corporate social responsibility (CSR) plays an important role in our company.
- CSRS2: The implementation of the CSR concept has a positive effect on the future of SMEs.
- CSRS3: CSR helps us to gain new business partners.
- CSRS4: CSR has a positive impact on a firm's financial performance.

2.3 Statistical Hypotheses, Methods, and Structure of Respondent

As part of the research, we established the following statistical hypotheses:

- H1: There are no statistically significant differences in the attitudes of owners/manager towards CSRS1 in terms of gender in PL, CR, SR and HU.
- H2: There are no statistically significant differences in the attitudes of owners/manager towards CSRS2 in terms of gender in PL, CR, SR and HU.
- H3: There are no statistically significant differences in the attitudes of owners/manager towards CSRS3 in terms of gender in PL, CR, SR and HU.
- H4: There are no statistically significant differences in the attitudes of owners/manager towards CSRS4 in terms of gender in PL, CR, SR and HU.

Statistical hypotheses were verified through chi-square at the significance level α = 5 % (0.05). If the chi-square p-value was lower than 0.05, the hypothesis was rejected. If the chi-square p-value was greater than 0.05, the hypothesis was accepted. Calculations were made using a statistical software IBM SPSS Statistics.

The demographic characteristics of owners/managers and SMEs (n = 1,090 SMEs) were as follows: i. size of enterprise: 64.6 % micro-enterprises, 24.2 % small enterprises, 11.2 % medium enterprises; ii. legal form: 54.0 % sole trader, 37.2 % limited liability company, 6.4 % join-stock company, 2.4 % another form of business; iii. time period in business: 21.9 % less than or equal to 3 years; 24.1 % more than 3 years and less than to 5; 20.5 % more than 5 years and less than to 10; 33.5 % more than 10 years; iv. position of SMEs in business environment: 90.2 % domestic market; 9.8 % foreign market; v. nationality of respondent: 27.6 % Polish respondent, 33.2 % Czech respondent, 14.9 %Slovak respondent, 24.3 % Hungarian respondent.

3 Empirical Results

Table 1 presents results of comparison between owners and managers regarding the statement "the concept of corporate social responsibility (CSR) plays an important role in our company (CSRS1)" according to the gender.

Table 1. Evaluation CSRS1 statements according to the gender of owners/manager.

CSRS1	Poland				CSRS1	Slovak Republic			
	W	M	W	M		W	M	W	M
1	50	42	37.3 %	25.1 %	1	12	18	15.8 %	20.9 %
2	35	59	26.1 %	35.3 %	2	30	34	39.5 %	39.5 %
3	38	52	28.4 %	31.2 %	3	25	30	32.9 %	34.9 %
4	7	9	5.2 %	5.4 %	4	7	3	9,2 %	3.5 %
5	4	5	3.0 %	3.0 %	5	2	1	2.6 %	1.2 %
SUM	134	167	100 %	100 %	SUM	76	86	100 %	100 %
CSRS1	Czech Republic				CSRS1	Hungary			
	W	M	W	M		W	M	W	M
1	9	23	8.7 %	8.9 %	1	50	30	28.4 %	33.7 %
2	51	126	49.5 %	48.6 %	2	71	32	40.3 %	36.0 %
3	34	82	33.0 %	31.6 %	3	44	19	25.0 %	21.3 %
4	8	23	7.8 %	8.9 %	4	9	5	5.1 %	5.6 %
5	1	5	1.0 %	1.9 %	5	2	3	1.2 %	3.4 %
SUM	103	259	100 %	100 %	SUM	176	89	100 %	100 %

Note: W – women; M – man. Source: own data collection.

The results (see Table 1) showed that more than 50 % of respondent from each country confirmed that the CSR concept plays an important role in our company. The are not significant differences in the perception on the CSRS1 according to the gender in PL (Chi-sqaure = 3.458; p-val. = 0.241), CR (Chi-square = 6.118; p-val. = 0.147), SR (Chi-square = 3.872; p-val. = 0.381), HU (Chi-square = 7.458; p-val. = 0.111). Hypotheses H1 was confirmed for each group of respondents according to the nationality.

Table 2 presents results of comparison between owners o the statement "the implementation of the CSR concept has a positive effect on the future of SMEs (CSRS2)" according to the gender.

Table 2. Evaluation CSRS2 statements according to the gender of owners/manager.

CSRS2	Poland				CSRS2	Slovak Republic			
	W	M	W	M		W	M	W	M
1	36	24	26.9 %	14.4 %	**1**	9	15	11.8 %	17.4 %
2	48	79	35.8 %	47.3 %	**2**	33	33	43.4 %	38.4 %
3	42	50	31.3 %	29.9 %	**3**	27	35	35.5 %	40.7 %
4	5	7	3.7 %	4.2 %	**4**	5	3	6.6 %	3.5 %
5	3	7	2.2 %	4.2 %	**5**	2	0	2.6 %	0.0 %
SUM	134	167	100 %	100 %	**SUM**	76	86	100 %	100 %
CSRS2	**Czech Republic**				**CSRS2**	**Hungary**			
	W	**M**	**W**	**M**		**W**	**M**	**W**	**M**
1	6	19	5.8 %	7.3 %	1	50	21	28.4 %	23.6 %
2	45	109	43.7 %	42.1 %	2	68	32	38.6 %	36.0 %
3	48	120	46.6 %	46.3 %	3	49	32	27.8 %	36.0 %
4	4	8	3.9 %	3.1 %	4	7	3	4.0 %	3.4 %
5	0	3	0,0 %	1.2 %	5	2	1	1.1 %	1.1 %
SUM	103	259	100 %	**100 %**	**SUM**	176	89	100 %	100 %

Note: W – women; M – man.
Source: own data collection.

The results (see Table 2) showed that more than 50 % of respondent from each country confirmed that the implementation of the CSR concept has a positive effect on the future of SMEs. The are not significant differences in the perception on the CSRS2 according to the gender in PL (Chi-square = 8.184; p-val. = 0.084),

CR (Chi-square = 5.227; p-val. = 0.246), SR (Chi-square = 5.669; p-val. = 0.232), HU (Chi-square = 7.758; p-val. = 0.108). Hypotheses H2 was confirmed for each group of respondents according to the nationality.

Table 3 presents results of comparison between owners o the statement "CSR helps us to gain new business partners (CSRS3)" according to the gender.

The results (see Table 3) showed that more than 50 % of respondent from each country confirmed that the CSR helps us to gain new business partners. The are not significant differences in the perception on the CSRS3 according to the gender in PL (Chi-square = 8.287; p-val. = 0.096), CR (Chi-square = 8.227; p-val. = 0.146), SR (Chi-square = 7.583; p-val. = 0.132), HU (Chi-square = 2.758; p-val. = 0.588). Hypotheses H3 was confirmed for each group of respondents according to the nationality.

Table 3. Evaluation CSRS3 statements according to the gender of owners/manager.

CSRS3	Poland				CSRS3	Slovak Republic			
	W	M	W	M		W	M	W	M
1	38	32	28.4 %	19.2 %	1	9	14	11.8 %	16.3 %
2	43	57	32.1 %	34.1 %	2	25	25	32.9 %	29.1 %
3	40	62	29.9 %	37.1 %	3	26	31	34.2 %	36.0 %
4	10	11	7.5 %	6.6 %	4	10	14	13.2 %	16.3 %
5	3	5	2.2 %	3.0 %	5	6	2	7.9 %	2.3 %
SUM	134	167	100 %	100 %	SUM	76	86	100 %	100 %
CSRS3	Czech Republic				CSRS3	Hungary			
	W	M	W	M		W	M	W	M
1	5	11	4.9 %	4.2 %	1	49	21	27.8 %	23.6 %
2	34	79	33.0 %	30.5 %	2	70	34	39.8 %	38.2 %
3	45	111	43.7 %	42.9 %	3	36	26	20.5 %	29.2 %
4	17	48	16.5 %	18.5 %	4	15	5	8.5 %	5.6 %
5	2	10	1.9 %	3.9 %	5	6	3	3.4 %	3.4 %
SUM	103	259	100 %	100 %	SUM	176	89	100 %	100 %

Note: W – women; M – man.
Source: own data collection

Table 4 presents results of comparison between owners o the statement "CSR has a positive impact on a firm's financial performance" according to the gender.

Table 4. Evaluation CSRS4 statements according to the gender of owners/manager.

CSRS4	Poland				CSRS4	Slovak Republic			
	W	M	W	M		W	M	W	M
1	36	35	26.9 %	21.0 %	1	76	86	6.6 %	20.9 %
2	41	57	30.6 %	34.1 %	2	25	25	36.8 %	25.6 %
3	43	58	32.1 %	34.7 %	3	26	31	32.9 %	37.2 %
4	10	10	7.5 %	6.0 %	4	10	14	15.8 %	12.8 %
5	4	7	3.0 %	4.2 %	5	6	2	7.9 %	3.5 %
SUM	134	167	100 %	100 %	SUM	76	86	100 %	100 %
CSRS4	Czech Republic				CSRS4	Hungary			
	W	M	W	M		W	M	W	M
1	5	8	4.9 %	3.1 %	1	41	20	23.3 %	22.5 %
2	27	79	26.2 %	30.5 %	2	71	28	40.3 %	31.5 %
3	51	108	49.5 %	41.7 %	3	44	29	25.0 %	32.6 %
4	17	54	16.5 %	20.8 %	4	13	8	7.4 %	9.0 %
5	3	10	2.9 %	3.9 %	5	7	4	4.0 %	4.5 %
SUM	103	259	100 %	100 %	SUM	176	89	100 %	100 %

Note: W – women; M – man.
Source: own data collection.

The results (see Table 4) showed that more than 50 % of respondent from each country confirmed that the CSR has a positive impact on a firm's financial performance. The are not significant differences in the perception on the CSRS4 according to the gender in PL (Chi-sqaure = 9.044; p-val. = 0.097), CR (Chi-sqaure = 7.058; p-val. = 0.129), SR (Chi-sqaure = 5.844; p-val. = 0.204), HU (Chi-sqaure = 7.458; p-val. = 0.111). Hypotheses H4 was confirmed for each group of respondents according to the nationality.

4 Conclusion

Aim of the article is comparison the attitudes of owners of SMEs on the corporate social responsibility according to the gender.

The findings confirmed that the are no significant differences between man and women in the perception of CSR in the SMEs segment V4 countries.

This research has some limitations. The findings cannot be generalized for any country, as the authors focused only on V4 countries. Information about the attitudes of owners and managers was obtained by completing an online questionnaire, which means that it was not possible to ascertain the responses of the respondents at a given time and place. On the other hand, the respondents were not influenced by the researchers and the need to answer the questions immediately; the anonymity of the respondents was also an advantage.

Authors findings and consequences are important for better understanding of support the national agencies and institutions which help the segment of small and medium-sized in the areas as is a education, prevention and future in business.

In the future, the authors are interested in comparing whether there are significant differences in the perception of personnel management in the company, the level of digitization, business ethics, business risks (e.g., market, financial, operational) according to gender in the SME segment in the V4 countries.

Acknowledgments

This article was published with support of institution research of Faculty of Operation and Economics of Transport and Communications, University of Zilina, KE/2023: The influence of gender disparities of owners and managers of small and medium-sized enterprises on business risk management in V4 countries.

References

Adams, R. B., & Ferreira, D. (2009). Women in the boardroom and their impact on governance and performance. *Journal of Financial Economics, 94*(2), 291–309.

Adams, R. B., & Funk, P. (2012). Beyond the glass ceiling: Does gender matter? *Management Science, 58*(2), 219–235.

Agyemang, O. S., & Ansong, A. (2017). Corporate social responsibility and firm performance of Ghanaian SMEs: Mediating role of access to capital and firm reputation. *Journal of Global Responsibility, 8*(1), 47–62.

Ahmad, N., Ullah, Z., AlDhaen, E., Han, H., & Scholz, M. (2022). A CSR perspective to foster employee creativity in the banking sector: The role of work engagement and psychological safety. *Journal of Retailing and Consumer Services, 67*, 102968.

Bahta, D., Yun, J., Islam, M. R., & Ashfaq, M. (2021). Corporate social responsibility, innovation capability and firm performance: Evidence from SMEs. *Social Responsibility Journal, 17*(6), 840–860.

Belas, J., Çera, G., Dvorský, J., & Čepel, M. (2021). Corporate social responsibility and sustainability issues of small- and medium-sized enterprises. *Corporate Social Responsibility and Environmental Management, 28*(2), 721–730.

Cera, G., Khan, K. A., Bláhová, A., & Belas, J. (2022). Do owner-manager demographics in SMEs matter for corporate social responsibility? *Equilibrium. Quarterly Journal of Economics and Economic Policy, 17*(2), 511–531.

Doh, J. P., Littell, B., & Quigley, N. R. (2015). CSR and sustainability in emerging markets: Societal, institutional, and organizational influences. *Organizational Dynamics, 44*(2), 112–120.

Glavas, A. (2016). Corporate social responsibility and employee engagement: Enabling employees to employ more of their whole selves at work. *Frontiers in Psychology*, 7(MAY), 796.

Godfrey, P. C. (2005). The relationship between corporate philanthropy and shareholder wealth: A Risk Management perspective. *Academy of Management Review, 30*(4), 777–798. https://doi.org/10.5465/amr.2005.18378878

Le, T. T. (2022). Corporate social responsibility and SMEs' performance: Mediating role of corporate image, corporate reputation and customer loyalty. *International Journal of Emerging Markets.*

Martínez-Martínez, D., Herrera Madueño, J., Larrán Jorge, M., & Lechuga Sancho, M. P. (2017). The strategic nature of corporate social responsibility in SMEs: A multiple mediator analysis. *Industrial Management & Data Systems, 117*(1), 2–31.

Nagy, M., Valaskova, K., & Durana P. (2022). The effect of CSR policy on earnings management behavior: Evidence from Visegrad publicly listed enterprises. *Risks, 10*(11), 203.

Nazir, O., Islam, J. U., & Rahman, Z. (2021). Effect of CSR participation on employee sense of purpose and experienced meaningfulness: A self-determination theory perspective. *Journal of Hospitality and Tourism Management, 46*, 123–133.

Okoye, A. (2012). Exploring the relationship between corporate social responsibility, law and development in an African context: Should government be responsible for ensuring corporate responsibility? *International Journal of Law and Management, 54*(5), 364–378.

Pfajfar, G., Shoham, A., Małecka, A., & Zalaznik, M. (2022). Value of corporate social responsibility for multiple stakeholders and social impact – Relationship marketing perspective. *Journal of Business Research, 143*, 46–61.

Platonova, E., Asutay, M., & Dixon, R. (2018). The impact of Corporate Social Responsibility disclosure on financial performance: Evidence from the GCC Islamic Banking Sector. *Journal of Business Ethics, 151*, 451–471.

Prochazkova, K., & Micak, P. (2023). CEO gender and its effect on Corporate Social Responsibility and the perception of business ethics. *Ekonomicko-manazerske spektrum*. 17(1), 29–38.

Sial, M. S., Zheng, C., Cherian, J., Gulzar, M. A., Thu, P. A., Khan, T., & Khuong, N. V. (2018). Does corporate social responsibility mediate the relationship between boardroom gender diversity and firm performance of Chinese listed companies? *Sustainability*, *10*(10), 3591.

Sikyr, M., Skypalova, R., & Vavrova, J. (2023). What HR decisions are crucial in turbulent times? An analysis of differences in manufacturing and non-manufacturing companies. *Problems and Perspectives in Management*, *21*(2), 618–629.

Tao, W., Song, B., Ferguson, M. A., & Kochhar, S. (2018). Employees' prosocial behavioral intentions through empowerment in CSR decision-making. *Public Relations Review*, *44*(5), 667–680.

Michal Dzian[1,*], Hubert Paluš[1], Ján Parobek[1],
Martina Nosáľová[1] and Marek Hlodák[1]

Analysis of Global Drivers for Sawnwood Demand in Slovakia: An Econometric Perspective

Abstract:

Research background: Globalisation of bio – based economies and trade has led to a new era of complexity and change in the demand for timber. Globalisation has driven the economic growth and urbanization, particularly in emerging economies, leading to an increase in demand for wood and wood products. The rapid expansion of construction, infrastructure development and consumer goods manufacturing has created a demand for timber, which has become an integral raw material in global supply chains.

Purpose of the article: The main goal of the study is to determine a set of factors affecting the development of demand for sawnwood in Slovakia. The results identified and quantified demand drivers for coniferous and non-coniferous sawnwood.

Methods: To create the models of sawnwood demand in Slovakia, the econometric modelling was applied. The study base on analysis of the development of economic and social factors between 1990 and 2020. Specific econometric models and their parameters, that optimally describe the development of the sawnwood demand variables were constructed and estimated using econometric methods

Findings & Value added: The results showed a number of significant explanatory variables for both types of sawnwood (coniferous and non-coniferous). The demand for coniferous sawnwood was determined by the number of completed buildings and tíhe price of coniferous sawnwood. On the other hand, the demand for non-coniferous sawnwood was determined by the GDP per capita and the price of non-coniferous sawnwood. The estimated demand models are the basis for forecasting the development of sawnwood demand in Slovakia.

Keywords: *demand drivers, econometric models, sawnwood,*

JEL Classification: *C5, F60, L73,*

* Corresponding author: michal.dzian@tuzvo.sk

1 Technical University in Zvolen, Faculty of Wood Sciences and Technology, Department of Marketing, Trade and World Forestry, T. G. Masaryka 24, 960 53 Zvolen, Slovak Republic

1 Introduction

Globalisation is defined as the increasing interconnection and interdependence of countries and their economies (Cassimon et al., 2018; Yameogo et al., 2021), consisting of various political, social, economic, cultural, ecological and technological dimensions (Khosravi et al., 2018). Over the previous decade, the globalization has had an enormous influence on society, the environment, and the economy (Zhang et al., 2022). It had a profound impact on various industries worldwide. Over the last few decades, globalisation caused significant changes in industry. These changes affected both producers and consumers in different ways (Hammudeh et al., 2020; Kandil et al., 2020). Globalisation drove economic growth and urbanization, particularly in emerging economies, leading to an increase in demand for wood and wood products. Leszczyszyn et al. (2022) claim that new technological possibilities and environmental concerns have raised demand for wood in recent years. The rapid expansion of construction, infrastructure development and consumer goods manufacturing created a demand for timber, which became an integral raw material in global supply chains. Globalisation had a significant impact on the timber trade, particularly in terms of consumption and market trends. According to a study by Paluš et al., (2021), globalisation led to changes in the use of wood from traditional to new ecological and sustainable use. Within the industrial sector in Slovakia, the wood processing industry has a significant position. The wood processing industry plays an important role both on the domestic market and on the international market of wood products. There are only a few large and medium sawmills. On the other hand, there are a large number of small sawmills on the market. (Paluš et al., 2018). Globalization is equally worshiped and disputed, according to Deacon et al., (2003). So also regarding the wood processing industry, globalisation brings both positive and negative consequences to the wood processing industry. Globalisation, especially in countries such as Slovakia, has played a significant role in improving the economic performance of the wood processing industry. Exports of wood-based products have a positive impact on the industry's economic performance (Demir et al., 2020; Paluš et al., 2021). On the other hand, despite its economic benefits, globalisation also brings significant environmental challenges to the wood processing industry. The increased movement of goods and services across borders leads to higher carbon emissions, deforestation and depletion of natural resources (Adhikari & Ozarska, 2018; Wang et al., 2021).

The main goal of the study is to determine a set of factors affecting the development of demand for sawnwood in Slovakia. The demand drivers for coniferous and non-coniferous sawnwood are identified and quantified in the study. To create the models of sawnwood demand in Slovakia, the econometric approach of modelling is applied. The results are based on data analysis of dozens of economic and social factors. Parameters are estimated and econometric models used are quantified and verified based on derived demand theory using a set of available economic indicators. Demand for sawnwood is therefore derived from the demand for the final products such as houses, flats and furniture (Borzykowski, 2017; Hurmekoski et al., 2015; Kangas & Niskanen, 2003; Paluš, 2002).

2 Material and Methods

The study focuses on determine a set of factors affecting the development of demand for sawnwood in Slovakia. To create the models of sawnwood demand in Slovakia, the econometric approach of modelling is used. The models are constructed as linear, dynamic and exponential. Dynamic models include time-lagged variables (with a lag of one year). These are assumed to have an impact from the previous period and affect the current level of demand. The study is an analysis of the development of dozens of economic and social factors between 1990 and 2020. Consumption (C) is the final goal of production. This applies to any productive activity and any type of product. The demand for products is therefore, in one way or another, the demand for consumption, and the theory of consumer demand is at the heart of all the theories of demand. Absolute variables such as production, imports and exports are used to explain the consumption of sawnwood in Slovakia. Consumption is calculated as follows:

$$C = Production + Import - Export \quad (1)$$

Sawnwood is mainly used as an input raw material in various manufacturing activities such as construction of residential and non-residential buildings, furniture manufacturing, industrial production, etc. The demand for sawnwood is based on what is known as the derived theory of demand. Demand for sawnwood depends on the development of demand for final products and reflects economic factors such as income, product price, demographics and possible substitution of sawnwood by other materials. The overall economic growth of a country is the most important factor that influences the demand in the timber market (Baudin, 2003).

A set of the following factors was examined: GDP, GDP per capita (GDPC), population (POP), index of industrial production (IIP), new construction including modernization and renovation (NCON), number of completed dwellings

(CD), price of furniture (PF), price of coniferous (PCS) and non-coniferous sawnwood (PNCS) and price of construction materials (PCM). The final general form of the ad hoc model has been defined in the following way:

$$C = f\left(GDP, GDPC, POP, IIP, NCON, CD, PF, PCS, PNCS, PCM\right) \quad (2)$$

where consumption is a function of the above variables. The ordinary least squares method is used to estimate the parameters of the given model. Durbin-Watson test is used to exam autocorrelation of residuals. Moreover, Variance Inflation Factors (VIF) tests multicollinearity. Both tests are calculated in a statistical package SPSS. The following general forms of log function was used:

$$\ln C_{CSW} = \beta_0 + \beta \ln X + \varepsilon_t \quad (3)$$

$$\ln C_{NCSW} = \beta_0 + \beta \ln X + \varepsilon_t \quad (4)$$

Where CCSW is consumption of coniferous sawnwood CNCSW is consumption of non-coniferous sawnwood ß0 is a constant, X is a vector of explanatory variables, and εt is the error term. All data have been log transformed in order to interpret the estimated model parameters directly as elasticities.

3 Results and Discussions

The individual demand models for coniferous and non-coniferous sawnwood are examined in the next step of the analyses. In order to identify the most important variables, the regression model included significant price and income variables. In the case of the non-coniferous sawnwood model, also GDP per capita is included to the regression model. Table 1 describes the estimated parameters of the models for the consumption of coniferous sawnwood. Other statistical characteristics are also included in Table 2.

Table 1. Model of consumption of coniferous sawnwood.

Model of consumption of coniferous sawnwood				
	Constant	CD	IIP	PCS
C_{CSW}	-1.718	0.866***	2.23***	-0.575***

Source: own research (2023)

Where *** – statistical significance of coefficient at the significant level 1 %, CCSW coniferous sawnwood consumption, CD – completed dwellings, IIP – index of industrial production, PCS – price of coniferous sawnwood.

Table 2. Statistical characteristics of model C_{SCW}.

Statistical characteristics				
	R^2	S_e	DW	F
C_{CSW}	0.673	0.5	0.515	28.857***

Source: own research (2023)

Where *** – statistical significance at the significant level 1 %, R2 – coefficient of determination, Se – standard error, DW – Durbin Watson, F – F test.

In general, demand for coniferous sawnwood is more dependent on the number of completed dwellings and index of industrial production than on the price of coniferous sawnwood. Changes in the number of completed dwellings have a greater impact on changes in the consumption of coniferous sawnwood than changes in prices of sawnwood. Based on the results, we can conclude that demand for coniferous sawnwood would increase by 0.87 % if the number of completed dwellings increased by 1 %. Increasing index of industrial production by 1 % would increase demand for coniferous sawnwood by 2.2 %. A one per cent increase in the absolute price of coniferous sawnwood would have a 0.58 % decrease in the demand for coniferous sawnwood.

On the other side, there are significant differences on demand models for non-coniferous sawnwood. The estimated parameters of the non-coniferous sawnwood model are elasticities, which reflect the percentage change in the value of the explanatory variable for a 1 % change in the explanatory variable. A one per cent increase in GDP per capita would increase the demand for non-coniferous sawnwood by 1.16 per cent. Demand for non-coniferous sawnwood would be decreased by 0.55 % if the absolute price of non-coniferous sawnwood increased by 1 % (Table 3). Demand is elastic to GDP per capita and inelastic to the absolute price of non-coniferous sawnwood.

Table 3 shows the estimated parameters of the models for the consumption of non-coniferous sawnwood.

Table 3. Model of consumption of non-coniferous sawnwood.

Model of consumption of non-coniferous sawnwood			
	Constant	GDPPC	PNCS
C_{NCSW}	4.618	1.156***	-0.546***

Source: own research (2023)

Where *** – statistical significance of coefficient at the significant level 1 %, CNCSW non-coniferous sawnwood consumption, GDPPC – gross domestic product per capita, PNCS – price of non-coniferous sawnwood.

Table 4. Statistical characteristics of model C_{NSCW}.

Statistical characteristics				
	R^2	S_e	DW	F
C_{NCSW}	0.647	0.4	0.92	25.675***

Source: own research (2023)

Where *** – statistical significance at the significant level 1 %, R2 – coefficient of determination, Se – standard error, DW – Durbin Watson, F – F test.

An analysis of the overall evolution of the model variables can be carried out to better understand the impact of different determinants on sawnwood consumption (Figure 1).

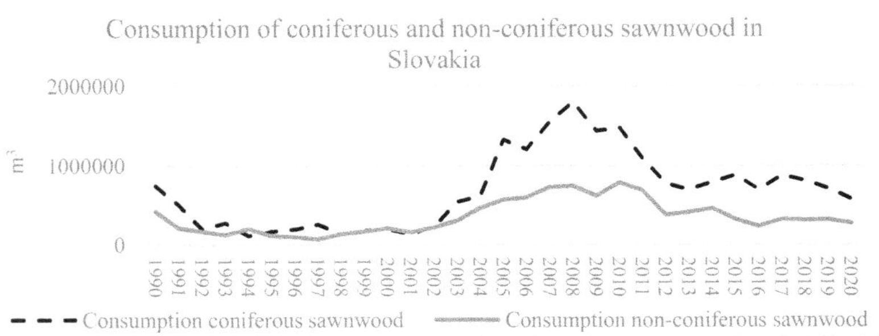

Figure 1. Development of consumption of coniferous and non-coniferous sawnwood in Slovakia.

Source: FAOSTAT (2023)

Slovak sawmills produced over 1.40 mil. m3 of coniferous and 0.38 mil. m3 non-coniferous sawnwood in 2022. The total exports of coniferous sawnwood accounted for almost 1.06 mil. m3 and of non-coniferous sawnwood over 0.20 mil. m3. The total value of coniferous sawnwood imports was almost 0.48 mil. m3 and non-coniferous sawnwood over 0.05 mil. m3.

Based on FAO's (Food and Agriculture Organization of the United Nations, n.d.) officially available data, sawnwood consumption in Slovakia has generally increased between 1995 and 2008, with fluctuations more pronounced in coniferous sawnwood during economic crisis years. The highest consumption of coniferous sawnwood is reported in 2008 with more than 1.8 million m3. The consumption of non-coniferous sawnwood peaked at 0.7 mil. m3 in 2010. In the current year, the overall consumption of sawnwood increased by more than double in comparison to 1990. The issue of lack of information on domestic price developments is solved by approximating domestic prices of basic wood products with average unit prices of foreign trade, calculated from the value and volume of exports or imports. This approach has also been applied in other studies (Hurmekoski & Hetemäki, 2013; Michinaka et al., 2011). The prices of both types of sawnwood are subject to fluctuation over time. Nonetheless, it is generally evidenced that the cost of non-coniferous sawnwood is higher than that of coniferous sawnwood. In 2001, the price of coniferous sawnwood reached a peak almost 800 € per m3 (Figure 2).

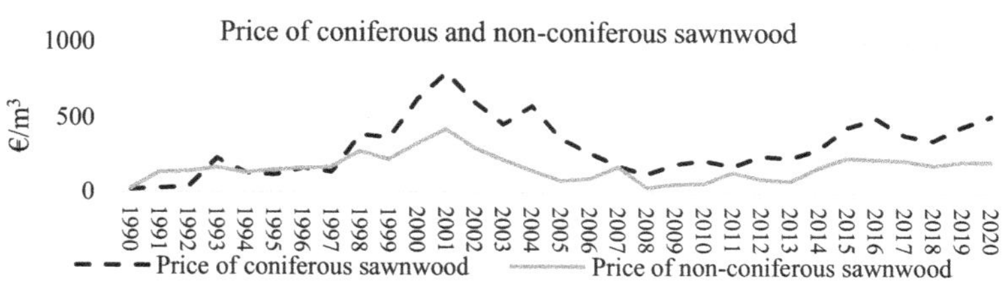

Figure 2. Development of prices of coniferous and non-coniferous sawnwood in Slovakia.

Source: FAOSTAT (2023)

Most of the sawnwood used is for residential construction. The situation in this sector directly affects the sawnwood consumption. The study has shown that the quantity of completed dwellings has the most significant impact on the consumption of coniferous sawnwood in Slovakia. Figure 3 shows the increase in the number of completed dwellings constructed in Slovakia over the period under consideration. In 1990, the number of completed dwellings in Slovakia exceeded 24000 units. This was the highest value ever recorded. A positive development trend can be observed over the period 1995–2009. And also during the period between 2014 and 2020. Since 1994, there has been an increase of almost 320 % in the number of completed dwellings. This trend reflects the general state of the socio-economic environment. It has a significant correlation with other macroeconomic indicators such as GDP growth, unemployment and population growth.

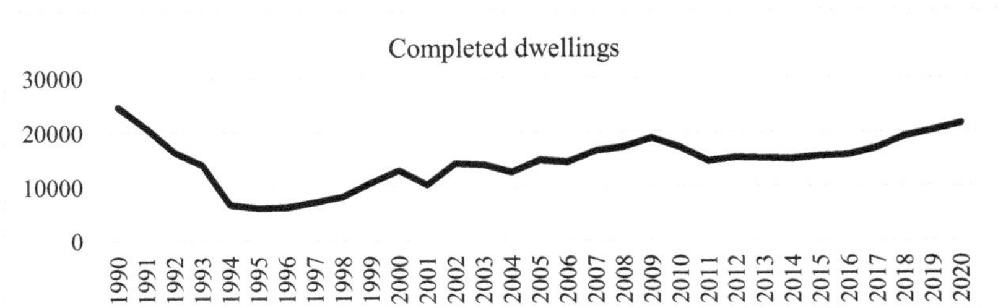

Figure 3. Development of number of completed dwellings in Slovakia.
Source: Statistical office of the Slovak republic (2023)

The results of the study showed several implications. Nevertheless, while analysing the estimates, it must be noted that this research provided country-specific results that reflect standard production and usage conditions within the domestic market.

4 Conclusions

The activity of the construction industry and the economic situation of the country are reflected in the demand for sawnwood in Slovakia. In particular, consumption of coniferous sawnwood is almost twice as high as that of non-coniferous sawnwood. The results show that demand for non-coniferous sawnwood is elastic to GDP per capita and inelastic to the absolute price of non-coniferous sawnwood. In the case of coniferous sawnwood, changes in the number of completed dwellings have a greater impact on changes in the consumption of coniferous sawnwood than changes in prices of sawnwood.

Acknowledgments

The authors are grateful for the support of the Woodema i.a. – Roy Damary Scholarship, the Scientific Grant Agency of the Ministry of Education, Science, Research, and Sport of the Slovak Republic, Grant No. 1/0494/22 Comparative Advantages of the Wood Based Sector under the Growing Influence of the Green Economy Principles and Grant No. 1/0495/22 Sustainability of Value Supply

Chains and its Impact on the Competitiveness of Companies in the Forest and Forest-Based Sectors.

References

Adhikari, S., & Ozarska, B. (2018). Minimizing environmental impacts of timber products through the production process "From Sawmill to Final Products." *Environmental Systems Research*, *7*(1).

Baudin, A. (2003). Modeling and forecasting the demand for sawnwood in western Europe from an end-use perspective. *Seminar on STRATEGIES FOR THE SOUND USE OF WOOD.*

Borzykowski, N. (2017). *The Swiss market for construction wood : Estimating elasticities with time series simultaneous equations* (Issue 258659).

Cassimon, D., Engelen, P.-J., & Van Cappellen, H. (2018). Globalization. In A. Marciano & G. B. Ramello (Eds.), *Encyclopedia of law and economics* (pp. 1–9). Springer New York.

Deacon, B., Ollila, E., Koivusalo, M., Stubbs, P. (2023). GLOBAL SOCIAL GOVERNANCE- Themes and Prospects. Avaible at: https://um.fi/documents/35732/48132/global_social_governance_%E2%80%93_themes_and_prospects.pdf/aa979ac0-5bce-47fe-72d4-61b7205941f5?t=1560452959004

Demir, I., Canakci, M., & Egri, T. (2020). Globalization and economic growth. In W. Leal Filho, A. M. Azul, L. Brandli, A. Lange Salvia, & T. Wall (Eds.), *Decent work and economic growth* (pp. 1–11). Springer International Publishing.

Food and Agriculture Organization of the United Nations, FAOSTAT. (2023). Food and Agriculture Organization of the United Nations, Statistics Division. Forestry Production and Trade. [online] [cit. 2023]. Available at: http://www.fao.org/faostat/en/#data/FO

Hammudeh, S., Sohag, K., Husain, S., Husain, H., & Said, J. (2020). Nonlinear relationship between economic growth and nuances of globalisation with income stratification: Roles of financial development and governance. *Economic Systems*, *44*(3), 100761.

Hurmekoski, E., & Hetemäki, L. (2013). Studying the future of the forest sector: Review and implications for long-term outlook studies. *Forest Policy and Economics*, *34*, 17–29.

Hurmekoski, E., Hetemäki, L., & Linden, M. (2015). Factors affecting sawnwood consumption in Europe. *Forest Policy and Economics*, *50*, 236–248.

Kandil, N., Battaïa, O., & Hammami, R. (2020). Globalisation vs. Slowbalisation: A literature review of analytical models for sourcing decisions in supply chain management. *Annual Reviews in Control*, *49*, 277–287.

Kangas, K., & Niskanen, A. (2003). Trade in forest products between European Union and the Central and Eastern European access candidates. *Forest Policy and Economics*, *5*(3), 297–304.

Khosravi, S., Maleknia, R., Adeli, K., Mohseni, R., & Hodges, D. G. (2018). The effects of globalization on the imports of wood products in Iran. *Journal of Forest Economics*, *32*, 116–122.

Leszczyszyn, E., Heräjärvi, H., Verkasalo, E., Garcia-Jaca, J., Araya-Letelier, G., Lanvin, J. D., Bidzińska, G., Augustyniak-Wysocka, D., Kies, U., Calvillo, A., Wahlströmh, M., & Kouyoumji, J. L. (2022). The future of wood construction: Opportunities and barriers based on surveys in Europe and Chile. *Sustainability (Switzerland)*, *14*(7).

Michinaka, T., Tachibana, S., & Turner, J. A. (2011). Estimating price and income elasticities of demand for forest products: Cluster analysis used as a tool in grouping. *Forest Policy and Economics*, *13*(6), 435–445.

Paluš, H. (2002). *Modelovanie dopytu po výrobkoch z dreva na trhu v SR*. Technická univerzita vo Zvolene.

Paluš, H., Dzian, M., Parobek, J., & Supin, M. (2021). Globalisation impacts on timber consumption in Slovakia. *SHS Web of Conferences*, *129*, 8014.

Paluš, H., Parobek, J., Dzian, M., & Šupín, M. (2018). Determinants of Sawnwood consumption in Slovakia. *BioResources*, *13*(2).

STATISTICAL OFFICE OF THE SLOVAK RREPUBLIC, 2023. DATAcube [online]. Available at: https://slovak.statistics.sk

Wang, Q. J., Geng, Y., & Xia, X. Q. (2021). The impact of globalization on forest growth: Evidence from multinational panel data. *International Journal of Environmental Research and Public Health*, *18*(24).

Yameogo, C. E. W., Omojolaibi, J. A., & Dauda, R. O. S. (2021). Economic globalisation, institutions and environmental quality in Sub-Saharan Africa. *Research in Globalization*, *3*(May 2020), 100035.

Zhang, L., Xu, M., Chen, H., Li, Y., & Chen, S. (2022). Globalization, green economy and environmental challenges: State of the art review for practical implications. *Frontiers in Environmental Science*, *10*.

David Fořt[1], and Miloslav Hub[1,*]

The Influence of Global Challenges on Fleet Optimization

Abstract:
Research background: Increasing prices of fuels and electricity and pressure on minimizing carbon footprint on transport presents managers with a question: How to organize the fleet so that it not only reduces emissions, but also does not limit business and does not radically increase the Total Cost of Ownership (TCO)? There does not exist any global approach that would work globally as the electricity carbon footprint differs anywhere in world, besides fleets are assembled based on purchase prices and operational costs determined by Worldwide harmonized Light Vehicle Test Procedure.
Purpose of the article: This paper shows the model to use in fleet optimization based on successful case studies of increased utilization combined with TCO optimization. Operational costs and carbon footprint are calculated on real consumption based on driving behaviour by fossil fuel vehicles and driving behaviour, distance travelled, and so on. This approach enables the optimization of the vehicle fleet with higher utilization, lower costs, and carbon footprint even when using vehicles of a higher standard.
Methods: For such a model, driver habits and local conditions need to be collected and processed through the model, where these vehicles are rated upon same conditions in real traffic. Data for the valuation model can be collected from telematics black boxes in older fleets and connected cars by new cars.
Findings & Value added: The paper presents a model of organization the fleet so that it not only reduces emissions, but also does not limit business and does not radically increase the TCO.

Keywords: *carbon footprint, fleet optimization, telematics, transport*

JEL Classification: *L86; L92; L96*

1 Introduction

With increasing prices of conventional fuels and electricity in last years and long-term exciting pressure on minimizing carbon footprint of transport presents

* Corresponding author: miloslav.hub@upce.cz
1 University of Pardubice, Faculty of Economics and Administration, Studentská 84, 532 10 Pardubice, Czech Republic

fleet managers with a difficult question: How to organize the fleet that not only reduces carbon emissions, but also does not limit the business and does not radically increase Total Cost of Ownership?

In European Union, transport sector accounts more than 27 % of total CO2 emissions (Marrero at al., 2021). However, fleets and number of cars are increasing, the global trend has been improving in recent years. Mainly due to tightening the EURO standards. Even so, transport sector remains one of the largest producers of CO2. From this comes the pressure to minimize the carbon footprint towards a zero-carbon footprint. This is a long term run and first step needs to be done by fleet managers as these changes radically affect the costs of the vehicle fleets.

Fleet management is an administrative approach that allows companies to organize and coordinate work vehicles with the aim to improve efficiency, reduce costs, provide compliance with government regulations (TechTarget Contributor, 2017) and plan, and fulfil carbon footprint goals (Wilberforce et al., 2017). The best methodology for comparing costs of fleet is Total Cost of Ownership (TCO) which includes all costs aspects of running a fleet for whole ownership period.

2 Methods

To make the TCO model relevant it is very important to identify and calculate the necessary costs for given product or service. In this paper a TCO model, defined by Hagman et al. (2016) in Total cost of ownership and its potential implications for battery electric vehicle diffusion (El Amarini et al., 2019; Jiang et al., 2021), will be used. Similar approach will be used in the distribution of the costs. Direct costs associated with vehicle usage will be isolated from costs related to ownership. Indirect costs such as opportunity costs of charging and refueling will be ignored in calculation. Only prices will be compared.

$$TCO = (PP - RP) + TEC + TIC + IC + MR + T + \quad (1)$$

PP - purchasing price
RP - reselling price
TEC - total energy/fuel cost
TIC - total interest cost
IC - insurance cost
MR - maintenance and repairs
GT - government taxes
GS - government substitutes

The difference between purchasing and reselling price of a product is deprecation and it's with almost 50 % of TCO by cars with conventional fuel. Deprecation depends on various factors such as brand, model, purchasing price, maintenance costs, quality and others. Vehicle loses its value at an exponential rate, when in the first year vehicle loses almost 25 % of its value and deprecation rate decreases in following years. In general petrol vehicles depreciate slower than diesel vehicles in 5 year period by 42 %, compared to 54 % by diesel personal vehicles (Imaweb, 2023). EV depreciates faster than vehicles with conventional fuel. According to comparison by Betriebskosten eSUVs, 2023 loose EV cars 46,5 % – 52,7 % in first three years, besides that is lower mileage used in the calculation and using purchase prices subsidy included. Similar comparison for conventional fuel vehicles by Redaktion der Fuhrpark&management (Betriebskostenvergleich, 2023) reported 56,4 %–64 % deprecation in 3 years period, but with 40k km per year mileage versus 15k km per year by EV (45k km by EV versus 120k km by conventional fuel in total mileage). Moreover, current trend is faster dropping price of used EVs due to increasing offer on the market of used electric cars.

Fuel/electricity cost is second most significant cost in TCO of vehicles (Jeong and Oh, 2002). There are many aspects affecting energy costs. Price of the petrol, diesel and electricity is affected by global influences (Pohonné hmoty dál zdražují, 2023). By petrol and diesel leads choice of refueling places according to the price to minor savings. Besides by electricity choice of charging place and type will radically influence the charging costs. According to actual CCS price list (CCS Česká republika s.r.o., 2023) the price per kWh for slowest AC charging starts at 10 Kč incl. VAT (without parking fee) and ends by 23 Kč incl. VAT for fastest UFC charging in E.ON Drive charging network. Home charging and charging in company garages is cheaper and according to TZBINFO, 2023 are prices in September 2023 between 5.13 and 8.42 Kč incl. VAT (monthly fix fee is excluded).

From the global perspective is consumption calculated based on results of Worldwide harmonized Light Vehicle Test Procedure (WLTP) for all kinds of vehicles. WLTP, introduced in 2017, reduced the consumption gap to 20–24 % by vehicles according to Dutch study made in 2020 on data from Travelcard Netherland BV analyzing over 259,000 petrol vehicles, of which 33,000 (plugin) hybrids, and 277,000 diesel vehicles, of which 4,000 (plug-in) hybrids, (Van Gijlswijk et al., 2020) against previous New European Driving Cycle (NEDC) with almost 40 % consumption gap in 2017 (Ktistakis et al., 2022). If there aren't any real traffic data collected from fleet, consumption gap should be counted in fuel/energy costs for conventional fuel vehicles but also for electric vehicles and their combinations (hybrids).

By electric charged vehicles (EV and PHEV) the charging loss should be part of the calculation. Charging loss, according to German ADAC study, reaches 5–30 % depending on the charging method and vehicle (Adac, 2022).

Total interest costs is the cumulative of interest a car buyer pays on a debt obligation over the time of lease time by standard leasing. For purpose of this work will be used standard car finance leasing without any additional like maintenance or insurance packages.

Basic Total interest formula used for calculations:

$$TIC = c * N - (PP - DP) \tag{2}$$

TIC - total interest costs
c - monthly payment
N - number of monthly payments
PP - vehicle purchase price
DP - down payment

For this work were leasing conditions set as follows, initial payment 25 % on vehicle purchase price, interest rate 6 % and time period 36 months.

Vehicle insurance is affected by various factors related to the vehicle and the owner. Specific vehicle factors are: vehicle value, annual mileage, performance, age, brand, safety ratings, antitheft-system and many others. Owner specific factors include age, gender, location, years without accidents and others.

In order not to distort the insurance calculation, we defined an owner profile which was used to calculation for each vehicle. Owner profile was defined as: Woman, 38 years, full-length accident free period (full bonuses), living in small city Pardubice. Other insurance specifics are set as follow: annual mileage limited do 20,000km, All-risk product without any additional packages, participation 5 % (minimum 5,000Kč). Insurance was calculated by Kooperativa insurance company.

New cars are sold with 3 or more years warranty which covers any malfunctions. Therefore, cost of repairs are zero in calculation (López-Arquillos, 2015). Warranty is valid under manufactures conditions including specific service intervals for each car which must be fulfilled. Maintenance costs are calculated based on costs of planned service intervals. Additional costs like tires and other consumables are similar by cars with conventional fuel and electric cars.

There are no government substitutes for electric vehicles in Czech Republic now. The only benefit of electric vehicle is lower tax for employee if vehicle is used not for business purposes only and employee can use vehicle for private journeys. In that case vehicles with CO_2 emissions under 50 g/km are taxed 0,5 % from purchase price, 1 % for vehicles with emissions over the limit. This benefit does not affect TCO.

3 Results

Electric cars are much more energy efficient on intermittent journeys in cities and suburbs than on long highway journeys. Many real-life EV tests, e.g., Keine Angst vorm Liegenbleiben: die E-Autos mit der größten Reichweite (Czajka, 2023), showed significant loss of battery range on highways. To verify this point of view we choose two vehicles to do same trips to compare fuel/electric consumption. First vehicle is EV Hyundai Kona electric, second is diesel vehicle Škoda Octavia 2.0 TDi, both produced in 2022. In comparison [Chyba! Nenašiel sa žiaden zdroj odkazov.] where WLTP values and actual market fuel and electricity were used. Despite the high price of diesel, the price per km for a diesel car is lower than for an electric one. On the other hand, electric Hyundai has 0g carbon footprint compared to almost 11 kg per 100 km.

Table 1. TCO comparison (WLTP).

	Škoda octavia 2.0TDi	**Hyundai Kona electric**	
KW/HP	85/116	100/136	
Fuel	Diesel	Electric	
CO2 emissions	108g/km	0g/km	
Annual mileage	15000 km	15000 km	
Time period (months)	36	36	
Consumption (WLTP)	4,1 l/100km	14,3 kWh/100km	
		Home charging	UFC charging
Fuel price	39 Kč/l	6 Kč	23 Kč/KWh
Purchase price	619900 Kč *	959990 Kč *	
Reselling price	430000 Kč **	530000 Kč **	
Rest value	69.4 %	55.2 %	
Deprecation	30.6 %	44.8 %	
Total insurance cost	49779 Kč	55785 Kč	
Total interest cost	37124.6 Kč	57544.2 Kč	
Total fuel cost	71955 Kč	38610 Kč	148005 Kč
Monthly payment	13 945,82 Kč	21 598,24 Kč	
Total Cost of Ownership	348758.6	581929.2 Kč	691324.2 Kč
Cost per Km	7.8 Kč	12.9 Kč	15.4 Kč
* – **from the manufacturer's configurator**			
** – **from tipcars.com portal**			

Source: author (2023)

As WLTP test cycle represents average values given by its specific conditions does include different efficiency or consumption gap, therefor two specific routes were defined to test both vehicles in real conditions. First route is a urban and suburb route with length of 15.8 km from center Prague to outskirts at Figure 1. Route 1: Prague

Source: author (2023) and second route from Prague to Pardubice with length of 121.4 km mainly on highway at Figure 4. Route 2: Prague – Pardubice

Source: author (2023). Both vehicles were tested in similar conditions, time of the day, summer, traffic, and driver. Due to traffic and local speed limits speed profile are speed profiles similar regardless different vehicle performance.

3.1 Test Route 1

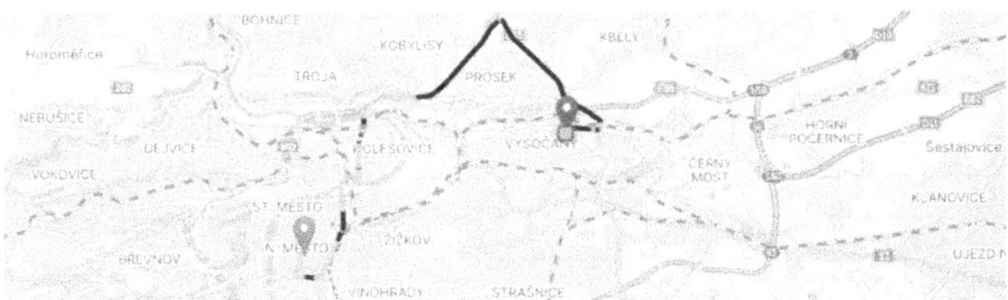

Figure 1. Route 1: Prague.
Source: author (2023)

Figure 2. Route 1 speed profile of Hyundai Kona Electric.
Source: author (2023)

Figure 3. Route 1 speed profile of Skoda Octavia 2.0TDi.
Source: author (2023)

On Route 1 has showed up higher energy efficiency of electric vehicles leading to better consumption results of Hyudai Kona Electric by 12.6 %, compared to worse result of diesel vehicle Skoda Octavia by 36 %. See results of Route 1 in vehicles with conventional fuel are much more dependent on driving style than electric vehicles. That significantly affects consumption in urban and suburb trips.

Table 2. Route 1 results.

	Škoda octavia 2.0TDi	**Hyundai Kona electric**
Consumption (Route 1)	5.6 l/100km (+36.6 %)	12.5kWh/100km (-12,6 %)
TCO per km	8.3 Kč	12.8 Kč

Source: author (2023)

3.2 Test Route 2

Figure 4. Route 2: Prague – Pardubice.
Source: author (2023)

Figure 5. Route 2 Speed profile of Hyundai Kona Electric.
Source: author (2023)

Figure 6. Route 2 Speed profile of Skoda Octavia 2.0 TDi.
Source: author (2023)

The opposite results were achieved on a long route along the highway. On long highway journey has diesel engine better consumption by 7 % compared with WLTP values. Electric Hyudai Kona consumption increased by 38.5 % to almost 20kWh. Electric vehicles are more dependent on speed than driving style which negatively affects electric consumption on highways.

Table 3. Route 2 results.

	Škoda octavia 2.0TDi	**Hyundai Kona electric**
Consumption (Route 2)	3.8 l/100km (-7 %)	19.8kWh/100km (+38,5 %)
TCO per km	7.6 Kč	13.2 Kč

Source: author (2023)

4 Discussion

The way to zero CO2 emissions transport is a long run. CO2 emissions are calculated for conventional fuel long time by constants (2,37kg CO2 per liter of petrol and 2.65kg CO2 per liter of diesel) no matter if it is E5 or E10, quality or anything else. Electric vehicles are presented as zero CO2 emissions vehicle without relation to local electric energy mix. According to latest calculations at NowTricity (CO2 emissions per kWh in Czech Republic, 2023) based on data from Entsoe was in 2022 one kWh responsible for 444g of CO2 emissions.

Table 4. Carbon footprint.

	Škoda octavia 2.0TDi		**Hyundai Kona electric**	
	Consumption	**CO2**	**Consumption**	**CO2**
WLTP	4.1 l/100km	108 g/km	14.3kWh/100km	63 g/km *
Route 1	5.6 l/100km	148 g/km	12.5 kWh/100km	55 g/km *
Route 2	3.8 l/100km	100 g/km	19.8 kWh/100km	87 g/km *
* – CO2 emissions from electricity production in the Czech Republic				

Source: author (2023)

5 Conclusion

This paper introduces basic approaches for composition of company fleet based on Total Costs of Ownership taking into account the carbon footprint of the vehicles. It shows that WLTP values are a good indicator for selecting vehicles, but may vary compared with real life values. The real-life vehicles test showed the differences in energy effectiveness between EV and conventional fuel vehicles in operation in urban, suburb and highways. TCO results showed that EV is still more expensive compared to vehicles with conventional fuel even with home charging due to actual high electricity prices. Home charging is limited with 2.3kW (1.2kW in real test) which limits the daily reach of EV without using faster public chargers. Therefor the ideal vehicle fleet composition is using EVs for urban and suburbs, where EVs has zero local emissions, and diesel (eventual petrol) vehicles for greater distances, where thanks to actual energy mix has these vehicles similar carbon footprint with much lower costs. Sharing cars among employees thus enables not only to reduce costs but also to reduce the carbon footprint of the vehicle fleet and is the first step to increasing utilization to reduce overall costs.

Acknowledgments

This paper was supported by grant No. SGS_2023_010 supported by the Student Grant Competition.

References

Adac. (2022, September 13). Elektroauto und Ladeverluste: So können Sie Kosten vermeiden. ADAC. ADAC.de. https://www.adac.de/rund-ums-fahrzeug/elektromobilitaet/laden/ladeverluste-elektroauto-studie/

Betriebskostenvergleich. (2023, September 18). *REDAKTION BFP FUHRPARK & MANAGEMENT. FUHRPARK.DE. FUHRPARK*. https://www.fuhrpark.de/sites/default/files/2021-09/betriebskosten-esuvs-tabelle-gross.pdf

Betriebskosten eSUVs. (2023, September 18). *REDAKTION BFP FUHRPARK & MANAGEMENT. FUHRPARK.DE. FUHRPARK*. https://www.fuhrpark.de/sites/default/files/2021-09/betriebskosten-esuvs-tabelle-gross.pdf

CCS Česká republika s.r.o. (2023, September 1). *Registrovaný zákazník služby E.ON Drive CZ*. Tankovací karty a vše pro správu vozového parku CCS. https://www.ccs.cz/files/4vop_aceniky/230801_cenik-dobijeni-e.on-drive-.pdf

Czajka, G. (2023, September 3). *Keine Angst vorm Liegenbleiben: die E- Autos mit der größten Reichweite. Autobild*. https://www.autobild.de/artikel/e-auto-reichweite-20977681.html

El Amarini, S., Chennani, M., & Belkhayat, D. (2019). *Comparative Study of Electric Vehicle Energy Consumption between Trunk Roads and Highways*. Online. In: 7th International Renewable and Sustainable Energy Conference (IRSEC). IEEE, 2019, s. 1–7. ISBN 978-1-7281-5152-6.

Hagman, J., Ritzén, S., Stier, J. J., & Susilo, J. J. (2016). Total cost of ownership and its potential implications for battery electric vehicle diffusion. *Research in Transportation Business & Management*, *18*, 11–17. ISSN 22105395.

Imaweb. (2023. October 18). *Vehicle depreciation: not all equal.* https://www.imaweb.com/article-depreciation-vehicle/

Jeong, K. S., & Oh, B. S. (2002). Fuel economy and life-cycle cost analysis of a fuel cell hybrid vehicle. *Journal of Power Sources*, *105*(1), 58–65.

Jiang, L., Diao, X., Zhang, Y., Zhang, J., & Li, T. (2021). Review of the charging safety and charging safety protection of electric vehicles. *World Electric Vehicle Journal*, *12*(4), 184.

Ktistakis, M. A., Pavlovic, J., & Fontaras, G. (2022). *Developing an optimal sampling design to monitor the vehicle fuel consumption gap. Science of the Total Environment*, *832*. ISSN 00489697.

López-Arquillos, A., Rubio-Romero, J. C., Súarez-Cebador, M., & del Carmen Pardo-Ferreira, M. (2015). Comparative risk assessment of vehicle maintenance activities: Hybrid, battery electric, and hydrogen fuel cell cars. *International Journal of Industrial Ergonomics*, *47*, 53–60.

Marrero, Á. S., Gustavo A. M., Gonzáles, R. M., & Rodríguez-López, J. (2021). Convergence in road transport CO2 emissions in Europe. *Energy Economics*, 99. ISSN 01409883.

NowTricity. (2023, September 22). *CO2 emissions per kWh in Czech Republic.* https://www.nowtricity.com/country/czech-republic/

Pohonné hmoty dál zdražují. Litr benzinu přesáhl hranici 40 korun. (2023, September 14). https://www.idnes.cz/ekonomika/domaci/benzin-nafta-ropa-barel-opec-pohonne-hmoty-zari.A230914_085000_ekonomika_vebe

TZBINFO. (2023, October 1). *Cena elektřiny 2023 – srovnání E.ON, PRE, ČEZ.* https://www.tzb-info.cz/ceny-paliv-a-energii/14-ceny-elektriny

Van Gijlswijk, R., Paalvast, M., Ligterink, N., & Smokers, R. (2020). *Real-world fuel consumption of passenger cars and light commercial vehicles: TNO 2020 R11664* [online]. 30 October 2020, 2020, 21–23 [cit. 2023-09-19].

WhatIs.com (2023, September 17). *TechTarget Contributor.* (2017) Fleet management. https://www.techtarget.com/whatis/definition/fleet-management

Wilberforce, T., El-Hassan, Z., Khatib, F. N., Al Makky, A., Baroutaji, A., Carton, J. G., & Olabi, A. G. (2017). Developments of electric cars and fuel cell hydrogen electric cars. *International Journal of Hydrogen Energy*, *42*(40), 25695–25734.

Shahla Gahramanova[1,*]

Corporate Social Responsibility Practice and Sustainability Strategy of Small and Medium-sized Enterprises in Developing Economies: The Case of Azerbaijan

Abstract:
Research background: In the beginning of XXI Century overwhelming majority of companies and organizations in post-soviet countries including Azerbaijan were not fully aware of the essence of corporate social responsibility (CSR) – one of the most important factors required for the sustainable development and successfulness of modern business activity. Now the social responsibility of businesses became crucial in this geography and has been more or less integrated into the strategy of the majority of large firms. However, this positive tendency is almost not visible in the activity of small and medium size enterprises.
Purpose of the article: The main purpose of this research work is to give an overview of the development of CSR practice in modern Azerbaijan with a focus on CSR activity of SMEs and obstacles they face to integrate this concept in their activity. Government support to SME development and sustainability in the country, the way the government can influence and encourage SMEs to become more socially responsible, the benefits of CSR orientation for ensuring SMEs sustainable development are also among issues discussed in the paper
Methods: Used methods include logical reasoning based on the analysis of scientific literature and of statistical data, analysis of CSR reports and other publicly available sources.
Findings & Value added: Conclusions and recommendations in this research work can be used by businesses, particularly SMEs interested in practicing consolidated CSR strategy and sustainable development. It may also be useful for the related government agencies. The content of the study can also be used for teaching purposes.

Keywords: *CSR, socially responsible business, sustainable development, business and society, SMEs.*

JEL Classification: *A10; A11; D90; M14*

---

* Corresponding author: shahla.gahramanova@unec.edu.az; gahramanovas@gmail.com
1 Azerbaijan State University of Economics (UNEC), UNEC Business School, Department of Economics and Business Administration, 6 Istiglaliyyat Str., Baku, Azerbaijan

1 Introduction

21st century entrepreneurship adopted new colours and tendencies becoming more stakeholder oriented, environmentally friendly, and focused on sustainability. Corporate social responsibility (CSR) in its turn became one of the important components of sustainable development and marketing strategy of large businesses and has been acknowledged as an indicator of the ethicalness of business. As concluded by Spence and Perrini, to some extent the fields of corporate social responsibility and ethics started to exist in parallel (Spence & Perrini, 2009).

Socially responsible entrepreneurship is traditional for Azerbaijan and commitment to it used to be a part of the nation's culture having been deeply rooted in its historical past. The manifestation of philanthropy, which is considered the predecessor of CSR was part of the activity of Azerbaijani entrepreneurs at all times in the form of charity (Yilmaz, 2014). In the late 19th and early 20th centuries Azerbaijan experienced more systematic socially responsible business activity – the traditional Maecenas activity was upgraded into more impressive in size and mature in character social investments made by oil magnates and other rich people of Azerbaijan to healthcare, education and other urgent social needs laying the foundation of responsible and ethical business in Azerbaijan (Gahramanova, 2019; Amrahov & Gafarova, 2012). However, their noble initiatives could last until the establishment of the soviet system in the country which put an end to the existence of private sector.

Becoming independent in 1991 Azerbaijan went through the difficult period of the political and social transformation and state-building period extremely complicated by the involvement in the Armenian-Azerbaijani Nagorno-Karabakh conflict and demographic crisis inherited from the soviet era. The poor socio-economic environment had its negative impact on sustainable approach to business development; entrepreneurs in the country were mainly trying to set up a business to somehow survive and improve their livelihoods (Gahramanova, 2023). As proposed in Maslow's hierarchy of needs, businesses focused on satisfying their basic physiological needs and were not mature enough to think of their stakeholders.

It worth to note that 60 years long history of CSR concept and practice shows that the attention to the social responsibility of business increases in parallel to the economic growth of a country or an entire region. This was the case in the United States, in developed countries of Europe and Asia. The same tendency was also observed in Azerbaijan: the economic conditions started to gradually improve in the country, particularly with the signing of "The Contract of the

Century" in 1994 aimed at using country's potential resources for its [country's] sustainable development. The outcomes of this project had its effect on all areas of the economy and social life in Azerbaijan. The situation with CSR activity also started to change in parallel to the economic development in the country as the reviving private sector now had the opportunity to think of its social responsibilities and sustainable development.

Now after almost 30 years later, we witness different picture: CSR that was not familiar to the overwhelming majority of newly established business organizations in early post-soviet Azerbaijan, now is integrated into the strategy of the majority of large firms while this positive tendency is less visible in the activity of small and medium size enterprises (SMEs). Research studies revealed that CSR activity of SMEs in Azerbaijan, as well as their focus on sustainable development is far behind compared to large businesses in the country and SMEs in developed economies. To note that situation with SMEs is different in developed countries where SMEs are becoming the backbone of the economy (Oldham & Spence, 2021; Del Baldo, 2018) representing more than 90 % of all businesses and providing more than 50 % of employment worldwide (World Bank, 2021). For the EU economy, SMEs constitute 99.8 % of all EU enterprises employing more than 74 million people (Statista.com, 2021; OECD, 2021).

Though SMEs in Azerbaijan are still far from becoming the backbone of the country's economy, their role in economic development and share in GDP is gradually growing. Currently SMEs representing various business spheres provide 56 % of the employment in the country (The State Statistical Committee of the Republic of Azerbaijan, 2022). Growing indicators allows expecting that positive world tendency in terms of SMEs' growing significance and CSR implementation will soon be observed in Azerbaijan too.

This study aims to summarize SMEs growing role in the economy of Azerbaijan, current situation with their socially responsible behaviour and sustainable development.

1.1 CSR and Its Role in the Sustainability of Businesses

Reviewing historical background to the CSR concept we see that as a conception CSR has around half-century history of formation and development and its role in sustainability of businesses has been proved both theoretically and empirically. First introduced by American scientist Howard Bowen in 1953 as a concept necessary for business's relations with society and other stakeholders (Bowen, 1953) this concept later gained popularity and some other significant theories were developed under its umbrella. Among them stakeholder approach proposed by E. Freeman, CSR Pyramid of A. Carroll, Corporate sustainability and Triple Bottom Line by J. Elkington to name a few.

One of the theoretical approaches developed under the umbrella of CSR theory is the concept of corporate sustainability. Various peer reviewed articles and other related sources surveyed by the author in an attempt to summarize the interrelation between CSR and sustainable development allowed to conclude that corporate sustainability refers to an approach that aims to create long-term value through a strategy that encompasses the ethical, social, environmental, cultural and economic aspects of business (Camillieri, 2017; Jansson et al., 2017).

CSR became particularly popular in the early years of the 21st century which was marked by serious corporate scandals stemming from unethical behaviour of reputable business giants in respect to the society and the environment. The collapse of large companies such as Enron, World Com, Lehman Brothers, Swiss Air and plenty of other business giants was a shock for the entire economy of developed economies such as the United States, Canada, as well as of the developed countries of Europe and Asia. These economic and social "earthquakes" have forced governments and commercial organizations to reconsider their attitude towards the society and environment and adopt more serious and responsible behavioural norms.

In modern economic conditions, the sustainable development of any business is interrelated with the sustainable development and social welfare of the society in which it operates and there is a close relationship between the CSR activity, reputation and sustainability of an organization (Porter & Kramer, 2006). 21st century business cannot afford to ignore its social responsibilities and the significance of social responsibility in the sustainable development of business and society has repeatedly been emphasized by practitioners and theorists.

An excellent empirical study in this connection was contributed by American scientists M. Porter and M. Kremer where they described CSR as a strong tool for improving competitiveness of a business. In the example of the world's leading sustainable and competitive business giants such as Volvo, BMW and Whole Foods Market authors proposed effective ways of using CSR policy as an opportunity for public welfare and business' own growth and sustainability (Porter & Kramer, 2006).

2 Materials and Methods

In this research work both primary and secondary sources were utilized to collect necessary data. Wide range of secondary sources such as peer reviewed journal articles, statistical information, media publications, expert analyses, reports of international organizations, conference materials and sustainability reports of target companies were studied.

In-depth interviews, involving representatives of selected large companies and SMEs were conducted to examine the existence of CSR policy and practice in companies. Interview questions were prepared to find out whether worldwide CSR practices applied in Azerbaijani companies, to learn about the perception of the CSR concept, drivers of CSR, level of involvement in CSR implementation and challenges faced, CSR policies and strategies developed and used, positive impact of CSR for company performance, application of global CSR standards in non-financial reports, future CSR related plans, etc.

Methods used include logical reasoning based on the analysis of scientific literature, statistical and interview data, analysis of reports of international organizations and publicly available data.

3 Results

3.1 SME's Growing Significance in the Country's Economy

SMEs role in Azerbaijan's economy is gradually growing and its impact is becoming important. Along with large companies now, medium and small enterprises make significant contributions to the economic development of the country.

According to the State Committee of Statistics, as of January 2022 there are around 1245000 officially registered SMEs representing various business fields. Table 1 demonstrates the size classification of SME's in Azerbaijan which is set by the Decree 555 of the Cabinet of Ministers of Azerbaijan in 2018 taking the global criteria indicators as a foundation.

Table 1. Size classification of SMEs in Azerbaijan.

Category of Enterprise	Employees	Annual revenue in Azerbaijani manat
Medium-sized	51 – 250	3.000000 – 30.000000
Small	11 – 50	200.000 – 3 000 000
Micro	Up to 10	Up to 200.000

Source: Prepared by the author using available statistics

As of January 2021 share of SMEs in the country's GDP is around 15 %. Share of SMEs in non-oil sector GDP is around 25 %. Constituting 87 % of all registered business entities in Azerbaijan SMEs provide more than 52 % of the total employment in the country which is quite impressive while still well behind the indicators of the developed countries. According to the Small and Medium Business Development Agency (SMBDA) their share in non-oil exports is also quite significant having around 53 % (SMBDA, 2021). From this perspective, it is difficult to overestimate the role of small and medium-sized businesses in the country's economy. However, in Azerbaijan SMEs are still far from becoming a backbone of the country's economy, as it is a case in EU and other developed geographies.

Although the share of SMEs in non-oil sector is close to normal, its share in total GDP of the country is small having only around 15 % share. One of the reasons for this insignificant share is because a large part of Azerbaijan's economy is based on oil revenues. However there are other problems and at present, this issue is in the focus of the government and serious strategic measures are being taken to increase the share of SMEs in the country's economy up to 40 % by 2025. Necessary measures related to increasing the share of SMEs in the country's economy is also underlined in the Decree of the President of the Republic of Azerbaijan on "Socio-economic Development Strategy of the Republic of Azerbaijan during 2022–2026". Mechanisms implemented within this state support program are aimed at ensuring the increase of SME share in the country's economy.

The strategic goal includes to strengthen the role of SMEs in the country's economy by supporting their development, boosting competitiveness, facilitating access to markets through the supply of daily consumer goods, achieving significant increase of SMEs share in the non-oil sector and national GDP. Providing more employment opportunities with the involvement of SMEs is also among the strategic goals to reach (SMBDA, 2021). Figure 1. demonstrates the current position of SMEs in the country's economy.

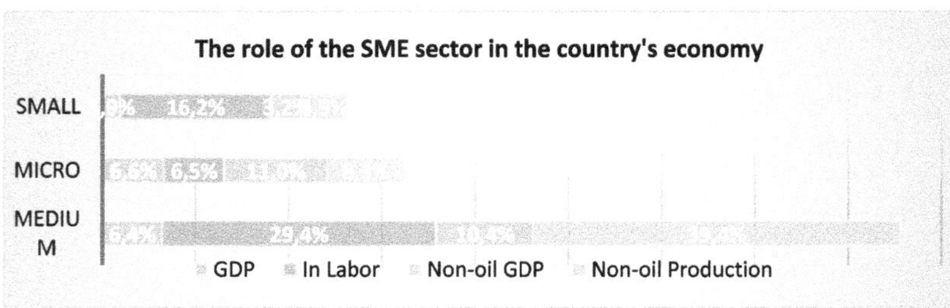

Figure 1. The role of the SME sector in the country's economy.

Source: Prepared by the author using the available statistics

3.2 CSR Practice of SMEs in Azerbaijan and Its Impact on Their Sustainable Development

Based on the literature review of CSR related activities of SMEs worldwide certain expectations/assumptions were developed about possible CSR practices of SMEs in Azerbaijan. The assumptions was proved while studying available secondary sources and then during the interviews with the representatives of both SMEs and large businesses.

Perception of CSR. There is a serious misunderstanding related to the perception of CSR concept. Random questioning of people working for SMEs and even in some large companies revealed their unawareness of CSR conception and activity. The term "CSR" sounds strange to them and they recognize the expressions such as "social responsibility," "moral responsibility toward society," "voluntary charity" and in most cases are involved in those initiatives in the way they consider appropriate and affordable to implement.

Level of involvement in CSR related activities. While the result of interviews showed the absence of mechanism for the systematic CSR implementation, answers to the specific questions demonstrated that CSR related activities are taking place all the time. Feedback received from the interviewed SME representatives demonstrated that majority of them already exhibit socially responsible initiatives and activities similar to what is meant by CSR. In this circumstances, conclusion by D'Andrea and Montanini for the Italian context is applicable also in Azerbaijani context – CSR practices of SMEs in the country is hidden in the daily behaviours (D'Andrea & Montanini, 2015) and is more a "sunken CSR" (Perrini et al., 2007). The outcomes of this study also proved the conclusion made more than a decade ago by Moore et al for UK context stating that SMEs are engaged in CSR related activities "without necessarily viewing such activity in this way" (Moore et al., 2009).

Drivers of SMEs' CSR practices in Azerbaijan. It was not possible to clearly identify the drivers of social responsibility initiatives of SMEs while the results of the interviews demonstrated that community focus is dominating for all SMEs and for large business as well. All the interviewed within this study considered social responsibility activities very noble and important engagement that makes them feel morally satisfied. Interview also revealed that the virtue, goodwill and the good citizenship feelings of a particular entrepreneur are the main factors encouraging business for social investments. In other words, if socially responsible behaviour is desired by the owner it then will be translated into the operations of the company.

CSR policies and strategies developed and used. Interviews with SME representatives demonstrated that majority of firms do not have CSR policy and strategy or at least a scheme of CSR implementation programs. They do not have neither a CSR unit nor a particular person responsible for coordinating CSR related activities. This reality dictates that managers and employees of private sector need training in order to acquire the necessary skills and competence to integrate CSR in their day-to-day activities and report on them.

CSR reporting. Publishing CSR activity and sustainability report is a major problem to be addressed. Currently SMEs do not publicize non-financial reports and they find doing it quite challenging. Unawareness of globally recognized CSR reporting standards negatively affects integration and regular implementation of CSR. From this perspective developing and promoting national non-financial reporting standards based on the globally recognized reporting systems such as GRI (The Global Reporting Initiative), ISO26000, *AA1000* (Assurance Standard) and other social reporting mechanisms would be a step forward in promoting CSR activities in the country. However, these standards should be worked and applied in a way not to become a burden for SMEs (Sheehy & Farneti, 2021).

Do SMEs think of any positive impact CSR may bring for their businesses? Major problem in this regard is that both large businesses and SMEs are mainly oriented for profit-sacrificing CSR and are far from thinking of profit-making CSR (Lee et al., 2015). CSR impact on organizational performance and profitability, talent acquisition and prevention of staff turnover, improved customer loyalty, good relationships with stakeholders, attracting investors and partners, achieving access to international markets and other potential benefits are not yet the part of the strategic thinking of businesses in this geography, particularly of SME's. Borrowing a conclusion from Camilleri it can be concluded that reducing pollution, improving waste management and implementing practices to minimize environmental impacts act as a reputation signalling exercise, which becomes crucial in terms of opening new markets (Camilleri, 2021).

4 Conclusion

This study analyzed the CSR practices of businesses in Azerbaijan with a particular focus on SMEs. Summarizing the research outcomes it can be concluded that CSR activity of businesses in Azerbaijan including SMEs is gradually developing though it differs from the practice in developed countries of the West where CSR has been institutionalized since decades. CSR activity is situational and spontaneous while there are positive intentions that needs to be directed. Expert support is required to help businesses to develop a CSR strategy that is comprehensive and stakeholder oriented.

There is unawareness of how well developed CSR strategy and improved community image can be linked to better business returns and improved customer and employee loyalty. Entrepreneurs somehow feel obliged to be socially responsible but cannot make a link between corporate social performance (CSP) and corporate financial performance (CFP) and do not use CSR policy in their strategy of growth and development.

The most important conclusion is connected to the importance of recognition of CSR on the governmental level and the necessity of developing national CSR strategy and CSR reporting standards in conformity with internationally recognized standards such as GRI reporting system, Dow Jones Sustainability Indices (DJSI), SA 8000, ISO 26000 and considering and adapting certain cultural and historical specificities. We think that the current positive dynamics in the national economic development of Azerbaijan, the reforms carried out in various fields of the economic, political and social life allows to predict positive changes in CSR field in the near future.

References

Amrahov, M., Gafarova G. Haji Zeynalabdin Tagiyev's school for girls – An educated girl means an educated family. 2012. Availbale at: http://www.visions.az/en/news/388/aca96e32/

Bowen, H. Social Responsibilities of the Businessman. Harper & Row. New-York, USA, 1953

Camilleri, M. A. (2021). Strategic attributions of corporate social responsibility and environmental management: The business case for doing well by doing good!. *Sustainable Development.*

Camillieri, M. A (2017). Corporate sustainability and responsibility: Creating value for business, society and the environment. *Asian Journal of Sustainability and Social Responsibility*, *2*, 59–74.

D'Andrea, A., & Montanini, L. (2015). Corporate Social Responsibility practices in Italian SMEs. *Journal of Business and Economics*, 6, 12, 2040–2053.

Del Baldo, M. (2018). Integrated Reporting in Small and Medium Enterprises: Issues and Perspectives from Italy. Current Issues in Corporate Social Responsibility, An International Consideration, 195–216.

Gahramanova, S. (2019). The role of the Corporate Social Responsibility in sustainable development of small and medium enterprises in Azerbaijan. Book of Proceedings, 37th International Scientific Conference on Economic and Social Development, pp. 1254–1260.

Gahramanova, S. (2023). Prospects of development of the strategic policy of corporate social responsibility and sustainable business in Azerbaijan. *Business Strategy & Development*, 1–10.

Jansson, J., Nilsson, J., Modig, F., & Hed Vall, G. (2017). Commitment to sustainability in small and medium sized enterprises: The influence of strategic orientations and management values. *Business Strategy and the Environment,* 26(1), 69–83.

Lee, K. H., Herold, D. M., & Yu, A. L. (2015). Small and medium enterprises and corporate social responsibility practice: A Swedish perspective. *Corporate Social Responsibility and Environmental Management*, 23(2), 88–99.

Moore, G., Slack, R., & Gibbon J. (2009). "Criteria for responsible business practice in SMEs: An exploratory case of U.K. fair trade organizations". *Journal of Business Ethics*, *89*(2), 173–188.

OECD SME and Entrepreneurship Outlook. 2021

Oldham, S., & Spence, L. J. (2021). A typology of small-and medium-sized supplier approaches to social responsibility. *Business Ethics, the Environment & Responsibility*, 33–48.

Perrini, F., Russo, A., & Tencati, A. (2007). CSR strategies of SMEs and large firms. Evidence from Italy. *Journal of Business Ethics*, *74*, 285–300.

Porter, M. E., & Kramer, M. (2006). Strategy and society: The link between competitive advantage and corporate social responsibility. *Harvard Business Review, 84*(12), 78–92.

Sheehy, B., & Farneti, F. (2021). Corporate Social Responsibility, sustainability, sustainable development and corporate sustainability: What is the difference, and does it matter? *Sustainability*, 13, 5965.

Small and Medium Business Development Agency (SMBDA). Review of small and medium-sized businesses in Azerbaijan. January 2021. Available at: https://smb.gov.az/storage/KOB%C4%B0A%20%C4%B0CMAL%202020.pdf

Spence, L. J., & Perrini, F. (2009). Practice and politics: Ethics and social responsibility in SMEs in the European Union. *African Journal of Business Ethics*, *4*, 20–31.

Statista. (2021). *Number of SMEs in the European Union 2008-2021, by size*. https://www.statista.com/statistics/878412/number-of-smes-in-europe-by-size/

The State Statistical Committee of the Republic of Azerbaijan. (2022). Entrepreneurship in Azerbaijan. https://www.stat.gov.az/source/entrepreneurship/?lang=en

World Bank (2021). World Bank. https://www.worldbank.org/en/topic/smefinance

Yilmaz, H. Zeynalabdin Tağıyevin qızlar məktəbi və I Dünya Müharibəsi (Zeynalabdin Tagiyev's school for girls and World War I.) 2014. Availabale at: http://www.bbc.com/azeri/azerbaijan/2014/08/140814_ww1_school_for_girls.shtml

Zsuzsanna Győri[1,*], Anita Kolnhofer-Derecskei[1], and Regina Zsuzsánna Reicher[1]

The Impact of Regulation on the Sustainability of SMEs

Abstract:

Research background: Sustainable operation of small and medium-sized enterprises (SME) is motivated by different factors which can be categorized to internal and external, or business case and moral case categories. National and international regulation – which, in a globalized world, is often more decisive than the national one – as an external factor have a huge impact on the sustainability related attitude, motivation and behavior of enterprises. It imposes both a challenge to comply and a positive motivational factor to change the logic of doing business, which means that it is linked to both the business and the moral case.

Purpose of the article: This study observes how the legal system and regulations impact sustainability according to the Hungarian SME leaders. The impact of laws and regulations will be studied on three level, so the attitudes, the motivations and the behavior of enterprises will be presented.

Methods: In May and June 2022, we conducted three focus group interviews with SME leaders, mainly professionals in the field of sustainability issues in business. In the summer of 2023, we surveyed this topic on a nationally representative sample with a questionnaire based on the qualitative results. We used different analyzing tools as methods, e.g., NVivo and SPSS software.

Findings & Value added: The results of the focus groups proved the significant impact of the legal system on the sustainability of entrepreneurial activity as a regulative framework and prominent incentive. Preliminary research from the representative survey showed that (1) the demographic characteristics of managers e.g., gender; (2) the position and decision making level of the manager; and finally (3) the size of the company can have a significant impact on the perception of regulation and solutions for coping with it.

Keywords: *SME sector, Sustainability, Responsibility, Impact of Regulation*

JEL Classification: *Q01; Q56; G38*

* Corresponding author: gyori.zsuzsanna@uni-bge.hu

1 Budapest Business University, CESIBUS, 1055 Budapest, Markó u. 29–31. Hungary

1 Introduction

The harmful impacts of business activity on society and environment were already evident in the early modern period, in the XVIII–XIX centuries. The industrial revolution brought about a major change in both the scale of corporate activity, and in the structure of political systems. Meanwhile, society was evolving, including the emergence of organisations and institutions that worked for the enforcement of social and human rights (Carroll, 2008) and environmental protection (Crane et al., 2008).

Yet, the idea of corporate social responsibility (CSR) appeared explicitly only in the mid-twentieth century, mainly in the USA. Europe's lag of a few decades can be explained by the historical and political differences between the two continents. The European welfare states and a more formalised legal system had for a long time fulfilled the functions that are now largely the responsibility of the companies. Moreover, the interests of stakeholders had implicitly been part of European capitalism's principles (Matten & Moon, 2005, Mitnick et al., 2023). Compared to the American way, where companies typically take on social responsibility voluntarily based on the business case or on moral commitment, the enforcement of corporate social responsibility and sustainability concepts is much more the role of states and international organisations in Europe (Bouckaert, 2006a, 2006b, Guo & Yu, 2022). Nowadays, CSR is a global phenomenon regulated and self-regulated by many international organizations.

Among the many definitions of CSR, ISO 26000 defines it as the "responsibility of an organization for the impacts of its decisions and activities on society and the environment, through transparent and ethical behaviour that contributes to sustainable development, including health and the welfare of society; takes into account the expectations of stakeholders; is in compliance with applicable law and consistent with international norms of behaviour; and is integrated throughout the organization and practised in its relationships" (ISO, 2010: 3). On this basis, it is reasonable to conclude that considering the social and environmental impacts of a business at the micro level means taking into account the macro-level, global sustainability objectives. This linkage is vividly highlighted by the latest acronym and framework for corporate sustainability movements and regulation, ESG (Environmental, Social and Governance), which defines corporate responsibility and contribution to sustainability in relation to the three dimensions of sustainability (EP and EC, 2022).

2 Theoretical Background

2.1 The Role of National and International Regulation in Corporate Responsibility and Sustainability

Just after the introduction of Sustainable Development (SD) concept (UN, 1987), since the early 1990s, CSR has taken on a new focus, both thematically and geographically. The focus shifted to the activities of global corporations, particularly in developing countries, to the enforcement of labour and human rights, to corruption, and to the voice of environmental concerns. Europe, especially Germany and the UK, rather than the USA became the new centre of theoretical and practical development (Vogel, 2006). The European Eco-label was established in 1992, EMAS in 1993, and organizations that remain significant today, such as Transparency International in 1993, the World Business Council for Sustainable Development in 1995, and the Global Reporting Initiative in 1997, were founded. Since the second half of the 1990s, the tasks, responsibilities and challenges of economic and social actors in Europe have changed significantly, and the history of CSR and sustainability issues is a reflection of this. In the 2000s, CSR was generally accepted by the business as a tool that could become profitable for companies (Crane et al., 2008). As a form of quality assurance, international organisations (such as the UN, OECD, ILO, or GRI) have developed recommendations and guidelines aimed at measure CSR performance and make it comparable. This can be seen in the four phases of European CSR policy that will be described below. While initially, in the first phase the aim was to unify CSR, in the second phase CSR was seen as a means to increase European competitiveness, and in the third, after the economic crisis CSR was seen as a crisis management tool and an innovative economic model (EC, 2001, 2011).

Now, in the identifiable fourth phase, European policy is increasingly emphasizing the primacy of the environmental dimension of sustainability, increasingly referring to international guidelines, including the UN's Sustainable Development Goals (2015), and fully embraced the ESG approach (Holmes, 2023). The regulatory framework approaches explicitly from the perspective of accountability, transparency, explicitly reporting and emphasizes the intermediation role of financial sector. Within the frame of Europe 2020 strategy (EC, 2010), the first step of extensive regulation was the Non-Financial Reporting Directive (NFRD) 2014/95/EU, which required the largest European companies to disclose non-financial information in their annual reports from 2018. In 2019 the European Green Deal (EP and EC, 2019b) was launched and relatedly the Sustainable Finance Disclosure Regulation (SFDR, EP and EC, 2019a) and

EU Taxonomy (EP and EC, 2020) provided a new sustainability framework for financing European companies (Balcerzak et al., 2023). Non-financial reporting for European companies reached a new level on 28 November 2022, when the EP adopted the Corporate Sustainability Reporting Directive (CSRD) 2022/2464/EU, which will make non-financial reporting mandatory for all large companies from 2025. In addition, the CSRD will take significant steps towards the creation of a single European Sustainability Reporting Standard (ESRS), which will require companies, even SMEs (as listed companies and as suppliers of large companies) to share significantly more sustainability information with stakeholders from 2024 (Dinh et al., 2023).

As we can see, in Europe national and international regulation as an external factor have a huge impact on the responsibility and sustainability related attitude, motivation and behaviour of companies, even small-, and medium-sized enterprises (SMEs). It imposes both a challenge to comply and a positive external motivational factor to change the logic of doing business linking to both the business and the moral case.

2.2 The Special Features of Responsibility and Sustainability of SMEs and Their Regulatory Implications

The emergence of CSR is traditionally associated with larger companies and have long been the focus of major international guidelines (ISO, 2010). However, the current social and ecological situation justifies the need for all social and economic actors, including SMEs, to act with the aim to promote sustainability, as declared in the UN SDGs (UN, 2015). SMEs are significant in taking CSR and achieving a sustainable business operation. Most companies belong to this sector, they play a crucial role in employment and their added value is significant and increasing.

There are significant differences between large companies and SMEs (Málovics, 2009), both in terms of challenges, the available resources (Radácsi, 2021), organisational activities, project management (Blaskovics, 2016), and therefore the characteristics of CSR activities of SMEs and large companies may differ in a number of aspects, e.g typical and prominent stakeholders or motivations (Molnár et al., 2023). Furthermore, SMEs tend to have much less opportunities to implement complex tools to improve their sustainability performance. Instead, they usually tend to focus on several key priority areas (Harangozo, 2008).

SMEs also differ from large companies in how they relate to legal regulations, which can be interpreted as an external motivation (Győri et al., 2019). They have a much smaller apparatus for compliance, so they often choose the simplest solutions that require the least energy in order to tick off legal obligations (Blaskovics et al., 2023). This activity is often outsourced, for example by soliciting lawyers or accountants. On the one hand, this is cost-effective, but on the other hand, it prevents employees or managers from truly integrating sustainability-related thinking and activities into everyday operations. However, the most important stakeholder group is the employees: it depends on them whether the responsibility is realized, and they are also the most common target group of the CSR activity (Vives, 2016, Marcinkowska & Sawicka, 2023).

SMEs usually start using explicit CSR tools, typically quality or environmental standards, when they are forced to do so, usually because they want to supply a large company that requires this (Stekelorum et al., 2023) or because of a legal regulation (Somoza, 2023). Most of the standards and guidelines already cover the supply chain (Stoian & Plakoyiannaki, 2023), with the aim of having measurable and accurate information on the largest share of the value created and the social and environmental impact associated with value creation, thereby improving performance. In this regard, the positive vision of a more than 20-year-old EU document, which has not yet been fully realized in the time that has passed, is interesting: "In the future, the most significant pressure on SMEs to adopt CSR practices is likely to come from their large business customers, which in return could help SMEs cope with these challenges through the provision of training, mentoring schemes and other initiatives." (EC, 2002: 12). To comply with the expectations along the supply chain, there is a set of simpler tools available for SMEs on the low-budget range (for instance free carbon footprint calculators). However, these tools usually raise validity and reliability issues (Harangozo & Szigeti, 2017).

3 Methodology

In our mix-method research we first used focus group interviews (3 occasions with 12 SME leaders) for identifying the terms and notions SMEs use related to their responsibility and sustainability. We used semi-structured technic, so the moderator used the same interview guideline based on the literature and our previous research pieces, but sometimes the sub-questions were formulated by the discussion and the topics the participants mentioned.

Based on the qualitative results, a questionnaire was formulated and surveyed in representative sample of Hungarian SMEs. In our representative national sample, we considered the following aspects: company size, region, sector classification. After the sample specifications, there were more group of questions related to the activities, motivations, organizational characteristics and leadership factors of CSR and sustainability. Questionnaire the questionnaire was interviewed by telephone by a professional research company, the respondent was the head of the company or, if there was one, the sustainability officer.

In this study we focus on the impacts of regulations. The impact of laws and regulations will be studied on three level, so the attitudes, the motivations and the ehavior of enterprises will be presented.

The research questions are:

1 What is the general attitude of Hungarian SME leaders related to the economic and sustainability-related legal regulations?
2 How strong the motivational impact of these regulations?
3 What are the behavioural implications of these regulations?
4 How the personal characteristics of SME leaders and executives (gender and personal sustainability commitment), as well as of the company (position of the respondent and company size) affect the previous questions?

4 Results

We primarily used the results from qualitative round to formulate the questions for the quantitative one, but we can say that the results of the focus groups proved the significant impact of the legal system on the sustainability of entrepreneurial activity as a regulative framework and prominent incentive. We indicate it here with some quotations from the participants: "In general, we are affected by the market and human resources, from the point of view of sustainability, I think it is policy. I think that is the most influential story" (Autosave); "I think policy is in everything." (Gábor); "As we talked about, policy has an incredible impact on our entire lives" (Oglu). Here we talked about entrepreneurial ecosystem, so policy as a notion was used by the definitions of Isenberg (2014), where it is related to legal regulations and environment of entrepreneurial activities.

In the quantitative sample 90 % of respondents were managers of domestically owned companies. 6.5 % were managers of wholly foreign-owned companies. The remaining respondents operate under a split ownership structure. The demographic breakdown of respondents is as follows: 177 men and 121 women (1 did not wish to specify their gender) took part in the survey. The average age of respondents is 50 years, and in terms of marital status, the majority of respondents are married or in a partnership. When we asked respondents to rate how environmentally aware they considered themselves to be, no one ticked box one, i.e., not at all, while 74 out of 300 people chose the highest level, 7, i.e., considered themselves to be fully environmentally aware and personally committed to sustainability. The average level was 5.66. It is worth noting that this reflects responses that are in line with societal expectations and is consistent with the 'halo effect' referred to in the literature (Lanero et al., 2021), which refers to a psychological bias that makes us feel that our choices are more sustainable and environmentally conscious than they actually are.

On the attitude, perception level, we have several questions about the personal evaluations of the respondents. Overall, the impact of legislation on sustainability, and compliance with it, was rated neutral to slightly positive across the sample, with no sense of the legal obligations being excessive or unenforceable. In this part we used a Likert scale from -3 to +3, where we got 0.87 for the statement: "Economic legislation severely limits what we can do for social and natural causes," and 0.07 for the following one: "Compliance with the Hungarian legislation on sustainability is not difficult." This is positive as shows the acceptance and legitimacy of regulation but may also indicate that the legislation is not sufficiently stringent.

Regarding their motivations, by their own admission, compliance with the law is an important aspect and externak motivation for taking their responsibility, and they strive to comply with it. It can be framed as a business case side motivation. But, in addition, the appearance of responsibility towards future generations and the expectation of this as an everyday social norm as 'normal' ehavior in line with general moral standards were also highly valued.

This is particularly risky if we move on from attitudes to ehavior, where in the second group of questions, on a Likert scale of 1 to 7, the following statement has an exceptionally high average of 6.34: "Our company meets natural and social expectations by complying with legislation." Most company managers therefore considered that their company was meeting natural and social expectations by complying with the law. At the same time, 80 % of the managers of the companies surveyed considered that sustainability is integrated into their strategy which goes well beyond simple legal compliance. However, only half (50.6 %) of the sample use international standards that go beyond legal obligations and 33 % do not have equipment or facilities that go beyond legal requirements to reduce the negative environmental impacts of their business.

5 Discussion

At the same time, preliminary research from the representative survey showed that some characteristics of the SME and its leader have significant impacts on the distribution of answers. We analyzed the impact of the leader's gender and personal commitment to sustainability, and from the company side the position and decision-making level of respondent (owner or manager), as well as the size of the company.

In the case of the abovementioned statement, we found a significant difference for the third one, i.e., compliance with the law showed significantly stronger agreement for women than for men ($F = 5.517$ and $p = 0.019$). For the other two statements, there was almost equal agreement across genders.

As a second key independent variable, the impact of personal commitment to sustainability was cross analyzed. There is clearly a strong relationship between individual commitment and legal compliance for the firm. The strongest effect was found for the third statement, i.e., personal commitment showed a significant relationship with compliance with company legal regulations ($n = 297$; $Phi = 0.592$ and $p < 0.001$ and Cramer's $V = 0.265$ and $p < 0.001$).

Table 1: Symmetric Measures for the question: "Our company meets natural and social expectations by complying with legislation."

		Value	Approximate Significance
Nominal by Nominal	Phi	0.592	<0.001
	Cramer's V	0.265	<0.001
N of Valid Cases		297	

Source: authors' own framing (2023)

The personal commitment is also reflected in the methods and equipment used by the firm, i.e., where the manager is more committed to sustainability in private life ($n = 298$; $Phi = 0.259$ and $p = 0.029$ and Cramer's $V = 0.183$ and $p = 0.029$), the firm has equipment and tools, in addition to the legal requirements, that reduce the negative environmental impacts associated with the firm's activities.

In one case, we found a significant difference (Kruskall Wallis = 8.503, df = 3, Assymp sig = 0.37). Apparently, the "non-owners" had stronger agreement with the statement. It raises again the risk that the legislation is not strong enough, at the same time, from the viewpoint of the company presumably, the owner is more interested in compliance with legislation and other requirements than a manager, for whom the future and operation of the company is less important. As owners, they also consider it more important to have equipment that meets or exceeds the requirements of legislation.

The size of the company also have a significant impact on the perception of regulation and solutions for coping with it. We found significant difference in two points explained by the size of the company in practical, behavioural applications: (1) only 26.83 % of managers of medium-sized companies said they do not use international standards, while the figure for small companies was 44.92 %; (2) 73.81 % of managers of medium-sized enterprises indicated that they had equipment and tools that reduce the negative environmental impacts associated with the company's activities beyond legal requirements, while for small enterprises the figure was 63.42 %.

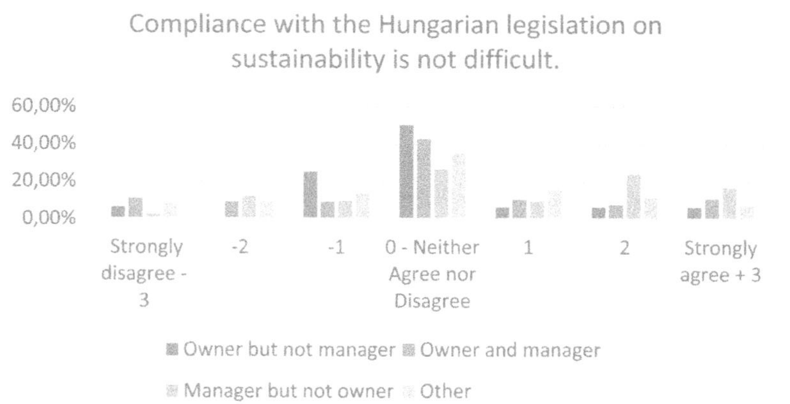

Figure 1. Results for the statement: "Compliance with the Hungarian legislation on sustainability is not difficult."

Source: authors' own framing (2023)

6 Conclusion and Limitations

Some of our results are in line with the previous studies. First, legislation and legal requirements mean real motivation for companies to be more responsible and sustainable, they shape the attitudes of SME leaders and have direct impacts on related ehavior as well.

Regarding the independent variables like size and ownership, we found similarities with the studied dealing with large companies, which means that handling sustainability issues in a company can be interpreted as a scale where companies have special characteristics, but there are also many similarities. For example, medium-sized companies have more explicit behavioural applications just as of large companies, whose responsibility and sustainability are more structured and institutionalized. Similarly, owners are more committed, which is very similar to the principal-agent problem which is usually mentioned related to large organizations.

An important addition to the results described above is that the managers surveyed share views to on their competitors' compliance with the law similar to their own. They largely agree with the statement that the expectations of market actors, such as partners or competitors, go as far as complying with legislation (5.41 on a Likert scale of 1–7), which, combined with the fact that they see themselves as having ticked off a large part of their own responsibility for complying with legislation, greatly underlines the responsibility of the state. Insufficiently stringent legislation does not sufficiently reinforce companies' attitudes and behaviour towards sustainability, as it does not provide a strong enough motivation to do so. Going further, on the question of whose responsibility it is to promote sustainability, there are two broad groups of responses: according to one, this is extremely important for every individual, but the other strong opinion points to the state as a regulator and catalyst. At the same time, it is worth to mention that the CSR literature emphasize that CSR is beyond legal requirements, as it is motivated by moral commitment besides business case. One of our focus group members also mentioned this view: "responsibility starts somewhere, where someone thinks beyond, beyond, to comply with the law" (Czafi).

As we indicated at the beginning these are the results of our preliminary analysis focusing on the legal system and regulations impact sustainability according to the Hungarian SME leaders. As the determinants of sustainability and responsibility are very much interrelated and interconnected, we will get more results either in relation to legislation when have more elaborated results for the whole research. And also, as sustainability is a global issue, investigation of other countries' experience would be a valuable following research direction after getting to know the opinions, attitudes, motivations and behaviour of Hungarian SMEs.

Acknowledgments

"This research was supported by the Ministry of Innovation and Technology of Hungary from the National Research, Development and Innovation Fund, financed under the Tématerületi Kiválósági Program 2021 (TKP2021-NKTA) funding scheme (Project no. TKP2021-NKTA-44)."

References

Balcerzak, A., MacGregor, R. K., MacGregor Pelikánová, R., Rogalska, E., & Szostek, D. (2023). The EU regulation of sustainable investment: The end of sustainability trade-offs? *Entrepreneurial Business and Economics Review, 11*(1), 199–212.

Blaskovics, B. (2016). Differences between managing projects in an SME and in a large company. In A. S. Sitar, D. Aleksic, J. Kovac, D. Peljhan, & R. Rozman (Eds.), *Corporate governance: Challenges and development* (pp. 159–176). Ljubljana, Slovenia: Slovenian Academy of Management.

Blaskovics, B., Maró, Z. M., Klimkó, G., Papp-Horváth, V., & Csiszárik-Kocsir, Á. (2023). Differences between public-sector and private-sector project management practices in Hungary from a competency point of view. *Sustainability 15*(14), Paper: 11236.

Bouckaert, L. (2006a). The ethics management paradox. In L. Zsolnai (Ed.), *Interdisciplinary Yearbook of Business Ethics, 1*(1), 191–194.

Bouckaert, L. (2006b). When more ethics create less ethics: Some further clarifications of the ethics management paradox. In Zsolnai, L. (Ed.), *Interdisciplinary Yearbook of Business Ethics, 1*(1), 207–210.

Carroll, A. B. (2008). A history of corporate social responsibility: Concepts and practices. In Crane, A., McWilliams, A., Matten, D., Moon, J. & Siegeé, D. S. (Eds.), (2008). *The Oxford handbook of Corporate Social Responsibility* (pp. 19–46). Oxford, UK: Oxford University Press.

Crane, A., McWilliams, A., Matten, D., Moon, J., & Siegeé, D. S. (Eds.). (2008). *The Oxford handbook of Corporate Social Responsibility*. Oxford, UK: Oxford University Press

Dinh, T., Husmann, A., & Melloni, G. (2023). Corporate Sustainability reporting in Europe: A scoping review. *Accounting in Europe, 20*(1), 1–29.

European Commission. (2001). Green Paper: Promoting a European Framework for CSR.

European Commission. (2002). Communication from the Commission concerning Corporate Social Responsibility: A business contribution to Sustainable Development.

European Commission. (2011). A renewed EU strategy 2011–14 for CSR.

European Council. (2010). EUROPE 2020 A strategy for smart, sustainable and inclusive growth.

European Parliament and Council. (2019a). Regulation (EU) 2019/2088 of the European Parliament and of the Council of 27 November 2019 on sustainability-related disclosures in the financial services sector (SFDR).

European Parliament and Council. (2019b). Communication from the Commission to the European Parliament, the European Council, the Council, the European Economic and Social Committee and the Committee of the Regions, The European Green Deal, COM(2019) 640 final.

European Parliament and Council. (2020). Regulation (EU) 2020/852 of the European Parliament and of the Council of 18 June 2020 on the establishment of a framework to facilitate sustainable investment, and amending Regulation (EU) 2019/2088 (EU Taxonomy).

European Parliament and Council. (2022). Directive (EU) 2022/2464 of the European Parliament and of the Council of 14 December 2022 amending Regulation (EU) No 537/2014, Directive 2004/109/EC, Directive 2006/43/ EC and Directive 2013/34/EU, as regards corporate sustainability reporting (CSRD)

Guo, J., & Yu, Y. (2022). CSR committees, politicians and CSR efforts. *Asian Review of Accounting. 30*(3), 297–313.

Győri, Zs., Svastics, C., & Csillag, S. (2019). Push and pull motivations of entrepreneurs with disabilities in Hungary. In D. Tipuric & D. Hruska (2019). *7th International OFEL Conference on Governance, Management and Entrepreneurship: Embracing Diversity in Organisations*. Dubrovnik, Croatia, Governance Research and Development Centre, CIRU, 351–366.

Harangozó, G. (2008). Mitől zöld egy vállalat-avagy mit is jelent a jó környezeti teljesítmény? (What makes a company green–or what does good environmental performance mean?). *Budapest Management Review, 39*(1), 27–36.

Harangozó, G. & Szigeti, C. (2017). Corporate carbon footprint analysis in practice–With a special focus on validity and reliability issues. *Journal of Cleaner Production, 167,* 1177–1183.

Holmes, S. (2023). Sustainability and competition policy in Europe: Recent developments, *Journal of European Competition Law & Practice.* https://ktk.pte.hu/sites/ktk.pte.hu/files/images/kepzes/phd/Malovics_Gyorgy_disszertacio.pdf

International Standard Organisation (ISO). (2010). ISO 26000: 2010 – Guidance on Social Responsibility. https://www.iso.org/standard/42546.html

Isenberg, D. J. (2014). What an Entrepreneurship ecosystem actually is. *Harvard Business Review,* May 2014, https://hbr.org/2014/05/what-anentrepreneurial-ecosystem-actually-is

Lanero, A., Vázquez, J.-L., & Sahelices-Pinto, C. (2021). Halo effect and source credibility in the evaluation of food products identified by third-party certified eco-labels: Can information prevent biased inferences? *Foods, 10*(11), art. no. 2512.

Málovics, Gy. (2009). A vállalati fenntarthatóság érintettközpontú vizsgálata. Doktori értekezés. Pécsi Tudományegyetem Közgazdaságtudományi Kar Regionális Politika és Gazdaságtan Doktori Iskola.

Marcinkowska, E., & Sawicka, J. (2023). CSR initiatives in SMEs: Employee perception and their influence on employment decisions. *Central European Management Journal,* Vol. ahead-of-print No. ahead-of-print.

Matten, D., & Moon, J. (2005). A conceptual framework for understanding CSR. In A. Habisch, J. Jonker, M. Wegner, & R. Schmidpeter (Eds.), *Corporate Social Responsibility across Europe* (pp. 335–356). Berlin – Heidelberg, Germany: Springer

Mitnick, B. M., Windsor, D., & Wood, D. J. (2023). Moral CSR. *Business & Society, 62*(1), 192–220.

Molnár, A., Vasa, L., & Csiszárik-Kocsir, Á. (2023). Detecting business cycles for Hungarian leading and coincident indicators with a Markov switching dynamic model to improve sustainability in economic growth. *Decision Making: Applications in Management and Engineering, 6*(1), 744–773.

Radácsi, L. (2021). *Felelős és fenntartható vállalat.* Saldo, Budapest.

Somoza, A. (2023). Voluntary sustainability assurance in small and medium-sized entities: The role of country origin in Europe. *Business Strategy and the Environment, 32*(1) 462–483.

Stekelorum, R., Courrent, J.-M., & Spence, M. (2023). Supply chain pressures and SMEs' CSR practices: The moderation effect of supply chain position. *International Journal of Logistics Research and Applications.*

Stoian, M.-C., & Plakoyiannaki, E. (2023). Understanding international CSR in SMEs. *Journal of Small Business Management.*

United Nations, UN. (1987). Our Common Future.

United Nations, UN. (2015). Transforming our world: The 2030 Agenda for Sustainable Development.

Vives, A. (2016). Responsible practices in small and medium enterprises. In G. Aras, & D. Crowther (Eds.), *A handbook of corporate governance and social responsibility* (pp. 107–130). New York: Routledge.

Vogel, D. (2006). *The market for virtue – The potential and limits of Corporate Social Responsibility.* Washington, D.C.: Brookings Institution Press.

Denis Juracka[1], and Katarina Valaskova[1,*]

Development and Perspectives of the Sharing Economy in the Global Environment

Abstract:
Research background: The world has changed significantly over the last decades, mainly due to the influence of globalization, internationalization, and digitization. Advancement in scientific and technical progress, technologies, the development of information and communication technologies, emerging web communities of people, social networks, but also the impact of globalization, multiculturalism, changes in common ideas helped to start a new economic model known as the collaborative (sharing) economy. The sharing economy has become a kind of more modern market, connecting supply and demand, providers and consumers, as the two basic groups entering the sharing system.
Purpose of the article: The aim of this contribution is to determine the theoretical aspects of the development of the shared economy in the conditions of European countries to identify the strengths and weaknesses of this phenomenon in the context of identifying the impacts of the sharing economy on the development of national economies.
Methods: The basic methods of synthesis, analysis, induction, deduction and comparation were used. Moreover, to visualize the results, we also focus on the bibliometric analysis which enables the processing of enormous amounts of data and the creation of sophisticated scientific maps.
Findings & Value added: It may be difficult to assess sharing economy and all its positive and bad elements since there is always a point at which something good crosses the line into becoming harmful. Although sharing can theoretically function even without technological support, the ongoing advancement of information and communication technologies facilitates its use for a large portion of the population that is interested in partaking in this business model, expanding its marketing, economic, and consumer reach and familiarity.

Keywords: *sharing economy, collaborative economy, bibliometric analysis, globalization*

JEL Classification: *D16; E26; F60*

* Corresponding author: katarina.valaskova@fpedas.uniza.sk
1 University of Zilina, Faculty of Operation and Economics of Transport and Communications, Univerzitna 1, 010 26 Zilina, Slovakia

1 Introduction

Innovation processes and innovations represent and indicate a rapidly changing environment in all (not only) economic aspects. Within enterprises of different sizes, focus, industry and various economic and financial indicators, it is possible to observe the intensifying competition and the effort to convince the customer that that particular product or service can be considered the best. However, companies do not operate in isolation in their business activities. In addition to internal company factors, external factors affecting companies must also be taken into account. Rising costs, the economic impact of the COVID-19 pandemic, and the uncertain situation caused by rising energy prices and high inflation (Vinod & Sharma, 2021; Hossain, 2021). The listed factors that affect the entire society and almost every sector of the country's national economy equally slow down growth and slow down the innovation process. In all kinds of innovations, from their birth, through the process itself, to finalization, the key is interest, creative thinking, and a sufficient number of stimuli and ideas. Adopting the search for innovative processes and procedures in all areas of human life is necessary and, in many ways, essential. The competitive struggle takes place in all sectors of the economy and also in various positions across the entire spectrum of the labour market (Tran et al., 2022). However, it is extremely important to realize that in practice and on the market itself, it is not ideas that are sold, but the products and services themselves. In practice, business entities must react to emerging situations. The economic models of individual countries are also undergoing changes. One such change is the sharing economy, which can be considered an innovative economic model. At the beginning, however, it is necessary to go through a brief historical development of this economic model. In essence, it is possible to generalize that sharing is as old as humanity itself. There was no precise and universally accepted definition in the past, and there is none today, that would clearly and precisely name this phenomenon (Kobis et al., 2021; Sadiq et al., 2023). Despite this, there are countless definitions taking into account the socioeconomic nature of this phenomenon.

The first attempt at a certain characteristic came from the authors Felson and Spaeth (1978), who introduced the term "collaborative consumption." These authors defined this term in 1978 as events in which one or more people consume economic goods or services in the process of engaging in joint activities with one or more other people. This term has practically been considered synonymous with the sharing economy until now. This term can be loosely translated as "joint consumption." Historically, the first official platform that allowed the development of sharing was eBay, whose activity began in 1995. The ground-breaking activity that this company mediated was the opening of a global online market where supply and demand were made by ordinary people or retailers. Operating 24 hours a day, 7 days a week, and with the possibility of shopping from around the world, it was possible to sell and buy at affordable, yet competitive prices (Keycafe, 2019). In the environment of the Slovak Republic, it is possible to observe the successful operation of several such portals, which function as intermediaries between the two parties. They are, for example, an internet portal that allows you to add specific advertisements to a website for free – Bazoš.sk. The Bazár.sk portal and various others, which primarily advertise consumer goods, work in a similar way. From a broader point of view, it is also possible to include the website Autobazar.eu and others, where mostly private individuals offer new, but mostly used, vehicles for sale.

A breakthrough in the understanding of sharing occurred with the book publication by the authors Botsman and Rogers (2010), who describe the sharing economy as "an economic model that supports the use of ownership and enables the optimization of consumption through the sharing, exchange, rental, and lending of products and even services." The innovation of these authors mainly consisted in the fact that they used the word combination, economic model. That is why this variant has been talked about more and more in recent decades, and more and more definitions describe this system as an "official and serious" alternative to the linear understanding of consumerism based on ownership. In terms of legal issues, according to experts, the most relevant definition is according to the European Commission, which refers to the sharing economy as business models in which activities are facilitated by collaboration platforms that create an open market for the temporary use of goods or services, often provided by private individuals. Transactions within the sharing economy generally do not involve a change of ownership and can be operated for profit or non-profit.

The aim of this contribution is to determine the theoretical aspects of the development of the shared economy in the conditions of European countries in order to identify the strengths and weaknesses of this phenomenon in the context of identifying the impacts of the sharing economy on the development of national economies.

2 Methods

To achieve the main aim of the paper, we used the basic methods of synthesis, analysis, induction, deduction and comparation. Moreover, to visualize the results, we also focus on the bibliometric analysis. The use of information and communication technologies has increased interest in bibliometric research because they enable the processing of enormous amounts of data and the creation of sophisticated scientific maps, which are commonly used to show the results (Durana et al., 2020).

It is possible to research historical trends in certain scientific fields using publications, bibliographic citations, and references. This allows one to frequently unearth unrecognized connections between different scientific fields, authors, or themes and illustrate these connections. On the other side, we may utilize bibliometric techniques to pinpoint the most current areas of scientific inquiry or the rate at which they are becoming outdated. The establishment of the data set for the study using bibliometric analysis begins with publications that have been specifically focused on the sharing economy or collaborative economy from their inception up until the present (1985–2023). This most recent time horizon is essential for the accurate determination of the latest trends.

The VOS viewer was then used to create the term/bibliometric maps based on the co-occurrence frequencies of words, which are a generally used measure of the relatedness of terms, using all the considered articles that had been downloaded from the journals (Van Eck et al., 2010).

In the visualization of a map, items with a higher weight are shown more prominently than items with a lower weight. There are two standard weight attributes, referred to as the links attribute and the total link strength attribute. For a given item, the links and total link strength attributes indicate, respectively, the number of links of an item with other items and the total strength of the links of an item with other items (van Eck & Waltman, 2020). Different colours are used to determine the clusters of the terms – the same colour means that terms within the cluster are more closely related than terms in different clusters. An item may belong to one cluster only. Items may have various attributes in VOS viewer. In the network visualization, items are represented by their label and by default also by a circle. The colour of an item is determined by the cluster to which the item belongs. Lines between items represent links. The bolder the line, the stronger the relation between the items. As asserted by Garcia-Machado (2018) VOS viewer is an excellent tool for the formation of maps of authors and journals based on co-citation data or keywords.

3 Results and Discussion

Chovanculiak (2019), an analyst at the Institute of Economic and Social Analysis, refers to sharing as a concept that is considered by the professional public to be an economic model that, unlike other traditional and conventional models, does not focus on the idea of ownership, but on the concept of using, sharing, and making available already available products. He expresses the opinion that it is not essential that everything falls into the sharing system. It is important that the general public know, in conversations about sharing, what this approach offers and what economic, environmental, personal, and other benefits it brings. Historically, sharing did not invent something revolutionary, but it enabled mutual exchange and the implementation of activities. Some platforms tried to develop their activity in market conditions with an effort to reach potential consumers, entered the market, but failed to apply it in practice. Others remained only at the level of unrealized ideas. However, many were able to be applied, first regionally, nationally, and later internationally and globally. The economic sphere also goes through various challenges as part of its development. Finding new ways of organizing economic transaction systems is an essential component of the functioning of the economy in practice, but mainly of the direction of the economy as a whole into the future. The genesis of sharing is discussed in his book publication by Sundararajan (2016), who points to the main factors that have enabled a system on a global scale where individuals, or even businesses, know how to use products owned by another individual more efficiently, and often for financially acceptable amounts or subjects. He reminds us that at the turn of the 20th and 21st centuries, there was a massive convergence of personal computers, and access to the Internet and its services became more and more common all over the world. Consumers began to use these new technologies for personal use, and market entities began to use available digital devices that transformed the approach to management, planning, organizing, communications, and the entire production process of enterprises. The development of sharing is also addressed in a study by the authors Gossling and Hall (2019), who point to a different concept of this business exchange decades ago and today. Since traditionally, sharing was an integral part of family, neighborhood, or other ties when the people concerned knew each other. Gradually, the form of exchange began to be established in larger communities, and evolutionarily, sharing passed from the local to the national level. The development of information and communication technologies has changed the links between geographic and social distance and economic exchange. Sharing provided new trajectories for more efficient use of manufactured products. Therefore, they state that instead of a community-oriented and non-profit-oriented approach, sharing has begun to portray itself as a profitable business model with the potential to decentralize production and consumption.

This corresponds to the analysis of available publications in the WOS database, which provided interesting results. In the Web of Science (WoS) database, we found 5214 publications for the current period, that are devoted to the issue of shared or collaborative economies in several spheres of research. The most publications in the subject area are recorded in the fields of business (18.24 %) and management (17.26 %), but there is also a large representation in the categories of hospitality, leisure, sport tourism (14 %), green sustainable science technology (10.36 %), economics (10.30 %), environmental studies (9.93 %), environmental sciences (9.65 %), computer science information systems (7.81 %), computer science theory methods (5.83 %), and engineering electrical electronic (4.79 %).

To make it clear that only relevant outputs are taken into account, we mainly focused on publications in journals (83.08 %) and conference proceedings (16.80 %). From the outputs in the WoS database, it is clear that the publications of 1985 (15 records) are mapped, while the phenomenon of the sharing economy has significantly come to the attention of researchers since 2015 (66 records), with the biggest boom in 2020 (944 records).

Figure 1 presents the cooperation among the countries. We analyze the countries with minimum 10 documents published in those articles that were extracted from the WoS database. Among all the 114 countries in the dataset, only 60 countries have published a minimum of 10 documents. Following the map, six different clusters were formed. The Slovak Republic, together with other Visegrad countries, belongs to the green cluster, with the strongest link (total link strength of 4.83) to the Czech Republic. Comparing all analyzed countries, the strongest publication link (161.83) is between the USA and the Republic of China, where shared services and consumption play a prominent role in economic development (Tham et al., 2022).

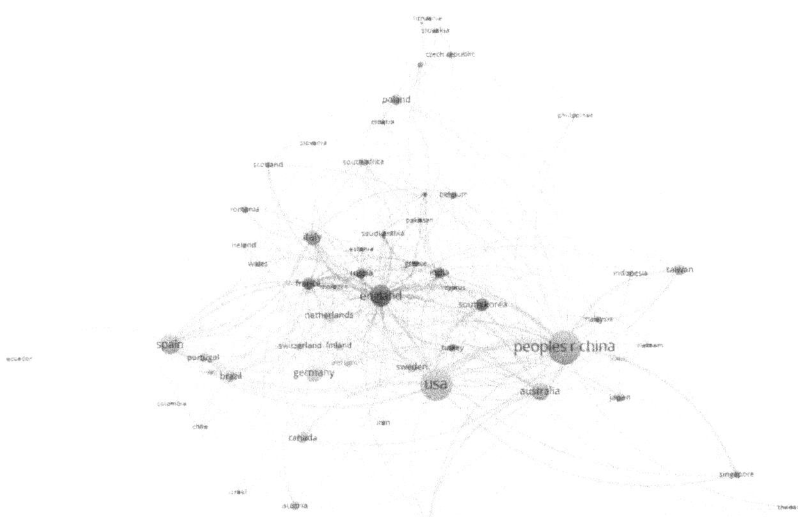

Figure 1. Bibliometric map of countries.

Source: own elaboration

Figure 2 is focused on the keywords that are closely linked to the issue of sharing or the collaborative economy. Of the 13,431 keywords, 588 met the threshold of the minimum number of occurrence of a keyword, which was set at 10. Similarly, to the previous figure, six clusters were formed. Cluster 1 (red colour) summarizes the basic principles of sharing economy, mobility, design and also includes one of the first platforms, Uber. The purple cluster is focused on tourism, accommodation, the impact of sharing platforms on the economy, and Airbnb. Cluster 3 (green colour) is devoted to collaborative consumption, consumption, trust, and satisfaction. The basic principles of circular economy, management, innovation, and stability create the core pillars of cluster 4 (dark blue colour). Cluster 5 (light blue colour) is for reciprocity and reputation. The last cluster, khaki colour, includes keywords related to the community, regulation, and collaborative principles of the economy.

Figure 3 highlights how the importance of the keywords linked to the sharing economy changes over time.

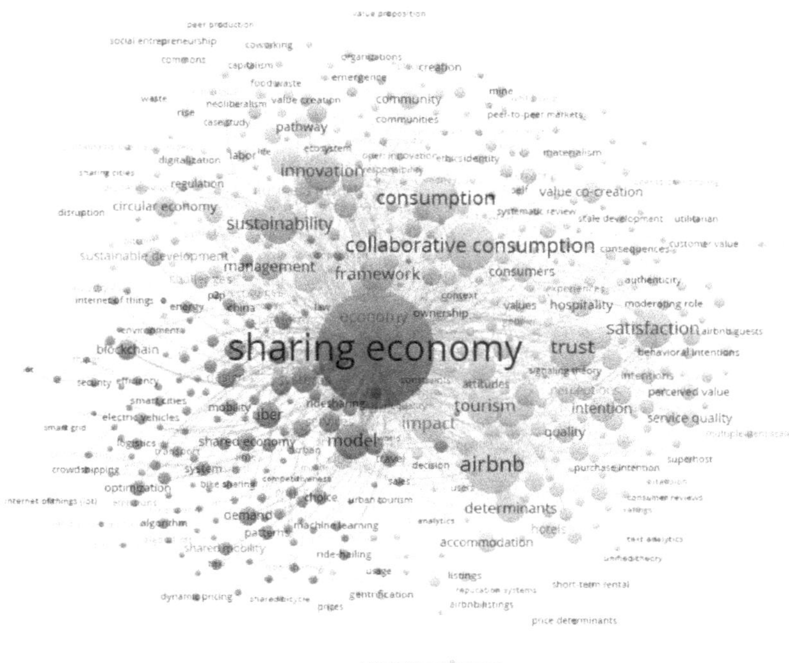

Figure 2. Bibliometric map of keywords.
Source: own elaboration

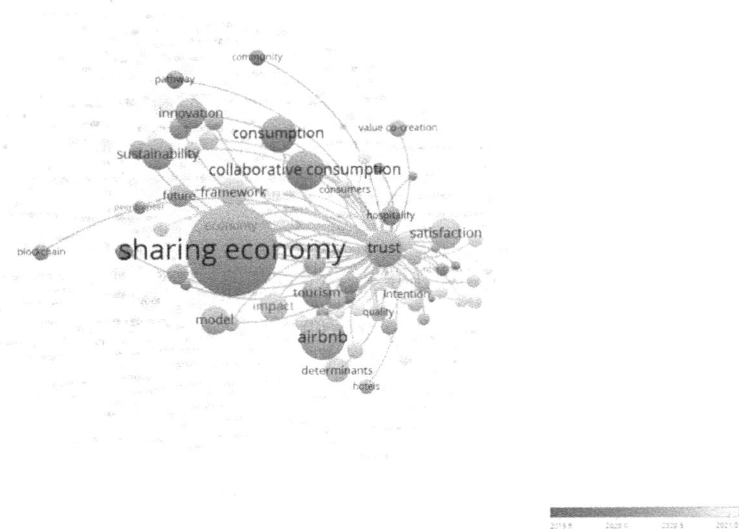

Figure 3. Overlay time visualisation of keywords.
Source: own elaboration

Evaluating the contribution of digital technologies and their benefits and negative aspects is a complex topic, as in every sphere of human life it would be necessary to take into account the boundary when useful becomes dangerous. In principle, sharing can work even without technological means, but the continuity of the development of information and communication technologies mediates the use of available forms of shared goods and services for a large part of the population that is interested in participating in this business model and thus increases its marketing, economic, and consumer reach and familiarity. This principle is also supported by the very concept referred to as P2P (peer to peer). Literally, this term can be translated as "equal to equal" (Kuhzady et al., 2022). In the field of computer technology, the term peer-to-peer refers to a type of computer network where there is no central server and users communicate directly with each other. The P2P economy, which also includes the sharing economy, is generally referred to as a decentralized model of providing, obtaining, or sharing access to goods or services, the operation of which is significantly facilitated by a community platform (Veber, 2018). However, we must point out that with the onset of the so-called digital economy, the pandemic accelerated. In their study, the authors Wynn and Jones (2022) characterize the digital economy or digital technologies as automatic systems and technological devices that process, store, and generate information. These technologies make it possible to store and compress large volumes of data. The authors Corejova and Chinoracky (2021) point to the significant impact of technological devices on the transformation of the economy and its transition to the digital space. They express the opinion that technological progress is synonymous with past and present changes. Through their findings, they came to the opinion that the scope of the economy, which received the attribute digital, is not conditioned by the geographical or economic dimensions of the state. Digitization is the introduction and use of specific digital technologies by a company or an entire industry. Companies can implement different kinds of technological innovations throughout their life cycle. These include, for example, digitization and subsequent automation of production processes, changes in the use of data, the transition from classic marketing tools to modern digital marketing tools, the introduction of an information system for various groups of suppliers, consumers, and various others.

The development of the sharing economy is also in the intentions of the European Union. Specifically, the functioning of digital platforms is dealt with by one of the bodies of the European Union – the European Parliament. From the point of view of statistics, in 2022, there were more than 500 platforms on the territory of the member states of the European Union, whose activities were included in the shared economy. At the same time, in the same year, more than 28 million people actively worked for the platforms, with the assumption that by 2025, this number should exceed the threshold of 43 million participating individuals. Revenues in the sharing segment have grown from €3 billion recorded in 2015 to €14 billion in 2020 (European Labor Authority, Directorate-General for Employment, Social Affairs and Inclusion, 2022). On the floor of the European Parliament, there are extensive professional discussions focused on the status and legal status of platform workers. The proposed directive of the European Parliament and the Council on the improvement of working conditions in the field of work for platforms presented in 2021 is widely supported in the professional debate. After the initial proposal and subsequent amendments, the members of the main legislative body of the European Union reached a mutual consensus at the end of 2022. The discussion primarily focused on issues related to the legal status of workers, i.e., classifying them as self-employed or employees and subsequently achieving the best protection for these workers. The initial proposal suggested reclassifying all workers as employees. The primary and focal objective of the Directive is to ensure that individuals participating in the system of digital work platforms are granted legal employment status. After reviewing and taking into account the official statistics, when up to 70 % considered work flexibility to be the most significant advantage, the leading representatives of the European Union states had to work and take into account the specifications, requirements of real users and the functioning of digital platforms in practice. The basic idea of this directive is that platform users are guaranteed basic security, labour, and social rights, such as: collective bargaining, paid vacation, health protection, working time, better access to protection against occupational accidents, unemployment benefits and sickness benefits, old-age pensions, and in the event that a minimum threshold is introduced in the given state, the minimum wage as well. In addition to the basic requirements, the secondary objectives of the directive are to ensure the monitoring of working conditions, increase transparency in the case of the use of automated algorithms, and give people the right to review these automated decisions. Concerns and conflicting opinions have led to debates, as a large number of platform workers could lose this kind of income. This fact led to a compromise that still leaves flexibility and choice. An example from Switzerland, which is not a member of the European Union grouping, points to the fact that in this country there has been a 42 % decrease in interest in platform services, and as a result, this decrease has caused up to 76 % of people working for platforms to lose this kind of income. Mandatory retraining would mean that these mostly technological companies would have to introduce fixed working hours, and the number of employees would also have to be reduced to meet these needs. The directive of the European Parliament and the Council of 21.12.2022 on the improvement of working conditions in the field of work for platforms evaluated, amended, and explained the contentious proposals and requirements (2021/0414(COD) Improving working conditions of persons working through digital labour platforms).

The opinions of experts (e.g., Wirtz et al., 2019; Hossain, 2020; Mi & Coffman, 2019; etc.), but also those of the lay public, differ. At the beginning of the operation, the use of platforms was almost unlimited from the point of view of providers and consumers. It is still possible to consider the platforms' own mechanisms important and effective. Among the most important ones, let's mention at least identity verification, evaluations based on previous experience, and a telephone line if necessary (Isaac, 2019). These means indicated that the platforms could deal with complex situations in practice. However, it should be kept in mind that the number of participants participating in any form of sharing exceeds the million marks. This is precisely why it is necessary to consider the guarantee of basic labour law rights and related tax obligations towards state budgets in the future. Flexibility, cost savings, and free choice when accepting orders represent significant benefits (Sadiq et al., 2023). However, with the ever-increasing expansion, there were incomes that were not regulated and subsequent tax evasion. The discussion in professional circles is also about how to control the activity of the platforms, individual stakeholders, while at the same time preserving the profitability and validity of this business model (Leoni & Parker, 2019). The Financial Directorate of the Slovak Republic amended the conditions for accounting for sales of digital platforms. According to the Financial Administration of the Slovak Republic, all drivers are required to document and record sales, either through a virtual cash register or an online cash register. In practice, this system works on certain principles. Passengers who use the application of the selected platform will pay the transport price after the service has been performed. The driver registers the sales through the selected sales recording system. The platform issues an invoice to the passenger on behalf of the driver and also sends to the driver's account an amount that represents the difference between the revenue for carrying out the transportation and the commission charged by the platform. The claim expires at the moment when the amount is credited to the driver's specific account. The last step, which may or may not result from the closed amount, is the declaration of the issuance of an invoice for commission. The driver is not obliged to issue a receipt, as the platform issues the document in electronic form.

In terms of European Union legislation, we must not forget the Directive of the Council of the European Union 2021/514 (Directive DAC7), which is applicable in all member states of the European Union (European Parliament, 2021). Implementation into Slovak legislation was carried out by Act No. 250/2022 Coll., which amends Act No. 442/2012 Coll. on international assistance and cooperation in tax administration, as amended. This directive introduces notification obligations for operators of digital platforms as 1 January 2023. Until this date, the Financial Administration of the Slovak Republic was able to find out information about income on the basis of a direct request. With the introduction of the directive and the registration of platforms, such information will be provided automatically through an automated system. It will concern digital platforms that mediate catering, transport, accommodation services, sales of goods, rental of means of transport, and real estate.

4 Conclusions

The trend toward sharing, also due to unpredictable exogenous influences and externalities, is difficult to predict. The economic situation in countries, political influences, conflicts in the world, or uncontrollably spreading viruses and diseases indicate that even in the area of sharing, it is only possible to predict. The COVID-19 pandemic only accentuated and deepened the differences in progress and in the use of available goods, products, and services between companies that had sufficient capital to handle this situation, to bridge the unfavourable situation, or to adapt. The system of shared services and products was developed with two different intentions. These intentions can be divided into two directions. The first is the development of a sharing system despite state regulations. The second direction pointed to developments that were in accordance with these regulations, or countries that considered this system as an alternative to the current, linear perception of the economic environment. The natural development of society and technological maturity show that stagnation in economic sectors is a highly undesirable phenomenon. It should be noted that law enforcement, the legal framework, laws, and regulations are necessary in all countries of the world, as relying on the "good and moral behaviour" of citizens seems like an illusion. However, technologies show that they can adequately help people in various fields. Smart applications, smartphones, tablets, computers, and laptops have started a shared system, regardless of which country they are in.

The current study is focused on the theoretical issues of the sharing economy which is its main limitation. The future research should include the quantification of impacts of this phenomenon on the gross domestic product of the national economies and thus identify the effects of the sharing economy. Moreover, it would be also beneficial to concentrate on the legal adjustments, riskiness of the platforms as well as the uncertainty linked to the exogenous effects of globalization.

Acknowledgments

This research was financially supported by the Slovak Research and Development Agency – VEGA 1/0121/20: Research of transfer pricing system as a tool to measure the performance of national and multinational companies in the context of earnings management in conditions of the Slovak Republic and V4 countries.

References

Botsman, R., & Rogers, R. (2010). *What's mine is yours: The rise of collaborative consumption*. Harper Business.

Corejova, T., & Chinoracky, R. (2021). Assessing the potential for digital transformation. *Sustainability*, *13*(19), 11040.

Chovanculiak, R. (2019). *Pokrok bez povolenia*. INESS.

Durana, P., Valaskova, K., Vagner, L., Zadnanova, S., Podhorska, I., & Siekelova, A. (2020). Disclosure of strategic managers' factotum: Behavioral incentives of innovative business. *International Journal of Financial Studies*, *8*(1), 17.

European Labor Authority, Directorate-General for Employment, Social Affairs and Inclusion. (2022, March 17). *EU proposes directive to protect the rights of platform workers*. https://eures.ec.europa.eu/eu-proposes-directive-protect-rights-platform-workers-2022-03-17_sk

European Parliament, Committee on Employment and Social Affairs. (2022, December 21). *Report on the proposal for a directive of the European Parliament and of the Council on improving working conditions in platform work*. https://www.europarl.europa.eu/doceo/document/A-9-2022-0301_EN.html

European Parliament, (2021, March 22). *Directive 2021/514 (DAC7) – Amendment of Directive 2011/16/EU on administrative cooperation in the field of taxation* https://eur-lex.europa.eu/legal-content/EN/ALL/?uri=CELEX%3A32021L0514

Felson, M., & Spaeth, J. L. (1978). Community structure and collaborative consumption: A routine activity approach. *American Behavioral Scientist*, *21*(4), 614–624.

Garcia-Machado, J. J. (2018). The latest streams in finance research: An updated bibliometric mapping based on co-occurrence data. *Forum Scientiae Oeconomia*, *6*(3), 7–23.

Gossling, S., & Hall, M. (2019). Sharing versus collaborative economy: How to align ICT developments and the SDGs in tourism? *Journal of Sustainable Tourism*, *27*(1), 74–96.

Hossain, M. (2020). Sharing economy: A comprehensive literature review. *International Journal of Hospitality Management*, *87*, 102470.

Hossain, M. (2021). The effect of the Covid-19 on sharing economy activities. *Journal of Cleaner Production*, *280*, 124782.

Isaac, M. (2019). *Super pumped: The battle for Uber*. W. W. Norton & Company.

Keycafe. (2019. August 1). *The History of the Sharing Economy*. https://medium.com/keycafe/the-history-of-the-sharing-economy-b139e55cdf47

Kobis, N. C., Soraperra, I., & Shalvi, S. (2021). The consequences of participating in the sharing economy: A transparency-based sharing framework. *Journal of Management*, *47*(1), 317–343.

Kuhzady, S., Seyfi, S., & Beal, L. (2022). Peer-to-peer (P2P) accommodation in the sharing economy: A review. *Current Issue in Tourism*, *25*(19), 3115–3130.

Leoni, G., & Parker, L. D. (2019). Governance and control of sharing economy platforms: Hosting on Airbnb. *British Accounting Review*, *51*(6), 100814.

Mi, Z. F., & Coffman, D. (2019). The sharing economy promotes sustainable societies. *Nature Communications*, *10*, 1214.

Sadiq, M., Moslehpour, M., Qiu, R. F., Hieu, V. M., Duong, K. D., & Ngo, T. Q. (2023). Sharing economy benefits and sustainable development goals: Empirical evidence from the transportation industry of Vietnam. *Journal of Innovation & Knowledge*, *8*(1), 100290.

Sundararajan, A. (2016). *The sharing economy*. MIT Press.

Tham, W. K., Lim, W. M., & Vieceli, J. (2022). Foundations of consumption and production in the sharing economy. *Electronic Commerce Research*.

Tran, T. T. H., Robinson, K., & Paparoidamis, N. G. (2022). Sharing with perfect strangers: The effects of self-disclosure on consumers' trust, risk perception, and behavioral intention in the sharing economy. *Journal of Business Research*, *144*, 1–16.

Van Eck, N. J., Waltman, L., Dekker, R., & Van der Berg, J. (2010). A comparison of two techniques for bibliometric mapping: Multidimensional scaling and VOS. *Journal of the American Society for Information Science and Technology*, *61*(12), 2405–2416.

Van Eck, N. J., & Waltman, L. (2020). *VOSviewer Manual for version 1.6.14.* https://www.vosviewer.com/getting-started

Veber, J. (2018). *Digitalizace ekonomiky a spolecnosti.* Management Press.

Vinod, P. P., & Sharma, D. (2021). COVID-19 impact on the sharing economy post-pandemic. *Australasian Accounting Business and Finance Journal*, *15*(1), 37–50.

Wirtz, J., So, K. K. F., Mody, M. A., Liu, S. Q., & Chun, H. H. (2019). Platforms in the peer-to-peer sharing economy. *Journal of Service Management*, *30*(4), 452–483.

Wynn, M., & Jones, P. (2022). Digital technology deployment and the circular economy. *Sustainability*, *14*(15), 9077.

Vladislav Kaputa[1,*], Erika Loucanova[1], Hana Matova[1], and Attila Racz[2]

Foreign Trade and Environmental Tariffs on Imports

Abstract:
Research background: In terms of the global environmental agenda, Europe wants to become the first climate-neutral continent by 2050. Foreign trade, namely the flow of goods into the customs territory of the EU, fundamentally affects the achievement of this ambition. Current initiatives result from one of the EU's priorities: building a climate-neutral, green, fair, and social Europe.
Purpose of the article: The objective of the paper is to evaluate the development of the foreign trade of Slovakia and, in accordance with the mentioned priority, to map the process of introducing the "Carbon Border Adjustment Mechanism" (CBAM). The consequences for international trade are discussed.
Methods: Methods such as data collection, foreign trade analyses, deduction, induction, and synthesis of findings were used to fulfill the purpose of the paper.
Findings & Value added: The milestone of the European Green Deal is to reduce greenhouse gas emissions in the EU by 55 % by 2030 compared to 1990 levels. The "Fit for 55" package is a set of legislative proposals to meet the goal. CBAM aims to change behaviour, specifically to stimulate producers from third countries to reduce emissions and to stimulate third countries to adopt green policies. The geographical scope of the mechanism covers imports into the EU from the rest of the world (except for goods originating in the EFTA countries). The declarant approved by the competent authority must purchase CBAM certificates corresponding to the value of the goods to be imported. Otherwise, goods may be stopped at the border, and sanctions may apply. CBAM also aims to discourage

* Corresponding author: kaputa@tuzvo.sk
1 Technical University in Zvolen, Faculty of Wood Sciences and Technology, Department of Marketing, Trade and World Forestry, T. G. Masaryka 24, 960 01 Zvolen, Slovakia
2 Technical University in Zvolen, Faculty of Ecology and Environmental Sciences, UNESCO Department for Ecological Awareness and Sustainable Development, T. G. Masaryka 24, 960 01 Zvolen, Slovakia

EU companies from moving their production to countries with less ambitious climate change policies.

Keywords: *foreign trade, EU Green Deal, CBAM certificates, import*

JEL Classification: *F10; F40; F50; F60*

1 Introduction

Foreign trade affects the level of a country's gross domestic product, as well as the performance of industries and businesses. When clarifying competitive advantages, especially at the level of industries and sectors, the balance of foreign trade is used as a starting point (Sujova et al., 2021). Slovakia's foreign trade is fundamentally influenced by the partnership in the EU and the fulfilment of European strategies and policies. Statistically, we report foreign trade, but in reality the producers allocated on the territory of the Slovak Republic are participants in the spacious Single European Market. Despite this view, the country creates strategies to support the domestic market and creates conditions for the foreign trade activities of domestic producers. By knowing the European ambitions and common goals of the member states, as well as by implementing the adopted strategies and tools, it is possible to achieve additional comparative advantages for the participation of the domestic business sectors in international markets.

The "Fit for 55" package is a set of legislative proposals to meet the goal anchored in the European Green Deal: to reduce greenhouse gas emissions in the EU by 55 % by 2030 compared to 1990 levels. The Carbon Border Adjustment Mechanism (CBAM) is a core part of the Fit for 55 package. In 2019, since the new President of the EU Commission took office, the implementation of CBAM was initiated as part of the Green Deal. Approaches to levying duties or taking other price adjustment measures on the embodied greenhouse gas emissions (GHG) of imported goods were explored. CBAM is the main instrument of EU climate policies and complements the European Emissions Trading System (EU-ETS).

2 Methods

The changes in foreign trade balance of the Slovak Republic are analyzed. The last 11 years of the development of the balance are presented. The fundamental changes that occurred in the last observed year (2022) are discussed. Data on foreign trade – export, import and balance values – are based on data published by the Statistical Office of the Slovak Republic, specifically from the DATAcube portal.

Foreign trade includes activities of all entrepreneurial entities, legal and natural persons involved in exports and imports in the form of merchandise. Foreign trade statistics generally cover the movement of goods in and out of the Slovak Republic intended for domestic consumption and for processing and subsequent re-exportation. In the total export, included are goods permanently leaving the territory of the Slovak Republic or goods leaving the territory for processing and subsequent re-importation (Slovak.statistics.sk, 2023a).

Further analysis continues to map the process of introducing the "Carbon Border Adjustment Mechanism" (CBAM). The consequences on international trade are discussed. The geographical scope of the mechanism covers imports into the EU from the rest of the world (except for goods originating in the EFTA countries: Iceland, Liechtenstein, Norway and Switzerland).

Trade openness indexes reported in the article represent exports plus imports as a percentage of GDP (based on The World Bank data). The methods used in this paper are:

- data/information collection,
- analyses (as a process by which the whole is decomposed into its individual elements and the relationship between them is examined),
- deduction (as a process by which new propositions are derived from certain assumptions and conclusions),
- induction (a logical method in which a conclusion about a generality or regularity is drawn from the observation of a certain number of specific cases),
- and synthesis (summarizes the information resulting from the analysis, on the basis of which it is possible to develop a proposal for measures to improve the situation in the future).

3 Results

According to data from The data.worldbank.org (2023), in 2018 the Slovak economy was the ninth most open in the world (190 %). Openness subsequently decreased due to the countries' anti-pandemic measures (to 168 % in 2020), but in 2021 the degree of openness of the economy exceeded the pre-pandemic period (185 %) and in 2022 it even increased to 204 % (Global Economy, 2023), which ranks Slovakia as the seventh most open economy in the world ranking.

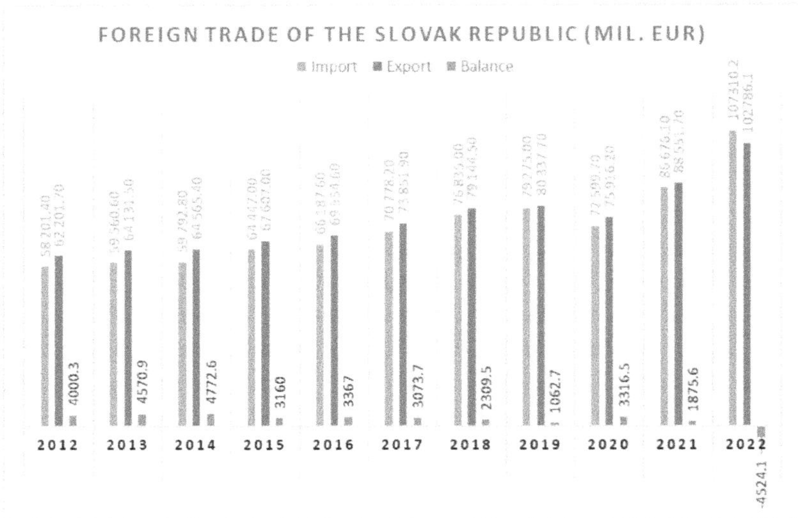

Figure 1. Foreign Trade Balance of the Slovak Republic (in mil. Euro).

Source: own elaboration based on Slovak.statistics.sk – data retrieved from the DATAcube portal (2023b)

The development of the Slovak trade balance including export and import values in the period 2012–2022 is evident from Figure 1. The Slovak Republic last reported an annual passive balance of foreign trade in 2008. However, after 14 years of active balance, it shows a negative balance of EUR 4.5 billion in 2022. This deficit occurs despite a significant increase in the value of exports in the given year. High values of imported natural gas, electricity and oil have a fundamental impact on the balance. This happened despite the fact that the value of exports grew over the last year in all 10 classes into which exports are structured. The class “Machines and transport equipment” was the most traded, as it also includes the export of cars. While anti-pandemic measures limited vehicle production in 2020 and 2021, in 2022 the Slovak automotive industry dealt with problems in supply chains (the global chip shortage for cars is cited as a major factor). The share of this class in total exports was 58 % in the given year. From the point of view of the territorial structure, foreign trade of the Slovak Republic is concentrated on EU countries. Imports from EU countries (as a share of total imports) are at the level of 62–67 % in the years 2019–2022, exports to EU countries are at the level of 79–85 % in the given period. The most important trading partners of Slovakia within the EU are Germany, the Czech Republic, Hungary, Poland, France and Italy. Outside the EU, these are China, the Republic of Korea, Vietnam and the Russian Federation.

A look at the development and structure (both commodity and territorial) of foreign trade implies the conclusion that Slovak exports are dominantly based on a sector that is currently quite sensitive to European climate goals (topics as emissions reduction, electromobility, transport transformation etc.). Other sectors of the economy are also significantly affected by these ambitions. We therefore want to draft the main challenges that Slovakia and other member states face from the implementation of CBAM as a tool for achieving climate goals.

The EU Emissions Trading System (EU ETS) covers emissions from power and heat generation, industrial production, chemical manufacturing, and other sources. The surrender of carbon certificates for imports is planned for the member states in January 2026. Expert studies within the topic focus mainly on the compatibility of CBAM with the rules of the World Trade Organization (WTO) and also on the effectiveness of this measure in limiting carbon leakage (McLure, 2014; Balistreri et al., 2019; Al Khourdajie & Finus, 2020; Banerjee, 2021; Smith et al., 2023). Smith et al. (2023) point out in their study that the EU's CBAM may lead to long-term trade disputes with major trading partners instead of facilitating the decarbonisation of the sector. They draw attention to the political feasibility of the intention, as this instrument may be considered unethical and the EU perceived as a normative power, which will weaken its position. The study points to the need to build strong coalitions with other countries of the emissions trading system (Canada, Iceland, Norway, UK, China, Japan, South Korea and the USA). The authors point out that the concept of political feasibility is closely related to efficiency (as Underdal, 2017 states in his work), or the effectiveness of the EU CBAM. From the point of view of justice (protection of the most vulnerable), the solution would be to exclude the least developed countries from the CBAM, but from the point of view of protecting competitiveness and reducing greenhouse gases, it will rather be emphasized, e.g., technology transfer to support decarbonisation of industry in such countries. Jacob (2023) sees the support of the transformation of sectors in third countries, the gradual introduction of CBAM and the removal of free emission permits for EU producers as a way to mitigate the political opposition of domestic as well as foreign industry. He suggests focusing diplomatic efforts on the small number of countries that will be most seriously affected by CBAM and not trying to extend the EU's climate policy to other countries.

4 Discussion and Conclusions

From the point of view of foreign trade, the automotive industry is still on the wave, but the situation in other sectors (which also depend strongly on other than market conditions) is not so favourable. It is possible to point to the level of processing and trade in wood-based industry. Here we have a comparative advantage in the products with lower added value (Parobek & Slastanova, 2020). Slovak timber trade development significantly depends on the globalization index (Dzian et al., 2020) and climate change mitigation strategies (Palus et al., 2020). The agricultural sector is also sensitive (due to its link to the country's food self-sufficiency). The study by Brodnanova et al. (2022) point to a deteriorated balance of foreign trade in fruit products between 2004 and 2020. The authors state that more innovations in fruit production are needed to strengthen competitiveness and increase benefits from foreign trade.

The high openness of the economy typical of Slovakia is a great advantage from the point of view of globalization. In this way, a small country with a small internal market participates in the international trade, reduces production costs, specializes production and intensifies the cooperation of market entities. On the other hand, it is subject to high economic dependence on foreign economies. This close relationship brings risks and exposes the domestic market to high vulnerability. Here we see the connection with the introduction of CBAM certificates and the impact on the open Slovak economy. This is not only a direct impact on domestic producers of steel, iron, cement, aluminium, fertilizers and electricity, but also on related sectors such as dominant automotive industry.

From the perspective of EU, the carbon price will cause an increase in the prices of energy inputs and thus disadvantage producers in the EU. Such a carbon pricing policy will not bring environmental efficiency, as market-behaving producers will shift production and emissions to territories outside the jurisdiction of the EU. This process is referred to as "leakage" for the prevention of which mechanisms have been proposed. The mechanism being implemented level the production conditions between producers in the EU and importers who do not pay the price for greenhouse gas emissions.

The WTO has a strong advocate in the EU of a multilateral trade system based on international rules. One of GATT's (General Agreement on Tariffs and Trade) non-discriminatory rules – national treatment – requires that no internal rules prescribe preferential treatment for domestic goods or production over imported products. The CBAM imposing an import tariff thus faces criticism.

The European Union claims that the tariff for importers will correspond to the cost of allowances paid by EU producers and thus the CBAM is not inherently discriminatory (Benson et al., 2023). Although the mechanism has only a limited economic impact on China's energy industry, Siy et al. (2023) state in their study that the EU's CBAM will have a broad and far-reaching negative impact on the social welfare and exports of China, the EU's largest trading partner.

The CBAM proposal omits the impact of the regulation on the downstream sector. It is clear that the increased cost of CBAM products will spread to industries such as automotive or construction. Manufacturers could shift imports to carbon goods. Possible negative impacts can thus be reflected in price increases, lack of supplies and leakage of production to third countries.

Acknowledgments

The authors thank the Scientific Grant Agency of the Ministry of Education, Science, Research and Sport of the Slovak Republic, grant No. 1/0475/22 "Environmental consumer and environmental citizen."

References

Al Khourdajie, A., & Finus, M. (2020). Measures to enhance the effectiveness of international climate agreements: The case of border carbon adjustments. *European Economic Review, 124*, 103405.

Balistreri, E. J., Kaffine, D. T., & Yonezawa, H. (2019). Optimal environmental border adjustments under the General Agreement on Tariffs and Trade. *Environmental and Resource Economics, 74*(3), 1037–1075.

Banerjee, S. (2021). Carbon adjustment in a consumption-based emission inventory accounting: A CGE analysis and implications for a developing country. *Environmental Science and Pollution Research, 28*(16), 19984–20001.

Benson, E., Majkut, J., Reinsch, W. A., & Steinberg, F. (2023, February 17). *Analyzing the European Union's Carbon Border Adjustment Mechanism.* https://www.csis.org/analysis/analyzing-european-unions-carbon-border-adjustment-mechanism

Brodnanova, R., Rovny, P., & Moroz, S. (2022). Competitiveness and innovations in foreign trade: A case of apples from Slovakia to Czechia. *Marketing and Management of Innovations, 2*, 43–54.

Data.worldbank.org. (2023). *Data.* The World Bank. https://data.worldbank.org/

Dzian, M., Palus, H., & Parobek, J. (2020). The impact of globalisation on the Slovak timber trade. *Sustainability of Forest-Based Industries in the Global Economy, Zagreb*, WoodEMA, 45–49.

Global Economy. (2023). *Trade openness – Country rankings*. The Global Economy. https://www.theglobaleconomy.com/rankings/trade_openness/

Jakob, M. (2023). The political economy of carbon border adjustment in the EU. *Oxford Review of Economic Policy*, *39*(1), 134–146.

McLure, C. E. Jr. (2014). Selected international aspects of carbon taxation. *American Economic Review*, *104*(5), 552–556.

Palus, H., Parobek, J., Moravcik, M., Kovalcik, M., Dzian, M., & Murgas, V. (2020). Projecting climate change potential of harvested wood products under different scenarios of wood production and utilization: Study of Slovakia. *Sustainability*, *12*(6), 2510.

Parobek, J., & Slastanova, K. (2020). Impacts of globalisation on the forest industry: Application of comparativeness analyses. *Sustainability of forest-based industries in the global economy, Zagreb*, WoodEMA, 71–76.

Siy, A. L., Wang, A., Zheng, T., & Hu, X. (2023). Research on the impact of the EU's carbon border adjustment mechanism: Based on the GTAP model. *Sustainability*, *15*(6), 4761.

Slovak.statistics.sk. (2023a). *Foreign trade*. Statistical Office of the Slovak Republic. https://slovak.statistics.sk

Slovak.statistics.sk. (2023b). *Foreign trade by month*. Statistical Office of the Slovak Republic. https://datacube.statistics.sk

Smith, I. D., Overland, I., & Szulecki, K. (2023). The EU's CBAM and Its 'Significant Others': Three perspectives on the political fallout from Europe's unilateral climate policy initiative. *JCMS-Journal of Common Market Studies*.

Sujova, A., Simanova, L., Kupcak, V., Schmidtova, J., & Lukacikova, A. (2021). Effects of foreign trade on the economic performance of industries – Evidence from wood processing industry of Czechia and Slovakia. *Economies*, *9*(4), 180.

Underdal, A. (2017). Climate change and international relations (After Kyoto). *Annual Review of Political Science*, *20*(1), 169–188.

Anita Kolnhofer-Derecskei[1,*], Regina Zsuzsanna Reicher[1], and Zsuzsanna Gyori[1]

Managerial Engagement in Sustainability Among Small and Medium-sized Enterprises Owners and Leaders

Abstract:
Research background: Sustainability is a crucial factor and driver for SMEs to access global business opportunities and resources. Regarding sustainability, many SMEs focus only on obligatory and regulatory compliance. Even on a personal level employers and employees are concerned about sustainability. Several SMEs are run by their owner-managers, who are personally engaged in the more sustainable approaches that can be implemented in business and entrepreneur actions.
Purpose of the article: Based on empirical studies, we investigated the bond between personal engagement in sustainability and SME leaders' business approach. Social, environmental, and economic responsibility are equally relevant, so each pillar has been observed.
Methods: Both secondary and primary data were analyzed. The European situation has been studied through Generali SME EnterPRIZE White Papers, and as for the primary research, a quantitative survey was carried out on a Hungarian representative sample in 2023.
Findings & Value added: Seemingly, the SME leaders are working for a more sustainable future unconsciously, they do more than they are aware of doing or communicating, especially in terms of social and local community aspects of sustainability. However, the global market requires SMEs to develop a better structured and formalized way of achieving sustainability, both in environmental and social aspects. To implement a well-structured sustainability strategy plan, leaders' motivations are among the key factors.

Keywords: *SME sector, sustainability, motivation*

JEL Classification: *D22 ; M12 ; M21 ; Q56*

1 Introduction

According to the Generali and Boccani Research (2021&2022), there are more than 25 million SME companies in Europe that account for 100 million jobs.

* Corresponding author: kolnhofer-derecskei.anita@uni-bge.hu
1 Budapest Business University, Faculty of Finance and Accountancy, CESIBUS, 1055 Budapest, Marko u. 29–31, Hungary

Smith et al. (2022) highlight that SMEs may be the link between global and individual sustainability, while SMEs view sustainable development as a "neighbourliness" that empowers local communities to address social and environmental needs. Therefore, sustainability may be possible access to the global market for them so it seems to be required in this sector to establish and maintain a more formalised and structured way, all from environmental, social and economic sides (Khan et al., 2023).

Saveanu et al. (2021) summarised the pros and cons of SMEs regarding sustainable practices (focusing on CSR).

Table 1. Pros and Cons regarding sustainable practices among SMEs.

Disadvantages	Advantages
SMEs are smaller and have fewer resources to allocate to CSR compared to large companies, their CSR action's impact is viewed as smaller; This sector is far from being homogenous, many differences are likely to affect their commitment towards CSR; Owner-managers of SMEs are often multitasking, along with other priorities they might not allocate time to deal with CSR SME owner-managers are often more distrustful of bureaucracies and less responsive to formal institutional pressures – such as those that promote CSR;	SMEs are more flexible and can respond much quicker to social and environmental problems; SMEs are directly connected to their community; SMEs are less inclined to formalize CSR-related aspects (develop strategies and set departments dealing with these aspects); The relationship with stakeholders tends to be rather informal and, consequently, so do the CSR-related initiatives regarding different stakeholders; The motivation towards CSR is less to respond to external pressures but to protect personal ethics, The managers of SMEs interested in CSR consider that they should pay attention to their social and environmental responsibilities

Source: own elaboration based on Saveanu et al. (2021)

Although as Vasquez et al. (2018) emphasized SMEs face three main barriers to adopting sustainable practices: (1) the perception of their small environmental impact, (2) lack of expertise and understanding of environmental strategies, and (3) the cost. These barriers hinder proactive sustainable behaviour in SMEs, as managers perceive little financial benefit from environmental, social or economically sustainable investments. Caldera et al. (2019) observed that SMEs striving for business sustainability must address barriers like financial constraints, time constraints, knowledge gaps, implementation risks, regulations, and organizational cultures that hinder sustainable practices, focusing on growth and reduced manufacturing consumption. Even Journeault and his colleagues (2021) called researchers' attention to the fact that despite a lot of effort, SMEs still struggle to integrate social and environmental concerns into their business practices. In this matter, barriers include limited awareness of sustainability impacts, lack of time and resources, and lack of skills and expertise.

That raised the question of whether the SMEs are interested in sustainability, and if so which are the key drivers of this decision? Research indicates that environmental management practices are influenced by various stakeholders, including legislators, environmental groups, financial institutions, and suppliers, as well as internal attitudes and knowledge (Saveanu et al., 2021). Generali and Boccani Research (2021, 2022) investigated numerous SME leaders and found that the owners' and managers' attitudes are essential for the adoption of sustainable practices (see Figure 1.).

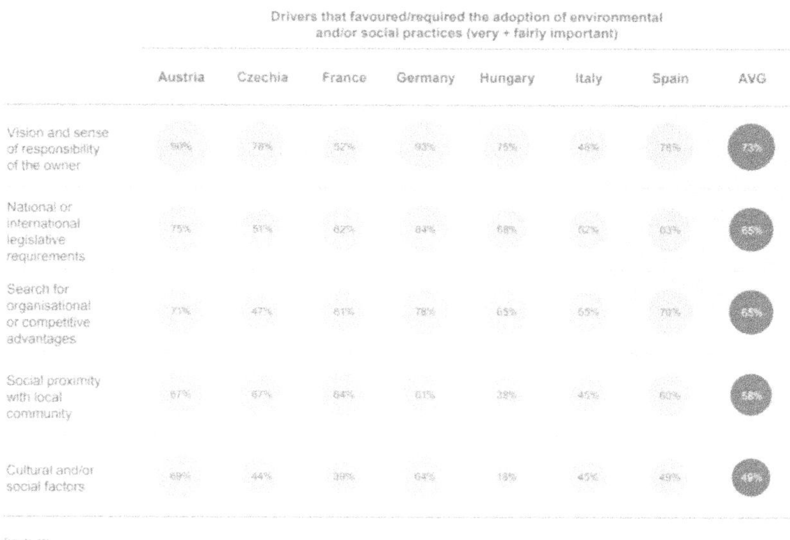

Figure 1. Drivers and motivations, European comparison.

Source: Generali and Boccani Research (2021)

Sustainability should be interpreted informally and introduced incrementally on this level. Artin's (2022) study reveals that SMEs are more likely to engage with sustainability if their owners/managers create a business culture that promotes environmental and social improvement. Also, Jenkins (2006) underlined that an owner–manager is closer to the organisation so can more easily manage sustainability. Additionally, the values and attitudes of owner–managers of SMEs largely define their companies' sustainability activities (Kiefhaber et al., 2020). Their values and attitudes, and their important position in the organisation, owner-managers have a major influence on the sustainability activities of their companies. However, according to Gyori et al. (2022), there are differences depending on the stage or status of entrepreneurs. While 30.8 % of the owner-managers who established their own firms were aware of the 17 United Nations Sustainable Development Goals, only 20.2 % of owner-managers of new firms answered the same. This characteristic showed a significant difference. It seems some gap among others between ownership and non-ownership.

2 Methodology

Individual beliefs, principles, and values, particularly the owner's attitudes, environmental orientation, and ethics, play a crucial role in preventing or favouring the adoption of sustainability initiatives. SME owner–managers' sustainability values and attitudes impact their company's sustainability activities. Individual motivations and the owner's sense of responsibility are the main drivers for the adoption of environmental and/or social practices. According to Generali and Boccani Research (2021 & 2022), Hungarian SMEs face challenges in environmental and social agendas due to lack of resources, lack of knowledge, and due to the high number of owner-managers who do not adopt modern management practices. So the question is given whether the Hungarian SME leaders are aware of conscious sustainable management approaches.

2.1 Hypotheses

H1. There are no differences between owners and managers on a personal level regarding sustainability awareness.

People who are concerned more about sustainability are more likely to be aware of the threats posed by environmental pollution and are willing to cooperate in eliminating the problem and to contribute to its solution. SME managers with greater environmental awareness are more likely to take responsibility for green technologies and are more likely to invest in sustainable tools and skills. (Polas et al., 2021)

H2. There are differences between owners and managers on the company level regarding sustainability awareness due to the agency problem.

At the same time acting in somebody else's interests can influence our values. Based on the principal-agent theory is concerned with how the principal (such as the owner) can motivate his agent (say the manager), to act in the principal's interests. This problem comes from different priorities and goals. While the owners are focusing on long-term profitability, assets and principal, the managers are interested in their own considerations. (Kolnhofer-Derecskei, 2017; Grossman & Hart, 1992) The attitudes and motivations of owners/managers have a crucial impact on business growth and are reflected in strategic decisions and the way the company is managed. (Sarwoko & Frisdiantara, 2016)

2.2 Samples and Procedures

In May of 2023, a phone survey was carried out on a representative sample of Hungarian SME leaders. In our representative national sample, we considered the following aspects: company size, region, and industrial classification. The survey contained several parts related to the activities, motivations, organizational characteristics and leadership factors of CSR and sustainability in the SME sector. In this study, seven statements were investigated and evaluated based on a main parameter (position of the subject). All statements measured on a 7-point semantic scale, subjects' beliefs, attitudes and understanding. Due to the representativeness, normal distribution was granted but items measured on an ordinal scale required non-parametric testing for comparing average values among subsamples.

3 Results

H1. There are no differences between owners and managers on a personal level regarding sustainability awareness.

As Figure 2 proves, results showed no differences among subsamples (regarding the positions of respondents). Regardless of their position of answerers, everyone was aware of sustainability on a similar level.

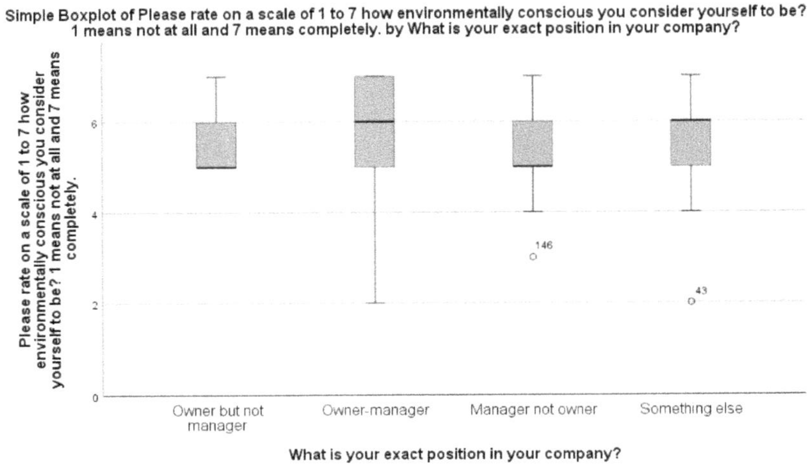

Figure 2. The similarity of each subsample's responses.
Source: own elaboration

H2. There are differences between owners and managers on the company level regarding sustainability awareness due to the agency problem.

In this section, six further statements were evaluated. Table 2 provides a broader understanding of our results and summarizes each statement whereas sustainability awareness covering the entire company showed a moderated difference between owners and non-owners. The owners were more concerned about the positive image of entrepreneurship both on local and international markets and paid a significantly higher account for the cost efficiency than non-owners. Conversely, non-owners kept more important personal development and training than owners.

4 Discussion and Conclusion

As for the importance of our study, we agree with Lawrence et al. (2006) that "While individually small and medium-sized enterprises (SMEs) may have small social, environmental and financial impacts, cumulatively their impact is significant." (Lawrence et al., 2006) Unfortunately, as the Generali and Boccani Research emphasized "due to their heterogeneity, there can be neither a 'gold standard', nor a 'one-size-fits-all' approach to fostering sustainability in SMEs" (Generali and Boccani Research, 2021).

Even though some assumptions can be formed, the general role of the principal-agent problem may cause some problems. As our results showed, the non-owner managers took the professional development and training for their employees more seriously, than owners. In reverse, the owners were more concerned about efficiency costs and the international market. Seemingly, the managers (agents) may have a clarified vision and better-structured business plan than owners who are running their business less deliberately. That is why it is crucial for SME owner-managers to see clearly how to resolve conflicts between their sustainability and other objectives. SME owners–managers should match identity and personal values in order to increase the reputation of the enterprise (Kiefhaber et al. 2020). Luckily, Blackburn et al. (2013) found that the size and age of the business, as well as a well-structured business plan, are more important determinants of performance than the entrepreneurial characteristics of the manager. Meanwhile, Ahinful et al. (2019) underlined the influences of the stakeholders, as well. According to them, primary stakeholder pressure, industry, and size significantly influence environmental management on sustainability by SMEs, while secondary stakeholders' pressure, firm age, and ownership type are not.

In sum, SME leaders adopt more informal strategies, but their approach to sustainability is still unplanned and moderated. However, European SMEs are achieving more than they are able and/or willing to communicate, such as in the welfare, environment and local engagement. It is reflected in the "sunk sustainability" phenomenon (Generali and Boccani Research, 2021, 2022) when owners do more than they are aware of, especially regarding employees or local communities. In terms of social and local communities' points of view, several Hungarian SMEs have improved working conditions, promoted diversity, inclusion, and equal opportunities; and have implemented initiatives for culture, education, youth, sport, and vulnerable groups in their local communities. All without doing or communicating these actions on a wide billboard. However, Eikelenboom et al. (2019) studied SMEs' ability to three pillars of sustainability and found that SMEs are able to simultaneously address social, environmental, and economic goals, whereby leaders can act as drivers of all three pillars. As results showed (Lawrence et al., 2006), most enterprises do not have formal reporting of their social and environmental practices. That means the lack of clearly communicated vision might cause the "sunk sustainability" phenomenon. That is why, in our following study, we are going to observe the way of communication and promotion of sustainable action by SMEs.

Table 2. Summary report of statistical analysis.

What is your exact position in your company?	Owner but not manager (n=16)		Owner-manager (n=145)		Manager not owner (n=41)		Something else (n=95)		Total (n=298)					
	Mean	Std. Deviation	Mean	Std. Deviation	Mean	Std. Deviation	Mean	Std. Deviation	Mean	Std. Deviation	Null Hypothesis	Test	Sig.	Decision
Please rate on a scale of 1 to 7 how environmentally conscious you consider yourself to be? 1 means not at all and 7 means completely.	5,5289	0,72065851	5,6472	1,18999929	5,5491	0,95830963	5,7082	0,92916034	5,6465	1,05671126	The distribution of Please rate on a scale of 1 to 7 how environmentally conscious you consider yourself to be? 1 means not at all and 7 means completely. is the same across categories of What is your exact position in your company?.	Independent-Samples Kruskal-Wallis Test	0,67	Retain the null hypothesis.
It is important that social responsibility permeates the entire way a company operates.	2,04	1,069	1,83	1,331	2,04	1,303	2,27	1,017	2,01	1,231	The distribution of It is important that social responsibility permeates the entire way a company operates. is the same across categories of What is your exact position in your company?.	Independent-Samples Kruskal-Wallis Test	0,07	Retain the null hypothesis.
It improves our bargaining power if our suppliers know that we care about social and environmental values.	3,25	1,893	3,52	2,075	3,43	1,796	4,29	2,054	3,74	2,049	The distribution of It improves our bargaining power if our suppliers know that we care about social and environmental values. is the same across categories of What is your exact position in your company?.	Independent-Samples Kruskal-Wallis Test	0,01	Reject the null hypothesis.
In the international market, stakeholders are much more demanding of social and environmental responsibility.	3,56	2,705	4,37	2,486	3,75	2,447	4,82	2,303	4,38	2,455	The distribution of In the international market, stakeholders are much more demanding of social and environmental responsibility. is the same across categories of What is your exact position in your company?.	Independent-Samples Kruskal-Wallis Test	0,03	Reject the null hypothesis.
To create a positive image of our company in the minds of the public, corporate social responsibility is now almost indispensable.	4,78	1,993	4,92	1,884	4,79	2,143	5,49	1,645	5,08	1,868	The distribution of To create a positive image of our company in the minds of the public, corporate social responsibility is now almost indispensable. is the same across categories of What is your exact position in your company?.	Independent-Samples Kruskal-Wallis Test	0,04	Reject the null hypothesis.
Our business is continuously reducing the amount of energy used in its operations	6,27	1,255	4,95	1,926	4,22	2,509	5,08	1,958	4,96	2,031	The distribution of Our business is continuously reducing the amount of energy used in its operations is the same across categories of What is your exact position in your company?.	Independent-Samples Kruskal-Wallis Test	0,02	Reject the null hypothesis.
It is important for our company to ensure the professional development of its employees, for example through professional training.	5,46	1,705	5,64	1,632	5,82	1,757	6,14	1,345	5,82	1,579	The distribution of It is important for our company to ensure the professional development of its employees, for example through professional training. is the same across categories of What is your exact position in your company?.	Independent-Samples Kruskal-Wallis Test	0,09	Retain the null hypothesis.

Source: own elaboration

Acknowledgments

This research was supported by the Ministry of Innovation and Technology of Hungary from the National Research, Development and Innovation Fund, financed under the Tématerületi Kiválósági Program 2021 (TKP2021-NKTA) funding scheme (Project no. TKP2021-NKTA-44)

References

Ahinful, G. S., Tauringana, V., Essuman, D., Boakye, J. D., & Sha'ven, W. B. (2019). Stakeholders pressure, SMEs characteristics and environmental management in Ghana. *Journal of Small Business & Entrepreneurship*, *34*(3), 241–268.

Artin, P. (2022). Critical sustainability factors of regional SMEs: A case study of regional Australia. *Current Research in Environmental Sustainability*, *4*, 100138.

Blackburn, R. A., Hart, M., & Wainwright, T. (2013). Small business performance: Business, strategy and owner-manager characteristics. *Journal of Small Business and Enterprise Development*, *20*(1), 8–27.

Caldera, H., Desha, C., & Dawes, L. (2019, May). Evaluating the enablers and barriers for successful implementation of sustainable business practice in 'lean' SMEs. *Journal of Cleaner Production*, *218*, 575–590.

Eikelenboom, M., & de Jong, G. (2019, October). The impact of dynamic capabilities on the sustainability performance of SMEs. *Journal of Cleaner Production*, *235*, 1360–1370.

Generali & SDA Bocconi Research. (2021). *Generali SME EnterPRIZE Fostering Sustainability in Small and Medium-sized Enterprises*. White Paper. 1st Edition https://www.sme-enterprize.com/

Generali & SDA Bocconi Research. (2022). *Generali SME EnterPRIZE Fostering Sustainability in Small and Medium-sized Enterprises*. White Paper. 2nd Edition https://www.sme-enterprize.com/

Grossman, S. J., & Hart, O. D. (1992). An analysis of the Principal-Agent problem. *Foundations of Insurance Economics*, 302–340.

Gyori, Z., Kasa, R., & Szegedi, K. (2022). Hungarian entrepreneurs' sustainability motivations based on GEM 2021 results. *Prosperitas*, *9*(4), 1–16.

Jenkins, H. (2006). Small business champions for Corporate Social Responsibility. *Journal of Business Ethics*, *67*(3), 241–256.

Journeault, M., Perron, A., & Vallieres, L. (2021). The collaborative roles of stakeholders in supporting the adoption of sustainability in SMEs. *Journal of Environmental Management*, *287*, 112349.

Khan, S. A. R., Sheikh, A. A., & Ahmad, Z. (2023). Developing the interconnection between green employee behavior, tax avoidance, green capability, and sustainable performance of SMEs through corporate social responsibility. *Journal of Cleaner Production*, *419*, 138236.

Kiefhaber, E., Pavlovich, K., & Spraul, K. (2020). Sustainability-related identities and the Institutional environment: The case of New Zealand Owner–Managers of Small- and Medium-Sized Hospitality Businesses. *Journal of Business Ethics*, *163*(1), 37–51.

Kolnhofer-Derecskei, A. (2017). The indifferent, the Good Samaritan, the brave and the agent in Allais Paradox situation – or How endowment effect influences our decision in case of Allais Paradox? *Organizacija*, *50*(4), 299–313.

Lawrence, S. R., Collins, E., Pavlovich, K., & Arunachalam, M. (2006). Sustainability practices of SMEs: the case of NZ. *Business Strategy and the Environment*, *15*(4), 242–257.

Polas, M. R. H., Tabash, M. I., Bhattacharjee, A., & Davila, G. A. (2021). Knowledge management practices and green innovation in SMES: The role of environmental awareness towards environmental sustainability. *International Journal of Organizational Analysis*.

Sarwoko, E., & Frisdiantara, C. (2016, January). Growth determinants of Small Medium Enterprises (SMEs). *Universal Journal of Management*, *4*(1), 36–41.

Saveanu, T., Badulescu, D., Saveanu, S., Abrudan, M.-M., & Badulescu, A. (2021). The role of owner-managers in shaping CSR activity of Romanian SMEs. *Sustainability*, *13*(20), 11546.

Smith, H., Discetti, R., Bellucci, M., & Acuti, D. (2022). SMEs engagement with the Sustainable Development Goals: A power perspective. *Journal of Business Research*, *149*, 112–122.

Vasquez, J., Bruno, G., Settineri, L., & Aguirre, S. (2018). Conceptual framework for evaluating the environmental awareness and eco-efficiency of SMEs. *Procedia CIRP Global Web Conference-Envisaging The Future Manufacturing, Design, Technologies And Systems In Innovation Era (Cirpe 2018)*, *78*, 347–352.

Jaroslava Kosarova[1,*], and Marta Urbanikova[1]

Is Food Waste in Slovak Primary Production a Real Threat to Food Security?

Abstract:
Research background: Food waste has a global impact not only on the environment but also on the economic development and food security of poor people. In recent years, more time has been devoted to food waste, but very few studies have been published on food waste in primary production.
Purpose of the article: The aim of this study was to quantify the amount of food waste by product group and estimate the food waste rates in Slovak primary production.
Methods: The amount of food waste in primary production is calculated on the basis of a methodology set by the European Commission that defines what needs to be measured as food waste. By calculating the food waste rate, it was determined how much food is wasted in relation to the total amount of food produced.
Findings & Value added: In 2014–2019, Slovakia's primary production was at most 54 % cereals, 20 % legumes, and 12 % raw milk. It was shown that the amount of food waste in Slovak primary production was, on average, 67.4 thousand tonnes per year. Food waste from cereals was estimated at approximately 23 thousand tonnes per year, which represents 0.46 % of the total amount of cereals produced. Food waste from meat production represented an average of 1.6 thousand tonnes of live weight, which represents 2 % of the total meat production. For every ton of food produced, nine kilograms are wasted, which represents approximately one percent of the total food production in Slovak primary production.

Keywords: *food waste, food losses, primary production, product group, agriculture*

JEL Classification: *Q18; Q53; Q56*

1 Introduction

The United Nations Food and Agriculture Organisation estimated that one-third of the global food supply gets lost or discarded every year (Food and Agriculture

* Corresponding author: jkosarova@ukf.sk
1 Constantine the Philosopher University in Nitra, Institute of Economics and Management, Faculty of Natural Science, Trieda A. Hlinku 1, 949 74 Nitra, Slovakia a

Organization of the United Nations, n.d.). Inefficiency use of resources increases greenhouse gas emissions as well as the quantity of food waste generated. From 2022 onward, under the EU Waste Framework Directive, Member States are required to collect and provide data on food waste to the European Commission (2020). The European Commission supports the United Nation target of halving the amount of food waste at all stages food supply chain, by 2030 (Martin, 2023). Although in industrialized countries the greatest potential for reducing food waste is in the last stages of the supply chain, especially in households, it is necessary to consider all stages of the food supply chain, including primary production and processing (Parfitt et al., 2021). Therefore, strategies to prevent food waste should take into account all phases of the food supply chain, and not focus on a specific phase of the supply chain. Therefore, dividing the food chain into individual phases is useful for identifying specific measures and targeted reduction strategies (Priefer et al., 2016).

2 Literature Review

Over the last decade, a number of studies on the quantification of food waste, but few studies have been carried out in European countries in first stage of food supply chain representing primary production (Redlingshofer et al., 2017; Hartikainen et al., 2018; Caldeira et al., 2021; Eicaite et al., 2022; O'Connor et al., 2022). Most studies on the quantification of food waste in primary production focus on case studies focusing on a food group or several food groups, such as plant products as potatoes, vegetables and fruits, or animal products such as milk and other product groups (Pereira et al., 2022; Beausang et al., 2017; Baker et al., 2019; Schneider et al., 2019; March et al., 2019; Johnson et al., 2019; Joensuu et al., 2021; Laba et al., 2022). Another type of study focuses on food waste in the entire supply chain, including primary production (Caldeira et al., 2019; Jeswani et al., 2021; Parfitt et al., 2021; Amicarelli et al., 2021; Karwowska et al., 2021).

Although many studies have investigated the measurement or monitoring of food waste in primary production, these studies are not directly comparable due to the use of different measurement methodologies. Therefore, monitoring food waste is very difficult, and also the common definition and quantification of food waste is still an open challenge. To prevent food waste and reduce food waste in the future, it is important to have an overview of the path of food from field to fork. Before food reaches the final consumer, it passes through several stages in the food supply chain, with each stage generating food waste. Estimates of food waste at different stages of the food supply chain are quite uncertain, whether at the national or sub-national level. In industrialized countries, the largest amount of food waste is generated in the last stages of the supply chain, especially in households. In underdeveloped countries, food waste occurs to a greater extent in primary production. This is due to inefficient collection technologies, insufficient transport infrastructure and poor storage facilities. Slovakia is characterized primarily by the cultivation of grain, which it also exports.

Although the share of food waste in Slovakia is the highest in households of all phases of the food supply chain, the share of food waste from primary production in the entire supply chain is among the highest among European countries for export reasons. In recent years, interest in publishing studies on total food waste has increased, but in primary production few studies on food waste have been published. The article aim is to quantify food waste and to estimate the food waste rates in Slovak primary production by product group, which mainly includes food products of plant production such as cereals, root crops and milk production from total animal production.

3 Data and Methods

In the literature focused on food waste or food loss, different definitions of food waste are used, which complicates the comparison of the amount of waste between countries, sectors and regions. In this article, we do not distinguish between food losses and food waste, so we will use the term food waste in primary production.

In this study, food waste in the primary production is defined as food waste generated in the section A, NACE code Agriculture, aquaculture and fisheries, from the time the plants are ready to harvest, animals are born and milk is drawn. Food waste refers to food as a whole and it also includes inedible parts that were not separated from edible parts during production. Thus, foods may contain elements consisting of parts of foods intended for human consumption and parts of foods not intended for human consumption (EC, 2019). Unlike the FUSIONS study (Stenmarck et al., 2016), food products that were originally intended for human consumption but are used as animal feed are included in the food waste in this study.

Data of waste are obtained from the Ministry of the Environment, which draws data from the Regional information system on waste for the period 2014–2019. Every year, Slovak companies report to the waste database the various types of waste generated, the amount of waste and the way they dispose of it. Thus, the reported amount of food waste may tend to underestimate the actual amount. This data does not contain information about what belongs and what does not belong in food waste.

Each type of waste is included in the NACE code, according to the establishment, is listed in the European Waste Code. Food waste measurement is carried out by means of waste codes assigning, which contain food waste into individual NACE categories (EC, 2019). The attribution of food waste to the different stages of the food supply chain should be made in accordance with the common statistical classification of economic activities in the European union set out in the regulations and NACE Rev. 2. The amount of food waste in primary production is calculated on the basis of a methodology set by European Commission in the delegated act, that defines what needs to be measured as food waste at each stage of the food supply chain (EC, 2019). The amount of food waste in primary production in Slovakia is calculated as follows:

$$FW_{primy\ production,i} = \sum_i FW\ 020102, i + \sum_i FW\ 020103, i \qquad (1)$$

where $FW_{primy\ production}$ is amount of food waste in phases primary production in 1000 tonnes in the given period in Slovakia, $FW\ 020102, i$ is the amount of food waste in Slovakia primary production in NACE activity A1, A3 of waste code animal-tissue waste for NACE classes (i) and $FW\ 020103, i$ is the amount of food waste in Slovakia primary production in NACE activity A1, A3 of waste code plant-tissue waste for NACE classes (i). Food waste values were calculated for each production group. The amount of food waste is calculated at relevant stages of the food chain through following NACE codes: Growing of cereals, leguminous crops and oilseeds; growing of vegetables and melons, roots and turbes,; other-non perenninial crops; growing of spices, aromatic, drug and pharmaceutical crops; plant propagation; growing of pome fruits and stone fruits; grapes; raising of dairycattle; raising of other cattle and buffaloes; raising of pigs; raising of sheep and goats; raising of poultry; mixed farming – other; aquaculture.

The food waste rate in Slovakia primary production, typically expressed as a percentage, was calculated as a share of total food waste in primary production and the sum of produced amount of food for product group:

$$\%\ FW_{primary\ production} = \frac{FW_{primy\ production}}{\sum_j Produced\ amount\ of\ food, j} \qquad (2)$$

where $Produced\ amount\ of\ food, j$ is the total amount of food in Slovakia primary production for food sector (j). The quantities produced per tonne of foods for food sector (j) are obtained from Eurostat. Data series from Eurostat used include production in meat as slaughtering in slaughterhouses [apro_mt_pann], production and utilization of milk on the farm [apro_mk_farm], crop production [apro_cpsh1] harvested cereals, grains, fruit and vegetables, and production from aquaculture excluding hatcheries and nurseries [fish_aq2a].

Crop production expressed in thousands of tons includes cereals for the production of grain, dry pulses and protein crops for the production of grain, root crops, oilseeds, fresh vegetables and strawberries, permanent crops for human consumptions and aromatic, medicinal and culinary plants. Dairy production expressed in thousands litres includes raw milk, total available on farms. Production of meat expressed in thousand tonnes includes data from animal production that was converted to approximate live weight using the following live weight to carcass weight coefficients. Coefficient for bovine meat is 0.59, coefficient of pigmeat is 0.7, coefficient of meat of sheep and goats is 0.47 and coefficient of poultry meat is 0.76 (Stenmarck et al., 2016).

This study for quantifying food waste uses a common methodology and minimum quality requirements for the uniform measurement of food waste. As countries are at different levels of development and implementation of a national strategy to measure food waste, it is difficult to compare the results with other studies.

4 Results and Discussion

As a small country in terms of population, Slovakia produces a large amount of food for export purposes. The highest share of agricultural land is used by grain, and wheat is the major grain planted. From the total amount of produced food in primary production, 54 % of cereal is produced in Slovakia (Table 1). Among the agricultural production of Slovakia, almost half of the grain grown is exported (Pittman et al., 2020). Countries with a higher share of food waste in primary production have a large agricultural production sector. A large part of the food produced is exported and therefore not consumed in the country. Therefore, in industrialized countries, food waste in the primary production phase is minimal.

Table 1 shows the corresponding NACE code and the waste registered for each of the codes. These data of NACE code also include several types of waste from products that are not included in the food sector. Therefore, these wastes from NACE codes include EAK categories only for numbers 020102 and 020103, which contain food waste.

Table 1 shows the selection of food sectors in the primary production, their representativeness in food production and food waste as an average representation of the years 2014–2020 for the plant and animal food sector. Fresh vegetables in food sector too include permanent crops as aromatic, medicinal and culinary plants due to low values. All types of meat are converted to live weight through coefficients expressing the share of live weight. The representativeness of the food waste of the given food sector expresses the share of individual foods, expressed using NACE classes, from the total food waste in primary production. The representativeness of the food production of the given food sector expresses the share of individual foods, from the total produced amount of food in primary production. From the total amount of produced food in primary production, 54 % of cereal is produced in Slovakia. It is followed by milk production, which represents 12 % of the total amount of food produced in primary production (Table 1). On average, up to 45 % of food waste was created during dairy farming. However, the data on waste includes food waste related to dairy farming, therefore we assume that this

Table 1. Selection of food sectors in the first stage of food supply chain their representativeness in food production and food waste in average years 2014–2019.

<table>
<tr><th>Food sector</th><th>Representativeness of food production</th><th>NACE classes (EWC Code – 02 01 02, 02 01 03)</th><th>Representativeness of food waste</th></tr>
<tr><td>Cereals</td><td>53.7 %</td><td rowspan="4">Growing of cereals, leguminous crops and oilseeds</td><td rowspan="4">34.10 %</td></tr>
<tr><td>Dry pulses</td><td>0.28 %</td></tr>
<tr><td>Root crops</td><td>19.64 %</td></tr>
<tr><td>Oilseeds</td><td>9.41 %</td></tr>
<tr><td rowspan="4">Fresh vegetables</td><td rowspan="4">1.19 %</td><td>Growing of vegetables and melons, roots and turbes</td><td>0.37 %</td></tr>
<tr><td>Other-non perenninial crops</td><td>0.06 %</td></tr>
<tr><td>Growing of spices, aromatic, drug and pharmaceutical crops</td><td>0.01 %</td></tr>
<tr><td>Plant propagation</td><td>0.10 %</td></tr>
<tr><td rowspan="2">Pernament crops -fruits</td><td rowspan="2">1.14 %</td><td>Growing of pome fruits and stone fruits</td><td>0.03 %</td></tr>
<tr><td>Grapes</td><td>0.25 %</td></tr>
<tr><td>Raw milk-dairy</td><td>11.99 %</td><td>Raising of dairycattle</td><td>44.72 %</td></tr>
<tr><td>Bovine meat (59 % live weight)</td><td>0.18 %</td><td>Raising of other cattle and buffaloes</td><td>0.83 %</td></tr>
</table>

Table 1. Continued

Food sector	Representativeness of food production	NACE classes (EWC Code – 02 01 02, 02 01 03)	Representativeness of food waste
Pigmeat (70 % live weight)	0.92 %	Raising of pigs	0.52 %
Meat of sheep and goats (47 % live weight)	0.02 %	Raising of sheep and goats	0.01 %
Polutry meat (76 % live weight)	1.24 %	Raising of poultry	1.04 %
-	-	Mixed farming – other	17.75 %
Fish	0.03 %	Aquaculture	0.06 %

Note: Within NACE classes represents NACE activity A -Agriculture, forestry and fishing

waste consists mainly of unconsumed feed. In the case of dairy raising, food waste from primary production is most often used as animal feed. It is followed by growing of cereals, leguminous crops and oilseeds, which 34 % of total food waste in primary production.

The differences in food waste for plant-based products, which are generally higher than for animal-based products, are due to differences in the characteristics of the two categories. Waste from plant-based products is difficult to control due to the biological nature, product properties and environmental conditions. Unlike animal-based products such as meat, milk and fish, plant-based products are still alive and therefore have a shorter shelf life and lower overall quality after harvest. The total amounts of produced food expressed in thousand tonnes are presented in Table 2. On average 2014–2019 the total amount of produced food in primary production in Slovakia is 7 659 thousand tonnes per year.

Table 2. Total produced food amounts in Slovakia food primary production (thousand tonnes).

Product group	Mean	Std. Dev.	Max	Min
Cereals	4147.6	455.2	4745.5	3484.1
Dry pulses	21.9	4.3	26.2	14.1
Root crops	1516.8	147.3	1739.6	1356.4
Oil crops	727.0	84.0	803.5	563.0
Vegetables	108.4	11.2	127.1	94.4

(*continued on next page*)

Table 2. Continued

Product group	Mean	Std. Dev.	Max	Min
Fruits	88.3	14.4	104.0	62.0
Other crop	3.9	1.7	7.3	2.3
Crop total	6613.9	625.4	7431.6	5860.6
Dairy	926.2	11.5	942.5	915.7
Bovine meat	14.0	0.5	15.0	13.2
Pigmeat	70.7	13.1	89.7	48.2
Meat of sheep and goats	1.2	0.1	1.3	1.1
Poultry meat	96.1	2.0	98.1	94.1
Meat total	117.2	56.0	197.8	64.5
Fish	2.0	0.6	2.7	1.2
Total production	**7659.3**	**617.0**	**8433.5**	**0.0**

Source: own estimation based on data from Eurostat

Results for the year 2014–2019 show (Table 3) that between 40 and 100 thousand tonnes of food was waste in primary production sector. The total amount of food waste from the respective NACE groups in primary production sector was estimated on average 67 thousand tonnes per year corresponding to 12 kilograms per person per year in Slovakia. Comparing the amount of food waste per capita in the primary production and production phase can be debatable, as each country has a different production profile.

Table 3. The amount of food waste in Slovakia primary production (thousands tonnes).

Product group	Mean	Std. Dev.	Max	Min
Cereals, Pulses And Oilseeds	23.0	11.0	42.5	12.0
Vegetables And Root Crops	0.3	0.4	1.1	0.1
Fruit	0.2	0.1	0.3	0.1
Meat	1.6	1.1	3.6	0.6
Dairy	30.2	5.2	37.5	22.7
Fish	0.0	0.0	0.1	0.0
Mixed Farming	12.1	9.9	26.6	1.2
Total	**67.4**	**25.7**	**100.8**	**39.3**

Source: own estimation based on data from the Ministry of the Environment

When monitoring the efficiency of food waste management, it is useful to calculate the food waste rate. The food waste rate represents the percentage of food waste from the total amount of food produced for a certain period.

The percentages of food waste for the amount of food produced in each category are shown in the Table 4. These main categories, entered by the relevant NACE code, are recorded in waste statistics. Missing values in some years were averaged.

Table 4. Food waste rates from total produced amount of food.

Product group	2014	2015	2016	2017	2018	2019	Average
cereals	0.51 %	0.64 %	0.76 %	0.28 %	0.29 %	0.28 %	0.46 %
vegetables root crops	0.06 %	0.01 %	0.01 %	0.01 %	0.01 %	0.01 %	0.02 %
fruit	0.25 %	0.24 %	0.37 %	0.10 %	0.08 %	0.10 %	0.19 %
meat	5.56 %	3.28 %	1.29 %	1.14 %	0.31 %	0.45 %	2.01 %
dairy	3.60 %	3.55 %	4.09 %	2.77 %	3.05 %	2.48 %	3.25 %
fish	1.10 %	1.89 %	2.06 %	1.67 %	2.35 %	2.89 %	1.99 %
Total	**1.02 %**	**1.31 %**	**1.20 %**	**0.58 %**	**0.61 %**	**0.52 %**	**0.87 %**

Source: own estimation

In Slovakia dairy sector in primary production was estimate of in average 3.25 % food waste. According to Hartikainen et al. (2018) food waste of the milk production was due to milk with antibiotic residues due to antibiotic treatment of the cows. Other reasons for milk waste are poor milk quality, problems with the cooling system in the milk tank and milk stuck in the tank filter. Recycling food waste in animal nutrition is a regular way in some sectors, like in the dairy sector discarded milk is used as feed to calves.

The food waste from cereals was estimated at about 23 thousand tonnes per year, or 0.46 % of the total produced amount of cereals. Food waste from cereals most often arises due to post-harvest losses, due to improper handling and storage.

The smallest share of waste is generated in growing vegetables, which represents only 0.02 % of the total production of vegetables. Very little vegetables are grown in Slovakia, they are mostly imported, so the share of food waste is also low. However, food waste from vegetables is generated in other stages of the food supply chain. Food waste from vegetables arises due to quality standards, also due to post-harvest losses, due to improper handling and poor storage. On the other hand, in the first phase of the food supply chain, it is typical that part of the waste is disposed of on site and is not included in the waste statistics. It consists of post-harvest and root residues of the main crops, which are plowed into the soil as an important link in the biological cycle of substances in the system. Therefore, there seems to be a very low amount of food waste.

Food waste from meat in primary production are estimated due to animal mortality and the entire carcass weight at slaughter for all dead animals (Karwowska et al., 2021). The meat potential for premature death, mortality among animals of all age groups and pre-slaughter rejection is also counted as food waste. To be transported to the slaughterhouse, the animal must be healthy and able to stand on all four legs. An animal that has suffered injuries during transport, but is otherwise healthy, can only be killed in exceptional cases. Instead, the animal is destroyed, although the quality of the meat is probably intact. Food waste from meat production represented an average of 1,600 tonnes of live weight, which represents 2 % of the total meat production. The most waste was generated during poultry farming, approximately 700 tonnes. A total of 14 thousand tonnes of food waste from bovine meat, 70.7 thousand tonnes from pigmeat and 96.1 thousand tonnes from poultry meat.

The food waste amounts to 9 kg for every tonne of food being produced on average. According to study FUSIONS, in primary production in EU countries is wasted 7 to 17 kg per tonne of food produced (Stenmarck, et al, 2016).

Irregularities in the first stages of the food chain are caused by the underestimation of collected waste in waste statistics, since waste flows in earlier stages can be processed on site e.g., ploughed of residues into the soil, incineration of residues for energy production, anaerobic digestion or using as fodder, and therefore do not have to be reported in waste statistics. Also, it is complicated to compare these results with others (Redlingshofer et al., 2017; Beausang et al., 2017). Not least because until now there were no standard measurements, understandings, definitions of what is and what is not food waste.

Due to the imprecise methodologies, classifications and definitions of waste, the methodology of waste collection and classification improves every year. Also, a common methodology for measuring food waste was not adopted until 2019, as well as a precise definition of food waste, what to include and what not to include in food waste statistics. The amounts of waste in the given sectors differ in individual years due to possible incorrect classification in previous years. Although since 2019 it has been defined which categories of waste are included in food waste and on the basis of this a certain clarification can be made, there is still a lot of ambiguity in what was included in the given amounts.

5 Conclusions

Due to the growing awareness of resource efficiency, sustainability and the impact of food production on the environment, there is an increased emphasis on reducing and preventing waste in the food supply chain. This study deals with the quantification of food waste in the first phase of the food supply chain in Slovakia, total production of food in primary production and estimating waste coefficients for the total food production, and also providing important information for stakeholders in terms of food safety.

The amount of food waste in primary production was estimated at 67,000 tons per year. In total, less than one percent of the total food production at the primary production level becomes waste. We found out that the most food waste was in growing of cereals and raising of dairy cattle. We concluded that a relatively small percentage of the annual amount of produced food in primary production within each category is waste. In general, the most common causes of food waste at the level of plant-based products are infestations by pests and diseases, and at the level of animal-based products are animal morbidity and mortality during transport to the slaughterhouse. In the case of cereals and dairy, food waste is most often used as animal feed. In general, producers in primary production try to minimize waste or use waste to create additional economic value.

Although the EU Commission has adopted a common framework for measuring food waste, there is still a lack of relevant research and transparent data on food waste not only in primary production but in all phases of the food supply chain. Therefore, there is a need for further research into food waste quantification and improved food waste data collection for individual product groups. Measuring food waste and identifying problems in the food system are fundamental steps to reducing environmental impacts, managing the human food system, reducing food insecurity, and ensuring healthy, nutritious and sustainable food.

Acknowledgments

Scientific Paper was elaborated within the framework of the project KEGA 029UKF-4/2022: Preparation of the structure and content of the subject, textbook and e- learning course "Entrepreneurial skills" for non-economic study programs with a focus on the online environment.

References

Amicarelli, V., Lagioia, G., & Bux, C. (2021). Global warming potential of food waste through the life cycle assessment: An analytical review. *Environmental Impact Assessment Review, 91*, 106677.

Baker, G. A., Gray, L. C., Harwood, M. J., Osland, T. J., & Tooley, J. B. C. (2019). On-farm food loss in northern and central California: Results of field survey measurements. *Resources, Conservation and Recycling, 149*, 541–549.

Beausang, C., Hall, C., & Toma, L. (2017). Food waste and losses in primary production: Qualitative insights from horticulture. *Resources, Conservation and Recycling, 126*, 177–185.

Caldeira, C., De Laurentiis, V., Corrado, S., van Holsteijn, F., & Sala, S. (2019). Quantification of food waste per product group along the food supply chain in the European Union: A mass flow analysis. *Resources, Conservation and Recycling, 149*, 479–488.

Caldeira, C., De Laurentiis, V., Ghose, A., Corrado, S., & Sala, S. (2021). Grown and thrown: Exploring approaches to estimate food waste in EU countries. *Resources, Conservation and Recycling, 168*, 105426.

Eicaite, O., Balezentis, T., Ribasauskienė, E., Morkunas, M., Melnikiene, R., & Streimikiene, D. (2022). Measuring self-reported food loss in primary production: Survey-based insights from Central and Eastern Europe. *Waste Management, 143*, 46–53.

European Commission, (2020). *Guidance on Reporting of Data on Food Waste and Food Waste Prevention*. European Commission. https://ec.europa.eu/eurostat/documents/342366/351811/Guidance+on+food+waste+reporting/5581b0a2-b09e-adc0-4e0a-b20062dfe564

European Commission. (2019). *Commission Delegated Decision (EU) 2019/1597 of 3 May 2019 Supplementing Directive 2008/98/EC of the European Parliament and of the Council as Regards a Common Methodology and Minimum Quality Requirements for the Uniform Measurement of Levels of Food Waste*. European Commission. http://data.europa.eu/eli/dec_del/2019/1597/oj

Food and Agriculture Organization of the United Nations [FAO]. (n.d.). Food loss and waste. https://www.fao.org/nutrition/capacity-development/food-loss-and-waste/en/

Hartikainen, H., Mogensen, L., Svanes, E., & Franke, U. (2018). Food waste quantification in primary production–the Nordic countries as a case study. *Waste Management, 71*, 502–511.

Jeswani, H. K., Figueroa-Torres, G., & Azapagic, A. (2021). The extent of food waste generation in the UK and its environmental impacts. *Sustainable Production and Consumption, 26*, 532–547.

Joensuu, K., Hartikainen, H., Karppinen, S., Jaakkonen, A. K., & Kuoppa-Aho, M. (2021). Developing the collection of statistical food waste data on the primary production of fruit and vegetables. *Environmental Science and Pollution Research, 28*(19), 24618–24627.

Johnson, L. K., Bloom, J. D., Dunning, R. D., Gunter, C. C., Boyette, M. D., & Creamer, N. G. (2019). Farmer harvest decisions and vegetable loss in primary production. *Agricultural Systems, 176*, 102672.

Karwowska, M., Laba, S., & Szczepanski, K. (2021). Food loss and waste in meat sector – Why the consumption stage generates the most losses?. *Sustainability, 13*(11), 6227.

Laba, S., Cacak-Pietrzak, G., Laba, R., Sulek, A., & Szczepanski, K. (2022). Food losses in consumer cereal production in Poland in the context of Food Security and Environmental Impact. *Agriculture, 12*(5), 665.

March, M. D., Toma, L., Thompson, B., & Haskell, M. J. (2019). Food waste in primary production: Milk loss with mitigation potentials. *Frontiers in Nutrition, 6*, 173.

Martin. (2023, October 20). Sustainable consumption and production. United Nations Sustainable Development. https://www.un.org/sustainabledevelopment/sustainable-consumption-production/

O'Connor, T., Kleemann, R., & Attard, J. (2022). Vulnerable vegetables and efficient fishers: A study of primary production food losses and waste in Ireland. *Journal of Environmental Management, 307*, 114498.

Parfitt, J., Croker, T., & Brockhaus, A. (2021). Global food loss and waste in primary production: A reassessment of its scale and significance. *Sustainability, 13*(21), 12087.

Pereira, R. P. T., Galo, N. R., & Filimonau, V. (2022). Food loss and waste from farm to gate in Brazilian soybean production. *Journal of Agriculture and Food Research, 10*, 100431.

Pittman, R., Jandova, M., Krol, M., Nekrasenko, L., & Paleta, T. (2020). The effectiveness of EC policies to move freight from road to rail: Evidence from CEE grain markets. *Research in Transportation Business & Management, 37*, 100482.

Priefer, C., Jorissen, J., & Brautigam, K. R. (2016). Food waste prevention in Europe–A cause-driven approach to identify the most relevant leverage points for action. *Resources, Conservation and Recycling, 109*, 155–165.

Redlingshofer, B., Coudurier, B., & Georget, M. (2017). Quantifying food loss during primary production and processing in France. *Journal of Cleaner Production, 164*, 703–714.

Schneider, F., Part, F., Gobel, C., Langen, N., Gerhards, C., Kraus, G. F., & Ritter, G. (2019). A methodological approach for the on-site quantification of food losses in primary production: Austrian and German case studies using the example of potato harvest. *Waste Management, 86*, 106–113.

Stenmarck, A., Jensen, C., Quested, T., & Moates, G. (2016). *Estimates of European Food Waste Levels.* www.eu-fusions.org/phocadownload/ Publications/ Estimates%20of%20European%20food%20waste%20levels.pdf

Jana Kozakova[1,*]

Corporate Social Responsibility in Times of Crisis: A Comparative Analysis of Social Public Assistance in the Visegrad Region, with Focus on Slovakia, Czech Republic, and Poland

Abstract:
Research background: Corporate social responsibility (CSR) encompasses voluntary actions taken by businesses to integrate social and environmental considerations into their operations and relationships with stakeholders. Recent events, including the COVID-19 pandemic, the conflict in Ukraine, and the energy crisis, have highlighted the importance of CSR in crisis management and support for affected communities. In the Visegrad region, businesses actively engage in CSR initiatives focusing on social public assistance.
Purpose of the article: The purpose of this paper is to investigate and compare the extent to which companies in the Czech Republic, Slovakia, and Poland prioritize specific CSR activities of social public assistance related to the COVID-19 pandemic, conflict in Ukraine, and energetic crisis.
Methods: The study collected data through an online questionnaire distributed to companies in the Czech Republic, Poland, and Slovakia, focusing on their emphasis on crisis CSR activities. The sample included 100 companies from each country. Statistical analysis involved descriptive and inferential techniques, including Cronbach's alpha, the Kruskal-Wallis test, followed by Bonferroni post hoc testing, and Pearson's correlation.
Findings & Value added: The study's findings reveal the crucial role of corporate engagement and solidarity through CSR initiatives in supporting countries during crises, including the COVID-19 pandemic, conflict in Ukraine, and energy crisis. However, the research highlights no statistically significant differences in CSR approaches connected to these crises in monitored countries. These insights provide valuable guidance for policymakers and stakeholders in enhancing crisis-related CSR practices.

Keywords: *corporate social responsibility, crisis, social public assistance, Visegrad region, comparison*

JEL Classification: *M14; O35; P52*

---

* Corresponding author: jana.kozakova@uniag.sk
1 Slovak University of Agriculture in Nitra, Faculty of Economics and Management, Department of Management, Trieda A. Hlinku 2, 949 76 Nitra, Slovakia

1 Introduction

Corporate social responsibility (CSR) has attracted a lot of attention in recent years as businesses have begun to realize how important it is to consider social effects in addition to economic benefits. To support sustainable development and solve societal issues, firms that participate in CSR voluntarily commit to incorporating social and environmental considerations into their daily operations. But at times of crisis, when firms' resiliency and capacity to respond to social demands are put to the test, CSR is really put to the test.

The COVID-19 pandemic, the crisis in Ukraine, and subsequent energy crises have all been experienced by the Visegrad area, which is made up of Slovakia, the Czech Republic, Poland, and Hungary. These crises have had a significant impact on society's socioeconomic situation and have brought to light the crucial role that public assistance plays in reducing the negative consequences on people's lives and the well-being of communities.

This article's objective is to examine and compare the levels of emphasis placed by companies operating in the Czech Republic, Slovakia, and Poland on the implementation of specific crisis-oriented CSR public assistance activities to assist in overcoming global crises related to mobilizing the corporate sector in the fight against the COVID-19 pandemic (social CSR activities for society's protection); the corporate engagement and solidarity (supporting Ukraine in times of crisis through CSR initiatives); energy crisis and corporate engagement: (CSR initiatives for sustainable development). The results of this study will add to the body of knowledge on corporate social responsibility (CSR) and crisis management by illuminating the function of CSR during crises. A thorough understanding of the level of emphasis related to CSR practices in the Visegrad region will also be helpful for policymakers, business executives, and stakeholders to help form strategies and make educated decisions that will promote sustainable and socially responsible development.

Research gap: The research gap for this paper lies in the limited understanding of how corporate social responsibility (CSR) initiatives and their impact on social public assistance unfold in the context of crises, particularly within the Visegrad region encompassing Slovakia, Czech Republic, and Poland. While CSR has gained recognition as an important aspect of business conduct, its effectiveness during times of crisis and its contribution to public assistance remain relatively underexplored. Existing literature on CSR primarily focuses on its implementation in stable business environments, with fewer studies examining its role and outcomes in crisis situations. Furthermore, most of the research on CSR has been conducted in Western countries, leaving a gap in knowledge regarding its application and effectiveness in the specific context of emerging economies.

2 Literature Review

A multifaceted concept of corporate social responsibility (CSR) has its roots in the study of organizational behaviour and management. It alludes to the voluntarily chosen steps and methods used by businesses to incorporate social and environmental considerations into their operations and relationships with stakeholders (McWilliams et al., 2019). Stakeholder theory, institutional theory, and social exchange theory are only a few examples of the scientific ideas and frameworks impacting the topic of CSR.

The stakeholder theory is built on the premise that businesses must consider the needs and interests of all parties involved. According to this, businesses are entangled in a complex web of interdependencies and their decisions can influence a variety of stakeholders. Therefore, organizations work to produce value for society as well as for their shareholders (Waheed & Zhang, 2022). The institutional theory highlights that organizations are affected by the societal expectations, values, and norms that are prevalent in their institutional context. Thus, cultural norms for moral conduct and environmental sustainability have changed throughout time. If companies implement CSR initiatives in order to adhere to these standards, they achieve credibility, and uphold societal approval (Risi et al., 2023). Social exchange theory assumes that connections between firms and stakeholders include reciprocal transfers of resources and benefits. In accordance with this CSR acknowledges that fostering and preserving goodwill among stakeholders may have a long-term positive impact on the business, including improved reputation, customer loyalty, and staff dedication. As a result, businesses take part in CSR programs to develop connections that are advantageous to both parties and win over stakeholders' confidence and support (Lee, 2021). All these theories can be mirrored in one of the key areas of CSR which is dealing with societal problems including eradicating poverty, improving education and healthcare, and promoting diversity and inclusion in the workplace. These CSR practices include also corporate philanthropy by contributing money, resources, or knowledge to aid humanitarian endeavors and neighbourhood improvement. All these become crucial when the COVID-19 pandemic appears in 2019. The business sector played a significant role in managing the pandemic and minimalizing its impact on society. Post-COVID recovery was far from over when the conflict in Ukraine started. This requires a considerable effort to ensure humanitarian aid, the reception of refugees, and the elimination of risks and consequences of conflict, especially in neighboring countries, which are the countries of the Visegrad region. The conflict itself is an onslaught and requires various actions on the part of the business sector, but the involvement of entrepreneurs in socially responsible aid is essential to manage the crisis. Moreover, the effect of the conflict is also an increased interest in the allocation of strategic raw materials, which caused an energy crisis in countries energy dependent on Russia, which are again primarily the countries of the Visegrad region.

2.1 Social Public Assistance

A scientific concept found in the social pillar of corporate social responsibility (CSR), social public assistance (SPA), includes topics of social welfare and social support. To solve social issues and advance social well-being, refers to the giving of various types of support and help by businesses to people and communities in need (Burgoon & Fransen, 2018). Social public assistance acknowledges that businesses have a duty to support the larger social fabric and lessen social inequality. The concept emphasizes the significance of tackling social concerns and supporting sustainable development while acknowledging the connection between businesses and society. The term refers to a variety of projects and activities that fall under the social pillar of CSR (Hoi et al., 2018). These programs may involve providing money in the form of grants or scholarships to help underprivileged people pursue higher education and enhance their skills. It could entail encouraging preventative health practices, assisting community health efforts, or giving access to inexpensive healthcare services. It might include measures to provide cheap housing, food assistance programs, or aid with access to sanitary facilities and clean water. Businesses can take part in activities that support social inclusion and diversity, such as providing marginalized groups with job opportunities or putting in place programs that support equality and anti-discrimination (Barnett et al., 2020; Metzker & Streimikis, 2020). To address the most urgent social issues and provide workable solutions, corporations can collaborate with governmental bodies, non-profit organizations, and community groups (Tanimoto, 2019). Initiatives for social public assistance can be planned and carried out in a way that optimizes effect and sustainability by interacting with stakeholders, performing needs analyses, and relying on scientific research and evidence-based methodologies. These programs can be measured and evaluated using approaches such as effect assessments, result evaluations, and beneficiary and stakeholder feedback systems which assist in determining where improvements may be made, gauging how beneficial the efforts are, and guaranteeing accountability and openness (Yadava & Sinha, 2022).

2.2 Social Public Assistance in the Visegrad Region (CZ, PL, SK)

In the Visegrad region as in other regions, social public assistance gain importance with the spread of the COVID-19 pandemic. But the next crisis connects with the conflict in Ukraine targets Visegrad countries specifically as direct neighbours. Also, the ongoing energetic crisis, even if it is global, touches the Visegrad region specifically as they are transit countries strongly depending on energies from the turbulent region (Duggal et al., 2021; Napoli, 2023).

In Slovakia, the Czech Republic, and Poland, social public assistance initiatives are designed to support various aspects of society, such as education, healthcare, poverty alleviation, job creation, and environmental conservation efforts. Corporations actively engage in these initiatives by providing scholarships, contributing to educational infrastructure, supporting healthcare facilities, and collaborating with non-profit organizations. Initiatives include community development projects, environmental sustainability programs, and support for vulnerable groups (Przytula et al., 2019). But facilitating and regulating social public assistance programs in these countries are relatively low supported by their governments (Grazhevska & Mostepaniuk, 2021). Considering the size composition of the business sector in these countries, a very important role in the implementation of CSR public assistance plays small and medium-sized enterprises (Belas et al., 2021). Czech Republic, Poland, and Slovakia recognize the importance of social public assistance in addressing societal challenges. However, the emphasis and approaches differ based on somewhat different cultural, economic, and regulatory factors. Understanding the characteristics and approaches in the Visegrad region is of key importance since it has the potential to inform policymakers, corporations, and stakeholders in developing effective strategies, addressing societal needs, and fostering sustainable development.

2.3 Crisis Social Public Assistance in Monitored Countries

During the COVID-19 pandemic, businesses in the Visegrad region have actively engaged in corporate social responsibility (CSR) initiatives. They have supported healthcare institutions by donating medical supplies and equipment, such as personal protective equipment and ventilators. Additionally, businesses have collaborated with local authorities to develop innovative solutions, like producing hand sanitizers and repurposing facilities for medical equipment manufacturing. CSR efforts have extended to vulnerable communities, where companies have provided financial aid and hygiene products. Supporting employees, businesses have implemented measures like flexible working arrangements and mental health support. They have also launched public awareness campaigns to disseminate accurate information and encourage responsible behaviour. Economic stability has been challenged, with governments offering financial support for businesses most affected by the pandemic. Through these CSR activities, businesses in the Visegrad region have made significant contributions to community well-being and recovery (Rozsa et al., 2021; Hoffman, 2023).

In response to the conflict in Ukraine, businesses in the Visegrad region have actively embraced CSR initiatives to support affected communities. CSR efforts have focused on providing humanitarian aid and essential supplies to alleviate immediate hardships. Furthermore, governments with the cooperation of the business sector have rebuilt infrastructure, to restore essential services and promote community resilience. Businesses have also prioritized supporting internally displaced persons (IDPs) by offering job training, employment opportunities, and social support services. Through their CSR activities, companies have played a vital role in addressing social and economic challenges resulting from the conflict. Currently, their efforts also aim at the future well-being, recovery, and sustainable development of affected regions in Ukraine (Akimjak & Shcherbiak, 2023; Health–Europe, 2022; Trebesch et al., 2023).

During energy crises, businesses from the Czech Republic, Poland, and Slovakia are actively engaged in CSR initiatives by supporting affected communities, promoting energy conservation, exploring sustainable alternatives, and fostering partnerships. They provide support to vulnerable populations through financial assistance and energy-saving education. Businesses focus on reducing their own energy consumption and investing in renewable energy sources. CSR activities contribute to social and environmental responsibility, addressing the challenges posed by energy scarcity and fostering community resilience in times of crisis (Kochanek, 2021; Oxford Analytica, 2022).

3 Methodology

The goal of this study is to examine and compare the levels of emphasis placed by companies operating in the Czech Republic, Slovakia, and Poland on the implementation of specific crisis-oriented CSR public assistance activities to assist in overcoming global crises related to the COVID-19 pandemic, conflict in Ukraine and energetic crisis.

Data collection for this study involved the development of an online questionnaire, validation through a pilot group, and distribution through various channels to gather responses from companies in the Czech Republic, Poland, and Slovakia. The study included a sample of 300 companies from Czechia, Poland,

and Slovakia, with an equal representation of 100 companies from each country. The sample encompassed different company sizes, including microenterprises, small, medium-sized, large, and extra-large enterprises (more than 500 employees), with equal proportions (20 per category) across size categories.

The research included 3 socially oriented CSR activities (variables) and a questionnaire aimed at the level of emphasis placed by companies operating in the Czech Republic, Poland, and Slovakia on their implementation. The question regarding them was formulated as follows: „To what extent the monitored company engage in the following social CSR activities?": (i) assistance focused on the Ukrainian crisis; (ii) assistance focused on the COVID-19 pandemic; (iii) assistance focused on managing the energy crisis." Answers to these questions were designed as a Lickert's scale using the following structure: (i) very strongly; (ii) strongly; (iii) average; (iv) negligible; (v) not at all.

In regard to the aim of the study, the following hypotheses were tested:

H0: There is no statistically significant variance in the level of emphasis placed by companies operating in the V3 countries, on the implementation of specific socially oriented corporate social responsibility (CSR) activities with the aim of assisting in overcoming global crises.

Ha: There is a statistically significant variance in the level of emphasis placed by companies operating in the V3 countries, on the implementation of specific socially oriented corporate social responsibility (CSR) activities with the aim of assisting in overcoming global crises.

Regarding describing various aspects of socially oriented CSR activities of monitored companies, this general hypothesis was enlarged to three hypotheses respecting monitored socially oriented CSR activities (Table 1).

The data analysis for this study involved both descriptive and inferential analyses commonly used in this type of research. To assess the reliability of the test, Cronbach's alpha coefficient was computed, resulting in a substantial level of internal consistency (Cronbach's alpha = 0.718). The normality of the data was assessed using the Shapiro-Wilk test, which revealed a significant deviation from normality. Autocorrelation among the variables was examined using the Durbin-Watson test, which showed no evidence of autocorrelation. Given the non-normal distribution of the data, the Kruskal-Wallis test was used to explore statistically significant differences in CSR implementation among the monitored Visegrad countries. Post hoc analysis was conducted using the Bonferroni test to identify significant differences among variables. For verifying obtained results, the Pearson Correlation coefficient was applied.

Table 1. Research design – construction of specific hypotheses.

<table>
<tr><th>Ha</th><th></th><th>Country (sorting char)</th><th></th><th>Variables (Socially oriented CSR activities)</th><th></th></tr>
<tr><td>Ha1</td><td rowspan="3">There is a statistically significant variance in the level of emphasis placed by companies operating in the…</td><td>1. Czech Republic</td><td rowspan="3">on the implementation of specific socially oriented corporate social responsibility (CSR) activities:</td><td>1. Mobilizing the Corporate Sector in the Fight against the COVID-19 Pandemic: Social CSR Activities for Society's Protection</td><td rowspan="3">…with the aim of assisting in overcoming global crises.</td></tr>
<tr><td>Ha2</td><td>2. Poland</td><td>2. Corporate Engagement and Solidarity: Supporting Ukraine in Times of Crisis through CSR Initiatives</td></tr>
<tr><td>Ha3</td><td>3. Slovakia</td><td>3. Energy Crisis and Corporate Engagement: Social CSR Initiatives for Sustainable Development</td></tr>
</table>

Source: own processing

4 Results and Discussion

Corporate engagement and solidarity through Corporate Social Responsibility (CSR) initiatives have become increasingly important in supporting countries facing crises, such as the COVID-19 pandemic, conflict in Ukraine, and energetic crises. This article aims to explore the significance of CSR in times of crisis and specifically examines the extent to which companies in the Czech Republic, Slovakia, and Poland prioritize crisis-related socially oriented corporate social responsibility (CSR) activities.

4.1 Mobilizing the Corporate Sector in the Fight against the COVID-19 Pandemic

The COVID-19 pandemic has presented unprecedented challenges globally, demanding collective efforts to protect society. Businesses in the Czech Republic, Poland, and Slovakia have responded to the pandemic by undertaking various CSR initiatives aimed at assisting the public. These include financial contributions to healthcare systems, donations of medical supplies, support for frontline workers, provision of essential goods and services, and campaigns to promote preventive measures. Moreover, companies recognize the importance of supporting their employees and have implemented initiatives such as flexible work arrangements, mental health support programs, and employee assistance funds to foster resilience within their organizations. They also adapted operations to align with CSR by implementing safety protocols, promoting remote work, and adopting sustainable practices to minimize environmental impact and protect society while ensuring their own continuity.

Our results reveal varying levels of perceived COVID-19 response and recovery support among respondents from the Czech Republic, Poland, and Slovakia (Figure 1). In the Czech Republic, 9 % of respondents rated the support as "Very strongly," while 23 % rated it as "Strongly," 23 % as "Average," 21 % as "Negligible," and 24 % as "Not at all." In Poland, the highest proportion of respondents (28 %) rated the support as "Very strongly," followed by 20 % who rated it as "Strongly." Additionally, 19 % perceived the support as "Average," 4 % as "Negligible," and 29 % as "Not at all." In Slovakia, 10 % of respondents considered the support as "Very strongly," 25 % as "Strongly," 31 % as "Average," 15 % as "Negligible," and 19 % as "Not at all." Across all countries, the majority of respondents rated the support as "Average," followed by "Strongly" and "Very strongly." Poland had the highest proportion of respondents perceiving the support as "Not at all" (29 %), while the other countries had lower percentages.

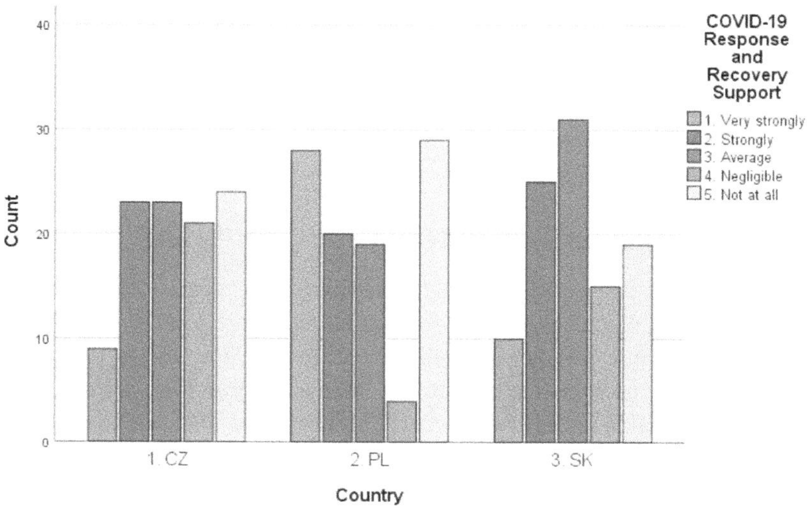

Figure 1. Mobilizing the Corporate Sector in the Fight against the COVID-19 Pandemic: Social CSR Activities for Society's Protection in the CZ, PL and SK.

Source: own processing

Table 2 presents the results of the Kruskal-Wallis Test conducted on Variable 1, which focuses on mobilizing the corporate sector in the fight against the COVID-19 pandemic through social CSR activities for society's protection. The asymptotic significance (p-value) for the two-sided test was 0.091 which indicates no statistically significant differences among the samples for Variable 1. Therefore, no further analysis or post-hoc tests were conducted for multiple comparisons.

Table 2. Independent-Samples Kruskal-Wallis Test Summary for Variable 1.

Total N	300
Test Statistic	4.794[a,b]
Degree Of Freedom	2
Asymptotic Sig.(2-sided test)	0.091
a. The test statistic is adjusted for ties.	
b. Multiple comparisons are not performed because the overall test does not show significant differences across samples.	

Source: own processing

The COVID-19 pandemic has led businesses to engage in social CSR initiatives, including financial support, resource donations, employee assistance, community outreach, and sustainable practices. Collaboration, impact measurement, and sharing best practices contribute to an effective response. Corporations play a vital role in protecting society and fostering resilience in every country. Therefore, it is no surprise, that no statistically significant differences were found in the assistance addressing global humanitarian crises related to COVID-19 in the Czech Republic, Poland, and Slovakia.

4.2 Corporate Engagement and Solidarity with Ukraine

Corporate social responsibility (CSR) initiatives have gained importance in neighboring countries of the Visegrad region in response to the conflict in Ukraine. These initiatives play a significant role in providing social public assistance to mitigate the impact of the conflict. Businesses from the Czech Republic, Poland, and Slovakia are actively involved in a range of CSR activities, including refugee support, financial contributions, humanitarian aid, infrastructure development, healthcare assistance, education programs, and employment opportunities. These initiatives demonstrate a commitment to social responsibility and contribute to the well-being and recovery of communities affected by the conflict. Effective corporate engagement involves partnerships with NGOs, government agencies, local communities, and international bodies to address the diverse needs of Ukraine and contribute to its long-term recovery.

The assistance addressing global humanitarian crises was evaluated using a 1 to 5 scale in the monitored countries. In the Czech Republic, out of 100 respondents, 12 indicated "Very strongly" assistance, 14 chose "Strongly," 27 selected "Average," 21 indicated "Negligible," and 26 chose "Not at all." For Poland, 21 respondents expressed "Very strongly" assistance, 23 selected "Strongly," 19 indicated "Average," 6 chose "Negligible," and 31 opted for "Not at all" out of 100 participants. In Slovakia, 13 respondents expressed "Very strongly" assistance, 17 chose "Strongly," 26 indicated "Average," 19 selected "Negligible," and 25 opted for "Not at all" out of 100 responses. The distribution of responses across the levels of assistance varies to some extent among the countries, highlighting potential differences in their approaches to addressing global humanitarian challenges (Figure 2).

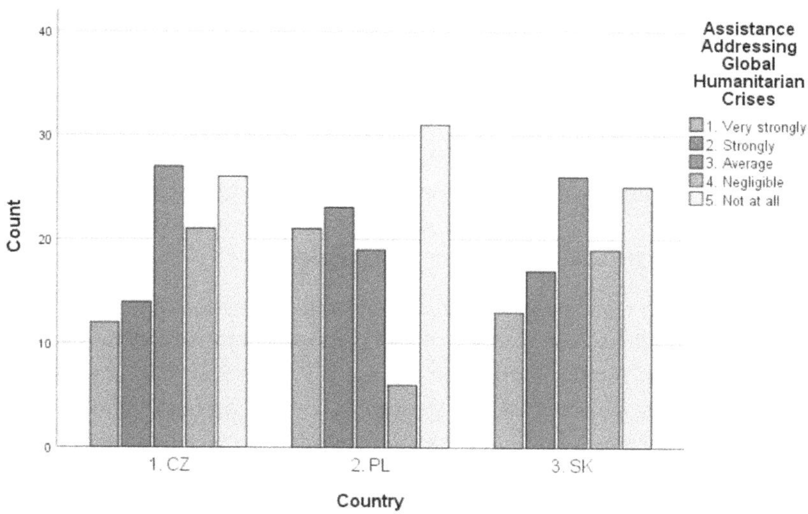

Figure 2. Assistance Addressing Global Humanitarian Crises in the Czech Republic, Poland and Slovakia.

Source: own processing

However, the Kruskal-Wallis test does not demonstrate significant differences across the samples. This means that there is no strong evidence to suggest variations in the levels of assistance provided by the Czech Republic, Poland, and Slovakia in addressing global humanitarian crises. The lack of significant differences implies that these countries exhibit similar levels of involvement and support in responding to such crises (Table 3).

Table 3. Independent-Samples Kruskal-Wallis Test Summary for Variable 2.

Total N	300
Test Statistic	2.307[a,b]
Degree Of Freedom	2
Asymptotic Sig.(2-sided test)	0.316
a. The test statistic is adjusted for ties.	
b. Multiple comparisons are not performed because the overall test does not show significant differences across samples.	

Source: own processing

Corporate engagement and solidarity through CSR initiatives are essential in supporting Ukraine during the armed conflict. Businesses from the Visegrad region actively participate in humanitarian efforts, sustainable development, and stakeholder collaboration to contribute to Ukraine's resilience. Overall, there is no evidence of statistically significant differences in the variable among the monitored countries, suggesting their similar general approach in addressing the crisis.

4.3 Energy Crisis and Corporate Engagement

The global energy crisis poses significant challenges to sustainable development in the Czech Republic, Poland, and Slovakia as transit countries are heavily reliant on resources from Russia. The business sector plays a crucial role in promoting sustainable energy practices and mitigating the energy crisis through social CSR initiatives. Companies invest in renewable energy projects, advocate for energy efficiency, support research and development in clean technologies, and promote policies for a low-carbon economy. These efforts contribute to long-term sustainable development and reduce dependence on fossil fuels. Collaboration among corporations, governments, academia, and civil society is essential to address the energy crisis and accelerate the adoption of sustainable energy practices.

The findings of this study reveal levels of emphasis placed by V3 companies on the implementation of specific crisis-oriented CSR public assistance activities to assist in energetic crisis. In the Czech Republic, 8 % expressed a strong emphasis, while 15 % showed significant support. Meanwhile, in Poland, 6 % expressed strong emphasis, and 10 % expressed support, but a substantial 39 %. In Slovakia, 3 % expressed strong emphasis, while 22 % showed significant emphasis. The majority of respondents across all countries rated the emphasis as average, with Poland having the highest proportion (39 %) of companies don't engage in these activities at all (Figure 3).

Table 4 presents the results of the Kruskal-Wallis Test conducted on Variable 3, focusing on the Energy Crisis and Corporate Engagement: Social CSR Initiatives for Sustainable Development. The p-value for the two-sided test was 0.152, indicating no statistically significant differences among the samples for Variable 3. Thus, no further post-hoc tests or multiple comparisons were conducted.

The energy crisis poses a significant challenge to sustainable development, and corporate engagement through social CSR initiatives plays a crucial role in addressing this crisis. By investing in sustainable energy practices, fostering collaboration and partnerships, engaging communities, and supporting research and development, businesses in V3 can contribute to sustainable energy solutions and mitigate the impact of the crisis. The business sector plays a vital role in driving the transition towards a more sustainable and resilient energy future and our study suggests no differences in this effort across monitored countries.

A similar outcome also provided the correlation analysis. Table 5 revealed weak and statistically non-significant relationships between the variables. There were no strong linear

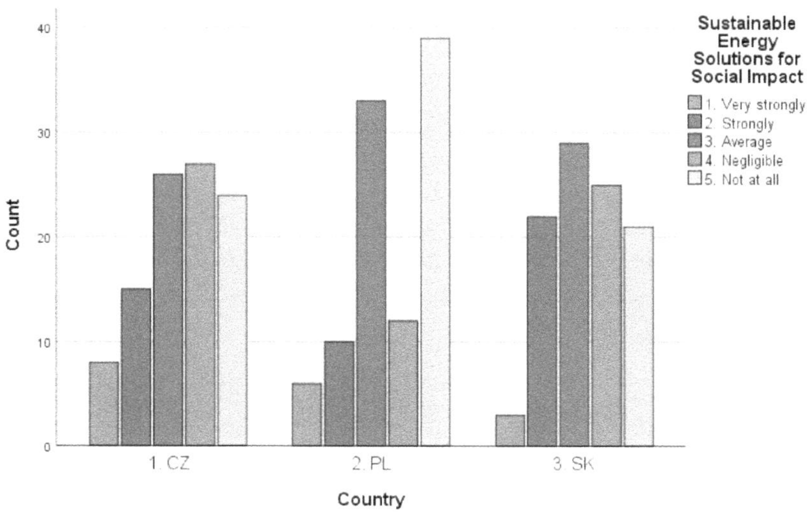

Figure 3. Energy Crisis and Corporate Engagement: Social CSR Initiatives for Sustainable Development in the Czech Republic, Poland and Slovakia.

Source: own processing

associations found between Assistance Addressing Global Humanitarian Crises, COVID-19 Response and Recovery Support, and Sustainable Energy Solutions for Social Impact. The correlation coefficients ranged from -0.059 to -0.017, indicating weak negative relationships, but these associations were not statistically significant ($p > 0.05$). Therefore, based on the available data, there is insufficient evidence to suggest meaningful connections between these variables. However, it is crucial to acknowledge that these conclusions are based on the specific dataset and the limitations of the study. Further research and analysis may be necessary to gain a more comprehensive understanding of the factors influencing assistance levels and to explore potential variations across different contexts or time periods.

Table 4. Independent-Samples Kruskal-Wallis Test Summary for Variable 3.

Total N	300
Test Statistic	3.768[a,b]
Degree Of Freedom	2
Asymptotic Sig.(2-sided test)	0.152
a. The test statistic is adjusted for ties.	
b. Multiple comparisons are not performed because the overall test does not show significant differences across samples.	

Source: own processing

The challenge of estimating the precise number of participants or return rate due to the use of multiple distribution channels may affect the representativeness of the sample. Relying on self-reported responses through an online questionnaire raises the possibility of social desirability bias, where participants may provide answers, they believe align with expected CSR practices. Additionally, the study's focus on the Visegrad region, specifically the CZ, PL, and SK which limit the generalizability of the findings.

Table 5. Correlations between country and Variables 1–3.

		Country	Assistance Addressing Global Humanitarian Crises	COVID-19 Response and Recovery Support	Sustainable Energy Solutions for Social Impact
Country	Pearson Correlation	1	-0.026	-0.059	-0.017
	Sig. (2-tailed)		0.654	0.312	0.771
	Sum of Squares and Cross-products	200.000	-9.000	-20.000	-5.000
	Covariance	0.669	-0.030	-0.067	-0.017
	N	300	299	300	300

**. Correlation is significant at the 0.01 level (2-tailed).

Source: own processing

5 Conclusions

The Visegrad region has faced multiple crises, including the ongoing COVID-19 pandemic, conflicts in neighbouring countries, and challenges related to energy supply. These crises have generated significant social impacts, highlighting the crucial need for effective public assistance measures. However, the extent to which CSR practices contribute to social public assistance, and the specific strategies employed by organizations within the Visegrad region during crises, have received limited scholarly attention.

The study highlights the important role of corporate engagement and solidarity through CSR initiatives in supporting countries during crises like the COVID-19 pandemic, the conflict in Ukraine, and the energy crisis. The research examined CSR activities in the Czech Republic, Slovakia, and Poland, revealing their attitudes towards these crises. While businesses demonstrated commitment, no significant differences were found among the samples, indicating a similar level of involvement and support across the countries. However, study found diverse perspectives on sustainable energy solutions. Poland had a notable proportion of monitored companies don't involve these initiatives at all. Moreover, the correlation analysis showed no significant connections between country and Assistance Addressing Global Humanitarian Crises, COVID-19 Response and Recovery Support, and Sustainable Energy Solutions for Social Impact. Further research is needed to explore the interplay between these factors in CSR practices.

Acknowledgment

This research has been supported and this paper was prepared within the project "Corporate Social Responsibility in Business Practice of the Visegrad Region (Visegrad Grant no. 22220149)." The project is co-financed by the Governments of Czechia, Hungary, Poland, and Slovakia through Visegrad Grants from International Visegrad Fund.

We would like to express our gratitude and acknowledge that this paper represents a segment of a comprehensive study conducted as part of the mentioned project. We extend our appreciation to the project team, funding agencies, and all individuals who contributed to the successful execution of this study.

References

Akimjak, A., & Shcherbiak, I. (2023). *Transformational processes of the social and humanitarian sphere of modern Ukraine in the conditions of war*. Ruzomberok, VERBUM–vydavatelstvo Katolickej univerzity v Ruzomberku.

Barnett, M. L., Henriques, I., & Husted, B. W. (2020). Beyond good intentions: Designing CSR initiatives for greater social impact. *Journal of Management*, *46*(6), 937–964.

Belas, J., Cera, G., Dvorsky, J., & Cepel, M. (2021). Corporate social responsibility and sustainability issues of small-and medium-sized enterprises. *Corporate Social Responsibility and Environmental Management*, *28*(2), 721–730.

Burgoon, B., & Fransen, L. (2018). Might corporate social responsibility hollow out support for public assistance in Europe?. *British Journal of Industrial Relations*, *56*(1), 128–163.

Duggal, K., Rangachari, R., & Gupta, K. (2021). Consequences of crisis and the great re-think: COVID-19's impact on energy investment, sustainability and the future of international investment agreements. *Journal of world energy law & business*, *14*(3), 133–146.

Grazhevska, N., & Mostepaniuk, A. (2021). The Development of Corporate Social Responsibility in the Context of Overcoming a Welfare State Crisis: A Theoretical and Empirical Analysis. *Comparative Economic Research. Central and Eastern Europe*, *24*(1), 123–140.

Health–Europe, T. L. R. (2022). The regional and global impact of the Russian invasion of Ukraine. *Lancet Regional Health-Europe, 15.*

Hoffman, I. (2023). Local development policies in the V4 countries-in the light of the impact of the COVID-19 pandemic. *Journal of Comparative Politics, 16*(1), 64–79.

Hoi, C. K., Wu, Q., & Zhang, H. (2018). Community social capital and corporate social responsibility. *Journal of Business Ethics, 152*(3), 647–665.

Kochanek, E. (2021). The energy transition in the Visegrad group countries. *Energies, 14*(8), 2212.

Lee, Y. (2021). Linking internal CSR with the positive communicative behaviors of employees: The role of social exchange relationships and employee engagement. *Social Responsibility Journal, 18*(2), 348–367.

McWilliams, A., Rupp, D. E., Siegel, D. S., Stahl, G. K., & Waldman, D. A. (Eds.). (2019). *The Oxford handbook of Corporate Social Responsibility: Psychological and organizational perspectives.* Oxford University Press.

Metzker, Z., & Streimikis, J. (2020). CSR activities in the Czech SME segment. *International Journal of Entrepreneurial Knowledge, 8*(1), 49–64.

Napoli, M. (2023). *EU social policies implementation through the European semester: Changing priorities from the pandemic to the war in Ukraine* [Master's Thesis].

Oxford Analytica. (2022). Ukraine crisis will muddy eastern EU energy transition. *Emerald Expert Briefings.*

Przytula, S., Formankova, S., Ubreziova, I., & Dunay, A. (2019). Corporate social responsibility in visegrad countries (Poland, Czech Republic, Slovakia, Hungary) overall landscape. *Corporate Social Responsibility in Poland: Strategies, Opportunities and Challenges*, 325–353.

Risi, D., Vigneau, L., Bohn, S., & Wickert, C. (2023). Institutional theory-based research on corporate social responsibility: Bringing values back in. *International Journal of Management Reviews, 25*(1), 3–23.

Rozsa, Z., Belas, J., Khan, K. A., & Zvarikova, K. (2021). Corporate social responsibility and essential factors of personnel risk management in SMEs. *Polish Journal of Management Studies, 23*(2), 449–463.

Tanimoto, K. (2019). Do multi-stakeholder initiatives make for better CSR?. *Corporate Governance: The International Journal of Business in Society, 19*(4), 704–716.

Trebesch, C., et al. (2023). *The Ukraine support tracker: Which countries help Ukraine and how?* (No. 2218). KIEL working paper.

Waheed, A., & Zhang, Q. (2022). Effect of CSR and ethical practices on sustainable competitive performance: A case of emerging markets from stakeholder theory perspective. *Journal of Business Ethics*, *175*(4), 837–855.

Yadava, R. N., & Sinha, B. (2022). Enhancing agro-environment and socio-economic condition of rural poor: The case of Lupin corporate social responsibility. *Social Responsibility Journal*, *18*(4), 825–838.

Stanislava Kristakova[1], Blanka Giertliova[1,*], and Iveta Hajduchova[1]

Challenges in Slovak Forestry Due to External Influences

Abstract:
Research background: At a time of constantly changing conditions in the market economy, the constant influence of the global economy, as well as new challenges brought by the COVID-19 pandemic and the war in Ukraine, all of these factors have a direct impact on the Slovak forestry performance. Moreover, forestry plays an important role in the transition to a sustainable society and also faces many challenges caused by climate change.
Purpose of the article: The aim of the paper is to investigate the socio-economic impact on forestry by testing the dependence of forestry performance on the development of the Slovak Republic macro-economic environment.
Methods: Methods of regression and correlation analysis were used to test the dependence of the gross value added of forestry and gross domestic product. The regression model of the trend tested the dependency in time.
Findings & Value added: The development of recent years strengthened the recreational function of forests but also increased the pressure on the efficient use of renewable natural resources in accordance with the principles of sustainable forestry management. Our findings confirmed the linear dependence of Slovakia's forestry gross value on the development of Slovakia's GDP.

Keywords: *forestry, performance, climate change, global economy*

JEL Classification: *E01; F63; Q23; Q57*

1 Introduction

Undoubtedly forests are among the most diverse and widespread ecosystems that must be preserved for future generations, and therefore the introduction of green economy principles in the forestry industry is essential (Yakovleva et al., 2019). In this case Yakovleva et al. (2019) mean efficient use of resources with sustainable forest management, preservation, protection, and adaptation of

---

* Corresponding author: giertliova@is.tuzvo.sk
1 Technical University in Zvolen, Faculty of Forestry, T. G. Masaryka 24, 96001 Zvolen, Slovakia

forests to climate impacts and their contribution to the absorption of greenhouse gases, moreover, raising the standard of living of the population through the creation of green jobs and the introduction of payments for ecosystem services too. Forestry also must consider the changing traditional market for forest products, which specifically means increase demand for innovative wood use and for ecologically sustainable products (Morland & Schier, 2020). Van Den Bergh and Botzen (2018) also concluded in his research that the consequences of climate change are likely to be the main environmental challenge for future economic growth, as climate damage is expected to generate significant economic costs and bring with it many challenges and measures. But not only climate change has negative affect on forestry. Besides this the external influence since 2020 has significant negative impact on forestry, especially pandemic COVID-19 as well as war in Ukraine (Zhang et al., 2021). Due to negative impact of above mentioned external factors the performance of the Slovak economy and consequently forestry decreased. After a period of economic growth, Slovak economy must face new challenges that also reflected in forestry. On the other hand, after reduction of anti-pandemic measures as well as with the lack of wood on the market and besides the energy crisis the forestry performance grew again since 2022. An increase of forestry performance will reflect in a higher level of the gross value added (GVA) and the entire industry and its complex downstream processing chain (Chen & Yao, 2020). Further improvements in forest management and investments in research and development activities are the answer for the long-term sustainability and increased economic efficiency of forestry (Neykov et al., 2021). Moreover, the transition of the entire forestry-timber complex to a sustainable industry on a societal scale becomes a hopeful answer to global challenges that will increase the demand for improving efficiency and performance not only for forestry but for whole economy (Hempel et al., 2019).

2 Methodology

In general, economists gauge the economy's performance through the evaluation of GDP (Gross Domestic Product), which represents the cumulative value added by various sectors within a country's economy (Lundmark et al., 2021). In our research, we conducted an analysis focused on testing a hypothesis related to the development of Gross Value Added (GVA) in the forestry sector and its impact on the Slovak GDP. The study covered a decade, spanning from 2012 to 2021. Our primary data sources for this research included DATAcube and Green Forest reports, both provided by the National Forestry Centre. To substantiate our hypothesis, we employed various statistical methods. In this instance, we specifically employed regression analysis, correlation analysis, and a regression trend model.

Firstly regression analysis was used to search for and confirm the existence of dependence between the quantitative features of the constructed optimal regression model describing its essence. The basis is a mathematical equation expressing the relationship between independent characters *x* and dependent characters *y* (Kumari & Yadav, 2018). Depending on the number of variables, it can be a simple regression analysis that describes the dependence of one dependent variable y on one independent variable *x*. Whereas a multiple regression analysis considers a larger number of independent variables *y*. On this occasion the simple linear regression equation according to the following relationship estimates the regression coefficients β_0 and β_1:

$$y_i = \beta_0 + \beta_1 x_i + \varepsilon_i, \tag{1}$$

where y_i – a value of the dependent variable *y* in the *i*-th observation, x_i – a value of the independent variable *x* in the *i*-th observation, β_0 – a locating constant (intersection of the regression line with the x-axis), β_1 – a regression coefficient (directive of the regression line), ε_i, – random error of the *i*-th observation.

Given these points the regression coefficient is interpreted depending on the type of research. In the case of an experiment, it expresses how much the expected value of the variable *y* increases/decreases on average if the value of the variable *x* increases/decreases by 1 unit.

Secondly correlation analysis assesses statistical dependencies between the investigated variables. In fact the strength of a correlation coefficient is often judged by context. The Pearson correlation coefficient (PCC) ρ_{xy} measures the tightness of the two-sided linear dependence between two random variables *x* and *y* and applies (Senthilnathan, 2019):

$\rho_{xy} = 0$ – variables *x* and *y* are linearly dependent,

$\rho_{xy} > 0$ – there is a direct linear relationship between the variables *x* and *y*,

$\rho_{xy} < 0$ – there is an indirect linear dependence between the variables *x* and *y*.

$$\rho_{xy} = \frac{cov(x,y)}{\sqrt{var(x) \cdot var(y)}} \tag{2}$$

where the expression $\sqrt{var(x)}$ is the standard deviation of ρ_x. PCC takes values from the interval $\langle -1;1 \rangle$ and the closer the absolute value is to the value 1, the closer the linear dependence is, in other words, it is a direct linear dependence, which means that if one variable grows, then the other variable also grows and vice versa. If ρ_x acquires the value 1, which means absolute indirect linear dependence. Finally if ρ_x reach the value 0 then variables are independent.

Finally a time series analysis was used to describe the characteristics of the development of changes in the variables values over time. Commonly a time series is a chronologically ordered sequence of materially and spatially comparable data on any quantitative random variable. Generally speaking the basic characteristic development of a variable is a trend that causes long-term stable effects. The time series trend model represents a functional relationship between the variable of interest and the time variable *t*. The most common trend model, which also was applied in our research, is the linear trend model, which is written using the linear regression function of *t* (Pacakova et al., 2009):

$$Tr_t = \beta_0 + \beta_1 t \tag{3}$$

where Tr_t is the trend of the time series modelled by a regression line depending on time t, β_0, β_1 are the unknown parameters of the linear trend.

3 Results

It is necessary to concern the fact that Slovak Republic is strongly connected to exports to the European market and opened to foreign investors. With regards to Slovak market specialization in the automotive industry it also reflected in the development of the Slovak GDP (Figure 1).

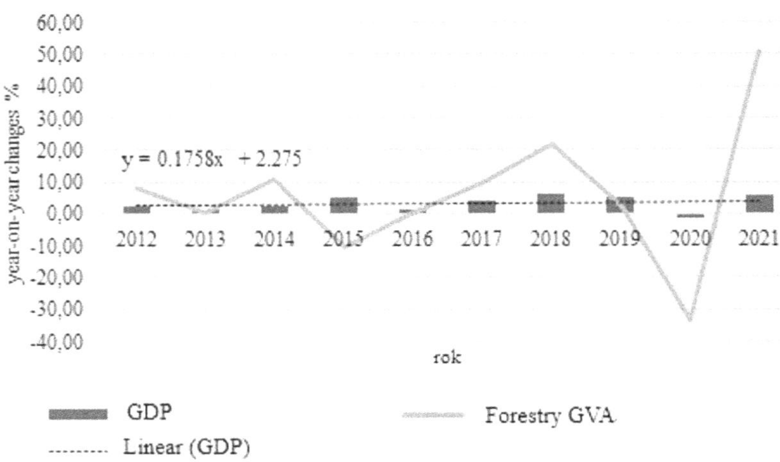

Figure 1. Development of the annual change in GDP and Forestry GVA.
Source: own processing

The peak of GDP was achieved in 2018 and 2019, caused mainly by record sales of cars, was replaced by a sharp decline caused by the COVID-19 pandemic, and the global situation dampened the activity of the Slovak economy and its foreign business partners. Even though the Slovak economy revived after the second wave of the pandemic and the GDP grew. The average annual change in GDP for the monitored period is 0.18 times. The economy supported by domestic demand for goods and increased investment by foreign investors, restarted Slovakia's economy. And yet the evolution of the change in the Forestry GVA, through the basic numerical characteristics of the time series analysis, is presented in Table 1.

Table 1. Basic numerical characteristics of Forestry GVA.

Year	**Forestry GVA** *mil. €*	**Absolute increase** *dt*	**Growth coefficient** *kt*	**Relative increment** *kdt*	**Rate of increment** *Tmdt*
2012	241.10				
2013	241.80	0.7	1.003	0.003	0.290
2014	267.50	25.7	1.106	0.106	10.629
2015	239.71	-27.79	0.896	-0.104	-10.389
2016	241.21	1.5	1.006	0.006	0.626
2017	265.21	24	1.099	0.099	9.950
2018	322.60	57.39	1.216	0.216	21.639
2019	330.41	7.81	1.024	0.024	2.421
2020	219.13	-111.28	0.663	-0.337	-33.679
2021	329.92	110.79	1.506	0.506	50.559

Source: own processing

As table above showed the largest relative increase based on the time series results in the monitored period was achieved in 2021 compared to 2020, increased by almost 51 %. Absolutely, this change represents an increase of Forestry GVA by 111 million €. This increase was caused by the reduction of anti-pandemic measures, the lack of wood on the market and as a result of the energy crisis. In 2020, the most significant relative annual decrease of 33.68 % compared to 2019 was recorded which in relative terms represents a reduction of GVA by 111 million €, which was caused by the effect of the anti-pandemic measures taken, which resulted in a reduction in wood harvesting. As reported by MPRV SR (n.d.), the forestry share of GDP has been below 1 % for a long time, and during the monitored period, Forestry GVA reached an average value of 0.52 % Slovak GDP. Based on the development of the Forestry GVA on GDP, the hypothesis H3 was tested. Thus the results of the regression analysis of Forestry GVA dependence on GDP are shown in the following table (Table 2).

Table 2. The result of the regression analysis of the Forestry GVA dependence on GDP.

	Coefficients	t Stat	P-value	Lower 95 %	Upper 95 %
Intercept	-53.480	-1.071	0.320	-171.505	64.544
Regression	0.004	6.408	0.000	0.002	0.005

Source: own processing

Due to the regres1sion coefficient which is statistically significant (p=0.000) at the chosen significance level of 5 % thus the hypothesis was confirmed. From the interpretation of the regression coefficient, it follows that with an increase in GDP by a measurement unit, the Forestry GVA increases by 0.004 €. The dependence of Forestry GVA on GDP is significant. The linear dependence of the investigated quantities is graphically shown on the following chart (Figure 2).

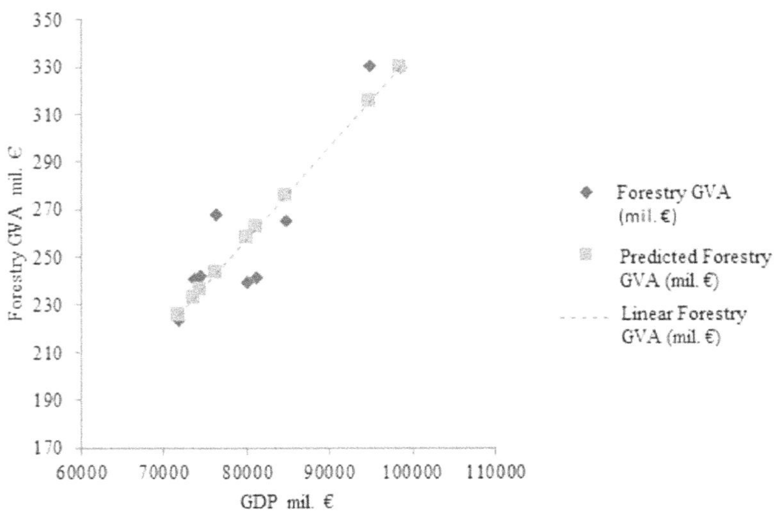

Figure 2. Forestry GVA dependence on GDP.
Source: own processing

Accordingly to the Figure 2, Forestry GVA grows linearly with the growth of GDP and has the shape of a linear regression curve. Furthermore, the dependence of Forestry GVA on GDP was further tested by correlation analysis.

Clearly the correlation coefficient in Table 3 reached a high value of 0.924, which indicates a strong positive dependence of Forestry GVA and GDP. The value of the R Square says that the given model explains almost 85 % of the variability of GVA due to the influence of changing GDP. It is important in connection with the results of the dependence of Forestry GVA and GDP to state that the extreme values from the regression analysis were excluded. Obviously outliers are years 2018, which as we mentioned above, was affected by the peak of GDP, and the year 2020, which represented a slump in both investigated quantities due to the COVID-19 pandemic.

Table 3. Regression statistics.

Statistical variable	Value
Multiple R	0.9243
R Square	0.8543
Standard Error	16.1551
Observations	8

Source: own processing

4 Discussion

By default, GDP growth causes an increased demand for wood products, which results in an increase in the prices of wood assortments, which contributes to the growth of the Forestry GVA (Nepal et al., 2021, Daigneault et al., 2022). Another research performed by authors (Brodrechtova & Halaj, 2014) created an econometric model that explains an elastic increase in the demand for wood by 1.17 % for a change in GDP by 1 % at a constant price. The authors found that while GDP was an exogenous variable in the model, the parameters of the volume of planned logging and the share of accidental logging were endogenous variables. Based on this fact, it is possible to define a wood demand model using regression equations based on GDP at a constant price. As was the case with the impact of the volume of random logging on the price of wood, the impact of GDP on the Forestry GVA is an inelastic change, as it is affected by a number of other parameters. Several authors dealt with modelling the impact of GDP on the price of wood (Kolo & Tzanova, 2017). Gejdos and Trenciansky (2021) created models for softwood and hardwood, according to which a 1 % increase in GDP causes the market price of softwood to increase by 0.85 % and the price of hardwood to increase by 0.08 %.

5 Conclusions

Altogether specifics of forestry and peculiarities of forest production also significantly reflected in the performance of forestry. Moreover an increasing pressure on the efficient use of renewable natural resources in accordance with the principles of sustainable forestry, forces forestry enterprises to improve their performance. Above all the results it can be sum up that forestry faced many challenges. Moreover it necessary to take into account that Slovak forestry market is very small in global context and it is significantly influenced by global market and external factors which are reflected in Slovak GDP as well as in forestry.

Acknowledgments

This research work was supported by the Slovak Research and Development Agency under the contract No. APVV-18-0520 and No. APVV-19-0612.

References

Brodrechtova, Y., & Halaj, M. T. D. (2014, June). Dynamics of Slovakian timber market in retrospect. *57th SWST International Convention 7th Wood Structure and Properties Conference 6th European Hardwood.*

Chen S., & Yao S. (2020). Evaluation of Forestry ecological efficiency: A spatio-temporal empirical study based on China's Provinces. *Forests*, *12*(2), 142.

Daigneault, A., Baker, J. S., Guo, J., Lauri, P., Favero, A., Forsell, N., Johnston, C., Ohrel, S. B., & Sohngen, B. (2022). How the future of the global forest sink depends on timber demand, forest management, and carbon policies. *Global Environmental Change*, *76*, 102582.

Gejdos, M., & Trenciansky, M. (2021). Ekonometricky model ceny ihlicnatej gulatiny v SR. *LH a DSP v podmienkach zelenej ekonomiky: zbornik vedeckych prac*, 145–152.

Hempel, C., Will, S., & Zander, K. (2019). Societal perspectives on a bio-economy in Germany: An explorative study using Q methodology. *International Journal on Food System Dynamics*, *10*(1), 21–37.

Kolo, H., & Tzanova, P. (2017). Forecasting the German forest products trade: A vector error correction model. *Journal of Forest Economics*, *26*, 30–45.

Kumari, K., & Yadav, S. (2018). Linear regression analysis study. *Journal of the practice of Cardiovascular Sciences*, *4*(1), 33–36.

Lundmark, R., Lundgren, T., Olofsson, E., & Zhou, W. (2021). Meeting challenges in forestry: Improving performance and competitiveness. *Forests*, 12(2), 208.

Morland, C., & Schier, F. (2020). Modelling Bioeconomy scenario pathways for the forest products markets with emerging lignocellulosic products. *Sustainability*, *12*(24), 10540.

MPRV SR. (n.d.). *Lesne hospodarstvo – Zelena sprava 2020 – Ministerstvo podohospodarstva a rozvoja vidieka SR*. Ministerstvo Pôdohospodárstva a Rozvoja Vidieka SR. https://www.mpsr.sk/zelena-sprava-2020/123---16162/

Nepal, P., Johnston, C. M., & Ganguly, I. (2021). Effects on global forests and wood product markets of increased demand for mass timber. *Sustainability*, Volume 13(24), 13943.

Neykov, N., Kristakova, S., Hajduchova, I., Sedliacikova, M., Antov, P., & Giertliova, B. (2021). Economic efficiency of forest enterprises – Empirical study based on data envelopment analysis. *Forests*, *12*(4), 462.

Pacakova, V., Labudova, V., Sipkova, L., Soltes, E., & Vojtkova, M. (2009). *Statisticke metody pre ekonomov*. Wolters Kluwer.

Senthilnathan, S. (2019). *Usefulness of correlation analysis*. Social Science Research Network.

Van Den Bergh, J. C., & Botzen, W. W. (2018). Global impact of a climate treaty if the Human Development Index replaces GDP as a welfare proxy. *Climate Policy*, *18*(1), 76–85.

Yakovleva, A. E., & Subhonberdiev, SH. A. (2019). Implementation "Green" economy principles in the forest sector. *IOP Cenference Series: Earth and Environmental Science, 392*(1), 012016,

Zhang, X., Zhang, Y., & Zhu, Y. (2021). COVID-19 pandemic, sustainability of macroeconomy, and choice of Monetary Policy targets: A NK-DSGE analysis based on China. *Sustainability*, *13*(6), 3362.

Radka Kubalova[1,*], Petra Chmielova[1], and Eva Kotlanova[1]

A Comparative Analysis of Municipal Waste Management Practices in Visegrad 4 Countries

Abstract:
Research background: Waste management is a critical aspect of environmental sustainability, and it varies significantly across European Union (EU) member states due to diverse socioeconomic, cultural, and geographic factors.
Purpose of the article: This conference paper presents a comprehensive comparative analysis of municipal waste management practices in V4 countries, shedding light on the strategies, policies, and outcomes that have emerged across this region.
Methods: The study employs a multi-dimensional approach, incorporating quantitative data, legislative and policy analysis. Key aspects such as waste generation rates, recycling rates, landfill diversion, and circular economy initiatives are explored to identify patterns, trends, and disparities among the countries.
Findings & Value added: The analysis offers valuable insights into the state of waste management in the region, emphasizing the need for coordinated efforts to address common challenges while accommodating national differences. By fostering knowledge exchange and policy harmonization, the region and the EU can move closer to achieving its ambitious waste reduction and circular economy targets, ultimately contributing to a more sustainable future.

Keywords: *circular economy, environmental protection spending, recycling, V4 countries, waste generation and waste management*

JEL Classification: *Q01; Q53, Q58*

1 Introduction

Waste management plays a pivotal role in realizing the circular economy's goals by ensuring that discarded materials are properly collected, sorted, and processed to be reintroduced into the production cycle (Baki & Ergun, 2021).

* Corresponding author: kubalova@opf.slu.cz
[1] Silesian university in Opava, School of Business Administration in Karvina, Univerzitni namesti 1934/3, 733 40 Karvina, Czechia

By integrating waste management practices into the circular economy framework, waste can be minimized, the environmental impact of resource extraction reduced, energy conserved, and the development of innovative and sustainable products and processes promoted. Thus, the topic over years gained an increasing recognition not only in connection to its links to circular economy as found in Buch et al. (2021) or Savini (2021), but also towards assessing implementation circular economy policies in different regions within the EU (Fagerholm et al., 2023; Loncaric et al., 2021; Erceg et al., 2017) and outside of the EU (Aycin & Kaya, 2021; Baki & Ergun, 2021) or for specific waste types such as electronic waste (Ali & Shirazi, 2023), food waste (Tamasiga et al., 2022; Tarhini et al., 2022), construction and demolition waste (Mahpour, 2018), etc.

Within the EU, waste management practices exhibit considerable diversity as found in the study of Vitenko et al. (2021), just as waste generation highly depends on factors as local consumer habits, type of industry or commerce, living conditions, and type of buildings (Iuga, 2016). This diversity underscores the need for comprehensive comparative analyses to understand the successes, challenges, and opportunities within different regions of the EU.

The V4 region, consisting of the Czech Republic, Hungary, Poland, and Slovakia, represents a distinct subset of EU member states located in Central Europe. These countries, while sharing geographic proximity and historical ties, exhibit notable differences in their approaches to waste management. As the EU endeavours to achieve its ambitious waste reduction and circular economy targets, understanding the experiences and outcomes of V4 countries becomes increasingly pertinent.

In the context of waste management in V4 countries, several studies have been conducted in past. For example, Alwaeli (2015) points out that source separation and collection, composting of biodegradable waste and recycling and resources recovery have not yet been implemented entirely effectively in Poland. Pikon et al. (2021) brought the attention to the negative impact of COVID-19 on the waste management system and the circular economy advances on the example of Poland, shedding the light on the changes in waste collection system, in the increasing volume of packaging waste and incineration due to fear of virus transmission.

This conference paper seeks to contribute to the existing body of knowledge by conducting a comprehensive comparative analysis of waste management practices with the focus on the municipal waste in the V4 countries. The primary objectives are to elucidate the strategies and policies that have evolved in response to waste management challenges, analyze the quantitative data related to waste generation and recycling rates, assess landfill diversion efforts, and examine the extent of circular economy initiatives within these nations. By doing so, this study aims to uncover patterns, trends, and disparities among the V4 countries, offering valuable insights into the state of waste management in this region.

2 Methods

The research methodology employed in this study incorporates a multi-dimensional approach. Legislative and policy analysis is conducted to examine the regulatory frameworks and incentives that shape waste management practices within the V4. This dual approach ensures a holistic understanding of the factors influencing waste management outcomes. Additionally, quantitative data on waste generation, recycling, and landfill diversion are gathered and analyzed, providing a foundation for understanding the scale of waste management efforts in each country.

3 Results and Discussions

The chapter is divided into two parts, the first one includes the descriptions and comparison of legislative frameworks and the general municipal waste management systems and fees. The second chapter then includes the analysis of quantitative data on waste generation, recycling and landfilling.

3.1 Legislative Framework and Waste Management Systems

The general framework for waste management within the EU is provided by the Council Directive 2008/98/EC on waste (the Waste Framework Directive). The document provides a list of substances that can be classified as waste, and individuals or organizations are required to bear the costs of their disposal (the polluter pays). This establishes a hierarchy of the desired waste management methods from most preferred to least as following: prevention of generation or minimization of sources, reuse, processing into raw materials and products, composting, incineration or burial with energy recovery, burial without energy recovery and incineration without energy recovery.

Moreover, the Directive (EU) 2018/851 amends Directive 2008/98/EC on waste to include the principles that govern the transition to a circular economy and for guaranteeing the European Union's long-term competitiveness.

European Commission's proposed Circular Economy Package with specific targets and objectives for five waste streams: municipal waste, e.g., from households, packaging waste, food waste, bio-waste and residues and critical raw materials (CRMs).

The EU Directives and the circular economy goals of EU are to certain degree accounted for in the respective national frameworks and legislation of the V4 countries as well. In every country the waste management is based on the national Waste Act, Packaging Waste, EPR legislation and respective national waste plans.

In Czech republic, the primary waste management authorities are the Ministry of Environment, Czech Environmental Inspectorate, regions and municipalities. According to the Supreme Audit Office in 2020, 48 % of municipal waste in the Czech Republic ended up in landfills, 39 % of the waste was recovered, i.e., reused or recycled, and only 13 % of the waste was used for energy. However, the priorities of the Czech Republic are set in the opposite direction: efforts to prevent waste come first, followed by reuse and recycling. Below is the energy recovery, and only the last place is the landfilling itself. The practice in the Czech Republic is therefore just the opposite of the set priorities (NKU, n.d.). The municipalities impose local fees for operation of a system of collection, which is mostly implicated transport, separation, recovery and disposal of municipal waste. The municipal waste fees according to the Act on Local Fees consist of: (i) a fee for the municipal waste management system; and (ii) a fee for the disposal of municipal waste from immovable property. A fee for the municipal waste management system cannot exceed 1.200 CZK (around 50 EUR) during the charge period (a year).

In Hungary, the waste management was nationalized in 2012–2013. Currently, as Hungary has no separate Ministry of Environment the environmental responsibilities are divided between The Ministry of Agriculture, the National Council of Sustainable Developments, The Herman Otto Institute (non-profit organization of The Ministry of Agriculture), The National Inspectorate for Environment and Nature, The National Waste Management Directorate and The Hungarian Energy and Public Utility Regulatory Authority recommends national fees for collection of municipal waste from households. For the concession period of 35 years starting on July 1, 2023, company MOL Plc. as the concessionaire is in charge of collecting and managing waste throughout Hungary.

In Poland, waste management responsibilities are shared among various authorities, including the Ministry of Climate and Environment, regional authorities, and local municipalities. The fees for the management of municipal waste are calculated in accordance with the Act on maintaining order and cleanliness in municipalities. There are several methods of calculating the fee rate: (a) method of calculating the number of inhabitants living in a given real estate, (b) method of calculating the amount of water used, (c) method in relations to real estate, d) calculation method for the area of a dwelling and e) the method with regard to real estate where residents do not live. The obtained revenues cover the costs of the municipal waste management system, which include the costs of: collection, transport, acquisition, recovery and disposal of municipal waste; creating and maintaining separate collection points for municipal waste; administrative support of this system and environmental education in the field of proper handling of municipal waste.

In Slovakia, including the Ministry of Environment, the Slovak Environmental Inspectorate, regional administrations, and local municipalities which impose local fee for municipal waste. According to Local Taxes and Local Fee for municipal Waste and Minor Construction Waste Act No. 582/2004 Coll., a flat fee rate per person per calendar day is set between 0.02 EUR and 0.2 EUR; the municipality may also express the flat rate of the fee in an amount per calendar year.

Table 1 displays the system of collection of municipal waste recyclables based on the capital city of the country.

Table 1. Collection of municipal waste recyclables (based on the capital city).

Country	Separate door-to-door collection	Mixed door-to-door collection	Bring points
CZ	Biowaste	-	Glass, paper, plastic
HU	Paper, biowaste	Plastic, metal	Glass
PL	-	-	Glass, paper, plastic, metal
SK	-	-	Glass, paper, metal, biowaste

Source: own processing based on data from Eurostat (2023)

The V4 countries predominantly use bring-point systems for collecting recyclables. Poland and Slovakia use only bring points and neither of the door-to-door collection (besides regular residual waste). Hungary uses all three systems, separate and mixed door-to-door systems as well as bring points. In Czechia a separate door-to-door collection is used only in the case of biowaste while glass, paper and plastic need to be brought to the bring points and the other recyclables are not collected. All other V4 countries have a system for metal as well.

3.2 Waste Generation and Treatment in V4 Countries

In 2020, the population of V4 countries made for less than 15 % of total EU population and generated 11.08 % of total waste in the EU. Specifically, the V4 region generated less than 11 % of EU's municipal waste.

Although the V4 countries contribute to the EU waste generation by only about 11 %, the share of disposal and recovery facilities operated within the countries was higher than that in 2018. In V4 region, there was located about 21 % of EU's incineration and recycling facilities, 15 % of landfill facilities and 11 % of energy recovery facilities as displayed in the Table 2.

Table 2. Share of V4 on waste generation (total and municipal) and the number of disposal and recovery facilities in the EU (2018; 2020).

	Population (mil.)	**Total waste generation (tonnes)**	**Municipal waste generation (tonnes)**	**Disposal facilities**		**Recovery facilities**	
				L	**I**	**ER**	**R**
EU	448.4	2,153,950,000	233,199,000	6,162	650	2,906	33,341
CZ	10.7	38,486,186	5,814,000	189	21	59	2,578
HU	9.75	17,150,400	3,780,000	105	11	28	766
PL	37.9	170,233,670	12,753,000	541	102	229	3,095
SK	5.46	12,775,926	2,299,000	109	3	17	644
V4	63.81	238,646,182	24,646,000	944	137	333	7,083
%	**14.23 %**	**11.08 %**	**10.57 %**	**15.32 %**	**21.08 %**	**11.46 %**	**21.24 %**

Note: L – Landfill; I – Incineration; ER – Energy recovery; R – Recovery
Source: own processing based on data from Eurostat (2023)

The Figure 1 shows that each V4 country generates less volume (kg per capita) of total waste than is the EU average in the observed period 2004–2020. However, only Hungary managed to significantly decrease the volume of total waste generated by 27,91 % in this period. Whereas the volume of total waste generated in Czechia (+25,32 %), Poland (+24,74 %) and Slovakia (+17,82 %) significantly increased.

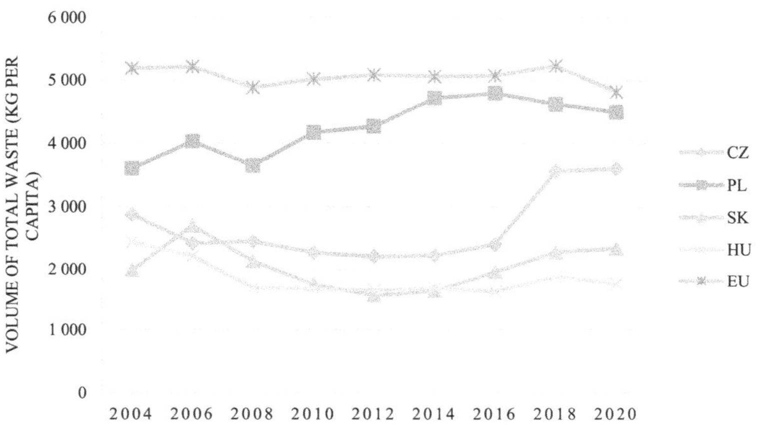

Figure 1. Total waste generation per capita (kg per capita).
Source: own processing based on data from Eurostat (2023)

While Poland had the highest volume of total waste generated per capita in 2020 (4 492 kg per capita), the share of its recyclable wastes per capita makes up only 9,6 % of total waste per capita. Czechia accounted for the highest volume of recyclable wastes generated per capita (654 kg per capita) and it makes up only 18,18 % of its generated total wastes. In Slovakia, the share of recyclable wastes in total wastes reaches 22,31 % (522 kg per capita). Hungary which had the lowest volume of total waste per capita generated in 2020 also had the lowest volume of recyclables generated (216 kg per capita). Despite the differences in the volumes of recyclable wastes generated, the composition of the materials is similar in the V4 countries with metal being the most dominant recyclable material in the generated waste as shown in Figure 2.

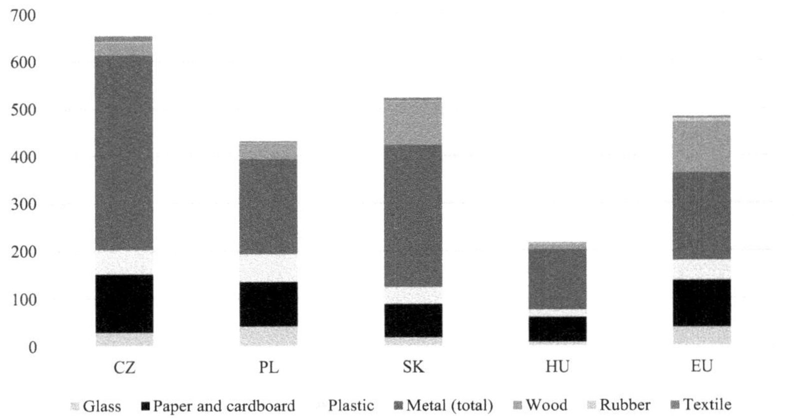

Figure 2. Total waste generation in 2020 – composition by main recyclable materials (kg per capita).

Source: own processing based on data from Eurostat (2023)

In 2020, the municipal waste accounted for less than 10 % of total waste generated in the whole EU as shown in Table 3. In Poland, the share of municipal waste was even lower, reaching less than 8 %, and the highest share of the waste was generated in mining and quarrying process (36,6 %). In Czechia, construction and demolition activities generated over 40 % of the waste, followed by the households (15,9 %) and waste water (15,5 %). In Hungary, the highest share of waste was generated by households (27,6 %), followed by construction and demolition industry (25,4 %). In Slovakia, the most waste was generated in other economic activities such as agriculture, commerce, tourism, and hospitality, etc. (32,5 %) followed by manufacturing (24,0 %). Municipal waste in Slovakia accounted for only 18,5 %.

Table 3. Generated waste composition by economic activities and households (%, 2020).

Country	Mining and quarrying	Manu-facturing	Energy	Waste water	Construction and demolition	Other economic activities	Households (municipal waste)
CZ	0.3	12.1	1.1	15.5	42.9	12.2	15.9
HU	0.8	15.2	11.4	12.1	25.4	7.5	27.6
PL	36.6	16.1	6.6	13.4	13.0	6.6	7.8

Table 3. Continued

Country	Mining and quarrying	Manu-facturing	Energy	Waste water	Construction and demolition	Other economic activities	Households (municipal waste)
SK	1.6	24.0	5.5	8.9	9.0	32.5	18.5
EU	23.4	10.6	2.3	10.8	37.5	5.9	9.4

Source: own processing based on data from Eurostat (2023)

The high proportions of the municipal waste do not necessarily equal to a bad waste management if they are accompanied by sustainable waste management practices such as reduction of waste generation, maximizing recycling rates and minimizing the environmental impact of waste disposal. Therefore, the next Figure 3 shows how the volume of municipal waste per capita generated in the V4 and the EU itself changed since 2004.

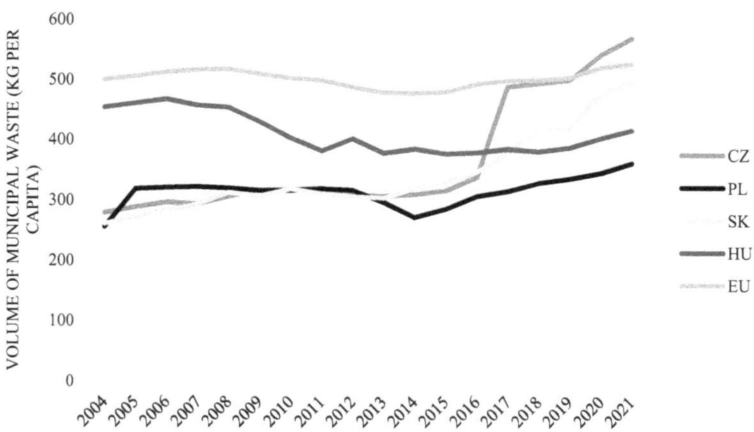

Figure 3. Municipal waste generation per capita (kg per capita).
Source: own processing based on data from Eurostat (2023)

Although the households in Hungary generated the highest proportion of waste in relation to other waste sources (compared to the other V4 countries), the Figure 3 shows that in 2021 the country generated less municipal waste per capita than Czechia and Slovakia. Also, Hungary is the only observed country which managed to in fact lower the volume of municipal waste generated per capita between 2004–2021 by 8,4 %. For all other V4 countries as well as the whole EU the volume of municipal per capita increased. While the EU average increased only by 5,4 %, the increase is very significant for Czechia which generated more than double the volume of municipal waste per capita in 2021 than in 2004 (+104,3 %) and the volume of the waste per capita in Czechia is higher than the EU average value since 2020. The volume of municipal waste per capita also significantly increased by 90,4 % in Slovakia and by 41,4 % in Poland.

The next important determinant in assessing the waste management is the recycling rate which is displayed in Figure 4. This determinant shows that the recycling had dynamically increased in the whole region since 2004 and the national recycling rates grew faster than the EU trend. Despite Hungary reducing the volume of municipal waste per capita its recycling rate by 2021 was in fact the lowest among the V4 countries since the recycling rates of Czechia, Slovakia and Poland got higher than the Hungarian in 2018–2019. Slovakia got the highest increase in recycling rates, from recycling 6,1 % of municipal waste in 2004 to recycling almost 50 % of it in 2021, catching up to the EU trend.

To assess the treatment of the collected municipal waste and the impacts on the environment the Figure 5 shows the volume of municipal waste disposed by the countries, e.g., by landfill, biodegradation, release into a water (including sea/oceans), etc. In 2021, about 23,0 % of municipal waste in the EU got disposed and the trend was decreasing in the past years. The data shows that all V4 countries, except Czechia, were in fact decreasing the

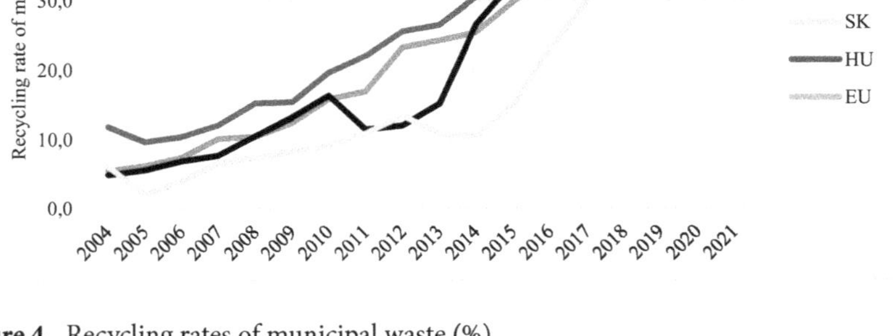

Figure 4. Recycling rates of municipal waste (%).
Source: own processing based on data from Eurostat (2023)

amount of municipal waste that was being disposed in land or water similarly to the EU trend. Poland managed to decrease the volume by 34,0 %, Hungary by 19,4 % and Slovakia by 9,8 % since 2012. Czechia on the other hand increased the volume of disposed municipal waste by 51,2 % which cannot be considered a long-term sustainable waste management practice.

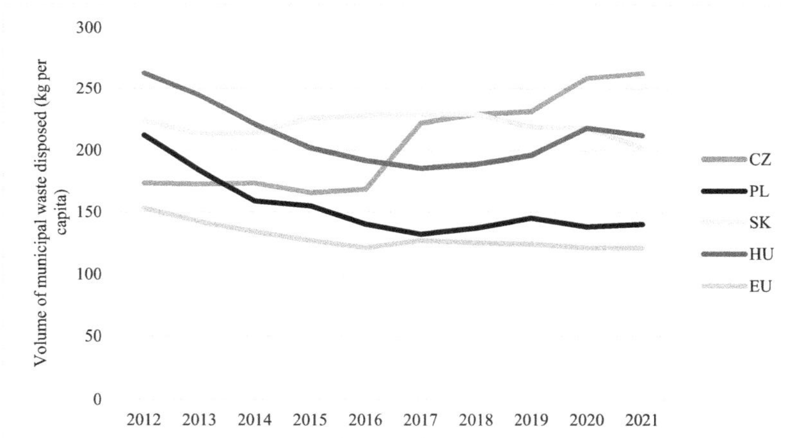

Figure 5. Volume of municipal waste disposed (landfill and others; D1-D7, D12) (kg per capita).

Source: Eurostat (2023)

When it comes to government spending on waste management, the comparison displayed in Figure 6 shows that the highest proportion of general government expenditure on 'environmental protection' is dedicated to waste management in Hungary (0, 41 % of GDP), Slovakia (0,37 % of GDP) and Czechia (0,31 % of GDP). Poland is the only country where the expenditure on waste water management (0,17 % of GDP) is in fact higher than the expenditure on the waste management (0,11 % of GDP).

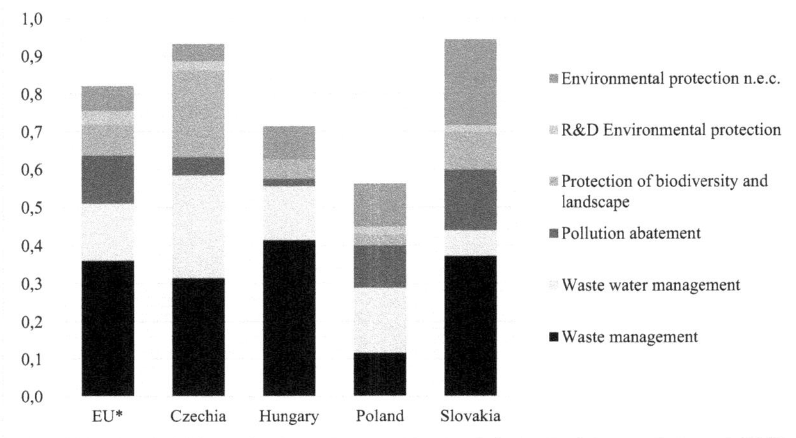

Figure 6. Total general government expenditure on 'environmental protection', 2021 (% of GDP).

Source: Eurostat (2023)

4 Conclusions

The study provide insights into the waste management practices and trends within the V4 countries (Czechia, Hungary, Poland, and Slovakia) as compared to the (EU) as a whole. The analysis of data from 2020 and historical trends spanning from 2004 to 2021 sheds light on several key aspects of waste generation, recycling rates, disposal methods, and government spending on waste management.

In 2020, the V4 countries collectively accounted for less than 15 % of the total EU population but generated approximately 11.08 % of the total waste in the EU. Notably, the V4 region was home to a significant portion of EU's incineration, recycling, landfill, and energy recovery facilities. Despite some variations among V4 countries, the dominant recyclable material in the generated waste was metal.

While each V4 country generated less total waste per capita than the EU average, there were significant disparities in waste generation trends. Hungary achieved a notable 27.91 % decrease in total waste generation from 2004 to 2020. Conversely, Czechia, Poland, and Slovakia saw significant increases of 25.32 %, 24.74 %, and 17.82 %, respectively.

The recycling rates in the V4 countries increased dynamically since 2004, surpassing the EU trend. Slovakia exhibited the most substantial improvement, increasing its recycling rate from 6.1 % in 2004 to nearly 50 % in 2021. However, Hungary had the lowest recycling rate among V4 countries in 2021, with Czechia, Slovakia, and Poland surpassing its rate in recent years.

Waste disposal practices significantly impact environmental sustainability. The data showed that all V4 countries, except Czechia, followed the EU trend of reducing the volume of municipal waste disposed in land or water. Notably, Poland, Hungary, and Slovakia made considerable progress in reducing disposal volumes.

Government expenditure on waste management as a percentage of GDP varied across V4 countries. Hungary, Slovakia, and Czechia allocated the highest proportions of their general government expenditure on 'environmental protection' to waste management. Poland, however, allocated a higher percentage to waste water management than waste management.

Overall, the V4 countries have made notable strides in waste management, with improvements in recycling rates and reductions in waste disposal volumes, aligning with broader EU trends. However, challenges remain, particularly in achieving more uniform recycling rates across the V4 region and further reducing waste generation in some countries. The findings underscore the importance of continued efforts to implement sustainable waste management practices, which are critical for environmental protection and resource conservation in the region. Additionally, the allocation of government expenditure to different aspects of environmental protection, as seen in Poland, warrants further investigation to ensure effective resource allocation in the pursuit of environmental sustainability. Future research and policy initiatives should aim to address these challenges and build on the positive trends observed in this study.

Acknowledgments

This paper was supported by the Ministry of Education, Youth and Sports Czech Republic within the Institutional Support for Long-term Development of a Research Organisation in 2023.

References

Ali, S., & Shirazi, F. (2023). The paradigm of circular economy and an effective electronic waste management. *Sustainability, 15*(3), 1998.

Alwaeli, M. (2015). An overview of municipal solid waste management in Poland. The current situation, problems and challenges. *Environment Protection Engineering, 41*(4), 181–193.

Aycin, E., & Kaya S. K. (2021). Towards the circular economy: Analysis of barriers to implementation of Turkey's zero waste management using the fuzzy DEMATEL method. *Waste Management & Research, 39*(8), 1078–1089.

Baki, O. G., & Ergun, O. N. (2021). Municipal solid waste management: Circular economy evaluation in Turkey. *Environmental Management and Sustainable Development, 10*(2), 79–92.

Buch, R., Marseille, A., Williams, M., Aggarwal, R., & Sharma, A. (2021). From waste pickers to producers: An inclusive circular economy solution through development of cooperatives in waste management. *Sustainability, 13*(16), 8925.

Erceg, A., Erceg, B. C., & Bozic, A. (2017). Toward circular economy – Impact and legal regulation – Example of Croatian plastic packaging producer. *6th International Scientific Symposium Economy of Eastern Croatia – Vision and Growth, Croatia,* 473–483.

Fagerholm, A.-S. Haller, H., Warell, A., & Hedvall, P. O. (2023). What a waste – A norm-critical design study on how waste is understood and managed. *Resources, Conservation & Recycling Advances, 19*, 200178.

Iuga, A. N. (2016). Waste management in the circular economy. The case of Romania. *IOP Conference Series Materials Science and Engineering, 161.*

Loncaric, R., Sudaric, T., & Milkovic, S. J. (2021). Circular economy and agricultural waste management in Croatia. *10th International Scientific Symposium Region, Entrepreneurship, Development, Croatia*, 787–803.

Mahpour, A. (2018). Prioritizing barriers to adopt circular economy in construction and demolition waste management. *Resources Conservation and Recycling, 134*, 216–227.

NKU. (n.d.). *Waste management in the Czech Republic: Subsidies in billions of CZK did not effect a change, landfilling still plays a crucial role.* SAO Czech Republic. https://www.nku.cz/en/for-media/press-releases/waste-management-in-the-czech-republic:-subsidies-in-billions-of-czk-did-not-effect-a-change--landfilling-still-plays-a-crucial-role-id12664/

Pikon, K., Poranek, N., Czajkowski, A., & Lazniewska-Piekarczyk, B. (2021). Poland's proposal for a safe solution of waste treatment during the COVID-19 pandemic and circular economy connection. *Applied Sciences, 11*(9), 3939.

Savini, F. (2021). The circular economy of waste: Recovery, incineration and urban reuse. *Journal of Environmental Planning and Management, 64*(12), 2114–2132.

Tamasiga, P., Miri, T., Onyeaka, H., & Hart, A. (2022). Food waste and circular economy: Challenges and opportunities. *Sustainability, 14*(16), 9896.

Tarhini, M., Turcea V. C., Zapucioiu L. F., & Ion, R.-A. (2022). Food waste status and reduction through the circular economy. *Scientific Papers Series Management, Economic Engineering in Agriculture and Rural Development, 22*(4), 731–742.

Vitenko, T., Marynenko, N., & Kramar I. (2021). European experience in waste management. *Environmental Sciences Proceedings, 9*(17).

Svitlana Luchyk[1,*], Vasil Luchyk[1], Yulia Manachynska[2], and Marharyta Luchyk[3]

The Forecasting and Analytical Model of Ensuring the State's Intellectual Security

Abstract:
Research background: In the conditions of Russian aggression and the large-scale destruction of the Ukrainian economy, the effective management of organizations should be based on the constant analysis of data on available human and intellectual resources, the search for new strategies and approaches to the recovery of the economy on a new, technological level. Forecasting socio-economic processes is an integral attribute of the management system at all its levels – from a small firm to the national economy as a whole.
Purpose of the article: The purpose of the article is to form an idea about ensuring the intellectual security of the Ukrainian state until 2025 based on an intellectual analysis of data on the development of intellectual capital in Ukraine in 2000–2021, the impact of the war in Ukraine, the demographic crisis related to it, the COVID-19 pandemic, as well as active development of digital technologies and artificial intelligence.
Methods: The article analyzes the level of intellectual security of the Ukrainian state in terms of its individual components and simulates an integrated indicator of intellectual security. Possible threats and dangers are defined for each component of intellectual security. For the integral indicator of intellectual security in Ukraine, a forecast until 2025 was calculated under three scenarios: pessimistic, realistic and optimistic using software and analytical platforms.
Findings & Value added: The authors have formulated conclusions and suggestions on increasing the level of ensuring the intellectual security of the country.

* Corresponding author: luchiksvitlana@gmail.com
1 Kharkiv National University of Internal Affairs, Faculty № 4, Department of Combating Cybercrime, 61080, Lva Landau Ave., Training Corps No. 2/1, Kharkiv City, 27, Ukraine
2 Chernivtsi Institute of Trade and Economics of SUTE, Department of Finance and Banking, 58002, 7 Tsentralna Square, Chernivtsi, Ukraine
3 JSC Credit Agricole Bank, Sales Network Department, 9 Instytutska Str., Kyiv, Ukraine

Keywords: *intellectual security, intelligent data analysis, statistical analysis, modeling, forecasting*

JEL Classification: *C53; C87; H56; O15; O32*

1 Introduction

The rapid expansion of knowledge and the increasing dependence of economic development on computerization, automation, and artificial intelligence, shape the modern economy into a knowledge economy that depends primarily on intellectual capital and skills and less on the production process. Knowledge provides the basis for the necessary practical experience with computer technology, data collection and analysis skills, and innovative management techniques that allow companies to compete with each other. Specialized knowledge and skills can serve as both productive assets for a business and products for marketing and sales.

The World Bank (Chen & Dahlman, 2006) defines the knowledge economy with the help of four pillars:

- institutional structures that provide incentives for entrepreneurship and the use of knowledge;
- the availability of a qualified workforce and a strong education system;
- access to infrastructures of information and communication technologies (ICT);
- a vibrant innovation landscape that includes academia, the private sector, and civil society.

Therefore, the knowledge economy primarily demonstrates the intellectual capital and intellectual potential of the state. However, the catastrophic reduction of the population in Ukraine (as of the end of August it is only 27.8 million people) (Decyk & Alekseev, 2022), exacerbated by the Russian-Ukrainian war, led to a demographic danger in the country and also created a threat to intellectual security. Significant losses of the young, working-age population in the war, the forced migration of women and children abroad, and the extremely high probability that youth population may stay abroad as permanent residents, narrow the intellectual potential of the Ukrainian state, threaten the loss of the scientific and educational potential of society, economic sub-entities, individuals.

The definition of "intellectual security" emerged relatively recently. However, the research on this topic raised considerable interest from scientists. The foreign researchers (Almahaireh et al., 2021; Al-Dajah, 2019; Alvino et al., 2021) define intellectual security as the ability of people to protect their minds and ideas from deviations and misconceptions that may pose a threat to the life of an individual, and society, as well as to achieve security and stability in all spheres of life.

While foreign researchers interpret intellectual security as the security of human development in general, the Ukrainian scientists emphasize the security of people as carriers of knowledge and their intellectual achievements. This approach (Marchenko, 2012) is focused on protecting workers' intellectual end products, including intellectual properties. Revak (2008) proposes to consider intellectual security as a set of socio-cultural, spiritual, moral-psychological, economic, demographic, ecological, and other factors that exert a corresponding influence on the intelligence of the nation and each citizen in particular, forming an established worldview, individual and public culture of behavior. The social consequences of intellectual insecurity include poverty, family and social disintegration, weak social control, disintegration and destruction of the principles of society, emigration of national competencies due to terrorism, the spread of violence, and changes in the economic and social development of the state, accompanied by instability. All of them affect people's life satisfaction, starting with a sense of security.

Based on the Marchenko (2012) approach, intellectual security consists of several components:

- security of intellectual labor resources as carriers of knowledge;
- safety of intangible assets as objects of intellectual property rights of the firm;
- security of intellectual capital as a state of security of the firm's investments in knowledge resources;
- security of knowledge movement in the organization, which includes creation, attraction, distribution (diffusion), mastering of knowledge, transformation, exchange, preservation, and use of knowledge as its objectification in the company's products and services;
- cyber security – security of information and communication technologies (ICT).

Therefore, intellectual security is a complex subject matter, characterized by a system of qualitative indicators of intellectual development. It includes not only the protection of intellectual work and products, but also the rational use, capitalization, reproduction, and improvement of the quality of innovative capital (Bamel et al., 2022; Konno & Schillaci, 2021; Osinski et al., 2017). Assessing the intellectual potential and intellectual security of the state domestically and internationally is one of the basic conditions for ensuring the country's national security (Bryhinets et al., 2021; Elmahjub, 2015; Kim et al., 2020; Mishchuk et al, 2022; Ramcharan, 2005; Kashyap & Agrawal, 2020). A special role in this case belongs to predictive conclusions, which are likely to significantly increase the certainty of the main goal when making decisions. High-quality and effective forecasting for the short and long term (Speigel, 2021) enables the state to implement economic and social policy taking into account positive and negative factors of the domestic or international environment, to take preventive measures, to make rational decisions that minimize costs.

2 Methods

The basis of the mechanism for ensuring the intellectual security of the state is the protection of scientific, educational, and innovative potential of society, business entities, and individuals. However, state intellectual security combines not only the preservation of intellectual resources, objects of intellectual property, and products of intellectual activity but also its protection aimed at the effective functioning of the entire intellectual sphere. The study of the level of ensuring the intellectual security of the Ukrainian state can be conducted through an integral assessment of such components as intellectual potential, intellectual capital, and the influence of the state on the formation of its intellectual potential and capital for a certain period of time, for example, from 2000 to 2021. Each of these indicators, as well as the integral indicator of intellectual security, can be considered as time-series data that can be analyzed and evaluated using modern data analysis technologies.

Therefore, we will try to determine the level of ensuring the intellectual security of the Ukrainian state through an integrated assessment of such components as intellectual potential; intellectual capital; the influence of the state on the formation of its intellectual potential and capital, as well as to obtain predictive trends of intellectual security for the next 5 years. Some of the best software packages for conducting this analysis include Sisense, Zoho Analytics, Xplenty, DataMelt, Inetsoft, SPMF, and SSDT. Such programs as Minitab, StatSoft, SAS, and SPSS are used for statistical data analysis. The most effective predictive analytical systems include RapidMiner, SAS, EViews, and Microsoft Excel.

Let's start with the description of a mathematical model for calculating the integral indicator of the state's intellectual security. Suppose that the intellectual security of the state can be described by n indicators that can be combined into s separate groups. Let's denote them G1, G22, …, Gs. In our study, the intellectual potential of the state, its intellectual capital, and the level of the state's influence on intellectual security were selected as constituent groups. Each component is described by its indicators:

$$G_1 = \left(P_1^1, P_2^1, \ldots, P_{r_1}^1\right); G_2 = \left(P_1^2, P_2^2, \ldots, P_{r_2}^2\right); \ldots, G_s = \left(P_1^s, P_2^s, \ldots, P_{r_s}^s\right) \quad (1)$$

where $r_j, j = \underline{1,s}$ – is the number of indicators of the jth group,

$P_k^i, i = \underline{1,s}, and\ k = \underline{1,r_i}.$ – is the k-th indicator of the i-th group

Indicators in groups can have different dimensions, so we normalize indicators using the linear scaling method and determine the minimum and maximum values of the general set of data for the period under study. We must take into account whether the indicator is a stimulator or not.

The integral index of each constituent group Gj, j=1,s is described by the equality:

$$IS_{G_j} = \sqrt{(P_1^j)^2 + (P_2^j)^2 + \ldots + (P_{r_j}^j)^2},\ j = \underline{1,s}. \quad (2)$$

The integral index of intellectual security of the state is calculated using the formula below:

$$IS = \sqrt{\sum_{j=1}^{s} IS_{G_j}^2} \quad (3)$$

We have included the following indicators in the system of intellectual security of the state:

- group "intellectual potential" as the share of people among the economically active population aged 15–70 who have a complete higher education, %; the number of higher education students per 10,000 people; the effectiveness of graduate school work, (the share of graduated graduate students with a dissertation defense to the total number of graduates), %; effectiveness of doctoral studies (the share of graduated doctoral students with a dissertation defense to the total number of graduates), %; the share of expenses for the implementation of the R&D by the higher education sector in the total amount of expenses for the implementation of the R&D, %; coefficient of scientific activity (the number of scientists to the number of organizations performing scientific works); the number of specialists performing scientific and technical work, % of the total number of people employed in the country's economy (per 1,000 people);

- the "intellectual capital" group – the number of industrial enterprises that implemented innovations per 1,000 population; the volume of realized innovative industrial products (goods, services) per 1 million people, thousand hryvnias; innovation costs, % of the total volume of sold products (goods, services) of industrial enterprises; the number of existing industrial property objects per 1,000 population; regular Internet users, % (use the Internet once a month or more often); the share of intangible assets in the invested capital of enterprises, %;
- group "influence of the state on intellectual security" – the share of expenses for the implementation of scientific and scientific and technical works in GDP, %; the share of state budget expenditures for the implementation of scientific and scientific and technical works, % in GDP; the share of expenses for scientific and technical (experimental) works to expenses for the GDR, %; consolidated budget expenditures on education, % of GDP; % for education in the consolidated budget.

We will describe the model of intellectual security as a time series model and present it as:

$$IS(t_i) = f\left(IS(t_{i-1}), IS(t_{i-2}), \ldots,\right) + \varepsilon(t_i). \tag{4}$$

The function f reflects the nature of the relationship between the next and the previous value of the indicator $IS(t_i)$.

The strategy for developing a lean model for ensuring the intellectual security of the state will include the following stages:

- definition of the model, which involves testing the time series for stationarity, and definition of the general characteristics of the model;
- estimation of model parameters using, for example, the nonlinear least squares method;
- checking the model for fit and adequacy;
- forecasting based on the obtained model.

Microsoft Excel 2016 and EViews packages will be used to forecast the intellectual security of the Ukrainian state in the short term.

3 Results

Our evaluation of the intellectual security of Ukraine in terms of such components as "intellectual potential," "intellectual capital," and "influence of the state on intellectual security" for 2000–2021 using the mathematical model (1)–(3) made it possible to obtain integral indicators and present them graphically in Figure 1.

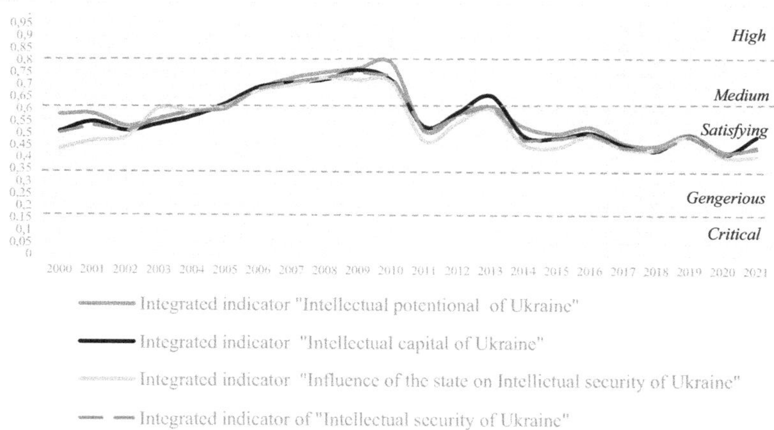

Figure 1. Integral indicators of the intellectual security of Ukraine for 2000–2021 yy with the allocation of security zones according to the Harrington scale.
Source: authors

The results of the integrated assessment of Ukraine's intellectual potential for 2000–2021 showed that its level was in the zone of satisfactory security for almost the entire period, although in 2012–2013 it reached an average level of security. It was in 2011–2014 that the highest values were reached by such indicators as the number of students per 10 thousand people – 557 people (2011), the performance of postgraduate programs – 26.4 % (2013) and doctoral programs – 33.3 % (2012). In Ukraine, the proportion of the population covered by complete and basic higher education is constantly growing. Among the economically active population aged 15–70, 77–79 % have a complete higher education. At the same time, in the short and medium term, the number of highly educated people in the country will continue to grow due to the natural decline of older, less educated age groups. It is the level of education that is a powerful means of predicting a country's wealth in the long term. According to experts of the Organization for Economic Cooperation and Development, (Cochlan, 2015) the GDP growth potential of the Ukrainian economy is 316 %, provided that all 15-year-olds in the country have a basic level of education.

Consolidated budget expenditures on education (Ministry of Education and Science of Ukraine, 2023) in 2021 amounted to 5.7 % of GDP compared to 8.4 % in 2010. In the state budget of Ukraine for 2022, 153.7 billion UAH were allocated for education, and in the 2023 budget, this sum dropped by 142.8 billion UAH (i.e., 10.9 billion less than last year). In 2022, education was financed less by 7.1 % in nominal terms and by 26.7 % in real terms. In 2022, spending on education decreased by UAH 21 billion or by 12 %. Comparing the budgets for 2022 and 2023, there is a significant reduction in the educational subvention (97.2 billion to 87.5 billion UAH) and the subvention to support persons with limited educational problems (0.45 billion – 0.30 billion UAH). Instead, two new subsidies appeared: UAH 1.5 billion for the provision of safe conditions in schools in connection with the state of war in the country and UAH 1 billion for the purchase of school buses.

The intellectual potential is an integrated set of interconnected and complementary components, such as education and science, the interaction between which causes a synergistic effect, which should be aimed at strengthening the intellectual security of the state. In Ukraine, the higher education sector works quite productively in the area of research and development. Its share of expenses for the implementation of the R&D in the total amount of expenses for the implementation of the R&D in recent years is 7 %. Scientific and technical (experimental) initiatives make up a significant share of R&D, their share in 2015–2016 in the total volume of R&D expenditures was 58–60 %. In recent years, this indicator has decreased to 53.3 %. The ratio of scientific activity (i.e., the number of scientists to the number of organizations performing scientific work) also dropped. For example, between 2018 and 2019 it was 10.8–12 %, then in 2021 it was 8.9. This situation is primarily explained by the decrease in funding of scientific programs and, as an outcome of it, the reduction of young, creative, and highly qualified personnel taking part in them. These trends are vividly demonstrated by the graph of the integrated indicator "The influence of the state on intellectual security," which combines indicators of state expenditures on education, science, and innovation for 2000–2021.

The graph presented in Figure 1 shows a downward trend since 2013. The share of expenses for the implementation of scientific and R&D initiatives decreased from 0.75 % of GDP in 2010 to 0.4 % of GDP in 2021. Similarly, the share of state budget expenditures for the performance of scientific and R&D initiatives during the same period decreased from 0.33 % to 0.17 %.

In the 2023 budget (Ministry of Finance of Ukraine, 2023), UAH 11.9 billion is allocated to finance scientific and R&D activities. Funds are going to be aimed at the following core initiatives:

- UAH 8.5 billion – for “academic science” (about 72 % of the total amount of expenditures is directed to the National Academy of Sciences of Ukraine and five national sectoral academies of sciences);
- UAH 1.1 billion – for “university science” (about 10 % of the volume of expenditures on higher education institutions and scientific institutions under the management of the Ministry of Education and Science of Ukraine);
- UAH 0.6 billion – for “industry science” (about 5 % of the total amount of expenditures on scientific institutions in the sphere of management of other executive authorities).

Support for the activities of the National Research Fund of Ukraine, grant support for scientific research, and R&D research have also been increased with 2 billion allocated for 2023 against 1.5 billion that was funded in 2022. Intellectual security also represents society’s ability to enhance creative activities and innovative development. The knowledge economy requires non-standard thinking, generating ideas, formulating new theories, laws, and technological inventions, and creating unique products. Scientific discoveries and technical inventions lead to the accumulation and development of intellectual capital.

Figure 1 graph of the development of intellectual capital in Ukraine between 2000 and 2021 shows positive trends, especially in 2020 and 2021. Thus, in recent years, the values of such indicators as the share of regular Internet users who use the network once a month or more has increased; the share of intangible assets in invested capital; the number of industrial enterprises that implemented innovations per 1,000 population. In the modern information society, intangible assets are determined by their specific value compared to real assets. For example, such cost items as software account for 70 % of the cost of intellectual labor and 10–30 % of the cost of used equipment (computers, etc.), electricity, buildings, and communications. Business Week published (Klymenko et al., 2021) an estimate of the most expensive brands in the world: Coca-Cola – $70 billion, Microsoft – $65 billion, IBM – $52 billion, GE – $42 billion, Intel – $31 billion.

The knowledge economy is a market to produce and monetize scientific and engineering discoveries. These knowledge end products are converted into a commodity as patents or other means of intellectual property protection. According to the results of the annual ranking of the Global Innovation Index by the World Intellectual Property Organization (WIPO, 2022), which is part of the United Nations, in 2022, Ukraine took 57th place in the world ranking, surpassing South Africa and Georgia, and 34th among European countries. Compared to 2021, Ukraine worsened its result: from 49th place to 57th place. According to the Ukrainian Institute of Intellectual Property, the number of registered patents for inventions in 2010–2021 decreased by 56.3 %, and for utility models – by 46.3 %. However, the number of registered applications for industrial designs (by 22.4 %), trademarks (34.6 %), and registered copyrights (93.0 %) increased (Annual report, 2022). In 2022–2023, the situation did not improve. As of February 2023, the number of registered objects of industrial property decreased by 33.5 % compared to 2022, mainly due to industrial designs (by 67.7 %) and patents for inventions (by 25.1 %).

The integrated assessment of the influence of the state on intellectual security for the period between 2000 and 2021 revealed downward trends that took place in 2011, 2014–2017, and also in 2020–2021. This was mainly associated with political crises that took place in Ukraine, which harmed the reduction of funding in the fields of science, culture, and innovation. Also, since 2014, Ukraine was forced to carry out an anti-terrorist operation in the east of the country to protect its territories, which also changed the structure of the state budget and negatively affected the financing of the country's intellectual resources.

4 Discussion

We will begin the construction of the predictive model by examining the numerical series of the intellectual security of the state for stationarity and determining the main characteristics (Figures 2 and 3).

Null Hypothesis: IS has a unit root
Exogenous: Constant
Lag Length: 0 (Automatic - based on SIC, maxlag=2)

		t-Statistic	Prob.*
Augmented Dickey-Fuller test statistic		-1.500534	0.5137
Test critical values:	1% level	-3.788030	
	5% level	-3.012363	
	10% level	-2.646119	

*MacKinnon (1996) one-sided p-values.

Augmented Dickey-Fuller Test Equation
Dependent Variable: D(IS)
Method: Least Squares
Date: 06/13/23 Time: 22:43
Sample (adjusted): 2001 2021
Included observations: 21 after adjustments

Variable	Coefficient	Std. Error	t-Statistic	Prob.
IS(-1)	-0.231628	0.154364	-1.500534	0.1499
C	0.128188	0.088664	1.445771	0.1645

R-squared	0.105950	Mean dependent var	-0.002640
Adjusted R-squared	0.058894	S.D. dependent var	0.076112
S.E. of regression	0.073836	Akaike info criterion	-2.283541
Sum squared resid	0.103584	Schwarz criterion	-2.184062
Log likelihood	25.97718	Hannan-Quinn criter.	-2.261951
F-statistic	2.251602	Durbin-Watson stat	2.121747
Prob(F-statistic)	0.149911		

Figure 2. The result of the study of the numerical trend of the intellectual security of the state (IS) on stationarity.

Source: authors

The results of the study of the time series of intellectual security of the state revealed its non-stationarity under the null hypothesis, however, it is stationary in the levels of the series (Figure 2). The construction of the correlogram of the IS time series (Figure 3) made it possible to select the parameters of the autoregression model (Figure 4).

Date: 06/13/23 Time: 21:56
Sample: 2000 2021
Included observations: 22

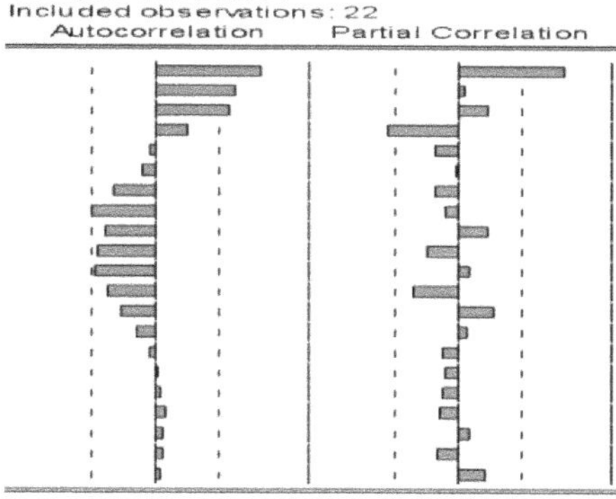

	AC	PAC	Q-Stat	Prob
1	0.727	0.727	13.305	0.000
2	0.546	0.035	21.168	0.000
3	0.502	0.199	28.180	0.000
4	0.216	-0.490	29.544	0.000
5	-0.028	-0.172	29.569	0.000
6	-0.097	-0.010	29.882	0.000
7	-0.283	-0.158	32.700	0.000
8	-0.437	-0.085	39.916	0.000
9	-0.346	0.202	44.792	0.000
10	-0.395	-0.223	51.652	0.000
11	-0.413	0.069	59.859	0.000
12	-0.324	-0.296	65.387	0.000
13	-0.234	0.240	68.610	0.000
14	-0.135	0.058	69.814	0.000
15	-0.045	-0.111	69.968	0.000
16	0.014	-0.095	69.985	0.000
17	0.038	-0.110	70.142	0.000
18	0.066	-0.118	70.716	0.000
19	0.056	0.075	71.265	0.000
20	0.047	-0.141	71.844	0.000
21	0.027	0.184	72.219	0.000

Figure. 3 Correlogram of the time series of intellectual security of the state (IS).
Source: authors

Dependent Variable: IS
Method: ARMA Maximum Likelihood (OPG - BHHH)
Date: 06/13/23 Time: 22:27
Sample: 2000 2021
Included observations: 22
Convergence achieved after 14 iterations
Coefficient covariance computed using outer product of gradients

Variable	Coefficient	Std. Error	t-Statistic	Prob.
C	0.541591	0.084725	6.392328	0.0000
AR(1)	0.745512	0.178870	4.167890	0.0005
SIGMASQ	0.004755	0.001911	2.488917	0.0223

R-squared	0.567869	Mean dependent var	0.559455
Adjusted R-squared	0.522381	S.D. dependent var	0.107370
S.E. of regression	0.074203	Akaike info criterion	-2.201008
Sum squared resid	0.104616	Schwarz criterion	-2.052230
Log likelihood	27.21109	Hannan-Quinn criter.	-2.165961
F-statistic	12.48405	Durbin-Watson stat	2.073333
Prob(F-statistic)	0.000345		

Inverted AR Roots	.75

Figure 4. Model of the IS numerical series with an autoregressive component.
Source: authors

The model of intellectual security of the state can be represented as an equation (5):

$$IS_t = 0{,}746 \cdot IS_{t-1} + 0{,}138 + \varepsilon_t \qquad (5)$$

Figure 5 presents a forecast model of ensuring the intellectual security of Ukraine until 2025 with the selection of pessimistic, realistic, and optimistic scenarios and security zones according to the Harrington scale.

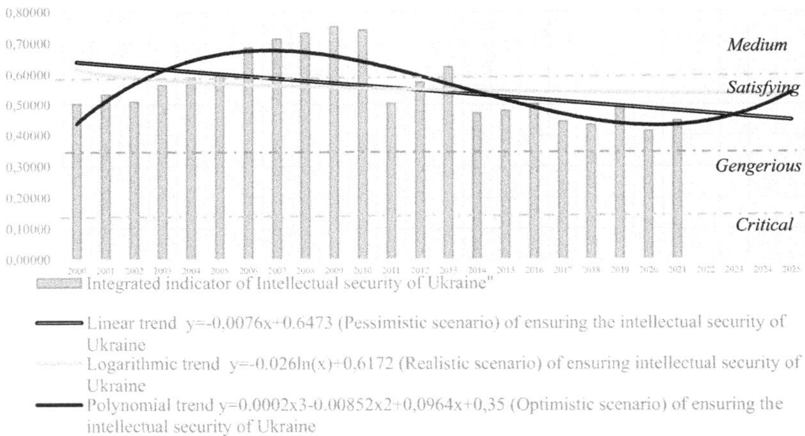

Figure 5. Forecasting model of the level of intellectual security of Ukraine until 2025 with the selection of pessimistic, realistic, and optimistic scenarios and security zones according to the Harrington scale.

Source: authors

According to pessimistic and realistic scenarios, the level of intellectual security in Ukraine will decrease and fall into a dangerous zone, as Ukraine bears irreversible economic, financial, and social losses in the war against Russian aggression. Human losses are especially irreparable. The forced migration of mostly young people abroad also significantly reduces the intellectual potential of the country. However, agreeing with the opinion of many scientists (Olshanska et al., 2022), after the end of the war, Ukraine will be able to recover and will recover at a new higher level of intellectual and socio-economic development based on the production and implementation of smart solutions and the consolidation of all subjects of the national economic system. Therefore, the optimistic scenario takes into account the improvement of the economic situation in Ukraine in 2023–2024, the return of migrants to the country, and the development of education and science.

5 Conclusions

Therefore, the use of specialized information technologies for statistical analysis has many advantages: it can increase the effectiveness and efficiency of work, can easily process large data sets, model social and economic processes, and make predictions. In order to strengthen the intellectual security of the state, it is necessary to create and implement conditions for the accumulation and use of intellectual potential and capital, which are, on the one hand, a source of replenishment of the scientific and industrial domains with highly qualified personnel, and on the other hand, a determining element in ensuring the growth of the state economy. The degree of intellectual security will depend on the presence of highly productive scientists, the effective organization of scientific and R&D initiatives, a developed system of commercialization of scientific ideas, modern information support and technological equipment capable of ensuring the production of domestic competitive products.

The country's intellectual potential and capital require constant protection by security entities, in particular by state institutions, since they accumulate intellectual resources and unused potential, which could be used for the benefits of the national economy. This efficient use of the intellectual potential of state institutions will not only positively impact the structural transformations in the national economy, but also drive required reforms of ensuring Ukrainian national security.

References

Almahaireh, A., Alzaben, M., Aladwan, F., & Aljahan M. (2021). The level of intellectual security and its relationship with life satisfaction among Mutah University students. *Journal of Social Studies Education Research Sosyal Bilgiler Eğitimi Araştırmaları Dergisi*, *12*(3), 28–46. https://jsser.org/index.php/jsser/article/view/3444

Al-Dajah, H. A. (2019). Contemporary theory of intellectual security. *Canadian Social Science*, *15*(3), 11–22.

Alvino, F., Di Vaio, A., Hassan, R., & Palladino, R. (2021). Intellectual capital and sustainable development: A systematic literature review. *Journal of Intellectual Capital*, *22*(1), 76–94.

Annual report. (2022). State Enterprise. Ukrainian Intellectual Property Institute (UIPI). https://ukrpatent.org/uk/articles/rzvit

Bamel, U., Pereira, V., Del Giudice, M., & Temouri, Y. (2022). The extent and impact of intellectual capital research: A two decade analysis. *Journal of Intellectual Capital*, *23*(2), 375–400.

Bryhinets, O., Shapoval, R., Bakhaieva, A., Pchelin V., & Fomenko, A. (2021). Problems of intellectual property in the national security system of the country. *Entrepreneurship and Sustainability Issues*, *8*(3), 471–486.

Chen, D. H. C., & Dahlman, C. J. (2006). The knowledge economy, The KAM Methodology and World Bank Operations, *The International Bank for Reconstruction and Development/The World Bank*, Washington, 2006, 42.

Cochlan, S. (2015). World rating of education: Ukraine became the 38th. *BBC News Ukraine*. https://www.bbc.com/ukrainian/science/2015/05/150513_vj_education_rankings_it

Decyk, O., & Alekseev, V. (2022). Return what was lost. What threatens Ukraine with population decline? *LB.ua*. https://lb.ua/economics/2022/09/22/530166_povernuti_vtrachene_chim_ukraini.html

Elmahjub, E. (2015). Situating intellectual property policy into a human development paradigm. *World Intellectual Property*, *18*, 245–269.

Kashyap, A., & Agrawal, R. (2020). Scale development and modeling of intellectual property creation capability in higher education. *Journal of Intellectual Capi*tal, *21*(1), 115–138.

Kim, H.L., Hovav, A., & Han, J. (2020). Protecting intellectual property from insider threats: A management information security intelligence perspective. *Journal of Intellectual Capital*, *21*(2), 181–202.

Klymenko I. S., Taranukha, O. M., & Zhuravel, O. V. (2021). Intellectual capital and the market of intellectual property in the conditions of the information economy: Problems of identification and evaluation. *Economy and the State*, *5*, 38–43.

Konno, N., & Schillaci, C. E. (2021). Intellectual capital in Society 5.0 by the lens of the knowledge creation theory. *Journal of Intellectual Capital*, *22*(3), 478–505.

Marchenko, O. (2012). Intellectual security in the dimension of knowledge economy. *Bulletin of the National University "Law Academy of Ukraine named after Yaroslav the Wise"*, *1*(8), 278–279. https://dspace.nlu.edu.ua/handle/123456789/1904

Ministry of Finance of Ukraine. (2023). Almost UAH 12 billion will be allocated to finance science in 2023. *Government portal.* https://www.kmu.gov.ua/news/minfin-na-finansuvannia-nauky-u-2023-rotsi-spriamovano-mai zhe-12-mlrd-hrn

Mishchuk, I., Riabykina, Y., Ushenko, N., Hamova, O., Tkachenko, S., & Yastremska, N. (2022). Intellectual capital as a factor forming economic security of enterprises in society 5.0. *Wseas transactions on business and economics, 10,* 269–277.

Olshanska, O. V., Oleshko, A. A., & Shatska, Z. Ya. (2022). Intellectualization of socio-economic development of Ukraine in the perspective of post-war recovery: monogr., Kyiv: KNUTD, 340. https://er.knutd.edu.ua/handle/123456789/20411

Osinski, M., Selig, P.M., Matos, F., & Roman, D.J. (2017). Methods of evaluation of intangible assets and intellectual capital. *Journal of Intellectual Capital, 18*(3), 470–485.

Revak, I. (2008). Intellectual security is an integral component of Ukraine's national security. *Management of Development: A Collection of Scientific Articles, 6,* 70–73.

Ramcharan, R. (2005). Intellectual property and security: A preliminary exploration. *Contemporary Security Policy, 26*(1), 126–159.

Speigel, I. (2021). Adopting and improving a new forecasting paradigm. *Intelligence and National Security, 36*(7), 961–977.

Ministry of Education and Science of Ukraine. (2023). *State budget for 2023: Expenditure on education and science.* https://mon.gov.ua/ua/news/derzhbyudzhet-na-2023-rik-vidatki-na-osvitu-ta-nauku

WIPO. (2022). Global Innovation Index 2022 published. State Enterprise "Ukrainian Intellectual Property Institute" (UIPI). https://ukrpatent.org/uk/news/main/wipo-global-innovation-index-2022-29092022

Mihajril Nikolaev[1,*], and Ilgiz Nurtdinov[1,2]

The Relationship of Globalization with the Mechanisms of Economic Growth in the World Economic System

Abstract:
Research background: The relationship of globalization with the mechanisms of economic growth has been studied by many authors who have obtained important results. However, the conditions of the growing imbalance in the world economy, provoked by the growth of international tension, require new approaches to the problem and form the basic premise of the study. Other prerequisites are related to the contradictory nature of the impact of globalization itself on economic growth, which depends on many uncertain factors.
Purpose of the article: Is to study and describe the mechanism of the impact of globalization on economic growth.
Methods: Historical analysis, abstract-logical approach, economic analysis.
Findings & Value added: The nature of the impact of globalization on economic growth is determined by the unity of its internal components mentioned above. A new equilibrium model of globalization should be built on this basis. Today, the correlation between the economic and political components of globalization is broken, the economies of many countries have become "hostages" of political decisions. In the new model of globalization, the place and role of each of the components should be strictly defined. The positive and negative impact of globalization on economic growth is determined by the level of its internal imbalance. The higher it is, the more pronounced the contradiction between globalization and the integral properties of economic systems, which has a negative impact on economic growth.

Keywords: *globalization, economic growth, world economy, factors of globalization, inconsistency of globalization*

JEL Classification: *F15; F63; O19; P51*

* Corresponding author: mnikolae@yandex.ru

1 Russian University of Cooperation, Kazan Cooperative Institute (Branch), Faculty of Economics and Customs, Department of Economics and Management, 420081, Kazan, Russia

2 Kazan State Medical University, Department of Economic Theory and Social Work, 420012, Kazan, Russia

1 Introduction

At the end of the XIX century, the rapidly developing trade relations between the countries began to integrate rapidly into the world economy, into the sphere of production and finance, marking essentially a new stage in the development of internationalization processes – the economic component of globalization which was in particular one of the main factors not only of development, but also of recovery in the post-war period in the XX century of many national economic systems, and later – the determining factor of their economic growth. Their integral part has become international trade not only in goods, but also in a variety of services important for peoples and states, the reduction and elimination of relevant economic and legal barriers, the widespread attraction of foreign investment, international cross-country financial flows. The processes of regionalization as well as the creation of bodies and institutions of supranational governance began to expand more and more clearly (Dix-Carneiro et al., 2023; Xu, 2023).

One of the main drivers of the economic component of globalization was technological progress combined with innovations which made it possible to significantly reduce the cost of international transportation and communications. This decline in turn has made it possible for today to actually change the status of many goods that could not be traded on a global scale until recently. Now trade between countries can go perishable vegetables and fruits, freshly cut flowers, live fish, etc. At the same time, the significant role in the development of the economic component of globalization is still played by the geographical, spatial, location of States and the distance between them (Babina et al., 2023; Akcigit et al., 2022).

And it's not just about the cost of transportation. Much depends on the presence of historical, linguistic and cultural proximity and community of countries and peoples inhabiting them (the cultural component of globalization), on the stability of not only their economic, but also socio-political ties. If such are the case, then the information barriers of the economic component of globalization are decreasing which leads in particular to the emergence of geographical agglomerations in industry, to regional concentration of production and ultimately to a significant increase in productivity and labor efficiency (Saittakari et al., 2023; Hajro et al., 2023).

If the above-mentioned proximity is absent, then there are more or less pronounced barriers to further deepening of globalization. Thus, the abundance of languages and language groups as well as diverse national cultures in the EU countries is undoubtedly one of the significant reasons for the incompleteness of its full economic integration (Do et al., 2023).

In this regard, we also note the important role of the political component of globalization which manifests itself primarily in the deepening and comprehensive development of bilateral and multilateral relations as well as in the improvement of diplomatic ties between States. Today globalization is a phenomenon that covers almost all aspects of people's lives and society which certainly contributes to the simplified movement of goods, services and finance in the world, cultural exchanges, the free dissemination of political and other ideas and knowledge. In this world any shocks and events, economic, cultural or political, developing in one country, inevitably affect the processes taking place in the entire world economy and other countries and determine their economic and political stability.

There is still no consensus in science on the problems, contradictions and the future of globalization. There are disputes in particular about how and through what mechanisms globalization affects economic growth in developed and through which in developing countries, what are the ways of its influence on the political and social stability of various countries. The issues of resolving the complications those are possible in the process of forming a unified world economy as well as those world problems that only globalization can solve are considered (Cui et al., 2023; Mihaylova & Buyanova, 2008).

The purpose of the article is to study and describe the mechanisms of the impact of globalization on economic growth (Nikolaev & Belyakin, 2016; Makarova & Nurtdinov, 2018).

In the course of the study, a number of tasks were considered:

- clarification of the essence of the globalization process from the point of view of the topic under consideration;
- analysis of the nature of the impact of globalization on the process of economic growth in conditions of economic balance and imbalance;
- identification of mechanisms of influence of integration processes on economic growth and global competitiveness;
- analysis of institutional changes (on the example of the Russian economy) necessary to ensure economic growth.

2 Methods

A number of scientific research methods were used in the work:

- the method of historical and economic approach and analysis which allowed us to consider the impact of globalization in the world economic system and individual countries on the processes of economic growth both in a logical and temporal sequence;

- the method of system–functional analysis, including the use of graphs and diagrams for a more visual illustration of economic patterns, relationships between individual variables related to issues of economic growth;
- a method of scientific abstraction that allows the researcher to distract from all the secondary, insignificant aspects of the phenomenon under study in order to identify the main thing in the interaction and interrelation of globalization and economic growth.

3 Results and Discussion

3.1 Mechanisms of the Impact of Globalization on the Processes of Economic Growth, Depending on the Level of Economic Balance

The impact of globalization on the processes of economic growth until about the 1980s focused mainly on the accumulation of physical capital through the penetration of foreign enterprises into the national economy and partly also capital.

The purpose of such penetration was firstly to achieve maximum profit through investment and then production activities. Secondly, obtaining indirect utility from access to research and development, potential opportunities and information resources of the host country (Rumyantseva & Welch, 2023; Butek & Spuchlakova, 2017).

However, the role of the main "commodity" in the XXI century has shifted from physical capital to knowledge which is very different from physical capital. It usually has a non-competitive nature since its use by an individual or a firm does not exclude the possibility of either simultaneous or subsequent use by other entities, new characteristics for them either to improve existing ones or to create even the same benefits but with significantly lower costs; secondly, the process of developing integration processes in commodity markets, together with the improvement of international trade, creates new incentives for innovation which may increase or decrease depending on whether the scale effect or the effect of competition will be more powerful.

Economists are now creating new models for the global dissemination of knowledge and several possible links between globalization and economic growth are highlighted:

- Firstly, globalization greatly simplifies the flow of knowledge across State borders and barriers. At the same time, foreign ideas become very useful for

creating fundamentally new products, for improving existing ones or creating the same benefits, but at a lower cost;
- Secondly, the development of integration processes in commodity markets together with the improvement of international trade creates new incentives for innovation which may increase or decrease depending on whether the scale effect or the effect of competition will be more powerful (Shenkar et al., 2022; Contractor, 2022);
- Thirdly, globalization and its accompanying international integration affect not only the formation of incentives for the creation of new knowledge and innovations, but also incentives for the spread of new technologies that directly affect the growth of productivity and production efficiency (Len & Winberry, 2023).

The most direct and tangible impact of globalization on the processes of economic growth appears when the knowledge gained in one country can be immediately used to simplify or develop scientific research in another country. Scientists exchange new ideas during meetings at regularly held international conferences. New ideas and knowledge are also disseminated in the process of business operations and in other interactions of specialists.

As for the direct flow of ideas and knowledge from other foreign countries, it can be carried out without personal contacts, but with the help of relevant publications as well as reverse engineering. At the same time it should be noted that the process of international dissemination of new ideas and knowledge is still far from its full completion which means that it can be further developed and increase the stock of ideas and knowledge around the world.

To date, a number of models have been proposed that analyze either exogenous, that is, associated with a set of external factors, or endogenous, that is, associated with a set of internal factors, the impact of innovations on economic growth rates.

This is due to the fact that a higher level of human capital development makes it relatively cheaper. With the creation of new technologies, a country has a comparative advantage in the manufacture of differentiated products which it exports in exchange for homogeneous goods, ultimately contributing to the acceleration of economic growth. If similar subsidies occur in a country where the sphere of innovation is less developed and the manufacture of final products prevails, then the pace of economic growth may decrease.

The analysis of the model also shows that if the trade policy of a country with less developed Research & Development has a pronounced protectionist orientation, then it contributes to its economic growth. But the effect will be negative if the country has advantages in Research & Development.

The model also takes into account the permissibility of capital overflow for the purpose of investing in Research &Development, and also predicts under certain conditions, the possibility of the formation of even transnational corporations as they approach the equilibrium trajectory of economic growth.

In recent years, a number of studies have been conducted aimed at studying the patterns and features of the spread of advanced technologies. In particular, it was shown that their constant spread is similar to the creation of new ones, and under certain conditions can be a source of sustainable economic growth. At the same time international integration contributes to the creation of new incentives for investment activity and ensures a strong interaction of globalization with economic growth which largely and directly depends on the degree of economic and political balance of the economic system (Leppaaho et al., 2023).

So, fixing the undoubted positive impact of globalization and its individual components on the processes of economic growth in various countries, we note at the same time the significant complication and disruption of a number of these links in recent years due to the growth of political tension in the world and the actual destruction of the political component of globalization (Miller, 1981).

3.2 Directions of Development and Prospects of Globalization in the Modern World

As you know, the global economy has been experiencing a steady trend of positive economic growth for a very long period of time with a significant impact from globalization. Based on the analysis of the materials of a long-term scientific study conducted by Angus Maddison, the results of which were presented in his work "The World Economy – a thousand-year perspective" (Maddison, 2001), he identified some important long-term global trends in the growth of average income in the world economic system per capita for the period from 1500 to almost 2000 (Figure 1) which clearly shows the nonlinear nature of the dependence. This figure shows the dynamics of global GDP per capita over the selected years 1500, 1820, 1870, 1913, 1950, 1973 and 1998 (in US dollars). This figure shows the dynamics of global GDP per capita over the selected years 1500, 1820, 1870, 1913, 1950, 1973 and 1998 (in US dollars).

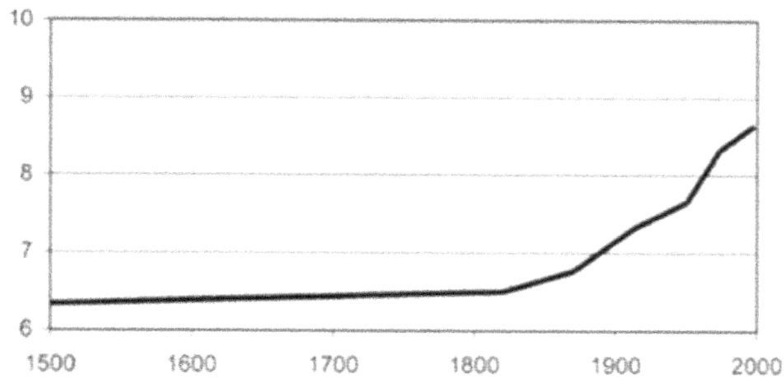

Figure 1. World GDP per capita.
Source: Maddison (2001)

Most of this period is characterized by development with relatively small growth. But already at the very beginning of the XIX century the world economy entered the path of steady and soon accelerating growth. This growth over the period 1500–1820 amounted to 18 %, and from 1820 to the present time has grown by more than 750 %. And this growth has not been sustainable. It averaged 0.53 % from 1820 to 1870, and then more than doubled to 1.30 % from 1870 to 1913. Growth declined to 0.91 % during a volatile period that lasted from 1913 to 1950, and then accelerated to an unprecedented 2.93 % from 1950 to 1973. Since that, time growth has declined to 1.33 %, although this period still continued to be the best in the history of mankind. This economic growth was not evenly distributed across various regions of the world economy. In most countries of Western Europe, as well as in its Western colonies (Australia, Canada, New Zealand, USA), economic growth began in the XIX century and has not stopped.

Other regions took a little longer to transition to sustainable economic growth. Thus, many Asian countries were in stagnation until 1950 which was then replaced by rapid development and became one of the fastest growing regions of the world. However, many African countries are still unable to decisively change the situation in their favor and provide more acceptable growth rates that could be considered at least modest for other countries and regions. Therefore, another characteristic feature of the process of economic growth is its uneven geographical distribution: in each period there are some lagging regions.

Thus, we see that one of the most important features of economic growth is its unevenness in geographical terms which is associated with many specific economic and political reasons.

3.3 Interaction of Traditional and Non-traditional (Non-equilibrium) Factors of Economic Growth

The most important task of the modern world economy is to ensure optimal rates of its economic growth. The problem of its transition to a new development trajectory must necessarily correspond to two key priorities:

- the first one is connected with the stability of the new trajectory, which must necessarily have significant innovative potential, including in the medium and long term, which is necessary to prevent new global crises (Abel, 1981; Okuno & Yakita, 1981);
- the second is the ability of the named new trajectory to ensure high rates of economic growth. This condition provides first of all for the effective development of entrepreneurship and the creation of an appropriate favorable environment. Simultaneous compliance with these priorities is a complex task that requires the search for fair solutions.

The traditional approach to the structure of world GDP is the main basis for determining the four current and future potential growth areas of the modern world economic system:

- agriculture based on digital modernization of production;
- industry based on the formation of a new industry 4.0;
- innovations, the prospects of which are aimed at high-tech production (Makarova & Nurtdinov, 2018);
- the service sector, the future prospects of which are tied to the development of e-commerce.

These areas should be considered through the prism of growth potential, growth sustainability, risk level and probability. They do not necessarily have to be alternative, their comprehensive implementation will make it possible to achieve the greatest efficiency of economic growth and development of the modern world economy. Thus, the described model of multipolar development is designed to ensure the emergence of a synergetic effect as a factor of additional acceleration and balance of economic growth (Erero, 2021).

Balanced growth of the world economy is one of the main global goals today. However, the current trends in its development not only do not stimulate, but even hinder the achievement of this goal, in particular, increasing the imbalances in the economy and growth trends of developed and developing countries. An example here is the lack of financial resources with developing countries. Although many of them have financial (technological, natural, human) resources, however, their effective use is not achieved due to insufficient investment attractiveness. Another trend is the interest of international organizations in interacting primarily with developed countries. Because of this developing countries do not receive additional preferences. Full-scale cooperation with international organizations is difficult for a developing country which narrows their economic growth potential.

The third trend is the growing differences in the rates of innovative development of these countries. Developed countries are actively implementing breakthrough technologies creating competitive advantages for themselves while many developing countries are not involved in the fourth industrial revolution 4.0 at all. Developing within the boundaries of the old technological way, they are increasingly losing their global competitive advantages. This also includes the imbalance in the growth rates of developed and developing countries as well as the lack of prospects for its reduction (Lee et al., 2023).

4 Conclusions

The research done including theoretical research as well as the analysis of practical materials allows us to draw a number of the following conclusions:

- The impact of globalization on economic growth is a complex and multifaceted process that is implemented through a variety of mechanisms and institutions. Until the mid1980s. it was largely carried out through the mechanisms of accumulation of physical capital, but by now this role has shifted to the accumulation of knowledge. In addition, today it is largely determined by the balance (equilibrium) between the internal components of the globalization process – economic and political globalization.
- In today's world, the normal correlation between the economic and political components of globalization is distorted and sharply disrupted, so that the economies of many countries have actually become "hostages" of not always justified and justified political decisions that cause damage to all states.
- The positive and negative impact of globalization on economic growth is also determined by the dynamics of its interaction with the fundamental (integral) characteristics of economic systems: their integrity, the violation of which is fraught with the possibility of inefficient systems with an oligarchic structure; the uncertainty of their initial quantitative parameters and the property of factuality (self-similarity), which consists in the formation of stable characteristics of the system, invariant with respect to any transformations, which can be interpreted as preserving the self-identity of the system under any conditions.

References

Abel, A. B. (1981). A dynamic model of investment and capacity utilization. *The Quarterly Journal of Economics, 96*(3), 379–403.

Akcigit, U., Grigsby, J., Nicholas, T., & Stantcheva, S. (2022). Taxation and innovation in the twentieth century. *The Quarterly Journal of Economics, 137*(1), 329–385.

Babina, T. et al. (2023). Changing the structure of world trade: Immediate and long-term consequences of bank failures. *Quarterly Journal of Economics, 137*(4), 895–954.

Butek, M., & Spuchlakova, E. (2017). The role of nation state in globalized economy. *Conference Globalization and Its Socio-economic Consequences.* 234–239.

Contractor, F. J. (2022). The world economy will need even more globalization in the post-pandemic 2021 decade. *Journal of International Business Studies*, 1–16.

Cui, V., Vertinsky, I., Wangyi, Y., & Zhou, D. (2023). Division in international business: The "new" vulnerability of globalization and MNE response strategies. *Journal of International Business Research, 54*(8), 1562–1576.

Dix-Carneiro, R., Pessoa, J. P., Reyes-Heroles, R., & Traiberman, S. (2023). Globalization, trade imbalances, and labor market adjustment. *The Quarterly Journal of Economics, 138*(2), 1109–1171.

Do, J. P., Eden, L., Cui, A. S., & Zahir, S. (2023). Developing international business scholarships for global impact on society. *Journal of International Business Research, 54*(5), 757–767.

Erero, J. L. (2021). Contribution of VAT to economic growth: A dynamic CGE analysis. *Journal of Economics and Management, 43*(1), 22–51.

Hajro, A., Brewster, C., Haak-Saheem, W., & Morley, M. J. (2023). Global migration: Implications for international business scholarship. *Journal of International Business Studies, 54*(6), 1134–1150.

Lee, J. Y., Kim, D., Choi, B., & Jiménez, A. (2023). Early evidence on how Industry 4.0 reshapes MNEs' global value chains: The role of value creation versus value capturing by headquarters and foreign subsidiaries. *Journal of International Business Studies*, 1–32.

Len, T. C., & Winberry, T. (2023). Investment network, industry interaction, and the changing business cycle in the United States. *Journal of Economics and Management, 137*(4), 387–433.

Leppaaho, T., Mainela, T., & Paavilainen-Mäntymäki, E. (2023). Opportunity beliefs in internationalization: A microhistorical approach. *Journal of International Business Studies*, 1–15.

Maddison, A. (2001). *The World Economy – a thousand-year perspective.* ОЭСР. 383.

Makarova, E. S., & Nurtdinov, I. I. (2018). Evaluating the innovative capacity of the region as a regional growth tool. *Conference Globalization and Its Socio-economic Consequences.* 2220–2228.

Mihaylova, V. A., & Buyanova, V.S. (2008). *Globalization.* 543.

Miller, S. (1981). The nonequilibrium macroeconomic model: A correction. *Journal of Economics and Management, 96*(4), 197–198.

Nikolaev, M., & Belyakin, A. (2016). Impact of globalization on the sustainable development of economic systems in the context of economic disequilibrium. *Conference Globalization and Its Socio-economic Consequences.* 1512–1520.

Okuno, N., & Yakita, A. (1981). Public investment and income distribution: A note. *The Quarterly Journal of Economics, 96*(1), 171–176.

Rumyantseva, M., & Welch, C. (2023). Redefining the born global and international new enterprise: An alternative explanation for early and rapid internationalization. *Journal of International Business Research, 54*(8), 1193–1221.

Saittakari, I., Ritvala, T., Piekkari, R., Kähäri, P., Moisio, S., Hanell, T., & Beugelsdijk, S. (2023). A review of location, politics, and the multinational corporation: Bringing political geography into international business. *Journal of International Business Studies*, 1–27.

Shenkar, O., Liang, G., & Shenkar, R. (2022). The last frontier of globalization: Trade and foreign direct investment in healthcare. *Journal of International Business Studies*, 53(2), 362–374.

Xu, C. (2023). Changing the structure of world trade: Immediate and long-term consequences of bank failurespp. *Quarterly Journal of Economics, 137*(4), 2107–2161.

Andrey Novikov[1,*], Elena Korostyshevskaya[1], and Natalya Gagulina[2]

Increasing the Sustainability of Development of Organizations in the Context of Global Instability

Abstract:
Research background: The slowdown in the world economy, which has been occurring over the past few years, is a consequence of global instability. Global problems: peace and war, interaction between man and nature, growth in the consumption of natural resources and their exhaustibility, wealth and poverty, have become a kind of hotbed of instability and require more and more attention from society and business. The relevance of the chosen topic is due to the need to find tools that can improve the state of the organization in the face of increasing pressure from problems that give rise to global instability.
Purpose of the article: The purpose of the study is to form a methodological basis for creating conditions in the organization that prevent the influence of global instability conditions on its state or mitigate the consequences of this instability.
Methods: The work was accompanied by the use of general scientific methods: analysis and synthesis, deduction and induction, detailing, comparison, analogy, scientific abstraction, and logical laws. The methodological base of the study is based on the use of a systematic approach, causal and functional-structural analysis, on the application of the methodological approach of the economy of quality, integrating standardization, metrology, and quality management.
Findings & Value added: In the course of the research, the application of ESG principles to improve the sustainability of organizations was substantiated. An approach was proposed and substantiated for the formation of an organization's sustainable development strategy the and analysis of its implementation by indicators.

Keywords: *economy, global problems, sustainable development, organizations, quality of life*

JEL Classification: *L2; R13; Q56*

* Corresponding author: a.novikov@spbu.ru

1 St. Petersburg State University, Faculty of Economics, 7/9 Universitetskaya nab., St. Petersburg, 199034 Russia

2 Institute for Regional Economic Studies, Russian Academy of Sciences Leading researcher 38, Serpuhovskaya str., Saint Petersburg, 190013, Russia

1 Introduction

According to the International Monetary Fund, in 2023, there is a decline in global economic growth to 3 % (World Economic Outlook Update, 2023). The slowdown in the world economy, which has been occurring over the past few years, is a consequence of global instability. Global problems have become peculiar centers of instability: peace and war, interaction between man and nature, growth in the consumption of natural resources and their exhaustibility, wealth and poverty. Human activities have a huge impact on the planetary balance: the average air temperature, sea level changes, which in the future can seriously change the conditions of life on Earth. Today it has been proven that the causes of the observed changes lie in the economic and anthropogenic activities of mankind, and inaction in this area leads to natural disasters, social crises, and increases the mortality rate (Carleton, 2022; Yu et al., 2023).

Global problems require more and more attention from the scientific community, society and business, as well as people who are not indifferent to the prospects for future development. To solve them, the joint efforts of different countries, companies and each person individually are needed. We mentioned earlier about the search for a solution on a global scale, which has more than half a century of existence and takes place within the framework of the concept of sustainable development (Zhulega et al., 2018).

Sustainable development is one of the paradigms on which the institutional mechanism of intercountry cooperation is based. A new step in the implementation of the principles of the concept of sustainable development was made in 2015, which was marked by the year of the adoption of 17 sustainable development goals (hereinafter referred to as SDGs, Goals) by the UN General Assembly (196 countries) (Promoting sustainable development, 2023). Measures to achieve the SDGs by 2030 are included by the participating countries in their internal national programs and involve a significant contribution of business to sustainable development.

As shown in a study (Catalin et al., 2022), for transition and developing countries, the contribution of business communities to the SDGs is of great importance. At the business level, the UN Global Compact has been developed – an international initiative in the field of corporate social responsibility and sustainable development. The agreement includes 10 principles divided into 4 groups: human rights, labor relations, environment, anti-corruption, which describe the responsibility of business in the field of sustainable development. These principles become decisive when criating a sustainable development strategy for companies.

2 Working-out of a Strategy for Sustainable Development in the Organization

In the generally accepted understanding, a sustainable development strategy for organizations is a component basis of the company's overall strategy, reflecting the compliance of individual business processes, as well as the overall result of the company's activities, with the key principles of sustainable development. Global instability threatens the activities of companies (Altunyan & Kotcofana, 2022) and contributes to the emergence of unstable forms and structures, which, if they arise, do not persist in the long term. Both the state and business are interested in reducing the level of uncertainty and in finding solutions to the problems of global instability.

At the institutional level in Russia, a number of documents have been developed and adopted aimed at defining the key principles of sustainable development and creating conditions for sustainable business development:

- GOST R 54598.1-2015. National standard of the Russian Federation. Management of sustainable development. Part 1. Guidelines (GOST R, 2015);
- GOST R 58531-2019. National standard of the Russian Federation. Organization management. Guidelines for the implementation of sustainable management in small and medium-sized enterprises (GOST R, 2019);
- Decree of the Government of the Russian Federation of September 21, 2021 No. 1587 "On approval of the criteria for sustainable (including green) development projects in the Russian Federation and requirements for the verification system for sustainable (including green) development projects in the Russian Federation";
- Decree of the Government of the Russian Federation of July 14, 2021 No. 1912-r "On approval of the goals and main directions of sustainable (including green) development of the Russian Federation";- Decree of the Government of the Russian Federation of October 29, 2021 N 3052-r "On the Strategy for the Social and Economic Development of the Russian Federation with Low Greenhouse Gas Emissions until 2050";
- Letters of the Bank of Russia No. 06–52/2463 dated April 10, 2014 "On the Corporate Governance Code" and No. 06-52/2825 dated March 30, 2015;
- -•Information letter of the Bank of Russia No. IN-06-28/111 dated July 15, 2020 "On recommendations for implementing the principles of responsible investment";
- Information letter of the Bank of Russia dated 12/16/2021 No. IN-06-28/96 "On recommendations for the board of directors of a public joint-stock

company to take into account ESG factors, as well as sustainable development issues";- Information letter of the Bank of Russia dated December 27, 2021 No. IN-06-28/102 "On disclosure in the annual report of a public joint-stock company of a report on compliance with the principles and recommendations of the Corporate Governance Code."

Following the principles of sustainable development and the provisions contained in the regulatory framework in this area is necessary to maintain the competitive position of business and use growth opportunities in the face of global instability, which for organizations is expressed in the growth of uncertainty in the external environment. The risks associated with increased uncertainty are expressed in the orientation of the company's activities to a greater extent on short-term goals than on long-term ones, in the fragmentation of the interests of decision-makers, a decrease in the efficiency and competitiveness of the business. The desire to prevent the negative consequences of associated risks motivates businesses to develop a sustainable development strategy.

The sustainable development strategy, like any document of a strategic orientation, has a certain target orientation, strategic priorities in the field of urgent problems of sustainable development. Based on the three-component measurement of these problems accepted in world practice, in our study, under the problems of sustainable development, we understand the problems of an economic, social and environmental nature (Falk et al., 2018).

Methodologically, when choosing the goals, objectives and composition of strategic measures, financial, logistical, organizational, legal and other conditions are taken into account. In the future, with the emergence of new factors (in our case, factors aimed at sustainable business development), the scenario conditions for the implementation of the company's strategy are adjusted. The need to take into account in detail a large number of factors and conditions that affect the position of the company and the implementation of the strategy in the future causes corresponding methodological difficulties.

To overcome the difficulties that arise in the development of strategic planning decisions, the cause-and-effect approach helps, the implementation of which in practice comes down to three procedures:

1 full and coordinated consideration of the factors influencing the solution of the problems of sustainable development;
2 establishing the relationship and synergy of the factors to be taken into account;

3 differentiated, coordinated and adequate choice of methods for solving problems, taking into account the influencing factors.

The application of the cause-and-effect approach makes it possible to systematically combine all the procedures and documents of strategic planning, align them and obtain the optimal solution to management tasks in line with sustainable development (Bierbrauer & Boyer, 2016).

All the variety of factors that must be taken into account in a company's sustainable development strategy in order to achieve the maximum positive effect from its implementation is subject to the influence of objective processes occurring in nature and society (the simplest example is weather and climate conditions), as well as institutional conditions that determine priorities and mechanisms for their implementation, etc. Accounting for these factors allows you to take strategic measures in advance to prevent damage to the reputation or competitive status of the company. In addition, establishing the relationship and cumulative influence of factors affecting the solution of sustainable development problems contributes to the formation of the company's strategic advantages based on a synergistic effect (Novikov & Gregova, 2017). An example of this is network structures, large diversified companies, etc.

The next step is the development of activities and the implementation of specific steps aimed at following the principles of sustainable development in the strategy of organizations. This is where the sustainability experience of foreign companies such as NVIDIA, Best Buy, Microsoft (with the highest AAA rating in the MSCI rating), which are considered standard setters in the ESG direction (High ESG-rated stocks, 2023), can come in handy. The top 5 ESG ranking of Russian companies (at the beginning of 2023) of the rating agency RAEKS-Analytics LLC are headed by NLMK PJSC, Polyus PJSC, Enel Russia PJSC, Uralkali PJSC, Polymetal JSC (Ranking : ESG ranking of Russian companies, 2023).

In the course of this study, the authors conducted a survey among representatives of Russian business and identified the main problematic points present in the development of a sustainable development strategy. As the analysis of the obtained data showed, the development of a sustainable development strategy for a single organization requires solving problems related to the formation of the theoretical basis of such a strategy, determining the need for a sustainable development strategy and the need to coordinate it with the main activities of the company, and, finally, with the formation of this strategy, substantiating its economic result (Franzi, 2018).

Respondents identified the main activities that they focus on when creating sustainability. Among them:

- allocation of sustainable development into a separate line of business of the company and fixing it at the structural and functional level;
- making changes to the current business strategy of the company, taking into account the provisions of the strategy developed, adopted and approved by ESG;
- making new time values, such as diversity, equality of opportunity and inclusiveness, among the company's priorities, reflecting them in the company's portrait;
- formation of a portfolio of projects aimed at reducing the company's social and environmental risks;
- creating an additional competitive advantage by making ethically impeccable business decisions in accordance with the principles of openness and transparency;
- development of a set of measures to optimize the resources used on the basis of the introduction of an automated system for collecting initial data;
- formation and implementation of flexible business models capable of adapting under the influence of factors that determine sustainable development in the future;
- interconnection of business areas and increasing the efficiency of cross-functional interactions when using resources and optimizing investment flows.

Thus, the practice of implementing the principles of sustainable development is becoming increasingly important for companies striving for sustainability. As international studies in the field of management methodology show (Bergh et al., 2022), at the methodological level, a significant role is played by the choice of tools that allow you to competently approach the choice of strategic tasks.

3 Selection of Indicators for the Sustainable Development Strategy and Evaluation of the Effectiveness of Its Implementation

Evaluation of the effectiveness of the strategy involves a set of indicators by which one can judge the achievement of strategic goals and the solution of tactical tasks. At the same time, the company is guided by the "coordinate system" of sustainability in which it is located. The problem is that in the practice of Russian companies there are three similar in essence, but different in content approaches to understanding achievements in the field of sustainable development (Figure 1).

Figure 1. Classification of sustainable development goals in the framework of non-financial reporting systems.

Source: Own processing

The Sustainable Development Goals replaced the Millennium Development Goals and outlined the priorities for the global transformation of the world until 2030 at the level of 17 goals that ensure a balance of economic, social and environmental sustainable development on a global scale.

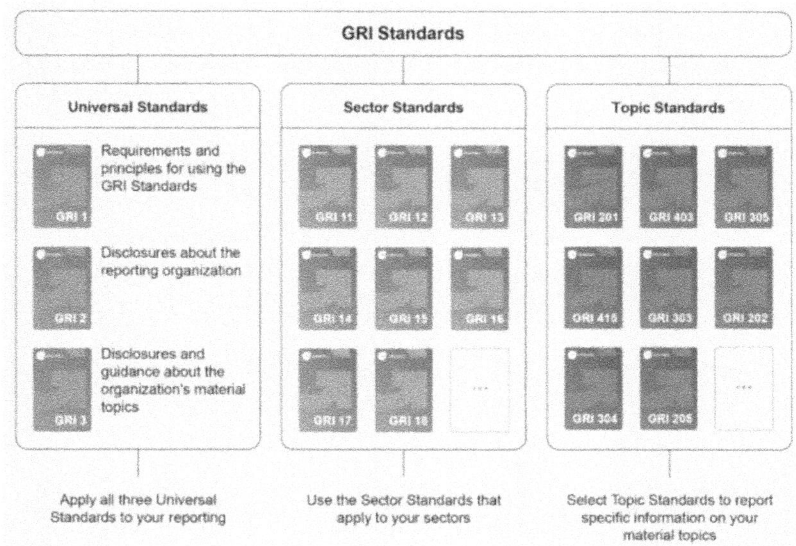

Figure 2. GRI Standards System (GRI – Standards).

Source: www.globalreporting.org

The Global Reporting Initiative (GRI) reporting system does not have such a long history as the SDGs – its practice begins in 2000. GRI standards are of great importance for investors, politicians and civil society (GRI, n.d.). The system of these standards is built on the principle of "from general to specific" and allows you to form a complete picture of the most significant areas of activity for the company, the impacts associated with them and their management (Figure 2).

The global standards for sustainability impacts make it possible to detail certain aspects of the impact on sustainability, which makes information about the company more transparent and makes it easier for investors and other stakeholders to make decisions. Among such aspects are economics, management, ecology.

Often the principles of sustainable development are identified with the ESG principles, which in a broad sense mean sustainable business development, which is based on the principles of a responsible attitude to the environment, social responsibility and a high level of corporate governance (Zhulega et al. 2019).

In our opinion, a good help for companies in the field of sustainable development characteristics is ISO Guide 82: 2019 – Guidelines for addressing sustainability in standards (ISO Guide 82, 2019). Here are some concepts of this guide that are necessary for developing a strategy for sustainable development of the company (Figure 3).

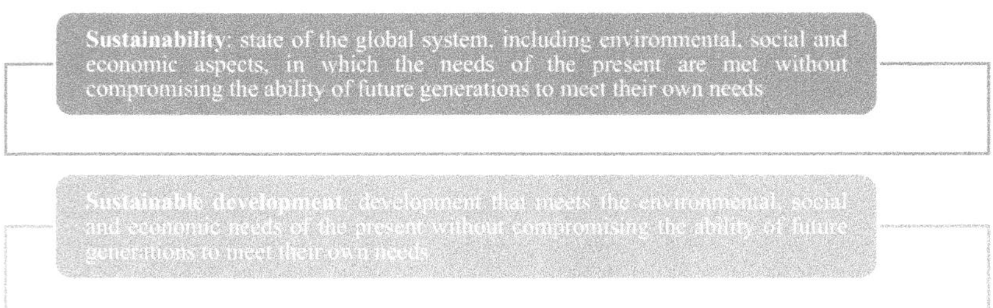

Figure 3. Sustainability according to ISO Guide 82:2019.
Source: Own processing according to ISO Guide 82

ISO Guide 82:2019 (ISO Guide 82, 2019) provides a step-by-step process for identifying and addressing sustainability issues in three dimensions: social, environment and economic. Each measurement is detailed by composition (Figure 4).

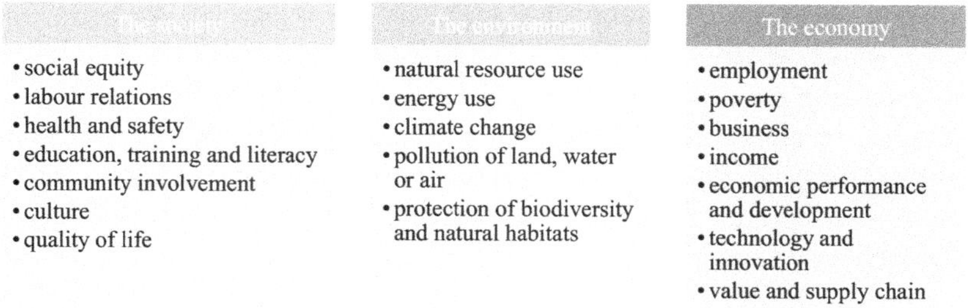

Figure 4. Potential areas for shaping a company's sustainability strategy.
Source: Own processing according to ISO Guide 82

Stakeholders today expect companies to have targets as a sign of commitment to results. As shown in Figure 4, companies have a very wide choice of areas to shape their sustainability strategy. This is both an advantage and a problem. On the positive side, it is possible to concentrate in the area where the company can get the best result, while maintaining sustainability in its activities. The reverse side of the wide possibilities of choice can be the problem of the optimality of choice. In both cases, it is necessary to choose your key performance indicators, which are the basis for evaluating the effectiveness of the strategy, which must be formulated and adopted.

For the purposes of the study, the authors developed the following definition. The company's sustainable development strategy is a set of goals, objectives and activities that does not contradict the main mission of the company, consistent with the development strategy and focused on achieving balance in three dimensions: social, environment and economic. Based on this definition, the company's sustainable development goals are set and indicators corresponding to them are developed. In this case, the industry affiliation of the company is very important, as it affects the choice of resources and technology, determines the impact on the environment and, in some cases, social aspects. Of particular importance in developing and following a sustainable development strategy is the use of a quality economy methodology focused on the unity of metrology, standardization and quality management (Okrepilov, 2021; , 2022).

In the Russian Federation at the beginning of 2023, among the top five sustainable development leaders (according to the rating agency RAEKS-Analytics LLC): PJSC NLMK, PJSC Polyus, PJSC Enel Russia, PJSC Uralkali, JSC Polymetal . In our opinion, LUKOIL Group is a good example of successful activity in the formation and implementation of a sustainable development strategy. From the company's reporting (LUKOIL – Sustainable Development, 2023) it follows that sustainable development is not only organically integrated into the mission and policy of the LUKOIL Group, but is also consistent with the Sustainable Development Goals (SDGs). As shown in Figure 5, the company's internal sustainable development goals systemically affect the achievement of the global Sustainable Development Goals.

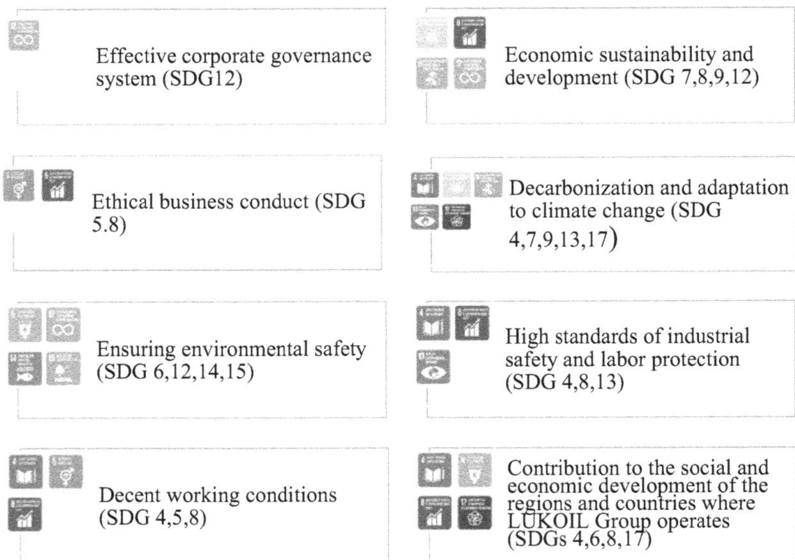

Figure 5. Sustainable Development Goals of the LUKOIL Group.

Source: www.lukoil.ru

The LUKOIL Group uses several reporting systems. Among them are both international and Russian reporting systems recommended by the Russian Union of Industrialists and Entrepreneurs (RSPP). Among the international ones are the Global Reporting Initiative (GRI) mentioned above, as well as Sustainability Accounting Standards Board (SASB), International Petroleum Industry Environmental Conservation Association (IPIECA), United Nations Conference on Trade and Development (UNCTAD). In addition, the World Bank Initiative "Zero Routine Flaring of Associated Petroleum Gas by 2030" was taken into account.

Such a wide coverage of reporting systems made it possible to group the indicators in the LUKOIL Group's sustainable development strategy into four sections: Climate, Environmental and industrial safety, Social aspects, Management. Each section has subsections with a corresponding set of indicators, in total – 604 units. (Table 1). The period for which the monitoring and calculation of indicators of the sustainable development strategy in the company was carried out: 2018–2022. Note that not all indicators have complete data series, which is associated with the constant improvement of their accounting system in the company.

Table 1. Grouping of ESG data of the LUKOIL Group.

Section	Section	Number of indicators
Climate	Greenhouse gases	34
	Energy	56
Environmental and industrial safety	Integrated control system	23
	Water	107
	Emissions	60
	Land and Waste	76
	Industrial safety	22
Social aspects	Labor protection	29
	Information about employees	164
Governance	Corporate governance	33

Source: authors

Summing up the analysis of the sustainable development strategy in a single company, we can draw the following general conclusions:

- in the context of global instability, following the principles of sustainable development is the key to maintaining market positions and improving performance;
- the development and implementation of a sustainable development strategy in the company is not limited to any one system of non-financial reporting;
- to assess the company's contribution to the achievement of the global Sustainable Development Goals, it is necessary to carry out large-scale work on the formation of systems of indicators, their monitoring and analysis.

4 Results and Discussion

Global instability means for organizations an increase in the uncertainty of the external environment and the need to take into account the risks associated with it. The state has developed an institutional mechanism that facilitates the choice of sustainable business development solutions. However, the very reduction of greenhouse gas emissions may be almost impossible without a green transition – a significant transformation of consumption and production patterns (Besley & Persson, 2023). It is in this direction that the sustainable development strategy developed and adopted by companies should find application. As the study conducted by the authors showed, the need to take into account in detail all the factors and conditions that determine the future of the company in the coordinate system of sustainable development causes methodological difficulties. To overcome the identified difficulties, the application of the cause-and-effect approach, as well as the theoretical and methodological approach of the economy of quality, seems to be the most appropriate.

The authors propose a definition from which a company should build on when forming its strategic priorities in the context of global instability. The company's sustainable development strategy is a set of goals, objectives and activities that does not contradict the main mission of the company, consistent with the development strategy and focused on achieving balance in three dimensions: social, environment and economic.

As the analysis of sustainability reporting by Russian companies, including the LUKOIL Group, has shown, it is expedient to solve emerging methodological difficulties in a complex, based on the recommendations of existing non-financial reporting systems. Such an approach is further useful in the formation of a set of indicators for assessing the effectiveness of a company's sustainable development strategy, and for assessing its consistency with the global Sustainable Development Goals.

5 Conclusion

The formation of a sustainable development strategy as a component of the main strategy will allow the company to strengthen its position due to intangible benefits, which in the future will serve as the foundation for improving its economic performance.

The approach to developing a sustainable development strategy formed in the course of the study can be recommended for practical application in companies that comprehensively analyze all areas of their activities. In the context of global instability that has gripped the entire world economy, this approach will reduce risks and costs, strengthen the brand of the organization, increase efficiency and increase the overall value of the company.

References

Altunyan A., & Kotcofana, T. (2022). The year 2022: The economic policy in the new reality. *Proceedings of the 22th International Scientific Conference of Globalization and its Socio-Economic consequences. Rajecke Teplice, Slovak Republic*, 11–18.

Bergh, D. D., Boyd, B. K., Byron, K., Gove, S., & Ketchen, D. J. (2022). What constitutes a methodological contribution? *Journal of Management*, *48*(7), 1835–1848.

Besley, T., & Persson, T. (2023). The political economics of green transitions. *The Quarterly Journal of Economics, 138*(3), 1863–1906.

Bierbrauer, F. J., & Boyer, P. C. (2016). Efficiency, welfare, and political competition. *The Quarterly Journal of Economics, 131*(1), 461–518.

Carleton, T., Jina, A., Delgado, M., Greenstone, M. Houser, T. Hsiang, S. Hultgren, A., Kopp, R. E., McCusker, K. E., Nath, I., Rising, J., Rode, A., Seo, H. K., Viaene, A., Yuan, J., & Zhang, A. T. (2022). Valuing the global mortality consequences of climate change accounting for adaptation costs and benefits. *The Quarterly Journal of Economics, 137*(4), 2037–2105.

Catalin, D. R., Negescu-Oancea, M. D., Cretu C. R., & Burlacu, S. (2022). Sustainable development and globalization. *Proceedings of the 22th International Scientific Conference of Globalization and its Socio-Economic consequences. Rajecke Teplice, Slovak Republic,* 202–209.

Falk, A., Becker, A., Dohmen, T., Enke, B., & Huffman, D. (2018). Uwe Sunde global evidence on economic preferences. *The Quarterly Journal of Economics, 133*(4), 1645–1692.

Franzi, S. (2018). The great convergence: Information technology and the new globalization. *Journal of Politics*, *80*(1), 40–51.

GOST R 54598.1-2015. National Standard of the Russian Federation. Sustainability management. Part 1. Manual: Approved By order of Rosstandart dated 18.11.2015 No. 1858. Consultant Plus (2023, May 6). https://www.consultant.ru/cons/cgi/online.cgi?req=doc&base=OTN&n=10903#l35r8mTqZWx0UZtx

GOST R 58531-2019. National Standard of the Russian Federation. Organization management. Guidelines for the Implementation of Sustainable Management in Small and Medium Enterprises : Approved By order of Rosstandart dated 12.09.2019 No. 664. Consultant Plus. (2023, May 6) https://www.consultant.ru/document/cons_doc_LAW_ 335226/

GRI. *The global standards for sustainability impacts.* https://www.globalreporting.org/standards/

ISO Guide 82: 2019 – Guidelines for addressing sustainability in standards 07.08.2023. ISO International Organization for Standardization https://www.iso.org/cms/%20 render/live/ru/sites/isoorg/contents/data/standard/07/65/76561.html.

LUKOIL – Sustainable Development. (2023, August 9) https://lukoil.ru/Sustainability

Novikov, A., & Gregova, E. (2017). Institution features of economic development during globalization. *Proceedings of the 17th International Scientific Conference of Globalization and its Socio-Economic consequences. Rajecke Teplice, Slovak Republic,* 1757–1764.

Okrepilov, V. V. (2021). Components of the quality economy as a factor in improving the quality of planning the development of the territory. *Northwest Economy: Challenges and Development Prospects, 3*(66), 52–60.

Okrepilov, V. V. (2022). Quality economics is the most important direction in the development of economic science. *Forecasting Problems, 33*(5), 519–528.

Promotion of sustainable development. (2023, January 17). United Nations. https://www.un.org/ru/our-work/support-sustainable-development-and-climate-action

Ranking: ESG-ranking of Russian companies (at the beginning of 2023) (2023, January 17). RAEX-Analytics LLC https://raex-rr.com/pro/ESG/ESG_companies/ESG_rating_ companies/2023.1/

Shares with a high ESG rating: Where to watch how to choose. BCS Company LLC (2023, January 17). https://bcs-express.ru/novosti-i-analitika/aktsii-s-vysokim-esg-reitingom-gde-smotret-kak-vybirat

World Economic Outlook Update. (2023, July). Near-Term Resilience, Persistent Challenges https://www.imf.org/en/Publications/WEO/Issues/2023/07/10/world-economic-outlook-update-july-2023?CID=sm-com-homepage-WEOET2023004

Yu, H., Bansal, P., & Arjaliès, D. L. (2023). International business is contributing to environmental crises. *Journal of International Business Studies, 54*(6), 1151–1169.

Zhulega, I. A., Gagulina, N. L., & Samoylov. A. V. (2018). Sustainable development under conditions of the sanction world order. *Proceedings of the 18th International Scientific Conference of Globalization and its Socio-Economic consequences. Rajecke Teplice, Slovak Republic*, 468–475.

Zhulega, I. A., Gagulina, N. L., Samoylov, A. V., & Novikov, A. V. (2019). Problems of corporate economics and sustainable development in the context of the sanction world order: Living standards and live quality. *Ekonomicko-manazerske spektrum, 13*(1), 83–95.

Vadim Yurievich Pashkus[1,*], Natalia Anatolievna Pashkus[2], Anna Aleksandrovna Koltsova[1], Ilya Savelyev[1]

Smart City: Development of the Concept and Problems of Implementation in the Global World

Abstract:
Research background: The article discusses the evolution of the concept of the Smart City and the requirements that are imposed on cities at different stages of evolution in order to comply with this concept. The paper shows the prerequisites for the creation of smart cities. The main parameters of a smart city (according to Giffinger) and the intersection of the concept of a smart city with a digital city, a global city, etc. are analyzed. The article provides examples of smart cities (both positive and negative). The paper shows that in the context of urban growth, the most promising cities were cities that actively used natural recreational areas.
Purpose of the article: Evaluation of the competitiveness factors of smart cities and identification of dominant characteristics that affect the competitive position and the possibility of effective promotion in the global world.
Methods: Matrix methods of strategic analysis, competitiveness matrices, Smart City assessment methodology.
Findings & Value added: Various concepts of territorial and urban management, such as "smart city," digital city, global city, and digital urbanism have some elements that unite them. It is emphasized that the integrated use of these intersecting elements of territorial development can ensure the growth of the economic potential and marketing attractiveness of the territories. It is noted that the ratings of smart cities and their competitive positions today do not quite coincide, which requires new approaches to their assessment.

Keywords: *Smart City, city administration, Moscow, city development*

JEL Classification: *O18, M31, M15*

* Corresponding author: v.pashkus@spbu.ru
1 St. Petersburg State University, Universitetskaya nab., 7–9, St. Petersburg, Russia
2 Herzen State Pedagogical University, the Moika river emb., 48.St. Petersburg, Russia

1 Introduction

Today, in the territorial market, as in other markets, there is a fierce competitive struggle for dominance in the minds of consumers and the capital that regions can attract due to the effective positioning of their territories. Moreover, there is competition both at the global level and at the level of countries and even individual regions. Consequently, when developing a development strategy, it is necessary to pay attention not only to the development of the territorial infrastructure of Russian regions, but also to its correct positioning in inseparable connection with the development of a comfortable environment for their territories (Scott, 2016).

The concept of a "smart city" is a global trend, which in turn involves the introduction of innovative technologies into a unified system of urban governance. It can be argued that the concept of a "smart city" is a proven method of more rational use of the resources available in the city, creating a comfortable and safe environment for living in the city, as well as expanding the availability of various services for residents, eliminating inequality and increasing the involvement of residents in the city processes.

The emergence of the smart city concept was largely due to the rapid processes of urbanization and the development of telecommunications technologies. Technological progress in the 1980s and 1990s contributed to an increase in the standard of living and well-being, first of all, of urban residents, which, in turn, attracted even more people to cities and exacerbated existing problems in them (Karagulian et al., 2020).

For example, according to the UN, now about 56 % of the world's population lives in cities. Almost all of the population growth in the future will be due to an increase in the number of urban residents, who, according to forecasts, will account for 60 % of the world's population in 2030, and approximately 68 % by 2050. It should be emphasized that the steady growth of the population of cities is not the determining criterion that influenced the development and dissemination of the concept of a "smart city" on a global scale.

2 Methods

Rapid population growth, in addition to significant pressure on the infrastructure of the city, creates serious threats, which leads to an increase in demand for services, housing facilities exceeding the capacity of cities, as well as irreparable damage to the environment (Attaran, 2022).For this reason, in the early 1990s, the concept of a "smart city," or smart city, began to develop, which became a reaction of society to the growing socio-economic and infrastructural problems of cities associated with traffic congestion, air pollution, loss of open space, overcrowding of schools and the rapid increase in the cost of public services. It was supposed to solve these problems by using a large number of various kinds of sensors embedded in the urban economy, intelligent technologies, applications, big data (Karagulian, 2020). But it is worth paying special attention to the fact that cities are also centers of attraction for people and a platform for both creativity and exchange of opinions. Cities are a condition of cooperation, which is the basis of the greatest success of mankind. Since people learn a lot from others, we learn more when there are more people around. The density of urban life creates a constant flow of new information that arises from observing the successes and failures of others. Cities make it easier to watch, listen and learn (Glazer, 2013).

In addition, the structure of the modern economy is changing. So, for example, in the modern conditions of the restructuring of economic systems caused by the exhaustion of their extensive development factors, the change of technological patterns and, as a consequence, the priorities of social development becomes an objective necessity. There is a return to protectionism all over the world. As a result, the fundamental foundations of the development of national economies are changing. The city becomes the "point of growth" of the modern economy (Ganin & Ganin, 2014).

The COVID-19 pandemic and the subsequent start of the special operation led to significant restrictions on the movement of the population and a decrease in demand from the previously established target groups of visitors and investors of the Russian territories. In these conditions, people especially acutely felt the need for a comfortable urban environment that allows them to spend their free time in harmony with nature without leaving the city. There is an urgent need for the development of new interesting locations for city residents and their visitors, which allow Russian regions to occupy new attractive positions in the territory market and even enter the global market, covering new target segments. For example, this is Kazan, which uses the image of Innopolis in close relationship with the cultural traditions of the region for its development. Further effective development of Russian regions requires a systematic and integrated approach to regional governance. In this regard, the use of the tools of the "smart city" concept opens up fundamentally new opportunities for regional management.

Let's focus on the main aspects of the "smart city" concept. The concept assumes the integrated development of information and communication technologies with the use of "Internet of Things" technologies for the management of urban space and urban property. At the same time, there is a concept of marketing territories, which involves the active use of information and communication technologies for the development of urban infrastructure. This concept involves the use of mechanisms for positioning and promoting territories for all groups of current and potential consumers (residents, potential migrants, enterprises and organizations; tourists and business visitors; investors of regional projects) and stakeholders of the territory interested in its high competitiveness.

The tools of these concepts are largely common. Both concepts are based on similar prerequisites, which made their application acutely necessary. The prerequisites for using the concept of a "smart city" were the following:

- there was an increase in the population of the city, which led to the emergence of transport problems;
- environmental problems have begun to increase, especially with regard to environmental pollution;
- open accessible spaces (parks, squares, squares, etc.) began to shrink and disappear in cities;
- problems often arise in the provision of social services (overcrowded schools, queues at polyclinics, etc.);
- the cost of paid public services began to grow rapidly;
- there has been a complication of city management processes and the transition of processes to the information environment;
- the territories of the city have lost their original purpose.

Prerequisites for the widespread use of modern tools for branding territories are:

- a high level of influence on the competitiveness of the territory of media support and representation of the territory in all media;
- lag in the development of the territory's infrastructure, including its transport, social, environmental components, from the level of their media promotion, leading to gaps in the perception of the territory and urgent negative effects of promotion;
- high dependence of the competitive status of the territory on the presence of a large volume of open spaces and the level of their media competitiveness;
- the high role of intangible assets in the competitiveness of territories;
- rapid growth in the price of a territorial product for all categories of consumers;
- increasing the role of creative and information technologies in the effectiveness of strategic positioning and promotion of the territory;
- high influence of information and digital technologies and tools for promoting the territory on its competitive status.

The identified prerequisites for the use of these concepts of regional development largely contribute to the development of general requirements for the territory and the possibility of choosing a strategy for its development. Because of this, the most competitively successful territories systematically apply a set of tools proposed within the framework of the concepts being studied.

Highlighting the main conceptual provisions of the development of a "smart city," it can be argued that from the point of view of the theory of a smart city:

- "Involves the active use of information and telecommunication technologies to improve the quality of life of urban residents, all groups of visitors to the city and active stakeholders based on the creation of a high-tech and comfortable urban environment" (Karagulian et al., 2020);
- it is considered as a "city of people," and even more – a city characterized by human-centricity (Hollands, 2008);
- involves the use of innovative methods of data collection and analysis in the management of the so–called "Smart City" (digital twin of the city) (Karagulyan et al., 2020);
- focuses on the decentralization of management and the creation of situations that promote the use of the potential of citizens in the development of the city, building relationships of trust and cooperation between urban management bodies and the population (Giffinger et al., 2007).

Thus, the following "smart" factors become the main parameters of a "smart city" (Townsend, 2013; Giffinger et al., 2007):

- economy (competitive intellectual economy – ICT, advanced production, dominance of high-tech and knowledge-intensive services);
- mobility (SMART Mobility) – intelligent mobility with devices, innovative and safe transport systems;
- people (developed social capital, high creativity, cooperation, high level of trust in society);
- management (active participation of the population in decision-making for state and municipal services, the city as a single organism with a high level of digital support);
- environment (intellectual) environment – "sustainable resource management," smart energy, smart buildings, environmental planning;
- lifestyle – high quality of life, security, social cohesion and a high level of trust in society.

These smart city factors are key to the formation of an undeniable competitive advantage and ensuring the strategic competitiveness of the territory (Hollands, 2008; Townsend, 2013). The growing attractiveness of the territory, innovations form the conditions for economic growth (Segerstrom, 1991). The ability to adapt to the conditions of uncertainty and high dynamism of the environment gives the territory a great advantage in the conditions of global competition, and in the future facilitates its further development of urban infrastructure and allows it to form a strong territorial brand (Sassen, 2005).

Based on the above factors determining the competitive status of a "smart city" among cities using the same development concept, it is possible to develop a system of criteria for the competitiveness of a "smart city." The use of such a system of criteria in assessing the marginal coefficients of substitution of each vector criterion will reveal the reciprocal position of "smart cities" on the competitiveness matrix. At the same time, these characteristics will be included in the system of criteria for assessing the competitive status of a "smart city" and will be fixed along the horizontal axis of the matrix, and the vertical axis characterizing the attractiveness of choosing a strategy for the development of the territory will determine the characteristics of the severity of the concept used. Evaluation of the main parameters of the model involves the use of matrix methods of strategic analysis, in particular, the modified methodology of hierarchy analysis.

3 Results: Application of the "smart city" Concept

It should be noted that the proclamation of the territory as a "smart city" and the choice of an appropriate development strategy does not yet mean achieving a targeted effect. Moreover, one of the most important factors hindering the effective integration of all urban structures and digital support systems is the lack of trust between all participants in the system of functioning and management of the territory and their stakeholders. There are also problems with the "possession effect" – their investments seem more valuable, which makes consensus problematic. (Hartzmark et al., 2021) Opposition to integration and conflicts between participants hinder the implementation of the smart city strategy and significantly distort its original intent (Griffiths, 2013).

For example, the strong desire for independence of Catalonia, its policy of reducing unpromising tourists has led to a significant rise in the price of the territory's services while reducing their quality. As a result, there was a decrease in tourist flows, and not only from the category of the least desirable for the territory. At the same time, the disorder in the service sphere began. But Barcelona proclaimed its technological sovereignty and was aimed at increasing the opportunities of citizens in the digital environment. Promising ideas for the development of the territory with the formal application of the concept of a "smart city" turned into a decrease in the competitiveness of the territory and a drop in the strength of its brand.

Another controversial project for the development of a "smart city" is the Sidewalk Toronto project. In accordance with this project, it was planned to:

- "Increase the availability of housing for the majority of citizens" (Garas, 2020);
- "Reduce family transportation costs by $4,000 per year" (Garas, 2020);
- "To abandon the use of own cars inside the city to reduce CO2 emissions" (Karagulian et al., 2020);
- "To introduce eco-friendly and energy-efficient technologies in urban environment" (Garas, 2020);
- "To create thousands of jobs through the development of the high-tech sector" (McCord & Becker, 2019).

Unfortunately, the success of the project is not so indicative. Currently:

- the availability of housing in the city has decreased even more;
- transportation costs of families have increased or have not changed compared to the previous ones;
- when implementing the project, the management of the city is transferred to Google, which pursues exclusively commercial purposes;
- "Digital technologies are used to collect information for the benefit of IT companies without improving the quality of life of citizens" (Garas, 2020).

"Sidewalk Labs tested technologies that nobody needed, the cost of which was quite high for the budget" (McCord & Becker, 2019). As a result, there were simply no funds in the budget for the implementation of other important projects for the city. This had a very negative impact on the functioning of urban systems during the COVID-19 pandemic. Many problems of the city were simply ignored, and data on diseases and deaths were artificially underestimated. It should be noted that "the Sidewalk Labs company, which is a subsidiary of Google, was engaged in the implementation of the smart city technology implementation project. Thus, in this project, Sidewalk Labs focused on Google's goals, and not the needs of the city at all" (Garas, 2020). It can be argued that Sidewalk Labs has turned Toronto into a "test bed" for new technologies, materials, and Google processes, according to which it is used to achieve sustainable growth and prosperity of cities. Thus, Google simply used Toronto as a test site for the development of its technologies with potentially high commercial potential (McCord & Becker, 2019).

A more successful example of the implementation of the "smart city" concept was the new positioning of Moscow. Over the past decade, a new concept of strategic development of the territory has been implemented in Moscow. It is based on the development and implementation of information and communication technologies both in city management and in all areas of city life (Karagulian et al., 2020). Moscow has spent huge sums on the introduction of smart city technologies, as a result, the city has turned into a single information space, and the city's infrastructure has grown and improved significantly.

The Smart City – Moscow – 2030 project is currently being implemented. The mission of the Smart city project is the following:

1 Muscovites should become happier.
2 The city is safe.
3 There should be more green spaces in the city.
4 A prosperous environment should be created for the development of business, the implementation of entrepreneurial activities, the work of scientific and educational communities.
5 Muscovites should become healthier, which implies the implementation of programs aimed at ensuring active longevity of people, including, inter alia, the creation of a genetic passport of a Muscovite.
6 Development of transport and information infrastructure of the city.
7 The city should unite people to improve their quality of life.

Currently, many elements of the project have already been partially or completely implemented. So, for example:

- in 2018, one of the best (according to PricewaterhouseCoopers) intellectual transport systems in the world was launched, which constantly continues to develop, on March 1, 2023, the world's largest metropolitan ring (BCL – the big ring line) was launched;
- in 2011, EMIAS (unified medical information and communication system) was launched analytical system, largely improved during the COVID-19 pandemic;
- a facial recognition system has been launched, modified during the pandemic;
- high camera coverage has been achieved to implement effective information support for the city.

The success of the implementation of the urban concept of the "smart city" of Moscow is also connected with the implementation of constant interaction with Muscovites and guests of the city in search of joint solutions for the development of urban infrastructure and the implementation of the system of urban communications. One of the promising directions of the implementation of the "smart city" concept in Moscow is connected with taking into account the aspirations of residents and guests of the city to enjoy nature without the need to travel outside the city limits. This direction is closely intertwined with one of the priorities of the Smart city project related to the greening of the city. Recently, especially during the COVID-19 pandemic, this component of the project has had a very positive impact on the effective positioning of the city and the strengthening of its brand.

It should be noted that the characteristics of the "smart city" perfectly match the developing needs of the last decade, which were formed and intensified during the pandemic and the period of mass restrictions that followed it, which relate to labor relations, social development, and free time. (Ivanova, 2020; Koshkin, 2021)

These needs include:

- admiring nature;
- striving for a healthy lifestyle;
- visiting ecozones, nature reserves, modern zoos, arboretums and forming a new paradigm of leisure for citizens, which has become commercially attractive;
- an increase in the desire to travel, including for a long-term stay in nature, immersion in a "new" reality for travelers (a different culture, a different environment that provides strong emotional experiences);
- the need for year-round contact with nature and increased accessibility of natural recreation areas and other open spaces that provide a wide variety of experiences.

These needs are based on the previous increase in the standard of living of the population, the release of time for recreation of citizens, as well as the effective use of information and remote technologies (for example, "smart home" or technologies used in housing and communal services). (Kislyakova et al., 2019). As a result, people increasingly want to be able to stay in nature without leaving the city, or to be able to quickly get to nature due to a developed transport system. And this component of urban life is gaining more and more influence in assessing the attractiveness of the territory and forming its strong brand.

The Ministry of Construction of the Russian Federation, together with Moscow State University, has developed an integral index for assessing the progress and effectiveness of the digital transformation of urban economy ("IQ of cities"). This index is used to assess the effectiveness of measures implemented within a specific project and the entire project.

This index includes an analysis of the implementation of the following indicators: urban governance, innovations for the urban environment, intelligent public safety systems, intelligent social services systems, intelligent environmental safety systems, network infrastructure, tourism and service, smart housing and communal services, smart urban transport, economic condition and investment climate. This index also takes into account the population of various cities.

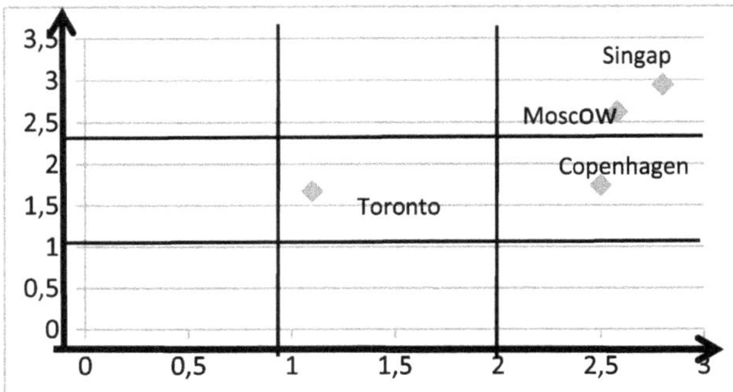

Figure 1. Smart Cities Competitiveness Matrix.
Source: Compiled by the authors

As can be clearly seen, Singapore, Copenhagen and Moscow took the leading positions. Toronto found itself in the most intermediate position, which means that the city either has to abandon the use of the smart city concept and move to some other development strategy, or in the case of further use of the smart city concept, the city should make efforts to move into more attractive areas of the matrix. If Toronto is unable to move into more attractive areas of competitiveness of "smart cities," then in the near future its uncontrolled fall into the field of losers will begin.

Singapore's position coincides with the city's high position in the world rankings of "smart cities," where it is in second place behind Copenhagen. But Copenhagen, although it is in the zone of leaders, but for it the smart city strategy is beginning to lose relevance, which is explained by the increasing price level of public services and the associated drop in their accessibility for residents and visitors of the city. At the same time, Moscow, which is not included in the world rankings of "smart cities," is only slightly inferior in competitive positions to Singapore.

4 Discussion

It is worth noting that within the framework of the topic under consideration, the scientific literature does not pay enough attention to the problems and discussion points that the implementation of the concept of a "smart city" in practice carries.

Firstly, with the declared tasks of a smart city that reduce inequality and increase the availability of services for all residents, regardless of their social status, financial situation, etc., in practice it turns out that inequality between people persists and even increases.

Even today, programmers serving the same Sberbank or Yandex website, within the same qualification category, with the same working day, labor and other conditions, create a relatively equal amount of intellectual product / intellectual services can receive completely different wages (Koshkin & Mokretsov, 2022, p. 4). And for example, electronic registration in the same polyclinics and hospitals is not available for older people who, due to age restrictions, cannot fully master electronic gadgets. A similar problem is also relevant for people with outdated smartphones who cannot afford to purchase more advanced gadgets. Consequently, they also cannot fully be participants in the "smart city."

Secondly, according to Egine Karagulian, Olga Zakharova, Maria Batyreva, David Dusseault, the next aspect that is critically assessed is the ability of smart cities to create conditions for taking into account the opinion of citizens in the implementation of urban development projects, including the implementation of the concept itself. It should be noted that at the initial stages of the development of the smart city concept, more attention was paid to the development of technologies and infrastructure, but as technologies developed, it became obvious that most of them did not resonate with citizens, did not have a noticeable impact on everyday life, did not take into account their opinions regarding the elements being implemented (Karagulian et al., 2020, p. 669).

Thirdly, smart cities are vulnerable to cyber attacks on critical infrastructure, which can paralyze the work of public transport, city services, etc., as well as sow panic among the population and reduce the manageability of urban space. In addition, attackers can spread viruses and malicious software through cyber attacks to spy on the population or individual citizens, etc. Also, smart cities significantly increase their dependence on electricity consumption and, if uninterrupted access to electricity is stopped for some reason, a significant number of devices and city services will cease to function stably.

Fourth, very often the "smart city" is implemented solely for the sake of marketing. It is difficult to implement a real project, especially since the main problem hindering the implementation of the smart city concept, both within the post-Soviet space and in cities of other states, is the high depreciation of housing and social infrastructure facilities. For example, being built in the Soviet period (the era of the predominance of a different technological way of life), these facilities are poorly susceptible to modern technologies, which does not allow them to be woven into a single network of "smart" city management. That is why only disparate sites on the territory of cities are considered for the formation of a "smart city." At the same time, the issue of turning the entire city into a single Smart City system remains unresolved. Separately, as a problem, it should be noted the considerable cost of "smart" technologies (and the insufficiency of budget funds for their operational implementation in cities), however, the price of their integration into the projected objects is always lower than the attempts of implementation in the old fund (Ivanova, 2020, p. 25). Unfortunately, the introduction of such technologies may be necessary for politicians to grow their image, according to Dani Rodrik (2018) and Bård Harstad (2020). Hugo Hopenhayn and Francesco Squintani (2021) talk about biased criteria for investing in innovations based on populist criteria, biased estimates and fake information (Massey et al., 2018; Rubin & Rubin, 2021), which leads to the failure of projects and discrediting the "smart city."

Fifthly, the smart city system, no matter how smart, technologically advanced and integrated into city management systems, is not immune from disruptions in the event of emergencies. The example of the COVID-19 pandemic illustrated this well when urban systems failed during the "peak" of the disease (Diez Roux, 2020).

Andrey Koshkin (2021), in his work on the economic aspect of Russian federalism, as well as inter-budgetary transfers during the outbreak of the COVID-19 pandemic, notes that many regional leaders, as well as heads of regional health departments, resigned due to the growing burden on the system.

Sixth, technologies can be used to spy on citizens and contribute to repressive coercion on the part of the state to comply with certain regulations. For example, in Moscow, as part of the fight against crime, smart cameras are being actively installed that can recognize faces and immediately compare them with the database of persons who are wanted, of course, technologies in this case are aimed at catching criminals, but the same technologies can be used to arrest or pressure on dissidents and creates serious dangers for the private life of a person who, in the conditions of the ubiquitous presence of technology, actually loses the right to private and private life from commercial companies or the state.

5 Conclusions

The concept of a "smart city," being a global trend that is actively implemented in many countries of the world, really contributes to the creation of a comfortable and safe urban environment, where residents get the opportunity to use various urban services with convenience for themselves. Today, every person, having only a smartphone with Internet access, can make an appointment with a doctor and choose a day and time convenient for himself, can see when the right bus arrives, plan a route through city electronic maps, calculating the time for the road, and covering courtyards and streets with cameras allows you to track in a short time and detain criminals. However, it is important to understand that in order to create such a comfortable urban environment, significant sums are required, which not every city has. For example, Moscow demonstrates the highest technological indicators among all Russian cities. And this is understandable, because having significant financial resources, the city authorities can afford to direct funds to the technological modernization of the urban environment. However, the smaller the city and the smaller its budget, the lower the technological indicators it demonstrates.

In general, despite the significant risks that the concept of a "smart city" entails, we can say that the introduction of technologies into the public administration system is an inevitable process that will continue and expand in any case. In Russia, this concept has received its institutional formalization relatively recently, but it is worth emphasizing that in all regions of the country, the city authorities have begun work on the introduction and integration of innovative technologies into the urban management system. Of course, the imposed sanctions and restrictions on technology imports to Russia can slow down the process of "technologization" of Russian cities, but not stop it completely. It can be concluded that the introduction of technologies into the processes of urban governance is a global trend that will actively develop both in the world and in Russia.

Thus, the analysis of territorial development projects shows that the concepts being implemented are not a panacea in themselves. When implementing smart city concepts, it is necessary to pay attention to the real needs of all consumers of the territory and take into account their strategic perspective. It is important to take into account the existing problems of territorial development and the wormholes hidden in beautiful projects in order to avoid the development of serious problems and achieve the stated goals of urban development projects.

References

Attaran, H., Kheibari, N., & Bahrepour, D. (2022). Toward integrated smart city: A new model for implementation and design challenges. *GeoJournal, 87*(4), 511–526.

Diez Roux, A. V. (2020). Population Health in the Time of COVID-19: Confirmations and Revelations. *The Milbank Quarterly, 98*(3), 629–640.

Ganin, O. B., & Ganin, I. O. (2014). "Smart city": Prospects and development trends. *Ars Administrandi (Art of Management), 6*(1), 124–135.

Garas, L. N. (2020). “Smart city”: Features of political management (on the example of the city of federal significance Sevastopol). *Society: Politics, Economics, Law*, *5*, 21–26.

Giffinger, R., Fertner, C., & Kramar H. (2007). *Smart cities. Ranking of European medium-sized cities*. http://www.smart-cities.eu/download/smart_cities_final_report.pdf

Glazer, E. L. (2013). Triumph of the City: How our greatest invention makes us richer, smarter, greener, healthier and happier. *Journal of Economic Sociology*, *14*(4), 75–93.

Griffiths, D. N. (2013). *City Cynic: “Against the Smart City”*. https://www.forbes.com/sites/danielnyegriffiths/2013/12/02/city-cynic-against-the-smart-city-by-adam-greenfield-review/#746fb1e3b190.

Harstad, B. (2020). Technology and time inconsistency. *Journal of Political Economy*, *128*(7), 2653–2689.

Hartzmark, S. M., Hirshman, S. D., & Imas, A. (2021). Ownership, learning, and beliefs. *The Quarterly Journal of Economics*, *136*(3), 1665–1717.

Hollands, R. G. (2008). Will the real smart city please stand up? *City*, *12*(3), 303–320.

Hopenhayn, H., & Squintani, F. (2021). On the direction of innovation. *Journal of Political Economy*, *129*(7), 1991–2022.

Ivanova, O. (2020). Problems of implementation of the Smart City concept in the largest cities of Russia (analysis on the example of the city of Yekaterinburg). *Modern City: Power, Management, Economy*, *1*, 20–30.

Karagulian, E. A., Zakharova, O. V., Batyreva, M. V., & Dussault, D. L. (2020). Smart City – Well-being for everyone? *Journal of Economic Theory*, *17*(3), 657–678.

Kislyakova, Yu. G., & Kazakova, O. Yu. (2019). Innovative technologies of “Smart city” in the field of housing and communal services. *Socio-economic Management: Theory and Practice*, 3(38), 57–58.

Koshkin, A., & Mokretsov, N. (2022). Between management and political economy: A system of accounting and evaluation of cognitarian in modern digital ecosystems. *Ecosystems Without Borders: Opportunities and Challenges, Switzerland,* 1–8.

Koshkin, A. V. (2021). The economic aspect of Russian federalism: Interbudgetary transfers during the beginning of the COVID-19 pandemic. *Marketing MBA. Marketing Management of the Enterprise*, *12*(1), 69–81.

Massey, G., Kliestikova, J., Kovacova, M., & Dengov, V. V. (2018). The perceived accuracy of fake news: Mechanisms facilitating the spread of alternative truths, the crisis of informational objectivity, and the decline of trust in journalistic narratives. *Geopolitics, History and International Relations, 10*(2), 37–43.

McCord, C., & Becker, C. (2019). *Sidewalk and Toronto: Critical systems Heuristics and the Smart City*. Toronto. https://www.arxiv.org/abs/1906.02266

Rodrik, D. (2018). Populism and the economics of globalization. *Journal of International Business Policy, 1*, 12–33.

Rubin, Am., & Rubin, A. (2021). Systematic bias in the progress of research. *Journal of Political Economy, 129*(9), 2666–2719.

Sassen S. (2005). When national territory is home to the global: Old borders to novel borderings. *New Political Economy, 10*(4), 523–541.

Scott, K. (2016). Smart City Seattle and geographies of exclusion. *The Digital City and Mediated Urban Ecologies*, Jan., 119–160.

Segerstrom, P. (1991). Innovation, imitation, and economic growth. *Journal of Political Economy, 99*(4), 807–827.

Townsend, A. M. (2013). *Smart cities: Big data, civic hackers, and the quest for a new Utopia*. W. W. Norton & Company.

Carmen-Valentina Radulescu[1,*], Sorin Burlacu[2], Sorin Perică Angheluta[3], and Florin Uta[4]

The Role of Public Administration in Shaping the Sustainability of Agriculture: An Analytical Perspective on Globalization and Sustainable Development

Abstract:
Research background: Globalization is influencing agriculture in numerous ways, creating both opportunities and challenges for sustainable practices. The role of public administration in this context is often underexplored and can vary widely between different regions and countries.
Purpose of the article: This study seeks to understand the relationship between globalization, sustainable development in agriculture, and the role of public administration within a specific national or regional context. The focus is on identifying existing policies, their effectiveness, and the gaps that may exist in promoting sustainable agricultural practices.
Methods: A qualitative approach was used, primarily relying on case studies, interviews with key stakeholders, and a review of existing literature and policy documents. The research focused on one country, offering an in-depth analysis of the interplay between globalization, sustainable agricultural development, and public administration.
Findings & Value added: The findings reveal a complex relationship between these elements, with public administration playing a crucial role in balancing global economic pressures and local sustainable needs. The study highlights specific areas where policy could be improved or refocused to better support sustainable practices within the context of globalization. The value added by this research lies in its focused examination of these

* Corresponding author: carmen-valentina.radulescu@eam.ase.ro
1 Bucharest University of Economic Studies, The Faculty of Agrifood and Environmental Economics, Professor Ph.D, Romania Russia
2 Bucharest University of Economic Studies, The Faculty of Administration and Public Management, Associate Professor, Ph.D, Romania
3 Bucharest University of Economic Studies, Associate Professor, Romania,
4 University of Wallachia, Phd Student, Targoviste, Romania

themes within a specific context, offering insights and recommendations that could be applied to similar settings or used to inform broader policy discussions.

Keywords: *Globalization, Sustainable Development, Agriculture, Public Administration*

JEL Classification: *Q01; Q15; R58; H11*

1 Introduction

Agriculture is a fundamental component of global societies, being a primary source of food, energy and raw materials. At the same time, it is also an area under considerable pressure due to the challenges of climate change, population growth and the globalization of markets. In this context, it is essential to analyze and understand the role of public administration in shaping the sustainability of agriculture, a crucial aspect for achieving the goals of sustainable development at the global level (Rădulescu et al., 2019).

Globalization has led to increased interconnectedness of economies and societies, profoundly influencing agricultural structures and production patterns (Rădulescu et al., 2020). This has fostered increased competitiveness, but at the same time it has also brought several disadvantages, such as price volatility, dependence on imports and increased inequality. Therefore, the sustainability of agriculture is becoming a major concern for governments and international organizations, requiring an integrated and coordinated approach (Vanloqueren & Baret, 2017).

The public administration plays a crucial role in shaping the sustainability of agriculture, by creating an appropriate regulatory framework, promoting effective public policy and ensuring a conducive environment for the sustainable development of the agricultural sector (Mexmonov, 2020). This research article aims to analyze the role of public administration in shaping the sustainability of agriculture, providing an analytical perspective on the impact of globalization and sustainable development. Emphasis will be placed on the importance of adopting coherent and globally coordinated public policies capable of addressing emerging challenges and promoting sustainable, resilient and competitive agriculture.

2 Literature Review

The study of specialized literature reveals that the dynamics of the evolution of sustainable agriculture is not only based on cultivation methods and climatic conditions, but is deeply interconnected with public administration and global forces (Clune, 2021). As the world comes closer together through globalization, the policies we develop and the strategies we adopt become more and more significant (Profiroiu et al., 2020a). Yunlong and Smit (1994) describe the symbiotic relationship between sustainability and agriculture, emphasizing the deep connection between them. However, Brand (2010) suggests that our traditional understanding can sometimes limit the achievement of truly sustainable goals. In this era of global interconnection, Alpopi et al. (2018) describe how ecological considerations are becoming central amid global economic expansion.

In the digital age, public administration is not only about governance, but also about harnessing technology for sustainable purposes (Ionita et al., 2009). Burlacu et al. (2021, 2022a) highlight the fusion between digital governance and sustainable goals, arguing for a future where technology becomes a catalyst (Burlacu et al., 2019).

Agriculture in Romania, explored by Gâf-Deac et al. (2022) and Rădulescu et al. (2022), provide a detailed picture of the challenges and opportunities presented by globalization. Mountainous lands, once considered barriers, now present themselves as refuges for sustainable agri-food practices.

Governance, as discussed by Kettl (2000), is in the midst of a metamorphosis, shaped by global forces, urging administrations around the world to evolve and adapt. Burlacu et al., (2022b) emphasize the need for cities to grow smart, businesses to be aware and governance to be agile. The strength of collaboration, particularly between the private and public sectors, is highlighted by Glasbergen et al. (2007) and Spielman et al. (2010). Partnerships combine expertise and resources to navigate the sustainability maze (Profiroiu et al., 2020b).

However, not everything is simple. Burlacu et al. (2022c) present the delicate balance between economic ambitions, resource management and the shadow of global food security. In a world driven by innovation, Levy and Newell (2005) and Seyfang and Smith (2007) make a strong case for businesses and communities to become leaders in sustainability initiatives. Taoumi and Lahrech (2023) remind us of the balance that must be achieved between economic objectives, environmental imperatives and social responsibilities, rounding out our understanding of sustainable agriculture in the face of public administration and global forces.

3 Methodology

In order to carry out an in-depth analysis of the interaction between globalization, sustainable agricultural development and public administration, a qualitative approach was adopted, which included several methods of data collection.

Case studies: The analysis included detailed case studies that provided deep insight into how public administration influences agricultural sustainability in the context of globalization. The case studies were selected to provide a variety of contexts and approaches, in order to obtain the most complete understanding of the researched topic.

Stakeholder interviews: Interviews with key actors in the agricultural sector, public administration and international organizations provided valuable information on current policies, challenges and opportunities related to sustainable agricultural development. The interviewees were selected based on their expertise in the field and the role they play in shaping agricultural policy.

Review of literature and policy documents: The review of existing literature and policy documents provided a theoretical and conceptual framework for the research. This included academic studies, research reports, policy papers and reports of international organizations.

The research focused on a single country, providing an in-depth analysis of how globalization, sustainable agricultural development and public administration interconnect and influence each other. The choice of the country was based on its relevance to the researched topic and the availability of the necessary data and information.

The collected data were analyzed using qualitative data analysis methods, which included thematic coding, content analysis, and discourse analysis. This enabled the identification of key themes, trends and relationships between different factors influencing agricultural sustainability in the context of globalization and public administration.

4 Results

In the context of a rapidly changing world, our study explores the interplay between globalization, sustainable agriculture and the influence of public administration. We analyze a specific national context, highlighting the implications of these global changes at the local level.

Agriculture and its challenges: Agriculture, essential to society, faces challenges related to climate change, population growth and the impact of globalization.

Table 1. Concepts and insights on agriculture and its challenges.

Concept/ Insight	Related Challenge	Recommendations	Potential Causes	Anticipated Effects
Interplay between sustainability and agriculture	Adapting to modern sustainable practices	Integration of innovative and sustainable techniques	Climate change; outdated farming practices	Enhanced resilience; better crop yields
Limitations of traditional understanding	Resistance to modern methodologies	Regular training and upskilling of farmers	Reliance on ancestral farming practices	Stagnation or decline in agricultural output
Ecological considerations amid global expansion	Balancing growth with eco-friendliness	Implementation of eco-agricultural practices	Rapid globalization; loss of biodiversity	Restoration of ecosystems; sustainable growth
Digital governance & agricultural sustainability	Incorporating technology in farming	Digital training for farmers; use of AI in agriculture	Technological advancements; changing governance models	Improved farm management; data-driven decisions
Globalization's dual-faced nature	Vulnerability to global market fluctuations	Diversification of crops; local market strengthening	Dependence on global markets; economic policies	Stable local economies; reduced import dependency
Evolution of governance under global pressures	Ensuring policies support sustainable agriculture	Policy reforms; global collaborations	International trade agreements; globalized economy	Enhanced international cooperation; better policy framework
Importance of public-private collaboration	Fragmented efforts and resources	Strengthening of public-private partnerships	Limited resources; varied interests	Cohesive efforts; shared expertise and resources

Source: Author's contribution

The Table 1 presents a comprehensive breakdown of critical concepts and insights in contemporary agriculture, encompassing global challenges and dynamics. Let's delve into a deeper analysis of each:

- *Interplay between Sustainability and Agriculture:* This concept highlights the crucial connection between sustainable practices and modern agriculture. As the world grapples with the pressing issue of climate change, the agricultural sector must adapt rapidly to maintain optimal yields and reduce environmental impact. The reliance on outdated methods exacerbates the problem, hence the emphasis on integrating innovative practices.
- *Limitations of Traditional Understanding:* An interesting insight into the gap between traditional agricultural knowledge and contemporary challenges. This suggests that while ancestral farming practices have value, they may not be sufficient to address today's agricultural demands and challenges. Upskilling becomes a prerequisite for progress.
- *Ecological Considerations amid Global Expansion:* With globalization expanding its reach, agriculture faces the dilemma of maximizing production without compromising ecological balance. This highlights the importance of ecological agriculture that synergizes production with biodiversity conservation.
- *Digital Governance & Agricultural Sustainability:* In the digital age, agriculture can't remain an exception. The potential of technology, especially AI, to revolutionize farming practices is vast. But for that to materialize, the farming community needs to be digitally literate, emphasizing the significance of training.
- *Globalization's Dual-Faced Nature:* A potent insight into the double-edged sword that is globalization. While it offers opportunities for market expansion, it also makes local agriculture vulnerable to global market dynamics. Strengthening local markets and diversifying crops can serve as a buffer against such volatilities.
- *Evolution of Governance under Global Pressures:* Governance structures need to evolve, reflecting global challenges and trade intricacies. The emphasis on policy reforms and international collaborations underscores the need for a dynamic governance framework capable of navigating global pressures.
- *Importance of Public-Private Collaboration:* This concept points out the fragmentation in agricultural efforts due to a lack of coordinated initiatives between the public and private sectors. The emphasis on strengthened partnerships indicates the vast potential of pooling resources and expertise for a common agricultural goal.

Globalization: A Double-Edged Sword: While increasing competitiveness, globalization also brings price fluctuations, greater dependence on imports and rising inequality.

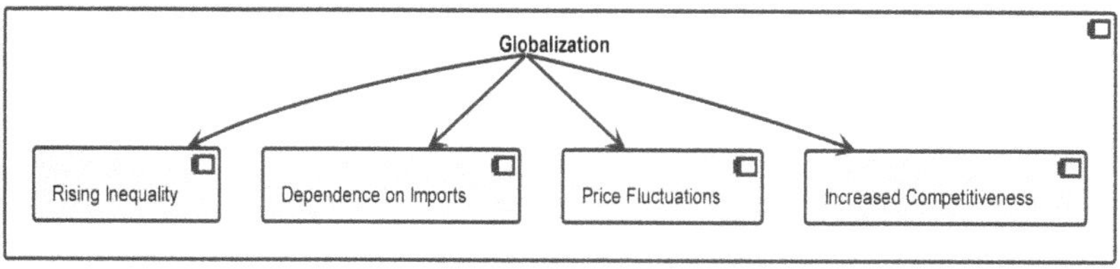

Figure 1. Globalization and its subcomponents.
Source: Author's contribution

This Figure 1 visualizes globalization as a component, with four sub-components representing the different aspects. The arrows indicate the relationship between globalization and each aspect.

The role of public administration: Public administration has a key role in defining the future of sustainable agriculture by setting the appropriate policies and strategies.

Table 2. Comparative analysis of prevalent policies, their yield, and identified voids.

Policy Name/ Category	Key Objectives	Policy Yield/ Outcomes	Identified Voids/Gaps
Green Agro Initiatives	- Reduce carbon footprint - Promote organic farming	- 20 % reduction in emissions - 30 % increase in organic farms	- Lack of widespread awareness - Insufficient subsidies for organic farming
Water Conservation	- Efficient water usage - Promote rainwater harvesting	- 15 % decrease in water wastage - 10 % increase in rainwater adoption	- Insufficient infrastructure for rainwater collection - Lack of training in water conservation techniques
Agro-tech Advancements	- Introduce modern farming technologies - Increase yield	- 25 % yield increase with tech - 40 % farmers adopting tech	- High initial costs - Resistance to technology adoption by older farmers

(*continued on next page*)

Table 2. Continued

Policy Name/ Category	Key Objectives	Policy Yield/ Outcomes	Identified Voids/Gaps
Biodiversity Protection	– Protect native species – Reduce use of harmful pesticides	– 30 % increase in native flora and fauna – 20 % reduction in harmful pesticide use	– Lack of clarity on pesticide alternatives – Insufficient local species seed banks
Fair Trade Practices	– Ensure fair prices for farmers – Strengthen local economies	– 15 % increase in farmer income – Stronger local trade networks	– Global market competition – Lack of universal fair-trade standards

Source: Author's contribution

Table 2 provides a structured assessment of prominent agricultural policies, their key objectives, the results derived from their implementation, and the identified voids or gaps that might be undermining their full potential.

- *Green Agro Initiatives:* This policy has been introduced to counter the pressing concerns related to global warming and environmental degradation. The policy's efficacy is reflected in significant reductions in emissions and an encouraging rise in organic farms. However, gaps like insufficient awareness among the masses and inadequate subsidies for organic farming are challenges that need addressing for the policy to have an even broader impact.
- *Water Conservation:* With water scarcity becoming a global issue, efficient water management practices are vital. The policy has seen some success, as indicated by decreased water wastage and increased adoption of rainwater harvesting. Still, there's room for improvement. Infrastructure for rainwater collection is lagging, and there seems to be a deficiency in training farmers in advanced water conservation methods.
- *Agro-tech Advancements:* The inclusion of modern technology in farming practices is inevitable for sustainable and efficient agriculture. The policy's success metrics, such as enhanced yield and a substantial portion of farmers adopting new tech, are promising. However, the significant initial costs can be prohibitive for many farmers, especially smallholders. Additionally, there's resistance from older generations, signaling a need for more inclusive training and outreach programs.
- *Biodiversity Protection:* The alarming rate of biodiversity loss has made it imperative to protect native species and cut down on the use of harmful

pesticides. The policy seems to have a positive effect, seeing an increase in native species and a decline in detrimental pesticide usage. Yet, challenges persist, such as the need for a clearer roadmap to pesticide alternatives and the establishment of local species seed banks.

- *Fair Trade Practices:* A crucial policy to ensure that the backbone of agriculture – the farmers – receive their due. By ensuring fair prices and strengthening local economies, there's been a noticeable boost in farmer income and robust local trade networks. Nevertheless, the challenges presented by global market competition and the absence of universally accepted fair-trade standards still loom large.

Results and perspectives: Our findings highlight both gaps in current policies and opportunities to advance sustainable agriculture.

Table 3. Identification of challenges and opportunities in the Romanian agricultural context.

Aspect	Challenge	Underlying Causes	Opportunity	Potential Benefits
Topography	Difficult terrains in mountainous areas	Natural landscape; limited accessibility	Development of terraced farming or niche crops	Utilization of previously underused land; unique crops leading to niche markets
Climate	Erratic weather patterns; potential for droughts or floods	Climate change; deforestation	Implementation of climate-resilient crops and farming techniques	Enhanced crop yields; reduced susceptibility to weather-related losses
Globalization	Price volatility; increased import dependence	Global market fluctuations; trade agreements	Strengthening local markets; promoting "Made in Romania" products	Economic stability; reduction in import costs
Technology	Limited technological integration in traditional farming	Lack of infrastructure; limited digital literacy	Introduction of digital farming tools; training programs for farmers	Increased crop yield; efficient farm management

(*continued on next page*)

Table 3. Continued

Aspect	Challenge	Underlying Causes	Opportunity	Potential Benefits
Policy & Governance	Outdated agricultural policies	Legacy systems; lack of policy reform	Policy overhaul to incorporate sustainable and modern farming techniques	Encouraged sustainable practices; improved sector growth
Economic Factors	Dependence on a few cash crops; lack of diversification	Historical trends; market demands	Diversification of agricultural products; exploration of organic farming	Risk distribution; tapping into global organic markets
Societal Factors	Urban migration leading to reduced labor in farms	Economic disparities; urban allure	Promotion of agro-tourism; incentivizing youth participation in agriculture	Revitalized rural economies; generational continuity in farming practices

Source: Author's contribution

This table elucidates challenges and opportunities intrinsic to Romania's agricultural context, offering an overview of potential benefits that can be reaped with appropriate interventions. Regarding *topography,* challenging terrains in mountainous areas stem from the natural landscape and limited accessibility. Yet, this allows for opportunities in terraced agriculture or niche crops, potentially unlocking underutilized land and unique market segments. *Climate* presents concerns with unpredictable weather patterns, often tied to climate change and deforestation. Adopting climate-resilient crops can lead to improved yields and reduced weather-related losses. In the era of *globalization,* price volatility and import dependence arise from global market shifts and trade pacts. However, fortifying local markets and endorsing "Made in Romania" products can offer economic stability. From a *technology* perspective, traditional farming's limited tech integration, attributed to inadequate infrastructure and digital literacy, can be counteracted by introducing digital tools and farmer training, resulting in better yields and farm management. *Policy and governance* face the hurdle of antiquated agricultural policies. Modernizing these, by addressing legacy systems and promoting sustainable practices, can spur sector growth. Economically, reliance on select crops restricts diversification. Exploring varied products and organic farming can mitigate risks and access the global organic market. Lastly, *societal factors* indicate urban migration reducing farm labor, driven by economic disparities and urban appeal. Initiatives like agro-tourism and youth engagement in farming can rejuvenate rural economies and ensure farming's generational continuity. In essence, while Romanian agriculture has its challenges, each holds an embedded opportunity. Tapping into these can position Romania for sustainable agricultural growth.

Our findings emphasize the importance of an integrated approach. A cohesive and holistic strategy is needed to properly navigate the interaction between agriculture, global trends and public administration in an interconnected world.

5 Discussion and Conclusion

In an increasingly interconnected world, agriculture is at the crossroads between the promises and pitfalls of globalization. As our exploration revealed, the trajectory of sustainable agricultural practices is not only at the mercy of global market forces; it is also deeply influenced by the actions and inactions of public administration within certain regional and national contexts.

This study looks at the complexity of the relationships that unite globalization, sustainable agricultural development and the roles that public entities assume. The narrative that unfolds is a compelling one: public administration acts as a fulcrum on which the balance between global economic dynamics and local sustainability aspirations tilts. Rather than being mere passive spectators, public institutions hold the reins that can steer agricultural practices toward a more sustainable paradigm, even in the face of mounting global pressures.

Our findings are a call to action. There are tangible areas within policies that, when fine-tuned or reimagined, can become powerful catalysts for change. These can serve to amplify the benefits and mitigate the challenges that globalization brings, ensuring that sustainable practices are not only encouraged but thrive.

In this context, we must not forget digitization either. The introduction of digital technologies in agriculture can facilitate the transition to more sustainable practices by providing innovative solutions for resource management, crop monitoring and production optimization. Digitization comes not only as a response to the needs of the global market, but also as an essential tool for public administration to promote and support sustainability.

On the grand stage of global interaction, this research underscores a significant proposition: Although globalization sets the stage, the nuanced choreography of public administration will determine whether the act of agriculture is a tragedy or a triumph of sustainability. As nations grapple with their place in this global narrative, the findings and recommendations of this research provide a guiding light, suggesting that a harmonious combination of global perspectives and localized action can indeed chart a sustainable path forward for agriculture.

References

Alpopi, C., Burlacu, S., & Iovițu, M.. (2018). Procesul de globalizare și politicile ecologice. *Competitivitatea și Inovarea în Economia Cunoașterii, Moldova, 2*, 317–324.

Brand, U. (2010). Sustainable development and ecological modernization–the limits to a hegemonic policy knowledge. *Innovation–The European Journal of Social Science Research, 23*(2), 135–152.

Burlacu, S., Alpopi, C., Mitrită, M., & Popescu, M. L. (2019). Sustainable e-Governance and human resource development. *European Journal of Sustainable Development, 8*(5), 16–20.

Burlacu, S., Crețu, C. R., Crețu, R. F., Spiridon, C. E., & Gombos, S. P. (2022a). Lack of economic and food security on a global scale. *Revista de Management Comparat International, 23*(5), 686–693.

Burlacu, S., Georgescu, R. I., Moise, D., Cretu, R. F., Platagea Gombos, S., Buzoianu, O. A. C., & Rotaru, C. (2022b). The tension between adjusted net savings, sustainable growth and resource depletion. *Economic Computation & Economic Cybernetics Studies & Research, 56*(3).

Burlacu, S., Gutu, C., Marinela, F., Gombos, C. C., & Biner, M. (2021). Resilience in Public Administration and sustainable development. *Proceedings of Administration and Public Management International Conference, Romania, 17*(1), 104–108.

Burlacu, S., Pargaru, I., Iacob, O. C., & Gombos, S. P. (2022c). Digital Public Administration and the perspectives of sustainable development in Romania. *European Journal of Sustainable Development, 11*(4), 230–230.

Burlacu, S., Popescu, M. L., Diaconu, A., & Sârbu, A. (2021b). Digital Public Administration for sustainable development. *European Journal of Sustainable Development, 10*(4), 33–40.

Clune, T. (2021). Conceptualising policy for sustainable agriculture development. *Australian Journal of Public Administration, 80*(3), 493–509.

Gâf-Deac, I., Bran, F., Radulescu, C. V., Burlacu, S. (2022). Short and proximity value chains in the agri-food economy in Romania. *Competitivitatea și inovarea în economia cunoașterii: Culegere de rezumate, Moldova,* 6.

Glasbergen, P., Biermann, F., & Mol, A. P. (Eds.). (2007). *Partnerships, governance and sustainable development: Reflections on theory and practice.* Edward Elgar Publishing.

Ionita, F., Ursacescu, M., & Burlacu, S. (2009). Public services as poles of regional competitiveness in sustainable development. *Revista de Management Comparat International/Review of International Comparative Management, 10*(3), 552–565.

Kettl, D. F. (2000). The transformation of governance: Globalization, devolution, and the role of government. *Public Administration Review, 60*(6), 488–497.

Levy, D. L., & Newell, P. J. (Eds.). (2005). *The business of global environmental governance*. MIT press.

Mexmonov, S. (2020). The ways to ensure the financial stability of agriculture under conditions of modernization of the economy. *Архив научных исследований, 33*(1).

Profiroiu, C. M., Bodislav, D. A., Burlacu, S., & Rădulescu, C. V. (2020a). Challenges of sustainable urban development in the context of population growth. *European Journal of Sustainable Development, 9*(3), 51–57.

Profiroiu, C. M., Rădulescu, C. V., & Burlacu, S. (2020b). The challenges of Smart City in the context of globalization and the health crisis. In *Proceedings of Administration and Public Management International Conference* (Vol. 16, No. 1, pp. 4–11). Research Centre

Rădulescu, C. V., Burlacu, S., & Bodislav, D. A. (2019). E-Government-a paradigm of sustainable governance. *Collaborative Research for Excellence in Economics and Social Sciences*, 48.

Rădulescu, C. V., Burlacu, S., Bodislav, D. A., & Bran, F. (2020). Entrepreneurial education in the context of the imperative development of sustainable business. *European Journal of Sustainable Development*, 9(4), 93–93.

Rădulescu, Carmen Valentina, Gâf-Deac, Ioan I., Burlacu, Sorin, Bran, Florina (2022). The development of the agri-food sector in the mountainous areas of Romania. *Competitivitatea şi inovarea în economia cunoaşterii: Culegere de rezumate*, Moldova, 24.

Seyfang, G., & Smith, A. (2007). Grassroots innovations for sustainable development: Towards a new research and policy agenda. *Environmental politics, 16*(4), 584–603.

Spielman, D. J., Hartwich, F., & Grebmer, K. (2010). Public–private partnerships and developing-country agriculture: Evidence from the international agricultural research system. *Public Administration and Development, 30*(4), 261–276.

Taoumi, H., & Lahrech, K. (2023). Economic, environmental and social efficiency and effectiveness development in the sustainable crop agricultural sector: A systematic in-depth analysis review. *Science of the Total Environment, 901*, 165761.

Vanloqueren, G., & Baret, P. V. (2017). How agricultural research systems shape a technological regime that develops genetic engineering but locks out agroecological innovations. *Food Sovereignty, Agroecology and Biocultural Diversity*, 57–92.

Yunlong, C., & Smit, B. (1994). Sustainability in agriculture: A general review. *Agriculture, Ecosystems & Environment*, *49*(3), 299–307.

Regina Zsuzsánna Reicher[1,*], Zsuzsanna Győri[1], and Anita Kolnhofer-Derecskei[1]

Entrepreneurship for a Sustainable World

Abstract:
Research background: Integration of entrepreneurial thinking and sustainable business operations is a pillar of globalisation. Sustainability refers to the impact of business practices on the social, natural and economic environment. Only successful businesses can support both social and economic sustainability goals. To achieve this, companies need to build an appropriate strategy. However, the external environment in which a business operates and the conditions under which it operates and promotes sustainability are strongly influenced by the company's external environment.
Purpose of the article: The study examines entrepreneurial attitudes towards sustainability regarding the tasks and responsibilities that can be taken on. We investigated the entrepreneurs' responsibility-task orientation towards sustainability and analyzed how the management of Hungarian SME entrepreneurs perceive their role in sustainability.
Methods: In May and June 2022, we conducted three focus group interviews with professionals representing the target group. In the summer of 2023, we surveyed this topic on a nationally representative sample. The qualitative research results were analyzed using NVivo software, while the quantitative analysis was carried out using SPSS software.
Findings & Value added: As a result of our study, respondents identify two broad categories of responsibility. Many entrepreneurs consider the state's role crucial in addition to their commitment. They feel and understand their responsibility for sustainable development as private individuals and company managers. However, they operate within the limits of the legal environment, and few businesses operate beyond it.

Keywords: *SME sector, sustainability, leadership, responsibility, role of the state*

JEL Classification: *M12; M5; Q01; Q56*

1 Introduction

The emergence of CSR has traditionally been associated with larger companies (Jansson et al., 2017) and has long been the focus of major international

---

* Corresponding author: reicher.regina@uni-bge.hu
1 Budapest Business University, Faculty of Finance and Accountancy, 1055 Budapest, Markó u. 29–31. Hungary

guidelines. However, the current social and ecological situation justifies the need for all social and economic actors, including SMEs, to act to promote sustainability, as declared in the UN Sustainable Development Goals (UN, 2015).

Surveys on CSR that include SMEs tend to be more pessimistic than those that focus only on large companies. The literature agrees that CSR activities are less visible in SMEs than in large companies (Bikefe et al., 2020; Metzker and Streimikis, 2020). SMEs tend to start using explicit CSR instruments, typically quality or environmental standards, when they are forced to do so, mainly because they want to supply to a large company that requires it.

As SMEs have unique characteristics and capabilities, the study of the characteristics of small business practices has led to a new field of research on CSR and corporate sustainability (Magrizos et al., 2021).

However, there is also the possibility that SMEs have less opportunity and less need to make CSR, particularly CSR communication, a prominent and emphasized part of their operations. SMEs often engage in 'implicit' CSR activities (Matten and Moon, 2007). Because of their high degree of social embeddedness, they act as responsible citizens of their local environment, recognizing their impact and resulting responsibilities, addressing the interests of their stakeholders (e.g., employees, consumers, business partners, local communities and the natural environment) (Vives, 2016), but not using the term CSR and related terminology, tools and standards (Szlávik et al., 2006), do not carry out conscious stakeholder management or communication.

Bajdor et al. (2021) indicate in their study that some companies only implement sustainable business at a declarative level. That is, they talk about it, and incorporate it into their communication, but actively, sustainability is less tangible. However, the research concludes that environmental goals are a bigger problem for businesses than social goals. They also find that businesses most likely to implement sustainable business practices often use advanced IT solutions.

In business, IT tools, including software, applications, and AI, are becoming increasingly widespread. This can increase customer satisfaction, customer retention, build a more efficient business model and improve the long-term efficiency of SMEs. The use of such technological tools also has the potential to maintain competitiveness (Rakshit et al., 2021). Sustainable businesses strive to ensure that their operations are unified, improve collaboration between employees, simplify processes within the organisation and introduce innovative solutions as often as possible. In this type of enterprise, the 'managers' are also more inclined to implement ecological and social activities (Bajdor et al., 2021).

The embedding of green sustainability in SMEs has received increasing attention in research, yet the environmental knowledge base of SMEs remains relatively unclear. Baggia et al. stress the importance of SMEs adopting an information system to support their sustainable development efforts. They introduce the concept of a Green Information system, which is an information system that contributes to building a sustainable future in business operations, limits resource use and encourages the adoption of energy efficient solutions (Baggia et al., 2019).

Multilateral FinTech Platforms (MSPs) have also gained significant traction among green entrepreneurs as an innovative tool to support their green new product development plans. In order to support green entrepreneurship and social welfare at the same time, some governments are promoting the use of MSPs (Reza-Gharehbagh et al., 2022).

Several studies have investigated the impact that the personality of corporate leaders can have on company operations, employee behaviour and organisational performance. It has been found that female CEOs behave more ethically compared to their male counterparts (Ismail et al., 2020). In general, gender diversity promotes the existence of CSR in companies. For business ethics, it is a cornerstone of corporate transparency. A woman is more likely to perceive the importance of business ethics if she is the leader (Prochazkova & Micak, 2023)

On one occasion, it was found that firm size was a significant moderating factor in the effect of structural characteristics on intrinsic corporate trust. The effect of interactiveness on corporate trust was larger for large firms than for SMEs. Individuals do not expect large firms to 'talk' to them, while they expect SMEs to do so. It is interesting that when large companies initiate individual communication, people value this more than in the case of SMEs (Kang & Par, 2018). It can also be shown that knowledge of systems alone, the amount of knowledge alone, cannot predict responsible environmental behaviour. However, there is no doubt that knowledge about environmental problems can be used to overcome fear and anxiety and lead to long-term protest actions (Kamal et al., 2022).

Microenterprise managers also appear to be prepared to integrate personal environmental concerns into their business activities. We see differences in the adoption of green practices at both the SME and individual level, mostly related to firm size and profit, but also to the gender of the manager. Research shows that SMEs learn best from their peers and informal networks, which are mostly related to firm size and profit, but also to the gender of the manager (Maniu et al., 2021)

Empirical analysis data from Laila et al. (2023) suggest that knowledge and attitude have a significant effect on SME owners' intention to participate in donations, while religiosity does not significantly affect SME owners' intention to participate in donations and grants.

The choice of instruments for corporate CSR activities can be influenced by the location in the industry. For example, in the travel and tourism services sector, action to protect the natural environment is more common. Corporate factors related to business management processes or the search for markets are also present in explaining the positioning of these companies in their approach to CSR, but there are also other types of factors, such as altruism or lifestyle, which explain more precisely the differences in motivations and behaviours (Ibarnia et al., 2020)

Baker and co-authors (2020) examined government policy, the role of government subsidies, organizational attitudes and organizational ethics in the light of sustainable technologies for SMEs. In their view, organizational attitudes and ethics are the key elements that complete the process of sustainable technology adoption. Their framework provides a well-thought-out structure for exploring how government roles play a vital role in the sustainable technology adoption behaviour of SMEs (Bakar et al., 2020).

2 Methods

In May and June 2022, three focus group meetings were organized, where the same moderator asked the same questions based on the same guidelines and guidelines. Before this, the guide was validated in a pilot round, and a screening questionnaire was used to collect information about the participants and the businesses they represent. In selecting the sample of experts, we considered it important to ask representatives of the SME sector who also consider sustainability and responsibility as a private individual and an entrepreneur important in their work. The focus group discussion was based on the concept of responsibility and sustainability and was structured using a funnel technique – i.e., the questions moved from the general to the specific. Our qualitative research findings were analyzed using NVivo 12 software.

The second phase of the research involved a nationally representative sample of SMEs in Hungary during July-August 2023. The sample of 300 respondents was carried out by the market research company IPSOS, and our sample was representative of the size of the enterprise, its geographical location and sectoral classification. Our quantitative analyses were conducted using IBM SPSS 29 software.

The survey's target population is the small and medium-sized enterprise stratum of the SME sector as defined by the European Union, i.e., enterprises with more than 49 employees (Table 1).

Table 1. Size of enterprise by number of employees.

Number of employees	Sample rate	Country rate
10–49 person	86,00 %	86,3 %
50–249 person	14,00 %	13,7 %

Source: own research

The results of our qualitative research have been presented in several publications, so in this paper, we will only summarise them to show the build-up of quantitative results.

The results of our focus group interviews confirmed the finding in the literature that SME actors have a local relationship with consumers and employees, the two most important stakeholders. They also pay attention to the natural environment and future generations. Sustainability is associated with environmental issues, while responsibility is typically linked to interpersonal relationships and future value creation. There is both explicit and implicit responsibility, but in virtually all cases there is a strong emphasis on the role of the owner-manager, with a strong co-existence and interaction between the values of the owner and those of the company. Strongly linked to the awareness and the prominent role of the leader, the interviewees have a very strong sense of personal motivation and responsibility for stakeholders and sustainability. They feel a sense of moral obligation, which strongly determines whether these issues are elevated to a strategic level or are reflected in everyday practice, in the core business and the business model.

From the responses, it can be seen that the positive or negative motivational factors (content theory) that influence sustainability and responsibility can be grouped according to the typology of short-term business interest, long-term business interest and moral obligation accepted in the literature. The questionnaire questions on motivation were formulated accordingly.

If we assign to them the stakeholders to whom these motivations are directed or who may be the sources of these motivational elements, we can draw a logic model in the combination of the target groups and the motivating factors. This formed the basis of our questionnaire survey (Table 2).

Table 2. Logical model underlying the questionnaire.

Target groups	Motivating factors
– Family and individual – Internal o Owner, manager, leader o Employee – External o Suppliers o Consumers o Wider market environment – Strategic partners – Competitors o Legal environment, stakeholders, government o Local, local environment o International, global environment – Natural environment – Future generation	1. profit/profit, success factorn energy prices, profits fall F 2. image / corporate image, communication B 3. social or stakeholder pressure, expectation B 4. legal environment (competition, tax, finance, tendering, employer, environmental), F 5. future responsibility, long-term thinking M 6. market expansion, new customers, suppliers, growth F 7. operational, day-to-day running of the company, problem solving B 8. individual conviction family values M

Source: own research

To formulate the questions, we also incorporated questionnaires from the research conducted by Málovics (2009) and Benedek and Takács (2016). In addition, we also took into account the core themes of ISO 26000, which were already included in the coding process for the evaluation of qualitative responses.

3 Results

This study aims to analyze the results of a questionnaire survey to find out who the SME manager thinks has the responsibility to address the issue of sustainability and responsibility. Based on the qualitative research, we started from the assumption that the managers' answers will be influenced by their attitudes and gender.

In the case of the quantitative research survey, it was considered important that the respondents' answers contained relevant information. Therefore, only responses from respondents who were involved in some form of proposal formulation or decision-making process affecting the operation of their business were accepted. Almost 36 % of the respondents were in the position of owner, and 30 % were in the position of the company director. The remaining 34 % were also in management positions, mostly in economic, financial or commercial fields.

90 % of respondents were managers of domestically owned companies. 6.5 % were managers of wholly foreign-owned companies. The remaining respondents operate under split ownership. 52 % had an annual net turnover of less than €2 million. 28 % had an annual net turnover of between €2 million and €10 million, and only 9 % said they had an annual net turnover of more than €10 million. Nearly 10 % of respondents did not wish to or could not answer this question.

The demographic breakdown of respondents was as follows: 177 men and 121 women (1 person did not wish to specify their gender) took part in the survey. As the respondents work in management positions, their average age was close to 50 years. In terms of marital status, the majority of respondents were married.

Before the professional questions were asked, we asked, "In general, who do you think has the responsibility to act for environmental (natural) and social issues?." We did this so that subsequent questions would not influence their answers. As can be seen from the word cloud, respondents identified two broad categories of responsibility. One is the individual, i.e., everyone is responsible for their environment. The other is the responsibility, responsible action and regulation of the state or government (Figure 1).

Figure 1. Responsibility – word cloud.

Source: own research

Sustainability can only be achieved in the long term, and a time perspective plays an essential role in this, as we need to preserve or maintain the environment for future generations and adapt our social and economic activities accordingly.

This paper focuses on three of the questions in the survey that deal with responsibility and sustainability. Respondents were asked to describe each statement in a list of statements with a score between -3 and +3, where -3 meant strongly disagree, 0 meant neutral, and +3 meant strongly agree. The three statements were as follows:

1. Each individual is responsible for not reducing the life chances of future generations of humanity through their actions.
2. Every business is responsible for social and natural issues to the extent of available resources.
3. Each individual has a responsibility to do as much as reasonably possible to protect the natural environment.

We have examined whether there are differences in the perception of the above statements between different types of businesses in terms of sectoral classification, size differences, and geographical location alternatively, whether respondents are influenced by their gender or marital status.

Since the sample of respondents did not show a normal distribution for any of the questions, we chose to use non-parametric procedures instead of traditional statistical methods for correlation analysis. Non-parametric procedures do not require any particular assumptions about the distribution of the variables, nor even an interval scale. However, the median plays an important role here. Non-parametric procedures do not work with the actual values, but with the order of values, which is captured by the so-called ranks. The rank of a value means its magnitude in the sample.

Table 3. Company size test.

Null Hypothesis	Sig.a,b	Decision
1	0,075	Retain the null hypothesis.
2	0,443	Retain the null hypothesis.
3	0,731	Retain the null hypothesis.

Source: own research

The results of the Mann-Whitney test showed that company size did not significantly affect the answers for the three questions (Table 3), but it can also be seen that the difference between the means of the two groups was the largest for the first question. On this question, smaller sized enterprises have a much stronger view on individual responsibility than larger sized enterprises (Figure 2).

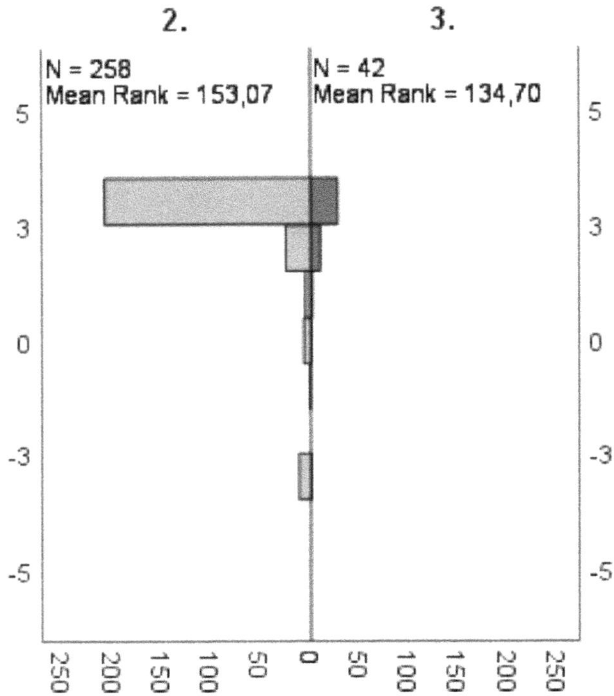

Figure 2. Independent-Samples Mann-Whitney U Test.
Source: own research

A similar result was seen when examining geographical location. Since the variable giving the categories was an 8-item variable, the Kruskal-Wallis (K-W) test was applied. The procedure is essentially a generalisation and extension of the Mann-Whitney test to three or more independent samples. Our results showed that the most significant difference between businesses in different areas was for the first question. This question showed an exceptionally low mean value. Hungary is characterized by the fact that the western part of the country is more economically and socially developed than the eastern region. The detailed data analysis showed that the low scores were given by respondents in the western parts of the country, so that this is considered less of an individual responsibility in that area.

Industry affiliation did not influence the respondents, with apparently almost identical responses from each group. We examined whether any differences could be found for the ownership structure. We found that no significant difference was observed, but if we split the ownership into 2 groups and put the companies with at least 60 % Hungarian ownership in one group and the others in the other, we observed a difference in opinion between the two groups for the second question. More Hungarian-owned companies tend not to think that businesses have a serious responsibility for natural and social issues

As mentioned in the literature, individual motivations and gender influence our attitudes, behaviours and responses to certain aspects of sustainability. Our research results showed no significant differences between groups by marital status, nor were there significant differences by age. Respondents below the average age of the first question were less likely to consider individual responsibility important. But the difference is negligible. However, gender also showed significant differences (Table 3).

Independent-Samples Mann-Whitney U Test:

Table 4. Gender research.

;Null Hypothesis	Sig.a,b	Decision
1	0,044	Reject the null hypothesis.
2	0,064	Retain the null hypothesis.
3	0,350	Retain the null hypothesis.

Source: own research

Women answered all questions with a higher average score. For question one, there is a significant difference between the responses of men and women, with women having a significantly higher average response, i.e., they were more likely to agree with the statement than their male counterparts. For question two, although the difference is not significant, there is a significant difference in the means. There was a smaller difference for the third question, but again women scored higher.

4 Discussion and Conclusion

The SME sector is often seen as lagging behind in terms of sustainable or green business, mainly due to the management and resource problems SMEs face. However, the lack of action in the company only sometimes reflects the personal attitude of the owner-manager.

Our study aimed to verify whether individual motivations and gender influence managerial attitudes towards sustainability and social responsibility. Our research found that smaller firms place more emphasis on the role of individual responsibility than their larger counterparts. However, companies operating in more developed regions tend to place less emphasis on individual responsibility and tend to see the role of companies as the dominant one. Looking at the issue of Hungarian majority-owned companies, we can see that they perceive the issue of sustainability and responsibility as a societal rather than an individual responsibility.

We also examined the role of the individual, such as marital status, age and gender. We found that marital status did not influence the responses. When controlling for age, we found similar results. However, we did see a significant difference between women and men on the issue of individual responsibility. According to women, each individual has a responsibility not to reduce the life chances of future generations of humanity through their actions. Entrepreneurs feel a sense of responsibility for sustainability, but their individual motivations and attitudes strongly influence their role as managers and their decisions.

Our results confirm the research hypothesis and offer new perspectives for the analysis of the green behaviour of SMEs.

Acknowledgments

This research was supported by the Ministry of Innovation and Technology of Hungary from the National Research, Development and Innovation Fund, financed under the Tématerületi Kiválósági Program 2021 (TKP2021-NKTA) funding scheme (Project no. TKP2021-NKTA-44).

References

Baggia, A., Maletič, M., Žnidaršič, A., & Brezavšček, A. (2019). Drivers and outcomes of Green IS adoption in small and medium-sized enterprises. *Sustainability, 11*(6), 1575.

Bajdor, P., Pawełoszek, I., & Fidlerova, H. (2021). Analysis and assessment of sustainable entrepreneurship practices in Polish small and medium enterprises. *Sustainability, 13*(7), 3595.

Bakar, M. F. A., Talukder, M., Quazi, A., & Khan, I. (2020). Adoption of sustainable technology in the Malaysian SMEs sector: Does the role of government matter? *Information, 11*(4), 215.

Benedek, A., & Takácsné György, K. (2016). A felelős vállalatirányítás személyi tényezői: A CSR-központ felelős vállalatvezetők attitűdjének vizsgálata a kis- és középvállalatok körében. *Vezetéstudomány – Budapest Management Review, 47*(1), 58–67.

Bikefe G., Zubairu, U., Araga, S., Maitala, F., Ediuku, E., & Anyebe, D. (2020). Corporate Social Responsibility (CSR) by small and medium enterprises (SMEs): A systematic review. *Small Business International Review, 4*(1), 16–33.

Ibarnia, E., Garay, L., & Guevara, A. (2020). Corporate Social Responsibility (CSR) in the travel supply chain: A literature review. *Sustainability, 12*(23), 10125.

Ismail, I., Shafie, R., & Ismail, K. N. I. K. (2020). Current trends and future directions on women CEOs/CFOs and financial reporting quality. *The Journal of Asian Finance, Economics and Business, 7*(11), 679–687.

Jansson, J., Nilsson, J., Modig, F., & Hed Vall, G. (2017). Commitment to sustainability in small and medium-sized enterprises: The influence of strategic orientations and management values. *Business Strategy and the Environment, 26*(1), 69–83.

Kang, M., & Park, B. (2018). Sustainable corporate social media marketing based on message structural features: Firm size plays a significant role as a moderator. *Sustainability, 10*(4), 1167.

Kamal, M. M., Mamat, R., Mangla, S. K., Kumar, P., Despoudi, S., Dora, M., & Tjahjono, B. (2022). Immediate return in circular economy: Business to consumer product return information sharing framework to support sustainable manufacturing in Small and Medium Enterprises. *Journal of Business Research, 151*, 379–396.

Laila, N., Ratnasari, R. T., Ismail, S., Mohd Hidzir, P. A., & Mahphoth, M. H. (2023). The intention of Small and Medium Enterprises' owners to participate in waqf: The case of Malaysia and Indonesia *International Journal of Islamic and Middle Eastern Finance and Management, 16*(3), 429–447.

Magrizos, S., Apospori, E., Carrigan, M., & Jones, R. (2021). Is CSR the panacea for SMEs? A study of socially responsible SMEs during economic crisis. *European Management Journal, 39*(2), 291–303.

Maniu, I., Costache, C., & Dumitrașcu, D. D. (2021). Adoption of Green Environmental practices in Small and Medium-Sized Enterprises: Entrepreneur and business policies patterns in Romania. *Sustainability, 13*(9), 4968.

Metzker, J., & Streimikis, J. (2020). CSR activities in the Czech SME segment *International Journal of Entrepreneurial Knowledge, 8*(1), 49–64.

Prochazkova, K., & Micak, P. (2023). CEO gender and its effect on Corporate Social Responsibility and the perception of business ethics, *Ekonomicko-manazerske spektrum, 17*(1), 29–38.

Rakshit, S., Islam, N., Mondal, S., & Paul T. (2021). Mobile apps for SME business sustainability during COVID-19 and onwards. *Journal of Business Research 135*. 28–39.

Reza-Gharehbagh, R., Arisian, S., Hafezalkotob, A., & Makui, A., (2022). Sustainable supply chain finance through digital platforms: A pathway to green entrepreneurship. *Annals of Operations Research.*

Matten, & D. Moon, J. (2007). 'Implicit' and 'Explicit' CSR: A conceptual framework for a comparative understanding of corporate social responsibility. *Academic Management Review, 33*(2), 404–424.

Málovics, G. (2009). A vállalati fenntarthatóság érintettközpontú vizsgálata. *Doktori értekezés.* Pécsi Tudományegyetem Közgazdaságtudományi Kar Regionális Politika és Gazdaságtan Doktori Iskola.

Szlávik, J. Pálvölgyi, T. Csigéné Nagypál, A., & Füle, M. (2006). CSR in Small and Medium-sized companies: Evidence from a survey of the automative supply chain in Hungary and Austria. *Rhetoric And Realities: Analysing Corporate Social Responsibility in Europe (RARE).*

Vives, A. (2016). Responsible practices in small and medium enterprises. In G. Aras & D. Crowther (Eds.), *A handbook of corporate governance and social responsibility* (pp. 107–130). *Routledge.*

UN. (2015). *Transforming our world: The 2030 Agenda for Sustainable Development.*

Jaroslav Setek[1,*], Jiri Alina[1], and Stanislav Simbartl[2]

Economic Aspects of the Sustainability of the System of Providing Gerontological Social Services in the Context of Population Aging on the Example of the Czech Republic

Abstract:
Research background: The article is focused on the current issue of economic belonging in accordance with the aging of the population on the example of the Czech Republic after 2030. The mentioned issue greatly affects the burden on public resources. The purpose of the research is to identify possible potential risks of an economic nature within the framework of the provided specialized gerontological social services.
Purpose of the article: Point out the importance of the forecast of human resources in the framework of ensuring the sustainability of appropriate standards in the context of population aging. For this reason, the article is prepared through an interdisciplinary approach of social sciences (especially economics, economic and social policy, demography, sociology).
Methods: For the study of the monitored problems, the method of analysis prevails, with the help of which the mentioned issue can be clarified within the dimension of the social sciences involved. Other supporting methods are comparison (finding similarities and differences of observed phenomena) and synthesis (to reveal the structure, mutual processes and relationships of individual aspects of the studied phenomenon).
Findings & Value added: The article deals with current issues that will be faced by the social and health system of the Czech Republic in the near future, an integral part of which is the provision of expert georontological social services. In connection with the aging of the population, it is necessary to pay attention to the issue of optimal staffing of social care for the group of senior citizens.

* Corresponding author: jsetek@ef.jcu.cz
1 University of South Bohemia, Faculty of Economics, Department of Applied Economics and Economy, Studentská 13, 370 05 České Budějovice, Czech Republic
2 Ministry of Defense of the Czech Republic, Prague, Czech Republic

Keywords: *population aging, staffing of gerontological social services, sustainability of public resources*

JEL Classification: *A13; F01; I23*

1 Introduction

The era of the 21st century has brought completely new requirements to the lives of all individuals. The European region is undergoing significant demographic changes of an unprecedented scale, bringing with it relevant problems of interrelated economic and social dimensions. The ever-increasing human lifespan represents a significant achievement of the sciences involved. From an economic point of view, the aging of the population is understood as a negative change in demographic factors. It results from the long-term trend of reducing the number of economically active population in the economy. This disproportion affects various areas of society's life, it even tends to reduce macroeconomic growth. The issue of population aging is dealt with at the world level by, among others, the Organization for Economic Cooperation and Development (Cavanagh et al., 2021). According to her report, population aging represents an increase in the ratio of the population aged 65 and over to the population aged 20–64. Due to the ongoing rapid processes of economic globalization and changes in the demographic structure of the population of individual countries, the effects on the economy, social environment and all-round development of society are gaining importance.

Based on the facts cited above, the article deals with the economic context of the current issue of demographic aging on the example of the Czech Republic, with a focus on staffing within the growing demand for special gerontological social services. The starting point for processing are changes in the age structure of the population of the national economy. It is the age structure, as a reflection of long-term population development and the related reproductive behavior and movement of the population, that ranks among the basic characteristics of monitored population development. This is one of the most significant demographic processes, which is characterized by the changing representation of age groups in the population (Jackson et al., 2023).

The argument about the negative impact of population aging on the economies of current countries (including the Czech Republic) is derived from the reality that the main burden of financing welfare state programs is borne by the productive employed generation (Duernecker & Vega-Redondo, 2018). While the main beneficiaries of the most important programs of the social and health system are seniors. From the negative effects of population aging on the current economy of the Czech Republic, the necessity of fundamental reforms is deduced, namely in the area of sustainability of the social services system (Faltová Leitmanová et al., 2021). This also results in the requirement for the creation of social policy plans, which is an integral part of public and regional economic policy.

2 Materials and Methods

Demographic aging in the Czech Republic is monitored as part of the article by measuring the shares of age groups from the total population, further on the basis of indices, i.e., relative comparative numbers (index of old age, indices of load on the productive component) and using the average age or median age. The share of the three main age groups of the population in the population is most often monitored, which are defined according to the expected economic activity of the majority of people of a given age. It is therefore a pre-productive component of the population, which is mostly defined stereotypically by ages 0–14 (respectively 0–19 years). The productive component of the population consists of persons aged 15–64 (respectively. 20–64 years) and the age group of post-productive persons aged 65 and over (age group 65+). Based on the age categories divided in this way, the aging process of the population is interpreted through indicators in the form of average age and the index of old age (number of people aged 65+ per 100 children aged 0–14) dependency index I (number of children aged 0–14 per 100 persons aged 15–64), dependency index II. (number of persons aged 65 and over per 100 persons aged 15–64), and the economic burden index (number of children aged 0–19 and number of persons aged 65+ per 100 persons aged 20–59) (Hajek & König, 2022).

The most commonly used characteristic in international comparisons is the proportion of persons aged 65 and over in a given population. The realization of forecasts of the future demographic development of the Czech economy is considerably unclear due to the events of February 24, 2022 – the aggression of the Russian Federation in Ukraine. From this date, as a result of the wave of migration from Ukraine, it is difficult to establish longer forecasts of the future development of demographic development for 10 years or more. With regard to the specifics of monitoring the economic and social impacts of the aging population in the Czech Republic, processing primarily requires the application of methods of analysis, comparison, synthesis, observation and generalization. Processing also requires an interdisciplinary approach of interested social sciences and humanities on the issue. These are mainly economics, demography, sociology, theory of economic and social policy, gerontology (Blakey et al., 2020).

3 Results and Discussions

3.1 Default Philosophy of the Issue

The theoretical concepts of population aging and gerontological science are quite broad. They can be observed from the aspect of: economic, medical, psychological, demographic, sociological, pedagogical, legal, etc… Based on the analysis of demographic changes in the context of social and economic aspects of population aging, it is perceived as a change in the age structure of the population, which manifests itself due to an increasing number or higher population compared to other age groups (Eaton, 2000). Determinants of population aging are presented in two main groups, namely demographic and non-demographic (Firman, 2023). The demographic group includes: age, decline in birth rate, migration, mortality, increase in average life expectancy. The non-demographic group mainly expresses the quality of life in old age. This is expressed by financial security in real terms (amount of income after deduction of inflation), leisure activities, medical level, scientific and technological innovations. Although the importance of a group of non-demographic factors on the aging of the population cannot be denied, unlike demographic factors, it is difficult to measure quantitatively, with the exception of financial security (Clark, 2020).

According to some sources of scientific interest, the growth of longevity represents a considerable achievement for humanity, it is one of the most remarkable achievements in human history (Gaugler, 2023). As a result of the growth of the elderly population, changes occur not only in the life of an individual, but also in the framework of interpersonal relationships. The social group of seniors presents a considerable reserve of human capital in society (Kafková, 2022). At the same time, the aging of the population has major economic consequences, such as the impact on public budgets, the aging of the workforce with a subsequent reduction in the growth rate of the labor supply (LaBarge and Pyle, 2020). The growing number of older people (aged 65 and over) is likely to have a significant impact on a wide range of policy areas: most directly, taking into account the different needs of specialist gerontological social services. Permanent changes in demographic processes thus affect the economic system and the material well-being of the population. An aging society, changes in the distribution of the population by age groups have significant social and economic consequences (Davison et al., 2022).

3.2 The Current Situation and the Expected Development of the Aging of the Czech Population

At the beginning of 2018, almost 6.9 million people aged 15 to 64 lived in the Czech Republic, which was half a million less than in 2009. At that time, their number was the highest since the end of the Second World War. According to the documents of the Czech Statistical Office, a further reduction in the number of inhabitants at this age can be assumed. According to the results of his demographic projection, the largest numerical reduction of the population of the Czech Republic between the ages of 15 and 64 should occur between 2035 and 2045, by 4.5 % (Šetek et al. 2019). In 2055, 53.7 % of the population of the Czech Republic should belong to this age category. As a result of the aging of individual generations, the centre of gravity of the economically active age population, which represents the strong cohorts born in the 1970s, will gradually shift to older ages and thereby naturally change the age composition of the population. From 2022, the centre of gravity of the population will be the age group 45–49, from 2027 then the age group 50–54, etc. In 2037, the position of the numerically strongest age group 60–64, i.e., people of pre-retirement age, should take over, and by the middle of the century maintain the position (Šetek et al., 2019).

From the above-mentioned facts, it is almost certain that a fundamental problem will arise after 2035. In this period, it is precisely the strong years of the mentioned 70s of the 20th century that will begin to retire. If we want to deal with the effects of the expected demographic development on the economy of the Czech Republic, the longer-term dynamics of the development of the age structure of the population, including their relevant predictions, must be taken into account as a very important starting point (Wilckens et al., 2023). These facts are evident from the following table 1 with demonstrated milestones from 2020 to 2050 in five-year intervals and a forecast of the demographic aging process until 2065 (table 2) through the old-age index (expressing how many people in the population aged 60 and over per 100 children aged 0–14 years), dependency index I (expresses the number of children aged 0–14 per 100 persons aged 15–59), dependency index II (indicates the number of persons aged 60 and over per 100 persons aged 15–59 years) and the economic burden index (shows the number of children aged 0–14 and the number of inhabitants aged 60 and over per 100 persons aged 15–59):

Table 1. Size of the population and selected age groups of senior citizens in the Czech Republic until 2050.

Year	Population total (in millions)	Population aged 65+ (in millions)	Population aged 80+ (in millions)	The share of people aged 65+ in the total population (in %)	The share of people aged 80+ in the total population (in %)
2020	10,67	2,13	0,44	19,99	4,14
2025	10,76	2,29	0,54	21,31	5,04
2030	10,78	2,40	0,71	22,29	6,56
2035	10,76	2,50	0,84	23,21	7,76
2040	10,74	2,60	0,88	25,12	8,18
2045	10,74	2,96	0,90	27,55	8,39
2050	10,74	3,08	0,95	28,65	8,81

Source: Czech Statistical Office 2018 and own processing

Table 2. Characteristics of the age structure and indexes of the economic burden of the productive component of the population of the Czech Republic between 2000–2065, selected years (in %).

Demographic indicator	2015	2020	2025	2035	2045	2055	2065
Average age	41,6	42,7	43,9	46,3	47,5	48,3	49,0
Age index	117.1	128,7	145,6	187,8	222,5	232,7	243,6
Dependency Index I.	22,5	24,2	23,5	20,8	23,4	25,9	24,2
Dependency Index II.	26,3	31,2	34,2	39,1	52,0	60,2	58,9
Load index	59,0	66,9	72,0	74,0	89,7	103,3	100,8

Source: Czech Statistical Office 2018 and own processing

3.3 Current Analysis of the Age Structure of the Elderly

The number and proportion of elderly people does not change only as a whole, the age structure within this component is also developing, which is especially a subject of interest in the framework of the sustainability of the interest system and the subsequent planning of specialized gerontological social services (Drobne and Bogataj, 2022). The most numerous age group in the senior population remains the youngest group in the age range of 65–69 years, representing a third of all seniors in the long term. Between 2007 and 2017, the group of people aged 90–94 years strengthened relatively the most, more than doubling (absolutely by 28 thousand), its percentage share in the senior population increased from 1.4 to 2.4 %. Of the younger age groups, the number of people in the 70–74 age group increased relatively the most (by 57 %, in absolute terms by almost 207 thousand), followed by the number of people in the 65–69 age group (by 44 %, in absolute terms by almost 211 thousand). The growth of these two groups demonstrates the shift of the strong post-war years in the senior years in recent years.

As part of a comparison over a longer time horizon (selected years 1987 and 1997) to 2017, the youngest age groups (65–69 years and 70–74 years) grew the most in absolute terms, but in relative terms, the oldest ones increased the most dynamically. Compared to 1997, there are currently more than twice as many people aged 90–94 and over 95. Compared to 1987, the number of people in the 90–94 age group has almost quadrupled, and the number of people in the 95+ age group has even increased by 4.6 times compared to 1987. However, the percentage representation of the oldest two groups in the senior group has been very low for a long time (over the last thirty years monitored) (for the 90–94 age group between 1.0–2.5 %, for the 95+ group between 0.2–0.4 %).

3.4 Staffing the Growing Demand for Social Services

A sliding scale approach is applied to the processing of the staffing model to cover the growing demand for specialized gerontological services, i.e., flexible adaptation to all changes in the system environment in the provision of social services, for a time horizon of 10 years (Cavanagh et al., 2021). The output document will be the proposal of the Human Resources Plan program for the provision of social services in the field of gerontology for the mentioned time horizon (Iglesias Souto et al., 2021). In essence, it will be a comprehensive plan at the macro level. During the processing, the method of system dynamics will be applied with appropriate simulations based on input variables (i.e., documents of the Czech Statistical Office on the demographic development of the population, departments of health, labor and social affairs, education….). It can be assumed that the end users of this program will mainly be the authorities of the interested ministries (labour and social affairs, youth education and physical education, health…), the Association of Social Service Providers, or other participating institutions. Based on the information obtained in this way, they can implement appropriate strategic decisions and measures.

In 2016, over 70,000 people worked in social care services in the Czech economy. persons, of whom approx. 67 % worked directly in gerontological services (Czech Statistical Office, 2018). Legislatively defined standards of the number of users of social services per worker in residential facilities, as for example in Slovak Act No. 448/2008 Coll., as amended. According to the aforementioned law, the appropriate standards for staffing the operation of specialized social services are established (for example, in a facility for the elderly with a year-round stay, where more than 50 % of the clients are in IV-VI degrees of dependency, there must be a maximum of 2 clients per employee, in the case, that it is a facility with a weekly stay, there must be a maximum of 2.3 clients per employee, and if it is an outpatient social service, then there must be a maximum of 3 clients per employee). At the same time, in all types of these facilities, at least 52 % of the total number of employees must be professional.

In 2017, there were a total of 355,000 recipients of the care allowance in the Czech Republic, of which 107,285 people received the care allowance in the first degree of dependency, and in the second degree of dependence 115,466 persons, in III. degree of dependence of 83,295 persons and in IV. the degree of dependence of 48,636 persons (Czech Statistical Office, 2018). In a time comparison of ten years (from 2007 to 2017), the number of recipients of this benefit increased by more than 63 thousand. persons, while the structure of beneficiaries increased significantly during this period (especially in the III stage it increased by 8 % in 2017, in the IV stage it increased by 5.9 and 13.7 %). From the aforementioned expected development of the number of care allowance recipients in individual degrees of dependency, it is clear that the existing capacities of individual types of social services will not be sufficient in the coming years (shown in Table 3). It is obvious that the development of all forms of field, outpatient and residential facilities should become an integral part of all development plans at the general and regional level. A necessary prerequisite for responding in time to the changed demographic situation is an increased emphasis on the analysis of changes in the demographic situation of the population in individual regions.

At the same time, it is necessary to set session standards through the ratio of social care workers to clients, similar to the one in the Slovak Republic in accordance with legislation (Act no. 448/2008 Coll. on social services). The potential risk of a lack of professional staff in social care can significantly reduce the quality of services and threaten the fulfillment of the basic human rights of the client (Tsao et al., 2020).

Table 3: Expected number of employees in individual types of social care services to the year 2035, while maintaining the level of facilities at the 2016 level.

Social Services	2016	2025	2030	2035
Homes for the elderly	25 275	32 072	41 805	49 394
Homes with special services	12 410	15 748	20 526	24 253
Care service	8 294	9 321	9 769	10 156
Daily services centres	2 105	2 365	2 479	2 577
Homes for people with disabilities	10 925	10 925	10 925	10 925
Protected housing	2 367	2 367	2 367	2 367
Respite services	2 484	2 792	2 926	3 042
Personal assistance	3 806	4 277	4 483	4 661
Support for independent housing	140	157	165	172
Guiding and reading services	57	64	67	70
Social services provided in health -care facilities	764	858	900	935
Emergency care	80	90	94	98
Daily care services	597	671	704	732
Total	70 052	82 549	98 091	110 298
Increase		12 497	28 039	40 245

Source: Czech Statistical Office 2018 and own processing

4 Discussion and Conclusion

The limits of the study of the issue of sustainability of staffing of specialized gerontological social services must be monitored within the critical infrastructure of the national economy. Its violation would have an impact on the provision of the basic life needs of the population, the health of people and, consequently, on the security of the state. The possible future direction of the investigated problem is determined by a number of factors. Among the most significant are the time-consuming process of acquiring employees as a result of the required higher professional standards, the accelerating growing demand for the mentioned social services and the implementation of Industry 4.0 technologies (especially digitization) in the mentioned sphere.

For the above-mentioned reasons, the expected acceleration of population aging in the Czech economy and with it the expected increase in demand for gerontological services in the context of sustainability is a challenge for the creation of the concept of a strategic document for the planning of gerontological social services. The human resources plan for the area of social services must be an essential part of the document. The starting point for the processing is the analysis of input variables (Ye and Post, 2020). This is the overall demand for these specific services and the future structure of human resources (in the educational process within professional social and health education, including potential job applicants in this sphere).

The onset of the Industry 4.0 era is also expected, some of whose technologies are also applicable to the sphere of social services. In this context, emphasis is placed on the growing importance of the innovation trend, the basis of which can be created in some cities and regions on the basis of connected programs Smart region (city, municipality) and Smart technologies (Zacher & Rudolph, 2019). In this way, the technical means of programs of direct personnel communication between the client (senior) and the social service provider through the application were created, which could ultimately mean significant personnel transfers within the social service professions.

References

Act no. 448/2008 Coll. on social services. (n.d.). 448/2008 Z. z. Zákon o sociálnych službách | Aktuálne znenie. epi.sk. https://www.epi.sk/zz/2008-448

Blakey, E., Durante, A., Malfait, S., Panayiota, K., Thilo, F., & O'Connor, S. (2020). Involving older people in gerontological nursing research: A discussion of five European. *International Journal of Older People Nursing, 15*(2), e12311.

Cavanagh, J., Pariona-Cabrera, P., & Halvorsen, B. (2021). In what ways are HR analytics and artificial intelligence transforming the healthcare sector?. *Asia Pacific Journal of Human Resources.*

Clark, P. G. (2020). Potentials and pitfalls of networking in interdisciplinary education: Taking on the challenges in Gerontology and Geriatrics. *Gerontology & Geriatrics Education, 41*(3), 264–272.

Czech Statistical Office. (2018). Population projection of the Czech Republic 2018–2100. https://www.czso.cz/csu/czso/projekce--obyvatelstva-ceske-republiky-2018-2100-.

Davison, T. E., McCabe, M. P., Busija, L., Martin, C., & Graham, A. (2022). Trajectory and predictors of mental health symptoms and wellbeing in newly admitted nursing home residents. *Clinical Gerontologist, 45*(5), 1103–1116.

Drobne, S., & Bogataj, M. (2022). Migration flows through the lens of human resource ageing. *Business Systems Research: International journal of the Society for Advancing Innovation and Research in Economy, 13*(3), 47–62.

Duernecker, G., & Vega-Redondo, F. (2018). Social networks and the process of globalization. *The Review of Economic Studies, 85*(3), 1716–1751.

Eaton, S. C. (2000). Beyond 'unloving care': Linking human resource management and patient care quality in nursing homes. *International journal of human resource management, 11*(3), 591–616.

Faltová Leitmanová, I., Alina, J., Šetek, J., & Bajer, D. (2021). Risks of unfavorable demographic development of population aging on public finances of the Czech economy. *The International Scientific Conference INPROFORUM, Czech Republic*, 173–180.

Firman, A. (2023). Knowledge management implementation and human resource development on employee performance. *Jurnal Manajemen Bisnis, 10*(1), 221–234.

Gaugler, J. E. (2023). Gerontology as transdisciplinary endeavor. *The Gerontologist, 63*(5), 799–802.

Hajek, A., & König, H. H. (2022). Grandchild care and loneliness among older Europeans: Longitudinal evidence from the Survey of Health, Ageing and Retirement in Europe. *International Journal of Geriatric Psychiatry, 37*(8).

Iglesias Souto, P. M., Real Deus, J. E., Dosil Maceira, A., Mayo Pais, M. E., & Taboada Ares, E. M. (2021). Suitability of social services for the older persons: Analysis of degree of fit between needs and services. *Journal of Aging & Social Policy, 33*(3), 285–304.

Jackson, E. M., O'Brien, K., McGuire, L. C., Baumgart, M., Gore, J., Brandt, K., … & Lamont, H. (2023). Promoting healthy aging: Public health as a leader for reducing dementia risk. *Public Policy & Aging Report, 33*(3), 92–95.

Kafková, M. P. (2022). Active ageing index as a tool for country assessment and comparison: The case of the Czech Republic and Slovakia. *Sociológia-Slovak Sociological Review, 54*(2), 168–185.

LaBarge, M. C., & Pyle, M. (2020). Staying in "the works of living": How older adults employ marketplace resources to age successfully. *Journal of Consumer Affairs, 54*(2), 742–774.

Šetek, J., Alina, J., Vlčková, M., & Poláčková, E. (2019). Economic dimension of aging of the population on the example of the Czech Republic. *The 13th International Days of Statistics and Economics, Czech Republic*, 1479–1488.

Tsao, H. H., Lei, X., & Patrick Rau, P. L. (2020). Design, development, and evaluation of a virtual aging simulation system. *Educational Gerontology, 46*(6), 317–330.

Wilckens, M. R., Wöhrmann, A. M., Deller, J., & Finsel, J. (2023). Health and the intention to retire: Exploring the moderating effects of human resources practices. *The International Journal of Human Resource Management, 34*(18), 3520–3554.

Ye, Z., & Post, T. (2020). What age do you feel?–Subjective age identity and economic behaviors. *Journal of Economic Behavior & Organization*, *173*, 322–341.

Zacher, H., & Rudolph, C. W. (2019). Just a mirage: On the incremental predictive validity of subjective age. *Work, Aging and Retirement*, 5(2), 141–162.

Renata Skypalova[1,*], and Martin Sikyr[1]

Current Attitudes of Business Enterprises Towards Corporate Social Responsibility Activities in the Czech Republic

Abstract:
Research background: Corporate Social Responsibility (CSR) has become a trend in many business strategies in recent years. Many business enterprises invest in various CSR activities to meet diverse social, environmental, and economic goals benefiting the entire society as well as the business enterprises themselves.
Purpose of the article: The article analyzes the current attitudes of selected business enterprises towards CSR activities to find out why they invest in CSR activities and how they organize them.
Methods: The analysis is based on the results of a questionnaire survey of 152 business enterprises running their business activities in the Czech Republic. The evaluation of responses on the size of surveyed business enterprises measured by the number of employees (small, medium-sized, large, and extra-large enterprises) is included in the analysis.
Findings & Value added: The results showed that the majority of surveyed business enterprises have a specific CSR strategy implemented by an HR department in line with the business strategy to contribute to the "public good." CSR activities become a natural part of business activities, and investments in CSR activities benefit both the business enterprises themselves and related stakeholders. The results demonstrate why CSR activities are important for business enterprises and how they incorporate them into their business activities.

Keywords: *corporate social responsibility, business enterprises, public good, stakeholder interests, Czech Republic*

JEL Classification: *M10; M12; M14*

1 Introduction

Corporate Social Responsibility (CSR) is generally known as a business concept including socially, environmentally, and economically beneficial activities

---

* Corresponding author: renata.skypalova@ambis.cz
1 AMBIS College, Department of Economics and Management, Lindnerova 575/1, 180 00 Prague 8, Czech Republic

implemented by business enterprises to achieve the general good of nature and community, including major stakeholders, such as investors, founders, managers, employees, customers, suppliers, and other business partners, government institutions, and community groups (Mi et al., 2018).

Business enterprises implement CSR activities to play a positive role in the environment around them. CSR efforts of business enterprises are founded on the belief that business enterprises may contribute to the improvement of the world through socially, ecologically, and economically beneficial activities (Koseoglu et al., 2021). CSR efforts of business enterprises can be driven by many different reasons, such as the altruism of founders, strategies of managers, demand of customers, expectations of job seekers and employees, or requirements of investors, suppliers, and subscribers (Saxton et al., 2019).

Being socially, environmentally, and economically responsible can be beneficial not only for the world but also for business enterprises themselves (Awaysheh et al., 2020). CSR activities of business enterprises can improve their business reputation and competitiveness, even if they require significant additional costs (Bernal Conesa et al., 2017). Social CSR activities of applying an ethical and fair approach to business can attract and retain both employees and customers, whose loyalty is crucial for the success of the business (Srisuphaolarn & Assarut, 2019). Environmental CSR activities of reducing and recycling waste can lower costs and improve financial results (Magee, 2019). Economic CSR activities of investing in effective and efficient products (goods and services) that bring a reasonable profit to the business and corresponding value to the society can lead to new market gains (Bian et al., 2021). Potential risks of unsuccessful implementation of CSR activities include lack of engagement, impracticable plans, unfulfilled promises, or inappropriate management (Chollet and Sandwidi, 2018).

The successful implementation of CSR activities should be established on a considered CSR strategy vertically integrated with the overall business strategy (Roy et al., 2021). This integration ensures the connection of CSR activities with business activities. This is how CSR activities can benefit both the business enterprises themselves and related stakeholders, namely employees and customers who value the socially, environmentally, and economically responsible efforts of business enterprises (Swiatkiewicz, 2017). The CSR goals must be in line with business goals and vice versa, the business goals must include the CSR goals. CSR activities must be incorporated into core business policies and practices. In other words, CSR activities must be combined with suitable business policies and practices (Maury, 2022). The implementation of CSR activities should be a strategic issue supported by top management and managed by the responsible organizational unit, a CSR or HR department. The success of CSR activities can be measured by the operational, market, and financial results of the company, such as reducing produced waste, increasing recycled material, acquiring new markets and customers, attracting and retaining new employees, improving relations with the local community and so on (Siltaloppi et al., 2021).

The implementation of CSR activities depends on the voluntary decisions of the business enterprises. Individual business enterprises usually implement CSR activities in line with their business strategies to achieve both business and CSR goals (Tourky et al., 2020). However, business enterprises may choose to follow certain standards for CSR activities, such as ISO 26000 issued by the International Organization for Standardization (ISO), which helps implement CSR activities effectively and efficiently (Herciu, 2016).

If business enterprises implement successful CSR strategies and activities, it should be publicly demonstrated and recognized. Various CSR certifications and awards issued by various governmental and non-governmental institutions are used to certify and award the most successful CSR strategies and activities. Such certification and recognition can enhance all the benefits of socially, environmentally, and economically responsible strategies and activities of business enterprises (Benjamin & Biswas, 2022).

However, despite all the potential CSR benefits and awards, the foundation of effective and efficient CSR efforts is an honest and open approach to everything the business enterprises do, especially concerning the outside world. Therefore, this article analyzes the current attitudes of selected business enterprises towards CSR activities to find out why they invest in CSR activities and how they organize them. Within the analysis, answers to three research questions are sought:

RQ1: What motivates surveyed business enterprises to invest in CSR activities?
RQ2: Do surveyed business enterprises have a specific CSR strategy integrated with the business strategy?
RQ3: Who is responsible for implementing CSR activities in surveyed business enterprises?

2 Methods

The analysis of the current attitudes of selected business enterprises towards CSR activities is based on the results of a questionnaire survey of 152 business enterprises running their business activities in the Czech Republic. The questionnaire survey was carried out within a project Corporate Social Responsibility in Business Practice of the Visegrad Region (Visegrad Grant no. 22220149) co-financed by the Governments of Czechia, Hungary, Poland, and Slovakia through the Visegrad Grants from International Visegrad Fund. The project surveys the current state of implementation of CSR activities by business enterprises in the Visegrad region, namely in Slovakia, Czechia, and Poland. This article uses data collected for the Czech Republic from January to May 2023.

The original online questionnaire used to collect data related to the implementation of CSR activities by business enterprises in the Visegrad region included fifty-three questions in five sections. For this article, nine questions in the CSR Generally section were used. The questions asked (1) how do the surveyed business enterprises have CSR integrated into the organizational structure, (2) what was the main motive of the surveyed business enterprises for starting the implementation of CSR activities, (3) whether the surveyed business enterprises have a specific CSR strategy, (4) whether the implementation of CSR activities is related to business activities in the surveyed business enterprises, (5) how much the surveyed business enterprises invested in CSR activities in 2021 (in euros), (6) whether the surveyed business enterprises have ever been awarded for their CSR activities, (7) what was the award if the surveyed business enterprises have been awarded for their CSR activities, (8) whether CSR activities of the surveyed business enterprises are certified, and (9) what is the certification, if CSR activities of the surveyed business enterprises are certified.

The set of 152 business enterprises included 11 % of microenterprises (0–9 employees), 17 % of small enterprises (10–49 employees), 13 % of medium-sized enterprises (50–249 employees), 24 % of large enterprises (250–499 employees), and 35 % of extra-large enterprises (500+ employees). The respondents included 5 % of owners, 4 % of executive directors, 2 % of CSR or PR managers, 37 % of other managers, 43 % of regular employees, and 9 % of other respondents.

The data collected was analyzed through Microsoft Excel. The analysis involved the calculation of relative frequencies of responses and the evaluation of responses on the size of surveyed business enterprises measured by the number of employees (micro, small, medium-sized, large, and extra-large enterprises). Within the analysis, a Pearson's correlation analysis with a significance level of 0.05 was applied.

The results of the analysis are limited by a relatively small number of surveyed business enterprises

3 Results

The current attitudes of 152 business enterprises running their business activities in the Czech Republic towards CSR activities are analyzed to find out why they invest in CSR activities and how they organize them.

The first analyzed question asked how the surveyed business enterprises have CSR integrated into the organizational structure. The responses showed that in the surveyed business enterprises, the implementation of CSR activities is mostly the responsibility of the HR department (26 %) and subsequently the marketing department (20 %), the CSR department (17 %), and the compliance department (14 %). In 23 % of enterprises, CSR is not organizationally integrated. A CSR department is more common in extra-large (54 %) and large (27 %) enterprises than in medium-sized (15 %) and small (4 %) enterprises. In medium-sized and small enterprises, CSR is mostly not organizationally integrated.

The second analyzed question asked what was the main motive of the surveyed business enterprises for starting the implementation of CSR activities. The responses showed that for most surveyed business enterprises, it was an effort to contribute to the "public good" (28 %) followed by an effort to strengthen marketing activities (18 %), an effort to follow current trends (14 %), an effort to compete with the competitors carries out these activities (13 %), and an effort to meet the requirements of the parent company. For 19 % of surveyed business enterprises, CSR is not purposeful, there is no effort. The motives for starting the implementation of CSR activities are similar regardless of the size of the enterprise.

The third analyzed question asked whether the surveyed business enterprises have a specific CSR strategy. The responses showed that only 24 % of surveyed business enterprises have a specific CSR strategy. The remaining enterprises have their CSR activities included in the business strategy (37 %) or have an "action plan" for their CSR activities (5 %) or implement their CSR activities spontaneously, without a strategy or plan (34 %). A specific CSR strategy is more common in extra-large (55 %) and large (25 %) enterprises than in medium-sized (14 %) and small (6 %) enterprises.

The fourth analyzed question asked whether the implementation of CSR activities is related to business activities in the surveyed business enterprises. The responses showed that only in 12 % of surveyed business enterprises the implementation of CSR activities is related to business activities. These enterprises include mostly extra-large (50 %) and medium-sized (22 %) enterprises. On the other hand, in 18 % of surveyed business enterprises, the implementation of CSR activities is not related to business activities. These enterprises include mostly large (36 %) and micro (21 %) enterprises. In the remaining 70 % of enterprises, the implementation of CSR activities is more or less related to business activities.

The fifth analyzed question asked how much the surveyed business enterprises invested in CSR activities in 2021 (in euros). The responses showed that 65 % of surveyed business enterprises were unable to determine how much they invested in CSR activities in 2021. The remaining enterprises invested from 10,000 to 5,000,000,000 euros. The average investment of micro-enterprises was 203,333 euros, small enterprises 362,000 euros, medium-sized enterprises 483,333 euros, large enterprises 837,619 euros, and extra-large enterprises 43,038,000 euros.

The sixth analyzed question asked whether the surveyed business enterprises have ever been awarded for their CSR activities. The responses showed that only 20 % of surveyed business enterprises have been awarded for their CSR activities. These enterprises included mostly extra-large enterprises (71 %). Following this, the seventh question asked what was the award, if the surveyed business enterprises had been awarded for their CSR activities. Most of the awards were from the "Enterprise of the Year" category.

The eighth analyzed question asked whether the CSR activities of the surveyed business enterprises are certified. The responses showed that the CSR activities of only 22 % of surveyed business enterprises are certified. These enterprises included mostly extra-large enterprises (50 %). Following this, the ninth question asked what is the certification, if CSR activities of the surveyed business enterprises are certified. Most of the certifications were from the "Global Reporting Initiative," "International Organization for Standardization" or "Fairtrade" categories.

Table 1 summarizes the results of Pearson's correlation analysis. The analysis revealed some significant associations between responses. First, there is a moderate positive association between the existence of a CSR strategy and the size of the enterprise ($r = -0.357$). The larger the enterprise, the more likely it is to have a CSR strategy. Second, there is a strong positive association between the existence of a CSR strategy and the organizational integration of CSR ($r = -0.539$). The existence of a CSR strategy is the foundation for the implementation of CSR activities under the responsibility of the HR department or the CSR department. Third, there is a strong positive association between the connection of CSR activities with business activities and the organizational integration of CSR ($r = -0.447$). The implementation of CSR activities under the responsibility of the HR department or the CSR department is the foundation for the connection of CSR activities with business activities. Finally, there is a strong positive association between the connection of CSR activities with business activities and the existence of a CSR strategy ($r = -0.527$). The connection of CSR activities with business activities is the result of the existence of a CSR strategy integrated with the business strategy. To sum up, effective and efficient CSR efforts require a specific CSR strategy implemented by an HR or CSR department in line with the business strategy.

Table 1. The associations between responses.

	Pearson's correlation coefficients (r)				
	Enterprise Size	**Organization of CSR**	**Motives for CSR**	**CSR Strategy**	**CSR and Business Fit**
Enterprise Size	1				
Organization of CSR	0.237	1			
Motives for CSR	-0.051	-0.201	1		
CSR Strategy	0.357	0.539	-0.210	1	
CSR and Business Fit	0.241	0.447	-0.329	0.527	1

Source: own calculations

4 Discussion

The analysis of the current attitudes of 152 business enterprises running their business activities in the Czech Republic towards CSR activities revealed that most of the surveyed business enterprises invest in CSR activities to contribute to the "public good" (RQ1), which is one of the main purposes of socially responsible behavior of any enterprise (Bradly & Nathan, 2019).

More than a third of surveyed business enterprises have their CSR activities included in the business strategy. However, less than a quarter of surveyed business enterprises, mostly extra-large and large enterprises, have a specific CSR strategy (RQ2). Regardless of the existence of a specific CSR strategy, any investment in CSR activities should be a strategic matter, and therefore CSR activities should be integrated with the business strategy and should be in line with business activities (Swiatkiewicz, 2017). This is true for most surveyed business enterprises where the implementation of CSR activities is more or less related to business activities. The strategic importance of CSR activities requires a responsible organization of their implementation (Maury, 2022). In more than forty percent of surveyed business enterprises, the implementation of CSR activities is the responsibility of the HR department or the CSR department (RQ3), which is a certain guarantee of professional implementation of strategic CSR activities (Risi et al., 2023).

The results demonstrate why CSR activities are important for business enterprises to maintain their competitiveness and how they incorporate them into their business activities by achieving a strategic fit between CSR and business activities.

5 Conclusions

The analysis of current attitudes of selected business enterprises running their business activities in the Czech Republic towards CSR activities aimed to find out why they invest in CSR activities and how they organize them. The results showed that CSR activities become a natural part of business activities in most of the surveyed business enterprises. They invest in CSR activities to contribute to the "public good." The strategic importance of CSR activities for most surveyed business enterprises is demonstrated by the inclusion of CSR activities in the business strategy and the implementation of CSR activities under the responsibility of the HR department or the CSR department. The strategic investments in CSR activities can benefit both the business enterprises themselves as well as related stakeholders.

The results of the analysis are limited by a relatively small number of surveyed business enterprises as well as the location of the Czech Republic. However, they encourage further research on the implementation of CSR activities by business enterprises within the Visegrad Region (Czechia, Slovakia, Poland, and Hungary) as well as elsewhere within the European Union. Further research could be aimed at specific CSR strategies and ways of their effective and efficient implementation in different conditions of business enterprises.

Acknowledgments

This research has been supported and this paper was prepared within the project "Corporate Social Responsibility in Business Practice of the Visegrad Region (Visegrad Grant no. 22220149)." The project is co-financed by the Governments of Czechia, Hungary, Poland, and Slovakia through Visegrad Grants from the International Visegrad Fund. The mission of the fund is to advance ideas for sustainable regional cooperation in Central Europe. We would like to express our gratitude and acknowledge that this paper represents a segment of a comprehensive study conducted as part of the mentioned project. We extend our appreciation to the project team, funding agencies, and all individuals who contributed to the successful execution of this study.

References

Awaysheh, A., Heron, R. A., Perry, T. & Wilson, J. I. (2020). On the relation between corporate social responsibility and financial performance. *Strategic Management Journal*, *41*(6), 965–987.

Benjamin, S. J., & Biswas, P. K. (2022). Does winning a CSR Award increase firm value? *International Journal of Disclosure and Governance*, *19*, 313–329.

Bernal Conesa, J. A., Briones Peñalver, A. J., & de Nieves Nieto, C. (2017). Impacts of the CSR strategies of technology companies on performance and competitiveness. *Tourism & Management Studies*, *13*(4), 73–81.

Bian, J., Liao, Y., Wang, Y. Y., & Tao, F. (2021). Analysis of firm CSR strategies. *European Journal of Operational Research*, *290*(3), 914–926.

Bradly, A., & Nathan, G. (2019). Institutional CSR: Provision of public goods in developing economies. *Social Responsibility Journal*, *15*(7), 874–887.

Chollet, P., & Sandwidi, B. W. (2018). CSR engagement and financial risk: A virtuous circle? International evidence. *Global Finance Journal*, *38*, 65–81.

Herciu, M. (2016). ISO 26000 – An integrative approach of corporate social responsibility. *Studies in Business and Economics*, *11*(1), 73–79.

Koseoglu, M. A., Hon, A., Kalargyrou, V., & Okumus, F. (2021). Hiring people with disabilities as a CSR strategy in the tourism industry. *Tourism Analysis*, *26*(1), 41–55.

Magee, R. G. (2019). Environmental worldview beliefs and CSR advertising. *Social Responsibility Journal*, *15*(3), 379–394.

Maury, B. (2022). Strategic CSR and firm performance: The role of prospector and growth strategies. *Journal of Economics and Business*, *118*, 106031.

Mi, C. M., Chang, F. K., Lin, C. T., & Chang, Y. H. (2018). The theory of reasoned action to CSR behavioral intentions: The role of CSR expected benefit, CSR expected effort and stakeholders. *Sustainability*, *10*(12), 4462.

Risi, D., Wickert, C., & Ramus, T. (2023). Coordinated enactment: How organizational departments work together to implement CSR. *Business & Society*, *62*(4), 745–786.

Roy, T.K., Al-Abdin, A., & Quazi, A. (2021). Examining the CSR strategy of MNCs in Bangladesh. *Sustainability Accounting, Management and Policy Journal*, 12(2), 467–490.

Saxton, G. D., Gregory, D., Gomez, L., Ngoh, Z., Lin, Y. P., & Dietrich, S. (2019). Do CSR messages resonate? Examining public reactions to firms' CSR efforts on social media. *Journal of Business Ethics*, *155*(2), 359–377.

Siltaloppi, J., Rajala, R., & Hietala, H. (2021). Integrating CSR with business strategy: A tension management perspective. *Journal of Business Ethics*, *174*, 507–527.

Srisuphaolarn, P., & Assarut, N. (2019). Winning CSR strategies for the talent war. *Social Responsibility Journal*, *15*(3), 365–378.

Swiatkiewicz, O. (2017). Linking CSR to strategy: A practical view. *Foundations of Management*, *9*(1), 299–316.

Tourky, M., Kitchen, P., & Shaalan, A. (2020). The role of corporate identity in CSR implementation: An integrative framework. *Journal of Business Research*, *117*, 694–706.

Camila da Penha Souza[1,*], and Selma Regina Martins Oliveira[1]

What We (Do Not) Know About Mental Health in Organizations? A Lens for Sustainable Development Goal 8

Abstract:
Research background: One of the pillars of international relations and human rights is the implementation of the Sustainable Development Goals (SDGs) of the United Nations (UN), which in its objective 8 highlights the need to promote sustained, inclusive and sustainable economic growth. sustainable.
Purpose of the article: Although the relationship between professional activities and their effects on the mental health of professionals in organizations is widely reported in the literature, little is known about the relationship between professional activities of accounting professionals and the main symptoms of stress promoted by professional activities in Brazil, an emerging economy. This study shows the main stress symptoms caused by professional activities in the context of organizations.
Methods: Using a questionnaire, a survey was carried out with professionals from accounting firms, higher education institutions and city halls in the South Fluminense region of Brazil, an emerging economy.
Findings & Value added: This study fills a gap in the existing literature and makes significant contributions. This work was conclusive in showing that stress does have an impact on the daily lives of professionals, causing inconvenience for both workers, companies and customers. This study was also conclusive in highlighting that the greatest intensity of stress is related to the pressure to deliver work on time.
Implications: Target 8 of Goal 8 of the UN 2030 Agenda for Sustainable Development calls for "safe working environments for all workers" – ensuring safe workplaces goes beyond protecting workers' physical safety, extending to their well-being mental and psychological. Therefore, this study serves as a guide for managers in promoting safer environments for workers. This study also extends the existing literature on decent work and economic development.

* Corresponding author: selmaregina@id.uff.br
1 Fluminense Federal University, Department Accounting, R. Des. Ellis Hermydio Figueira, 783 – Bloco A – Aterrado, Volta Redonda – RJ, 27213-145, Brazil

Keywords: *decent work, mental health, activities professionals, Brazilian organizations, Brazil*

JEL Classification: *A11; A14; B16*

1 Introduction

One of the pillars of international relations and human rights is the implementation of the Sustainable Development Goals (SDGs) of the United Nations (UN), which in its objective 8 highlights the need to promote sustained, inclusive and sustainable economic growth. One of the most challenging objectives for the Brazilian reality (SDGs) is (8) decent work and economic growth. This is what the Sustainable Development Report 2020, published by the University of Cambridge, points out (Sachs et al., 2022). The ILO-Brazil (2022) argues that the concept of Decent Work is central to achieving the Sustainable Development Goals (SDGs) defined by the United Nations. Anholon et al. (2021) highlight that the development of actions aligned with the goals of SDG 8 generates more than just economic gains, as they contribute to the construction of a more fair, egalitarian and inclusive society. Goal 8 of Goal 8 of the UN 2030 Agenda for Sustainable Development calls for "safe working environments for all workers" – ensuring safe workplaces goes beyond protecting workers' physical safety, extending to their mental and psychological. Although the effects of professional activities on the mental health of professionals in organizations are widely reported in cutting-edge literature, little is known about the relationship between stress symptoms caused by professional accounting activities in the context of organizations in Brazil, an emerging economy.

Finding the perfect career and having professional success is the dream of most young people in large urban centers. However, this incessant search for professional success can end up becoming dangerous for the mental health of the population. Ryder (2016) states that this work-related stress ends up affecting professionals in all areas, without distinguishing between developed and developing countries. He also states that this stress harms not only the worker's health, but also the family's well-being. Very intense routines, accumulation of tasks and especially too much social pressure to present a "happy and perfect life" increase the effect of stress to truly dangerous and, in some cases, even lethal levels. The most common causes of stress at work are psychosocial risks related to work organization, work projects, work and its conditions, as well as external conditions that can influence worker performance, job satisfaction and health.

Although the impact of workplace stress varies from one individual to the next, it is known to have health consequences ranging from mental disorders to cardiovascular, musculoskeletal and reproductive diseases. Work stress can also lead to behavioral problems, including alcohol and drug abuse, increased smoking, and sleep disturbances (PAHO, 2016). The symptoms are quite diverse and can cause both physical and psychological discomfort. Illnesses present themselves little by little and are generally ignored because they seem common and unimportant, and are even not perceived as symptoms, but rather "lack of willpower, or nonsense." Simple symptoms such as excessive drowsiness or insomnia, irritability, constant heartburn, which can evolve into gastritis, migraine attacks, joint pain are some examples of the effect that stress has on the body.

When these symptoms are ignored, serious and potentially fatal diseases can arise, such as Diabetes, Hypertension, Cancer, Depression, Panic Syndrome and Anxiety Disorder, which can be aggravated by lack of knowledge about the disease and recurrent social prejudice. to mental disorders. "One of the worst consequences of depression is the stigma that surrounds it" (Barros, 2019). This study will emphasize the psychological illnesses that, because they cannot be proven by clinical and laboratory tests, many people refuse to seek professional help when they feel weak and ashamed of themselves. In addition to pressure from family and friends who believe that positive thinking and willpower are enough to free them from these ailments. Sendin (2016) states that within the Brazilian labor market, nine out of ten workers present symptoms of anxiety at some level, with approximately half of these workers suffering from some level of depression. According to PAHO (Pan American Health Organization) (PAHO, 2016), "In Brazil, a study on absence due to occupational accidents and illnesses found that 14 % of annual health benefits were related to mental disorders." Even with this data, it is still quite evident that entire communities disregard mental health and the impact that stress can cause.

There are professions that are more prone to stress, as they live with pressure to meet goals, meet demands or even increase productivity, thus leading to a picture of psychological illnesses that can become even greater illnesses. Its consequences affect several professional areas, sometimes leading to daily incapacitation of workers. From the perspective inherent to accounting and accounting professionals, it is believed that the situation is no different, one or another activity is related to a greater or lesser degree to the symptoms of stress promoted by the profession. Some professions are more physically and mentally demanding than others, such as the accounting profession, where professionals need to work with high levels of attention, caution and concentration for long periods of time. In the accounting profession, a small error can have a substantive and irreversible impact on the business. Therefore, in this area, there is a great mental workload for professionals. It is evident that such a heavy mental workload can result in various negative perceptions, attitudes and behaviors (Ozkan et al., 2015).

In fact, the accountant holds a lot of vital information for the entities they represent, but most of the time, it is not possible for them to move the market and make the results satisfactory. For the economy to develop correctly, it is essential to create solid companies that generate jobs, pay taxes and generate income for the population. For these entities to survive in the highly competitive market, the accounting professional is the most qualified to provide intelligent decision-making. In this sense, the pressure on this professional is much greater than what could be considered healthy, since a single wrong comma can, in more extreme situations, lead a company to bankruptcy (UNITED STATES BANKRUPTCY COURT DISTRICT OF DELAWARE, 2020).

Added to this, there is also the lack of knowledge of the profession on the part of clients, who demand results that in most cases do not depend on the professional, such as a positive response from the market or a reduction in taxes. This set of factors ends up leading professionals to suffer from stress. In this way, both sides end up placing their professional expectations, whether men or women, who dedicate themselves daily to maintaining the market, often at the cost of their own health. This research aims to correlate the professional activities of different groups such as: Professionals from Accounting Offices, Higher Education Institutions and City Hall; and the main symptoms of stress caused by the before mentioned activities of these professionals. For this, the research was carried out in the largest cities in the South Fluminense region, state of Rio de Janeiro. We highlight that implementing the SDGs requires in-depth scientific analysis, continuous monitoring and political action (Bilek et al., 2022). Some studies have already been developed on the impact of stress in different professions, such as:

- Khalique et al. (2020) investigated the incorporation of workforce diversity, equal opportunities and inclusive growth of their employees in multinational companies in India.
- Rai et al. (2019) takes an approach related to SDG target 8: Decent work and economic growth – A gender analysis.
- Stewart and Barling (1996) presented a model suggesting that daily job stress influences daily job performance through its influence on mood was developed and tested.
- Prado (2016) related occupational stress to its causes and consequences.
- Mothé (2006) addressed stress in the workplace.

- Stocco and Bortholuzzi (2006) showed the influence of stress on the executive secretary's work environment.
- Nascimento (2017) showed consequences and strategies of the relationship between Stress and Teachers in the Accounting Area.

However, none of the studies referenced the objective addressed in this research. In this way, this research gains emphasis, by highlighting a topic that is so relevant for professionals and also for corporations, which is a field that at each moment produces one or another professional with different symptoms promoted by professional activities and their environment, which often have an effect multiplier. It is also hoped that this research can serve as an instrument in the hands of company managers, highlighting a topic as evident as this and that it can support them in defining strategies and/or measures opposing substantial numbers of symptoms of stresses related to activities and their work environments. In this way, this study is aligned with target 8 of the Sustainable Development Goals: providing quality jobs and a safe working environment, while reducing in-work poverty, are important preconditions for sustainable economic development (Dokic & Jovanovic, 2019). On the other hand, it is also expected that accounting professionals will consider activities that may not be so harmful to their health and that may make them so unproductive that they withdraw from the job market at an early age. This work is structured according to the following chapters: 2 – Literature review; 3 – Methodology; 4 – Underlying Results and Analysis; 5 – Final words.

2 Literature Review

The Sustainable Development Goals are a way to change the world, representing the most ambitious plan to promote the sustainable development of people and the planet (Jones et al., 2017). The UN's SDG 8 defines its main objective as: "Promoting sustained, inclusive and sustainable economic growth, full and productive employment and decent work for all." Formalized in 1999 by the International Labor Organization, Decent Work can be defined as "adequately remunerated work, carried out in conditions of freedom, equity and security, capable of guaranteeing a dignified life." The UN goals highlight in Section 8.8 "Protect labor rights and promote safe and secure working environments for all workers, including migrant workers, in particular migrant women, and people in precarious employment." Decent work and economic growth are considered essential elements for the sustainable development of countries (Carlsen, 2021). This study lists the symptoms of stress caused by professional activities in organizations. Therefore, this study is directed towards this goal.

Recently, the term stress has been used more and more frequently, and this more continuous use is thanks to the lifestyle that has been developed over recent years. When this term is isolated into a specific niche, it becomes easier to understand the impact that this small word has on the lives of thousands of people. With this fact in mind, this article aims to explore a little the impact that stress has on the lives of professionals who work in the accounting area in their most diverse roles. To make these factors easier to understand, you must first understand what accounting is. When activating an online search engine, the first definition that appears is "theoretical and practical science that studies the methods of calculating and recording the financial transactions of a firm or company" (Niyama & Silva, 2011). Marion (2015) says that it covers the study of an entity's assets and the variations in this equity, evidenced in the balance sheet, in the income statement for the year, in the statement of accumulated profits or losses, in the statement of cash flows and in other more specific reports, which serve for decision making. However, when you experience the day-to-day life of a professional in this area, you realize that this definition is very technical and do not understand the human reality of these professionals. Working in the accounting field goes far beyond studying equity. According to Iudicibus (2010), "Accounting is a model, and models are, by definition, simplifications of reality. This, in essence, is the biggest limitation of accounting." In practice, workers need to balance the scales and form a bridge between the tax authorities and the taxpayer, in addition to being constantly trained and updated to maintain this healthy relationship. Professionals are still able to create a clinical picture of the entity, show its financial health, make future projections, and talk to all sectors and potential investors through the financial statements.

This entire range of functions requires a wide variety of professionals who will work from tax bookkeeping to the closing of important statements for the financial market. A company, whether micro, small, medium or large, is not capable of functioning perfectly and legally without the work of at least one good accounting professional. Not to mention the investment market, which is entirely based on financial statements that say where it is more safe to invest and where it is better not to. In addition to its functions in the private sector, accounting also plays a very important role in the public sector. Kohama (2010) says that public accounting "is the branch of accounting that studies, guides, controls and demonstrates the organization and execution of the Public Treasury; public assets and their variations." Consequently, it bridges the gap between governments and taxpayers, making this science vital for the proper functioning of the

State's accounts, therefore, it is also vital for full social maintenance. The current world of work – given the challenges of industrial progress, globalization, technological development and virtual communication – imposes conditions on us that exceed the limits of our skills and capabilities. The result is stress in the workplace, which can cause physical, psychological and even social dysfunctions that harm our health, undermine our productivity and can even affect our families and social circles (PAHO, 2016).

Existing studies highlight several factors (anxiety, sadness, temper, monotonous speech, etc.) in a work environment that negatively affect the performance and health of individuals, which should be minimized in order to allow individuals to work without any exposure to heavy workloads and stress (Ozkan et al., 2015). Protecting the physical and mental health of workers and preventing the negative psychological and sociological impacts of working life on workers are among the basic objectives of modern science (Özgür et al., 2011). Now that an important concept of this study has been defined, it is necessary to seek definitions from the other side. What is stress? What causes it and what are its main impacts? "The word stress means 'pressure,' 'tension' or 'insistence,' therefore being stressed means 'being under pressure' or 'being under the action of an insistent stimulus' " (Tolentino et al., 1997). This definition becomes clearer when faced with different everyday situations. The body needs to adapt to conflicting situations such as unattainable deadlines, pressure from superiors, long queues and the constant balance between professional and personal life. These situations tend to increase the level of hormones such as adrenaline, which causes an increase in blood pressure, an increase in heart rate and prepares the body for quick action to save its own life. These reactions kept past generations alive, as they occurred sporadically in the face of some mortal danger. However, modern life, with all its hustle and bustle, causes these same reactions with a frequency that is extremely harmful to the body. This constantly repeated enhancement of organic reactions leads to a weakening of the organism, which, in turn, leads to a series of "small defects." Stress is essentially a degree of wear and tear on the body and mind, which can reach degenerative levels (Ozkan et al., 2015).

Impressions of being nervous, agitated, neurasthenic or debilitated may be perceptions of subjective aspects of stress. However, stress does not necessarily imply a morbid change: normal life also causes wear and tear on the body's machinery (Tolentino et al., 1997). Understanding is made easier if the human body is compared to a machine that works at a constant pace. If subjected to a greater volume of work than recommended for a long period of time, this machine will invariably have a reduction in its useful life. In humans, excessive exposure to stress causes serious problems for the body, such as hypertension, diabetes, bruxism, cardiovascular diseases, sleep disorders, gastrointestinal problems, etc. It's difficult to talk about stress without mentioning the work relationships that permeate modern life. In ancient times, people worked to earn a living. With the advent of the industrial revolution and the emergence of new labor relations, work created another meaning and began to take center stage in the lives of thousands of people. First with exploitation, where men and women, from childhood onwards, were subjected to working hours of up to 18 hours a day without security, rights or rest, which led to hundreds of workers dying from exhaustion or work accidents. On the other hand, the rise of the bourgeoisie brought a reality where the elite accepts working and even encourages and glamorizes this act for as long as possible, in addition to the reward for considering that more work means more income.

In 2016, the theme for World Health and Safety at Work Day was "Stress at Work." This was also the title of a report that year by the ILO (International Labor Organization). According to PAHO (2016) there is still no global data that talks about the impact and prevalence of stress in the workplace, but there are studies carried out in the Americas and other regions that show that this is a relevant problem. PAHO also states that in 2012 a survey was carried out on health and work conditions in Central America and one of the data was that "more than 10 % of those interviewed reported feeling constantly pressured and stressed at work, sad or depressed, with problems of insomnia due to concerns about their working conditions." These distorted relationships have created clinical conditions where excessive work, whether through exploitation or glamorization, is responsible for the emergence of syndromes, such as Burnout, and the "proliferation" of serious illnesses, such as depression, anxiety disorders and hypertension, for example. Sendin (2016) states that the granting of sickness benefits has increased almost 20 times in the last ten years due to illnesses caused by stress, and that patients are often away from work for more than 100 days. On a global scale, it is speculated that expenses related to psycho-emotional disorders by 2030 could reach 6 trillion dollars. This value is greater than the combined costs of treating diseases such as diabetes, respiratory diseases and cancer, according to the World Economic Forum. He also states that this prediction may be underestimated since, on average, two thirds of people do not seek specialized medical help. In a general analysis, Sendin states that the reason for workers' nervousness, irritation, tiredness, sadness and lack of energy is the work itself, and that moments of economic recession increase this situation as the demand for results, fear of layoffs and downsizing in the workforce is present.

In addition to the obvious losses to the employee who falls ill, another factor deserves to be highlighted: The activities previously carried out by the professional who fell ill must continue to be carried out, which creates a greater burden of stress among teammates who need to make up for this lack in some way. Sendin (2016) states that mental disorders are the third cause of absence from work due to illness in Brazil and that in 2011 it is estimated that more than 211 million reais were paid to new beneficiaries. She also points out another strong consequence of these absences, the impact on colleagues who remain working. Sendin found that SHRM (American Society of Human Resources) did a study showing that, on average, supervisors spend more than four hours a week dealing with unscheduled absences, which involves making reallocations, reorganizing tasks and training those who will take over. the position that day. It is estimated that approximately half of absences become overtime for those who remain, and that superiors lose 15 % of their productivity while colleagues lose up to 30 % of their productivity. "The latest Statistical Yearbook of Occupational Accidents, from Dieese, a public department of socioeconomic studies, reveals that the number of people away from work and who received assistance from the INSS reached 16,381, in June 2015. Depressive episodes, anxiety disorders, reactions to severe stress and adjustment disorders were the main diagnoses" (Sendin, 2016). Even with such alarming data, there is still a strong reluctance to talk about mental health in the professional environment and a real resistance to admitting that stress is rising to disorder levels.

3 Methods

A personal contact with Burnout Disorder at the beginning of 2017 brought a question to be answered: "What is the impact of stress on the daily lives of accounting professionals and what are their perceptions on the subject?." Based on this question, the theme, problem and objective of the research were developed, before starting the search for bibliographic material. Little is said among Brazilian accounting academics about the mental health of professionals, so the most natural path was to turn to other areas of knowledge. Initially the search was carried out in the history of the accounting profession, society as a whole, and records of stress as a social evil. Next, it was necessary to understand what stress is, what biological processes generate it and its effects on the human body. The third part of the search for bibliographic material consisted of uniting the first two stages and understanding how society understands stress and deals with it. To achieve this, a multidisciplinary study was once again necessary, combining accounting sciences, medicine and psychology, as accounting studies alone would not meet the demand for information.

The search and reading of all the material on the topic to be worked on took approximately 12 months, only after this careful analysis of all the topics that deal with the subject did the structure of the research begin to be designed. It was decided that an exploratory study would be necessary to understand the local scenario and it was determined that building a judgment matrix would be an efficient way of understanding how the different accounting sectors felt and dealt with stress. Initially, a draft of what the matrix would be based on articles and books on medicine and psychology that talked about symptoms related to stress and on articles and accounting books that identified professionals from different areas and denoted their main occupations. This was submitted to three professionals involved in the main areas researched: A doctor in accounting, a psychiatrist and a psychoanalyst. This submission was important to ensure the seriousness and veracity of the data obtained, in addition to guaranteeing the ethics of the data collection procedure. The matrix was structured into five distinct tables, each with a specific focus. The first table asked about the functions performed by professionals, their areas of activity, divided into four subgroups:

A – Accountant at the company.
B – Independent Accountant.
C – Accountant in Education.
D – Accountant at a public agency.

In each subgroup, the various functions within the accounting area were specified and professionals were asked to mark only the boxes corresponding to the functions performed. In the second table, 12 practices and varied facts from the daily lives of these professionals were listed with the aim of identifying which item generates the highest level of stress in respondents. To do this, each item was asked to rate from zero, not at all stressful, to five, very stressful, according to their daily perceptions. The third table, composed of 25 items, also presented the respondents' judgment, but this time, the items in question were common symptoms in people suffering from exacerbated stress, such as insomnia, anxiety and migraines. For each item, participants assigned a rating from zero, I never feel it, to five, I feel it very often, according to their daily perceptions. The fourth table listed eleven measures and/or consequences of stress, such as going to the doctor or missing an important appointment, therefore, respondents were asked to mark only what suited their reality. The fifth and final table asked about the personal characteristics of the respondents, such as whether they were married, age and perspectives so that it was possible to define a profile of the professionals and relate this profile to the other tables. The matrix was subjected to 3 pre-tests before application, all carried out with students, teachers and accounting professionals. In the first, it was found that the language used was very technical and difficult to understand, which compromised data capture.

To solve this problem, the matrix language was replaced by a more generic one. The second pre-test found that the matrix was too long and not very objective, which led to it being reduced as much as possible so as not to lose the necessary information. With this, the final result was reached, which was approved in the third pre-test. To start the application, the matrix was transferred to the website encuestafacil.com and the link to answer it was sent to a series of electronic addresses of accounting offices in the South Fluminense region. More than 50 emails were sent, but we only received 8 responses. The low number of responses required a new strategy: A list was created with the telephone numbers of the main offices in the largest cities in the South Fluminense region – Barra Mansa, Resende and Volta Redonda. Each of them was called to explain the survey and asked for an email address so it could be sent to be answered.

The results were also not satisfactory as the number of respondents after more than 20 calls increased by only 2 points. Finally, the solution found was to print the judgment matrix and take it personally to the respondents. Approximately 130 copies of the matrix were printed, of which approximately 90 were responded to. To reach this number of respondents it was necessary to go to various offices, city halls and colleges, explain what the survey was about, the objective and relevance of the research, ask for a few minutes to administer the questionnaire and, often, explain to the respondents in a hurry each frame. However, considering some events that occurred, with major damages, there was a loss of approximately 20 responses that corresponded to the questionnaires administered in one of the undergraduate courses in accounting sciences offered by university centers in the region. As there was no time to repair this loss, the total number of responses obtained was approximately 70. To achieve the objective of this research, it was initially defined that the questionnaire would be applied in the South Fluminense Region, South of the State of Rio de Janeiro and the possible respondents were divided into four groups:

- Independent accountants and accounting office employees.
- Public accountants working in city halls in the region.
- Teachers and students from the main accounting courses in the region.
- Accounting professionals from multinational companies located in the region.

However, it proved to be a very complicated task to cover the entire South Fluminense region and a new delimitation was made for the three largest cities in the South of the State: Resende, Barra Mansa and Volta Redonda. The research was carried out from October 2018 to May 2019, using printed material taken personally to the respondents, which resulted in greater knowledge about the professionals and their perspectives. In general, when arriving at an office to carry out the survey, it was necessary to convince an employee that the time to respond would be very short and would not be wasted. This process took an average of 10–15 minutes. This employee then distributed the survey to those who knew who would respond. Many respondents showed sympathy for the topic, while others refused to respond, citing too much work and no time to waste. It was noted that the apparently most stressed employees did not want to respond. Unlike offices and city halls, it was easier to obtain answers at higher education institutes, since they are environments that promote diverse research. This field was also where the greatest diversity of people was found, including teachers of different ages and very young students who had never had professional experience and others who are already in the job market in different sectors.

The sample indicates that less than half of all respondents declare themselves married and the vast majority are between 20 and 35 years old, a quarter of them are between 36 and 50 years old, a fifth are between 51 and 65 years old and the smallest age group is of people under 20 years old. Furthermore, approximately 70 % of respondents have worked in the accounting industry for less than 10 years. The majority of respondents identify as female. Figure 1 highlights the respondents' areas of concentration.

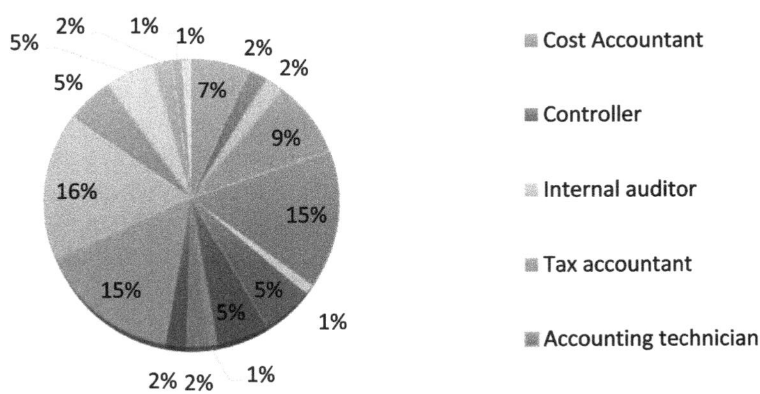

Figure 1. Main areas of activity.

It can be seen that the largest group is students in the middle of the course and accounting technicians, followed by students at the end of the course and general accountants. The following section presents the results of the research with all the aggregated results: private accountants and accounting professionals from accounting firms; accountants and accounting professionals in the public sector; and professors and undergraduate students in accounting sciences.

4 Results and Discussion

4.1 Expected Results

This section presents the results of the impact that stress causes on accounting professionals globally. Figure 2 highlights the relationship between stress and the main activities of professionals.

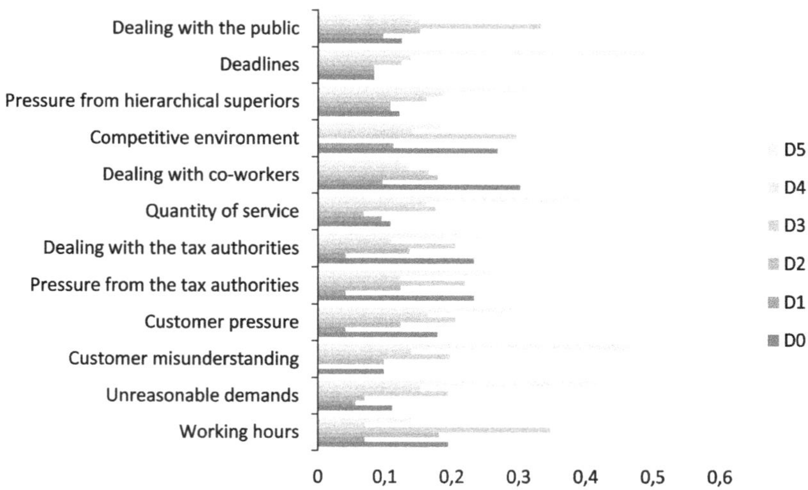

Figure 2. Stress in main activities.

In general, the intensity of stress in activities is concentrated between zero, three and five, which indicates a balance between no stress, moderate stress and intense stress. Even with greater balance, factors such as Deadlines, Quantity of Services, Unreasonable Demands and Customer Misunderstanding still suggest very high levels of stress incidence. This increase shows that greater attention is needed to these factors, as they may be responsible for the deterioration of professional health. Figure 3 shows an overview of the main symptoms of excessive stress and its incidence on respondents.

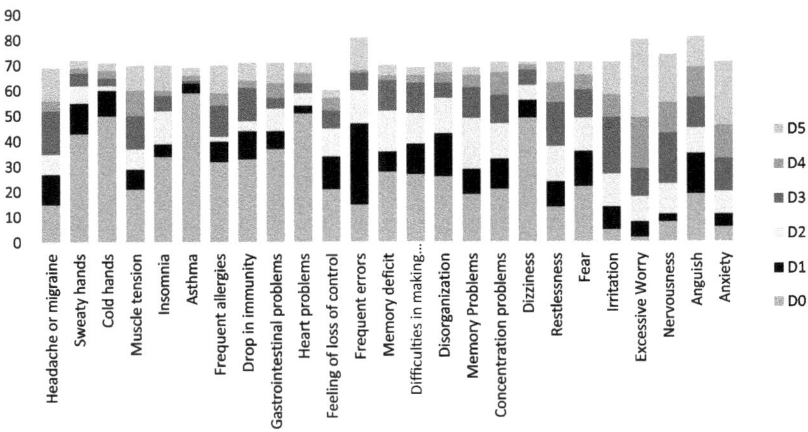

Figure 3. Symptoms of Stress.

Excessive worry is clearly one of the factors that most affects respondents, followed by anxiety and nervousness. Factors such as headache, restlessness and irritation do not present high levels, but are present at moderate levels. Concentration and memory problems are low, but present. The results also indicate that half of those interviewed have already researched the symptoms on the internet and/or have self-medicated as a result. Approximately half of these people have already sought medical help because of one of these symptoms, but only approximately a third of them receive medical care and/or use medication. As in the group analyses, more people have missed family events due to stress than have missed professional events.

4.2 Unexpected Results

As mentioned previously, most of this research was collected in person, going to the respondents, talking to each of them and asking them to kindly respond to the matrix. During this process, some facts were observed that were not initially part of the scope of the work. It was noted that a factor that worries and stresses students and accounting professionals in the region is the implementation of a program called e-social. E-Social is an information provision program for the Federal Government that aims to unify labor information and make business processes more transparent and less complicated. However, it is clear that accountants are having a lot of difficulty implementing this system, partly due to the deadlines for installation and full operation and partly to make their clients understand the importance of this tool and deliver the documents correct within the stipulated deadline. In all offices visited, there were complaints from professionals regarding this new way of presenting information to the Federal Government. Therefore, it was felt that a new interview would be necessary in one or two exercises to check the data from this work again and identify whether or not the implementation of E-Social created an atypical scenario of stress for professionals.

Another point that drew attention was the restlessness of undergraduate accounting students. In general, most students show clear signs of restlessness during classes, moving their feet, legs or hands in repetitive and continuous movements. These movements become even more intense on test days. Knowing that you will be evaluated brings a level of tension much higher than regular class days. This agitation is great in the first period of the course, where excitement about entering college is natural, but it is very worrying in the final periods of the course. It is also observed that a number of students who are about to graduate do not consider themselves capable of entering the job market. Even though I am studying at a renowned institution and have gone through all the learning processes, which increases the agitation even more. However, the perception of time in the last periods of graduation is so intense that most of the time these students completely neglect the symptoms of stress caused by this supposed "inability" and end up creating roots for stress-related problems in the future. One issue that drew attention during the research was the existence of FOMO (Fear of Missing Out), a type of social anxiety that mainly affects people with great involvement in social networks and which has grown dramatically in recent years.

Understanding FOMO in students was not the objective of this research, but in conversations with them it was possible to identify some signs of this anxiety. FOMO is a big cause of stress, and its increase needs more attention. Finally, one last unexpected observation: There is still a huge amount of prejudice when it comes to mental health. In general, people feel uncomfortable talking about the subject and cannot relate stress to mental health. This strong prejudice has a devastating effect as it causes people to refuse to seek medical help when discomfort due to stress begins to appear, which can worsen symptoms and, in more serious cases, lead to potentially fatal illnesses. It can be said without fear of misunderstanding that, if people were as concerned about their mental health as they are about their physical health, they would have a much higher quality of life and save time and resources on various treatments throughout their lives.

5 Final Remarks

The objective of this research was to correlate the professional activities of different groups such as: Professionals from Accounting Offices, Higher Education Institutions and City Hall; and the main symptoms of stress caused by the aforementioned activities of these professionals. For this, the research was developed in the South Fluminense region, state of Rio de Janeiro. We expected to find evidence that was easy to translate into numbers to prove the hypothesis that stress ends up causing a major inconvenience for professionals and students which, over time, causes financial impacts and even influences the local economy. Sendin (2016) states that talking about mental problems is still a taboo in society, so much so that of the 260 strikes on worker health that took place in 2012, none addressed psychological and emotional illnesses. Topics such as leisure, stress and quality of life and work are not discussed by unions and employers. However, as the research took shape and the questionnaires were answered, it was discovered that, although it is clear that stress has a significant impact on these people's lives, it would be very complicated to measure this impact, mainly due to the great difficulty faced by the respondents. in understanding that stress is a mental health problem and as such, ends up having an impact on physical health. Another major difficulty was the prejudice against talking about mental health, as one of the survey panels directly asked whether respondents had already sought medical help due to any symptoms caused by stress.

When structuring the research, it was assumed that respondents already knew what stress is and its impacts on health and would be able to answer questions on the subject easily. This principle was induced by the fact that there is a lot of talk about stress in everyday life and that it is a common complaint among urban workers (Cabral et. al., 1997) "Stress reactions result, therefore, from adaptation efforts. However, if the reaction to the aggressor is very intense or if the stress agent is very powerful and/or prolonged, the consequence may be illness or a greater predisposition to the development of illnesses." However, the reality turned out to be very different from what was supposed. In general, the people who agreed to answer the questionnaires did not treat stress as a health risk factor but as something every day, routine. And when it was mentioned seeking medical treatment from psychologists and/or psychiatrists, the answers were elusive or absent. Finally, it was possible to observe that professionals relate the stress they feel more to facts than to symptoms. It was much simpler to identify that deadlines for submitting work and impossible demands caused stress than to relate this same stress to some physical symptom such as a headache, for example. This work was conclusive in showing that stress does have an impact on the daily lives of professionals, which can cause problems for both workers and companies and clients, in addition to showing that this same stress is already high in the graduation of future accountants, which, In the long term, it will introduce professionals increasingly harmed by stress and with their capacity affected at an increasingly earlier age into the job market. It was also conclusive when it showed that in all sectors surveyed the highest level of stress is related to work delivery deadlines. A likely measure that would mitigate this impact would be to work with more comfortable deadlines and with less pressure and demands. These are apparently simple measures, but they would have great effects in the long term. Target 8 of Goal 8 of the UN 2030 Agenda for Sustainable Development calls for "safe working environments for all workers" – ensuring safe workplaces goes beyond protecting workers' physical safety, extending to their mental well-being and psychological (Ryder, 2016). Another suggestion is to invest extensively in campaigns to prevent diseases related to mental health, especially those caused by excess stress. It is extremely important that prejudice about mental health is overcome and that everyone can have access to information and prevention.

5.1 Limitations and Ways Forward

This study is not free from limitations. One of the biggest difficulties is related to the difficulty in obtaining answers. In general, people did not want to stop their work to answer a questionnaire, even after the full importance of the project had been explained. There was also a major restriction on financial resources for traveling between cities to increase the scope of the research. As there was no type of financing, it was necessary to use our own resources for transportation within and between cities and for food in the process. There was also a time constraint. A more complete research would take much more time than is available to carry out, given the scarcity of other resources. Another restriction that limited this work was the delay in obtaining responses. Large offices and a city hall asked to leave a certain number of questionnaires to be answered, but they never delivered the answers. Due to time and protocols, it was not possible to obtain responses from accountants from multinationals based in the region. This fact forced us to work with only three of the four groups initially proposed. Finally, before starting to collect responses, we already imagined that talking about stress in a deeper way outside the health sector would be a challenge. However, the lack of understanding about the topic and even a certain prejudice in relation to mental health have proven to be a barrier that prevents a deeper dialogue and, therefore, more precise research on the subject. We suggest that future studies expand the scope of the sample and highlight that funding bodies, government, institutions, etc. help to enhance research through financial incentives. Despite the limitations, this research opens the way for several others that would further complement the topic. Throughout the development, several questions arose such as:

- What is the economic impact of a professional suffering from exacerbated stress?
- What is the financial impact that the lack of prevention of mental illnesses has on the SUS?
- What is the difference in profitability in reais between a stressed professional and a healthy professional?
- If the high level of stress is "accepted as normal" within undergraduate accounting courses, what will be the impact on the job market?
- What can companies and offices do to protect the mental health of their employees, what would be the financial result?
- What is the difference in response to major challenges between a stressed professional and a healthy professional?
- Knowing that many undergraduate students are already working in the job market, what is the impact of studying and working on people's mental health?
- Which social class suffers most from mental health problems and what is the economic impact of these variables.
- How to combat prejudice against mental health in the corporate world?
- What is the impact of stress on the lives and work of accountants and controllers of large multinationals.
- How much does the economic crisis affect the mental health of workers and what is the impact of this result on the economy?
- Is it possible to eliminate excessive stress from the daily lives of accounting professionals?
- What is the salary/mental health relationship of accounting science workers?
- Does higher pay positively influence the mental health of accountants?

As you can see, this work was just a starting point for many relevant questions to be answered. It is important to remember that there is no accounting without an accountant and that there is no degree in accounting sciences without students and teachers. Understanding and worrying about the mental health of these professionals and students is to guarantee the future of the profession in a sustainable way. It is important to highlight the contribution of accounting sciences in all work activities, being a fundamental cog for the full functioning of the economic machine. It is important to emphasize the presence of the accounting professional at every scale of production, actively participating in all types of business.

References

Anholon, R., Rampasso, I. S., Martins, V. W. B., Serafim, M. P., Leal Filho, W., & Quelhas, O. L. G. (2021). COVID-19 and the targets of SDG 8: Reflections on Brazilian scenario. *Kybernetes*, 50(5), 1679–1686.

Barros, D. (2019). *O grande desafio na depressão – superar o preconceito*. Emais. https://emais.estadao.com.br/blogs/daniel-martins-de-barros/o-grande-desafio-na-depressao-superar-o-preconceito/

Bilek-Steindl, S., Kettner, C., & Mayrhuber, C. (2022). Special issue: Sustainability, work and growth in the context of SDG 8. *Empirica*, *49*, 277–279.

Cabral, A.P.T., Luna, J. F., Souza, K. N., Macedo, L. M., Mendes, M. G. A., Medeiros, P. A. S., Gomes, R. M. (1997). *O Estresse e as Doenças Psicossomáticas*. Labs. http://labs.icb.ufmg.br/lpf/mono1.pdf

Carlsen, L. (2021). Decent work and economic growth in the European Union. A partial order analysis of Eurostat SDG 8 data. *Green Finance, 3*(4), 483–494.

Đokić, M., & Jovanović, M. (2019). Productive employment and working conditions as determinants of sustainable economic development in Serbia. *Studies in Business and Economics, 14*(3), 84–96.

Iudicibus, S. (2010). *Contabilidade Introdutória: 11 ed.* Editora Atlas S.A.

Jones, P., Wynn, M., Hillier, D., & Comfort, D. (2017). The sustainable development goals and information and communication technologies. *Indonesian Journal of Sustainability Accounting and Management*, *1*(1), 1–15.

Khalique, F., Madan, P., Puri, G., & Parimoo, D. (2020). Incorporating SDG 8 for decent work practices: A study of MNC subsidiaries in India. *Australasian Accounting Business and Finance Journal, 15*(5), 99–114.

Kohama, H. (2010). *Contabilidade Pública: Teoria e Prática: 11 ed.* Editora Atlas S.A.

Marion, J. C. (2015). *Contabilidade Básica: 11 ed.* Editora Atlas S.A.

Mothé, C. B. (2006, December 8). *Stress no ambiente de trabalho – Migalhas*. Migalhas. https://www.migalhas.com.br/depeso/33425/stress-no-ambiente-de-trabalho

Nascimento, E. M. (2017). *Estresse e docentes na área de ciências contábeis: consequências e estratégias* (Doctoral dissertation, Universidade de São Paulo).

Niyama, J. K.; Silva, C. A. T. (2011). *Teoria da Contabilidade* (2 ed.). Editora Atlas S.A.

Ozkan, A., Ozdevecioglu, M., Kaya, Y., & Koç, F.Ö. (2015). Effects of mental workloads on depression–anger symptoms and interpersonal sensitivities of accounting professionals, *Revista de Contabilidad-Spanish Accounting Review, 18*(2), 194–199.

Prado, C. E. P. (2016). Estresse ocupacional: causas e consequências. *Rev Bras Med Trab, 14*(3), 285–289.

Rai, S. M., Brown, R., & Ruwanpura, K. N. (2019). Decent work and economic growth – A gendered analysis. *World Development, 113*, 368–380.

Ryder, G. (2016). *Estresse no local de trabalho: É hora de aliviar o fardo.* Ilo. https://www.ilo.org/brasilia/noticias/WCMS_475248/lang--pt/index.htm

Sachs, J. D., Kroll, C., Lafortune, G., Fuller, G., & Woelm, F. (2022). *Sustainable development report 2022.* Cambridge University Press.

Sendin, T. (2016). *Precisamos falar sobre estresse.* Exame. https://exame.abril.com.br/negocios/precisamos-falar-sobre-estresse/

Stewart, W., & Barling, J. (1996). Daily work stress, mood and interpersonal job performance: A mediational model. *Work & Stress, 10*(4), 336–351.

Stocco, J. A. P., & de Lara Bortoluzzi, C. (2006). A influencia do estresse no ambiente de trabalho do secretario executivo. Secretariado Executivo em *Revist@, 2*.

Tolentino, BGJ. (1997) Accounting for Partnership and Corporation.

UNITED STATES BANKRUPTCY COURT DISTRICT OF DELAWARE, (2020). https://document.epiq11.com/document/getdocumentsbydocket/?docketId=776200&projectCode=ABR&docketNumber=358&source=DM

Renata Stanley[1,*], Demetra Demetriou[2], Renata Paksiova[1], and Anton Marcin[1]

Overview of the European Union Legislative Framework for Sustainable Reporting in 2023

Abstract:
Research background: In 2014, the first directive on non-financial reporting (NFRD) was approved, which required large entities of public interest to provide information in their annual report on their sustainability practices for the first time in 2018, covering the financial year 2017. The development of regulation is currently turbulent about sustainability, which also results in the creation of the so-called regulation EU taxonomy and another directive guidance on reporting information on social responsibility (CSRD). The most recently approved regulation is the European Sustainability Reporting Standards (ESRS) adopted in July 2023. Due to the high actuality of this topic and the rapidly increasing regulation, it is important to provide an overview of existing standards for better orientation when preparing sustainability reports not only for business entities.
Purpose of the article: The aim of this paper is to provide an overview of the existing regulation and to stimulate the discussion in the field of sustainability for business entities operating in the EU. The conclusions might have implications for policymakers whom they will be called upon to address concerns.
Methods: To achieve the set goal, an analysis of international sustainability standards, European legislation and published domestic and foreign sources was carried out. Synthetic-analytical and inductive-deductive methods were also used.
Findings & Value added: The contribution of this article is a comprehensive overview of the existing regulation and to stimulate discussion in the field of sustainable reporting within the EU.

* Corresponding author: renata.stanley@euba.sk
[1] University of Economics in Bratislava, Faculty of Business Informatics, Department of Accounting and Auditing, Dolnozemska 1, 852 35 Bratislava, Slovakia
[2] Neapolis University, Pafos, School of Economics, Business and Computer Science, Department of Accounting and Finance, 2 Danais Avenue 8042, Paphos Cyprus

Keywords: *sustainability, EU regulation, CSRD, EU taxonomy, ESRS*

JEL Classification: *Q01; M40; M48*

1 Introduction

Due to the impact of climate change and other significant events affecting existence on our planet, the topic of sustainability has become a priority among nations and individuals. Climate change, carbon emissions, deforestation, social inequality and unethical corporate management are just some of the problems around the world. More and more companies began to realize the importance of adopting new practices that would help ensure sustainability. Investors themselves are not only interested in the return on their financial investment, but also in the company's impact on the environment and social development. These naturally evolving requirements have created the need to create a framework for informing investors and other interested parties about the relevant sustainability practices of companies.

Various organizations and initiatives began to emerge that wanted to support informing companies and the general public in the field of sustainable development. One of the first was the creation of the international organization GRI (Global Reporting Initiative), which was founded in 1997 in the USA and, thanks to its activities, helps organizations take responsibility for their impact on the sustainable development of our planet. GRI collaborates with companies, investors, policymakers and other experts to develop practical guidelines, GRI standards and certified programs to help transparently report information about companies' environmental and social impact. The development of these activities has resulted in the establishment of basic criteria known under the acronym ESG, which represents environmental, social and governance criteria that have become a set of standards for the sustainable activities of companies and also the basis for reporting information on adopted sustainability practices. The GRI standards are the most widely used sustainability reporting standards worldwide.

An important milestone on a European scale was the Paris Agreement on climate change, following the adoption of the UN 2030 Agenda, establishing a general framework for all countries that aim to eradicate poverty and achieve sustainable development by 2030. The Paris Agreement on December 12, 2015 brought for the first time once the offer of a global agreement that all countries, including support for developing countries, take measures to combat climate change and adapt to its consequences. The Paris Agreement was opened for signature symbolically on Earth Day on 22 April 2016 at UN Headquarters in New York and entered into force on 4 November 2016.

2 Methodology and Data

The paper aims to analyze EU legislative framework and to stimulate the discussion in the field of sustainable reporting. We have drawn data mainly from the EU regulation (CSRD, 2022; NFRD, 2014; EC, 2019, 2023a, 2023b and SFDR, 2019) and articles with sustainability reporting topics from many different authors (Brogi & Lagasio, 2018; Krambia-Kapardis et al., 2023; Chalmers & Kliger-Vidra, 2023; Zeytinoglu & Tumpach, 2023) mostly published in the current period of 2023 or earlier (Majernik et al., 2022; Makarenko et al., 2022; Palinchak et al., 2021; Slavik, 2021; Knazkova & Ondrusova, 2020). The topic of ESG reporting and websites we took from the explanation of EU legislation or auditing companies providing surveys on the topic of sustainable reporting (KMPG, 2020; Plevova & Maxim, 2021).

Several studies deal with the actual sustainable development goals (Subramaniam et al., 2023; Kraetzschmar et al., 2023; Raman et al., 2023).

The latest information regarding the European guidelines for reporting sustainability information was obtained directly from the European Commission's website on the date of their publication on July 31, 2023, as their scope and detailed description of the content has not yet been elaborated in scientific articles.

The following deduction and synthesis of results will allow to provide an overall view of the existing legislation in the field of sustainable reporting within the EU.

3 Results

On the basis of the Paris Agreement on climate change, the EU responded to the needs of ESG reporting through the action plan for financing sustainable growth and the European Green Deal, where it committed, among other things, to the development of regulation, which the member states must subsequently incorporate into their legislation in order to support ESG goals in reporting sustainable practices of companies.

The EU action plan aimed at a faster and more efficient development of the circular economy, especially in resource-intensive sectors (textile industry, construction, electronics, and plastics) and to positively influence consumer behavior, which would offer customers the opportunity to purchase reusable durable products. It will also address energy-intensive areas such as construction and renovation of buildings or transport, whose share in greenhouse gas emissions is extremely high. The development and subsequent implementation of the "Farm to Table" Strategy should in turn lead to a more sustainable food policy by involving all phases of the food chain. (The Ministry of the Environment, 2023)

The European Green Deal represents the European Commission's plan aimed at the ecological transformation of the European Union's economy in the interest of a sustainable future of existence on our planet. The agreement includes several supporting elements. Among the most important are ambitions in the area of:

- climate, where the EU has set as its primary goal the reduction of greenhouse gas emissions by 55 % by 2030 and by 2050 to make Europe the first ever climate-neutral continent,
- ensuring the supply of clean and affordable energy, while the focus will be on strengthening the production of energy from renewable sources,
- expanding international cooperation in improving energy infrastructure or fighting energy poverty.

As you can see, the trends in the field of green transformation are not only related to the adoption of laws in individual member states, which companies must then comply with, but the essence is a change in thinking and the adoption of a sustainable business model. The European Commission, advisory bodies, and other professional organizations are trying to create a certain framework of procedures for transparent and comparable reporting of relevant information in the field of corporate sustainability.

Scheme 1 provides an overview of the selected legislative framework in the area of sustainability reporting for companies doing business in the EU in chronological order. In the centre of the diagram is the name of the specific guideline adopted by the EU, on the left side is the effective date of the given guideline, and on the right side is the number under which it was adopted. Individual guidelines will be the subject of processing in the following points of this article.

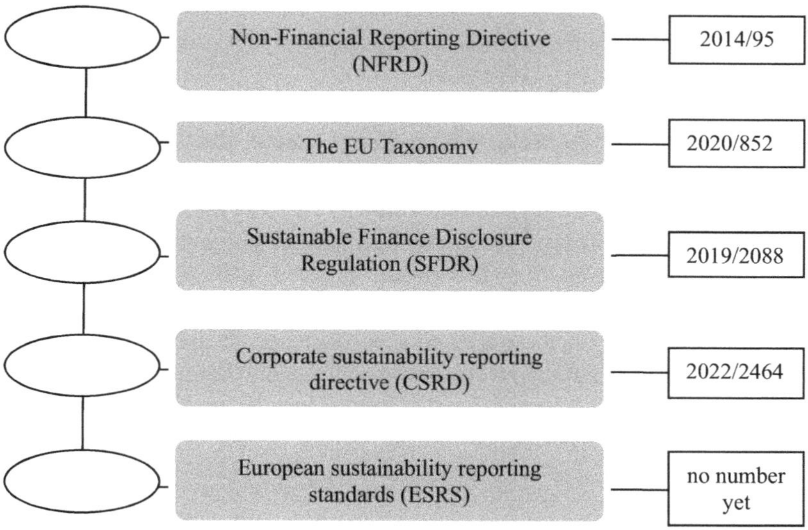

Figure 1. EU sustainability legislation frame for reporting.
Source: own processing

3.1 Non-Financial Reporting Directive (NFRD)

On 22 October 2014, the EU approved the Non-Financial Reporting Directive 2014/95/EU (NFRD), which requires large companies to report qualitative and quantitatively sufficient non-financial information in their annual reports or in a separate submission from 2018, covering financial year 2017 including information on:

- environmental protection,
- respecting human rights,
- fight against corruption and bribery,
- social responsibility and treatment of employees a
- diversity in company boards.

The Accounting Directive 2013/34/EU was modified by the NFRD directive. According to the NFRD, entities of public interest (hereinafter referred to as "SVZ") with more than 500 employees are considered large companies.

The disclosure asks companies to outline what their risks are with respect to these issues, the resulting policies the company has adopted to mitigate those risks, and the results of those policies. These detailed reporting requirements are an annual public reporting obligation.

As a first step towards sustainable reporting, the NFRD guideline was a recommended guideline, but it was not binding in nature. The obligation to report sustainable information comes with the new CSRD directive, which is already binding for the selected companies mentioned further in the text. When disclosing non-financial information under NFRD, these large companies could decide according to which guidelines they would proceed in their preparation, they could also use a combination of national, international and European guidelines. However, with the gradual development of regulation in the field of providing information on sustainability, companies will gradually have to follow the standards approved by the EU, which will subsequently be applied to the national legislation of the member states.

3.2 EU Taxonomy

The EU taxonomy is a fundamental pillar of a sustainable EU financial framework and an important tool for market transparency. It helps direct investment into economic activities that are most needed in line with the objectives of the European Green Deal. Taxonomy Regulation 2020/852/EU entered into force on 12 July 2020. It establishes the basis for an EU taxonomy based on 6 conditions that an economic activity must meet in order to qualify as environmentally sustainable, which are shown in scheme 2 below. (EC, 2023a)

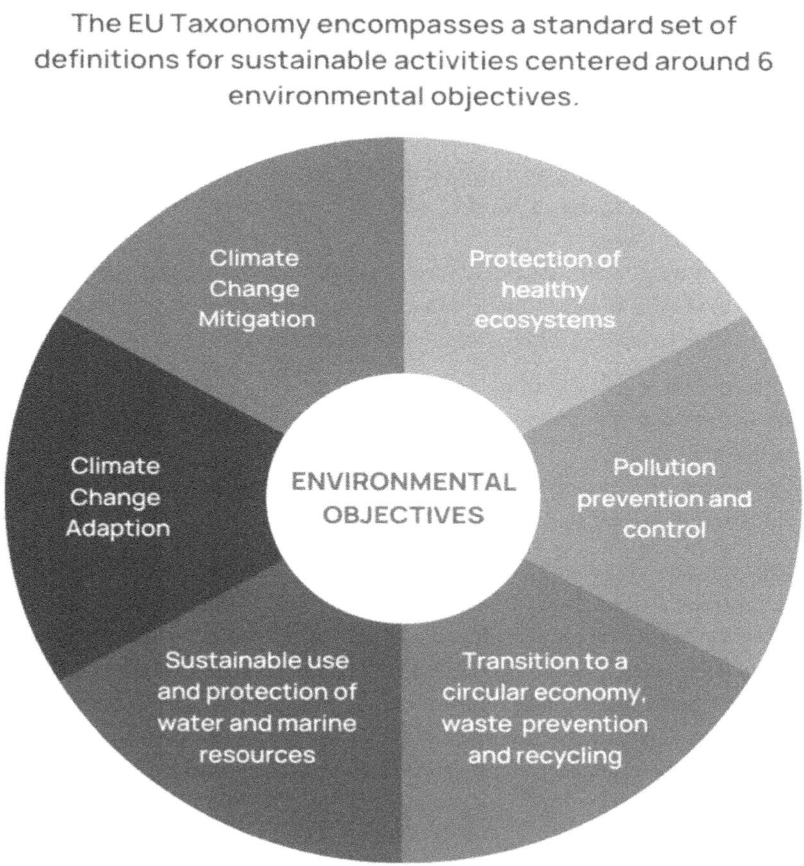

Figure 2. Objectives of the EU Taxonomy.
Source: Celsia (2022)

Given that there are already several guidelines regarding the reporting of information about their sustainability, the Taxonomy has the task of simplifying, clarifying, and unifying the information reporting procedure for companies. Clear rules should also strengthen the EU's fight against environmentally misleading statements, and the so-called greenwashing of some companies on the market.

3.3 Sustainable Finance Disclosure Regulation (SFDR)

Regulation (EU) 2019/2088 on Sustainable Finance Disclosure (SFRD) is a mandatory European Union regulation effective March 10, 2021 that aims to improve the transparency and standardization of ESG disclosures for financial products and services. It is binding on financial market participants (FMPs) and financial advisors (FAs) operating in the EU, who are required to provide reliable and comparable ESG data.

The most important aspect of this legislation is that fund managers are required to submit detailed quantitative data on behalf of their portfolio companies on a quarterly basis. SFDR has 3 main requirements:

1. Elimination of greenwashing and false claims,
2. Accountability for financial market participants (FMP) claims regarding sustainability,
3. Improving the transparency of sustainable investment products in the European financial sector.

In addition, the SFDR requires financial market participants to disclose information on the sustainability impact of investment decisions in pre-contractual information and on their websites. In the case of financial products with environmental or social features, the SFDR regulation sets out the rules that financial market participants must follow for these products. Access to sustainability information is intended to help clients clarify the policy of financial institutions and will enable comparison of product offerings on the market in terms of ESG criteria.

3.4 Corporate Sustainability Reporting Directive (CSRD)

The European Commission (EC) adopted in April 2021 a proposal for a new corporate sustainability reporting directive (CSRD), which fundamentally improves the current requirements for reporting information in accordance with the NFRD directive. The CSRD Directive approved on 14 December 2022 under the number Directive (EU) 2022/2464 is a European Union measure to strengthen and expand the existing scope of ESG reporting requirements for companies operating in the EU.

CSRD simplifies and brings sustainability reporting on par with financial reporting to standardize the disclosure of sustainability-related information. The concept of "double materiality" came to the fore, requiring that the information disclosed by a company be significant in terms of its consequences for the financial value of the company, as well as in terms of the company's impact on the environment, people and the economy.

CSRD introduces a requirement for a third-party audit of sustainability reporting information and requires statutory auditors to submit annual reports to the Competent Authority (to be defined by local laws) that specifically identify non-audit service revenue derived from sustainability reporting. The directive also specifies the information they must disclose and introduces new and more comprehensive sustainability reporting requirements.

CSRD directive applies to a larger number of companies and not only to companies based in the EU, but from 2028 also to companies based outside the EU that have a subsidiary in the EU. They will be obliged to report sustainability information with effect from 1st of January of the years mentioned in Scheme 3 below. The application of the requirements will be divided into 4 stages, which will come into effect gradually depending on the classification of the company which are listed in the following timeline scheme. In the centre of the scheme are listed the companies that are covered by the CSRD directive in a given year, and on the right, it is indicated when they are required to report 1x sustainability report.

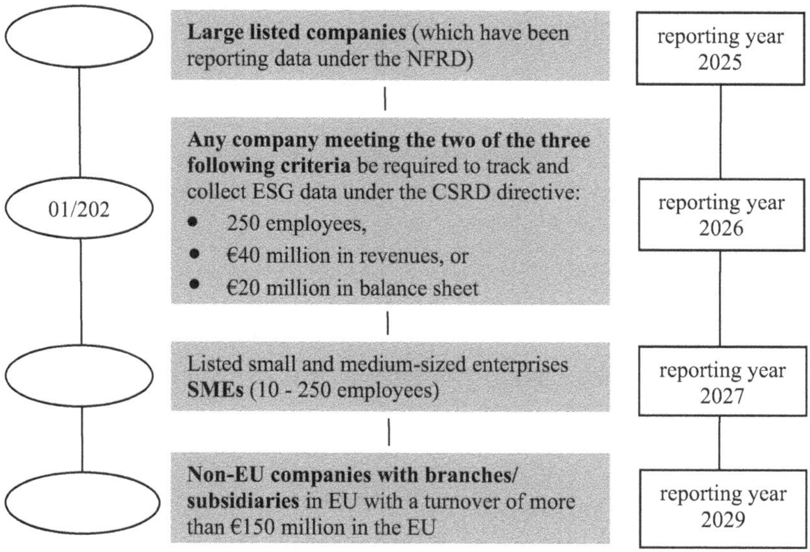

Figure 3. Classification of companies according to the stages of CSRD implementation.
Source: own processing

3.5 European Sustainability Reporting Standards (ESRS)

The creation of the European Sustainability Reporting Standards (ESRS) started already in June 2021 in accordance with the CSRD directive. Under the proposed CSRD directive, EFRAG (European Financial Reporting Advisory Group) has been appointed as technical advisor to the European Commission, which is drafting the ESRS. The EU Commission adopted the ESRS on 31 July 2023, which can be used by all companies covered by the CSRD Directive. ESRS aims to provide specific sustainability information that selected companies must disclose in accordance with the CSRD Directive.

There are 3 ESRS categories of standards (Annex 1 of ESRS standards from 31 July 2023):

1. Cross-cutting standards,
2. Topical standards (Environmental, Social and Governance standards), and
3. Sector-specific standards.

Cross-cutting standards and topical standards apply to all undertakings regardless of which sector or sectors the undertaking operates in. There is two cross-cutting standards, which provide general reporting concepts and include general disclosure requirements.

Cross-cutting standards:

- ESRS 1 General requirements,
- ESRS 2 General disclosures.

Ten topical standards supplement the cross-cutting standards with detailed disclosure requirements within environmental, social, and management topics.

Topical standards are divided by topic as follows:

- Environment:
  - ESRS E1 Climate change
  - ESRS E2 Pollution
  - ESRS E3 Water and marine resources
  - ESRS E4 Biodiversity and ecosystems
  - ESRS E5 Resources and circular economy
- Social:
  - ESRS S1 Own workforce
  - ESRS S2 Workers in the value chain
  - ESRS S3 Affected communities
  - ESRS S4 Customers and end-users
- Governance:
  - ESRS G1 Business conduct.

Together, these twelve ESRSs require companies to provide information on:

- their management and strategy to address material sustainability issues;
- the impacts, risks and opportunities arising from these topics; and
- established quantitative metrics and explain how to disclose related targets for each topic.

Sector-specific standards will be applied after a few years and after evaluating the effects of the recent directive entered into force.

4 Discussion and Conclusions

The topic of sustainability is among the most discussed topics at the moment, which is also the result of the EU's reaction in the form of regulation on the sustainable development of companies.

Over the past decade, the European Union, together with other organizations (such as EFRAG) has worked to develop a legislative framework that would require companies to provide credible and relevant information about sustainable practices. The NFRD directive was the first to be created, which only concerned large entities of public interest, was not mandatory and its intention was to provide information relating to ESG objectives within the framework of non-financial information.

In 2019, the SFDR directive was approved for financial market participants and financial advisors trading in the EU with effect from March 2021. However, in addition to these directives, other directives were developed within the EU and on a global scale. Based on the need to have a unified structured framework for sustainable reporting, the EU Taxonomy was created as a fundamental pillar of a sustainable EU financial framework and an important tool for market transparency in line with the objectives of the European Green Deal. Subsequently, the CSRD directive was approved, which is already mandatory for a larger number of companies within the individual implementation phases, focuses exclusively on providing information on sustainability and is the basis for the creation of ESRS standards.

They are all interconnected parts of the European Union's efforts to promote sustainable finance and fight climate change and greenwashing. All of these regulations aim at ensuring a sustainable financial system that supports the EU's goal of becoming neutral by 2050. Together, they provide companies and financial market participants to determine sustainability risk and impact disclosures and help investors to make the right decisions.

While standardization of the disclosure of sustainability-related information is crucial for promoting transparency, comparability, and accountability, is also a complex endeavor that aims to provide consistency and comparability in environmental, social, and governance (ESG) reporting across EU member states and raises several concerns and challenges to policymakers.

For instance, the EU encompasses a wide range of industries and sectors, each with unique sustainability challenges and material ESG factors. Standardization must account for this diversity to ensure that reporting requirements are relevant and meaningful for all companies. Also, balancing the need for consistency in reporting with the need for flexibility to accommodate industry-specific metrics and targets is a delicate task. In addition, determining what constitutes material ESG information can be challenging, as it varies from one industry to another and depends on the specific context of each company. A standardized approach may struggle to capture the nuances of materiality. Further, companies, particularly smaller ones, may face increased reporting burdens due to standardization efforts. This can strain resources and may lead to compliance challenges, especially if the reporting requirements are too complex or onerous. Finally, ensuring the accuracy and reliability of sustainability data is a key concern. Standardization should include mechanisms for data validation and verification to prevent greenwashing and maintain trust in reported information.

Addressing these concerns, on the part of the policymakers, requires a balanced and iterative approach to standardization, one that considers the needs of different stakeholders, supports innovation, and maintains flexibility to adapt to changing circumstances. The field of sustainability is dynamic and continually evolving, with new issues, risks, and best practices emerging. Policymakers should approach standardization from a forward-looking information approach and innovation in sustainable business practices.

References

Brogi, M., & Lagasio, V. (2018). Environmental, social, and governance and company profitability: Are financial intermediaries different?. *Corporate Social Responsibility and Environmental Management*, *26*(3), 576–587.

Celsia. (2022, November 17). *EU Taxonomy timeline: milestones and deadlines you should know.* Celsia. https://www.celsia.io/blogs/eu-taxonomy-timeline-tables-and-milestones

Chalmers, A., & Klingler-Vidra, R. (2023). European Sustainability Reporting Standards (ESRS): Interoperability as innovation? *Global Policy*.

CSRD. (2022, December 16). *Directive (EU) 2022/2464 of the European Parliament and of the Council of 14 December 2022 amending Regulation (EU) No 537/2014, Directive 2004/109/EC, Directive 2006/43/EC and Directive 2013/34/EU, as regards corporate sustainability reporting*. Eur-lex. https://eur-lex.europa.eu/legal-content/EN/TXT/?uri=CELEX%3A32022L2464

EC. (2019, December 11). *The European Green Deal*. European commission. https://ec.europa.eu/info/strategy/priorities-2019-2024/european-green-deal_en

EC. (2023a). *EU taxonomy for sustainable activities*. European commission. https://finance.ec.europa.eu/sustainable-finance/tools-and-standards/eu-taxonomy-sustainable-activities_en

EC. (2023b, July 31). *The Commission adopts the European Sustainability Reporting Standards*. European commission. https://finance.ec.europa.eu/news/commission-adopts-european-sustainability-reporting-standards-2023-07-31_en

Knazkova, V., & Ondrusova, L. (2020). Public interest entities in the context of accounting and auditing legislation in the wake of the globalization process. *Globalization and its Socio-Economic Consequences: Sustainability in the Global-Knowledge Economy, 74*.

KPMG International. (2020). *The KPMG Survey of Corporate Responsibility Reporting 2020*. Kmpg. https://home.kpmg/content/dam/kpmg/xx/pdf/2020/11/the-kpmg-survey-of-corporate-responsibility-reporting-2020.pdf

Kraetzschmar, E., Emin, D., Albert, J., Franke, J., Giraud, H., Treinsoutrot, D., Astola, H., & Seifert, F. M. (2023). EO4SDG Forest – Supporting the Reporting Process of the Sustainable Development Goals.

Krambia-Kapardis, M., Stylianou, I., & Savva, C. S. (2023). Ethical leadership as a prerequisite for sustainable development, sustainable finance, and ESG reporting. *Sustainable Finance and Financial Crime*. Springer.

Majernik, M., Stofkova, J., Malega, P., & Barilova, B. (2022). Standardisation of the social responsibility system as a tool for business sustainability. *Quality Innovation Prosperity, 26*(2), 39–54.

Makarenko, I., Plastun, A., Mazancova, J., Juhaszova, Z., & Brin, P. (2022). Transparency of agriculture companies: Rationale of responsible investment for better decision making under sustainability. *Agricultural and Resource Economics: International Scientific E-Journal, 8*(2), 50–66.

NFRD. (2014, October 15). *Directive 2014/95/EU of the European Parliament and of the Council of 22 October 2014 amending Directive 2013/34/EU as regards disclosure of non-financial and diversity information by certain large undertakings and groups*. Eur-lex. -https://eur-lex.europa.eu/legal-content/EN/TXT/?uri=CELEX%3A32014L0095&qid=1691753631362

Palinchak, M., Tsalan, M., Brenzovych, K., Kucher, A., Kajánek, T., & Grešš, M. (2021). Competitiveness as the basis of EU regional policy: Smart specialization and sustainability. *European Journal of Sustainable Development, 10*(4), 227–239.

Plevova, M., & Maxim, M. (2021, October 25). *Spoločenské, environmentálne a sociálne riadenie firiem.* Sohk. https://www.sohk.sk/download/eventDocuments/Prezentacia_KPMG%20Slovensko_ESG_25%2010%202021.pdf

Raman, R., Nair, V., Shivdas, A., Bhukya, R., Viswanathan, P. K., Subramaniam, N., & Nedungadi, P. (2023). Mapping sustainability reporting research with the UN's sustainable development goal. *Heliyon*, *9*(8), e18510.

SFDR. (2019, November 27). *Regulation (EU) 2019/2088 of the European Parliament and of the Council of 27 November 2019 on sustainability-related disclosures in the financial services sector.* Eur-lex. -https://eur-lex.europa.eu/legal-content/EN/TXT/?uri=celex%3A32019R2088

Slavik, S., Bednar, R., Misunova Hudakova, I., & Zagorsek, B. (2021). Business models of Start-ups and their impact on the sustainability of Nascent Business. *Entrepreneurship and Sustainability Issues*, *8*(4), 29.

Subramaniam, N., Akbar, S., Situ, H., Ji, S., & Parikh, N. (2023). Sustainable development goal reporting: Contrasting effects of institutional and organisational factors. *Journal of Cleaner Production*, *411*, 137339.

The Ministry of the Environment. (2023). *The European Green Deal.* Minzp. https://www.minzp.sk/klima/europska-zelena-dohoda/

Zeytinoglu, E., & Tumpach, M. (2023). Disclosure of sustainability information in banks: The case of Slovakia and Turkey. *OPUS Journal of Society Research, 20*(51), 43–55.

Vladimir Urazgaliev[1,*], Asadula Asadulaev[1], and Andrey Agashin[1]

The Global Energy Transition's Trends and Contradictions

Abstract:
Research background: The energy component is the material basis for the development of global processes in the economy. In theoretical and practical terms, the modern process of transformation of this component is represented by the concept of "energy transition" that does not have an unambiguous interpretation in international legislative and regulatory documents, as well as among scientists involved in the study of this phenomenon. However, according to most analysts, there is no alternative to the energy transition in order to create a green economy and achieve indicators of carbon neutrality.
Purpose of the article: The purpose of the article is to define the concept of the energy transition, classify the stages of its development, as well as quantitative verification of its parameters and assessment of possible options for achieving them in the short and medium term.
Methods: The authors carried out a comparative analysis of scenarios for the implementation of the energy transition, presented in the most authoritative international publications and in the expert conclusions of scientists and analysts.
Findings & Value added: Based on comparative assessments of international reports, reports and documents using the analysis of statistical data and indicators characterizing the existing processes in the field of international energy, the authors of the study identified and substantiated the positive and negative processes of the current stage of the energy transition and formulated possible predictive options for the transformation of these processes. The study substantiates the conclusion about the new qualitative specifics of the current international processes that consist in their force majeure nature, which, to a large extent, makes it difficult to predict the possible results and timing of the energy transition.

Keywords: *energy transition, decarbonization, climate neutrality*

JEL Classification: *Q32; Q42; Q47*

* Corresponding author: uvsh54@yandex.ru
1 St. Petersburg State University, Faculty of Economics, 7/9 Universitetskaya nab., St. Petersburg, 199034 Russia

1 Introduction

In the last decade, tensions have been intensified over the threats to the climate state of the planet in the process of the world economy development. In this regard, against the background of the fundamental changes development in the global energy system, the attention and interest of state and international structures, energy agents, experts, analysts and scientists to the analysis, evaluation and forecasting of these processes has sharply increased. This attention was embodied in the concept of "energy transition," which received quite heterogeneous interpretations of specific characteristics, along with an already well-established understanding of the essence of this phenomenon.

2 Definition and Methods

It is believed that the term "energy transition" was first proposed by the Czech-Canadian scientist Vaclav Smil (Smil, 2010). According to his concept, the energy transition is a change in the structure of primary energy consumption in the process of transition to a new state of the energy system, the quantitative criterion of which is a 10 % change in the share of the main energy resource in the energy balance over 10 years.

There are 4 stages of energy transition:

- the first – the transition from biomass (wood) to coal (from 5 % in 1840 to 50 % in 1900);
- the second – the spread of oil (from 3 % in 1915 to 45 % in 1945);
- the third is a significant replacement of coal and oil in consumption by natural gas (from 3 % in 1930 to 20 % in 2017);
- the fourth transition is currently taking place. It is based on the fight against global climate change through the introduction of low-carbon and carbon-free energy technologies into the economy. This process is often called the process of decarbonization of the economy, and the energy transition itself is called the decarbonized energy system.

When characterizing the current stage of the energy transition, the "mainstream" is present in almost all studies of experts, analysts and scientists; only the emphasis on certain aspects of the transition differs. Thus, a number of authors pay special attention to the political (Bashir et al., 2022) and geopolitical (Bazilian et al., 2019) meanings of the ongoing global energy transition, and reveal the institutional and socio-technical nature of the energy future. Longhurst and Chilvers (Longhurst & Chilvers, 2019) provide policy recommendations to overcome emerging challenges in building sustainable energy systems using renewable energy sources (Zakeri et al., 2022). Many papers present a specific analysis of the economic achievements of various countries on the path of the "green" transition: in Germany (Savio et al., 2022), Portugal (Carvalho et al., 2022), China (Chien et al., 2023), Russia (Rasoulinezhad et al., 2020; Mitrova & Melnikov, 2019), Vietnam (Siciliano, 2021), in Central and Eastern Europe (Apostu et al., 2022).

In our opinion, the energy transition is not associated with any technological revolution. It represents an emerging mechanism for the decarbonization of the economy through the constant increase of the "green" position in the global energy system, as opposed to changing its individual technologies or fuel sources. In many studies, it is the latter components that are the main focus.

The energy transition includes three parts and four components. The first ones are: the transition from the use of fossil energy resources and renewable energy sources (RES), the development of efficient technologies for energy saving and energy consumption, the transition from a centralized to a decentralized system of energy production. To the second: energy efficiency of the energy sector, its decarbonization, decentralization and digitalization. The main directions of the global energy transition are the path to sustainable and environmentally friendly energy.

3 Analytical Sources and Results

Let us turn to the data presented in the reports of analytical agents on the assessment of the global energy transition. Let's start with an analysis of its investment component. At the beginning of 2023, research company BloombergNEF (BNEF) presented its annual report on investments in green energy "Energy Transition Investment Trends" (NEF, 2023). It notes that in 2021 and 2022 there was a significant acceleration in the growth of investments in the energy transition (Figure 1).

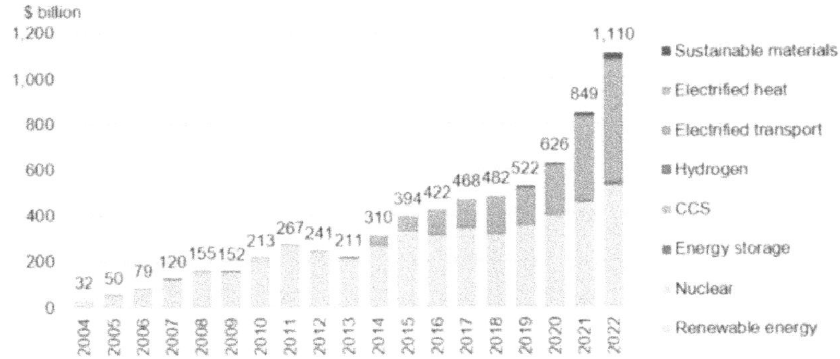

Figure 1. Global investment in energy transition.
Source: World Energy Investment (2023)

With the exception of investments in nuclear energy, which remained at the same level, all other renewable energy sectors reached a record level of $495 billion, which is 17 % more than in 2021. In 2022, investments in the production of electric vehicles and related infrastructure grew by 54 % to $466 billion. The fastest growing sector in terms of investment was the production of hydrogen, where investments increased 3 times over the year, but in absolute terms they amounted to only $1.1 billion, which corresponds to 0.1 % of the total investment in renewable energy.

The undisputed leader in investments in the energy transition is China, which more than doubled its investments over the year (from $266 billion in 2021 to $546 billion in 2022). The United States, which is in second place, lagged behind China in this indicator by almost 4 times. Germany retained third place in the top five countries, while the UK dropped to fifth place, ahead of France.

For comparison, the report provides data on global investment in fossil fuels, including exploration, transportation, processing and power generation. They, as well as investments in renewable energy, amounted to 1.1 trillion dollars in 2022.

Taking into account investments in the electrical network (274 billion), the total investment in the energy transition amounted to 1.38 trillion USD. However, according to BNEF, to achieve the world's net zero CO2 emissions trajectory by 2050 (BNEF Net Zero Scenario), these growth rates of global investment are insufficient; they must be increased by 3 times, i.e., by the end of the current decade to grow by an average of 4.55 trillion dollars per year

In May 2023, the International Energy Agency (IEA) also published a report on investments in the global energy sector ("World Energy Investment", 2023; IEA, 2023) containing a forecast for the current year. According to it, 2.8 trillion dollars will be invested in 2023. Out of them more than 1.7 trillion. will go to green energy: renewables, electric vehicles, grids, energy storage, nuclear power, low-emission fuels, heat pumps, efficiency improvements. Investments in coal, oil and gas increase slightly – just over 1 trillion USD (Figure 2).

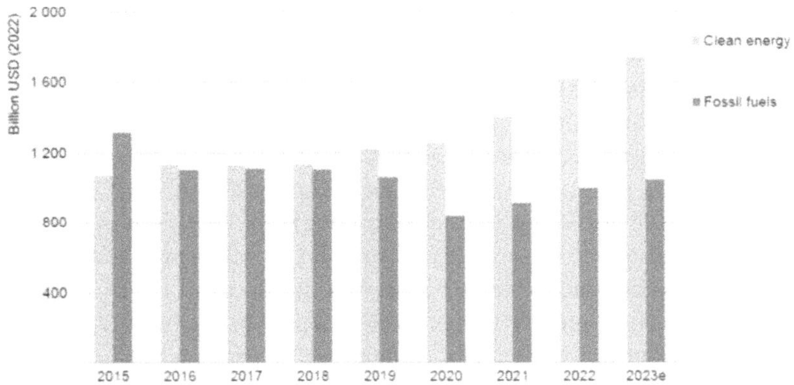

Figure 2. Global energy investment in clean energy and in fossil fuels, 2015–2023e.
Source: World Energy Investment (2023)

For every dollar of investment in fossil fuels, clean energy is now worth $1.7, and 5 years ago this ratio was 1:1. At the same time, investments in solar energy will exceed investments in oil production for the first time. It is predicted that 90 % of investments in 2023 will be in low-emission power generation technologies. As shown in the Figure 3, investments in solar energy alone will significantly exceed investments in gas, coal, nuclear and hydro combined.

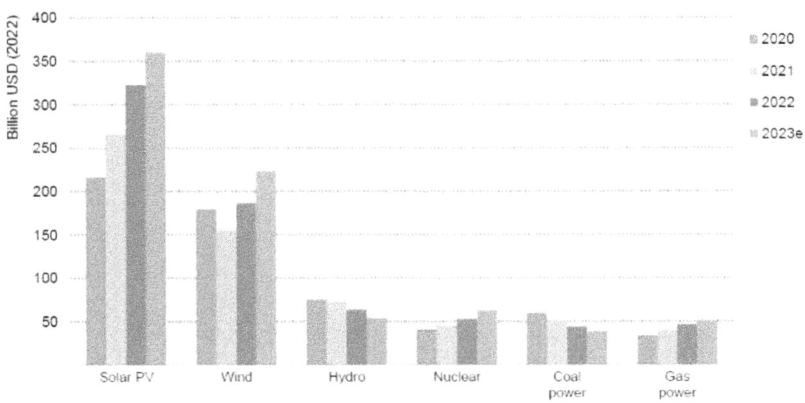

Figure 3. Global annual investment in the power generation by selected technology, 2020–2023e.
Source: World Energy Investment (2023)

However, despite a slight increase in investments in fossil fuels in absolute terms, they will more than double in 2023 – the amount needed to achieve the Scenario IRA "Net-zero emission by 2050 case" (NSF). At the same time, the consumption of the main air pollutant – coal, will exceed the planned parameters of this Scenario by almost 6 times.

In June 2023, the IEA released a special report "Renewable Energy Market Update. Outlook for 2023 and 2024" (IEA, 2023). According to the Agency's statistics, in 2022 the global renewable generation capacity increased from 340 GW (i.e., by 13 %). Of these, solar energy accounted for 220 GWh (35 % growth). But in 2023, this record statistic will be exceeded and, according to the base scenario, will be 440 GWh. The global installed capacity of renewable energy will be by 2024 4,500 GWh.

Renewable energy indicators are presented in the report of the think tank Ember "European Electricity Review, 2023" (Jones, 2023). In 2022, wind and solar co-generation outpaced gas for the first time, generating 623 TWh or 22 % of all electricity in the EU. Solar generation increased by 24 % (39 TWh), wind by 8.6 (33 TWh). On a solar basis, the generation was 203 TWh, corresponding to 83 % of the electricity produced in the EU. The share of gas in generation was 20 % (i.e., an increase of 1 % in 2021). Coal generation increased by 7 % or 28 TWh. This growth is associated with a sharp drop in electricity generation by nuclear power and hydroelectric power plants, which in total fell by 185 TWh (minus 119 TWh and minus 66 TWh, respectively), which is about 7 % of the generation of all EU electricity in 2022 (Figure 4).

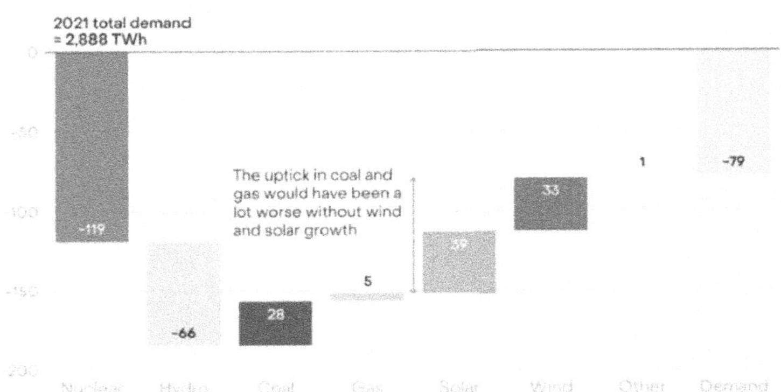

Figure 4. The EU's coal generation rose due to a sizeable nuclear and hydro deficit, year-on-year change in EU-27 generation for 2022 (terawatt hours).
Source: EMBER (2023)

The reasons for the failure of nuclear energy were a severe crisis in the aging French nuclear industry with its low-maneuverability capacities, as well as the closure of three nuclear power plants in Germany at the end of 2021. Ember forecasts EU fossil fuel generation to fall by 211 TWh or 20 % in 2023, while solar and wind power generation to rise by 86 TWh.

In 2023, The International Renewable Energy Agency (IRENA) released the annual compilation "Renewable Capacity Statistics, 2023" (IRENA, 2023). According to it, the capacity of power plants operating on the basis of world renewable energy increased by 295 GW, which is an absolute record in history. Of these, 60 % were introduced in Asia. The total capacity of RES power plants was 3372 GW. The total capacity of the world energy sector increased from 38.5 % to 40.2 %. At the same time, the share of RES in the growth of global generating capacities for 2022 amounted to 83 %

90 % of new renewable energy capacity comes from solar and wind power plants. Solar energy grew by a record 191 GW (installed capacity was 1,053 GW) and wind by 75 GW (installed capacity – 899 GW). Hydropower capacity increased by 21 GW, bioenergy by 7.6 GW. Hydropower in terms of installed capacity (1393 GW) still ranks first among renewable energy sources.

The material basis for the energy transition is the presence of a sufficient amount of minerals. In 2021, the IEA released a specialized report "The Role of Critical Minerals in Clean Energy Transitions" (IEA, 2021). It recorded significant differences in the number of resources required for the operation of traditional and "green" energy systems. For example, an electric car (in terms of kilograms per unit) requires on average 6 times more minerals than a conventional car, and an onshore wind plant (in terms of kilograms per MW) requires 9 times more minerals than a gas-fired power plant.

The types of mineral resources vary depending on the technologies used. Thus, rare earth materials are required for permanent magnets, without which the operation of electric motors and wind turbines is impossible. Nickel, cobalt, manganese, graphite, lithium are essential for battery performance, strength and durability. Electrical grids absorb huge amounts of copper and aluminum. At the same time, no technology related to electricity can work without copper.

According to IEA calculations in the Sustainable Development Scenario (SDS), the share of environmentally friendly technologies in the next 20 years will grow for copper and rare earth metals by more than 40 %, for nickel and cobalt – by 60–70 %, for lithium – by almost 90 %.

The Stated Policies Scenario predicts a 2-fold increase in total mineral demand for green energy technologies by 2040. In Scenario (SDS), by 2040 the demand for lithium will increase by more than 40 times, for graphite, cobalt, and nickel by 20–25 times, for copper for electrical networks by 2 times.

In July 2023, the IEA released a new report assessing the mineral base for the energy transition "Critical Minerals Market Review (IEA, 2023)." It notes the essential ones necessary for "green energy": in 2021 they increased by 20 %, in 2022 – by 30 %. The market for these minerals has doubled in 5 years and reached $ 320 billion. It is predicted (Scenario NZE) that by 2050, global consumption of lithium will grow 13 times from the level of 2021, cobalt more than 3 times, nickel more than 2 times.

The Report also provides short-term projections up to 2030. Some minerals, such as cobalt and lithium, will be abundant, while others (pure lithium, battery nickel, a number of rare earth elements) may become scarce. At the same time, despite the relatively high intensity of emissions from the extraction and processing of minerals, this does not negate the obvious climate benefits of clean energy technologies.

Analysis of forecasts for the development of the energy transition involves an assessment of climate risks for the functioning of the global financial system. There are 2 main climate risks: the physical risk arising from the negative costs of climate change and the transition risk associated with the process of transition to a low-carbon economy (for example, depreciation of the assets of companies in carbon-intensive industries). To predict them, 8 central banks in 2017 created the Network Central Banks and Supervisors for Greening the Financial System (NGFS) association. By the summer of 2019, it already consisted of 39 participants, including the Central Banks of most of Europe, China, as well as the supranational institutions of the OECD, the World Bank, the International Finance Corporation, the EBRD. At the beginning of July 2020, 94 central banks and financial regulators were already the members of the NGFS, as well as 15 observers (Network for Greening the Financial System, 2019).

In April 2019, NGFS released the first dedicated climate risk report in the history of financial regulation (A call for action, 2019). It presents a scheme of the physical (Figure 5) and transitional (Figure 6) climate risks algorithms.

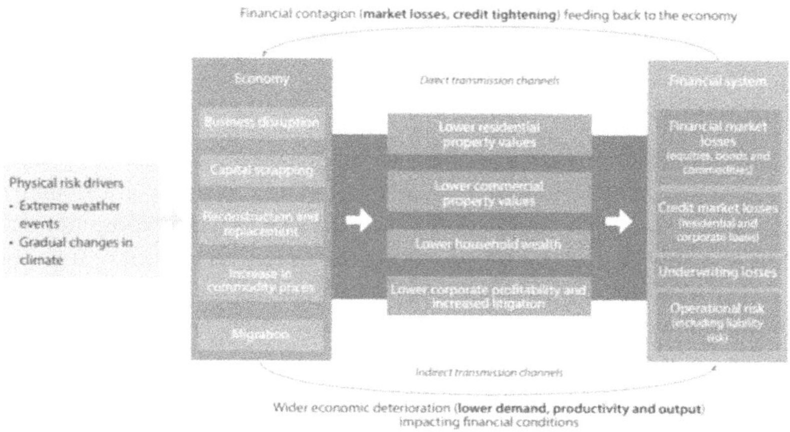

Figure 5. From physical risk to financial stability risks.

Source: A call for action Climate change as a source of financial risk (2019)

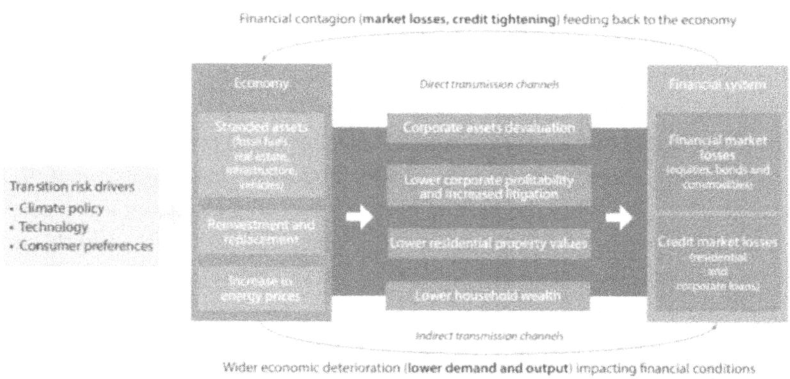

Figure 6. From transition risk to financial stability risks.

Source: A call for action Climate change as a source of financial risk (2019)

The approach proposed by the NGFS is of undeniable value as a conceptual basis for climate risks in the process of energy transition.

4 Discussion and Conclusions

The energy transition is not associated with any one technological revolution. The accumulated critical mass of a whole range of technological "green" innovations, both on the side of production and on the side of energy consumption, is leading to a gradual deep transformation of the entire energy sector. At its core, the energy transition is a mechanism for decarbonizing the economy through a constant increase of the "green" state in the global energy system, as opposed to changing its individual technologies or fuel sources.

From a conceptual point of view, energy transition is a way, form and result of the energy power transition, where the advantage of climate measurement of processes over economic ones will most likely lead to a redistribution of natural energy rent from energy exporting countries in favor of countries that do not have this rent.

The given data and assessments of the reports show that the share of RES in global energy is constantly growing and in 2020–2022 this process has accelerated to a record high.

It is problematic to assess the achievement of the energy transition goals in the medium term (by 2030) and even more so in the long term (by 2050).

The existing and projected problems of extraction and processing of minerals will not be able to have a significant negative impact on the development of the world energy sector along the path of energy transition. However, if the geopolitical situation reaches a force majeure level, which the world has recently come close to, then not only the energy transition, but the entire global economic system may plunge into massive crisis.

Force majeure of the world economy, stimulated by sanctions pressure. already leading to negative consequences. For normalization, it is necessary first of all to remove the force majeure of modern ecological processes through detente of international tension.

References

Apostu, S. A., Panait, M., Balsalobre-Lorente, D., Ferraz, D., & Radulescu, I. G. (2022). Energy transition in Non-Euro Countries from Central and Eastern Europe: Evidence from panel vector error correction model. *Energies*, *15*(23), 9118.

Bashir, M. F., Sadiq, M., Talbi, B., & Shahzad, L. (2022). An outlook on the development of renewable energy, policy measures to reshape the current energy mix, and how to achieve sustainable economic growth in the post COVID-19 era. *Environmental Science and Pollution Research, 29*(29), 43636–43647.

Bazilian, M., Bradshaw, M., Gabriel, J., Goldthau, A., & Westphal, K. (2019). Four scenarios of the energy transition: Drivers, consequences, and implications for geopolitics. *Wiley Interdisciplinary Reviews: Climate Change, 11*(2), e625.

BloombergNEF. (2023, January 26). *Global Low-Carbon Energy Technology Investment Surges Past $1 Trillion for the First Time*. Bloomberg NEF. https://about.bnef.com/blog/global-low-carbon-energy-technology-investment-surges-past-1-trillion-for-the-first-time/

Carvalho, A., Riquito, M., & Ferreira, V. (2022). Sociotechnical imaginaries of energy transition: The case of the Portuguese Roadmap for Carbon Neutrality 2050. *Energy Reports, 8*(3), 2413–2423.

Chien, F., Zhang, Y., Li, L., & Huang, Hiang-Chu (2023). Impact of government governance and environmental taxes on sustainable energy transition in China: Fresh evidence using a novel QARDL approach. *Environmental Science and Pollution Research, 30*(16), 48436–48448.

Critical Minerals Market Review. (2023, July). IEA. https://www.iea.org/reports/critical-minerals-market-review-2023

IEA. (2021). *The role of critical minerals in clean energy transitions*. IEA. https://www.iea.org/reports/the-role-of-critical-minerals-in-clean-energy-transitions/executive-summary

IRENA. (2023). Renewable capacity statistics. https://www.irena.org/Publications/%202023/Mar/Renewable-capacity-statistics-2023/

Jones, D. (2023, January 31). *European electricity review*. Ember. https://ember-climate.org/insights/research/ european-electricity-review-2023/.

Longhurst, N., & Chilvers, J. (2019). Mapping diverse visions of energy transitions: Co-producing sociotechnical imaginaries. *Sustainability Science, 14*(4), 973–990.

Mitrova, T., & Melnikov, Y. (2019). Energy transition in Russia. *Energy Transit, 3*(1), 73–80.

Network for Greening the Financial System First comprehensive report. (2019). *A call for action Climate change as a source of financial risk*. https://www.banque-france.fr/sites/default/files/media/2019/04/17/ngfs_first_comprehensive_report_-_17042019_0.pdf

Rasoulinezhad, Eh., Taghizadeh-Hesary, F., Sung, J., & Panthamit, N. (2020). Geopolitical risk and energy transition in Russia: Evidence from ARDL Bounds Testing Method, *Sustainability, 12*(7), 2689.

Savio, A., De Giovanni, L., & Guidolin, M. (2022). Modelling energy transition in Germany: An analysis through ordinary differential equations and system dynamics. *Forecasting*, MDPI, *4*(2), 438–455.

Siciliano, G., Wallbott, L., Urban, Fr., Dang, A. N., & Lederer, M. (2021). Low-carbon energy, sustainable development, and justice: Towards a just energy transition for the society and the environment. *Sustainable Development*, *29*(6), 1049–1061.

Smil, V. (2010). *Energy transitions: History, requirements, prospects*. ABC-CLIO, Santa Barbara.

World Energy Investment. (2023). https://www.iea.org/reports/world-energy-investment-2023

Zakeri, B., Paulavets, K., Barreto-Gomez, L., Gomez-Echeverri, L., Pachauri, S., Boza-Kiss, B., Zimm, C., Rogelj, J., Creutzig, F., & Ürge-Vorsatz, D. (2022). Pandemic, war, and global energy transitions. *Energies, 15*(17), 6114.

Simona Vojtekova[1], and Katarina Valaskova[1,*]

Impact of the Global COVID-19 Pandemic and Perspectives of the Hospitality Sector in Slovakia

Abstract:
Research background: The COVID-19 pandemic, which rocked the world in 2020–2021, was brought under control only after taking stringent and prompt action. This illness also had a big effect on the individual sectors and a demonstrable financial impact on whole economies. The local travel bans and lockdowns rocked the hospitality sector's performance, thus, the perspectives of this sector are analyzed in the paper.
Purpose of the article: The aim of the contribution is to describe the impact of the COVID-19 pandemic on a selected sector of the national economy – NACE I – in the conditions of the Slovak Republic and to point out changes in the financial stability of this sector, strongly dependent on direct consumption, which was impacted and significantly constrained by the COVID-19 pandemic crisis.
Methods: The Orbis database provided the data for the industry analysis for the years 2016–2021. 321 businesses' worth of data are accessible for examination. We employed various well-known ex ante models to evaluate the financial stability of a predetermined sample of enterprises.
Findings & Value added: To determine corporate strengths and weaknesses and choose the best financial management strategy, it is essential to evaluate the corporate business performance and financial health. Based on how well a company is doing, it is possible to predict whether it will be able to continue functioning in the future. Therefore, the main contribution is mapping of the financial soundness of businesses in the hospitality sector, strongly affected by the pandemic, and assessing the changes.

Keywords: *sharing economy, collaborative economy, bibliometric analysis, globalization*

JEL Classification: *D16; E26; F60*

* Corresponding author: katarina.valaskova@fpedas.uniza.sk
1 University of Zilina, Faculty of Operation and Economics of Transport and Communications, Univerzitna 1, 010 26 Zilina, Slovakia

1 Introduction

In 2020–2021, the world was shaken by the pandemic outbreak of the viral disease COVID-19, which could not be brought under control even with strict and timely measures. This disease had a significant impact not only on the healthcare industry and people's health conditions but also on the functioning of the economy throughout the world.

With the first confirmed case of COVID-19 in Slovakia in March 2020, it was necessary to take the necessary measures, even in our conditions (Csanyi & Kucharcik, 2023). In the course of days, hours, and even minutes, it was necessary to make decisions that would primarily protect us and our health. One of the first steps was to declare a state of emergency, close schools, and declare a state of emergency. When the pandemic did not subside and the virus spread more and many times faster, it began to appear that it would be necessary to act promptly and in such a way that decisions were also future-oriented (Veselovska et al., 2021; Gajdosikova et al., 2022). The situation in the form of a pandemic of such dimensions will not subside so quickly, and the economies of each and every state will very likely suffer greatly (Valaskova & Nagy, 2023). The pandemic of the viral disease COVID-19 had a great impact on the world economy and also on the employment of the population of the Slovak Republic (Cernenko et al., 2021). In order to survive, business companies reduced the number of employees, which increased the number of unemployed people. The first aid from the state for employees, self-employed, and entrepreneurs who were affected by the pandemic and anti-pandemic measures to such an extent that they had to limit their work or business activities were contributions replacing employees' wages up to 80 % of average earnings, but at the same time up to a maximum of 1 100 euros (Habanik et al., 2022; Svabova et al., 2021; Kramarova et al., 2022). The measures to prevent the spread of COVID-19 included the suspension of classes at all types of schools for a period of at least 14 days, restrictions on access to the country and the ability to travel, border controls, mandatory quarantines in various cases, and restrictions on the possibility of operating shopping centers, restaurants, and various centers and facilities that mainly offered services for final consumers (Grancay, 2020). Later, the government's decisions were tightened, a state of emergency was declared, and shops were closed except for food, pharmacies, internet services, etc. Not only economically weaker developed countries suffered, but also those that are among the most developed (Durana et al., 2022). In an effort to protect the health of the people of the countries, several measures were established regarding the quarantine of the population, which had an impact on the economic decline and the beginning of the economic crisis

(Waliszewski, 2022). The adopted measures of the countries partially, or in some cases in full, affected business activity. Demand decreased, thus the value of sales also decreased, and this also affected the business entity's economic results. The Slovak Republic had long-term anti-pandemic measures, which made us one of the countries whose economies were most affected (Kovacova et al., 2022). These measures affected business entities in different ways. There were measures across the board that applied to all entities and then measures exclusively for entities that are in the trade, transport, accommodation, catering, and other service sectors (Lesakova et al., 2022). The accommodation and catering industries were hit to the greatest extent, their activities being banned in full during the first wave of the pandemic. This also results from the fact that it belongs to the sectors that were restricted first, but the mitigation and relaxation of these measures for the given sector were among the last. Due to the great impact on business entities and employees, the government of the Slovak Republic also adopted measures that served as help and support (Bundzikova & Janosova, 2020). These measures can also be divided into nationwide measures and those intended for the most affected subjects. Across-the-board measures included employment support, help for entrepreneurs in the event of a loss of income, possible deferment of lease payments, taxes, loans, and insurance premiums, the possibility of subsidies for the payment of rent, and many others. For the most affected subjects, aid was provided in a targeted and special way. As such, the pandemic has affected demand, supply, mobility of people, decline in global consumption, decline in GDP, inflation rate, industrial production, and employment. The performance of the economy is best assessed using GDP. Already in 2019, a deterioration in the development of the economy could be observed. The pandemic had various impacts on the business economy of the Slovak Republic, which we can quantify with the indicators of gross production, added value, profit, number of employees, and the number of newly established or closed business entities (Slovak Business Agency, 2020).

The aim of the contribution is to describe the impact of the COVID-19 pandemic on a selected sector of the national economy – NACE I – in the conditions of the Slovak Republic and to point out changes in the financial stability of this sector.

In the conditions of the Slovak Republic, it was quite evident how business entities suffered as a result of the government's strict measures to prevent the spread of this viral disease. The functioning and operations of some entities were partially affected, and some had to be completely closed and their operations interrupted. In the current situation, those businesses that did not reach liquidation, bankruptcy, or cancellation due to the onslaught of strict measures are getting out of difficulties and are trying to return to the level of functioning they were at before the outbreak of the pandemic. Another of the stimuli for solving this problem was the opinion that, in the case of certain matters, greater intervention and assistance from the state could significantly affect the functioning and future of business entities doing business in the territory of the Slovak Republic, and thus their collapse, liquidation, and cancellation could be prevented.

2 Methods

According to the NACE statistical classification of economic activities of the European Communities, we focused on Section I – accommodation and catering services – which was most affected by a number of measures during the pandemic. This section is divided into two divisions: the first is accommodation, and the second is restaurant and hospitality activities. Our choice is Division 56: Restaurant and hospitality activities, which includes restaurant activities performed by traditional, self-service restaurants, restaurants selling across the street, and permanent or occasional stands. The condition is that the food and drinks provided must be completely ready for consumption at the given moment.

The data for analyzing the industry is for the period 2016–2021 and comes from the Orbis database, which has been sorted based on the necessary information and parameters that determine the essence of the work. We have data for 321 companies available for analysis. The reason for focusing specifically on SK NACE I was the fact that, in most cases, it is this sector that is dependent on direct consumption, which was affected and largely limited by the crisis caused by the pandemic of the viral disease COVID-19, which was also reflected in the decrease in employment.

To assess the financial stability of a selected sample of companies, we used some well-known ex ante models, specifically a model adapted to the conditions of the Slovak Republic, and we will compare the results with a model that is considered one of the most important models worldwide, the Altman model.

$$Z = 0{,}717\,x_1 + 0{,}847\,x_2 + 3{,}107\,x_3 + 0{,}420\,x_4 + 0{,}998\,x_5 \qquad (1)$$

Where:

$$x_1 = \frac{net\ working\ capital}{assets}$$

$$x_2 = \frac{retained\ earnings}{assets}$$

$$x_3 = \frac{EBIT}{assets}$$

$$x_4 = \frac{market\ value\ of\ equity}{liabilities}$$

$$x_5 = \frac{sales}{assets}$$

The classification scheme of other enterprises has adjusted weights (see formula). For other companies, we interpret Z at the following intervals: If Z has a value of 2.99 or more, then the financial situation is and will be very good and stable. If Z was in the interval from 1.2 to 2.99, it would be a grey zone, and if Z was from 1.2 or less, there would be a threat of bankruptcy and the company would be in a bad financial situation (Kliestik et al., 2021).

$$\begin{aligned} Z\ score &= 0{,}5 - 0{,}323.regionBA - 0{,}434.smallcompany \\ &-0{,}022.x_1 + 0{,}215.x_8 - 0{,}203.x_{10} - 0{,}469.x_{11} + 1{,}045.x_{12} \\ &+0{,}651.x_{20} - 0{,}054.x_{22} + 0{,}168.x_{25} - 0{,}097.x_{26} + 1{,}067.x_{27} \\ &+0{,}287.x_{28} + 0{,}016.x_{30} \end{aligned} \quad (2)$$

$$x_1 = \frac{sales}{assets}$$

$$x_8 = \frac{working\ capital}{assets}$$

$$x_{10} = \frac{(long-term + short-term\ liabilities)}{assets}$$

$$x_{11} = \frac{short-term\ assets}{assets}$$

$$x_{12} = \frac{cash\ and\ equivalents}{assets}$$

$$x_{20} = \frac{net\ profit}{sales}$$

$$x_{22} = \frac{cash\ and\ equivalents}{short - term\ liabilities}$$

$$x_{25} = \frac{current\ assets}{current\ liabilities}$$

$$x_{26} = \frac{(short - term\ assets - stock)}{short - term\ liabilities}$$

$$x_{27} = \frac{EBT}{assets}$$

$$x_{28} = \frac{net\ profit}{equity}$$

$$x_{30} = \frac{equity}{(long - term + short - term\ liabilities)}$$

3 Results and Discussion

Chovanculiak (2019), an analyst at the Institute of Economic and Social Analysis, refers to sharing as a concept that is considered by the professional public to be an economic model that, unlike other traditional and conventional models, does not focus on the idea of ownership, but on the concept of using, sharing, and making available already available products. He expresses the opinion that it is not essential that everything falls into the sharing system. It is important that the general public know, in conversations about sharing, what this approach offers and what economic, environmental, personal, and other benefits it brings. Historically, sharing did not invent something revolutionary, but it enabled mutual exchange and the implementation of activities. Some platforms tried to develop their activity in market conditions with an effort to reach potential consumers, entered the market, but failed to apply

With Altman's ex ante financial analysis model, we divide business entities into three groups based on the discrimination equation (1). In the first group, there are companies whose Z-score is less than 1.2 and have a very high probability of bankruptcy. The second group is for entities achieving a Z-score from the interval from 1.2 to 2.99, otherwise known as the grey zone of bankruptcy, and the third group is made up of entities achieving a Z-score higher than 2.99 and being in a good financial situation (Gregova et al., 2020). Based on these facts, we divided the business entities of the analyzed industry into three groups, in which we will evaluate the year-on-year development of their numbers (Table 1).

Table 1. Frequency of the Altman model categories.

	to 1.2	**from 1.2 to 2.99**	**over 2.99**
2021	50.5 %	31.2 %	18.4 %
2020	53.3 %	27.7 %	19.0 %
2019	45.2 %	27.4 %	27.4 %
2018	49.5 %	26.2 %	24.3 %
2017	49.2 %	24.9 %	25.9 %
2016	49.5 %	27.4 %	23.1 %

Source: authors

In Table 1, we find the percentage expression of the number of business entities in the industry located in individual groups of the distribution of the resulting values of the achieved Z-score. The category of subjects with a very high probability of bankruptcy had the highest occupancy during all the analyzed years, in which the occupancy by enterprises in the sector was the lowest in 2019 and the highest, i.e., 53.3 %, in 2020. It was positive that the number of enterprises in this group decreased in 2017 and 2019, but in 2020, the number of businesses with a high probability of bankruptcy rose to 53.3 %, which is an increase of 8.1 percentage points compared to 2019. In 2017, the second and third groups exchanged first place in occupancy, and in 2019, the occupancy of these two groups was even. The negative is the fact that, since 2017, the number of entities with the possibility of bankruptcy has been increasing year-on-year. The last group of enterprises in a good financial situation has had an alternating situation over the years; one year the number decreased, the next increased, and this continued until 2019. From 2020 on, the occupancy of this group decreased and reached its minimum in 2021. The increase in the number of companies with a very high probability of bankruptcy, companies in the grey zone, and the decrease in the number of companies in a good financial situation in 2020 can be attributed to a certain impact of the pandemic of the viral disease COVID-19.

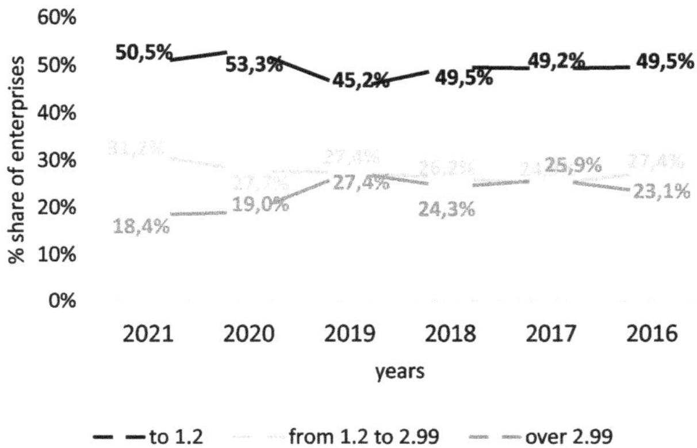

Figure 1. Development of the sector according to the Altman model (2016–2021).
Source: authors

Figure 1 shows the development of the sector according to the Altman model during the monitored period.

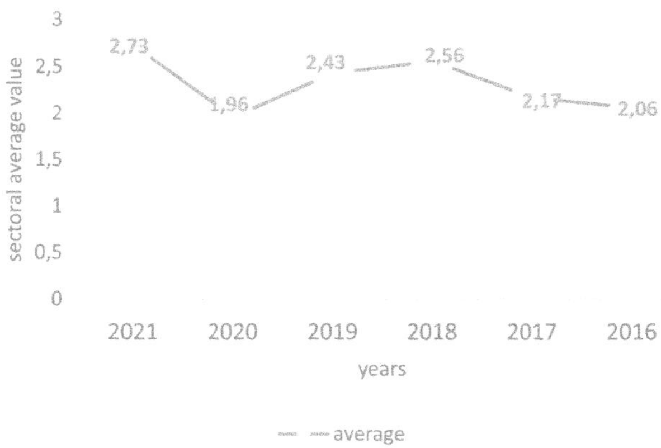

Figure 2. Development of the average Altman Z-score value (2016–2021).
Source: authors

For a better evaluation of the industry, we averaged the Z-scores achieved by all companies in the industry. During all the analyzed years, the industry was in the grey zone, i.e., the zone of possible bankruptcy. Until 2018, the trend of the average value increased; in 2019, there was a slight decrease of 0.13 units of the indicator, but in 2020, probably due to the impact of the pandemic of the viral disease COVID-19, the value of the Z-score reached the lowest value among the analyzed years. On the positive side, in 2021, there was an increase in the value of the Z-score of the industry to the highest value of the analyzed years of 2.73. At the same time, this value is approaching the minimum achieved by subjects in a good financial situation.

The second analyzed model was the model developed in Slovak conditions for the enterprises operating in the sector NACE I. We analyzed 321 business entities that made up the industry division we selected. The resulting Z-score values are divided into two groups based on whether their value was positive or negative. If the value of the Z-score of the business subjects of the industry was less than 0 and reached minus or negative values, these enterprises were prosperous in the given year. Otherwise, i.e., if the Z-score was higher than 0 and therefore in positive values, the subjects were unsuccessful (Table 2).

Table 2. Frequency of the Slovak NACE I model categories.

	prosperous	**non-prosperous**
2021	50.5 %	49.5 %
2020	53.0 %	47.0 %
2019	47.7 %	52.3 %
2018	51.4 %	48.6 %
2017	47.7 %	52.3 %
2016	52.0 %	48.0 %

Source: authors

Table 2 shows the number of either prosperous or non-prosperous enterprises in the sector for individual years, which are covered by the analysis, and in figure no. 3, we can use a line graph to see the represented percentage occupancy of the category.

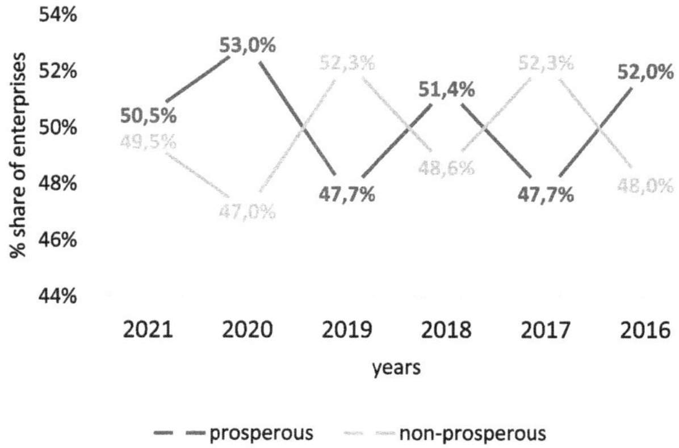

Figure 3. Development of the sector according to the Slovak NACE I model (2016–2021).

Source: authors

In 2016, the number of industry subjects in the prosperous group prevailed. The following year, however, it was the other way around, and the majority of enterprises, namely 52.3 %, were non-prosperous in the group, which indicates that most of the industry's subjects were on the verge of bankruptcy. The year 2018 also brought a change in which industry categories prevailed. Prosperous entities once again took the lead with 51.4 %. The fourth year analyzed was 2019, in which the most occupied category was again replaced. This year, there were again more business entities in the industry that were not prosperous, in the same number as in 2017. Although the COVID-19 pandemic broke out at the end of 2019, it did not affect Slovakia until 2020. An interesting fact is that in 2020, due to the pandemic, the number of prosperous entities did not decrease, but on the contrary, there were 5.3 percentage points more thriving business entities in the industry, putting the category back in the lead.

The next "covid" year, 2021, was relatively favorable. The number of thriving businesses still prevailed in the industry, albeit in a lower number than in 2020. However, it is necessary to pay attention to the fact that in 2021, the number of businesses in individual categories came dangerously close to being balanced.

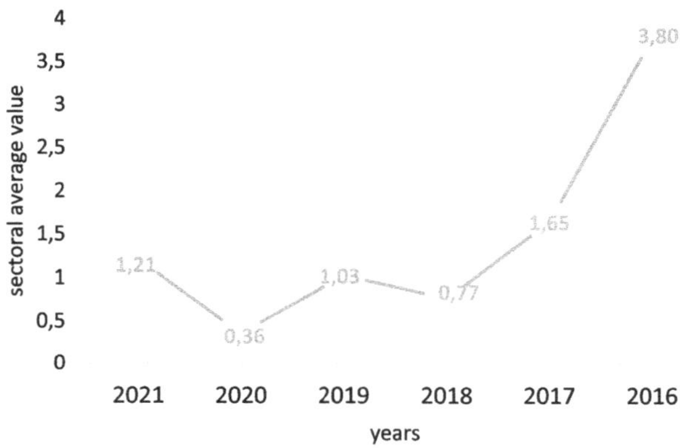

Figure 4. Development of the average Slovak NACE I Z-score value (206–2021).
Source: authors

In Figure 4, we graphically illustrated the development of the average value of the SR model achieved by the NACE I industry. We know that with this model, we divide subjects into prosperous ones if their Z-score is less than 0, and non-prosperous ones that have reached an indicator value greater than 0. We can evaluate that during all the years, the prediction of the situation of the industry would develop positively, and the industry could be called non-prosperous, but only in 2018 and 2020 did it come close to potential prosperity.

Ptak-Chmielewska (2021) of Valaskova et al. (2022) mapping the superiority of multidimensional discrimination over conventional linear multivariate discrimination, as proved by support vector machines, checked and validated the effect of the financial crisis on bankruptcy prediction. The results showed that operating profitability of sales, current liquidity, gross margin ratio, and asset turnover are the most significant explanatory variables in bankruptcy prediction, demonstrating the plausibility of the results obtained in the Visegrad environment. The association between greater gross margin values and bankrupt companies was confirmed, and this association is reflected in each generated prediction model. When analyzing the risk of bankruptcy by data envelopment analysis in the Slovak environment, Horvathova and Mokrisova (2018) emphasized the significance of return on assets, return on equity, collection period, asset turnover, quick liquidity, and current liquidity ratios in the bankruptcy prediction modeling used in this study. Low liquidity ratios and yearly profitability raise the chance of bankruptcy, according to comparisons between the results of this study and other pertinent studies (Lukason & Camacho-Minano, 2019).

4 Conclusions

Currently, businesses must study their operations and evaluate their performance more than ever before. Businesses take care of their financial well-being, are aware of their strengths and shortcomings, are able to act effectively, and can thus adjust quickly to changing circumstances. However, only businesses that are able to adapt to changes in their environment rapidly enough may thrive, succeed, and improve their performance. It is crucial to assess a company's corporate business performance and financial health in order to identify its strengths and weaknesses and select the appropriate financial management technique. It is feasible to foretell whether a corporate entity will be able to continue operating in the future based on how well the firm is performing. Thus, it is really important to measure the changes caused by the pandemic and map the financial stability of enterprises in the key sectors of national economy.

The current research was strongly focused on the hospitality sector, which can be considered also the main limitation on the study. Nonetheless, there is a need to search the changes in the financial stability of every sector of the country, using also different prediction models, to be able to quantify the differences in the development caused by the macroeconomic instability. However, the international comparison of the sectors also plays an important role in the process of implementation of new measures in current economic conditions.

Acknowledgments

This research was financially supported by the Slovak Research and Development Agency – VEGA 1/0121/20: Research of transfer pricing system as a tool to measure the performance of national and multinational companies in the context of earnings management in conditions of the Slovak Republic and V4 countries.

References

Bundzikova, R., & Janosova, D. (2020). The reaction of the Slovak Republic to the COVID-19 pandemic in the context of supporting regional development. *Marketing Identity: COVID-2.0*, 62–71.

Cernenko, T., Neubauerova, E., & Zubalova, A. (2021). Impact of the COVID-19 pandemic on the budget of Slovak Local Governments: Much cry and little wool? *Scientific Papers of the University of Pardubice – Series D – Faculty of Economics and Administration*, *29*(1), 1249.

Chovanculiak, R. (2019). Pokrok bez povolenia.

Csanyi, P., & Kucharcik, P. (2023). Slovakia and the Slovak local governments response to COVID-19 challenges. *Journal of Social Policy Studies*, *21*(1), 107–120.

Durana, P., Blazek, R., Machova, V., & Krasnan, M. (2022). The use of Beneish M-scores to reveal creative accounting: Evidence from Slovakia. *Equilibrium. Quarterly Journal of Economics and Economic Policy*, *17*(2), 481–510.

Gajdosikova, D., Valaskova, K., & Durana, P. (2022). Earnings management and corporate performance in the scope of firm-specific features. *Journal of Risk and Financial Management*, *15*(10), 426.

Grancay, M. (2020). COVID-19 and Central European tourism: The competitiveness of Slovak tourist guides. *Central European Business Review*, *9*(5), 81–98.

Gregova, E., Valaskova, K., Adamko, P., Tumpach, M., & Jaros, J. (2020). Predicting financial distress of Slovak Enterprises: Comparison of selected traditional and learning algorithms methods. *Sustainability*, *12*(10), 3954.

Habanik, J., Vyhnicka, J., Stefcikova, K., & Jakubcinova, M. (2022). The COVID-19 pandemic and its impact on the labor market in the Slovak Republic and the European countries. *Entrepreneurship and Sustainability Issues*, *10*(2), 189–206.

Horvathova, J., & Mokrisova, M. (2018). Risk of Bankruptcy, its determinants and models. *Risks*, *6*(4), 117.

Kliestik, T., Belas, J., Valaskova, K., Nica, E., & Durana, P. (2021). Earnings management in V4 countries: The evidence of earnings smoothing and inflating. *Economic Research – Ekonomska Instrazivanja*, *34*(1), 1452–1470.

Kovacova, M., Krajcik, V., Michalkova, L., & Blazek., R. (2022). Valuing the interest tax shield in the Central European Economies: Panel Data Approach. *Journal of Competitiveness*, *14*(2), 41–59.

Kramarova, K., Švábová, L., & Gabrikova, B. (2022). Impacts of the Covid-19 crisis on unemployment in Slovakia: A statistically created counterfactual approach using the time series analysis. *Equilibrium. Quarterly Journal of Economics and Economic Policy*, *17*(2), 343–389.

Lesakova, L., Vinczeova, M., & Kascakova, A. (2022). Measures supporting entrepreneurship in Slovak SMEs in the most vulnerable industries in times of the COVID-19 pandemic. *E & M Ekonomie a Management*, *25*(3), 4–18.

Lukason, O., & Camacho.Minano, M. (2019). Bankruptcy risk, its financial determinants and reporting delays: Do managers have anything to hide? *Risks*, *7*(3), 77.

Ptak-Chmielewska, A. (2021). Bankruptcy prediction of small- and medium-sized enterprises in Poland based on the LDA and SVM methods. *Statistics in Transition New Series*, *22*(1), 179–195.

Slovak Business Agency. (2020, July). *Adverse impact of the coronavirus pandemic on the corporate economy of the Slovak Republic*. https://monitoringmsp.sk/wp-content/uploads/2021/07/Nepriazniv%C3%BD-vplyv-pand%C3%A9mie-koronav%C3%ADrusu-na-podnikov%C3%BA-ekonomiku-SR.pdf

Svabova, L., Tesarova, E. N., Durica, M., & Strakova, L. (2021). Evaluation of the impacts of the COVID-19 pandemic on the development of the unemployment rate in Slovakia: Counterfactual before-after comparison. *Equilibrium. Quarterly Journal of Economics and Economic Policy*, *16*(2), 261–284.

Valaskova, K., Gajdosikova, D., & Pavic-Kramaric, T. (2022). How important is the business environment for the performance of enterprises? Case study of selected European countries. *Central European Business Review*, *11*(4), 85–110.

Valaskova, K., & Nagy, M. (2023). Macro-economic development of the EU countries in the context of performance and competitiveness of SMEs. *Business Management and Economics Engineering*, *21*(1), 124–139.

Veselovska, L., Zavadsky, J., & Bartkova, L. (2021). Consumer behaviour changes during times of the COVID-19 pandemic: An empirical study on Slovak consumers. *E & M Ekonomie a Management*, *24*(2), 136–152.

Waliszewski, K. (2022). The impact of the COVID-19 pandemic on the personal finance-a comparative analysis of Poles and Slovaks. *Financial Internet Quarterly*, *18*(3), 80–87.

Stanislav Zabojnik[1,*], and Marius Hricovsky[1]

Challenges of Potential E-mobility Revolution on the Electricity Production in Slovakia

Abstract:
Research background: The goals in the field of electromobility of the EU and the Slovak Republic are very ambitious and, according to several experts, unachievable. The policy will have fundamental impacts for the Slovak Republic as a significant importer of oil from the Russian Federation, especially in the area of the electricity production structure (with an expected increase in consumption).
Purpose of the article: To outline the increase in electricity consumption caused by the rapid growth of BEVs and PHEVs on Slovak roads.
Methods: Simulation of scenarios based on fleet changes and simulation of electricity consumption at the level of car owners (PHEVs and BEVs without trucks).
Findings & Value added: Based on the current policies and EU and Slovak Government goals, the authors indicated an additional minor increase in electricity demand at the level of 0.6 TWh per year by 2030. Possible scenarios for the production of this quantity include several generation options, possibly renewable energy sources and in the long term (by 2040, a need to complete the construction of a new nuclear source) for the purpose of covering the consumption of electricity caused by the electrification of the vehicle fleet and batteries production in Slovakia.

Keywords: *e-mobility, energy security, Slovak energy market*

JEL Classification: *F10; F13; F60*

1 Introduction

Electromobility is coming to the center of the EU decarbonization policy, but also aspects of the energy market, especially after the publication of the Fit for 55 package. Within the package, the European Commission committed to

* Corresponding author: stanislav.zabojnik@euba.sk
1 University of Zilina, Faculty of Operation and Economics of Transport and Communications, Univerzitna 1, 010 26 Zilina, Slovakia

significantly speeding up efforts to transform the EU vehicle fleet from cars with internal combustion engines to fleets of BEV-type electric cars, in a transitional period of hybrid drive type PHEV (combustion engines combined with electric motors). The Slovak Republic, as a member state of the EU, is obliged to adapt this strategy within the national economy of the Slovak Republic based on the resulting implementing regulations. Several specifics result from this, as the Slovak economy is one of the least developed economies of the EU (and the resulting lower demand for electric cars). The key challenge cover high energy costs (especially fuel and electricity), since Slovakia is one of most industrialized countries in the world, and the pace of electromobility is significantly behind the expected plan.

In line with EU legislation, at the end of 2022, the Action Plan for the Development of Electromobility in the Slovak Republic was approved with foundations and set goals until 2030. In connection to the war in Ukraine, a change in the energy paradigm of the Slovak Republic – a shift away from the import of fossil resources from the Russian Federation – represents the revolution in the electric car market. This is a great opportunity, but there are also many hitherto almost unsolved problems and challenges that the decision-making sphere and private energy companies will have to deal with. One of such challenges is the growth of electricity consumption associated with the sharp increase in the number of BEVs and PHEVs in the Slovak Republic until 2030. The research question of the submitted contribution is therefore to identify the basic trends of the electromobility development in the Slovak Republic through baseline scenarios and then to estimate the impact on the requirements for increasing the electricity production in the Slovak Republic.

2 Literature Review and Methods

In the case of the intensity of electromobility progress in Slovakia, the authors generally agree that it does not reach the set parameters and previously defined ambitions (Mikusova et al., 2018; Potkany & Lesnikova, 2019; Zábojnik et al., 2022). Some authors, especially in recent years, have directly examined the impact of electromobility on individual aspects of the economy or on energy security. Feckova Skrabulakova et al. (2021) point out that Slovakia is not ready for the growth of electromobility at the same level as in the EU countries with the fastest penetration of electric cars. At the same time, they state that the Slovak Republic (including the energy market) is relatively well prepared for the expansion of BEVs but does not reach the advantages of countries producing electricity from renewable energy sources (e.g., Germany).

Zivcak et al. (2020) deal with a critical analysis of the electric cars´ advantages and examine what impact electromobility and the massive increase in BEV vehicles in the Slovak Republic will have on areas such as energy sources. They come to the conclusion that the rapid growth of electromobility in the Slovak Republic will not have a fundamental impact on the energy balance of the Slovak Republic. Zábojník and Hričovský (2021) stated that several TWh of additional electricity available on the market will be needed after full roll-out of the e-mobility plans till 2050. Other scientific studies directly examining the impact on the energy balance or the electricity network in Slovakia are absent. Analytical materials on this topic are processed primarily by the Ministry of Economy of the Slovak Republic, distribution system operators in the Slovak Republic (DSOs), and energy market analysts. Despite the absence of such a key study, electromobility in the Slovak Republic is promoted centrally through the implementation of EU legislation, which, however, does not reduce the intensity of the need to investigate such impacts.

Authors examining the current trends and foundations of the development of electromobility in Slovakia point to five basic documents on which support for this transformation is built (Zábojník et al., 2022, in chronological order) in SR:

- Strategy for the Development of Electromobility in the Slovak Republic and its Impact on the National Economy of the Slovak Republic (2015) and transposition documents,
- National Policy for Deploying Infrastructure for Alternative Fuels in the Slovak Republic (2016),
- National policy framework for the development of the alternative fuel market (2016),
- Action Plan for the Development of Electromobility in the Slovak Republic (2019), and
- Slovakia Automotive Electric Vehicles Action Plan (2023).

The basic material and platform for evaluating the potential of electromobility in the Slovak Republic was the Strategy for the Development of Electromobility in the Slovak Republic and its Impact on the National Economy of the Slovak Republic (2015) under the auspices of the MHSR working group. This document evaluates the basic starting points, positives and negatives of electromobility in Slovakia, as well as the broad-spectrum impacts of a more massive transition to electromobility in passenger transport. The key conclusion is the estimation of the development of the electric cars number (BEV and PHEV together) in the Slovak Republic through a standard and technological (more optimistic) scenario. In the case of the standard scenario, the MHSR working group estimated this number of vehicles on Slovak roads at the level of 10,000 in 2020, in the case of the technological scenario, this estimate was up to 25,000 in 2020. This assumption turned out to be significantly optimistic over time and was not achieved. One of the reasons for the non-fulfilment was the incentives for the purchase of an electric car, which were evaluated as less intensive compared to several European states, even states at a comparable level of economic development. Without a significant increase in the MHSR's budget for this initiative and broader legislative favoring of electric car owners, significant changes in market share will be probably not achieved. These initial data were overestimated for a long time and were not significantly updated until the processing of European legislation and the need to submit the National Climate Plan of the Slovak Republic (European Commission, 2023). This changed only in June 2023, when the Automotive Electric Vehicles Action Plan (MHSR, 2022) was presented and approved. Since then, it has become a basic conceptual document in the Slovak Republic for comparing the electromobility rate of progress, but it already contains specific mandatory and recommended tools for supporting electromobility in the Slovak Republic.

In connection with the revolutionary changes in the electromobility market, it is necessary to examine the energy market, or electricity system, on two levels. The first is the actual consumption of electricity by BEV and PHEV owners (the expected increase in electricity consumption as a substitute for diesel and gasoline). Here, the rate of progress in the sale of new BEVs and PHEVs as a share of newly sold vehicles (priority in passenger transport) is questionable, which will decide the amount of additionally consumed storm electricity. On the one hand, the substitution of the import of fossil resources (oil) with electricity can contribute to a better external energy security (Misik, 2022), but at the same time generates questions regarding its availability and price. The second level is the consumption of electricity for the production of electric cars (BEV and PHEV), as the Slovak Republic is a significant producer of cars, including many models from the field of electromobility (Morvay, 2022). Studies examining the impact on electricity consumption, or the consumption profile is relatively widespread abroad (Chinoracky et al., 2022; Trebecki et al., 2022; Gryparis et al., 2020), or conditionality for increasing electromobility to engage additional capacities from renewable energy sources in the electricity network, primarily photovoltaic sources (Szymanski & Zurek-Mortka, 2022; Rivera et al., 2022; Malek et al., 2022).

The rapid growth in the number of BEVs and PHEVs could have an impact not only on the need for additional sources of electricity in the Slovak Republic but also on its price itself, which could ultimately affect the competitiveness of domestic producers vis-à-vis foreign competition and the price competitiveness of Slovak exporters on foreign markets (Zábojník et al., 2023).

The review of the literature clearly shows that after the approval of the new conceptual documents for electromobility in the Slovak Republic, there is a lack of serious studies published in prestigious economic journals. The impact of electromobility in the Slovak Republic on the additional demand for electricity in the Slovak Republic is particularly absent. The presented contribution therefore sets itself the primary goal of updating and quantifying the expected development of the electric vehicle market (BEC and PHEV) and specifically quantifying the additional need for electricity produced for these vehicles.

Methodologically, the contribution is divided into three parts: prediction of the development of electromobility in Slovakia (three scenarios), prediction of electricity consumption (BEV and PHEV), and then cumulative electricity consumption in Slovakia in 2030 caused by the increase in BEV and PHEV ownership.

Due to the scope of the contribution and its main goal of pointing out the development of electricity consumption caused by electric cars, the prediction of the development of the number of electric cars was based on the model of Zábojník et al. (2022). The prediction of the number of BEVs and PHEVs on Slovak roads is based on the model of these authors, based on updating: the numbers for the number of BEVs and PHEVs are updated for the year 2022 (actual situation), and, according to the model, cumulative increases until 2030 were calculated according to individual scenarios. Development scenarios include three alternatives: reference scenario, fossil scenario, and ecological scenario. The model equation for the BEV and PHEV fleet forecast was applied as follows:

$$\text{L\_new\_BEV} = \beta_0 + \beta_1 * \text{l\_Fast charging points} + \beta_2 * \text{l\_Normal\_charging\_points} + \beta_3 * \text{l\_GDP\_p.c.\_const} + u \quad (1)$$

Individual scenarios reflect statistically significant variables: classic (slow) chargers, growth in the robustness of the infrastructure in the form of fast chargers, growth in the standard of living in Slovakia as an accelerator of demand for electric cars, and the intensity of regulation as an important element determining consumer demand. The first scenario is based on the preservation of the current state and individual policies, the implementation of European legislation, and the mandatory tools of the Action Plan for Electromobility in the Slovak Republic. The fossil scenario is based on the weakening of the ambition of policies to support electromobility and the continuous support of internal combustion engines in the EU (which, despite the extension of EUR7 and the easing of its technical conditions, is unlikely). The ecological scenario is based on the rapid development of infrastructure, the standard of living in the Slovak Republic, as well as regulation and subsidies in favour of the BEVs and PHEVs purchases.

The prediction of electricity consumption is based on renowned analyses by authors investigating the consumption of BEVs and PHEVs. The authors assume a 100 % replacement of fossil resources (diesel and gasoline) in the case of BEVs and estimate consumption at an average annual BEV (14,200 km)/ PHEV (13,785 km) mileage and an average BEV consumption of 195 Wh/km (Concawe, 2023). In accordance with the assumptions of several authors publishing similar studies, the authors assume diesel/gasoline savings for BEVs at the level of 100 % of fossil resources and 48 % for PHEVs (Concawe, 2023). The authors anticipate an increase in efficiency by 2030, or battery capacity in BEVs and PHEVs by at least 10 %, which was also taken into account in the prediction of electricity consumption.

3 Results

Based on the methodology of Zábojník et al. (2022), three scenarios of the development of the number of electric cars (for this purpose, BEV and PHEV only) and their numbers until 2030 were estimated. It is necessary to emphasize that the critical foundation of development is the level of regulation and legislative measures at the level of the member states (individual incentives), which are likely to decisively impact the rate of advancement of BEVs and PHEVs in newly sold vehicles. The mentioned scenarios bring concrete results: in 2030, there will be approximately 50,034 BEVs and 58,931 PHEVs on Slovak roads in the case of the pessimistic fossil scenario. The market share of newly sold passenger vehicles in 2030 will be approximately 26.7 %. The reference scenario reflecting the current ambitious decarbonization plans of the European Commission assumes a 41.7 % share of "green" cars in the total fleet sold in 2030. The most optimistic scenario, environmental, assumes that in 2030, up to 74.3 % of cars will be sold with a fully electric or hybrid drive in Slovakia. This assumption would mean that more than 58,000 BEVs will be sold in 2030, and this share will increase thereafter. In the case of further escalation of European emission standards and pressure on European car manufacturers, these numbers are not utopian, but they have a questionable impact on the competitiveness of European car manufacturers. In terms of innovation capacity, they already lag behind Chinese manufacturers in the segment of a lower-class affordable cars.

Table 1. Forecast of BEV and PHEV fleet till 2030.

new cars		Annual increase								
Fossil Scenario	2022 (real)	2023	2024	2025	2026	2027	2028	2029	2030	Total fleet
New registrations		107 826	109 551	111 195	112 751	114 217	115 588	116 859	118 028	
New BEV registrations	*7 869*	**1 586**	**1 899**	**3 742**	**4 195**	**4 659**	**5 213**	**5 865**	**15 006**	50 034
New PHEV registrations	*3 931*	**2 200**	**2 900**	**3 850**	**4 400**	**5 900**	**7 900**	**11 400**	**16 450**	58 931
Reference Scenario		2023	2024	2025	2026	2027	2028	2029	2030	
New registrations		107 826	109 551	111 195	112 751	114 217	115 588	116 859	118 028	
New BEV registrations	*7 869*	**1 896**	**2 354**	**5 258**	**6 167**	**7 246**	**8 622**	**10 329**	**24 280**	74 021
New PHEV registrations	*3 931*	**2 800**	**3 950**	**4 950**	**6 900**	**9 700**	**14 720**	**19 500**	**24 950**	91 401
Ecological Scenario		2023	2024	2025	2026	2027	2028	2029	2030	
New registrations		107 826	109 551	111 195	112 751	114 217	115 588	116 859	118 028	
New BEV registrations	*7 869*	**2 651**	**4 008**	**6 787**	**9 400**	**16 500**	**28 500**	**37 900**	**58 249**	171 864
New PHEV registrations	*3 931*	**3 875**	**4 550**	**5 225**	**7 000**	**8 500**	**11 500**	**18 500**	**29 450**	92 531

Source: authors´ calculation and Zábojník et al. (2022)

The results in the field of electricity consumption are shown in Table 2. The projections show that in the environmental scenario, the most optimistic model of the advancement of electromobility in Slovakia, the "electrified" fleet will require an additional 557.6 GWh of electricity by 2030. In the fossil scenario, there will be only 208 GWh of additional electricity needed, which will have to be produced in Slovakia or imported. The reference scenario envisages additional consumption of electricity only at the level of 308.6 GWh.

Table 2. Additional electricity consumption in Slovakia by 2030.

electricity consumption		Annual increase of electricity consumption (in MWh/year)								
Fossil Scenario	2022 (real)	2023	2024	2025	2026	2027	2028	2029	2030	Total consumption
New registrations	32 674	7 317	8 840	14 860	16 417	19 290	22 940	28 566	57 074	207 977
New BEV registrations	21 789	4 393	5 101	9 947	10 920	11 997	13 280	14 778	37 396	129 601
New PHEV registrations	10 885	2 924	3 739	4 912	5 497	7 293	9 660	13 788	19 678	78 376
Reference Scenario	2022 (real)	2023	2024	2025	2026	2027	2028	2029	2030	
New registrations	32 674	8 973	11 414	20 293	24 672	30 649	39 965	49 612	90 354	308 606
New BEV registrations	21 789	5 251	6 322	13 977	16 052	18 659	21 966	26 027	60 508	190 550
New PHEV registrations	10 885	3 722	5 093	6 316	8 621	11 990	17 999	23 585	29 845	118 056
Ecological Scenario	2022 (real)	2023	2024	2025	2026	2027	2028	2029	2030	
New registrations	32 674	12 491	16 632	24 708	33 212	52 997	86 665	117 876	180 391	557 647
New BEV registrations	21 789	7 340	10 766	18 041	24 467	42 490	72 603	95 500	145 162	438 160
New PHEV registrations	10 885	5 150	5 866	6 667	8 746	10 507	14 062	22 376	35 228	119 487

Source: authors´ calculation based on Energy policy of Slovakia

4 Discussion

The pace of progress in the field of electromobility and diversion of fossil resource consumption in transport is continuous, but revolutionary changes cannot probably be assumed. Despite the fact that several mentioned authors critically evaluate the political dimension of the decision for electromobility rather than economic arguments, the substitution of relatively expensive imports of oil and oil products for electricity potentially produced by domestic (primarily nuclear) sources makes economic sense for the economy of the Slovak Republic (assuming amortized, but of powerful technology in the Jaslovské Bohunice and Mochovce nuclear power plants).

Based on the model and the current data on the starting foundations (infrastructure, standard of living, and level of regulatory intervention), it can be expected that no significant "revolution" in electromobility in the Slovak Republic will take place until 2030. It is related to the basic market fundamentals (consumer preferences, capital equipment), as well as the setting of legislation and regulation until 2030 (modification of EUR 7, measures and incentives in electromobility in the Slovak Republic, etc.).

Our most optimistic scenario predicts that only approximately 12.7 % of newly sold cars in Slovakia will be purely electric, and in the most optimistic scenario, only 49.4 % in 2030. Despite the continuously high interest of consumers in PHEVs, we have to state that, due to the varying degree of recharging from the electrical network, they do not contribute so significantly to the saving of fuels dependent on the import of oil (diesel, gasoline). It is also necessary to emphasize that the implementation of EUR 7, bans on diesel cars in cities, etc. may increase the purchase of BEVs and PHEVs, but we assume that only as a secondary car in the family or a car that will be used (with lower mileage). This applies on the condition that they are no new or increased current taxes impacting diesel or gasoline consumption or mileage on the Slovak highways.

The results of research in the field of electricity consumption led to a fundamental finding. In the most pessimistic fossil scenario, the increase in electricity consumption directly caused by the increase in the number of BEVs and PHEVs on Slovak roads will amount to only approximately 208 GWh in 2030. In the case of the reference scenario, it will be only 308.6 GWh, and in the most optimistic case of the development of electromobility in the Slovak Republic, only 557.6 GWh of electricity. For illustration, this volume represents the industrial consumption of approximately three larger automobile manufacturing plants in the Slovak Republic, and the shutdown of the production of the Slovak aluminum producer (Slovalco) from 2022 represented a saving of more than 1.5 TWh of electricity in the Slovak Republic. It can therefore be concluded that the increase in the volume of electricity due to the sharper growth in the number of BEV and PHEVs on Slovak roads will not result in any more massive consumption of electricity. On the contrary, with long-term planning and the conception of the plan for the development of transmission and distribution systems, this volume is undoubtedly manageable from the production point of view or cross-border import electricity. For an illustration, this volume represents approximately 200 to 550 MWh of the installed capacity of photovoltaic sources, or the volume of electricity produced by the nuclear reactors in Mochovce on one block in less than 50 hours of active operation.

In addition to the clear conclusion that electromobility itself – the operation of electric cars in 2030 – will not have a fundamental impact on the production and consumption of electricity in the Slovak Republic, the authors consider it necessary to emphasize several secondary impacts and some circumstances. Electromobility can potentially have a slightly negative impact on the stability of the network and also on electricity prices (through the necessary auxiliary services and mechanisms ensuring the stability of the electricity system).

Secondly, electromobility itself will most likely not have such a fundamental impact on the consumption of electricity, also due to the fact that the vehicle fleet in the Slovak Republic is considerably outdated and the effect of the emerging electromobility will be shown gradually, not at a high intensity already in 2030 (the average age of passenger vehicles in Slovakia is more than 13 years old). In the period after 2030, in combination with a more stringent regulation of car manufacturers, rapid growth in electricity consumption can therefore be expected.

Another challenge and secondary effect of electromobility is the fact that not only electric cars are on the roads, but the production of electric cars can have a fundamental impact on the consumption of electricity in Slovakia. In the Slovak Republic, a significant producer of batteries for BEVs and PHEVs is still absent, but in Hungary, there are already a large number of large producers of accumulators for the entire European automotive industry. At the same time, the first requirements for SARIO indicate that producers coming to the Slovak Republic will demand not only a high volume of electricity consumption in the energy-intensive production of accumulators but also "green" electricity from renewable energy sources. This indirect impact of the electromobility trend can cause its growth in the Slovak Republic, while the annual consumption can exceed 200 GWh in the case of a single larger producer.

In the case of the electricity system of the Slovak Republic, electromobility represents a challenge to ensuring the volume of electricity, but above all, its stability. However, direct use in passenger transport does not presuppose a fundamental increase and a problem with securing the volume of power electricity. From a macroeconomic point of view, electromobility represents a unique opportunity to reduce the volume of imports of oil and oil products from third countries (especially the Russian Federation), but only with a limited, minor effect. Therefore, the Government of the Slovak Republic and the relevant institutions must only secondarily reflect on the risk of a lack of electricity caused by personal automobile transport by 2030.

Potential areas for further research include a more accurate estimate of the fundamentals influencing the development of the number of BEVs and PHEVs, as well as updated penetration and consumption of the average BEV and PHEV in Slovakia. A fundamental incentive for further and more precise research in the period up to 2030 may be the updating of the action plan, or the reflection of more massive regulation, or incentives for the purchase of electric cars or charging infrastructure.

5 Conclusions

The first part of the authors' research was devoted to the question of predicting the development of the market for electric vehicles (BEV and PHEV), while the prediction is based not only on the current action plan in the field of electromobility of the Slovak Republic but also on the prediction of infrastructure, Slovak standard of living, and the strong degree of regulation in the EU. The authors' findings yield a concrete estimate of the share of electric cars in the case of BEVs and PHEVs at the level of more than a quarter of newly registered cars in 2030 in the case of a pessimistic scenario and more than three quarters of the market in the case of an optimistic scenario.

The presented research was devoted to answering the question of to what extent the expected expansion of electromobility in Slovakia (evaluated in three scenarios depending on the development of foundations) will affect the volume of electricity consumption. Answering this question is important both for the creation of policies in the field of electromobility until 2030 as well as for the concept of the new energy policy of the Slovak Republic until 2030, prospectively until 2050. The result of the authors' research is the finding that electromobility will have a minimal impact on the amount of electricity consumed in SR. The problem of the lack of electricity in the Slovak Republic is a secondary topic when supporting electromobility, as in the most optimistic scenario of the development of electromobility, the additional consumption caused by new BEV and PHEV vehicles represents only 557.6 GWh in 2030, and in the pessimistic scenario of preserving fossil resources, even at the level of 208 GWh, This amount of electrical energy can be covered by renewable energy sources, which would fulfill the purpose of electromobility, namely to minimize the emissions of CO2 and other undesirable gases produced by combustion engines as much as possible. The fundamental benefit of electromobility for the Slovak Republic is the substitution of the import of oil and oil products (the enormous dependence of the Slovak Republic) with electricity potentially produced domestically.

Acknowledgments

This research is a part of the research project VEGA No. 1/0270/22 "Growth of Slovakia´s innovative capabilities and competitiveness for foreign investors in post-covid deglobalization era from the aspect of knowledge creation and transfer."

References

Chinoracky, R., Stalmasekova, N., & Corejova, T. (2022). Trends in the field of electromobility – From the perspective of market characteristics and value-added services: Literature review. *Energies*, *15*(17), 6144.

Concawe. (2023, October 15). *BEV and PHEV database*. Concawe. https://www.concawe.eu/publication/evaluation-of-plug-in-hybrid-vehicles-in-real-world-conditions/

European Commission. (2023, October 15). Integrated National Energy and Climate Plan for 2021 to 2030. Energy. https://energy.ec.europa.eu/system/files/2020-03/sk_final_necp_main_en_0.pdf

Feckova Skrabulakova, E., Ivanova, M., Rosova, A., Gresova, E., Sofranko, M., & Ferencz, V. (2021). On Electromobility Development and the Calculation of the Infrastructural Country Electromobility Coefficient. *Processes, 9*(2), 222. https://doi.org/10.3390/pr9020222

Gryparis, E., Papadopoulos, P., Leligou, H. C., & Psomopoulos, C. S. (2020). Electricity demand and carbon emission in power generation under high penetration of electric vehicles. A European Union perspective. *Energy Reports*, *6*, 475–486.

Małek, A., Dudziak, A., Stopka, O., Caban, J., Marciniak, A., & Rybicka, I. (2022). Charging electric vehicles from photovoltaic systems – Statistical analyses of the small photovoltaic farm operation. *Energies*, *15*(6), 2137.

MHSR (Ministry of Economy of the Slovak Republic). (2022). Slovakia Automotive Electric Vehicles Action Plan. Available on: https://www.trade.gov/market-intelligence/slovakia-automotive-electric-vehicles-action-plan

Mikusova, M., Torok, A., & Brida, P. (2018). Technological and economical context of renewable and non-renewable energy in electric mobility in Slovakia and Hungary. In *International Conference on Computational Collective Intelligence* (pp. 429–436). Cham: Springer International Publishing.

Misik, M. (2022). The EU needs to improve its external energy security. *Energy Policy*, *165*, 112930.

Morvay, K. F. K. (2022). Economic Development of Slovakia in 2021.

Potkany, M., & Lesniková, P. (2019). The amount of subsidy for the electric vehicle in Slovakia through a strategic cost calculation. *Transportation Research Procedia*, *40*, 1168–1175.

Rivera, S., Goetz, S. M., Kouro, S., Lehn, P. W., Pathmanathan, M., Bauer, P., & Mastromauro, R. A. (2022). Charging infrastructure and grid integration for electromobility. *Proceedings of the IEEE*, *111*(4), 371–396.

Szymanski, J., & Zurek-Mortka, M. (2022). Industrial scenario of renewable energy-based electromobility. In *Advanced Energy and Control Systems: Select Proceedings of 3rd International Conference, ESDA 2020* (pp. 3–15). Springer Singapore.

Trebecki, J., Przybylska, J., Rydzak, W., Sellitto, M. A., & Oleśków-Szłapka, J. (2022). Activities related to an electromobility strategy as a part of low carbon energy transition: A survey in Polish Communes. *Energies*, *15*(11), 3934.

Zabojnik, S., & Hricovsky, M. (2021). Balancing the Slovak energy market after the adoption of "Fit for 55 Package". In *SHS Web of Conferences* (Vol. 129, p. 05015). EDP Sciences.

Zábojnik, S., Steinhauser, D., & Kráľ, P. (2022). E-mobility in Slovakia by 2030 – End of oil dependency?. *IET Smart Cities*, *4*(2), 127–142.

Zábojnik, S., Steinhauser, D., & Peštová, V. (2023). Decarbonisation: Do EU electricity costs harm export competitivness ?. *Amfiteatru Economic*, *25*(63), 522–540.

Zivcak, J., Kadarova, J., Puskar, M., Kocisova, M., & Lachvajderova, L. (2020). Expected impacts of the massive increase in electric vehicles in Slovakia. *Applied Sciences*, *10*(24), 8945.

Irina Zhulega[1,*], Andrey Novikov[2], and Natalya Gagulina[3]

Sustainable Development of Russia in the Global Innovation Index System

Abstract:
Research background: At the end of the 20th century, both foreign and domestic scientists substantiated the need for a transition from an industrial to an innovative economy. The introduction of innovations increases production efficiency, improves product quality, makes it possible to withstand market competition and thereby ensure economic security. On the other hand, ensuring economic security is the basis for sustainable development. Thus, innovative development and economic security are interconnected. Currently, the results of innovative development in Russia cannot be considered satisfactory for a number of indicators in comparison with developed countries of the world level.
Purpose of the article: The purpose of the study is to improve public policy in the innovation sphere to ensure sustainable development of the economy and protect it from real and potential threats. In this regard, the state of innovative development of Russia in the Global Innovation Index (GII) system is considered. A comparative analysis of the levels of innovative development of Russia and the leading countries in the GII ranking is given.
Methods: The work was accompanied by the use of general scientific methods: analysis and synthesis, deduction and induction, detailing, comparison, analogy, scientific abstraction and logical laws. The methodological basis of the study is based on the use of a practical approach, functional-structural analysis, and the use of the methodological approach of innovative economics.
Findings & Value added: The study analyzed institutional factors that influence innovation activity and are threats to Russia's economic security. Possible ways to increase the

* Corresponding author: zhulega@mail.ru
1 State University of Aerospace Instrumentation, Bolshaya Morskaya str. 67, Saint Petersburg, 190000, Russia
2 St. Petersburg State University, Faculty of Economics, 7/9 Universitetskaya nab., St. Petersburg, 199034 Russia
3 Institute for Regional Economic Studies, Russian Academy of Sciences Leading researcher 38, Serpuhovskaya str., Saint Petersburg, 190013, Russia

level of innovation activity that ensures the economic security of the Russian Federation are proposed.

Keywords: *innovative development, economic security, innovation index, institutional indicators.*

JEL Classification: *L2; R13*

1 Introduction

Based on historical experience, each state, under the influence of changing geographic information factors, has to introduce new or change old institutions of society in order to accelerate socio-economic development (Carleton et al., 2022). In the conditions of modern global economic activity, it is necessary to understand how to determine the requirements of the global economy, what impact can and should be expected if these requirements are met (Zhulega et al., 2018).

In the 21st century, innovative technologies are one of the key and most promising areas of competition for economic influence between countries. Positioning a country as competitive ensures economic security (Zhulega et al., 2021). National competitiveness, determined by socio-economic and political factors, ultimately determines the level of well-being of society that can be achieved by economic growth and innovation, which is a strategic growth factor. With the exhaustion of growth opportunities for each technological structure and a change in the structure of demand for scientific discoveries and inventions, the need for fundamentally new technologies arises, the competitive selection of which forms the basis of new technological trajectories (Sycheva et al., 2020).

Global competition poses completely new goals for the state in the field of ensuring economic security. The key one is the development of innovative technologies.

In the context of the global crisis and the strengthening of economic sanctions against the Russian Federation by the United States and the European Union, the innovative orientation of the state's economic policy is of paramount importance, since the achievements of science and technology, more than ever before, determine the dynamics of economic growth, the level of well-being of the population, the competitiveness of states and the degree of security their national security. This makes the study of problems of development of innovation activity in our country especially relevant.

2 Economic Security in the Context of Innovation Policy

The development of innovative technologies that affect the economic security of the country is included among the main directions of state policy in the field of ensuring economic security by the Decree of the President of the Russian Federation "On the strategy of economic security until 2030." section III, clause 15, clause 3. (Bergh et al., 2022). The study of Russia's position in the field of innovation in comparison with other countries contributes to decision-making on the management of innovation activities in areas of priority for the state, their support and financing.

Assessing the level of institutional factors of innovative development, including the political stability of the country, the efficiency of the government and legal system, and the degree of complexity of starting a business, largely determines the level of economic security and requires constant monitoring and comprehensive research (Bierbrauer & Boyer, 2016).

The purpose of the study in this case is to analyze the institutional aspects of innovative development based on indicators that are used when comparing innovation systems on the world stage to ensure the economic security of the country, taking into account current global changes and for future forecasts. The block of institutional indicators contains indicators that allow one to assess the quality of institutions, as well as indicators by which one can judge the effectiveness of institutions (Helliwell et al., 2023).

3 Selection of Indicators to Measure the Dynamics of Innovative Development

The methodology for measuring the level of use of innovative technologies that ensure economic security is reflected in the development and use of a system of indicators. There are currently no generally accepted criteria for assessing the level of innovative development. In Russian and international practice, there are different approaches used to monitor the dynamics of innovative development in modern conditions.

Based on the study of available statistical sources, it is proposed to use indicators for analysis – the Global Innovation Index (GII) innovation development indices (Global Innovation Index, n.d.). According to experts, GII is the most comprehensive set of indicators for assessing the effectiveness of innovation in the global economy. GII includes indicators of innovation activity, which are grouped into areas covering the main elements of the national economy.

The total number of points in the GII ranking received by a country is determined as the average of two sub-indices: the sub-index of innovation costs (institutions, human capital and research, infrastructure, domestic market development, business development) and the sub-index of innovation results (results of technology development and knowledge economy, results of creative activity) (Franzi, 2018).

According to the GII results in 2022, Russia ranked 47th out of 131. Based on modernization opportunities, according to Western experts, the Russian economy can be classified as a "catch-up" model. The results of the GII ranking of the ten leading countries and Russia are clearly summarized in Figure 1.

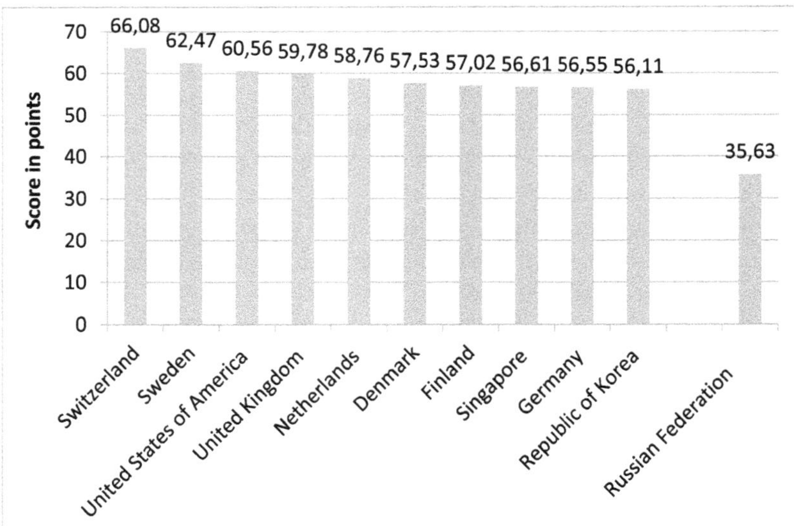

Figure 1. Comparative analysis of innovative development ratings 10 leading countries and Russia in the GII system.

Information on Russia's place in GII in the main areas of innovative development over the past five years is given in Table 1.

Table 1. Russia's place in the GII system for the period 2018–2022.

Indicators (directions of innovative development)	Place in the ranking				
	2018 г.	2019 г.	2020 г.	2021 г.	2022 г.
Place in Russia's ranking	43	45	46	46	47
1. Institutes	73	73	74	74	71
2. Human capital and research	23	23	22	23	30
3. Infrastructure	60	62	63	62	60
4. Market development	63	60	56	61	55
5. Business development	37	33	33	35	42
6.Results of technology development and knowledge economy	40	45	47	47	50
7. Results of creative activity	66	62	72	72	60

Source: author based on Global Innovation Index data.

Higher rankings indicate poor performance. An analysis of Russia's position in the GII for the period from 2018 to 2022 shows a slight change in innovation activity in almost all areas. According to Table 1, Russia in the overall ranking worsened its position by 4 points (in 2018 it took 43rd place, and in 2022 – 47th place out of 131). The worst in the ranking among the directions of innovative development is the direction "1.Institutions." Information about the indicators of the direction "1.Institutions" is presented in Table 2.

Table 2. Values of indicators of the institutional direction of innovative development in the GII system.

		Score/Value	Rank
	INSTITUTIONS	**61,5**	**71**
1.1.	Political environment	54,5	75
	1.1.1 Political and operational stability	66,1	76
	1.1.2 Government effectiveness	48,8	75
1.2	Regulatory environment	54,0	95
	1.2.1 Regulatory quality	27,5	105
	1.2.2 Rule of law	25,4	114
	1.2.3.Cost of redundancy dismissal, salary weeks	17,3	69
1.3	Business environment	76,1	45
	1.3.1 Ease of starting a business	93,1	38
	1.3.2.Ease of resolving insolvency	59,1	52

Source: authors based on Global Innovation Index data.

An analysis of Table 2 shows the weaknesses of the innovation system in the institutional direction according to the "Regulatory environment" criterion, occupying 95th place among 131 countries, according to the "Regulatory quality" and "Rule of law" indicators, occupying 105 and 114 places in the ranking, respectively (Armin et al., 2018).

A visual comparison of Russia and Singapore, the leader in the factors of institutional direction of innovation activity, in the GII system, is presented in Figure 2.

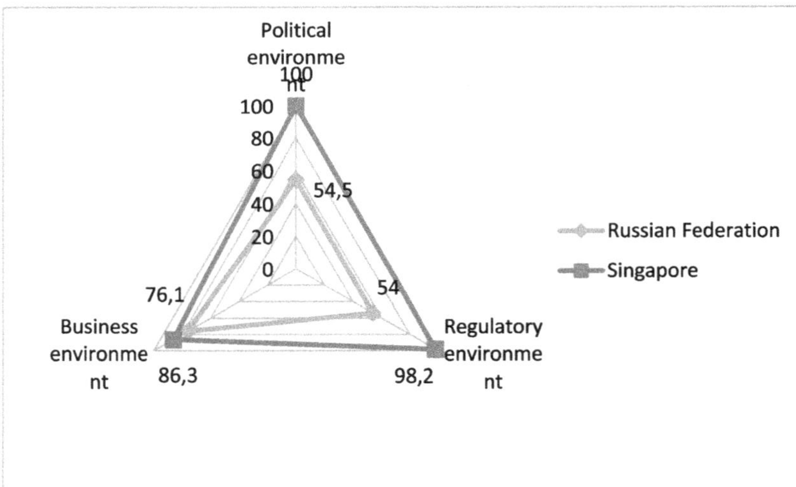

Figure 2. Comparative analysis of indicators of the institutional direction of innovative development of Russia and Singapore in the GII system.

Figure 2 clearly shows Russia's significant lag in terms of the "Political environment" and "Regulatory environment" indicators.

4 Results and Discussion

Thus, the results of the study make it possible to assess the current level of innovation activity in the Russian Federation in comparison with other countries. Indicators – indices of innovative development in the GII system allow you to see the weaknesses of institutional factors of innovative development and formulate priority development directions in the future to ensure sustainable economic development and thereby ensure economic security (Novikov & Gregova, 2017).

In the 21st century, positioning a country as competitive ensures economic security. The key and most promising areas of competition for economic influence between countries is the development of innovative technologies, provided for among the main directions of state policy in the field of ensuring economic security by Decree of the President of the Russian Federation No. 208 of May 17, 2017 "On the Economic Security Strategy of the Russian Federation for the period until 2030" (Decree of the President of the Russian Federation, 2017).

5 Conclusions

The results of innovative development in Russia cannot be considered satisfactory. Russia ranks 47th in the Global Innovation Index system. Particularly weak positions in the direction of institutional factors. Such indicators as "Regulatory quality" and "Rule of law" require attention, occupying 105 and 114 places in the ranking, respectively, out of 131 countries. This poses a threat to economic security. Therefore, it is necessary to intensify innovation activities, taking into account legislative and regulatory documents that regulate and stimulate innovation activities.

References

Armin, F., Becker, A., Dohmen, T., Enke, B., & Huffman, D. (2018). Uwe Sunde global evidence on economic preferences. *The Quarterly Journal of Economics, 133*(4),

Besley, T. & Persson, T. 2007. https://ideas.repec.org/p/nbr/nberwo/13028.html The Origins of State Capacity: Property Rights, Taxation, and Politics, https://ideas.repec.org/s/nbr/nberwo.html NBER Working Papers 13028, National Bureau of Economic Research, Inc.

Bergh, D. D., Boyd, B. K., Byron, K., Gove, S., & Ketchen, D. J. (2022). What constitutes a methodological contribution? *Journal of Management, 48*(7), 1835–1848.

Bierbrauer, F. J., & Boyer, P. C. (2016). Efficiency, welfare, and political competition. *The Quarterly Journal of Economics, 131*(1).

Carleton, T., Jina, A., Delgado, M., Greenstone, M., Houser, T., Hsiang, S., Hultgren, A., Kopp, R., McCusker, K. E., Nath, I., Rising, J., Rode, A., Seo, H. K., Viaene, A., Yuan, J., & Zhang, A. T. (2022). Valuing the global mortality consequences of climate change accounting for adaptation costs and benefits. *The Quarterly Journal of Economics, 137*(4), 2037–2105.

Decree of President of Russian Federation 208. (2017). On the Stratagy of Economic Security of the Russian Federation for the Period until 2030.

Franzi, S. (2018). The great convergence: Information technology and the new globalization. *Journal of Politics, 80*(1).

Global Innovation Index (n.d.) *What is the future of innovation-driven growth?* Global Innovation Index. https://www.globalinnovationindex.org/

Helliwell, J. F., Layard, R., Sachs, J. D., De Neve, J.-E., Aknin, L. B., & Wang, S. (Eds.). (2023). World Happiness Report 2023. New York: Sustainable Development Solutions Network.

Novikov, A., & Gregova, E. (2017). Institution features of economic development during globalization. *Proceedings of the 17th International Scientific Conference of Globalization and its Socio-Economic consequences*, 1757–1764.

Sycheva, E., Budagov, A., & Novikov, A. (2020). Urban infrastructure development in a global knowledge-based economy. *Globalization and its Socio-Economic Consequences 2019,* 74.

Zhulega, I. A., Gagulina, N. L., & Samoylov. A. V. (2018). Sustainable development under conditions of the sanction world order. *Proceedings of the 18th International Scientific Conference of Globalization and its Socio-Economic consequences*, 468–475.

Zhulega, I. A., Sycheva, E., & Samoylov, A. (2021). The use of innovative technologies to ensure economic security of the Russia in the context of globalization. *Proceedings of the 20th International Scientific Conference Globalization and its Socio-Economic Consequences, 92.*

Joana Zukauskiene[1,*], and Vytautas Snieska[1]

Sustainability of Economy in Countries with Different Levels of Development

Abstract:
Research background: The world is currently talking about the importance of sustainable development, and the need to achieve sustainable economic development that does not deplete natural resources or damage the environment. Many countries have chosen the path of sustainable development and they are moving towards a sustainable economy. Waste is being recycled, renewable natural resources are being used, attention is being paid to climate change, poverty reduction, energy efficiency, production, etc. A sustainable economy includes poverty reduction, better living conditions, better health care, nutrition, production using renewable natural resources, waste recycling, transport, and climate change, which is happening due to the greenhouse effect. A sustainable economy aims to promote political and economic sustainability, protect nature, and use renewable natural resources. Discussions are still going on about the factors crucial for the economy to become sustainable.
Purpose of the article: The study aims to find out why some countries in the European Union have higher or lower greenhouse gas emissions, in relation to their gross domestic product (GDP).
Methods: To perform calculations, the panel data analysis method was used.
Findings & Value added: The analysis has revealed a rather chaotic influence of GDP growth on greenhouse gas emissions. This may signal changes in the environmental policy in the analyzed countries and inefficient control of the emissions.

Keywords: *sustainable economy, gross domestic product, greenhouse gas emissions, panel data analysis*

JEL Classification: *Q54; Q57; F64*

* Corresponding author: joana.zukauskiene@ktu.edu

1 Kaunas University of Technology, School of Economics and Business Economics, Business & Management Centre, Gedimino g. 50, LT-44239 Kaunas, Lithuania

1 Introduction

Due to concerns about the Earth's ecosystem, the idea of sustainable development arose. Economic growth has a negative impact on the natural environment, thus concern for the natural environment and economic development has led to the need to seek balance (Rybak et al., 2021). One of the biggest problems in the world is climate change. Climate change is already happening, and its impact on us is increasing. Especially in economically developed, rich countries, climate change is happening due to the way people live. Factories producing goods, aeroplanes and cars, and heat-producing power plants are affecting climate change. For a person, one of the most necessary needs is energy. Energy production, like any human activity, is inseparable from the environment; when the energy source is fossil fuel and coal, its side effect is the emission of pollution into the environment (Bajno et al., 2021). The industrial sector is the largest consumer of energy (Wachnik et al., 2022). The current concentration of greenhouse gases in the atmosphere is the highest in the last 420,000 years. As a result, the climate is changing, and the greenhouse effect is intensifying. People are contributing to the release of these gases. Carbon dioxide is the main greenhouse gas: it accounts for 75 % of all greenhouse gas emissions. Gases are emitted together with steam, smoke from chimneys and other sources of fire. When coal, natural gas, and oil are burned, carbon dioxide is released. Businesses that carry out production should lower their energy consumption and adopt new climate-friendly technologies. Today the biggest focus is on CO2 emissions (Porzio et al., 2013). Companies that produce cars should reduce CO2 emissions. The development of climate-friendly technologies should open new markets and create new jobs. The sustainable use of limited resources on Earth implies the efficient use of raw materials (Tausova et al., 2021). Europe is committed to reducing CO2 emissions by about 20 % (Khouri et al., 2020). At the United Nations Climate Change Conference in 2015, it was proposed to reduce the global average temperature rise from 2 degrees Celsius to 1.5 degrees Celsius (Xu et al., 2022). Unfortunately, it is not clear how successful are the efforts of countries in achieving these goals are. The aim of this paper is to analyze and model how in line to the declared green goals, different countries are successful comparing their emissions and GDP dynamics.

2 Literature Review

The harmonious development of a country or region is a very complex process, which is influenced by many external and internal factors (Niklewicz-Pijaczynska et al., 2021; Mach et al., 2021). A sustainable economy includes poverty reduction, better living conditions, better health care, nutrition, production using renewable natural resources, waste recycling, transport, and climate change, which is happening due to the greenhouse effect. A sustainable economy has minimal or no impact on the economy (Alekna et al., 2019).

The Commission on Development and the World Environment describes sustainable development as development that does not endanger the future and meets current needs (Fong et al., 2022).

It depends on climate change whether the economy will be sustainable, harmonious, or not. The objective of a sustainable economy is to promote political and economic sustainable development, protect nature, and use renewable natural resources, thus, as not to harm future generations. The energy, industrial, and agricultural sectors emit the most greenhouse gases. If the transport, energy, forestry, industry, agriculture, and waste sectors are properly regulated, greenhouse gas emissions can be reduced. Waste management is associated not only with environmental protection but also with human health and the economy of the country, therefore, this led to a harmonious sustainable economy aimed at maintaining the value of materials in the market (Skorupskaite et al., 2017).

A lot of greenhouse gases and pollutants are emitted into the atmosphere due to the inefficient use of thermal energy by outdated heat supply systems and the poor thermal performance of houses built in the past. Due to the underdeveloped public transport system, the low use of alternative means of transport, the slow construction of infrastructure, and the growing number of cars in cities, greenhouse gas emissions are increasing, and the ambient air quality is deteriorating. Because of insufficient attention to regulation and control of pollution, intensive development of the road transport sector, and lack of encouragement to renew vehicles, air pollution is increasing. More primary energy is consumed, due to the high growth of consumption and production, which leads to emitting more pollutants into the atmosphere. Society will not change its habits in cities without the improvement of the public transport situation and the organization of road transport traffic, thus the growing traffic flows on the road can further deteriorate the air quality of cities. EU structural funds can be used to reduce air pollution caused by industry, transport, and energy companies. EU support will allow to modernize the heating sector and buildings, to use energy more efficiently. Wider use of renewable energy resources: water, wind, solar, and biomass, and wider use of biofuels in transport and energy sectors will make it possible to reduce the use of fossil fuels and related air pollution and that will reduce greenhouse gases (GHG). The introduction of green technologies, the promotion of social responsibility in companies, and the introduction of "green procurement" principles will help reduce air pollution. The philosophy of sustainability states that without changes in one's consciousness, the goals set cannot be achieved (Margeta et al., 2022). A sustainable economy is the goal of the green economy (Maran et al., 2017).

3 Methods and Data

To find out why some countries in the European Union have higher or lower greenhouse gas emissions compared to their gross domestic product, we used the statistics of gross domestic product for the period 2009–2021 and the greenhouse gas emissions statistics for the years 2009–2021, see Table 1 For calculations, we chose the Baltic countries with similar levels of development, i.e., Estonia, Latvia and Lithuania.

Table 1. Gross domestic product (GDP) at market prices, chain-linked volumes (2010), billion euro and greenhouse emissions, million tons, 2009–2021, Baltic countries panel data.

Date	Region	CO2mil.t	NO2 mil.t	CH4 mil.t	GDP€ Bn
2009	LTU	5.4685	0.0106	0.1472	27.5784
2010	LTU	3.3383	0.0103	0.1462	28.0338
2011	LTU	3.2966	0.0115	0.1407	29.7268
2012	LTU	3.7671	0.0108	0.1411	30.8695
2013	LTU	3.4703	0.0100	0.1384	31.9653
2014	LTU	3.9664	0.0105	0.1390	33.0960
2015	LTU	5.0050	0.0106	0.1380	33.7660
2016	LTU	5.8813	0.0105	0.1346	34.6165
2017	LTU	6.6289	0.0107	0.1318	36.0990
2018	LTU	7.7382	0.0102	0.1246	37.5406
2019	LTU	7.6844	0.0104	0.1224	39.2768
2020	LTU	6.8054	0.0111	0.1187	39.2682
2021	LTU	7.6319	0.0104	0.1179	41.6167
2009	LVA	2.6188	0.0060	0.0932	18.7740
2010	LVA	5.4843	0.0061	0.0907	17.9375
2011	LVA	4.3221	0.0061	0.0894	18.3992
2012	LVA	2.6512	0.0063	0.0917	19.6949
2013	LVA	3.7650	0.0064	0.0935	20.0903
2014	LVA	7.4362	0.0066	0.0972	20.4725
2015	LVA	6.2289	0.0068	0.0946	21.2679
2016	LVA	4.3068	0.0068	0.0971	21.7717
2017	LVA	2.8114	0.0069	0.0996	22.4928
2018	LVA	5.8516	0.0067	0.0991	23.3907
2019	LVA	3.9754	0.0070	0.0985	23.9918
2020	LVA	6.4069	0.0072	0.0980	23.4404
2021	LVA	8.2096	0.0072	0.0985	24.4429
2009	EST	9.2859	0.0034	0.0487	14.3894
2010	EST	13.1603	0.0035	0.0490	14.7411

Table 1. Continued

Date	Region	CO2mil.t	NO2 mil.t	CH4 mil.t	GDP€ Bn
2011	EST	13.4225	0.0035	0.0479	15.8118
2012	EST	13.8778	0.0037	0.0484	16.3222
2013	EST	16.6224	0.0037	0.0484	16.5602
2014	EST	18.2303	0.0038	0.0475	17.0589
2015	EST	14.7000	0.0039	0.0438	17.3750
2016	EST	16.9965	0.0039	0.0431	17.9233
2017	EST	16.9965	0.0040	0.0436	18.9614
2018	EST	19.7940	0.0039	0.0436	19.6790
2019	EST	13.1273	0.0042	0.0440	20.4728
2020	EST	11.4005	0.0042	0.0436	20.2751
2021	EST	12.9551	0.0042	0.0439	21.7449

Source: Eurostat (2023) data, authors calculations

We applied the panel least squares model for the evaluation of GDP influence on CO2 emissions million ton in the Baltic countries (Table 2). The evaluation has revealed that R-squared for this model is rather low, equal to 0.196498. So, the regression is not reliable for forecasting purpose.

Table 2. GDP influence on CO2 emissions million ton in the Baltic countries panel least squares model estimations.

Dependent Variable: CO2MLNT				
Method: Panel Least Squares				
Date: 10/04/23 Time: 00:24				
Sample: 2009 2021				
Periods included: 13				
Cross-sections included: 3				
Total panel (balanced) observations: 39				
Variable	Coefficient	Std. Error	t-Statistic	Prob.
C	15.34592	2.440600	6.287767	0.0000
GDPBLN	-0.287266	0.095499	-3.008063	0.0047
R-squared	0.196498	Mean dependent var		8.341525
Adjusted R-squared	0.174782	S.D. dependent var		5.025634
S.E. of regression	4.565361	Akaike info criterion		5.924793
Sum squared resid	771.1734	Schwarz criterion		6.010104

(*continued on next page*)

Table 2. Continued

Log likelihood	-113.5335	Hannan-Quinn criter.	5.955402
F-statistic	9.048441	Durbin-Watson stat	0.236074
Prob(F-statistic)	0.004709		

Source: authors calculations

Figure 1 reveals the reasons for this situation. When in Latvia we can observe normal seasonal fluctuations with the modest long-term growth of CO2 emissions, in Lithuania were no observable seasonable fluctuations and was significant long term growth tendency. Estonia had the fastest rate of growth in CO2 emissions.

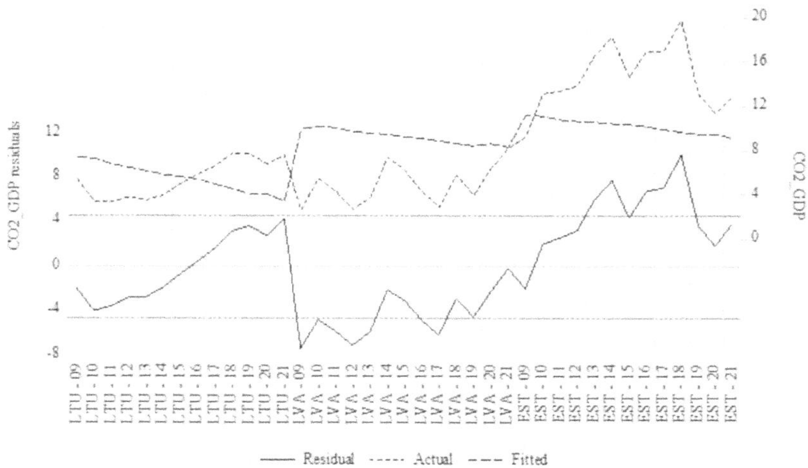

Figure 1. GDP influence on CO2 emissions million ton in the Baltic countries panel least squares model actual, fitted, and residuals graph.

Source: authors calculations

The influence of GDP on CH4 emissions million tons in the Baltic countries panel least squares model estimations (Table 3) achieved a rather high R-squared, but the probability of the coefficient C is close to one, suggesting that this calculated coefficient is not reliable.

Table 3. GDP influence on CH4 emissions million ton in the Baltic countries panel least squares model estimations.

Dependent Variable: CH4MLNT				
Method: Panel Least Squares				
Date: 10/06/23 Time: 21:58				
Sample: 2009 2021				
Periods included: 13				
Cross-sections included: 3				
Total panel (balanced) observations: 39				
Variable	Coefficient	Std. Error	t-Statistic	Prob.
C	-0.000181	0.012317	**-0.014665**	**0.9884**
GDPBLN	0.003769	0.000482	7.819964	0.0000
R-squared	0.623033	Mean dependent var		0.091718
Adjusted R-squared	0.612845	S.D. dependent var		0.037030
S.E. of regression	0.023041	Akaike info criterion		-4.653196
Sum squared resid	0.019642	Schwarz criterion		-4.567885
Log likelihood	92.73732	Hannan-Quinn criter.		-4.622587
F-statistic	61.15183	Durbin-Watson stat		0.048491
Prob(F-statistic)	0.000000			

Source: authors calculations

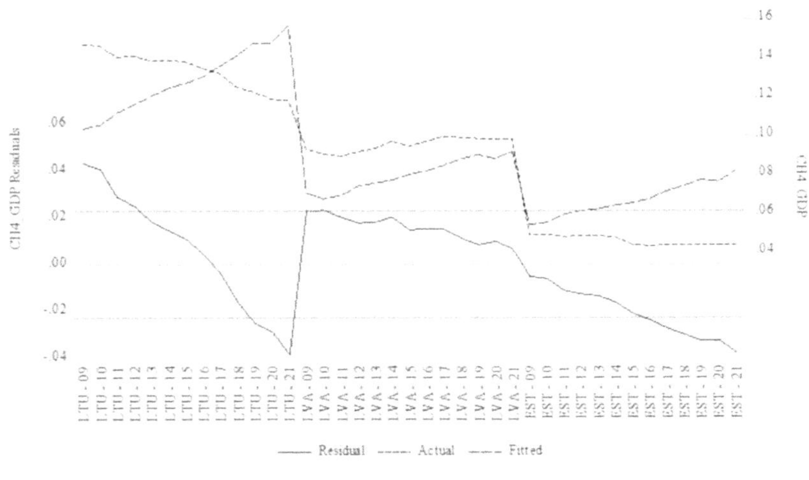

Figure 2. GDP influence on CH4 emissions million ton in the Baltic countries panel least squares model actual, fitted, and residuals graph.

Source: authors calculations

Figure 2 reveals the reasons of this model estimation result. Lithuania managed to decrease CH4 emissions, when in Latvia they grew up, and in Estonia were diminished. The logarithmic transformation (Table 4) ensured better results in model estimation, which were reflected in Figure 3.

Table 4. GDP influence on CH4 emissions million ton in the Baltic countries logarithms panel least squares model estimations.

Dependent Variable: LOG(CH4MLNT)				
Method: Panel Least Squares				
Date: 10/06/23 Time: 21:56				
Sample: 2009 2021				
Periods included: 13				
Cross-sections included: 3				
Total panel (balanced) observations: 39				
Variable	Coefficient	Std. Error	t-Statistic	Prob.
C	-6.228094	0.483312	-12.88627	0.0000
LOG(GDPBLN)	1.189842	0.152848	7.784500	0.0000
R-squared	0.620896	Mean dependent var		-2.482545
Adjusted R-squared	0.610650	S.D. dependent var		0.456562
S.E. of regression	0.284885	Akaike info criterion		0.376458
Sum squared resid	3.002901	Schwarz criterion		0.461769
Log likelihood	-5.340938	Hannan-Quinn criter.		0.407067
F-statistic	60.59845	Durbin-Watson stat		0.038519
Prob(F-statistic)	0.000000			

Source: authors calculations

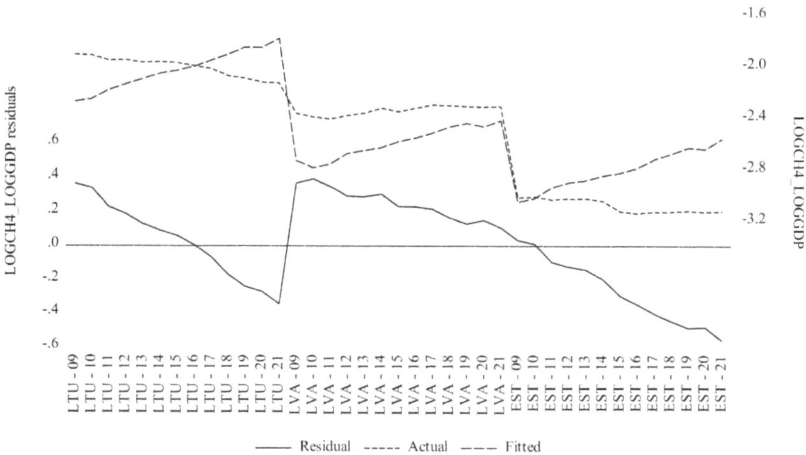

Figure 3. GDP influence on CH4 emissions million ton in the Baltic countries logarithms panel least squares model actual, fitted, and residuals graph.
Source: authors calculations

The influence of GDP on NO2 emissions million tons in the Baltic countries panel least squares model estimation results in Table 5 demonstrate rather high R-squared but reveal the unreliability of the coefficient C. Figure 4 shows quite a closeness of fitted by the model graph to the actual data.

Table 5. GDP influence on NO2 emissions million ton in the Baltic countries panel least squares model estimations.

Dependent Variable: NO2MLNT				
Method: Panel Least Squares				
Date: 10/06/23 Time: 22:00				
Sample: 2009 2021				
Periods included: 13				
Cross-sections included: 3				
Total panel (balanced) observations: 39				
Variable	Coefficient	Std. Error	t-Statistic	Prob.
C	-0.001028	0.000645	**-1.592430**	**0.1198**
GDPBLN	0.000329	2.53E-05	13.04784	0.0000
R-squared	0.821468	Mean dependent var		0.007006
Adjusted R-squared	0.816643	S.D. dependent var		0.002819

(*continued on next page*)

Table 5. Continued

S.E. of regression	0.001207	Akaike info criterion	-10.55127
Sum squared resid	5.39E-05	Schwarz criterion	-10.46596
Log likelihood	207.7498	Hannan-Quinn criter.	-10.52066
F-statistic	170.2462	Durbin-Watson stat	0.156165
Prob(F-statistic)	0.000000		

Source: authors calculations

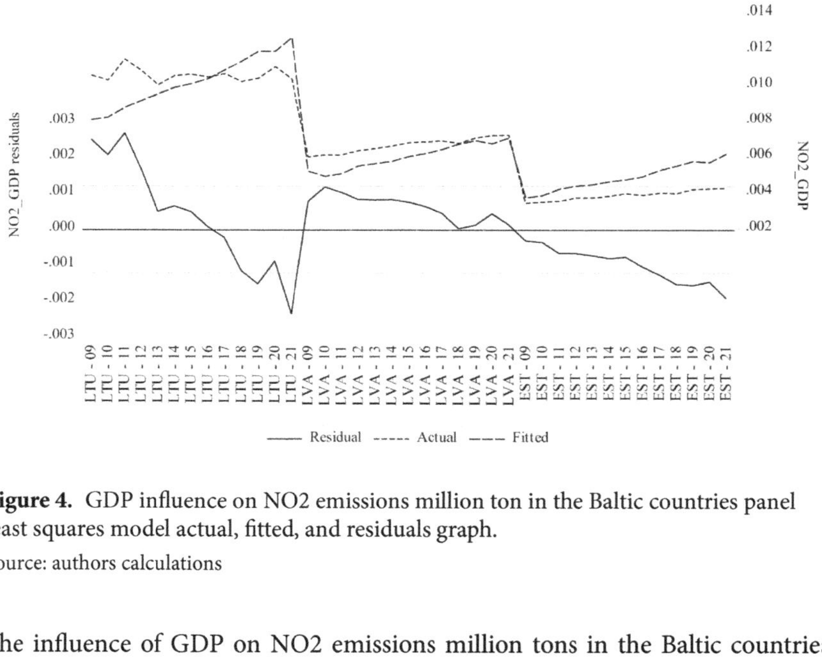

Figure 4. GDP influence on NO2 emissions million ton in the Baltic countries panel least squares model actual, fitted, and residuals graph.

Source: authors calculations

The influence of GDP on NO2 emissions million tons in the Baltic countries logarithm panel least squares model estimation results in Table 6 demonstrate rather high R-squared and the reliable coefficient C. Figure 5 shows quite a similar to Figure 4 closeness of the fitted model graph to the actual data.

Table 6. GDP influence on NO2 emissions million ton in the Baltic countries logarithms panel least squares model estimations.

Dependent Variable: LOG(NO2MLNT)				
Method: Panel Least Squares				
Date: 10/06/23 Time: 22:04				
Sample: 2009 2021				
Periods included: 13				
Cross-sections included: 3				
Total panel (balanced) observations: 39				
Variable	Coefficient	Std. Error	t-Statistic	Prob.
C	-9.047910	0.305668	-29.60049	0.0000
LOG(GDPBLN)	1.271467	0.096667	13.15301	0.0000
R-squared	0.823811	Mean dependent var		-5.045409
Adjusted R-squared	0.819049	S.D. dependent var		0.423556
S.E. of regression	0.180174	Akaike info criterion		-0.539872
Sum squared resid	1.201113	Schwarz criterion		-0.454561
Log likelihood	12.52750	Hannan-Quinn criter.		-0.509263
F-statistic	173.0017	Durbin-Watson stat		0.095735
Prob(F-statistic)	0.000000			

Source: authors calculations

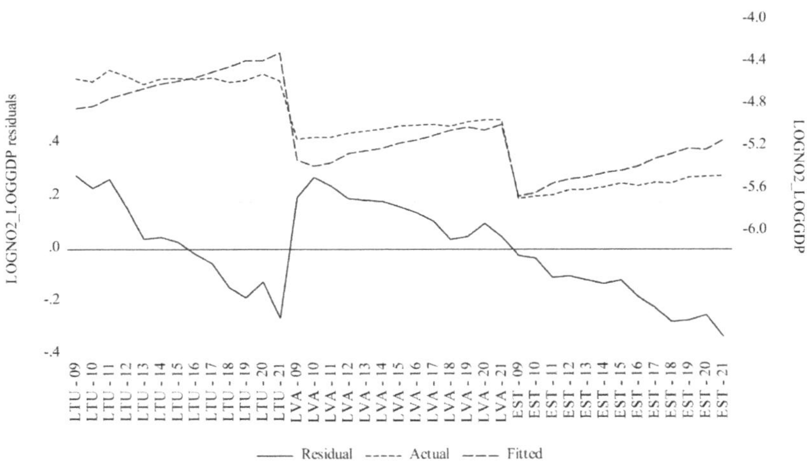

Figure 5. GDP influence on NO2 emissions million ton in the Baltic countries logarithms panel least squares model actual, fitted, and residuals graph.

Source: authors calculations

4 Results and Discussion

Estonia had the fastest rate of growth in CO2 emissions. Lithuania managed to decrease CH4 emissions, when in Latvia they grew up, and in Estonia were diminished. The study aims to find why some countries have higher or lower greenhouse gas emissions, in relation to their gross domestic product (GDP). Panel data analysis of the Baltic countries has revealed a rather chaotic influence of GDP growth on greenhouse gas emissions. This may signal changes in environmental policy in the analyzed countries and inefficient control of emissions, which was revealed in the panel data analysis.

5 Conclusions

A sustainable economy includes poverty reduction, better living conditions, better health care, nutrition, production using renewable natural resources, waste recycling, transport, and climate change, which is happening due to the greenhouse effect.

The study aims to find out why some countries in the European Union have higher or lower greenhouse gas emissions, in relation to their gross domestic product (GDP). Panel data analysis of the Baltic countries has revealed a rather chaotic influence of GDP growth on greenhouse gas emissions. This may signal changes in environmental policy in the analyzed countries and inefficient control of emissions, which was revealed in the panel data analysis.

References

Alekna, R., & Kazlauskiene, E. (2019). Žaliosios ekonomikos probleminės sritys globalioje rinkoje. *Science: Future of Lithuania, 11.*

Bajno, D., Bednarz, L., & Grzybowska, A. (2021). The role and place of Traditional Chimney System Solutions in environmental progress and in reducing energy consumption. *Energies*, *14*(16), 4720.

Eurostat. (2023). Eurostats. www.eurostatas.eu

Fong, W. C., Sun, Y., & Chen, Y. J. (2022). Examining the relationship between energy consumption and unfavorable CO2 emissions on Sustainable Development by going through various violated factors and stochastic disturbance-based on a three-stage SBM-DEA model. *Energies*, *15*(2), 569.

Khouri, S., Behun, M., Knapcikova, L., Behunova, A., Sofranko, M., & Rosova, A. (2020). Characterization of customized encapsulant polyvinyl butyral used in the Solar Industry and its impact on the environment. *Energies*, *13*(20), 5391.

Mach, L., Bedrunka, K., Dabrowski, I., & Fracz, P. (2021). The relationship between ROP funds and Sustainable Development-A case study for Poland. *Energies*, *14*(9), 2677.

Maran, R. M., & Nedelea, A. M. (2017). Green economy: Challenges and opportunities. *Ecoforum*, *6*(3).

Margeta, K., Glasnovic, Z., Logar, N. Z., Tisma, S., & Farkas, A. (2022). A Concept for solving the sustainability of cities worldwide. *Energies*, *15*(2), 616.

Niklewicz-Pijaczynska, M., Stanczyk, E., Gardocka-Jalowiec, A., Grodek-Szostak, Z., Niemczyk, A., Szalonka, K., & Homa, M. (2021). A strategy for planned product aging in view of Sustainable Development challenges. *Energies*, *14*(22), 7793.

Porzio, G. F., Fornai, B., Amato, A., Matarese, N., Vannucci, M., Chiappelli, L., & Colla, V. (2013). Reducing the energy consumption and CO2 emissions of energy intensive industries through decision support systems – An example of application to the steel industry. *Applied Energy*, *112,* 818–833.

Rybak, A., & Kolev, S. D. (2021). Analysis of the EU-27 countries energy markets integration in terms of the Sustainable Development SDG7 implementation. *Energies*, *14*(21), 7079.

Skorupskaite, K., & Junevičius, A. (2017). Atliekų tvarkymo politikos formavimas Lietuvojetaikant žiedinės ekonomikos modelį. *Public Policy and Administration*, *16*(1), 91–107.

Tausova, M., Culkova, K., Taus, P., Domarackaand, L., & Senova, A. (2021). Evaluation of the effective material use from the view of EU environmental policy goals. *Energies*, *14*(16), 4759.

Wachnik, B., Klodawski, M., & Kardas-Cinal, E. (2022). Reduction of the information gap problem in Industry 4.0 projects as a way to reduce energy consumption by the industrial sector. *Energies*, *15*(3), 1108.

Xu, X. Y., Wang, Y., Ruan, Y. J., Wang, J., Ge, K. L., Zhang, Y. M., & Jin, H. K. (2022). Integrated energy planning for near-zero carbon emission demonstration district in urban areas: A case study of Meishan District in Ningbo, China. *Energies*, *15*(3), 874.

www.ingramcontent.com/pod-product-compliance
Ingram Content Group UK Ltd.
Pitfield, Milton Keynes, MK11 3LW, UK
UKHW020258051026
15470UKWH00021B/1317

9 783631 924655